A SANTALI-ENGLISH DICTIONARY

A SANTALI – ENGLISH DICTIONARY

(In Two Volumes)

(VOLUME-2)
(L – Z)

A. CAMPBELL

GYAN

A Santali – English Dictionary

ISBN: 978-81-212-1193-2 (Set)
ISBN: 978-81-212-1196-3 (Vol. 2)
Price: Rs. 1800 (2 Vols. Set)

Reprinted in 2013 in India by
Gyan Publishing House
23, Main Ansari Road, Daryaganj,
New Delhi - 110002
Phones: (011) 23282060, (011) 23261060
Fax : (011) 23285914
E-mail : books@gyanbooks.com
Website: gyanbooks.com

Printed at: G. Print Process, Delhi

L

To dig.
La gadaeme. Dig deep, dig down.
La toťkedeako. They dug him out.
Ran lala senakanae. He is gone to dig medicinal roots.
La gaḍa. A pit that has been dug.

Lab. Profit.
Lab bań ńamlaǩa, boroh loksanenań. I did not get any profit, on the contrary I lost.
Ninạǩ labliń jomeda. We receive so much profit.

Labaǩ. Cf. legeć labaǩ, green and luxuriant, succulent.

Labaǩ cabaǩ. } Labuǩ cạbuǩ. } Talkative, unable to keep a secret, gossipping, blabbing.
Nui do alope lạiaea, labaǩ cabaǩ hoṛ kanae. Do not tell him, he is a blabbing person.
Nui samaṅre babon roṛa, lạbuǩ cạbuǩgeae. We will not speak before him, he is a blabber.

Labań lubuń. Leisurely, slowly, applied mainly to the leisurely movements of wild animals when undisturbed.
Labań lubuńe calaoena kul do. The tiger went away leisurely.

Labaṛ. Deceitful, given to exaggeration, false.
Labaṛ katha. A false statement.
Uni hoṛaǩ babon ańjoma, labaṛgeae. We will not listen to what that man says, he exaggerates.

Labaṛ atnaǩ. A species of forest tree mentioned in Santal tradition.

Labar labar. } Lạbur lạbur. } Garrulous, talkative, loquacious, perpetual chatter, applied to females.
Nui maejiu lạbur lạbure roṛa. This woman chatters perpetually.

Labar lobur. } Labar lubur. } Soft, as mud; squashy, sloppy, uliginous, oozy, pulpy, pappy.
Labar luburko daǩ mạndiakaťa. They have cooked the rice into pap.

Labas lubus. Applied to the walking of animals, mainly dogs and cats, just beginning to use their legs; flabby, weak on legs.
Labas lubuse daṛankana.
Labas lubuse ńeloǩkana. He looks flabby.

Labda. } Labdao. } Lebda. } To throw at, as a stick to hit or knock down anything.
Kulạị ma labdaepe. Throw your sticks at the hare.
Mase labda gur goťkaťpe. Throw at it and knock it down.
Labda bindạṛ goťkedeae. He threw (a stick) at it and knocked it down.

Labejan. To collapse, as a person suffering from some fatal disease; sick unto death, worn out.

Labejanenae. He has collapsed.
Ruạteye labejanena. He is at death's door through fever.

Labeko. Children.

Labhaeć lubhạić. A call to dogs when hounding them on, also a call to drive away jackals at night from crops.

With regard to jackals the idea seems to be that when they hear the cry they will think that dogs are at hand and from fear of them they will not dare to come near.

Labhae lubhại. To please, or quiet a child for the time being by giving it something, to deceive, to gull, to hoax.

Labhae lubhạikateko idikedea. They gulled him and took him away. (They gulled him into going with them.)

Labhaṅ lubhuṅ. Leisurely, slowly, without apparent effort.

Hundạrko dạra labhaṅ lubhuṅ. Wolves run leisurely, or go fast without apparent effort.

Labhe. }
Labhe labhe. } Profit, recompence.

Labhe labhe baṅ ńamlekhan noa ohoń goklea. Unless I get some recompence, I will not carry this.

Labhra. M. }
Lạbhri. F. } Deceitful, false, exaggerating.

Lạbiť. Soft, to become soft.

Lạbiť hasa. Soft soil.
Lạbiť kaṭ. Soft wood.
Dakakkhan lạbidoka. If you water it it will soften.
Lạbiťgea. It is soft.

Lablab. }
Lablaba. }
Laplapa. } Broad, wide, applied to anything very broad, or wide, to flap the wings, to expand.

Kicriċ lablaba osara. The cloth is very broad.

Lablạbi. }
Lablạbiạ. } Soft.

Hasa lablạbigea. The soil is soft.

Lablạbi. Trigger of gun.

Laboj. }
Loboj. } A flourish in music, a fanciful addition to a tune, a whimsical accompaniment to a tune, a humorous prelude designed to amuse before the introduction of more serious matters; to amuse, to tickle the fancy; to entertain.

Pahile laboj maṛaṅkedea, enkhaćte kathae ehoṕkeda.

Banam jokheć uniye labojaka.
Mocateye labojaka, dhạtiṛ dhatak tiṛdak, muoatreye labojeda.

Laboṛ. To deceive, to wheedle, to gull.

Nui doe lại laboreťgea. He is deceiving, he is telling lies.

Laboṛi. To stultify oneself, to make a false promise, deceitful.

Laboṛienaṅ. I have stultified myself.
Laboṛigeae, uniak katha babon añjoma. He is deceitful, we will not pay attention to what he says.

Laboṛiạ. Deceitful.

Ạdi laboṛiạ hoṛ kanae. He is a very deceitful person.

Labṛa. M. }
Lạbṛi. F. } Deceitful, untruthful.

Bebạṛiċ labṛageae nui hoṛ do. This man is very deceitful.

Labṛaṅ. }
Lạbṛuṅ. } To hang the head, to hang loosely, to droop, to become feeble.

Nui ḍahra bańcaok coe bacoe lạbṛuṅenae.
Setoṅte sakam sanam labṛaṅ lạṛbuṅena. Owing to the heat the leaves are all drooping.

Lạbṛi. F. }
Labṛa. M. } Deceitful, untruthful. Cf. labṛa.

Labṛe. On the chance of, in hope of, as best one can.

Heć labṛeakanae. He has come in hope of (getting work.)

Dapal labṛeakanae. She is clothed as best she can (with the clothes she has.)

Kạmi labṛekakkanaṅ, ado hoyok coṅ baṅ coṅ. I am planting my dhan on the chance of getting a crop, but I can't say whether it will succeed or not.

Lạbṛuk. To become feeble, to become poor, dejected.

Bae nunueť teṛoṅe lạbṛukena. It has become feeble because it does not suck.

Nui do nahake lạbṛukena. He is now poor.
Din kalom khone lạbṛukena. He has been in reduced circumstance since last year.

Bhagaoenteye lạbṛukena. He is dejected owing to his having been worsted.

Lạbṛuṅ. To hang the head, to hang loosely, to become feeble; ill, done up.

Lạbui. The pot which is hung on the palm tree to receive the liquid from which *tari* is manufactured.

Lạbuk cạbuk. }
Lạbur cạbur. } Given to exaggeration, loquacious.

Uni do lạbuk cạbuk hoṛ kanae. He is a person given to exaggeration.

Labus labus. Soft, as a ripe fruit, too easily bent, too pliant, too flexible, as a bow.

Ak labus labus ṣikṣukkana. The bow feels too pliant.

Laċ. The belly, the stomach, the abdomen, inmost parts, the womb.

Laċ haso. Stomach ache, any bowel complaint.
Ṭaka emkate laċ latarkedeae. He gave him money and made him his partizan.
Uni laċ latarre ṣsulokkanae. He is dependent on him for a living.

Miṭ laċ boeha. Own brother, own brothers, children of the same mother.
Laċ oḍok. Diarrhœa, any bowel complaint.
Laċre seakedae, bae lạilaka. He kept it to himself, he did not tell.

Miṭ bitạ laċ khạtirtebo haronokkana. We trouble about a span of a stomach.
Laċ jalate. Through stress of hunger.
Laċ jalatele heċena. We have come through stress of hunger.

Laċ dole aka oṭoakaṭa? bam emalea? Did we hang up our stomachs before leaving? Won't you give us food?

Laċ dole ạgu daraakaṭa, bale doho oṭolaka. We have brought our stomachs with us, we did not leave them behind us.
Laċ gaḍa sanam gaḍa khon marañgea. The belly-pit is the greatest of all pits.

Sul laċ oḍokokkanae. He has dysentery.
Laċre tahenrege apatteṭe goċena. His father died before he was born.
Laċ duhạu. To clean the entrails of an animal.

Laċ duhạu ạgunime. Clean and bring the entrails.
Laċrele eadmea, bam kạmikana. We will stint your victuals, you are not working.

Laċrege daṛe bañ aṭkareda. I am hungry.
Ale do laċ topakakantalea tehen do. We have no food for to-day.
Lajokkanae. Her pregnancy is becoming apparent.

Laċakanae. Her pregnancy is apparent.
Laċ daṛetem kạmia, se sopo daṛete? Do you work by the strength of your stomach, or your arm?

Laċrege bae pacao daṛeada. He could not digest it.
Laċ ñurakantiña. I am suffering from diarrhœa.

Biñ laċ tegeko calaka. Serpents crawl on their bellies.
Laċ oṛseċ. To contract the stomach, to apply one's whole strength.
Ma laċ oṛseċtam, bandekamañ. Draw in your stomach, I will bind on your cloth.

Laċ oṛseċkateñ ṭhelaokeda. I drew in my stomach and pushed. (I pushed with all my might.)

Moṭa laċ. } Entrails.
Nanha laċ. }

Munḍu laċ. A certain part of the entrails of a fowl.
Laċre do bako dohoea. They do not keep it to themselves, but blab it out.

Lacak lucuk. Not to put the ball of the foot to the ground when walking owing to the presence of a sore, thorn &c.

Lacak lucuke calakkana. He is walking on his heel.

Lacak pacak. Large drops of rain, large drops of rain falling from the leaves of a tree, &c.

Lacak pacake dakeda. The rain is falling in large drops.

Lacañ locañ. } Greedy, covetous, hankering after.
Locañ lucuñ. }

Ạḍi lacañ locañ baṛaeae. He is hankering after anything to eat going first to one place then to another.
Lacañ locañ baṛae kanae. He is always on the look out for something to eat.

Lacañ locoñ. Irregular in surface, opposed to plane or smooth, jagged, jagged or irregular outline.

Lacañ locoñko lakakaṭa. They have cut it (with an axe) and left the surface rough.

Lacar. To be helpless, to be without resource.

Ạḍi lacarre menaña. I am in a great difficulty.
Lacarenae, bhorsa bạnukanañ. He is helpless, there is no hope (of his rallying.)

Lacar. } Talkative, always chattering.
Lacra. }

Lacar lacar. To chatter, to gabble, quickly.

Lacar lacare roṛeda. She is gabbling.
Lacar lacare heċ goṭena. He came quickly.

Lacha. } A number of small bundles, mainly of *backom,* (q. v.) tied together.
Lacha lacha. }

Miṭ lacha backom. A bundle of backom (q. v.)
Lacha lacha menaka. It is in bundles.
Miṭ lacha uḅ. A handful of hair.

Lachan. } Bad habit, evil courses, bad behaviour.
Lochan. }

Lachman. A variety of the rice plant.

Lachman bhog. A variety of the rice plant.

Lạchmi. Cattle, live stock, wealth, fortune.

Ona atorege ạḍi lạchmiko gujukkana. In that village many cattle are dying.

Laclaca. Flat and broad, flat and wide, occupying much space, flat as opposed to steep.

Laclaca duṛuḅakanae. He sits spread out.
Laclaca benaoakana, onate jorokkana. (The roof of the house) has been made flat, for that reason it leaks.

Laclaca derentae. It has wide spreading horns.
Catom laclacagea. An umbrella is flattish and wide.
Haṭak laclacagea. A haṭak (q. v.) is flat.

Lacra. Cf. lacar.

Laṛcri. } Cf. lacar.
Larco.

Laṛcuk. } Said of women as lacak lucuk (q. v.) is applied to men.
Laṛcuk laṛcuk.

Laṛcuk laṛcuke calakkana. She is walking on her heel.

Lad. Cf. lat.

Ladać luduć. } Applied to the gait of a corpulent person, to waddle, flesh to shake when moving.
Ladhać ludhuć.

Ladać luduće calakkana. He waddles along.

Laḍak. } To shut, or pull-to a door.
Lagak.

Laḍak darakam. Pull-to the door after you.
Silpiń lagak darakam. Shut the door after you.

Ladak luduk. } Applied to the gait of a very corpulent person, to waddle, or roll.
Ladak luduk.

Ladak ludukе calakkana. He waddles along.
Bana hõ ladak ludukko calaka. Bears also have a heavy rolling gait.

Laḍap. } To pick up one by one, or a small quantity. Cf. laṭap.
Laṭap.

Aṭińkanae, se bah? Laḍap baṛaedae. Is it grazing? It is picking here and there.

Lada upar. One above another.

Lada upar dohoakana. They are placed one above another.

Laḍauri. Rubbish, droppings of goats, sweepings of a goats' house.

Ladbad. } To be soft, as a ripe fruit, to squash, as ripe fruit when it falls, to become soft, as paste, &c.; noise produced by the fall of any thing that is soft and squashes; to flop, to splatch.
Ladbadao.

Rukulekhan ladbad beleak ńuroka. If you shake (the branch) the ripe fruit will fall with a thud.
Ladbadko utuakaće. They have boiled the relish soft.
Muh dal ladbad le godoka. Mung dal dissolves readily.

Ladbad. } At its height, as an epidemic, or as the fruit season when the fruit is ripening all at once.
Ladbadao.

Ona atore aḍiko ladbadaoakana. Many people are dying in that village.

Kuinḍi ladbadaoakana. The fruit of the matkom (q. v.) tree is in full season.
Rokhoere khubko ladbadaoakana. Rice planting is in full swing.

Laḍbur. } Hanging down, bent down, as a branch with fruit.
Ladbur.
Laḍgur.
Laḍur.

Jo laḍburakana. It is bent down with fruit.

Lade. To load, to put one thing on another.

Ḍher do alope ladeakina, bakin or daṛeaka. Do not load them heavily, they will not be able to drag it.
Lade ḍaṅra. A pack bullock.
Khajna aḍiko ladeadiń. They imposed a heavy rent on me.
Kul gaire ladeĕnae. The tiger leapt on the cow.
Mak ḍharuak ledeanae. He has taken upon himself the guilt of another.
Ladenak. Clothes, garments.
Hoṛmore ladeak banuktińa. I have no clothes.
Dose ladeadea. He put the blame on him.
Eṭak hoṛ ṭhene ladeakana. He is another man's dependent.
Hasa lade baṛawakme. Heap on earth.
Noa hõ ladeka. This will also be loaded (on the cart.)

Laḍe. Slanting, off the perpendicular, leaning to one side.

Khunṭi laḍeakana. The post is off the perpendicular.

Laḍea. } Bent, crooked, of no great value.
Laḍea laḍea.

Laḍea laḍea ṭhenga kolalepe. Send us an crooked stick, or a stick of any kind however worthless.

It is customary for a man to send his stick or club when sending a message by another person. The person to whom the stick is brought recognises it and trusts the messenger.

Laḍea dare. A tree that has grown to one side, and then returned to the upright position.

Laḍgui. } To bend down, as an ear of ripe grain, branch with fruit. &c.
Laḍgui laḍgui.

Laḍgui geleakana. The ears of grain are bent.
Ceť hoṛokan bah laḍgui laḍgui ṭgeleakana. What sort of dhan is it, the ears are bent down.
Bhiḍi do laḍguigetakoa uḿ. Sheep having hanging wool.
Laḍguiakana. It is bent, as an ear of grain.
Laḍgui laḍgui joakana. It is bent down with fruit.

Laḍgum. Cf. ladgui.

Laḍgur. Hanging down, bent down. Cf. laḍbur.

Ladhar lodhor. } **Ladhar ludhur.** } To roll when walking, flesh hanging in folds and shaking during movement, as of a very fat man or animal.
Mota hor ladhar ludhurko calaka. Fat men roll heavily when they walk.

Ladhna ḍanra. } **Ladna ḍanra.** } A pack bullock.
Ladhna sadom. } **Ladna sadom.** } A pack horse.

Ladlad. } **Ladladao.** } A succession of rumbling or thudding sounds, continuous, one after the other, in a stream, thick.
Ladladao ńurena bhit. The wall fell rumbling down.
Daka ladlade upkeda. He poured out a large quantity of boiled rice.
Ladladko hijukkana. They are coming in large numbers.
Dak ladladao argo gotena. The water rushed down in a flood.
Dak mạṇḍi ladladko ạrićakata. They have poured off thick rice water.
Ladlad dak mạṇḍi. Thick rice water.

Ladladao. In crowds.
Ladladao calakkanako. They are going in crowds.

Ladlud. A succession of thuds, one after the other, in succession.
Iṭạ dhasao ńurhạena ladlud. The bricks have collapsed and fallen with a succession of thuds.
Ladludko donkeda. They jumped one after the other with a thud.
Ladludko don caḍoena. They plunged in one after the other with a splash.

Ladna ḍanra. Cf. ladhna ḍanra.

Ladoṗ. To be covered by the leaves of any climbing plant, as a tree.
Ladoṗ eseṭakana. It is hidden by the leaves of a climbing plant.

Laḍoṗ. To draw a door-to a little, to partly shut.
Silpiń laḍoṗ darakam. Draw-to the door after you.

Ladoṛ badoṛ. Quickly and indistinctly, having an impediment in one's speech, to stammer.
Ladoṛ badoṛe roṛeda. He stammers in his speech.

Laḍu. A kind of sweetmeat.
Jili laḍu. } **Jhili laḍu.** } A kind of sweetmeat.

Laḍui laḍui. Cf. lạḍgui.

Laḍur. To hang down, to bend over.
Ḍạr lạḍurakana jote. The branch is bent owing to the fruit on it.

Laḍur baḍur. } **Luḍur buḍur.** } Carelessly, thoughtlessly, negligently, perfunctorily.
Lạḍur bạḍure kạmikana. He is working carelessly.
Lạḍur bạḍur baṛakanae. He is going about neglecting his work.

Laḍwir. To hang down, to bend over. Cf. laḍur.

Lae. } **Laete.** } All, the whole.
Sińlae ńindạ lae dak idikedae. It rained all day and all night.
Koṛa lae kuṛi laeko jarwaakana. All the young men and maidens are assembled.
Hoṛ lae Diku lae sanamko calaoena. All the Santals and Hindus have gone away.
Gidrạ pidrạ laeteko heḍena. They have come with all the children.
Gidrạ pidrạ laeteń heḍena. I have come with my children.

Laelokṭha. } **Lạilukṭha.** } To quarrel, to be at variance with, to dispute. Cf. lokṭha.
Okoe tuluć hõ laelokṭha bae lagaoka. He quarrels with no one.
Laelokṭha banuktae. He does not quarrel.

Laea. Wide spreading, as horns.

Laeloṭha. Ill-feeling, disagreement, quarrel, dissension.
Uni tuluć laeloṭha bạnuktińa. I have no ill-feeling towards him.
Okoe soṅge hõ bae laeloṭhalena. He quarrelled with no one.

Lag. } **Lagloṭha.** } Ill-feeling, disagreement, quarrel, dissension, loggerheads.
Okoe tuluć hõ lag banuktińa. I bear no one ill-will.
Hoṛ tuluć ạḍi lagloṭhakae. He is greatly given to disagree with people.

Lag. Cf. lak.

Lạg. Sharp, pungent, acute, hot, strong, potent, fertile.
Lạg hasa. Fertile soil.
Lạg hạṇḍi. Strong, potent rice beer.
Lạg thamakhur. Strong tobacco.
Lạg so. A pungent smell.
Lạgak paurạ. Potent liquor.
Lạg ran. A powerful medicine.
Noa hasa bań lạga. This soil is not fertile.
Noa hạṇḍi bań lạga. This rice beer is weak.

Lạg. To be due, liability, obligation to pay.
Khajna lạgakana. The rent is due.

Laga. To drive, to chase, to pursue.
Ato khonko lagakedea. They drove him from the village.
Setako laga ńirkedea. The dogs chased it away.
Seta lagakedeae toyo. The dog chased the jackal.
Gạḍi lak̕gaić. The driver of the cart.
Laga lagakinme. Drive them faster.
Manḍa laga lạhuṭkedań. I drove (bullocks) over the grain on the threshing floor till it was threshed out.

Laga. Lagao. } To apply, fix, touch, come in contact with, to join, to occupy, to suit, to begin, to happen, to be occupied or busy in, to be owing, to be at variance with, to quarrel.
Guni guribko casko lagaoakaṭa. Poor people have planted (or sown) their corps.
Hoṛ tuluć alom lagaok̕a. Do not quarrel with people.
Ạḍi lagao seta kanae. He is a tight gripping dog.
Hoṛko kạmireń lagaoakaṭkoa.. I have started the people to work.
Ḍher din lagaok̕a. It will occupy many days.
Lagaok̕ hoṛ. A contentious, or quarrelsome person.
Seńgel lagaoena burure. The hill has taken fire.
Setoń lagaoadińa. The sun beat upon and affected me injuriously.
Ṭaka lagaoańkana. I am owing money.
Jomak̕ lagaoama. You will have to give food.
As lagaoena. There was hope.
Mõṛẽ ṭaka gonoń lagaoadińa. I paid five rupees for my son's bride.
Hoṛko lagaoadińa. They set men on me.
Peṛako lagaoena mạire. The daughter has had an offer of marriage, or marriage negotiations are in progress.
Bońga lagaoadeae. A spirit possessed him.
Lạgu lagaoena. Under a spell.
Lagak̕a, se bań? Will it succeed or not? will it be effective?

Lagae. Lagaete. } Including, along with.
Ape lagaete delabon sendraea. Let us along with you go a-hunting.
Niạ lagaete ponea hoyok̕a. Including this there will be four.
Niạ lagae pon dhao hoeena. Including this it will be four times.

Lagae logoe. Laga logo. } Slowly, leisurely, applied to females.
Lagae logoe calak̕kanae. She is going leisurely.

Lagak̕ lagak̕. Becoming large, increasing in size, as a sore.
Lagak̕ lagak̕entaea ghao do. His sore has increased in size.

Laga lạgi. Lega legi. } Near, close, about, with a short interval of time or space between.
Oṛak̕ laga lạgiko benaoakaṭa. They have built their houses close to each other.
Matkom ńurok̕ laga lạgiye goćena. He died about the time of the falling of the matkom (q. v.)

Laga logo. Cf. lagae logoe.

Lagam. A bridle, a bit.

Lagan. Logon. } Preparations for a marriage or for the Sohrae festival (q. v.), the knotted string intimating the date of a marriage, appointed time, crisis.
Bapla reak̕ lagan seṭerena. The marriage day has arrived.
Ohoń senlena Sohrae logon seṭerena. I cannot go as the time of the Sohrae (q. v.) is near.

Lagan bagan. To invest, to lend on interest, as money, or grain.
Ạḍi ṭheciń lagan baganakaṭa. I have invested money in many things, or in many places.
Mahajon reak̕ lagan bagan. The collecting and re-investing of money by a money lender.

Lagać. Lagić. } For the purpose of.
Kombṛo lagać. For the purpose of stealing.
Mańjan jom lạgić. For the purpose of eating dinner.
Am lạgidok̕kanae. He is searching for thee, or he wants thee.
Gại doe mihũ lạgidok̕kana, mihũ doe gại lạgidok̕kana. The cow wants its calf, and the calf wants the cow.

Lagać. Lagić. } About to, to be about to, to intend.
Calak̕ lagaće. He is about to go.
Calak̕ lạgidok̕kanako. They are on the point of going.
Hijuk̕ lạgićlenae, bako hec ocoadea. He intended to come, but they did not allow him.

Lage loṛẽ. To quarrrel, to be at enmity.
Okoe sońge hõ bae lage loṛẽa. He quarrels with no one.

Laghar. Lagher. } To be familiarized, to be in the habit of, to become bold through immunity, to prowl.
Onte alope calak̕a, kulko lagherakana. Do not go there tigers are prevalent.
Kombṛo lagherakanako. The thieves are prevalent at present.
Kombṛo reak̕ ạḍi lagher onte do. There is great danger from thieves there.

Lagiạ paṛao. Lagiạ̃ paṛao. } On the look-out for, on the trail of, to exert oneself. Cf. lagi bohao.
Nui bạhu lạgić ạdile lạgiạ paṛaoakana. We are doing our utmost to secure this marriageable damsel.

Lagibohao. On the look-out for, on the trail of, lying in wait for

Adi horko lagi bohaoakana, sabe lagic. Many people are on the look out for him to catch him.

Laglag. Luxuriant, to grow luxuriantly.

Laglag ñelokkana. It looks luxuriant.
Laglagakana. It is luxuriant.

Laglagao. To be on the look-out for an opportunity.

Kule laglagao baraekana. The tiger is on the look-out.

Goje lagite laglagaoakana. He is on the look-out for an opportunity to kill him.

Lagle. } With a short interval of
Lagle lagle. } time or space between.

Lagle lagleko heoena. They came one after the other.

Laglege perako heoena. Visitors came one after another.

Laglege uyukkedae. He struck blows in quick succession.

Lagle mar. With a short interval between, in quick succession.

Lagle marko jomkeda. They ate again in a short time.

Lagle marko emalekana. They give to us again after a short interval.

Lagna. Investment, as money or grain on interest, dues.

Hande nande lagna menaktaea. He has investments here and there.

Lagrẽ. } A dance so called.
Lagrẽ enec. }

This is the most common kind of dance, and can be danced on all odd occasions.

Lagrẽ sereñ. Songs sung during the dancing of the *Lagre* dance.

Lagrẽ ru. Time beaten on the drum, to which the *Lagre* dance is danced.

Lagti. Liability, obligation to pay. Cf. lag.

Lagti lagaoakawadiña. I have a liability to meet.

Lagu. A spell, charm, enchantment.

Lagu lagaoakana. A spell is in operation.

Lagui pagui. To mumble, to chew, or eat as a person without teeth.

Lagui paguiye jomeda, data banuktaete.

Laha. } Before, in front of; to be
Laha laha. } before or in front of.

Lahaenae. He is in front, or he is dead.
Lahare menaka. It is in front, or ahead.
Berec lahaenae. He rose first.
Bele lahaena. It is over-ripe.
Uni doko lahakedea. They put him forward, or put the responsibility on him.

Laha taeomre menaea. } He is next to the first,
Laha talare menaea. } or he is second.

Taeom lahare menaea. } He is before the last, or
Taeom talare menaea. } he is second last.
Isin lahaena. It is over cooked.
Alom rora laha laha. Do not speak without thought.

Mañjhi auriye rohoea, adge laha lahae rokhoekana. The Mañjhi (q. v.) has not yet begun to plant (his rice) and he is planting his before him.

Laha lahae tengo baraekana. He is standing out in front, (putting himself forward.)

Lahao. To succeed, to overcome.

Sahaoleñnecem lahaoka. You must suffer before you succeed.

Horak katha bae añjomlekhan ohoe lahaolena. If he does not attend to what people say to him he will not succeed.

Lahao. To suffer, to bear.

Sahaokak lahaokak.

Lahar cahar. Always to the front, always taking a leading part, officious.

Sanam ghuri do uniye lahar caharoka. He is always in front.

Lahas. A corpse, a dead body.

Lahãt. To excell, to vanquish, to conquer.

Kamire lahãtakanae. He excells in work.
Uni khone lahãtena. He conquered him.

Lahe cahe. Liberal, unstinting, generous; always to the front, officious.

Nui do adi lahe cahegeae. He is very liberal.
Lahe cahe ãrtiedae. He gives a second helping of food unstintingly.

Lahe caheko galmaraoa. They speak much, are talkative.

Laher. } To slice deeply, to cut.
Lahur. }

Jel laherme. Cut the meat into slices.
Ule laherkeda. He sliced the mango deeply (when paring it.)

Laher murmu. A sub-sept of the Santal sept Murmu. (q. v.)

Laher Hembrom. A sub-sept of the Santal sept Hembrom. (q. v.)

Lahi. The Lac insect, *Coccus Lacca*; lac in its crude state.

Lahia. An insect resembling the Lac insect found on certain kinds of cultivated crops.

Lahkao. To do anything with enthusiasm, with heart and soul, with great zest; to add to.

Lagrẽko lahkaoakada. They have warmed up to the lagrẽ (q. v.) dance.

Buru hor khube lahkaoakata. The person beating the drum is doing it with great zest.

Lahkao ñokkateye laikeda. He added a little in telling it.

Lahke lahke. Carefully, with discrimination, gently.
Lahke lahkete taṛamme. Walk carefully.

Lahna. To exaggerate, to draw the long bow, to spin a yarn. .
Lahna katha. An exaggerated story.
Ạdiye lahnaeda. He exaggerates greatly.
Eken lahna kathatae. His story is all a make-up.

Lahna. Cf. lagan bagan.

Lahra. Clouds, flying clouds.

Lahra. M. } Loquacious, talkative and
Lahri. F. } given to exaggeration.

Lạhuć lạhuć. Applied to the gait of a tall person, springy, as the top of a bamboo.
Lạhuć lạhuće calaḱkana. He goes striding and swinging.
Lạhuć lạhuć maće goḱ idia. The bamboo springs at either end as he carries it.

Lạhṭi. An armlet or bracelet made of lac.

Lạhur. To slice deeply, to gash, to cut. Cf. laher.

Lạhuṭ. To powder, to make fine, to crush.
Kathako lạhuṭkeda. They threshed out the matter.
Si lạhuṭ. To break by ploughing.
En lạhuṭ. To thresh.
Togoć lạhuṭ. To chew.
Riṭ lạhuṭ. To grind fine.
Dal lạhuṭ. To thresh by means of a flail or stick.
Huṛuń lạhuṭ. To pound fine in the dhinki.

Lạị. To tell, to say, to acquaint, to repeat, to inform.
Lạị sade. To make public, to proclaim.
Lạị sodor. To make public, to reveal.
Lạị pasnao. To publish, to spread by telling.
Lạị oṭo. To tell and go away.
Lạị tora. To tell as one goes, as soon as told.
Lạị bujhạu. To explain, to advise.
Uniń lạiaea. I will tell him.
Amiń lạimea. I will tell of you.
Lạị hapạṭińpe. Tell each other.
Lạị chuṭiańme, emoḱam se bań. Tell me finally whether you will give or not.
Lạị cal katha. A tradition, a tale told by a talebearer.
Lạị cal katha ar areć cal daḱ ạdi haḱsoa. Slander and water thrown on one are both very painful.
Lạị oeṭ katha. Hearsay, anything taught or communicated verbally.
Lạị puṭi. To stuff the belly, to gull, to hoax, to cajole, to deceive by false representation.
Mocate lạiaḱ. Word of mouth.
Lạị doho. To give information with a view to future eventualities.
Bań lạiogoḱ lekan katha kana. It is not a story that can be told.
Ma lạioḱpe. Come, tell who you are.
Lạị ṭhikadińae. He told me correctly, he gave me precise information.

Lạiha. An insect resembling the lac insect, found on certain cultivated crops.

Lạị labaṛ. False, deceitful.
Lạị labaṛ katha kana. It is a false statement.

Lạilukṭhạ. Cf. laelokṭha.

Laj. Shame.
Laj sorom bạnuḱtaea. He is shameless.
Laj hõ bạnuḱtama? Do you not even feel shame?

Laja lukạ. Shame, modesty.
Laja lukạ bạnuḱtaea. He has no shame.

Lajak lujuk. } Slow-paced, heavy,
Lajhak lujhuk. } opposite of nimble.
Lajak lujuk bae dạṛ daṛeaḱkana.

Lajao. } To be ashamed, to be con-
Lajao paṛa. } scious of shame, dis-
Lajao paṛao. } grace, or humiliation; shame, sense of shame or disgrace.
Lajao bạnuḱtaea. He has no sense of shame.
Lajaoḱkanae. He is ashamed.
Uni do bes lajaoḱ kuṛi kanae. She is a good modest girl.
Hoṛ talareń lajao paṛaoena. I am disgraced in the presence of other people.
Noa do ạdi lajao paṛa katha kana. This a shameful story.
Eken ti calaḱ ạdi lajao paṛań aṭkareda. I am ashamed to go empty handed.
Roṛ lajaoeako. They will expose and disgrace him.

Lajao baha. A sensitive plant.

Laj baj. Ill-will, ill-feeling, quarrel.
Lajbajre alom tahena. Do not harbour ill-feeling.

Lajbajhi. } To be ensnared, inveigled,
Lajbajhao. } decoyed, entrapped, seduced, entangled.
Lajbajhao tahẽenako. They got entangled (with boon companions) and remained behind.
Mokordomarekin lajbajhaoakana. They are entangled in a law suit.

Lajbij. To be ashamed, to feel disgraced.
Lajbijoḱae. He will be ashamed.
Lajbij bạnuḱtaea. He has no sense of shame.
Uniaḱ lajbij do setae jomkeṭtaea. A dog ate up all his sense of shame (he has none left.)

Lajhar. Busy, filled full, fully occupied, no time or space available for other purposes.
Ạdi lajhar menaḱtińa. I am very busy.
Noa khuṛpi ạdi lajhargea, ṭhão bạnuḱan. This room is packed full, there is no unoccupied space.

Lajhuṅ lajhuṅ. } Cf. lajuṅ lajuṅ.
Lujhuṅ lujhuṅ.

Lajkhauka. M. } Shameless, immodest.
Lajkhauki. F.

Lajuṅ lajuṅ. } Slow-paced, unweildy, heavy, inactive. Cf lajak lujuk.
Lujuṅ lujuṅ.

Laḱ. To dress or pare wood with an adz or axe, to cut, trim or pare with a kudali or hoe.

Are laḱ. To trim the ridges of rice fields.
Kharai laḱ. To pare the place intended for a threshing floor.
Kaṭ laḱ. To cut or pare wood.

Lak. A hundred thousand.

Lakać lukuć. Weak, applied to weakness of the loins.

Ḍanḍa lakać lukućiṅ ṣikauеda. I feel weak in the loins.
Ḍanḍa hasote lakać lukujoḱkanae. Owing to a pain he is weak in the loins.

Lakar lakar. To protrude the tongue with thirst, as a dog; to be faint with thirst.

Lakaṛ lukuṛ. } To tremble owing to nervousness, to totter, to tremble, to shake, as in ague.
Lukuṛ lukuṛ.

Lakaṛ lukuṛe taṛama. He trembles as he walks.
Ti lukuṛ lukuṛ hilauḱkantaea. His hand shakes owing to nervousness.

Lakar phakar. } Tired, wearied worn out or fatigued before work, &c. has been finished.
Lokor phokor.

Dāṛā dāṛātele lakar phakarena. We are tired out with walking and yet have not completed our journey.

Lakaṛ thakaṛ. Tired, fatigued.

Ṅir ṅirteṅ lakaṛ thakaṛena. I am tired with running.

Lakaṛ thukuṛ. } Weak through age or illness.
Lukuṛ thukuṛ.

Lakaṛ thukuṛ bae kami daṛeaḱkana, haṛam hoṛ do.

Lake lake.
Lakhe lakhe. } Carefully, with discrimination, gently.
Lake loke.
Loke loke.

Lake lake taṛamme. Walk carefully.

Lakelak. Hundreds of thousands.

Lakelak hoṛ. Hundreds of thousands of people.

Laker. } Habit, to be efficient, to master, to shew aptitude for anything, to be proficient in anything.
Lakir.

Kombṛo reaḱ laker bae bagi idia. He will not give up the habit of thieving.
Apattete kombṛoea, hopon hō ona laker hōe saba. The father steals, the son also contracts the same habit.
Bese lakirakaṭa. He is proficient.
Oloḱ bese lakirakaṭa. He has mastered writing well, (he is a proficient writer.)

Lakh. A hundred thousand.

Lakhao. To be apparent, to be visible, to be known.

Hoṛ then bae lakhaoḱa. He will not shew himself to people.
Auriye lakhaoḱa. She does not yet shew signs (of being with calf.)
Auriye lakhaoḱa. The signs of puberty are not yet apparent.

Lakhi. M. } Lucky, fortunate. Cf. lukhi'
Lukhi. F.

Lakir. Cf. laker.

Laki. } A brass vessel used to cook in.
Luki.

Laklak. } To grow luxuriantly, to grow quickly.
Laklakao.

Laklak naṛiḱkana. It is growing luxuriantly, as a climbing plant.
Laklak hara gotenae. He shot up.
Dare laklakaoena. The tree has grown luxuriantly.

Laklakao. To crave or long for, as for food or liquor.

Jel lagiṭe laklakaoḱkana. He is longing for flesh meat.

Laklakia. Tall and slim.

Laklakia hara goṭenae. He quickly grew tall.

Lakop. To roll food into a ball and take a large mouthful of it, a big mouthful.

Miṭ lakop gane emadiṅa. He gave me about a mouthful.

Lakophoko. } Applied to the sound produced when any thick substance is boiling and bubbling, to breathe heavily, as a person or animal out of breath with exertion.
Lokophoko.

Laṅga bana lokophokoe hećaṭlea. The tired bear came at us breathing heavily.
Jondra daka hedejoḱa lakophoko. The Indian corn porridge sounds *lakophoko* when boiling.

Lakphak. } To bubble when boiling, as of any thick substance.
Lakphakao.

Lakphak hedejoḱkana. It is boiling and bubbling producing the sound *lakphak, lakphak.*
Lakphakaoḱ kana. It is bubbling and making a sound resembling *lakphak, lakphak.*

Lakphak. } To be worn out, as through
Lakphakao. } hunger, thirst, &c.
Daḱ tetańte lakphakaoenań. I am worn out with thirst.

Lakṭha. } To be at variance, to dispute,
Lokṭha. } to altercate, to lay adverse claim to, to quarrel.
Nukin do matkom darerekin lakṭhaakana. These two are quarrelling over a matkom (q. v.) tree.
Nui do okoe tuluć hõ bae lokṭhaḱa. He never quarrels with any one.

Lakṭha. A long pole.
Lakṭha ḍań. A measuring rod.
Mać lakṭha. A bamboo pole, used mainly to knock down fruit from trees.

Lạkuć lạkuć. Applied to the jerking at both ends of a long, pliant body as a bamboo, to jerk, short sudden movement.
Lạkuć lạkuće tarama. He walks jerkingly, (as a person with a stiff thigh joint or a wooden leg.)
Mać lạkuć lạkuće goḱ idieda. The bamboo jerks at either end as he carries it away on his shoulder.

Lạkuć. To bend down, to hang over, to dangle.

Lạkuḱ phạkuḱ. Toothless, as having no teeth; to mumble, as a toothless person eating.
Lạkuḱ phạkuḱe jomeda. He mumbles (when eating.)
Ḍaṭa rạpuć cabaentaete lạkuḱ phạkuḱenae. Owing to his teeth having all fallen out he mumbles.

Lakum. To chew, to put into the mouth and chew.
Mihũ kicriće lạkumtama. The calf will chew your cloth.

Lal. A kind of precious stone.

Lala. A sub-division of the Hindu Writer-caste of Kayasths.

Lala. A drain, a ditch, a small water course. Cf. nala.

Lalae. Time, hour.
Tikin lalaekoteye seṭerena. He arrived about the hour of noon.

Lalak. } To shew off, as one shewing
Lolok. } what he can do in dancing, to cut a figure.
Lalake uduḱeda. He is shewing off.

Lalao. } To long for, to hunger for, to
Lalkao. } be tantalized, to be destitute.
Bengeéte lalaokećbona. He made us long for food (kept us waiting.)
Gidrań lalaokećkoań. I kept the children longing for their food.

Lala lạli. To long for, to hunger for, to be impatient, to be destitute.
Jom lạgić lala lạli baṛaekanae. He is impatient to begin to eat.

Lalạuwer. Cf. lawer.

Lalca lạlci. } Covetous, greedy, to be-
Lạlci. } covetous or greedy.
Ạḍi lalca lạlci hoṛ kanae. He is a very covetous person.
Alom lalca lạlcia. Do not be covetous.

Lalca. M. } Covetous, envious, greedy.
Lạlci. F. }

Lale. To force oneself in or forward, impelled by a strong desire.
Merom bhiḍiko laleakana The goats and sheep have forced a way in.
Sojheko laleḱkana. They are pressing forward.
Boge ọcoḱko laleḱkan tahẽkana. They were pressing forward to be healed.

Lalhar. To disproportion, disproportionately much, wide apart.
Buluńpe lalharkeda. You have put in too much salt.
Pạhilpe lalharkeda onate bań anṭaolena. At first you gave disproportionately, therefore there was not enough for all.
Lalharaḱ racreye aderkeda, onate kicrić do etańena. He passed (the threads of the warp) through a wide toothed reed, and therefore the cloth is thin (or open.)
Haḱṭińre lalharkedae. In dividing he gave disproportionately much.

Lalejańje. To hang about in hope of getting food.
Noakore ạḍi hoṛko lalejańje baṛaekana. Many people are hanging about here in hope of getting food.

Lalkao. To coax, to wheedle, to desire eagerly, to long for.
Jom lạgićko lalkaoḱkana. They are eagerly desiring food.

Lalkar. To coax, to wheedle, to inveigle, to cajole.
Lalkar idiećkoako hoṛ hanka nhanka ńamoḱa. They cajole people into going (saying) this and that will be received.

Laloc. To covet, covetousness.
Alom lalockoa. Do not covet them.
Am phedren hoṛaḱ oṛaḱ alom lalocaḱa. Do not covet thy neighbour's house.

Laloci. } Covetous.
Lalocịa. }
Lalocịa hoṛ kanae. He is a covetous man.

Lalsa lạlsi. To complain against each other.
Lalsa lạlsiḱkanakin. These two are complaining against each other.

Lamak'. The fruit of a large jungle climber, *Bauhinia Vahlii*, W. & A.

Lamak' lar. The bast fibre yielded by *Bauhinia Vahlii, W. & A.*
Lamak' here. One half of the inner empty pod of Bauhinia Vahlii.
Jom lar. } The huge jungle climber, *Bauhinia* Vahlii, *W. & A.*, which yields the *Lamak'* fruit.
Lamak' lar. }

Lamak'. To gash, to cut deeply.
Nok'če iń lamak'ena. See, I have got gashed.

Lambać lumbuć. Leisurely. Cf lambhać lumbhuć.

Lambao. To decay, to go bad, to begin to rot.
Ul bele lambaoena. The ripe mango has begun to decay.
Buḍhi doe lambaok'kana. The old woman has begun to decay (begun to break up.)

Lambe. Self-sown, growing from seed that has fallen from ripe grain in the field.
Lambe horo. Dhan that has grown from seed which has fallen at harvest.

Lambeć. To crouch, to couch, as a beast of prey.
Kulko lambedok'a. Tigers couch.

Lambhać lumbhuć. Leisurely.
Lambhać lumbhuće calak'kana. He moves leisurely.

Lambhuạ. Jocular, humorous, funny.

Lambo. To be over-ripe, to be middle aged and unmarried.
Bele lamboena. It is over ripe
Uni doe lambok'kana. She is passing the flower of her age (and is still unmarried.)

Lạmbri. Slow, tardy, falling behind, unable to keep pace with others.
Cećreye lạmbrikeda? What has detained him?

Lamjak'. Unserviceable, insipid, tasteless, savourless.
Sea lamjak'ena. It is so rotten as to be unserviceable.
Isin lamjak'ena. It has been cooked to insipidity.

Lamka. M. } Tall, tall and lank.
Lạmki. F. }
Lạmki ạimại. A tall lank woman.

Lamka lạkuć. To hang down or over.
Gurok' lamka lạkućena.
Mać lamka lạkućkedae. He cut the bamboo (half through) and made it hang over.

Lamkamarịạ. Idle, passing time idly and in fun, frivolous.
Lamkamarịạ hor kanae. He is a person given to frivolity

Lamkambạri. } Funny, hnmorous, jocular, idle.
Lamkambạrịạ. }
Lamkambạri katha. A funny joke.
Lamkambạrịạ hor. A humorist, a funny man.

Lamoṭ. Lazy and dissolute, lewd.

Lampoṭ. }
Lampoṭia. } Lazy and dissolute, lewd.
Lampoṭia. }

Lampoṭ eneć. A dance indulged in by men when passing the night in a hunting camp.

Lampoṭ sereń. Songs sung when engaged in the *Lampoṭ* (q. v.) dance.
These songs are of an objectionable character.

Lamṭa. Naked, destitute, poor.

Lanban. }
Landband. } To act as a money lender or grain lender, to trade, to buy and sell, to transact business, to act as steward or factotum.
Lonbon. }
Londbond. }
Landbandić. A steward, a trader.
Nuiak' ạdi lanban menak'taea. This man has much money (or grain) invested, or has large commercial transactions.
Ạdiye lanbaneda. He has large investments, or he lends money (or grain) largely.

Lanḍ. M. } A defiance used in answer to threats.
Lanḍi. F. }
Lanḍkedińae? Did he do for me?
Lanḍiledińam, okorem otaledińa? Did you do for me? did you press me down?

Land. } To laugh, to smile.
Landa. }
Landkanako. They are laughing.
Landa sạgại. The relationship between sister-in-law, and brother in law, grandparents and grand children, uncle and nephew or niece.
According to Santal ideas a sister-in-law may laugh at her brother-in-law, and a grand child at its grandsire, and a nephew or niece at his or her uncle, the relationship between these is, therefore, called the laughing relationship. Cf. sạgại.
Landa katha. A joke, anything not said in earnest.
Bor land. Frivolity, speaking and laughing.
Landawadeako. They laughed at him, they mocked him.
Landa landate sạriak'kedae. He took the joke in earnest.
Landa jońkanako. They are laughing.
Landa landae koeyekana. He is asking from her for a joke.

Lanḍa lonḍo. } To stare with wide open eyes, to have big staring eyes.
Lonḍo lonḍo. }
Landa londoe bengeṭadińa. He stared at me (angrily.)

Landbhand. } To defile.
Londbhond. }
Onde dak ohoń ńulea, sanamko landbhandkeda.

Landbhandao. To decay, to meet with adverse fortune, ruin, calamity, &c.
Noko hoṛko landbhandaoena. These people are decayed (become poor.)
Noa atoren sanamko landbhandaoena. All the people of this village have fallen on evil days.

Landha. Stubble, poor.
Landha hoṛ then cetem ńama? What can you get from a poor man?
Hoṛo landha. Rice stubble.

Landha phuciạ. Lazy, a sluggard, poor, destitute.
Nui landha phuciạ ạsulokae? Will this sluggard earn a living?

Landha galoć. A species of bird, a hunting term applied to small birds in general.

Lạndhiạ. }
Lạndhuạ. } Lazy, sluggish, inactive.
Londhiạ. }
Nui doe lạndhiạgea. This (person) is lazy.

Lạndhu. To lay low, to cause to lie flat, as growing grain, grass, &c., to break, or transgress, as a law.
Hapṛamkoak lebet lạndhutele hecena. We came following in the path our fathers trod.
Nokǒe nondeko lebet lạndhuakata. See here! they have trodden it down (as grass in a path.)
Hoṛo hoete lạndhuena. The dhan has been laid low by the wind.
An lạndhu. To break or transgress a law.
Noa kathae lạndhukeda. He did not respect this order.

Lạndhuạ. Lazy, sluggish, inactive.
Lạndhuạ hoṛ kanae. He is a lazy man.

Lạndup. To fall in, to collapse.
Lạndup micena. It has collapsed into a heap.
Tạru lạndupentaea.
Ot laṛaolenre ạdi then lạndup boloena. At the earthquake many places fell in.

Lạnduṛ. To fall down, to collapse as a wall, house, &c.; to throw down, as a house, wall, &c.
Oṛak lạnduṛentakoa. Their house has fallen in.
Lạnduṛ bhit. A collapsed wall.
Lạnduṛoka nahak. It will collapse presently.

Lạndur bhạndur. } To destroy, to ruin;
Lạndur bạndur. } careless, feckless, not putting one's mind to anything.
Sanam kạmiko lạndur bhạndurketina. They ruined all my work.
Lạndur bhạndurgeae, bes do bae kạmia. He is careless, he does not work well.

Lạndur dhiṅ. A stripling, a lad about 14 years of age.

Laṅ. Abbreviated form of alaṅ (q. v.)
Alaṅ calakalaṅ. } We two will go.
Alaṅlaṅ calaka. }
Dalketlaṅae. He struck us two.

Laṅcaṅ. }
Laṅcạṅgiạ. } Foppish and dissolute.
Jāhā seć dhol sadeko aṅjoma, onteko calaka laṅcạṅgiạ do. Wherever they hear the sound of a drum, there the dissolute fops go.

Laṅga. To be tired, to be fatigued, to be worn out, as an old person, to be very ill.
Laṅga haron. Fatigue and worry.
Reṅgećte laṅgaenae. He is worn out through hunger.
Kạmi kạmite laṅgaenae. He is fatigued with continued labour.
Uni haṛam doe laṅgaena. That old man is worn out.
Laṅgakedeaṅ. I fatigued him.
Laṅga marao. To rest, to drive away fatigue.
Niạ laṅga marao leka gele emamkana. We are giving you this (a small quantity of food or liquor) only to drive away fatigue.
Laṅgakako nahak. They will tire presently.
Ruạ laṅgaakanae. He is dangerously ill with fever.

Laṅgaṭ. To be in want of clothing, to be naked.
Kicriċtele laṅgaṭakana. We are in want of clothing.
Laṅgaṭgeae. He is in need of clothing.
Laṅgaṭokale. We will be in want of clothing.

Laṅka. }
Loṅka. } Distant, very far away.
Ạki laṅkatem senlena. You went very far away.

Laṅlaṅ. } Shirking work, standing idle
Loṅloṅ. } when others are working.
Laṅlaṅe teṅgoakana. She is idling when the others are busily engaged.

Laṅṭa. M. }
Laṅṭi. } F. } Naked, to become naked,
Luṅṭi. } to strip off clothing.
Laṅṭa sar. A featherless arrow.
Laṅṭakedeako. They stripped him of his clothing.

Laṅtiti. A small bird, the Indian Paradise Flycatcher, *Terpsiphone Paradise.*

Laolokṭa. } To quarrel, to dispute, to
Laolokṭha. } be at variance.
Alope laolokṭhaka. Do not quarrel.

Laoṭa. A net for catching birds.
This method of catching birds is resorted to in the hot weather when water is scarce. The net is fixed at a place where the birds come to drink.

Laowao. To divide, to share, to make into shares.

Khạsiko laowaoakadea. They have divided the (carcase of the) goat into shares.

Laḅ. } To catch with both hands, as
Laḅlaḅ. } a ball thrown.

Laḅ mente loka daramedae. He catches it ere it (a ball) reaches the ground.
Laḅlaḅe lokaeda. He catches (the balls) before they reach the ground.

Lapa dhopa. Large pieces, large clusters.

Lapa dhopako geṭakaṭa. They have cut it into big pieces.
Matkom lapa dhopa geleakana. The *matkom* tree has large clusters of flowers.
Ul lapa dhopa joakana. The mangoe fruit is in large clusters.

Lạpại. The Reciprocal form of lại (q. v.), to speak together, to consult, to discuss.

Oṛaḱre lạpạipe. Discuss this matter at home.
Lạpại joḿkanako. They are consulting together.

Lapaḱ capaḱ. To exaggerate, to squash or flatten, to flatten, as a ripe fruit, drop of water, &c. falling.

Onte note lapaḱ capaḱe lại baṛaedạ. He is spreading exaggerated reports every where.
Dare khon daḱ lapaḱ capaḱ ńuroḱkana. Large drops of rain are falling from the tree.
Bele kuindi lapaḱ capaḱ ńuroḱkana. The ripe fruits of the Mohwa tree are falling and squashing (on the ground.)
Lapaḱ capaḱ gạiko ić idiakaṭa.

Lapaḱ lapaḱ. } A thudding or flopping
Lapaḱ lopoḱ. } sound produced by something soft falling.

Lapaḱ lapaḱ ńuroḱkana ul bele. The ripe mangoes fall thudding.

Lapaḱ mente. } With a flop.
Lapaḱ marte. }

Lapaḱ mente ńurena. It fell with a flop.
Lapaḱ marte ńurhạena. It fell with a sudden flop.

Lapaḱ marạo. To strike with something soft, as a ball of clay.

Lapaḱ maraokedeae. He hit him flop (with a ball of soft clay.)

Lapa lopo. } To move slowly, as a young
Lipạ lape. } bird learning to fly, without confidence.

Lapa lopoe taṛameda. He walks slowly.
Lipạ lape udạuḱkanae. It is flying slowly (as a young bird unaccustomed in the use of its wings.)

Lạpạlis. The Reciprocal form of lạlis (q. v.)

Lạpạṛhại. The Reciprocal form of laṛhại (q. v.)

Lapaṛkaḱ. } Contracted stomach, shrun-
Lapaṛkaṭ. } ken stomach through hunger; with an empty stomach.

Lapaṛkaṭe gitićakana. He is lying with a shrunken stomach.

Lapar lapar. } Thin, thin and flapping,
Lạpur lạpur. } as an elephant's ears.

Hạthi lutur lapar lapar geṭakoa. An elephant's ears are thin and flapping.
Lapar lapar piṭhạ. Very thin cakes of bread.

Lapar loṅgaṭ. } Lanky, slim and feeble.
Lapaṛ loṅgaṭ. }

Lapaṭić. An affection of the eyelids, etropium or inversion of the eyelids.

Lapaṭićko jomekana. He is suffering from inversion of the eyelids.

Lapaṭ lupuṭ. To lift the feet slowly, as old people or as a woman wearing heavy anklets.

Lapaṭ lupuṭe taṛameda. She walks slowly.

Lapco. Loquacious, exaggerating, talkative.

Lapeć. To put into the mouth, as natives of India do food, a mouthful, a handful.

Mić lapećko emadińa. They gave me a mouthful.
Lapeć lapedme. Eat it up quickly.

Lapha. Profit, to make a profit.

Lapha bạnuḱan. There is no profit.
Ninạkiń laphaakaṭa. I have made so much profit.

Lapha dopha. Large pieces, large clusters. Cf. lapa dhopa.

Laphaṅ. High, long, round-about; to prolong, to protract.

Aḍi laphaṅre joakana. It has fruited on the high branches.
Aḍi laphaṅte ạcurakana. It goes round a long way (a road.)
Ukilko do mokordomako laphaṅ idieda. The lawyers protract lawsuits.

Laphao. To stretch out the arm. *Scottice*, 'rax'.

Ma laphao ṅogoḱme. Stretch out your arm a little.
Laphao tiogme. Stretch your arm and touch it.

Lạphuạ. Humorous, having the power of imitating others, entertaining, amusing, jocular.

Lapickak F. } Corpulent, broad, big
Lapockak. } M. } and flat, occupying
Lapocak. } much space, used mainly in abuse.

Kulai adi marah lapocake oborakana. The hare is lying big and flat.

Lapir jadir. Very stout, fat and squat, of females.

Adi lapir jadire benaoakana. She has become extremely fat.
Mase, uni aimai ńeleme, tinak lapir jadire motaakana. I say, look at that woman how extremely stout she is.

Lapit. A barber, the Hindu Barber caste of Napit or Lapit.

Lapka. } To fight in the air, as two
Lapkao. } birds; to throw a stick to hit another stick that has been thrown up.

Ńelme, cotrekin lapkaokkana. Look, they are fighting in the air.
Ma thengabo lapkaea. Come, we will throw up a stick into the air and throw our sticks at it.

Lap. } To catch with both hands,
Laplap. } as a ball.

Lap mente loka daramedae. He catches it ere it (a ball) reaches the ground.
Laplape lokaeda. He catches (the balls) before they reach the ground.

Laplap. To flap the wings as large birds when flying.

Phäkräke laplapeda. It is flapping its wings.

Laplapa. Broad and horizontal, to extend horizontally. Cf. lablaba.

Cërë phäkräke laplapaakata. The bird has stretched out its wings.
Laplapa patrako rokakata. They have pinned (the leaves together) into broad and flat leaf plates.

Laplonde. Slightly, to dirty with dust, as the body, clothes, &c.

Kicricko laplondeakata.
Cet lekae dakakata? dhuri laplondeakatae.
Huruh laplondeakatae.
Pithe gur tulue laplondekateko joma.

Lapondań. } Flat, flat and extended,
Lapordań. } covering a large area,
Lopodań. } occupying much space.

Lapondańe durupakana. He sits spread out.

Lapot. Dewlap of bullock, gills of turkey.

Lapot ghäs. }
Lapotiań ghäs. } A common grass, *Panicum humile, Nees.*
Lopotiań ghäs. }

Lapotiań up. } Fine hairs on the body.
Lopotiań up. }

Lapos. } Soft, as an overripe fruit,
Lapos lapos. } the feeling when eat-
Lopos lopos. } ing anything soft, pulpy.

Lapos lapos aikaukkana. It feels soft (to the eating.)
Lapos lapose jomeda. He eats it easily from its being soft.

Lapra. } M. }
Lapra. } } Having hanging ears, as a
Lapri. } F. } dog, goat, &c., lop-eared.
Lapri. }

Lapra kode. A variety of *Eleusine corocana, Gaertn.* Cf. kode.

Lapra horo. A species of tortoise so called.

Lapre. Slow, sluggish, inactive, lazy, applied to females only.

Nui aimai lapregese. This woman is slow.

Lapre hatak cërë. A small bird so named.

Lapri. } Lop-eared, having hanging
Lapri. } ears, as a goat, &c., applied to females only. Cf. lapra.

Lapsi. } A method of cooking the
Kode lapsi. } grain of *Eleusine corocana, Gaertn.* Cf. kode.

Lapta lapti. Rolling or tumbling over each other on the ground.

Lapta laptikin tapamena. They fought and tumbled over each other.

Laptao. To drag one in, as into a scrape; to become an accomplice, to get mixed up with.

Laptao mitkedeako. They dragged him into it along with themselves.

Lapuk. A method of sifting or winnowing.

Hatakteko lapuga. They sift with the *hatak'* (q. v.)
Lapuk gidikam. Sift it out.

Lapuk capuk. } Loquacious, unable to
Labuk capuk. } keep a secret, given to exaggeration.

Lapuk capuke galmaraoa. He exaggerates, or he tells everything.

Lapur lapur. To hang down or over the edge.

Lapur lapur aturakana. (The cloth) is hanging down over the edge.

Lar. A string, as of beads, once round, as a chain.
Bar lar mala. A necklace of two strings of beads.
Bar lar sikṛi. Twice round of a chain.
Mit̕ lar mala. One string of beads.
Lar upạr larko udạuk̕kana. } They are flying
Larke larko udạuk̕kana. } string upon string (as birds when migrating.)

Laṛ. *Membrum virile.*

Laṛ. Bast or bass fibre, the fibrous inferior layer of the bark of trees.
Baṛe laṛ. The bast fibre of the Banyan tree.
Jom laṛ. The bast fibre of Banhinia Vahlii.
Jom laṛ. A huge jungle climber, *Bauhinia Vahlii. W. & A.*
Cihũṭ laṛ. A large jungle climber, *Spatholobus Roxburghii, Benth.*
Noa reak̕ laṛok̕a, se baṅa? Will this yield a bast fibre, or not?
Laṛteć iń chạḍaoa. I will separate the bast fibre (from this bark.)
Laṛteko tola. They tie it with bast fibre.

Laṛ. A serpent.
Laṛ joteć̕akawadea. A snake has bitten him.

Laṛ biń. A species of snake inhabiting hills.

Laṛa. M. } Horns pointing downwards,
Laṛi. F. } having the hair tied in a knot at one side of the head instead of at the back.
Laṛa ḍaṅra. A bullock with drooping horns.
Lạṛi gại. A cow with drooping horns.
Laṛa sut̕akanae. He has his hair tied in a knot on one side of the head.
Lạṛi sut̕akanae. She has her hair tied in a knot on one side of her head.
Maejiu lạṛi laṛiko sut̕akana. The women have their hair knotted on the side of the head.
Herel laṛa laṛako sut̕akana. The men have the hair tied in a knot on one side of the head.

Laraha. Remaining lean although well fed.
Laraha ḍaṅra kanae. It is a bullock that will not fatten.

Laraṅ laraṅ. } Remaining lean although
Liriṅ liriṅ. } well fed, applied mainly to children.

Laṛaṅ laṛaṅ. To hang down, as the tongue of a bell, &c.
Laṛaṅ laṛaṅ ạturakana lạṛuteć. The tongue of the bell hangs down.

Laṛaṅka. Tall and stout.
Khub laṛaṅka juạn kanae. He is a fine tall, stout youth.

Laṛaṅkar. Fighting, quarrelsome.
Ạḍi laṛaṅkar hoṛ kanae. He is a great fighting man.

Laṛaṅ pataṅ. To sway backwards and forwards, as a pendulum, to be without a *bhagwa (q. v.)*

Laṛao. To shake, to move, to exert oneself.
Alom laṛaok̕a, thirkok̕me. Do not move, keep still.
Ato khon alom laṛaok̕a. Do not leave the village.
Nui kisạṛ ṭhen khon alom laṛaok̕a. Do not leave this employer.
Laṛaolenenam paṛaok̕a. You must first work before you can eat.
Jaṅga bae laṛao daṛeak̕kana. He cannot move his feet.
Nes calaoen din ot laṛaolena. Last year there was an earthquake.

Laṛbaṛao. To stammer, Cf. laṛkhaṛao; to become poor.
Laṛbaṛaoenae. He has become poor.

Laṛbaṛia. Deficient in stamina, or intelligence.
Laṛbạṛiạgeae, keṭeć do baṅ. He is deficient in stamina, he is not hardy.

Larbhad. Luck, fortune, fate.
Iṅak̕ larbhad menak̕tiṅkhan tahengea. If it is my luck it will remain (not be lost.)

Laṛbhad. Applied to the sound produced by a long, soft body falling, as a snake; also to that produced by a hard body striking something soft, as the hoofs of an animal on soft soil.
Laṛbhad maraoenae. He fell down with a flop.
Dạṛ idiedae laṛbhad laṛbhad. He is running away thud thudding.

Laṛbhad marte. } With a flop.
Laṛbhad mente. }
Laṛbhad marteye bindạṛena. He fell with a flop.

Laṛbuk̕. To be tired, wearied, fatigued.
Duṛuṕ lạṛbuk̕enae. He is tired sitting.

Laṛbuṅ. To hang the head, to hang loosely, to become feeble. Cf. lạbṛuṅ.

Laṛcaṛ. } To shake, to move, to use, to
Loṛcoṛ. } handle, to administer, to employ.
Alom laṛcaṛa. Do not move.
Kãc do ạḍi ṭhasạhagea, ona iạte bes okoćteko loṛcoṛa. Glass is very brittle, and for that reason it is handled carefully.

Laṛea. Crooked, applied to trees.

Laṛga. M. } Tall, long.
Laṛgi. F. }
Laṛga ḍaṅ. A long pole.
Laṛga bạnduk. A long gun.
Laṛga lạṛgikin heṅena. The tall man and the tall woman have come.

Laṛga.
Luṛga.
Luṛgau. } To poke with a stick or pole, as an animal in a den, cave or hole.

Laṛga toḱkedeako. **They poked him out with a long stick.**

Laṛhai. To fight, to quarrel, to be at feud with each other

Laṛhai kanakin. **They are fighting.**
Laṛhai do reḱhgeoa. **A feud brings poverty.**
Ạdi din khonkin laṛhaikana. **They have been at feud with each for a very long time.**

Laṛia paṛia.
Naṛia paṛia. } Reluctantly, with much beseeching, with great exertion.

Laṛia paṛia emoḱae. **He gives reluctantly.**
Laṛia paṛia miť goṭećiń ńamlaḱa. **I got one with much beseeching.**

Larjar.
Larjor. } Related by marriage. Cf. lorjor.

Laṛka baha. A favourite flower with Santals, *Amarantus paniculatus, Miq.*

Laṛka Munḍa.
Laṛka Kol. } A section of the Ho tribe who inhabit Singbhum in Choṭa Nagpur.

Laṛka paṛka. Children, children, and other such belongings.

Laṛkać luṛkuć. The feeling as of a swollen gland which when pressed moves, to move, as a broken limb when twisted.

Laére laṛkać luṛkuće ṡikạueda. **He feels a twisting in his stomach.**

Larkao. To fall behind.

Kạmi larkaoentaea. **His work has fallen behind.**

Laṛkuć. To move or bend, as a limb; to hang loosely, to dangle.

Ti laṛkućtam. **Move your arm.**
Maḱ laṛkućkedako. **They cut it (half through) and caused it to hang dangling.**

Laṛkhaṛao. To stammer, as one very much afraid when speaking.

Botorte laṛkhaṛaoḱkanae. **He stammers through fear.**
Harta luṭi miť ghaṛitege laṛkhaṛaoena.

Larlarao. To be eager for, to crave for.

Jom lagiť larlaraoḱkanae. **He is eager to eat.**
Jom lagiť larlarao baṛaekanae. **He is eager to get something to eat.**

Larlaṛia.
Larlaṛia. } Very slender, lanky.

Nui do larlaṛiae haraakana. **He has grown up very lanky.**
Larlaṛia hara goṭena. **It shot up very slender (a tree.)**

Laṛoe cakoe.
Laṛo cako.
Laṛoṕ cakoṕ } To move the jaws or mouth, as when eating, to munch.

Moca laṛoe cakoetege tahẹntaea. **His jaws keep moving continually.**
Jom kombṛoedae laṛoe cakoe.

Laṛpa. Lean, lank, tall and lanky, with depressed stomach, flat, as certain fruit pods.

Laṛpa hoṛ. **A tall, lanky person.**
Laṛpa jo. **A flat, thin pod.**

Laṛpań. Shrunken stomach.

Laṛpańe gitićakana. **He is lying with a shrunken stomach.**

Laṛu. The tongue of a bell.

Laṛuạ. To wither, to fade.

Sakam laṛuạena. **The leaf is withered.**

Laṛuć baṛuć. To shirk work.

Laṛuć baṛuć baṛaekanae bae kạmikana. **He keeps out of the way, he is not working.**

Laṛuć baṛuć.
Laṛuć paṭuć. } Naked, as a child.

Laṛum. To put a small quantity of food into the mouth.

Laṛuń. To dangle, to hang loosely, as the tongue of a bell, or the loose coupling of a wagon.

Laṛuń laṛuń. To dangle or sway backwards and forwards, as the tongue of a bell.

Lasaḱ pasaḱ. Sticky, uncomfortable feeling of the skin, mainly in the hot weather; over cooked, or over ripe, so as to be insipid.

Lasaḱ pasaḱ aṭkaroḱkana hoṛmo. **The body feels sticky.**

Lasaṅga.
Lasaṅgate. } On account of. Cf. losoń.

Gidrạ lasaṅgateń calaḱkan tahẽkana, gidrạ ma bạnugić.

Lasãṛhẽ.
Lasãṛhẽte. } On account of, for this reason, owing to, on the pretext of, through.

Am lasãṛhẽteń ńamkeda. **It is owing to you that I received.**
Kokoe lasãṛhẽteye hećakana. **He has come on the pretext of begging.**
Ceť lasãṛhẽte bań calaḱa? **For what reason should I go?**

Lasar lasar. Talkative, loquacious, garrulous, glib-tongued, applied to females.

Aége lasar lasaroḱkanạe. **She does all the talking herself.**

Laser. Sharp, keen, as the edge of a cutting instrument.
Laser sar. A sharp arrow.
Teṅgoć uruṭ laserme. Grind the axe sharp.
Ňu laserenae. The liquor has loosed his tongue.
Jom laserenae. He ate and is strengthened.
Adi moca laserok̕kantaea. His tongue is being loosed, he is becoming very talkative.

Lasgar. Good, juicy, savoury.
Khub lasgar jel kana. This is first class meat.
Lasgarge tekeme. Cook it so that the juice may be retained.
Aṛak̕ lasgargeko tekeakaṭa. They have cooked the vegetables in a savoury manner.

Laskal. To mate without the usual proprieties.
Ghanṭabaṛi laskalakin nukin do.

Laskao. To be entangled, to stick, to be caught, as a stick &c. that has been thrown into a tree.
Uni hoṛe laskao tahẽna. That man was caught and remained there.
Ulin̕ capaṭeṭ tahẽkana, ṭheṅga laskao tahẽntiña. I was throwing at mangoes, and my stick was caught and stuck (in the branches.)

Laskar. } **Lasker.** } Numerous, in crowds, a crowd, an army.
Adi laskarko heċakana bariat do. A very large marriage party has come.
Adi laskar menak̕lea jojomko. We are many mouths to feed.

Laslasa. Occupying much space, spread out.
Laslasae gitiċakana. He is lying stretched out.
Laslasae duṛupakana. He is occupying much space as he is sitting.

Lasok̕. } **Lasok̕ lasok̕.** } To bite, to take mouthfulls, to gobble, applied to animals.
Adi lasok lasok̕e jomeda. He is gobbling.
Pusi oċẽe lasok̕kedea. The cat seized the bird with its mouth.
Bana lasok̕kedeae. The bear bit him.

Laspas. } **Laspasao.** } Muddy, to make muddy.
Laspas aṭkarok̕kana. It feels muddy.
Lebeṭ laspasaokedako. They trampled it into mud.

Lasra M. } **Lasri.** } **Lasro.** } F. } Talkative, garrulous, loquacious.

Lasrao. To smear, to plaster, to daub.
Gidra dakako lasrao joma. Children smear themselves when eating cooked rice.
Bhit paṛak̕akan ṭhen lasrao eseṭkam. Plaster over the cracked place in the wall.

Lasri. } **Lasro.** } Talkative, garrulous, loquacious, applied to females.
Lasri mara simsi. A glib tongued hussy.

Laṭ. To wrap up in leaves for the purpose of cooking.
Laṭ jel. Flesh meat wrapped up in leaves and roasted in ashes.
Laṭ hako. Fish wrapped in leaves and roasted in ashes.
Laṭ aṛak̕. Vegetables wrapped in leaves and cooked in ashes.
Laṭ rapak̕kateko jomkeda. They wrapped it in leaves and then roasted and ate it.

Laṭ. To be tied, as the tongue; tied.
Alaṅ laṭentaea. He is tongue tied.

Laṭ. *Membrum virile.*

Laṭ. Cor, of the English word "lord."
Laṭ saheb. The Viceroy.
Hudiṅ laṭ saheb. The Lieutenant Governor.

Laṭ. } **Laṭlaṭ.** } To stick, sticky.
Laṭ marte iṅak̕ katha lagaoena. My word stuck at once, i. e. my statement produced an instantaneous effect.
Nuiak̕ katha laṭlaṭ lagaok̕taea. This (man's) words stick, i. e. have great effect.
Laṭlaṭge sikṛuk̕kana kicrić. The cloth feels sticky.

Lat. A creaper, a climbing plant.
Latre lopak̕re.

Laṭ Ṭudu. A sub-sept of the Santal sept Ṭudu (q. v.)

Laṭ Baske. A sub-sept of the Santal sept Baske (q. v.)

Laṭ Besra. A sub-sept of the Santal sept Besra (q. v.)

Laṭ Cõṛẽ. A sub-sept of the Santal sept Cõṛẽ (q. v.)

Lata. To be attached to, cling, cleave, adere to.
Nui gidra do goṛomteṭ tuluć adiye latawa. This child is greatly attached to its grandmother.

Laṭae ghoṭae. } **Laṭae goṭae.** } **Leṭae goṭae.** } **Leṭae ghoṭae.** } Dirty, towzled, dishevelled, ruffled, promiscuously, without care as to caste, &c.
Leṭae goṭaeko ńuńukana. They are drinking promiscuously.
Leṭae goṭaeẽnako. They are defiled (by marrying outside the caste.)
Sapha lugṛi sanam laṭae goṭaeye dhuṛikeda. He dirtied the clean cloth with dust.
Niṭkore laṭae ghoṭaeń tahena. I will remain hanging about here.
Laṭae ghoṭaeko baplaena. They contracted an unlawful marriage.
Paura ńukate laṭae ghoṭaeye heċakana. He has been drinking and has come all dishevelled.
Laṭae ghoṭae bań ganok̕ak̕ko gan ooкeda.

Laṭak'. Sticky, a fault, crime, to accuse.

Laṭak' bạnuk'taea. He has no faults.
Begor doste laṭak' lagaoadiñae. He blamed me though innocent.
Iñko laṭak'adiña. They accused me.

Laṭak. } Laṭok. } Hindrance, intervention, event.

Cet' laṭak lagaoente bae heĕlena? What has intervened to prevent his coming.

Laṭak' laṭak'. Sticky, viscous,

Laṭak' laṭak' aṭkarok'kana. It feels sticky.
Nuiak' katha laṭak' laṭak' lagaok'taea. His words stick, i. e. are effective.

Laṭak' paṭak'. Sticky, dry, as the mouth in illness.

Moca laṭak' paṭak' ṣikạuk'kana. My mouth feels dry.

Laṭaṅ. Cf. leṭaṅ.

Latao. To lie in wait, as a beast of prey, tiger, caṭ &c. Cf. lotao.

Laṭao. To grow luxuriantly and promising a good crop.

Khub laṭaoakana hoṛo do. The dhan has grown luxuriantly.

Laṭap. } Laḍap. } To pick up one by one, or in small quantity.

Nasenak'e laḍap baṛaeĕda. He is picking a little (eating very little.)
Ạtiñkanae, se baṅ? Laḍap baṛaeĕdae. Is it grazing, or not? It is picking here and there.

Latar. Under, underneath, below, to put under or underneath.

Dhiri latarre. Under a stone.
Dare latar. Under a tree.
Ot latarenae. He is under the earth, i. e. gone to the lower regions.
Latarkedeako. They put him undermost.
Hara latarkedeako. They outgrew him.
Amak' jaṅga latarreñ tahena. I will remain submissive to you.
Uniak' jaṅga latarenako. They are in subjection to him.
Ot latar dak'. The waters under the earth.
Laċ latarte boloenae. He has become his partizan.
Laċ latarkedeae. He reduced him to submission, or made him his partizan.
Cetan latar. Above and below.
Latar disom. The low country.
Cetan disom. The high country, from which the rivers run.
Latar luṭi. The under lip.

Laṭbalaṅ. All kinds, every kind, many kinds.

Laṭbalaṅe egera. She gives all kinds of abuse.
Laṭbalaṅko eneċa. They dance all kinds of dances.
Laṭbalaṅko teñ dareak'kana. They can weave all kinds (of cloth.)

Laṭea. } Laṭhea. } Lazy, slow in movement, sluggish, crooked.

Laṭea ḍaṅra. A sluggish ox.
Laṭea ṭhenga. A crooked stick.

Lateṛ. } Letaṛ. } Thick, dense, as a forest; clustered thickly, as cobwebs, &c., full, as an apartment of various articles.

Noa horte alope calak'a, ạḍi lateṛgea. Do not go by this road, it is through very dense jungle.
Cal lateṛakana. The roof is covered with clusters of cobwebs.

Laṭ ghaṭ. To mix, to intermix.

Iṣin bhajan alope laṭghaṭa. Do not mix up the cooking pots.

Laṭ ghaṭ. } Laṭ ghạṭi. } Unlawful sexual intercourse, adultery, fornication; to commit adultery or fornication.

Laṭha. To stick to, to be attracted and held.

Rabaṅ dinre seṅgel ṭhen hoṛko laṭhak'a. During the cold weather people are attracted to and held by a fire.

Lathak'. } Lathak' lathak'. } Thick, gummy, viscous.

Laṭha. Birdlime, sticky, adhesive; to catch, as with birdlime.

Susurbaṅko laṭhakoa. They catch wasps by means of birdlime.
Cĕṛĕko laṭha goćena. The birds were caught in the birdlime.
Laṭha ṭhoṅga. A piece of hollow bamboo in which birdlime is kept.

Laṭhe. A method of cooking *matkom* (q. v.) by mixing it with the flour of certain grains and seeds.

Cet' menak'tama? Matkom laṭhe. Cet'tepe laṭheakaṭa? Surguja.
Iñ do ḍiṅgạr laṭheñ ạguakaṭa. I have only brought pounded *matkom* (q. v.)

Laṭhea. Lazy, slow in movement, sluggish, crooked. Cf. laṭea.

Lạthiạu. To throw as on a wall, &c. any thing of the consistency of mud, mortar, &c. which sticks.

Pilasterko lạthiạu idia, khanko ṣariạua karnite. They throw the plaster on the wall, then they smooth (or spread) it with a trowel.
Bhitko lạthiạuakaṭa. They have thrown (soft clay) on the wall where it has stuck.

Lạti. A skein, to wind into a skein.

Lạti sutạm. A skein of thread.
Mić lạti emaeme. Give him one skein.
Sutạm lạtikateko basketa. They wound the thread into skeins and laid it past.

Lạṭiċ. To shrink back, to recoil, to flinch, to dodge, to tell, to bend, to give, as a branch laden with fruit.

Jom lạṭiċenae. He has eaten much, has laden himself.
Dal lạṭiċkedeañ. I struck and made him flinch.
Hante nhatem lạṭiċ baṛaeda. You are telling it here and there.
Ḍanḍom lạṭiċreḱkoako. They fined them so as to make them flinch.
Sadome lạṭiċena. The horse recoiled.
Kạṭiċ sadomre marañ hoṛe deolenkhan lạṭijoḱae. If a heavy man mounts a small horse, it recoils (with his weight.)

Lạṭiċ laḍar. To move the body, to posture, to wobble.

Hoṛ do hạnḍi ñu bulkate lạṭiċ laḍarko eneċa.

Laṭkao. To stick, to adhere.

Uni ṭheniñ laṭkaoakana. I am his servant.
Losoṭ laṭkaoadea. The mud stuck to him.

Laṭkar. Enthusiasm, enthusiastic.

Lạṭkiċ. Having a hollow back and prominent chest, depressed, having a depression in the surface.

Lạṭkiċ mara ạimại.
Lạṭkiċ ḍahra. An ox with a hollow back.

Laṭ kokor. A species of owlet.

Lạṭku pạṭku. To half do a thing, to partially break up soil by the plough, to mix up, to complicate, to do carelessly or inefficiently.

Noa kathape lạṭku pạṭkukeda. You complicated this matter.
Si lạṭku pạṭkukedako. They ploughed and only partially pulverised the soil.

Lạṭkuṭạ. Villanous, shameless, obstinate, inveterate.

Lạṭkuṭạ mara hoṛ. A villanous scoundrel.

Laṭlaha. Lean, shrivelled, emaciated, weak, poor, destitute.

Laṭlaha niạ hõ bam tul daṛeaḱa? You weakling, can't you even lift this?
Laṭlaha cabaenañ. I am utterly destitute.

Laṭlaṭ. Sticky, adhesive.

Hoṛmo laṭlaṭ aṭkaroḱkana. My body feels sticky (owing to perspiration having dried.)

Laṭlaṭiạ. } **Laṭpaṭiạ.** } Sticky, as the prickly seed case or head of certain plants, and awns of grasses which stick to the clothes.

Noa ghãs do laṭlạṭiạgea. The awns of this grass stick.

Laṭ marte. } **Laṭ mente.** } Immediately, instantly.

Laṭ marte katha lagaoentaea. His word instantly took effect.

Laṭpaṭ. } **Laṭpaṭao.** } To roll, or toss about, to wallow, give rein to the passion of love by young people, to be in an unseemly condition as one who has been tossing about or wallowing, to be in great straits.

Reṅgeċteñ laṭpaṭena. I am in great straits owing to poverty.
Reṅgeċteko laṭpaṭaoakana. They are in great straits through poverty.
Unkinkin laṭpaṭaoena. They two are guilty of unlawful intercourse.
Dhuṛireko laṭpaṭaoakana. They have rolled in the dust.
Kuṛi koṛako laṭpaṭena. The young folks have been unchaste.
Noa do laṭpaṭgea. This is sticky.

Laṭpaṭiạ. Sticky, as a burr. Cf. laṭlaṭiạ.

Lạṭu. Big or large, to make big or large.

Kạṭiċgem geṭeda, niạ khon lạṭuime. You are cutting it too small, cut it larger.

Lạṭu bhạnḍu. } **Lạṭu phạnḍu.** } Some occult adverse influence, danger, ill-fortune or affliction, the result of supernatural influence.

Noko do lạṭu phạnḍu menaḱtakoa, lạiakope birte aloko boloḱma. There is a presage of danger regarding them, warn them, so that they may not enter the jungle (along with the other hunters.)

Lạṭum. To put a full mouthful into the mouth after making it into a ball, a mouthful, as much as one would put into the mouth at once. Cf. lạkum.

Miṭ lạṭumge hoelentaea. It was just a mouthful for him.

Lạṭum. To fold, a fold.

Pon lạṭum hoeena. There are four folds.
Miṭ lạṭum. Two fold.
Kiriċ lạṭum goṭkam. Fold the cloth.

Lạṭumpaḱ. Very fat.

Lạṭumpaḱe moṭaakana. He is very fat.
Lạṭumpaḱe ñeloḱkana. He appears to be very fat.

Lạṭu phạnḍu. Cf. lạṭu bhạnḍu.

Latwaḱ. Worn out, weak, faint.

Reṅgeċte latwaḱenae. He is weak through hunger.

Lạuạ. A dish made from the hard shell of a pumpkin.

Lạuạ lagṭa. } **Lạuạ lokṭha.** } Quarrel, ill feeling, dispute.

Lạuạ lokṭha do bạnuḱan. There is no ill-feeling.
Okoe tuluċ hõ bae lạuạ lokṭhaḱa. He never quarrels with any one.

Lạujhạ.
Lạujhạṛ.
Lạujhạu.
Lạujhạ pạujhạ. } To be ravelled.

Sutạm lạujhạenа. The thread is ravelled.

Lạukạ. A boat, a dinghi.

Lạunḍi.
Lạunḍi era. } A concubine.

Lạuṛi. A stick which is twirled round on the fingers in much the same way as the Irishman twirls his shellalah, an oar.

Lạuṛiye ạcureda. He is twirling his shellalah.

Lạuṛiạ. One who can twirl a shellalah, an oarsman.

Lạuṛiạ kanae. He is a twirler of the shellalah.

Lạuṭạu. To return, to turn back.

Hoete seṅgel lạuṭạu ạcurkeda. The wind turned back the fire.

Mene lạuṭạu tiok̉mea. Look out, he will turn and reach you (a snake.)

Caba kathako lạuṭạu ruạṛkeda. They again brought up a matter that had been settled.

Iń seóko lạuṭạukeda. They turned it against me.

Lawak̉ lạtiń. To become weak, to lose the power of moving the limbs, as one at the point of death; to tremble as one weak, to sway from side to side.

Eneóre lawak̉ lạtińko hilạuk̉a. They sway from side to side when dancing.

Lawak̉ lạtiń hobor baṛaedekanae. He is carrying him in his arms and swaying.

Laé oḍokok̉te lawak̉ lạtińenae. He is weak through dysentery.

Lawak̉.
Lawak̉ lawak̉. } To dangle, to jerk up and down, to spring up and down, to hang loosely.

Lawań
Lawań lawań. } To dangle, to jerk up and down, to spring, to hang down, as anything almost cut through.

Lawań lawań ṭahraoakana. It is hanging by a shred.

Mat̉ do lawań lawańok̉kana. The bamboo is dangling (being half cut through.)

Lawao. To share, to divide.

Meromko lawaoakadea. They have divided (the carcase of) the goat.

Lawar lawar. To be springy, to bob up and down, as anything springy when carried.

Lawer. To bend or hang over or down, to incline.

Lawer ḍạr. A hanging bough.

Mone lawer. To influence, or incline the mind.

Ḍạr jo lawerena. The branch is bent with fruit.

Tikin siń lawer siń. Noon, or afternoon.

Baṛema lawerre gutrut̉ doe saheda. The Gutrut̉ bird (q. v.) calls from the hanging branch of the Banyan tree.

Lạwić.
Lạwić lạwić.
Liwić liwić. } To be springy at the extremities, to bob up and down.

Maṛāṛ bań lạwijok̉kantaea. His banghy pole is not springing.

Kạṭup̉ lạwićedae. He is beckoning by bending his finger again and again.

Layam luyum.
Luyum luyum. } Soft and thin, soft, as cottonwool.

Layo.
Layo gundli. } A cultivated millet, *Panicum antidotale, Retz.*

Layŏk̉.
Layŏk̉ layŏk̉. } Long, wide.

Usul hoṛ layŏk̉ko taṛama. Tall people take long steps.

Gạṛuṛ layŏk̉ layŏk̉ko uḍạuk̉a. The adjutant birds cover a long stretch (with their wings) when they fly.

Le. To melt, to dissolve, to be won over or convinced.

Leĕna. It has melted.

Hasa le cabak̉a. The earth will all dissolve (in water.)

Iṭạ le lanḍurena. The bricks have softened and collapsed.

Bhit le lanḍurentalea. Our wall (of clay) softened and fell down.

Ona kathategem leĕna. You are convinced by that statement.

Le. The abbreviated form of ale (q. v.)

Dalket̉-le-ako. They struck us.

Alele calak̉a. We will go.

Duṛup̉a-le. We will sit down.

Le.
Lei. } Paste.

Leao. To select, to choose a bride for another, to make a match, to couple the names of two marriageable persons.

Kuṛi koṛako leaokoa. They match the young men and maidens.

Mahajon leaoańme. Recommend a money lender to me.

Am dom leao idińkana, uni tulué iń jurikok̉a? You continue to couple my name with hers, now, would I be a fit match for her?

Lebda. To throw, to dash.
Lebda jal. A cast net.
Lebda bindaṛ goḱkedea. He threw (his stick) and knocked him down.
Jaṅga lebda goḱentaea. His foot was thrown forward.

Lebda libdi. To throw, sway or roll from side to side.
Lebda libdiye calaḱkana. He throws his feet from side to side as he goes.
Bul hoṛ lebda libdiko calaḱa. Drunk people sway from side to side when walking.

Lebe lebe. To waddle.
Geḍe lebe lebeko calaḱa. Ducks waddle when walking.

Leber leber. } Soft, thin, as paste or
Lubur lubur. } gruel, to chatter incessantly. Cf. labar lobur.
Leber lebere roṛa. He is very talkative.
Leber leberoḱkanae. She is chattering incessantly.

Lebeḱ. To tread, to trample.
Lenebeḱ. A pedal, a stirrup, &c.
Lebeḱ gasmanḍao. To trample under foot.
Lebeḱ haṭ. To step short.
Lebeḱ gejer. To trample to pieces.
Lebeḱ lahuḱ. To trample fine.
Lebet gañjao. To mix by trampling.
Noa katha alope lebeḱ paroma, Do not transgress this order.
Hapṛamkoaḱ lebeḱ laṇḍhuaḱre menaḱlea. We are in the paths our fathers trod.
Lebedoḱa. It will be trampled on.
Leḱbeḱić. A trampler.
Lebeḱaḱ. What has been trampled on.

Lebhaċ. } Used to hound on a dog.
Lebhai. }

Lebṛa. M. } Greedy, gluttonous.
Libṛi F. }
Lebṛa caṭa. M. } Ostensibly for something else,
Libṛi caṭi. F. } but really for food.

Lebṛeć. Soft, yielding, to become soft.
Lebṛeċgea. It is soft.
Lebṛejoḱa. It will become soft.

Le calao. To help, to assist.
Okoe hõ bako le calaoediña, iñtegeñ asuloḱkana. No one assists me, I earn my own living.
Iñ bañ le calaolekhan ohoe tahẽ daṛelena. If I did not assist him he could not stay.

Leceć. To give the haṭaḱ (q. v.) a peculiar tip so as to throw out undesirable matter from among the grain, to spill.
Leceć giḍikam.

Lece ceṛe. Talkative, garrulous, applied mainly to females.

Leceć leceć. Quickly, readily.
Leceć leceće calaḱkana. He goes very quickly.
Leceć leceće lai baṛaea. He readily tells everything (can't keep a secret.)

Lecelece. Unsteady, tottering, staggering.
Lece lece heo baṛaedeae. She totters under the weight of the child.
Lece lece calaḱkanae. He goes staggering.

Lecepece. Tired, unsteady through weakness, incoherent.
Lecepece galmaraoae. He speaks incoherently.
Dipil dipilte lece peceenae. She is tired with continued carrying on the head.
Ḍahra lecepeceenae. The bullock is fatigued.

Lecer lecer. Fluently, glibly.

Lecer pecer. } Tired, fatigued, unsteady,
Lece pece. } tottering.

Lecke. To squash, as a basket, hat, &c. if sat on, to dent.
Khaṇcaḱ leckeena. The basket is squashed.

Leclece. Flat and wide, flat and broad, occupying much space, flat as opposed to steep.
Leclece duṛupakanae. He sits spread out.
Leclece soṛhaakaḱae. She has made the leaf cup broad.
Ḍalić leclecegea. The basket is wide.

Lecoḱ. } One leg injured, to limp
Lecoḱ lecoḱ. } on one foot.
Lecoḱ lecoḱ calaḱkanae. He goes limping on one foot.
Lecoḱakanae. He is lame in one leg.
Lecogoḱae. He will become lame in one leg.

Lecṛe. To squash, as a hat by being sat on, to put out of shape.
Ṭukri cetanre alom duṛupa lecṛeḱa. Do not sit on the basket it will be squashed.
Ceḱlekape phuṛuḱkeḱ? lecṛeena. How have you made the leaf cup? it is out of shape.

Leḍ. Miry pool, muddy hole, the wet, marshy place immediately below the embankment of a tank.
Sukri do leḍre jobeenae. The pig is wallowing in the muddy hole.

Leḍ. } Excrement of horses, elephants,
Leṛ. } asses, &c.

Ledeć bedeć. } With short steps, as a
Ledeć pedeć. } child or dwarf, to walk falteringly, as a child beginning to use its legs, to move slowly, applied to females.
Ledeć pedeće taṛameda. She walks falteringly.
Nui gai do ledeć pedeenae. This cow walks slowly (being heavy with calf.)

Ledeć thekṛeć. Of varying ages and sizes, applied to children.
Noko ledeć thekṛeć gidrạ oekatem idikoa? How can you take these little ones?

Lede lede.
Ledlede. } To bulge, bulging.
Lede lede jom biakanae. He has eaten till his stomach is bulging.
Bhạri hoṛo led ledeëntama, baṅ jutem bhạrilaka. Your cart load of dhan is bulging, you did not load it properly.

Lede lede. With short steps, as a child or dwarf, to walk falteringly, as a child just beginning to walk, to move slowly, applied to males. Cf. ledeć bedeć.

Lede phede. Sound produced by a thick substance when boiling, to speak as anything bubbling.
Jonḍra daka lede phede hedejokkana. The Indian corn porridge boils and bubbles.

Lede poṭe. Little difference in age or size
Ạdi utạr lede poṭe gidrạ menakkotaea. He has a large family of small children.

Leḍer beḍer. Carelessly, inefficiently, to scamp.
Leḍer beḍer silpiṅko benaoakata. They have made the door very carelessly.

Leder peder. Poorly clad, clothed in rags, said of females.
Leder pedergeae. She is scantily clad.

Leḍga. M. } Having a hesitating gait,
Liḍgi. F. } as a child.

Ledgeć. Chubby, plump, applied to children.
Ledgeće moṭaakana. He is plump and fat.

Leḍha. M. } Lame, to become lame, to
Liḍhi. F. } limp.
Leḍha khoṛha. } Having some physical defor-
Leḍha khoṛda. } mity or other.
Reṅgeć orećko, ar ṭhunṭhạko ar kạṛạko ar leḍhako. The poor and maimed, and blind and lame.
Leḍhageae. He is lame.
Leḍhaenae. He has become lame.
Liḍhigeae. She is lame.
Leḍha liḍhiko jaoraena. The lame men and lame women are assembled.

Leḍhak.
Leḍhak leḍhak. } To be lame, to limp.
Leḍhakkanae. He is limping.
Leḍhak leḍhake calakkana. He goes limping.

Ledher bedher. Soft as clay mixed with water, the consistency of mud.
Hasa ledher bedherko sipiakata. They have mixed up the clay with water till it is of the consistency of mud.

Leḍho.
Leḍhok.
Leḍhok leḍhok. } To be lame to limp. Cf. leḍhak.
Leḍhok leḍhoke calakkana. He limps.

Ledhra. M. } Undersized with protu-
Lidhri. F. } berant stomach.

Leḍlede. Shaky on the legs, as a child who has not confidence in his power to stand.
Leḍlede teṅgoakanae.
Nonḍe oedak leḍledem teṅgoakana? Why are you standing shaking here?

Ledlede. To bulge, bulging.
Losoṭ thapo thapolekhanem ledledeka. If you pat soft clay it will bulge out.
Ledlede biakanae. He is full to bulging.

Ledlede. To carry away by percolation, as a dam by water percolating through it.
Hasa ledledekkana. The earth (of the embankment) is being carried away by the percolation of water.

Ledma. M.
Ledmi. }
Lidmi. } F. } Short of stature.
Ledma hoṛ kanae. He is a short man.

Ledoṛ pedoṛ. } Applied to the gait of
Pedoṛ pedoṛ. } a corpulent person whose excess of flesh shakes at every movement.
Ledoṛ pedoṛe calakkana.

Leg. A payment or perquisite allowed or sanctioned by custom.
Ạdi utạr leg lagaoka baplare. At a marriage many payments sanctioned by custom have to be made.
Hapṛamkoko legakata. The ancients have initiated the custom.
Baṅ legakle legkeda. What was not sanctioned by custom we made customary.

Lega. To test, to try, to attempt.
Jom lega. To test by eating.
Ṅu lega. To test by drinking.
Tunum lega. To test by feeling.
Roṛ lega. To test by speaking (as to whether one will be listened to or not.)
Sereṅ legakme. Sing and see if they will be pleased with it.
Ru lega. To test by beating, as a drum.
Mak lega. To test by hacking.
Eneć lega. To test one's ability to dance.
Tuṅ lega. To try to shoot, to test one's powers by shooting.
Horok lega. To test by putting on, as a garment.
Deć lega. To test by riding, to test one's ability to climb.
Em lega. To offer.
Sap lega. To test by seizing.
Oroṅ lega. To test by playing, as a flute.

Lega ligi. About, on the point of, one after the other.
Ayup legaligiko tiok keda. They arrived about evening.
Gujuk lega ligi. On the point of death, about to die.
Lega ligiko hecena. They came one after the other, (with a short interval of time or space between them.)

Legcar. Custom, to introduce a custom, to make customary.
Haprạmkoko legcarakaṭa. The ancients have introduced the custom.
Haprạmkoak legcarakrege menaklea. We follow the customs introduced by our forefathers.
Bạki bokoe cetko legcar menaka? What other customary usages are still to be observed?

Legeć labak. Fresh, green and tender, beautiful, as young, fresh leaves.
Mungạ arak legeć labak sarhecakana. The budding leaves of the Mungạ (q. v.) tree are green and tender.

Legeć legeć. Luxuriant and tender, as grass, dhan, &c.
Ghas legeć legeć ńelokkana. The grass looks luxuriant and tender.

Legem legem. Glidingly, as water with unruffled surface, to move slowly and gently, as an animal tracking its prey.
Dak calakkana legem legem. The water flows glidingly.
Naprak bin legem legemko calaka. Large snakes move glidingly.
Kul hõko calaka legem legem. Tigers also move glidingly.

Legesak. Huge, big and broad, bulky.
Legesake gitićakana, parkome perećakaṭa. He is lying with his huge bulk, he has filled the bed.
Legesake duruṭakana. She is stitting with her huge bulk.

Leglam. To carry off, to destroy.
Leglamkedeae, nitok ohope ńamlea. He carried it off (a wolf a goat) you will not find it now.
Dakte leglamkedae abar do. A flood carried away (or destroyed) the embankment.

Leglao. To apprehend and put in prison.
Uni hoṛko leglaoakadea, ạdiye kombṛoeṭ tahẽkana. They have apprehended and imprisoned that man, he was much given to thieving.

Legoe pegoe. Bulging on both sides, to chew, used mainly of old people, to mumble.
Legoe pegoe gochaakaṭae. She has her lap so full that one side after the other bobs out as she walks.
Legoe pegoeye jomeda. Both sides of his mouth bulge out as he chews (he has filled his mouth so full that his cheeks bulge each time he moves his jaws.)

Leh.
Leh leh. } A call to a dog to bring it near.

Lehaha. Said to a dog when hounding it on.

Leha lihi. About, nearly, only a little remaining.
Nitok leha lihiedabo. Now we are drawing to a close.

Lehedehe. Near the time of delivery.

Lehe guhe.
Lehe gure. } Of the consistency of well mixed clay, soft clay laid out in small heaps.
Lehe gure hasako sipiakaṭa. They have worked up the clay with water till it is soft.
Lehe gure leakana dạl do. The "dal" has dissolved to the consistence of soft clay.
Lehe guheko doho idiakaṭa.

Lehe lehe. To put oneself forward, to be officiously active.
Aćge lehe lehe baṛaedae. He is putting himself forward.

Lehe lehe. To break up and pulverise, as by the plough.
Si lehe lehekedako. They ploughed and broke up the soil.
Onkoko lehe lehekeda. They broke up the soil with the plough.

Leher.
Leher leher.
Leher bohor. } Semi-liquid, too much liquid mixed with it, thin, as gruel, softer or thinner than the usual or proper consistency.
Leher leherko dakaakaṭa. They have cooked the rice too soft.
Unạkem dakakkhan leheroka. If you put so much water in it will become too thin.

Lejek pejek. Slightly muddy, wet and slippery, as moist clay soil.
Lejek pejek losoṭakana.

Leje peje. Soft and sticky, viscous.

Lejer lejer.
Lejer pejer. } Soft, muddy, flabby.
Raca lejer lejer losoṭakana. The courtyard is muddy.

Lejoṛ lejoṛ. Lagging behind, hanging or slipping down, as a child not properly held astride the hip.
Ceṭ leka lejoṛ lejoṛem heoakadea?
Taeomtegem orokkana lejoṛ lejoṛ.

Lejra.
Lijra. } Not closely woven, as cloth.

Lejraha. Flabby, as the flesh of an unhealthy animal.

Lejraha. M. } Dirty, slovenly, sluggish.
Lejrahi. F. }

Lek. Capable, fit, worthy, fitting, becoming.

Nui hoṛe lekena. This man has become capable or able bodied.

Ạdi reṅgeće tahẽkana, lekenae. He was very poor, (but) is now well-to-do.

Onko lekte hoṛge baṅko metaṅkana. In their estimation I am not a human being.

Lekleka. } As is fitting or becoming, fittingly,
Leklekate. } becomingly.

Leklekate bam beoharlaka. You did not act becomingly.

Kạmi leke hoeṅa. He has become fit to work.

Leka. Like.

Niạ leka kạmime. } Do like this.
Niạ lekaeme. }

Alom uni lekaka. Do not be like him.

Joto lekako goćena. Almost all have died.

Okoe leka menaea? Who is he like?

Guti kisạṛ leka bae kạmia. The servant does not work like the master.

Khub leka. Efficiently.

Khub leka jotonem. Nurse him efficiently.

Ḍhạlu leka. Slopingly, with a slope.

Cet lekakedako? How did they do it?

Kul lekae tahẽkana. It resembled a tiger.

Lekan. Like, such.

Uni lekan hoṛko bạnuṅkoa. There is no person like him.

Uni lekan bạhu ḍhergeko ńamoka. Many brides such as she can be had.

Cet lekań disom kana? What kind of a country is it?

Nui lekanić okare ohope ńamlea. You will nowhere find such an one as he is.

Noa lekanakem emańkhanih hataokea. If you give me one such as this I would take it.

Nukin lekakin tahẽkantińakin. I had two (bullocks) such as these two.

Noko lekankoń ạcukoa. I will hire such as these (men) are.

Lekate. Like, by way of.

Jãhãlekate. In any way, by any way howsoever.

Ghosaldih lekate calakme. Go by way of Ghosaldih (village.)

Noa lekate kạmime. Do like this.

Sanam lekate. Altogether, in every way.

Leklekate. Worthily, fittingly, becomingly.

Cetlekate. How, in what way.

Cet lekatem ạsulokkana? How do you earn a living?

Lekate. Along with, in company with, taking.

Gidrạ lekatege tahenme. Stay along with the child.

Jiwi lekateko dạṛkeda. They fled to save their lives (leaving all else behind.)

Adha ghorkorna lekateye oḍok calaka. She will leave taking half of the goods and chattles with her.

Leke pheke. To bubble, as anything stiff when boiling. Cf. lokopoko.

Jonḍra daka leke pheke hecḍejokkana.

Lekha. To count, to number.

Lekha jokha. Account.

Lekha guṭ. To total, to add up.

Lekha mit. }
Lekha selet. } To include in the number.
Lekha joṛao. }

Lekha jokha emok hoyoktama. You must give an account.

Lekha guṭketkoale. We totalled them up.

Lekha seletkedeako. They included him in the number

Lekṛe taṛup. A leopard.

Lekṭha } To quarrel, to be at variance
Lekṭhi. } with each other, to dispute, to wrangle.

Hoṛ tulué alom lekṭhaka. Do not quarrel with people.

Lele boṅga. One of the many Santal godlets.

Dasãe jokhed Lele boṅgako rumoka, arko rum cabalenkhan tire ar jaṅgare backom baber uńkateko dalkoa.

Lele lele. Said to a dog when setting it on.

Leleṅget. Wearisome, as a long monotonous road.

Inạ ṭạnḍi ạdi leleṅgeta.

Ạdi marań ṭạnḍi kana leleṅget. It is a great wearisome plain.

Lelha. M. } Foolish, ignorant, stupid.
Lilhi F. }

Lelha koṛa. A foolish boy.

Lilhi ạimại. A foolish woman.

Lelha lekam roṛeda. You speak foolishly.

Lelipur. }
Lilipur. } Poetical form of lipur (q. v.)
Leolipur. }

Lembe tumbe. To gobble, to eat quickly or voraciously.

Lembe tumbeye jomeda. He devours his food.

Lembo. A lemon.

Lemeń. Fine, powdery, mealy, pulverised; to make fine, to pulverise.

Lemeń gitil. Fine sand.

Lemeń holoṅ. Finely ground flour.

Lemeń gitile tiokkeda. He is dead.

Lemer.
Lemer lemer. } To move the lips when grazing, peculiar to goats, horses, &c.

Merom lemer lemer baṛaeako. Goats move their lips when grazing.
Jom lạgitko lemer lemeroḱkana. They are moving their lips impatient to eat.
Lemer lemerko jomeda. They move their lips when eating.

Lemetuṛe. Never satisfied with flesh meat, greedy for flesh meat.

Lemetuṛeye jomeda. He eats as if he would never be satisfied.

Lemlem. Full and gliding, applied to a river when so full that the surface of the water is unbroken; irritating feeling in the throat after swallowing certain things.

Lemlem lạbić. Very soft.
Lemlem perećakana gaḍa do. The river is so full that the surface of the water is unbroken.
Lemlemge ṡikạuḱa. It has left an irritating feeling (in the throat.)

Lemṭoḱ. Over-ripe and tasteless, applied mainly to the fruit of the *jạnum, Zizyphus jujuba.*

Lemṭoḱ. To become lumpy, as meal or flour put into water without being stirred.

Jonḍra daka lemṭoḱa. The Indian corn meal porridge will be lumpy.

Len. To press, to express.

Ạk len. To express the juice from sugarcane.
Sunum len. To express oil in an oil press.
Lelenaḱ. A press, as an oil press, &c.

Kulhu.
Mahasal.
Rạksi.
Cạrkhi. } Varieties of sugar cane presses.

Sunum lenoḱ paṭa. An oil press.

Len. A line, cooly lines, (a tea garden term.)

Len len cạukidar menaḱkoa. There is a watchman for each line or row of huts.

Leń. To creep, to crawl, applied mainly to the mode of progression of snakes, earthworms, &c. &c.

Leń calaḱ. To move by crawling, as a snake.
Leńoḱko. Creatures unprovided with legs which progress on the ribs.

Leńboń. Tall, high.

Leńboń dareakana. The tree has grown very high.
Kuṛi koṛa leńbońko haraakana. The girls and boys have grown tall.

Leńca. M.
Lińci. F. } Lame of one leg, owing to injury of the thigh.

Leńcoḱ.
Leńcoć leńcoḱ. } To limp, limping, owing to one leg being injured.

Leńcoḱ leńcoḱe calaḱkana. He goes limping, or he is limping on one foot.
Leńcoḱakanae. He is lame in one leg.

Lenda. Small, young; the youngest of a family or the smallest in a brood, litter, &c., the booby of a class; dregs.

Lenda lendageako. They are small, or young.
Cabaena, lendateć menaḱa. It is finished, only the dregs remain.

Lendaṭuriạ. The youngest of a family, the smallest of a brood, litter, &c. poor, destitute. Scottice, *crit.*

Nui lendaṭuriạ do tinạḱe damoḱa? What will be the price of this *crit?*
Eken lendaṭuriạ porja menaḱkotińa. I have only poor tenants.

Lenḍe. To despise, to subject to contumely, to slight, to sneer at.

Lenḍekedińako. They subjected me to contumely.

Lenḍeć. To make oneself scarce, to hide, to keep out of the way.

Kạmi botorte lenḍećenae. He is keeping out of the way through fear of being put to work.

Lenḍer lenḍer. Carelessly, lazy, slow at work, inefficiently; as a learner.

Lenḍer lenḍere kạmikana. He is working carelessly.

Lenḍer penḍer. Shirking work, passing the time doing as little work as possible.

Thoṛa berhonko emaekanteye lenḍer penḍer baṛaea. He does as little work as possible as they pay him a small wage.

Lenḍeć. The earthworm.

Lenḍeć moca. Beginning to ripen, as grain.

Neḱe lenḍeć mocaḱkana. It is just beginning to ripen.

Lendha.
Leńjha. } A cultivated millet, *Pencilaria spicata, Lindl.*, synonym, *Pennisitum typhoideum, Rich.*

Lenḍker.
Lenḍker lenḍker. } Fat, plump, swollen, as a pea that has been steeped in water.

Lenḍkere ńeloḱkana. He looks plump.
Lenḍker lenḍkerko moṭaakana. They are plump and fat.

Lendoṅ.
Raimal lendoṅ.
Raima lendoṅ. } A very large centiped.

Lendur̥. To fall down, to collapse, as a wall, house, &c., to throw down, as a wall, house, &c. Cf. landur̥.

Lenebet́. Anything on which the foot is placed, as a stirrup iron, a pedal, rung of ladder, &c. Cf. lebet́.

Lenetep̆. The pulsation felt below the fontanel on an infant's head.

Leṅga. The left.

Leṅga ti. The left hand.
Leṅga lutur. The left ear.
Leṅga ti sen.
Leṅga ti seć. } To the left.
Leṅga ti senaḱ. The one to the left.
Leṅga nakha. The left side, to the left.
Leṅga titeye saba. She seizes it with the left hand.

Leṅget́.
Leṅget́ leṅget́. } To be frightened or startled, to start with fear.

Leṅget́adaṅ. I got a fright, I started.
Ona bir leṅget́ leṅget́le paromena. We were in great fear while passing through that jungle.

Leṅget́ leṅget́. Wearisome, as a long uninteresting road.

Leṅget́ leṅget́ aṭkaroḱkana. It feels wearisome.

Leṅget́ sopot́. To be in great fear.

Leṅget́ sopot́le paromena. We were in great fear while passing.
Leṅget́ sopot́lenale. We were in great fear.

Leṅgra. M.
Liṅgri. F.
Leṅgr̥a. M.
Liṅgr̥i. F. } Left-handed.

Leṅloṅ.
Liṅloṅ. } Long.

Ạdi jhala liṅloṅ. It is very long (a ball of twine.)
Ạdi leṅloṅ bandeakanae. She has bound her cloth round her waist so that it reaches far down to her feet.

Leńjer.
Leńjet́. } Smooth, slippery, to slip, to slide.

Dare daḱte leńjerakana, alope dejoḱa. The tree is slippery with the rain, do not climb up it.
Leńjet́ ńurenae. He slipped and fell (from a height.)

Leńjer.
Leńjer leńjer. } Viscous, mucilaginous.

Atnaḱ jer leńjer ṡikṛuḱa. The gum of the atnaḱ (q. v.) tree feels viscous.

Leńjer boroṛ. Viscous, soft and slightly gummy to the touch.

Leńjha. A cultivated millet *Pencilaria spicata, Lindl.* Cf. lendha.

Leńjhar̥. Accumulated rubbish.

Ạdi leńjhar̥gea, biṅ tanaḱko basaḱa. There is much rubbish, serpents and such like will take up their quarters.

Leńjhar. Unfinished, incomplete, connection, as between one duty and another or between one thing and another.

Ạdi kạmiye leńjharkeda. He left much of his work undone.
Noakore leńjhar menaḱa. There are connections here, no space between one thing and another.
Bapla reaḱ leńjhar menaḱtińa. I have still (one or more) to get married.

Leńjraha. M.
Leńjr̥ahi. F. } Weak, soft, sluggish, dirty, slovenly.

Lenthe.
Leoṭhe. } To copulate, as dogs, silk moths, &c. that remain a considerable time united.

Leobhaḱ.
Leoleo. } A kind of chorus sung at the end of the village street at the Sohrae (q. v.) festival.

The idea is that the Hanuman monkeys, whom it is desired to drive away, will think that dogs are being hounded on them, and leave the neighbourhood of the village.

Leoḍa.
Leoḍa liuḍi. } To stir up, to agitate, as water.

Hakoko leoḍakoa. They stir up and muddy the water in which the fish are. (a method of catching fish by making the water muddy, and when they come to the surface to breathe they are caught.)
Daḱ alom leoḍa boḍe ocoea. Do not agitate the water and make it muddy.
Lać leoḍaḱkantińa. There is a commotion in my belly.

Leoha.
Leoha liuhi. } To mix with liquid, to make of the consistence of gruel.

Sạtu leohaḱateḱo joma. They mix the flour with water and eat it.

Leoṅ. A movement of the hands made by a woman when returning the salutation of a younger who has made obeisance to her.

Bohoḱ cetanreko leoṅ got́aea.

Leoṛa. } The male organ.
Laṛ. }

Leoṭhe. To cleave to, to stick to, to remain, to assemble together, to stick together, to put together. Cf. lenṭhe.

Miť jawäe ṭhenkin leoṭheakana.
Sutąm leoṭhe miťena.
Nonḍe heċkateko leoṭheäna. They came here and stuck (remained.)
Sanamiń ṭhenko leoṭheäna. All have come and attached themselves to me.
Barea pea maejinko uni ṭhenko leoṭheakana. Two or three women have attached themselves to him.

Lep. To apply ointment, as a medicine.

Lep ran lagaoaeme. Apply a healing ointment.

Leṗ. To flap the wings, to bound, as a deer when shot; to skip as a kid, lamb, &c.

Leṗ goťkedae. It flapped its wings.
Leṗ ǩṛgo goťenae. It flapped its wings and swooped down.

Lepeć. } Of the consistency of
Lepeć lepeć. } curdled milk or soft paste.

Lepeć lepeć daǩ mąnḍiko ǩṛiċakaťa.
Lepeċgea. It is thick (as paste.)

Lepeḍher. Applied to the appearance of a fat person when sitting.

Lepeḍhere duṛuṗakana. He sits flattened out.

Lepekope. To put food into the mouth before it is empty, to eat greedily.

Lepekopeye jomeda. He keeps putting food into his mouth before it is empty.

Lepe leṅgoṛ. One of the Santal godlets, a female.

Lepe lepe. To flap the wings slowly.

Cẽṛẽ hopon lepe lepeko uḍąuǩkaną. The young birds fly slowly flapping their wings.

Lepen. The Reciprocal form of len (q. v.)

Lepen tepen. } To crush and elbow
Lepen tapakić. } each other as in a
Tapam tapakić. } crowd, to jostle.

Lepen tapakić hoṛko jarwaakana. So many people are assembled that they are jostling each other.

Lepe peje. Soft and sticky, viscous, gummy.

Lepeṛkať. Contracted stomach, stomach shrunken through hunger, with empty stomach. Cf. lapaṛkaǩ.

Leper leper. Thick, stiff, as porridge; of the consistency of thick paste. Cf. lepeć.

Leper leper jonḍrako dakaakaťa.

Lepes. } Soft.
Lepes lepes. }

Lepes lepes sebela. It is nicely soft.

Lepese. To bite each other, as two puppies playing, the Reciprocal form of lese (q. v.)

Lepesen. The Reciprocal form of lesen (q. v.)

Leṗleṗ. Flapping the wings.

Leṗleṗ uḍąuǩkanae. It is flapping the wings and flying.

Leplep. } Large in area, as a field,
Leťleť. } lake, &c.

Nąi ąḍi leplep ńeloǩkana. The river is very wide.

Lep lepe. Broad, flat; to flatten.

Leplepe duṛuṗakanae. He sits flattened out.
Leplepe pinḍąakaťako. They have made a broad verandah.

Leṛ. Semen.

Leṛ. } To eat.
Leleṛ. }

Leleṛkanae. He is eating.

Leṛań peṭań. Inferior quality, as flesh meat, poor, lean and weak.

Ceťlekan jel kana? leṛań peṭańgea. What sort of meat is it? It is of inferior quality.
Leṛań peṭańgeae. He is poor.

Leṛe beṛe. Mixed, all sorts and kinds.

Bul hoṛ leṛe beṛeko galmaraoa.
Leṛe beṛeko jomeda. They eat all kinds (good or bad.)

Leṛeć peṭeć. } Of inferior quality, as
Leṛeć tuṛeć. } flesh meat; poor.

Leṛem leṛem. Soft and beautiful, as a ripe fruit.

Leṛem leṛem beleakana, It has ripened soft and beautiful.
Leṛem leṛem ṡikąuǩkana. It feels soft.
Leṛem leṛem ul bele. A ripe, soft mango.

Leṛe theṛe. Tired, fatigued.

Kąmi kąmitele leṛe theṛeäna. We are tired with continuous labour.
Jomjomtele leṛe theṛeäna. We are tired eating.

Leṛgo. To eat.

Aċ eskare leṛgokeda. He ate it himself.

Leṛhoǩ. } To be lame, to limp.
Leṛhoǩ leṛhoǩ. }

Leṛhoǩ leṛhoǩe calaǩkana. He is limping.

Leṛka. A child.

Leṛosią. } Weak, feeble, lazy.
Lesoṛią. }

Leṛosiągeae. He is weak.
Nui leṛosią dakae jomeda, se bah? bae tul daṛeaǩkana. Does this weakling eat any food? he cannot lift.

Leṛwak̓. To incline to one side, as the neck; to lose control over the limbs, as a person near death.
Hoṭoke leṛwak̓keda. He held his head to one side.
Leṛwak̓enae. He has lost control of his neck. (can't hold his head straight.)

Leṛwak̓. To droop, to wither.

Leṛwa laṛwe. } Awkward, clumsy, lazy,
Leṛwa saṛwe. } feeble, exhausted.
Kạmire leṛwa saṛwegeae.

Leṛwe. To bend over, or down, to sulk.
Kagat leṛweĕna. The paper is folded over.

Les. } Semen.
Leṛ. }

Lese. To snap at, to bite, but without drawing blood, to beshrew, to execrate, to scold, to abuse.
Nitgeń heó goćena, adom lese daramińkana. I have just come, and you meet me with abuse.
Seta lesekodeae. A dog bit him.
Joto hoṛko leseĕdińa. All the people are against me, all snapping at me.

Lese lese. } To speak quickly, and in-
Lese pese. } distinctly.
Leṭe pese. }
Lese peseye galmaraoeda. He speaks quickly and indistinctly.

Lesen. To crush, crowd, trample under foot.
Lepesen. To crowd, to push each other, as in a crowd.
Gadel hoṛko ạḍiko lek̓sena. A crowd of people crush greatly.

Lese pese. Wet, moist, muddy.
Holanak̓ dak̓te racae lesepesekeda. The rain of yesterday made the court yard muddy.

Leser beḍer. } Muddy, thick and muddy,
Leske beḍer, } mixed, promiscuously.
Dak̓ko leske beḍerkeda. They muddied the water.
Paurạ gạdire leser beḍerko jom ńuieda. At a liquor shop they eat and drink promiscuously.

Leser leser. Talkative, fluent in speech.
Leser lesere galmaraoeda. He talks fluently, or he is loquacious.

Leske beḍer. Cf. leser beḍer.

Lesker. } Plump, fat, chubby, ap-
Lesker lesker. } plied to infants or young animals.
Sukri hopon lesker lesker henak̓koa. The piggies are very plump.
Nui gidrạ khub lesker goćakanae. This child has become very plump.
Khube leskerena. He is nice and plump.

Leslese. } Immodestly, with the knees
Laslasa. } wide apart.
Leslese duṛupakanae.
Leslese gitićakanae, onate bań sorlena.

Lesoṛịa. Feeble, weak, lazy. Cf. leṛosịa.

Lesraha. M. } Indolent, neglecting
Lesrạhi. F. } work through laziness, slovenly, slatternly.
Nui lesraha do oṛak̓ duạr bae juttaea. This sloven does not keep his house and its surroundings tidy.
Nui lesrạhi raca hõ bae joga. This slattern will not even sweep her courtyard.

Lesrao. To be unfinished, incomplete, to be to do.
Lesrao tahĕena kạmi. The work remains unfinished.
Kạmi nunạk̓ lesraoentaea, ar hạni torae calaoena. So much of the work remains to be done, and see he has gone and left it.

Lesrao. To smear, to plaster, to daub. Cf. lasrao.

Lesṛok̓. } To plump down, as a
Lesṛok̓ lesṛok̓. } tired person seats himself; to throw down, as anything one is too lazy or tired to carry.
Lesṛok̓ lesṛok̓e duṛup baṛaekana. He plumps himself down here and there.
Nịkorege lesṛok̓kadae. He threw it down about here (being too lazy to carry it further.)

Lesṛok̓ marte. } With a plump.
Lesṛok̓ mente. }
Lesṛok̓ mente gur goćenae. He fell down plump.

Leṭa. Dusty, covered with mud or dust, to plaster, to smear.
Dhuṛire leṭaenae. He is dusty through rolling in dust.
Khetre kạmi jokheć hoṛko leṭak̓a. When working in the rice fields people get covered with mud.
Gạikoak̓ cuńci hõ guricteko leṭaakoa. They also plaster cowdung on cows' dugs (to prevent the calves sucking.)

Leṭań. } Interruption, obstruction;
Leṭań letaṛ. } to impede, to retard, multiplicity of calls upon time or giving, many things to attend to.
Leṭańge ạḍi, bań kạmi daṛeak̓kana. There are so many interruptions, I am unable to do my work.
Leṭań tahĕena, bań cabaakana.
Leṭań letaṛge ḍhera.

Leṭao. To be dusty, as a person rolling on the ground.
Dhuṛire alom leṭaok̓a. Do not get dusty by rolling in the dust.

Letar. Interruption, obstruction, to impede, to retard, multiplicity of duties to attend to, many matters requiring attention.

Ạdi bapla reak̕ letar henak̕tiñ. I have many matters connected with the marriage to attend to.

Letea tarup.
Lekre tarup. } A leopard.
Potea tarup.

Leteć. To be able, to succeed, to overcome.

Letećkedañ. I succeeded in doing it.
Letećkedeañ. I overcame him.
Tutule senlena, bae letećlak̕a. He went to lift it, but he was not able.

Manwa then ona do beletejok̕gea, menkhan Isor then do jotoge letejok̕a. With men it is impossible, but with God all things are possible.

Leteć peteć. Weak, emaciated, feeble and lean.

Lete lete.
Lete pete. } Soft, mud-like, moist.

Bañ jutle rohoelak̕a, letepete.
Daka letepeteèna. The boiled rice is like mud.

Khub do bañ losoćlena lete pete. It was not well stirred up, simply moistened.

Letep letep. Weak, only able to breathe, moribund.

Ruak̕kanae, letep letepe gitiċakana. He is ill with fever and is lying only able to breath.
Rengećte letep letep menaea. He is weak from hunger.

Leter peter. Weak, feeble and emaciated.

Rengećtele leter peterena. We are weak through hunger.
Leter peter osok̕akanae. He is emaciated to feebleness.
Leter peter dahrateye siok̕kana. He is ploughing with a weak and emaciated bullock.

Letha.
Lotha. } To include, to implicate, to drag into.

Letha.
Letho. } To be at variance, to dispute, to altercate. Cf. laktha.

Horko songe lethaakanae. He is at variance with some people.

Letheć.
Lethreć. } To throw down with a flop, as anything soft, to fall with a flop or bump.

Letheć marte.
Letheć mente.
Lethereć marte.
Lethereć mente.
Lethreć marte.
Lethreć mente. } To fall with a flop.

Losoćte lethreć marte capak̕kedeae.
Lethereć marteñ gurena. I fell flop (into mud.)

Letho.
Lotho. } Obstinate, self-willed, disobedient.

Letho. To be on terms of great familiarity, as a child with an adult.

Letka. Children.

Letko. Sticky, adhesive, as some kinds of clay.

Letkom. To stick to, to adhere.

Matkom sature letkomkateko joma.
Hasa letkomlenkhan nahelre bañ lagaok̕a.
Jañgare hõ letkomok̕a.

Letlet. Wide, expansive, as a river or lake; long, as a road.

Letlet perećakana.
Letlet ñelok̕kana.

Leto. A method of preparing Indian corn, &c. for food, a method of preparing tripe, and flest meat.

Jondra leto. Indian corn flour boiled to the consistency of stiff porridge.
Kode leto. The flour of kode (q. v.) boiled like porridge.
Laċ leto. Tripe prepared in a particular way. The tripe is boiled, and then flour added and the whole well stirred.

Letok̕. Hindrance, interruption, obstruction.

Letok̕ lagaoena. An interruption has occurred.

Letra. M.
Litri F. } Small and lean, as children and the young of domesticated animals.

Letrok̕.
Letwet. } Lean, ill conditioned, as children and young domesticated amimals.

Noko letwet mara gidrą. These lean little rascals.
Merom hopon letrok̕enako netar. The kids have become thin now-a-days.

Letwet. Small, puny, lean, ill-conditioned.

Letwet mara gidrą. A puny little rascal.

Lewa. Pliant, soft, as mud; to render pliant, or skilful by exercise.

Kąmi kąmite hormoe lewaak̕ata. By continual work he has made his body pliant.
Thenga lewaakana. The stick is pliant.
Lewa aphor. Seed sown in mud.
Dhuri aphor. Seed sown on dry soil.

Lewak̕.
Lewak̕ lewak̕. } To shake, to hang dangling, to jerk up and down, to spring, to vibrate. Cf. lawak̕ lawak̕.

Lewa saré. Swaying the body and nodding the head, swaying and nodding.

Onko bul hor lewa saréko calak̕kana. These drunk men go swaying the head and body.

Lewe.
Lewe lewe. } To bend slightly, to be loose, to tremble, to shake, to be afraid.

Amak kathate bań lewekа. I will not tremble at your word.

Ḍaṭa lewe lewe hilạukkantaea. His tooth keeps moving (every time he speaks.)

Ḍaṭa leweakantaea. He has a loose tooth.

Lewere kodore.
Lewer kodor. } To shake or move the head and body, to nod the head.

Lewere kodoreko eneḍa, They move the head when dancing.

Lewer lewer. To shake up and down, to move up and down, opposite to moving from side to side, as a pendulum.

Ḍaṛ hilạukkana lewer lewer. The branch is shaking up and down.

Kuinḍiko rukuia lewer lewer They shake down the kuinḍi fruit by shaking (the branches.)

Leweṫ. To bend, to droop. Cf. liweṫ.

Libạ labe.
Liboć loboć.
Libo lobo. } Slow, sluggish in movement.

Libạ labe calakkanae. She is going slowly.

Libhrạ.
Lipsạ. } Pliant, easily bent.

Libhrạ ak. A too pliant bow.

Libir libir. Soft, as a ripe fruit, or as a marsh.

Liblib.
Liblibiạ.
Liblibạu. } Soft, to be soft, to give way under pressure through being soft.

Bele liblibạuena. It is ripe and soft.

Jarkao liblibạuena. (The soil) is water-logged and soft.

Ot liblib aṭharokkana. The soil feels soft.

Liboć loboć. M.
Libạ labe. F. } Slow, sluggish in movement. Cf. libạ labe.

Libo lobo. Slow, sluggish in movement.

Libṛi. F.
Lebṛa. M. } Greedy, gluttonous. Cf. lebṛa.

Libṛi caṭi. Ostensibly for something else but ṛeally for food.

Libṛuk.
Lạbṛuk. } To become weak, feeble, poor.

Uni hoṛe libṛukena. That man is cowed (he will not take the matter to court.)

Libuk. To deceive, to wheedle, soft.

Libukkedeae. He wheedled him.

Eṛe libuk.
Lại libuk. } To persuade, to entice, to wheedle, to coax, to talk over.

Lić.
Lać lić. } The entrails.

Lićteṫ bape emadea. You did not give him any of the entrails.

Licạ lace.
Licạ loco.
Lico loco. } Limping, walking on the toes.

Licạ lace calakkanae. She is limping.

Licạń picạń.
Ricạń picạń. } Without appetite, without relish, unwillingly, half-heartedly, reluctantly.

Licạń picạńe jomeda. He is forcing himself to eat, he eats with little relish.

Licạṛ. Pliant, yielding, soft, of tender age, not full grown, weak, feeble.

Nui hoṛ doe licạṛgea. This person is of underage.

Liḍạk. To shut, close to, almost shut close.

Silpiń liḍạkkam. Draw to the door.

Liḍạ laḍe. Tottering, as a child just beginning to walk, shaky, shoggly, as a post not firmly fixed.

Liḍạ laḍe cacokkanae. It walks shakily.

Lidạ lodo.
Lido lodo. } Applied mainly to the swaying movement of the bellies of animals which have eaten to repletion, or are heavy with young.

Jom lido lodoenako. They have eaten till their sides shake with every movement.

Liḍgạ laḍge. Cf. liḍạ laḍe.

Lidgoe lodgoe. Stout and heavily clad, as Marwari females.

Liḍhi. F.
Leḍha. M. } Lame.

Liḍhigeae. She is lame.

Lidhri. F.
Ledhra. M. } Undersized with protuberant stomach.

Lido lodo. Cf. lidạ lodo.

Liḍu. To become soft, as a fruit when ripe, to ripen.

Bele liḍuena. It is fully ripe.

Liduṛ piduṛ. Flesh of a fat woman shaking when she moves.

Liduṛ piduṛ moṭakanae.

Liḍwạ laḍwe.
Liḍwạ saḍwe. } Shaky, as a child beginning to walk, wobbly, as a post not firmly fixed.

Ligi.
Leg. } A payment or perquisite allowed or sanctioned by custom.

Ligi bhạgi. Custom, customary.

Ligi bhạgi tinạkе ńama, emkataeme. Give him as much as by custom he has a right to get.

Ligiṛ sigiṛ.
Ligṛi sigṛi. } All kinds, all sorts, many kinds, many sorts, various kinds or sorts.

Ligṛi sigṛim galmaraokana.

Noa disomre ạdi ligṛi sigṛi lagaokkana. In this country many kinds of cesses are collected.

Liha lahe. } Almost, very little remaining.
Liha lihi.
Leha lihi.

Liha lahebon tiokkeda. We have almost reached our destination.

Lijak. } Cloth, clothing, not closely woven, as cloth.
Lijak lijak.

Noa kicrić lijak lijakgea. This cloth is not closely woven.

Lijra. } Not closely woven, as cloth.
Lejra.

Lijraha. } Slovenly, dirty, inactive, sluggish.
Lejrahi.

Lijrak. To flop down.

Men, lijrak ńur ocoeam. Be careful, you will let him flop down

Lijrak marte. } With a flop.
Lijrak mente.

Lijrak marteń gur gotena. I fell flop.
Katić gidra lijrak mentem ńur ocokedea.

Likha. Writing, fate.

Likhal. } A writing, fate.
Likhon.

Likhal badal. } Fate.
Likhon lokhon.

Likhal badal inakge tahẽkantaea. Fate had only so much for him.

Likhon gorhon. Carving, representations of men, animals, trees, &c., &c., drawn on the walls of houses.

Likhon emalem, khane patiauka. Give us it in writing, then he will believe us.

Likhwatia. } Counting, estimating, as to how much work he should do.
Lekhwatia.

Adi likhwatia hor kanae. He is careful to estimate how much work he should do (for the pay he gets) and will do nothing more.

Likić likić. To spring up and down, jerk up and down, to vibrate.

Likir. } To spring up and down as anything long and pliant if unsupported in the middle, to shake, to vibrate.
Likir likir.
Likiť likiť.

Likir likir hilauk kana.
Orak likir likirokkana.

Likiť domok. To move or sway the body, as an enthusiastic dancer.

Khubko hilaukkana likiť domok.
Bir jel lekam likiť domogokkan.

Liki phiki. Frightened, panic stricken.

Botorteko liki phikikkana. They are panic stricken through fear.

Likoć lokoć. Cf. lirkoć lorkoć.

Liko lokó. To sway, or totter, as one carrying too heavy a load on the head.

Liko loko dipilakadae. She totters as she carries it on her head.

Bae dipil hewaakante liko lokok kanae. She is tottering not being accustomed to carry on the head.

Lil. } Blue, the Indigo plant, *Indigofera tinctoria, Linn.*
Nil.

Lila. An entertainment, a show, a spectacle, a sight, tamasa.

Ceť lilako lagaoakaťa? What is the *tamasa*?
Lilako uthaukeda. They got up an entertainment.

Oka lila hõ bań bujhaueda. I cannot understand the *rationale* of it (I see no tamasa in it.)

Lilam. An auction, to auction; to eat.

Dahrako lilamkeťkoa. They sold the bullocks by auction.

Lilamreń hataokeťkina. I got them at an auction.

Ceť pe senakkan sanamko lilam cabakeda.

Lilhi. F. } Foolish, ignorant.
Lelha. M.

Lilhi aimai. A foolish woman.

Liliau. To hound on, to set on, as a dog, to egg on.

Liliauadeako. They set a dog on him.
Horko liliauakadea. Other people hounded him to it.

Lilibici. } Beautful with coloured patterns or figures, as cloth, stained glass, &c.
Lilibichi.

Lilka lilki. To covet, to long for.

Reńgeće lilka lilki baraekanako. They are longing for food through being hungry.

Lilkathi. A small plant, *Polygala crotalarioides, Buch. & Ham.*

Lilkau. } To wheedle, to cause to long for, coax, covet, desire.
Lalkao.
Lilkar.

Asam Kacarte horko lalkao idiećkoa. They wheedle men into going to Assam and Cachar.

Gidra alom lilkaukoa. Do not cause the children to long for it.

Gidra samahre alom joma, lilkaukako. Do not eat before the children, they will long for some too.

Lilkar idikedeako. They wheedled him into going with them.

Lilmani. A precious stone of a blue colour.

Lilo loko. } Shaky in the loins, weak in the loins.
Liro loko.

Lilo lokoe dipilakaťa.

Liloj. Disobedient, obstinate, bad.

Lima̤ṅ lamaṅ. Long, reaching to the ground, as a garment; whole body clothed.

Limboć. To throttle with both hands, to put the forelegs on the neck of another, as dogs when fighting.
Limboćkedeae. He throttled him with both hands.

Lin. To press with the hands, to squeeze.
Hoṭoḱe linkedea. He throttled him.
Ghaoe linkećtiña. He pressed my wound.
Lin gejerkedeako. They used him roughly.

Linḍa̤. } A species of small fish
Linḍa̤ hako. } having a very minute mouth.

Linḍa̤r. } To become efficient, to be
Linḍor. } equal to, to be practised, accustomed to.

Linḍa̤r lapar. } Long and shaking, shak-
Linḍa̤r la̤pur. } ing, as tattered gar-
Lindla̤pur. } ments.
Lindla̤pure bandeakana. She is wearing her garment long.
Sanam kicrić lindla̤purentaea. All his clothes are tattered.
Ceć leka bae bandeakan lindla̤pur.

Linḍbhinḍ. Extremely, excessively, applied to corpulency.
Linḍbhinḍe moṭaakana. He is extremely fat.

Linḍhi. } The anus.
Linḍi. }
Linḍhi bhuḱ. The anus.

Linḍiḱ. To mock, to despise.

Lindla̤pur. Long and shaking, shaking, fluttering, as tattered garments.

Linḍor. To become efficient, to be equal to, to be practised, accustomed to. Cf. linḍa̤r.

Liṅgi. } To trickle, to drip, to flow or
Liṅji. } run gently, as liquid.
Daḱ liṅgi jarwaḱkana. The water is dripping and accumulating.
Liṅji oḍokoḱkana, It is oozing out.
Lenlekhan liṅji todoḱa. If it be pressed (liquid) will ooze out and trickle down.

Liṅgić. } To be startled or fright-
Liṅgić liṅgić. } ened, to palpitate. Cf. leṅgeć.
Liṅgić liṅgidoḱkanae.

Liṅgić liṅgić. Wearisome, uninteresting. Cf. leṅgeć leṅgeć.

Liṅgṛi. F. } Left-handed.
Leṅgṛa. M. }
Liṅgṛi a̤ima̤i. A left-handed woman.
Liṅgṛite jomedae. She eats with her left hand.

Lipa̤ lape. To fly slowly and hesitatingly, as a young bird just beginning to fly.

Lipa̤ lopo. Cf. lipa̤ lape.
Lipi cẽṛẽ da̤i lipa̤ lopo.

Lipa̤ṅ lapaṅ. Shorter than customary, loosely.
Kicrić lipa̤ṅ lapaṅe bandeakaća. She is wearing her cloth shorter than is customary.
Ceć lekae oyoakana lipa̤ṅ lapaṅ?

Lipa̤ṭ lapaṭ. Lagging behind.
Lipa̤ṭ lapaṭe ta̤ṛameda. He walks lagging behind.

Lipi cẽṛẽ. } The Ashy-crowned Finch
Gõeṭha lipi. } Lark, *Pyrrhulauda grisea.*
Kumba lipi. A small bird so named from the shape of the nest it builds.

Lipić peṭeć. } Light grain that has been
Peṭeć lipić. } removed by the process of winnowing.
Eken lipić peṭećko emadiña. They gave me only the light grain removed by winnowing.

Lipin. The Reciprocal form of 'lin' (q. v.)

Lipinḍić. Mica.
Lipinḍić hasa. Soil mixed with decomposed mica shale.

Lipir lipir. To quiver, as an aspen leaf, to ripple, as a wave on the shore.
Lipir lipir hila̤uḱkana. It is quivering.
Daḱ lipir lipiroḱkana. The water is rippling (on the shore.)

Liplap. To flap the wings, to shew off conceitedly, to give oneself airs, to sway.
Liplaboḱkanae. It is flapping its wings.
Liplap ba̤ṛaekanae. She is shewing off.
La̤uka liplaboḱkana. The boat sways from side to side.

Liplip. } To shine brightly, to be
Liplipa̤u. } glossy, to tremble, to shake, quiver, twinkle.
Sadom liplipe ñeloḱkana. The horse's skin is glossy.
Ipilko liplipa̤uḱa. The stars twinkle.

Lipoć lopoć. To walk slowly and painfully, as one tired and footsore.
Lipoć lopoće ta̤ṛameda. He walks slowly and painfully.

Lipsa̤. Too pliant, as a bow; weak, as the spring of a gun lock.
Lipsa̤ aḱ. A too easily bent bow.
Ba̤nduk reaḱ ghoṛa lipsa̤ena. The hammer of the gun is become weak.

Lipuk̕.
Libuk̕. } To deceive, to wheedle.

Jom lipuk̕ket̕koae.
Eṛe lipuk̕kedeae. He wheedled him.
Kạmi lipuk̕ ocokedeae. He wheedled him into working for him (and paid him nothing.)

Lipur. A band tied round the ankle to which are attached a number of little hollow globes of bell-metal with small stones or pieces of iron inside, worn when dancing.

The little hollow globes attached to the lipur are called "jhunkạ" (q. v.)

Liṛić.
Liṛić piṭić.
Liṛić piṛić. } Small, a small child, a number of small children.

Onko liṛić lagakom. Drive away those little children.
Noko liṛić piṭić nonḍe cet̕ko ñamkana? What do these children want here?

Liṛkoć loṛkoć.
Likoć lokoć. } Slack, loose, movement of head, as of a child whose neck is weak.

Alom liṛkoć loṛkojea, heo thirkaeme. Do not allow his (a child) head to sway from side to side, hold him steady.

Liṛoć loṛoć. Slack, aimlessly.

Cet̕ lekam bhagwaakana liṛoć loṛoć?
Am do kạmi bạgikate liṛoć loṛoć baṛaekanam.

Liṛok loṛok, Empty-handed, in vain, without purpose.

Liṛo loṛo. Loosely.

Liṛo loṛo bhagwaakanae. He has not tightened up his *bhagwa*, (q. v.)

Liṛoṅ loṛoṅ.
Loroṅ soroṅ. } Slack, aimlessly.

Liṛoṅ loṛoṅ ḍaṅrako joṛaoakadea.
Kạmi bạgikate liṛoṅ loṛoṅe dãṛãbaṛaekana.

Liṛwạ. To bend over, backwards or downwards.

Liṛwạ saṛwe.
Liṛwạ laṛwe.
Liḍwa saḍwe. } Weakly, feebly, half-heartedly, inefficiently, slack, unable to keep the body straight, as a drunk man, shaky, tottering, staggering.

Ceka liṛwạ laṛwe baṛaekan bam?
Onte note liṛwạ laṛwe baṛaekana. It is swaying to one side and the other.

Liṛwạ thaṛwe. Cf. liṛwa saṛwe.

Rengeġte liṛwạ thaṛweġnaṅ. I am shaky through hunger.

Liṛwić piṭić. Cf. liṛić.

Lisi.
Lisind.
Susi. } Opportunity, chance, excuse, pretence.

Ruạ lisindte bae kạmikana. He is not working on the pretence of having fever.
Lisinde ñam baṛaeda, Cet̕ lekate uniṅ girạuea.

Lisoe losoe.
Liso loso.
Losoe losoe. } Applied to the gait of a female who is stout, heavily clad, and wearing heavy anklets.

Lisoe losoe baṛaekanae. She is moving about slowly and heavily.

Lisot̕ losot̕.
Isot̕ osot̕. } Applied to the waddling gait of a very corpulent person.

Lisot̕ losot̕e calak̕kana. He waddles.

Lit.
Nit. } Now. Cf. nit.

Met̕ dak̕ lit joṛok̕rehõ. Although (my) tears were now to flow.

Liṭạ. A mythical hero.

Liṭạ ak̕. The rainbow, the bow of Liṭạ (q. v.)

Liṭạ tombṛe. A species of wasp.

Liṭhi. To be heavy with sleep, as the eyelids, to overcome, to take precedence.

Ạdak̕ kathage liṭhik̕kana. His word is to be law.
Met̕ liṭhik̕a dudṛum jokheć. The eyelids are heavy when one is sleepy.

Liṭhir.
Liṭhir liṭhir. } Crashing, as of a thunder peal, banging, of a gun, noise produced by an explosion of gunpowder, &c.

Men ceṭer ñurena liṭhir. The thunder bolt fell crashing.

Liṭhir marte.
Liṭhir mente. } With a crash, as of thunder or an explosion, with a bang, as of a gun.

Liṭhum.
Liṭhum liṭhum.
Luṭhum. } Smacking or thudding sound, sound of thumping.

Liṭhum liṭhumko dalkedea. They smacked him repeatedly (they struck him and produced a smacking sound.)

Liṭhum marte.
Liṭhum mente. } With a smack, thud, or thump.

Liṭhum menteko dalkedea. They hit him thump.

Liṭhur.
Niṭhur. } Pleasant, sweet, enticing, captivating, mellifluous.

Ạdi liṭhur galmaraotae. His conversation is pleasing.
Khub liṭhure ruieda. He beats the drum very pleasantly (in good time.)
Khub liṭhur tirioe oroṅeda. He plays the flute sweetly.

Liṭi. Gone bad, soured, mouldy, decomposition set in, used with regard to food.

Liṭi daka. Boiled rice unfit for consumption.
Utu liṭik̕a. The relish will go bad.

Liṭi birsi. All kinds, all sorts, many kinds, many sorts, all manner of, all, the whole.

Liṭi birsiye roṛeda. He talks all manner of stuff.

Aḍi kami menak̓tińa liṭi birsi. I have much work of many kinds to do.

Liṭi birsile jomeda, emanteak̓. We eat all kinds of things.

Liṭir piṭir. Weak, emaciated and feeble.

Dhere liṭir piṭirena. He has become very feeble.

Aḍiye osok̓ena liṭir piṭir. He has become very emaciated and feeble.

Liṭpiṭia. Lean, skinny.

Rengecte liṭpiṭiageae. He is skinny through hunger.

Lituṛ hako. A species of small eel found in rivers.

Liwar lawar. Dangling, hanging in folds.

Liwar lawar aturakana baṛe joro. The aerial roots of the Banyan tree hang dangling down.

Liwer lawar. } Long, or far reaching and
Liwer liwer. } nearly horizontal, as the branches of a Banyan tree.

Liwer lawer ḍarakana. The branches extend almost horizontally.

Liweć. To bend, to droop.

Ḍar or liwedme. Pull down the branch, (pull and bend the branch.)

Maćko liwećakaća. They have bent the bamboo.

Liwedok̓gea. It will bend.

Liwić. } To be springy at the
Liwić liwić. } extremities, to bob up and down.

Marāṛ bah liwijok̓kantaea. His banghy pole is not springing.

Liyoṛ loyoṛ. } To move zigzag, serpen-
Liyor loyor. } tine.

Bińko dāṛā baṛaea liyoṛ loyoṛ. Snakes move in a zigzag.

Lo. To draw water, to lift water by dipping a vessel into it, to take rice, &c., out of a pot with a ladle, &c.

Dak̓ loe senakana. She has gone to draw water.

Daka loeme. Take the boiled rice out of the pot.

Lo. To burn, to scald.

Oṛak̓ loentakoa. Their house is burned down.

Lo ḍigir. } To burn to ashes.
Lo toroć. }

Lo poṭak̓. To burn to ashes, to scald so as to form a blister.

Baske dak̓ manḍire lok̓ hoṛ. A person whom cold rice water would scald (a modest estimate of one's abilities.)

Lo bir. } The burnt jungle, the
Lo bir sendra. } burnt jungle hunt.

Lo birkedam, enhõ bam daṛelena. You took it (a complaint) to the burnt jungle, still you did not succeed.

Lo bir baisi. The court which assembles on the evening of an annual hunt.

At the beginning of the hot weather the hills and jungles are as a rule set fire to for the purpose of clearing away the wealth of under growth, grass, leaves, &c., which have accumulated during the year, so that hunting may be less dangerous and more easily prosecuted. For hunting purposes the hills and jungles are divided into sections each under a Dihri (q. v.). The court which assembles after the day's hunt is over is the supreme court of the Santals. Any Santal who considers himself aggrieved by any decision which has been given during the year may appeal to this court, which sits after the day's hunt in the burnt jungle is over, and his appeal is decided by his compeers under the presidency of the Pargana (q. v.) of the district. Questions that arise during the day connected with the hunt are decided by the hunters under the presidency of the Dihri (q. v.) or hunt master.

Loa. } A species of fig tree, *Ficus*
Loa dare. } *glomerata*, *Roxb.*, the fruit of *Ficus glomerata.*

Lob. } To covet, covetousness,
Lob laloc } avarice.

Lobab. } A great man, a prince.
Nobab. }

Loban. To offer the first fruits.

Loban. A mela held yearly at Buḍhai in the Santal Pargannas.

Loban. Frankincense.

Lobde eneć. A game so called.

Lobdhao. To attract, charm, allure, entice, entangle.

Lobdhao tahẽnae paura dokanre. He got entangled at the public house and remained.

Lobe. Cf. lob. [to entice.

Lobhao. To amuse, to divert, to charm,

Lobhao dohokedeako. They enticed him to remain with them.

Lobhatia. Covetous, avaricious.

Lobhi. Greedy, covetous.

Lobhok̓. } Fat, very obese and
Lobhok̓ lobhok̓. } flesh quivering with each movement of the body.

Lobhok̓ lobhok̓e calak̓kana.

Lobhor. Soft.

Lob laloc. Covetousness, avarice.

Lobo dhorok̓. Fat, very corpulent, extremely, applied only to fatness.

Lobo dhorok̓e moṭaakana. He is extremely corpulent.

Loboe. }
Loboe loboe. } Long and dangling.
Loboe loboele eneća. We will dance with long dangling or waving skirts.
Loboegea. It is long and dangling.
Loboe loboe ghãs bahaakana. The flowers of the grass are long and dangling.

Loboe ghãs. A common fodder grass, *Anthistiria Wightii, Nees.*

Loboe kharaṅ ghãs. }
Kharaṅ loboe ghãs. } A grass, *Aristida depressa, Retz,* the culms of which are used to make brooms.

Loboe bak. }
Loboe bãk. } The large, white Paddy bird.

Loboe gaya. A capon with very long feathers.

Loboe eneć. A dance by men during the Dasãe (q. v.)

Loboe sereń. The songs sung when the *Loboe* is being danced.

Loboe ru. The time beaten on the drum during the *Loboc* dance.

Loboj. Cf. laboj.

Lobojhor. Fat and big-bellied.
Duṛuḃakanae lobojhor.

Lobok̓. Flour, meal, made from any kind of grain, fruit, &c., food, to make into flour.
Hoṛo lobok̓. Rice flour.
Heṛe lobok̓. Flour made from rice husks.
Jạnum lobok̓. Flour made from the fruit of the Janum tree, *Zizyphus Jujuba.*
Terel lobok̓. Flour made from the fruit of the Terel tree, *Diospyros tomentosa, Roxb.*
Jondra lobok̓. Flour made from Indian corn.
Noa do lobogok̓a. This will be made into flour.
Lobok̓akaťae. She has made it into flour.

Lobok̓ kõk̓. The little brown-backed Paddy bird.

Lobok̓ muć. The Flour ant, a small red ant.
Lobok̓ muć gegerkanako, The Flour ants are biting, i. e. I feel the pangs of hunger.
Lobok̓ muć bako jạpiť ocoaekana. The Flour ants will not allow him to sleep, *i. e.* hunger prevents him sleeping.

Loć. }
Toć. } *Membrum virile.*

Loca. To lift with the hand, to take a handful.
Locawaeme. Take some up with the hand and give him.
Khajạṛi locakateko hapạṭińkana. They are dividing the parched rice by taking it up in handfuls (or with the hand.)

Lochon. }
Lachan. } Bad habits, evil courses, bad behaviour; motive, springs of action.
Noa lochon do bạgime. Leave off this bad habit.

Locloco. Long under lip, to pout, to sulk, to protrude the under lip.
Locloco baṛaekanae. She is pouting.
Luṭi loclocogetaea. His under lip is long, he is hanging his lip, *i. e.* he is sulky.

Locoe locoe. }
Locok̓ locok̓. } To spring up and down, as anything long and pliant if unsupported, to shake, to vibrate, springy. Cf. likir.

Locoṅ. Pointed, narrowing to a point, uneven, a cape, a promontory.
Miť seć locoṅakana. One side is pointed.
Bir reak̓ locoṅre. At the narrow point of the jungle.

Locor. }
Locor locor. } Unnatural craving for any delicacy which one sees without regard to whether one has had sufficient or not.
Locor bhaṅgao. }
Locor marao. } To appease the appetite.

Locor pocor. Unreliable, not to be depended on.
Locor pocore galmaraokana. He is talking rubbish.
Uniak̓ katha alope sabtaea locor pocorgea. Do not accept his statement, he is unreliable.

Locoť locoť. Numerous, in multitudes.
Locoť locoťko jaoraakana. They are assembled in multitudes.

Locra. M. }
Lucri. F. } Greedy, given to stealing eatables.
Locra ḍaṅra. A greedy bullock (always getting among the growing grain.)

Lodam. A small forest tree the bark of which yields a valuable mordant, *Symplocos racemosa, Roxb.*

Lodam. }
Buru lodam. } Level ground at the base or on the slope of a hill.
Lodam lodamreko berelakana. They have built their houses on the level spots on the slope of the hill.

Lodam. }
Odam. } The common Indian otter, *Lutra nair.*

Lodga. M. }
Ludgi F. } Stout, big-bodied, often also given as a name, Lodga to a male, and Ludgi to a female.

Lodhea. Fat, stout, big-bodied, also given as a name to a male who is stout, or fat.

Lodhor lodhor. } Fat, obese, corpulent.
Ladhar lodhor. } flesh hanging in folds and shaking during movement, as of a very fat man or animal. Cf. ladhar lodhor.

Lodhor lodhor. Thick, gummy, thick and frothy.

Lodhor lodhor meṭ khon beñjaḱ oḍokoḱkana. Thick matter is coming from his eyes.
Bele lodhor lodhor oḍokoḱkana. Thick pus is coming out.

Lodhra. A sapling, saplings about the thickness of a man's arm.

Lodhroḱ. } Fat, corpulent.
Lodhṛoḱ. }

Lodo dhoṛo. } Quivering, shaking, as a
Loto dhoṛo. } very nervous person anxious to get something, shaking with excitement.

Lodo dhoṛoḱ. Fat, corpulent, indistinctly.

Lodop̆. } Shaking, swaying.
Lodop̆ lodop̆. }

Lodop̆ lodop̆e hilạuḱkana.
Lodop̆ lodop̆e eneḱkana.
Lodop̆ lodop̆ko bahaakana.

Lodop̆ marte. } To flop down, to fall
Lodop̆ mente. } with a flop, as anything heavy and soft.

Lodop̆ mente ńurenae. He flopped down.

Loḍor boḍor. } Anyhow, as best one
Loḍor poḍor. } may, inefficiently.
Luḍur buḍur. }

Loḍor poḍoriń benaoakaṭa. I have made it anyhow.
Taeomlenale, loḍor poḍorle rohoeḱeda. We were late, we planted (our rice) as best we could.

Lodor bodor. Soft, of the consistency of porridge.

Lodṛo. Fat, chubby, speaking indistinctly.

Lodṛoe moṭaakana. He (child) is very fat.
Lodṛo kanae. He is an indistinct speaker.

Loe. To help, to assist, to accompany; together, along with.

Pạhile kạmi loeaekhan enoḱ iroḱre adoe ńama. If he assist him with his work at the beginning, at the time of reaping and threshing he gets (some of the grain.)
Ona dinre bam kạmi loelaḱa, ceṭ lekate tumạl tolsam ńama?
Jom loeko neotakope. Invite those who can eat in company, or along with us.

Loetoṛ. Long, very long.

Loetoṛ jeleńa. It is very long.

Logno. Strong, strong and well proportioned, beautiful.

Logno ḍahra kanae. It is a strong and well made bullock.

Logon. } Preparations or all things
Lagan. } necessary for the due celebration of an event, but mainly used with regard to a marriage or the Sohrae (q v.) festival, the knotted string fixing the date of a marriage, appointed time, crisis.

Bapla reaḱ logon tioḱakana.
Are mãhã reaḱ girạ se logonko tola.
Bapla reaḱ logonko tolkeda.
Logonte. Expeditiously.

Logoṭ logoṭ. Soft.

Tạkiạ logoṭ logoṭ aṭkaroḱkana. The pillow feels soft.
Logoṭ logoṭ aṭeṭkate gitićakanae. He spread a soft bed and is lying down.

Loha luti. Iron utensils and implements.

Lohạni. Noted, famous, clever, expert, able, of good report.

Kạmire ạdi lohạniakanae. He is very expert at work.

Lohke. } Carefully, gently.
Lohke lohke. }

Lohke lohkete taṛamme. Step carefully.
Lohkete tulme. Lift it gently.
Lohketeko oooḱeṭkana, alo caprạḱa mente. They remove it gently so that it may not flatten (a vessel from off the potter's wheel.)

Lohok. Slowly, leisurely.

Bejãe lohokem taṛameda. You are walking amazingly leisurely.

Lohok. Parabolic, proverbial.

Lohok roṛ. A parable, a proverb.

Lohok. To sway the body to the time of the music when dancing or beating the drum.

Noko ruru jokheḱko lohokaḱa. When beating the drums these (men) sway their body to the time.

Lohoḱ lohoḱ. } Wide, long.
Layoḱ layoḱ. }

Usul hoṛ lohoḱ lohoḱko taṛama. Tall people take long strides.

Lohom. To die, used by women when angry.

Lohomoḱme. Die (and rid me of yourself.)
Lohom hõ bae lohomoḱkana, dalińkanae. He is not dying (as I wish he would), he is beating me.

Lohor. To delay, to dilly dally.

Ạdi lohorkedae, uni hoṛ do. That man put off much time.

Lohoṛ. To dry. Cf. rohoṛ.

Lohor bohor.
Lohor lopor.
Lodor bodor. } Soft, of the consistency of porridge.

Lohor loporko utuakaṭa. They have cooked the relish too soft.
Sipi lohor loporakaṭako. They have mixed it with water till it is of the consistency of porridge.

Lohoṭ. To be wet, moist, damp.

Kicriċ lohoṭena. The cloth is wet.
Lohoṭ janena. It is too wet (it has been allowed to absorb too much moisture.)
Lohodoḱam. You will get wet.
Lohoṭ lugṛi. Wet cloth.
Lohoṭkedeae. He wetted him.
Lohoṭge aṭkaroḱkana. It feels wet.

Lohta. The lower part of a kanḍa or waterpot, which has been broken across through the middle, protuberant, as the stomach.

Loka. To catch in the hands, as a ball; to play with, as a cat with a mouse; to catch in the mouth, as a dog anything thrown to it; to bandy words, to dandle an infant on the hands.

Capaṭadeań bae lokalaḱa. I threw (the ball) to him, he did not catch it.
Gidṛako loka eneśkoa. They dandle infants on the hands.
Mase, pusi ńeleme ceṭ lekae lokaedekana. Come look at the cat, how she is playing with it (a mouse.)

Loka guṭi. A children's game.

Lokań. To break the arm.

Tiye dal lokańkedea. He struck and broke his arm.

Lokao.
Lotao. } To lie in wait, to watch for an opportunity.

Pusi hone lotaoedekana. The cat is lying in wait for a rat.
Kombṛo lạgiṭe lokao baṛaeda. He is watching for an opportunity to steal.

Lokhibar.
Lukhibar. } Thursday, the fifth day of the week.

Lok loko. To keep the fingers or wrist bent, until they become too stiff to move.

Tiye loklokoakaṭa. He has kept his fingers bent until they are now too stiff to move.

Lokomdoroḱ. Very stout, very corpulent.

Lokomdoroḱe moṭaakana. He is very corpulent.
Lokomdoroḱe ńeloḱkana. He appears very stout.

Lokomduri. Large, applied to the fruits of certain trees and the flowers of the Matkom (q. v.) tree.

Lokomduri matkom. Large Matkom flowers.
Lokomduri ńeloḱkana. The fruit appears of large size.

Loko phoko.
Lako phoko. } Applied to the sound produced when any thick substance is boiling and bubbling, to puff and blow, to breathe heavily, as a person or animal out of breath with exertion.

Kạmite lokophokoenae. He is puffing and blowing with working.

Lokoṛe. Having a stiff disabled arm.

Lokor phokor.
Lakar phakar. } Tired, worn out or fatigued before work, &c. has been completed.

Kạmi kạmitele lokor phokorena. We are worn out with working and still have not finished.
Dāṛā dāṛātele lakar phakharena. We are tired out with walking and yet have not completed our journey.

Lokoṭ.
Lokoṭ lokoṭ. } The throat to move with each respiration, as a hen panting.

Lokoṭ lokodoḱkanae.

Lokphokao. To puff, as a bear; to boil and bubble. Cf. lokophoko.

Onte lokphokaoḱkanae alope calaḱa. He (a bear) is puffing over there, do not go.
Bana leka rel gạḍi lokphokao calaḱkana. The engine goes puffing like a bear.

Lokṛe. Injured, hurt, wounded; deformed or crippled, as hand or foot through injury.

Ti lokṛeẽntaea. His hand is maimed (lost a finger through an injury.)
Jańga lokṛeẽntaea. His foot is deformed, (having been injured.)

Loksan.
Noksan.
Nuksan. } To destroy, to injure, to perish, to die; injury, scath, damage, havoc.

Pohoko cas ạḍiko loksankeda. The locusts greatly injured the crops.
Dinkalom ạḍi hoṛko loksanena. Last year many people perished (from starvation,)
Ạḍi loksankeṭtińam. You did much damage to my property.

Lokṭa.
Lokṭha. } To quarrel, to be at variance with each other, to dispute, mainly with regard to possession of land or trees.

Lokṭhako janamakaṭa. They have started a dispute (with regard to possesion of a field.)
Okoe tuluċ hõ alom lokṭhaḱa. Do not quarrel with any one.
Ot reaḱko lokṭhaḱkana. They are disputing about the possession of some land.

Lol. To wheedle, to cajole, to persuade.

Lolkedińae. He cajoled me.

Lolao.
Lalao. } To long for, to crave for, to be tantalised, to be destitute.

Lolo lolo. A lullaby sung by Santal mothers to cause a child to sleep.

Gidṛako lolo lolokoa.

Lolo. Hot, heated, to be envious, impatient.
Seṅgel lologea. The fire is hot.
Ot netar hõ lologea. The ground at this time of the year also is hot.
Calak lagitko loloakana. They are impatient to start.
Loloakem ńamkana? Do you wish hot (water, food, &c.)
Hape, thirokpe, loloakem ńamkan? Wait a bit, do you want something hot? (used by women when scolding.)
Lolo lologeń jomkeda. I ate it scalding hot.
Lolo dak. Hot water.

Lolok. } **Lalak.** } To shew off, as one shewing what he can do in dancing, to cut a figure.
Loloke udukeda. He is shewing off.
Aḍim lolokeṭkana. You are making a great show.

Lolopoto. Hastily, hurriedly.
Lolopotoko rohoe goṭkeda. They planted (the rice) hurriedly.

Lombor. } **Nombor.** } **Nomor.** } Cor. of the English word "number," to institute legal proceedings, to lay a complaint.
Uni ńutumteń nomborakaṭa. I have brought a suit against him.

Lomoń. } **Lomoń lomoń.** } Fine, as flour; soft, as a pillow.
Lomoń lomoń aṭkarokkana. It feels very soft.

Lomor. The foreskin.

Lomor lomor. } **Lemer lemer.** } To move the lips when eating as is peculiar to horses, goats, and several other animals.
Sadom lomor lomorko joma. Horses keep moving the lips in a peculiar way while grazing.

Lomosoro. To endeavour, to exert oneself to do or obtain; to wish, to desire.
Hathao lagit lomosorokkanae. He is anxious to obtain.
Olok lagit lomosoroenae, He is about to begin to write (has all in readiness.)

Lompoṭiạ. Lazy and dissolute.

Lona. That. Cf. ona
Lona mohnḍa. That direction.

Lonbon. } **Londbond.** } A steward, an agent; to trade, to perform the duties of a steward.
Aḍi londbondedae, He does much trade.
Amak londbond reak hisab emokme, ente ado bam londbond dareaka. Give an account of thy stewardship, for thou can'st no longer be steward.

Londbhonḍ. To defile, to transgress social customs.
Sanampe londbhonḍakaṭa ohoń jomlea. You have defiled all, I will not eat.
Begor baplatekin miṭentekin londbhonḍena.

Londbond. A steward, a trader. Cf. lonbon.

Lonḍhea. } **Lenḍhea.** } Lazy, careless, disobedient.
Lonḍhea hoṛ. A sluggard.

Londkoṭ. Having big, staring eyes, used mainly when fault-finding.
Londkoṭe beṅgeṭakaṭa. He is staring (when he should be doing what he is told.)
Londkoṭ, bam ńel ńameda? You staring fool, don't you see it?

Londoć. Hollow, to have a depression or depressions on the surface, to become depressed.
Ot laṛaolenre adom adom ṭhenre ot londoć boloena. At the earthquake the earth became depressed at some places, i. e. sank.
Ḍubhi londoćentaea. His hip has a depression in it.
Mak londoćkedae kaṭ do. He hacked a depression (hollow) in the surface of the log.

Londo londo. Staringly, having big, staring eyes.
Londo londoko beṅgeṭadea. They looked at him with wide open eyes.

Londphond. To tell tales, to make mischief by tale bearing, to create discord, to foment quarrels.
Unige londphonde joṛao baṛaeda. He it is who is fomenting the quarrel.

Londphondiạ. Mischief making, quarrel fomenting.
Londphondiạ hoṛ kanae. He is a mischief maker.

Loṅgor coṅgor. Frivolous, licentious, rakish, lecherous.
Loṅgor coṅgore dhutiakana. He is dressed with a view to captivate.

Loṅgra. M. } **Luṅgri. F.** } Unchaste, wanton, licentious, incontinent, impure.
Loṅgra luṅgrikin ńapamakana. The wanton he and the wanton she are mated together.

Loṅka. } **Laṅka.** } Distant, far off.
Aḍi loṅkagea. It is very far off.
Aḍi laṅkatem senlena. You went very far away.

Loṅka. Ceylon.

Loṅka gaṛ. The fort of Ceylon.

Loṅki. Weak or disabled in the arm, applied to females.

Lop. To elide, to be elided, to be lost.
Noa harop lopena. This letter is elided.

Lopak'. } A hollow, hole or cavity of
Lophak'. } no great depth in a bank, hill, hedge or other upright object.
Marah darah reak lopak. A cave in a large precipice.
Jhanti lopakre durupakan tahẽkanae. He was sitting in a hole in the hedge.

Lopion. } Soft, downy, as grass, feathers
Lopioṅ. } or hair.

Loplopo. To crouch or sit huddled up, as one very cold.
Rabah iste loplopoe durupakana. He is sitting huddled up on account of the cold.

Lopoć. To do, used chaffingly by brothers-in-law to sisters-in-law, and *vice versa*, when out of hearing of others. Cf. loć.
Lopoćkedam? You did it?

Lopok'. } A soft thudding sound,
Lopok' lopok'. } flop.
Lopok lopoke thaiakedea. He kicked him several times with a thud thud.

Lopok' marte. } With a soft, thudding
Lopok' mente. } sound, with a flop. Cf. lapak' lapak'.
Lopok mente ńur goćena. It fell with a flop.

Lopoṅ dare. A forest tree, *Terminalia belerica. Roxb.*
Lopoṅ tuti. An arrow with a fruit of the Lopong on the tip, used to shoot birds with.

Lopoṅ arak'. A wild pot-berb, *Ærua lanata, Linn.*

Lopoṅ herak'. A small plant, *Uraria lagopoides, D. C.*

Lopoṅ thopa. A bunch of Lopoṅ (q. v.) fruit, used sarcastically to one who has failed.
Cećem oekakeda, lopoṅ thopakedam? What did you do? Did you accomplish it?.

Lopor. } Of the consistency of
Lopor lopor. } soft mud, porridge, or moulten metal; viscous, pasty.
Loporgea. It is thin (like moulten lead.)
Lopor lopor jondrako dakaakaća. They have cooked the porridge of Indian corn meal too thin.

Lopoć. } Very fine dust, to make
Lopoć lopoć. } very fine, as dust.
Hutiko jom lopoćakaća. The wood weevils have eaten it into dust.
Lopoć hormore baisauka. The fine dust adheres to the body.
Lopoć lopoćkedako. They made it very fine.

Lopotiaṅ arak'. Reddish, tinged with red.

Lopotiaṅ ghãs. A common fodder grass, *Eragrostis bifaria, W. & A.*

Lopotiaṅ arak'. A kind of wild potherb.

Lopotiaṅ up. Fine hair on the back of the neck.

Lopotiaṅ il. Down on the body of a newly hatched bird.

Lor. Sense, ability, skill. Cf. lur.

Lora. Necessity, occasion.

Lorao. To become faint, weak or feeble, to lose heart, to collapse through fatigue.
Rehgećteye loraoena. He has become enfeebled through hunger.
Upasteń bidalekokhan horreko loraoka. If I dismiss them fasting they will faint in the way.

Lorbo sorbo. To do wrongly, or inefficiently.
Sanam kamipe lorbo sorbokeda. You did all the work wrong.

Lorcor. To move, to shake, to use, to handle, to employ, to administer.
Alope lorcorka. Do not move.
Alope lorcora. Do not shake it.
Kãc do adi thusaha jat kana, ona iate bes okoćteko lorcora. Glass is of a very brittle nature, therefore it is handled with care.

Lordhej. Sense, skill, ability.
Oka hõ lordhej banuktaea. He has no ability whatsoever.

Lordho. Fusionless, stupid, good for nothing.
Okatak hõ bae dhejana, lordho mara hor. He can do nothing whatsoever, the fusionless muff.

Lore. A thick, sticky, milky juice which exudes from certain trees and plants when an incision is made in the bark.
Uni do lorek lekanak kathae rora. He speaks words like the milky, sticky juice of a tree (words that stick like birdlime.)

Lorea. } Tall and slim, slim, lanky.
Lorea lorea. }
Lorea loreae haraakana. He has grown lanky.

Lorjor. }
Larjar. } Related by marriage.
Larjor. }

Lorkaeni. Empty-handed, in vain, without result.
Lorkaeniń hećakana. I am come empty handed.

Loṛkoć. To hang to one side, to hang down, as the hand when the wrist is broken, or the head of a child who can't hold its neck stiff.
Hoṭok'e loṛkoćkeda. His head hung to one side.

Loṛo. To have sexual intercourse.

Loṛo.
Loṛo loṛo. } Long and narrow.
Loṛo khet. A long narrow rice field.
Simạ loṛo loṛo calaoena, ondẹ hạbić. The boundary has gone in like a wedge up to there.

Loṛoć loṛoć. Immodestly attired, or unattired.

Loṛo dhoṛo. Cf. loṛo thoṛo.

Loṛok loṛok. Empty-handed, in vain, without reason or purpose.
Eken tiye hijuk'kana loṛok loṛok.
Loṛok loṛoke hećakana. He is come empty handed.

Loṛo loṛo.
Loṛo thoṛo. } To be in a hurry, to be impatient to begin, to bungle or miss through haste, hastily and inefficiently.

Loṛoṅ coṛoṅ. To move, to shake.
Ondẹkhon bae loṛoṅ coṛoṅok'a. He will not move from there.

Loṛoṅ phocoṅ. Carelessly, inefficiently, dawdling, faultily.
Loṛoṅ phocoṅ baṛaea. He dawdles.
Loṛoṅ phocoṅe joṛaoakadea. He has yoked it (bullock) carelessly.

Loṛoṅ posoṅ. Loose and shaking, as a tooth,
Sanam ḍaṭa loṛoṅ posoṅgetaea.
Loṛoṅ posoṅe roṛa. He speaks indistinctly through having lost some of his teeth and others being loose.

Loṛo thoṛo.
Loto thoṛo. } To be in a hurry, to be impatient to begin, to bungle or miss through haste or nervousness; hastily and inefficiently.

Loṛpe. Large lobed, as the ear, having the lobes ef the ears unusually large.
Loṛpe lutur. A large lobed ear.
Loṛpegeae. The lobes of his ears are unusually large.

Loṛyo. Tall and slim, slim, lanky. Cf. lorea.

Loṛyo.
Loṛyoć. } To stand speechless while wishing to speak through impediment in speech, simple, silly, silent through stupidity.
Loṛyoć mara hoṛ. A stupid dummy.
Cele loṛyoć kan coe, roṛ bõ bae roṛa. What dummy is he, he will not open his mouth.

Losak'. To bite, to take a mouthful, used mainly of dogs.
Losak' goćkedeae. It bit him at once.
Seta ḍherko losaga. Dogs are most given to biting.

Losoe losoe. Applied to the gait of a female who is stout, heavily clad and wearing heavy ornaments.

Losoṅ.
Losoṅga.
Lasaṅga. } On account of.
Gidṛạ losoṅgateṅ calak'kan tahẽkana, gidṛạ ma bạnugić. I was going on account of the child, but the child is not there (or is dead.)

Losopondo. Dusty, dirty.
Gidṛạ losopondo dhuṛireko eneća.

Losoć. Mud, to become mud, to be bespattered with mud.
Losoćense. He is bespattered with mud.
Khetle losoćakaća. We have ploughed the field into mud.
Losoć lekae japićkeda. He fell into a deep sleep.

Loṭ. A Government currency note.
Bar kiṭạ loṭ. Two currency notes.
Gel ṭaka reak' loṭ. A ten rupee note.
Loṭ bhaṅjao ạguime. Cash the note and bring the money.

Loṭ. A handful, as much as the hand held scoop-wise will contain.
Aṅjle. As much as the hands will hold when put together. Cf. aṅjle.
Cupuć. A fist full, as much as one hand can enclose. Cf. cupuć

Lot.
Lot paṅj. } A clew, part or whole of stolen property. Cf. bomal.
Uniak' oṛak' khon lot oḍokakana. Part of the stolen property was found in his house.
Ghor tolasikedako, menkhan lot paṅj baṅ ṅamlena. They searched the house, but no trace of the stolen property was found.

Lota. A creeping or climbing plant.

Loṭa. A brass vessel used for drinking purposes.
Loṭa dak'. A *lota* of water.
Mić loṭa dak'ante teṅgoena. He stood holding a *lota* of water (referring to the attitude of submission assumed by one who has been out-casted praying for re-admission.)
Hoponera misera mić loṭa dak' reak' asrage. From a daughter or sister (when married) one can only expect a cup of water.

Lota luti. To skulk about looking for an opportunity to pounce upon anything, as a leopard.
Tạrup lota luti baṛaekanae. The leopard is skulking about looking for a chance to pounce upon some prey or other.

Loṭa luṭi. Brass house-hold utensils in general.

Lotao. To lie in wait, as a beast of prey; to watch for an opportunity to approach a superior.

Lotao baṛaedekanae. He is lying in wait for him (to present a petition.)

Loṭ ghuṭi. Unlawful carnal knowledge, adultery, fornication, to commit adultery or fornication.

Loṭha. Cf. laṭha.

Loṭho. Not obeying at once, requiring to be repeatedly told or urged.

Ạdi loṭho hoṛ kanae.

Loṭhor poṭhor. Tired, as one who has sat a long time.

Duṛuṕ duṛuṕte loṭhor poṭhorenań. I am tired with continued sitting.

Lothro. M. } Stout, fat.
Luthri. F. }

Khub lothroe ńeloḱkana. He looks nice and fat.

Loṭloṭo. To sulk and refuse to eat.

Loṭloṭo baṛaekanae. She is in a sulky mood.

Loṭo. A small thorny tree, *Randia dumetorum, Lam.*

Loṭoaḱ. High cheek bones, full cheeked.

Loṭoaḱe ńeloḱkana. He has high cheek bones.

Loṭoć. A large fly very troublesome to cattle during the rains.

Loṭoć. Injured, hurt, bruized, sprained.

Ti loṭoćentaea. His hand is injured.

Loto dhoṛo. Cf. lodho dhoṛo.

Lotoe. } Soft feeling, as of a boiled
Lotoe lotoe. } potatoe, turnip, &c., when eaten.

Lotoegea. It is soft.
Lotoe lotoe aṭkaroḱkana. It feels very soft.

Loṭoḱ. } To reduce to fine pow-
Loṭoḱ loṭoḱ. } der, to raise dust.

Huṛuń loṭoḱ loṭoḱkedako. They have ground it in the dhińki to a very fine powder.

Lebeć loṭoḱkedako. They trampled it into dust.

Loṭok. } Hindrance, intervention,
Laṭak. } event.

Loṭok lagaoena. A hindrance has occurred.
Nitoḱ bań jutoḱkana loṭok lagaoena. It will not succeed now, some thing has intervened to prevent it.

Ceć loṭok lagaoente bako heělena. What has intervened to prevent their coming?

Loṭom. To cover over, to hide by covering, to subdue, to refute, to abrogate.

Duṛuṕ loṭom. To cover by sitting on.
Lebeć loṭom. To tread in another's foot prints.
Gur loṭom khạsi. A goat which has been set apart for sacrifice at the Jomsim (q. v.) festival, but before its celebration some older member of the family has died and rendered the goat unsuitable for that particular sacrifice.
Kathako loṭomkeda. They hushed the matter up.
Gidrạe gitić loṭomkedea. She overlaid the child.
Sereń banamte loṭomoḱkana. The fiddle drowns the singing.
Doho loṭom. To cover by placing something on the top.
Uni do onkoaḱ sanam kathae loṭomkeťtakoa. He refuted all their statements.

Loṭopoṭo. } To be distressed, to cling
Loṭorpoṭor. } to place of residence.

Reńgeće̅tele loṭopoṭoena. We are in straits through hunger.
Dukrehõ sukrehõ nondege loṭorpoṭor menaḱlea. In affliction or prosperity we remain fixed here.
Noakore loṭopoṭo menaḱlea. We are fixed in this neighbourhood,

Loṭor. } To reduce to powder, or
Loṭor loṭor. } dust, powdered.

Lebeć loṭor loṭorkedako. They trampled it into dust.

Loto thoṛo. } To be in a hurry, to be im-
Loṛo thoṛo. } patient to begin, to bungle or miss through haste or nervousness; hastily and inefficiently.

Jom lạgić loto thoṛo baṛaekanae. He is very impatient to get his food.

Loṭpoṭ. } To wallow, to tumble and
Loṭpoṭao. } toss, to indulge illicit love,
Laṭpaṭao. } to be in an unseemly condition as one who has been tossing and tumbling about or wallowing. Cf. laṭpaṭao.

Loṭpoṭo dare. The Teak tree, *Tectona grandis, Linn. fil.*

Loyom. A toad-stool.

Loyoń jalo. } A fox, a hunting term.
Loyoń kulạı. }

Loyoń jalo. A species of large hawk. Cf. jalo.

Loyoń. A toad-stool.

Loyoń marte. } Without warning, sud-
Loyoń mente. } denly.

Oka do bhugạḱ khon loyoń menteko oḍokoḱa.

Loyoṛ. } Very long.
Loyor. }

Loyoṛ loyoṛ ńeloḱkana. It appears to be very long.
Loyor mać. A very long bamboo.

Loyoṛ marte. } Without warning, sud-
Loyor mente. } denly.

Lubạn. The first fruits given to a Brahman.

Luban. } Incense, the rezin of *Boswel-*
Loban. } *lia serrata.*

Lubạs lubus. Cf. lubus lubus.

Lubhạí. } Said when hounding on a
Lebhaić. } dog.

Lubhạu. } To amuse, divert, charm,
Lobhao. } entice. Cf. lobhao.

Lubhi. } To be greedy, covetous, avari-
Lobhi. } cious, to filch through greed.

Jel gegṛere alom lubhia. When cutting up the meat do not filch through greed.

Lubhiạ. Greedy, covetous, avaricious, dishonest through greed.

Lubhiạ gese hạṛṭiń alope metaea. He is greedy, do not give him the dividing of it.

Lubhrạ. } Easily bent, as a
Lubhrạ lubhrạ. } bow, &c.

Lubhuń lubhuń. } Leisurely, slowly,
Labhań lubhuń. } without apparent exertion.

Lublubu. Protuberant, as the stomach, soft,

Laḋ lublubu ńeloṛkantaea. His stomach seems protuberant.

Lublubiạ. } Soft. Cf. liblibia.
Liblibiạ. }

Lubuń lubuń. } Leisurely, slowly,
Lubhuń lubhuń. } without appar-
Labhań lubhuń. } ent effort. Cf. labhań lubhuń.

Lubui. } Thin, fine, as grass,
Lubui lubui. } straw, &c., the opposite, of stiff.

Jonoṛ lubuigea, The broom is thin (and therefore not stiff.)

Lubui ghās. A common fodder grass, *Anthistiria Wightii, Nees.* Cf. loboe ghās.

Lubur. } Soft, boggy.
Lubur lubur. }

Lubur lubur beleakana. It is ripe and soft.

Baṛe sakam ṣuri keṭejoṛa lubur luburgea. The Banyan leaves have not yet hardened, they are very soft. i, e. they are young.

Lubur marte. } Quickly and easily, as
Lubur mente. } into anything soft, without warning, used only in connection with soft substances.

Lubur marteń thạli gośena.

Lubus lubus. } To toddle, as a child
Lubas lubus. } learning to walk;
Labas lubus. } slowly and hesitatingly, soft, too pliant, too flexible, as a bow.

Lucạ. M. } Blackguardly, scoundrelly,
Luci. F. } rascally, vicious, immoral, profligate, unprincipled, disreputable.

Lucạ mara hoṛ. An unmitigated scoundrel.

Lucạ lamoṭ. Lasciviousness.

Luci. Cf. lucạ.

Lucpuc. } To be frightened, ner-
Lucpucạu. } vous trembling through fear of spirits or ghosts, superstitious fear.

Lucpuciạ. Frightened, trembling, shaking, terrified, through dread of the supernatural.

Lucpuciạ hoṛ kanae. He is a person who is frightened at ghosts or bhuts, &c.

Lucupucu. Cf lucpuc.

Lucri. F. } Greedy, given to stealing
Locra. M. } eatables.

Lucrigeae. Shea is greedy (cow stealing a mouthful of growing grain.)

Ludgi. F. } Stout, big-bodied. Cf.
Lodga. M. } lodga.

Ludgup̣. } With a thud, a
Ludgup̣ ludgup̣. } thudding sound.

Ludgup̣ ludgup̣ ńuroṛkana. They are falling thud thud.

Ludgup̣ marte. } With a thud.
Ludgup̣ mente. }

Ludhur ludhur. Shaking as the flesh of a fat person or animal when moving.

Ludhur ludhure moṭaakana. He is so fat that his flesh shakes when he walks.

Lud lud. } A succession of thuds, one
Lad lud. } after the other in succession, with a thud. Cf. ladlud.

Ludludu. To bend as an ear of grain when full.

Hoṛo gele ludluduena. The ear of rice is bent down.

Jote perećakana ludludu. It is loaded to bending with fruit.

Ludluduakana oal do. The roof (supports have given way and it) is hanging down.

Ludludu. To bulge, bulging.

Hasako puńjiakaṭa ludludu. They have piled up the earth till it is bulging.

Ludludu oraṛtako. Their house is bulging.

Jom ludluduenae. He has eaten to bulging.

Luduk. } Applied to the move-
Luduk luduk. } ments of a very fat
Ludup̆. } or corpulent person
Ludup̆ ludup̆. } whose flesh shakes each time he stirs.

Ludup̆ ludup̆e doneda. Each time he jumps his flesh shakes. [as he walks.
Luduk luduke calaǩkana. His flesh shakes

Ludur budur. Anyhow, as best one may, inefficiently. Cf. loḍor poḍor.

Luḍur luḍurle rohoekeda. We planted it (rice) anyhow.

Luduṛyuť. Very fat, very corpulent, extremely, applied to fatness.

Luduṛyuťe moṭaakana. He is excessively fat.

Lugạ. } Cloth, clothing.
Lugṛi. }

Niạte dole lugṛi joha. With this we will provide ourselves with clothes.

Luhi. A small, shallow iron pan.

Luhiạ. } A small shallow, iron pan.
Luiha. }

Luhu cuhu. } To take precedence, to
Ruhu ṭuhu. } take the lead, to flatter.

Luhu cuhu baṛaekanae. He is taking the lead.

Luhui. Iron-stone sand.

This iron is obtained by washing the sand of river beds and nallahs.

Luhui. } Very fine, as flour, &c.,
Luhui luhui. } finely powdered.

Luhui luhuiko huṛuṅakaťa. They have pounded it very fine.

Luhui luhui. Gently and cold, as the blowing of a north wind.

Luhui luhuiye hoeẽda. It is blowing gently and cold.

Luhum suhum. In a friendly manner, freely, cheerfully, wheedling by a shew of friendship or interest.

Jom lạgiť luhum suhum baṛaekanae. He is wheedling to get something to eat.
Luhum suhume galmaraoeda. He speaks honeyed words.
Luhum suhume emoǩkana. He is giving freely (without constraint.)

Lujhuk lujhuk. } To trot, to run at a
Lujhuṅ lujhuṅ. } moderate pace and
Lujuṅ lujuṅ. } continue it.

Lujuṅ lujuṅe dạṛ idieda. He goes swinging along at a good round pace.

Lujuǩ. } To move the body and
Lujuǩ lujuǩ. } feet so as to keep time with the springing of the banghy.

Bae lujuǩlenkhan oho jutlena. If he does not move his body so as to keep time with the springing of the banghy it will not work well.

Lujuk lujuk. Cf. lujhuk lujhuk.

Lujuṅ lujuṅ. Cf. lujhuṅ lujhuṅ.

Lukạ chapa. A secret, to do secretly, to keep secret.

Lukạ chapaedae. He does it secretly.
Noko lukạ chapa bạnuǩtakoa. These (people) have no secrets.

Lukhi. } Farm produce, live stock,
Lạkhi. } wealth, prosperity, lucky, fortunate.

Lukhi bạnuǩantaea, ninạǩ hõ baṅ. He has no grain stored in his house, not so much as this.
Lukhi maejiu kanae, ghorkornae babaea. She is a lucky woman, she lays past wealth.

Lukhibar. Thursday, the fifth day of the week.

Luki. A brass vessel often used to cook [in.

Lukluk. } To shiver, to tremble.
Luklukạu. }

Ruạte lukluk̇ạuǩkanae. She is shivering through fever.
Leď lukluk̇ạuǩkantaea.
Lukluk hilạuǩkanae. He is shivering.

Lukṛe. } Bent and stiff, as an injured
Lukṛeť. } finger; injured, broken, as a limb.

Jaṅga lukṛeťgetaea. His leg is stiff.
Lukṛeť lukṛeťe calaǩkana. He limps owing to a stiff leg. [his arm.
Tiye dal lukṛeťkeťtaea. He struck and broke

Lukui ghãs. A tall grass of *Arundinella* sp.

The culms of this grass are used to make brooms.

Lukur. } To tremble, shake,
Lukur lukur. } quiver; trembling, shaking, quivering, quaking.

Ti lukurgetaea. His hand is shaky (through nervousness.)
Rabạṅte lukur lukurehilạuǩkana. He is shaking with cold, or he is shivering.
Lukur lukur baṅ sap̆ ṭabrao daṛeada. I could not hold owing to my hands shaking.

Lukur marte. } With a start.
Lukur mente. }

Lukur marte hilạu goťenae. He gave a start.

Lukur thukur. } Cf. lukur.
Lukur tukur. }

Lukuť. } To start, as from sudden
Lukuť lukuť. } fright, to palpitate.

Lukuť goťada. He started.
Ackareko lukuť godoǩa. People start at anything that comes upon them unawares.
Bhabnate lukuť lukuťiṅ ạṭkareda. My heart palpitates through sorrow.
Lukuť lukuť tinre coṅ aṅgaǩ, meť hõ baṅ japidoǩkantiṅa.

Lukuť marte. } To give a sudden start.
Lukuť mente. }

Lulhạ. The back of the hand.

Lulhạu. Cf. lulwạu.

Lulu bạchu. To coax.

Lulu bạchukate dakae jom ocokedea. She coaxed him to take his food.

Lulurkuć. Stiff and bent, as a joint that has been injured, and the muscles allowed to contract.

Tiye lulurkućakaťa. He holds his hand bent (it being painful or impossible to straighten the fingers.)

Luluạu. Cf. lulwạu.

Lulwạu. To wheedle, to induce by specious promises.

Kacharteko lulwạu idikedea. They induced him by promises to go to Cachar.

Lulwạukateko ạgukediňa. They wheedled me into coming.

Lumạm. } The Tusser silk worm and
Lumạń. } moth, *Antheraea mylitta;* the cocoon of the Tusser silk worm.

Tirạ. The male of *Antheraea mylitta*.
Pạtni. The female " "
Lumạmko kaṭaoena. The Tusser moths have emerged from the cocoon.
Lumạmko tolena. The Tusser silk worms have spun their cocoons.
Lumạm lekale dheanakana. We are fasting like Tusser silk worms. (Silk worms leave off eating for a certain time before moulting, which they do four times.)
Lumạm do pon dhao urkateko toloǩa. Tusser silk worms moult four times and then spin their cocoons.

Sagoe.	**Tusser silk worms**	**at**	**1st moult.**
Dojra.	,,	,,	**2nd ,,**
Ṭeka.	,,	,,	**3rd ,,**
Koela.	,,	,,	**4th and last moult.**

Lumạmkin joṛakana. The two silk moths are paired.
Lumạm peṭeć. To detach Tusser cocoons from the trees.

Lumạm peṭeć pujạ. A sacrifice offered when the Tusser cocoons have been gathered.

Lumbạǩ. } A little after nightfall,
Ạyuṗ lumbạǩ. } about one hour after sunset.

Ạyuṗ lumbạǩle seṭerena. We arrived a little after nightfall.

Lumti. To accompany a bride or bridegroom.

Lumti koṛa. A young man, preferably a cousin, who accompanies a bridegroom when going to be married.

Lumti budhi. } Old women who accompany a
Lumti budhiko. } bride from her own village where she has been married to her husband's house.

Lumtiǩe calaoena. He has gone as companion to a bridegroom, or she has gone to escort a bride to her new home.

Lumtiǩić leka iń taeomte daraekana. He follows me as if I were going to be married and he were my companion.

Lumu. } To bow the head when making
Numu. } obeisance, said of children.

Lumuń. } Soft, smooth, glossy
Lumuń lumuń. } as the coat of a well groomed horse.

Lunḍ. A length of cloth woven in one piece, a web of cloth.

Lunḍạ. } To apply rice flour in the
Lunḍạń. } shape of a ball to the person after an incantation to cure pain or to render poison innocuous, to plaster or smear with a little cow dung, as a floor, to cover any thing objectionable.

Pạhil doko jhaṛea, ado holońteko lunḍạea. First an incantation is said, then a ball of rice flour is gently rolled over the affected part.

Lunḍi. A large ball of twine.

Luṅgri. F. } Unchaste, wanton, licen-
Loṅgra. M. } tious, incontinent, impure.

Luṅkạ. } Having a stiff wrist or elbow
Luṅki. } joint.

Luṅkạṛ. } To be stiff, as an arm which
Luṅkeṛ. } has been injured, or which having been injured is permanently bent.

Ti luṅkeṛentaea. His arm is stiff.
Dal luṅkeṛkedeako. They struck and disabled his arm.

Lupạǩ. } To be dark, after sunset.
Ạyuṗ lupaǩ. }

Ạyuṗ lupạǩ. After sunset.
Lupạǩ goṭena. It has become dark.

Lur. }
Lurbhas. } Sense, skill, ability.
Lor. }

Lurbhas bạnuǩtaea. He has no ability.
Lur bạnuǩtaea. He has no skill.

Lur na bhas. Ill-conditioned, simple, the reverse of what is right and proper.

Lur na bhase ńeloǩkana. He looks the reverse of what he ought to be.

Luṛạ luṛi. Snatching or grabbing by several people, as apples, &c. from a basket, exerting oneself, as one of two or more trying to secure anything for oneself.
  Luṛạ luṛiko repeḿkana. Each is trying to secure it for himself.

Luṛgạ. } To poke with a stick &c., to
Luṛgạu. } drive out; a stick or anything to poke with.
  Luṛgạu toḱkedeae. He poked him out.
  Luluṛgạuak'. Anything to poke with.
  Luṛgạ ạgaime, adobon luṛgạea. Bring something to poke with and we will poke him out (of his hole.)

Luṛkạ. } Applied to a breed of sheep
Luṛki. } which has one or two soft protuberances under the chin, also to cattle whose horns are not fixed to the skull, but only attached by the skin and therefore shake.
  Luṛkạ bheḍa. A ram of the breed described above.
  Luṛki bhiḍi. A ewe of the breed described above.
  Luṛkạ ḍaṅgra. A bullock or bull having loose horns.
  Luṛki gại. A cow having loose horns.
  Deren̕ luṛkigetaea. Her horns are loose.

Luṛkuć. } To bend or move, as
Luṛkuć luṛkuć. } the hand at the wrist joint.
  Ti luṛkućgetaea. His wrist is bent.
  Ti luṛkućkeḱtaeae. He bent his wrist.
  Ti luṛkuć luṛkuć hilạuk'kantaea. His hand is bending backwards and forwards at the wrist.

Luṛuṅ luṛuṅ. } To sway backwards and
Laṛaṅ laṛaṅ. } forwards, as the tongue of a bell; to tinkle, as a bell.

Luṛuṅ buṛuṅ. } Idle, lazy, shirking
Luṛur buṛur. } work, anyhow, inefficiently.

Luskur. } Plump, applied to children
Lesker. } and the young of domesticated animals.
  Luskure moṭaakana. He is plumply fat.

Lusku lundur. Fat, plump, chubby.

Lusur lusur.
Lusur pusur. } To whisper, whisper-
Phasar phusur. } ingly.
Phusur phusur.
  Lusur lusurkin galmaraokana. They are talking in whispers.
  Lusur lusurok'kanae. He is whispering.
  Lusur pusurkin galmaraokana. They are whispering to each other.

Luṭ. } To pillage, to rob, to plunder.
Luṭpaṭ. }
  Sanamko luṭkeḱtaea. They pillaged all he had.
  Luṭpaṭkeḱkoako. They pillaged them.

Luṭạ. Unhealthy and stunted in growth and development, applied mainly to certain cultivated leguminous plants.
  Malhan luṭạgea.

Luṭa luṭi. Struggling to grab.

Luthri. F. } Stout, fat.
Lothro. M. }
  Khub luthriye n̕elok'kana. She looks very fat.

Luṭhu. To put oneself forward, to be officious, to commend oneself by word only, to hold the balance, as between two sides in a game helping whichever seems to be losing, to assist.
  Aćgeye luṭhuk'a. He puts himself forward.

Luṭhu kunḍạ. An odd player who assists whichever side appears to be losing.
  Dene banar ren luṭhu kunḍạ kanae. He helps whichever side appears to be losing.

Luṭhum. } A thud, a succes-
Luṭhum luṭhum. } sion of thuds, or thumps.
  Luṭhum luṭhume dalkedea. He thumped him several times.

Luṭhum marte. } With a thud or
Luṭhum mente. } thump.
  Luṭhum marte n̕urena. It fell with a thud.
  Luṭhum menteyo dal goḱkeda. He gave him one thump, he struck him with a thump.

Luṭhur. } Crashing, as of a thun-
Luṭhur luṭhur. } der peal, banging, as of a gun or an explosion. Cf. liṭhir liṭhir.

Luṭhur marte. } With a crash, as of
Luṭhur mente. } thunder. Cf. Luṭhur.

Luṭi. A lip, the lips.
  Cetan luṭi. The upper lip.
  Latar luṭi. The under lip.

Luṭi. } A hank, or ball of thread, as
Laṭi. } taken from the *natwa* (q. v.)

Luṭi. A small brass drinking vessel.

Luṭi. } Domestic utensils of iron.
Lohaluṭi. }

Luṭi. A small, wild honey bee.
  Luṭi rasa. The honey of the *luṭi* bee.

Luṭiạ. Given to pillaging, plundering, or robbing.

Luṭiạ hoṛ kanako. They are men given to plundering.

Luṭkum. Stout, chubby, fat, applied to children and young animals.

Luṭkume ńeloḱkana. He appears to be fat.

Luṭkuri. The part of the head in front of the ear and upwards to the hair.

Luṭluṭu. To rise, raised, as a blister.

Luṭluṭu phokaakana. The blister has risen high.

Luṭni. The mustard plant, *Brassica campestris, Linn.*

Luṭpuri. The side of the face.

Luṭuć. Under-done, insufficiently cooked, to take one in, to do for one.

Luṭuće isinakana. It is under-cooked.

Luṭućkedeako. They did for him (fined him heavily, or stole his goods, &c. &c.)

Luṭuć ocoenae. He was taken in.

Luṭuk. Cf. loṭok.

Luṭuḱ luṭuḱ. Watching, sleepless, owing to anxiety, fear. &c.

Mić ńindạ luṭuḱ luṭuḱiń tahẽena. I continued watching the whole night,

Lutur. The ear, to listen.

Jojom lutur. The right ear.

Leṅga lutur. The left ear.

Lutur bić. To cock the ears, to listen intently.

Lutur oḍao. To listen intently.

Ińaḱ katha luturaḱtińme. Listen to what I have to say, or have said.

Lutur peṭer. To twist, or wring the ear.

Lutur pạṭi. To bore the ear, as for earrings, &c.

Lutur hupạ. The mastoid process behind the ear.

Luyum luyum.
Luyuṅ luyuṅ. } Soft, very soft.

Luyuć.
Luyuć luyuć. } To start, as from fear, to be in terror, to be all in a tremble.

Luyućadae. He started (from sudden fear.)

Luyuć luyuće botorena. He is in great fear, all in a tremble through fright.

Luyuć marte.
Luyuć mente. } With a sudden start.

Luyuć cupuć. Terrified, in abject fear, trembling from fear, extreme trepidation.

Luyuć cupućiń botorena. I trembled with fear.

Luyuć cupuć noa biriń paromena. I passed through this jungle in a state of extreme trepidation.

M

Ma. A particle used regularly with the Optative of the verb; frequently with the Imperative, which it softens to an Optative sense; in speaking of future events, to indicate the confidence of the speaker; also in connection with clauses and even principal sentences which state facts to turn them into, or imply that they are statements of reason or cause.

Hẽ, ańjomtamãń, ma roṛme. Yes, I will hear you, come, speak.

Acha, enbõ ma se ente sae hạbić roṛme. Good, nevertheless come count up to a hundred.

Moṭakoḱmae. May he become fat.

Ituć boteḱkeae, husiạrkoḱmae. She may be *ituted*, let her be on her guard.

Ma heć hijuḱme. Do come.

Roṛmae. Let him speak.

Hõ ma hõge, menkhan ale seć do teṅgo ruạ ge tho ạḍi ãṭkana. Certainly, but famine is very acute over our way.

Ma senoḱme. Do go.

Ma dela. Come.

Ma enḍekhan calaḱme. Then go.

Em mae emoḱa, menkhan teheń do baṅ. Give he will, but not today.

Enbetar ma uṭuć puṭuć setohkećte babon kạmileć. At that time owing to the great heat we did not do our cultivating work.

Cedaḱko sen ocoadea? Bań baḍaea, unre ma bań tahẽkan. Why did they allow him to go? I do not know. I was not there at the time.

Macalka.
Mucilkạ.
Mucạlkạ. } Personal recognizance.

Mõmõṛ ṭaka mucạlka emoḱ hoyoḱtapea. Each of you must enter into his personal recognizance in five rupees.

Macan.
Maṛom. } A raised platform or scaffold.

Maceṛ. To gobble up, to eat.

Macha. Approximately, resembling, like, (used only in composition.)

Ponḍ macha. Whitish.

Hende macha. Blackish.

Okte macha.
Din macha. } At the proper time or season.

Mić machagẹakin. They are about equal.

Hoṛ machageye ńeloḱkana. He looks a little like a Santal.

Ńut machareko oḍokena. They left while it was yet a little dark (in the morning.)

Niạ macha kạmime. Do something like this.

Mache. The edge, border of cloth, lengthwise.

Mache mache. Along the edge or border.

Mache machete calakme. Go along the edge.

Machreṅka. } A kind of bird which
Machreṅṭa. } lives on fish, applied also to an expert fisher.

Uni do machreṅka kanae. He is an expert fisher.

Mạci andhar. Night fall.

Mabon bạgia mạci andharena. Come, let us leave off, it is now nightfall.

Mạci. A stool.

Ṭeṇḍar mạci. A chair with a back.

Mạci koṭha. Woven with a pattern, as the woven twine work of a bed, &c.

Mackao. To be sprained, cracked, twisted, painful.

Ohoń senlena jaṅgań mackaoakana. I will not be able to go, I have sprained my foot.
Niṅghạ mackaoakana, gạḍi alom joṛaoe. The axle is cracked, do not yoke the cart.
Onte alom dejoka, ḍạr mackaoakan leka ńeloḱkana. Do not climb up there, the branch looks as if it were cracked.

Mackundạ. A large forest tree, *Pterospermum acerifolium, Willd.*

Macmac. To squeak or creak, as boots when the wearer walks.

Panahī macmac saḍekana. The shoes squeak.
Nui khạsi reaḱ jaṅga macmac saḍekana. The feet of this goat creak, or make the sound of "machma h."

Macnothor. A variety of the rice plant.

Macṛa mạcṛi. Cf. mocṛa mucṛi.

Mạcuḱ. To eat up, to gobble.

Mạcuḱkedeale. We ate him all up.

Mạcur. To eat all, to finish.

Mạcurkedako. They ate up all.

Madhe. } From among, among, middle,
Modhe. } centre. Cf. modhe.

Madhãs. } Fat, corpulent, wealthy,
Mandhas. } influential, respectable.

Madhosiń. The name of a man mentioned in Santal tradition.

Madhosiń is said to have been the person who first broke up the unity of the Santal people.

Mạdhuạ. } To decrease, slovenly, fusion-
Mạndhuạ. } less, sluggish, discoloured or mildewed as anything stored damp.

Netar mạdhuạena. It is less now-a-days than it was.
Kicrić mạdhuạena. The cloth is discoloured.
Madhuạgeae. He is fusionless.

Mạdhur lata. A creeping species of fig, *Ficus scandens.*

Madoli. } A receptacle in which a
Maudoli. } charm is enclosed and worn round the neck, the upper arm or the waist.

A piece of bone of certain snakes is considered an effectual charm against lumbago. It is placed in the *mandoli* which is worn attached to a string round the waist.

Maeda. Flour, wheaten flour.

Maejiu. A woman.

Maejiu jạt. Female, females.

Maemạsi. Cousins by the female side, the relationship between the children of sisters.

Mãeṛa. }
Mãeṛa mũhã. } Having no hair on the
Mãeṛahã. } upper lip.

Mag. } The tenth Hindu month Jan.-
Magh. } Feby., the end of the agricultural year.

Mag boṅga. }
Mag cando. } The month of Magh, Jan.-Feb.
Mag mas. }

Mag sim porob. A festival observed in the month of Mag.

Mạgdur. } Power, strength.
Mạkdur. }

Cet́ mạkdur menaḱtama? What strength have you?

Magh. Cf. Mag.

Maghi. Of or belonging to the month Mag or Magh.

Maghi puja. The offering of sacrifices at the end of the year which occurs in Magh (q. v.)

Maghi raheṛ. A variety of raheṛ (q. v) which ripens in the month of Magh.

Magra. } A drain pipe, the ridge tiles
Maṅgra. } of a roof.

Magni. } Without payment, gratis, for
Maṅgni. } the asking.

Mạgni okoe emamae? Who will give to you for nothing?
Mạgniteń ạgukeda. I got it gratis.

Mãhã. A day.

Mit́ mãhã. One day.
Barpe mãhã. Two or three days.
Bạrsiń pe mãhã. Two or three days.
Pe mãhã hiloḱ. The third day.

Maha. Great.
Maha jal. A large fish net.
Maha sal. A large sugar cane press.
Maha jala. Great distress or anxiety.
Maha muskil. / Maha mәskil. } Very difficult, great anxiety.
Maha jalaenań. I am in great anxiety.
Maha muskilenae. He is in great difficulty.
Maha dan. To give liberally.

Maha bhәg. Great good fortune, great good luck.
Teheń әdi maha bhәg hoeakantakoa. To-day great good fortune has befallen them (enjoying themselves in feasting, &c.)

Mahadano. One of the numerous Santal godlets.

Mahadeb. / Mahadeo. } The Hindu deity Mahadeo.

Mahadeb. A variety of the rice plant.

Mahadeb. The centre of the yoke where it is attached to the plough beam (isi) or to a cart shafts.

Mahadebjaṭa. A variety of the rice plant.

Mahajan. / Mahajon. } A great man, a money lender.

Mahajәni. / Mahajoni. } Money lending, the business of a money-lender,
Mahajәniedae. He lends money.

Mahak. Pleasant odour, sweet scent.
Әdi mahak heó goćena. A very pleasant odour arose.

Mahakal. A time of great distress, danger, or anxiety; many days, a long time, a lengthened period, a long life time.
Mahakaliń ńelkeda. I passed through a time of great danger.
Mahakale ńelakaća. He has seen a long time, i. e. lived long.
Mahakalreliń ńapamlena. We met after many years and much suffering.

Mahal. / Mohal. } A large house, a palace.
Raj mohal. A king's palace.

Mahal. / Mahala. } Street, house or houses, district, department.

Mәhәlә. / Mәhlә. } The Palm-cat, *Paradoxurus hemaphroditus*, var *niger*.

Mahander. / Mahnder. } Day before yesterday.
On mahander. Three days ago.
Mahander hilok. The day before yesterday.

Mahańga. Dear, high priced, as rates. Cf. mahńga.

Mahara. / Mahra. } A Hindu caste, the Goalla, or cow keeping caste.

Mәhәrәu. Cf. mәhrәu.

Maharog. / Mahrog. } Dear, high priced, scarce and dear.
Әdi maharog ńamokkana. Prices are very high.
Netar maharoggea. It is very dear at present.

Mahatom. Quality, honour, good name, flavour, savouriness.
Noa reak mahatom bәnukәn. This has no flavour, it is insipid
Mahatom bәnuktaea. He is untrustworthy, he has no honour.
Mahatom ge calaoentaea. He is disgraced.
Olok paṛhaok reak mahatom әuriko bujhәua. They do not yet know the sweets of education.

Mahel. / Mahela. } Jurisdiction.
Noa bәgieә uni sahebak mahelre menaka. This garden is within that gentleman's jurisdiction.

Mәhimә. / Mohimә. } Glory, to glorify.
Otreń mohimәakawaćmea. I have glorified thee on the earth.

Mәhinә. / Mәhnә. } A month, a month's wages.
Mit mәhnә hoeńa. One month has passed.
Mәhinә atańe senakana. He has gone to draw his month's pay.

Mәhir. / Mәhír. } Gentle, to be gentle, patient, quiet.
Mәhirgeae. He is gentle.

Mәhirәu. Cf. mәhrәu.

Mәhit. Neat, tidy, handsome.

Mәhjid. A musjid, a Mohomedan mosque.

Mәhjud. / Muhjud. / Mәhjut. / Muhjut. } To be ready, prepared, ready at hand.
Sanamiń mәhjudakaća. I have all ready at hand.
Mәhjutenale nitok do. We have all now ready at hand, we are fully prepared now.

Mahka mәhki. Fragrant, sweet smelling, savoury.
Mahka mәhki sokana. (The flower) is fragrant.
Noko oṛakkhon mahka mәhki so odokokkana. A savoury smell is coming from their house.

Mәhkal. The Indian Crow-pheasant, *Centropus rufipennis*.

Mahkalom. Three years ago, three years hence.
Din kalom. Last year.
Hol kalom. The year before last.
Mahkalom ren gidrә kanae. He is a child of three years ago, was born three years ago.

Mahkao. } To smell sweetly, odor-
Mahkaok. } iferous. fragrant, to emit a perfume.
Cet baha ooń mahkaokkana? What flower is it that is emitting a perfume?

Mạhkup. } To be deferred, postponed,
Mạkup. } relinquished, delayed; to leave off, to abolish, to settle.
Calakið sapṛaolena, adoń mạhkupkeda. I was ready to go, but I relinquished the idea.
Noa mamla mạhkupena. This suit is postponed.

Mạhlạ. The Palm-cat, *Paradoxurus hemaphroditus*, var. *niger*. Cf. mạhạlạ.

Mahla. A story.
Bar mahla oṛak. A two storied house.

Mahlam. } Cf. mohlon.
Mahlan. }

Mahle. A tribe of aboriginies who speak a Kolarian dialect, and are by trade workers in bamboos.

Mahle kidiń. A species of centipede.

Mahnder. Two days ago. Cf. mahander.
Hola. Yesterday.
Mahnder. Two days ago.
On mahnder. Three days ago.
Mahnder hiloke goćena. He died two days ago.

Mahṅga. Dear, high priced, high, as rates.
Dorre ạḍi mahṅgagea nes. The rates are very high this year.

Mahra. A Hindu caste, the Goalla or cow keeping caste. Cf. mahara.

Mahra. } A small insect found in
Dak mahra. } water.

Mạhrạu. To demur, to refuse, to decline, to withhold one's assent.
Mạhrạukkanae, emok bae meneda. He demurs, he does not wish to give.
Emamkan khan jojomem mạhrạukkana. When I give it to you, you refuse to eat.

Mahre. After, difficulty.
Uniye calaoen mahre amem heċena. After he left you came.
Tinạk mahreń ńamakata. With how much difficulty I have procured it.
Tin mahrereye senakawatkoa. After how long a time he went to see them.

Mahrog. Dear, high-priced, high, as rates or prices, scarce.
Sahan ạḍi mahroggea. Firewood is very scarce.

Mah satom. Three years hence.

Mạhsul. } Rent, fare, freight, postage,
Mạsul. } royalty, toll.
Ḍak mạhsul. Postage.
Ghaṭ reak mạhsul. Cess levied on produce passing by a road.
Kaṭ reak mạsul. Royalty levied on timber.
Mat reak mạsul. Royalty levied on bamboos.
Oṛak mạsul. House rent
Rel gạḍi reak mạsul. Railway fare or freight.

Mạhur. An unusually large species of *Nematode* worm.
They are allied to the so called Eel-worms and vinegar-worms of Europe.

Mạhur. Poison, spirituous liquor, alchohol, intoxicating drink.
Mit phuṛuk mạhuriń ńukette ạkil do bań ńuakata. By having drunk one glass of liquor I have not drunk my sense.

Mạhut. A mahout, an elephant driver.

Mạhut. The scum which rises to the surface when sugarcane juice is being boiled, and which is skimmed off with a ladle.

Mại. Used in addresing a daughter, younger sister, younger female cousin, niece, and a female younger than the speaker; a daughter, a female, the female organ.
Mại kanae. It is a female child.
Mại dole ṭhạokedea nes. We gave our daughter in marriage this year.

Mạiku. Cf. mạku.

Mailạ. Dirt, filth, to be dirty, filthy.
Mạilạte bań chaḍaokkana. The dirt is not coming off.
Kiorić mạilạentaea. His clothes are dirty.
Oṛak mạilạ getaea. Her house is dirty.

Mạiri. A term of endearment, used when addressing a particular female friend.

Mạiri. A form of mild oath.
Mạirikateń metamkana. I swear to you.

Mạ̃j. } Hard heart-wood, centre wood
Mańj. } of some kinds of trees.
Terel mańj. Ebony.

Mạ̃jao. To scour. Cf. mańjao.

Majbut. } Right, proper, well, efficiently,
Majgut. } strong, substantial. Cf. mańjgut.

Majlis. } Conference, assembly. Cf.
Mạńjlis. } mojlis.

Majur. } Daily wages, a daily labourer.
Majuri. }
Mạjurikoń lagaoakatkoa. I have employed labourers.

Mak. } To slash, hack, chop, or hew with
Man. } any cutting instrument such as a sword, axe. &c.

Mak goc. To kill by slashing or hacking, to cut down.
Maktaṇḍi. To clear, as jungle, by cutting with an axe.
Mak gur. To hew down, as a tree.
Mak kundlah. To give a cut, as with a sword, and make to fall or lie down.
Mak gitic. To cut down.
Mak ñur. To cut and cause to fall, as a branch of a tree, &c.
Noa hõ magok'a. This will also be cut.
Mahgeme. Cut off his head, slash him.

Makaṛgạti. To cross over, to link; a method of wearing the upper loose garment when extra exertion is required.

Ado titakine makaṛgạtikeda. He linked their arms.

Makaṛkenda. A large forest tree, *Diospyros embryopteris, Pers.*

Makhan. } Ointment, to apply ointment.
Makhon. }

Mạklu. Cf. mạku.

Makmak. } To frolic, to romp, to lark.
Makmakao. }

Makmakao baṛaekanako. They are romping.

Mak mõṛẽ. A festival observed by Santals at intervals of five years or upwards. A white goat is sacrificed in the name of the village community to Mõṛẽko (q. v.)

Hana atoreko mak mõṛẽkkana. In that village they are observing the Mak mõṛẽ festival.

Makordama. } A suit, a case in a court
Mokordoma. } of justice.

Makordama khạrijentaea. His suit is dismissed.
Makordama makordamateñ lahgaena. I have become poor with continued law suits.

Makoṛi. } An ear ring.
Makṛi }

Pagra reak makoṛi. A ring on the inside of the ear to prevent an ear pendant from falling out.

Makṛe. The left side, incorrect, unidiomatic and mispronounced, applied also by Santals to the dialectic differences between the other Kolarian dialects and their own, assuming that theirs is the standard.

Makṛete ṣourokme. Turn to the left.
Makṛete toleme. Pass the rope to the left in tying him.
Kolhe do makṛe makṛe geko roṛa. Koles speak incorrectly (as judged by the standard of Santali.)
Nui hõ kạmi makṛe makṛegetaea. His work also is incorrect.
Makṛe makṛeko bicạrkeda. They judged wrongly.

Makṛi. Cf. makoṛi.

Makṭha. Refuse cotton after carding.

Mạku. A shuttle.

Mạku. A term of endearment applied to girls, also employed when according to Santal custom the speaker may not use the name of the female addressed.

Mạkup. } To be deferred, postponed,
Mạhkup. } delayed relinquished.

Cetre coe mạkupena. He is delayed by something or other.

Mạkur. } Sound of crunching,
Mạkur mạkur. } as when eating a raw carrot, &c.

Mạkur mạkure jomeda. He is crunching.

Mal. } Goods, effects, merchandise.
Maljal. }

Mit isi ṭakaren male kheanatentiña. I have lost property (a buffaloe) worth twenty rupees.

Mal. The driving band of a spinning wheel.

Mal. Rent paying, bearing full rent, as opposed to rent free, *khandit* (q. v.), &c.

Noa do mal jaega kantiña. This is land for which I pay full rent.
Mal ot. Land for which full rent is paid.

Mal soren. A sub-sept of the Santal sept Soren (q. v.)

Mala. A necklace, anything of the nature of an ornament worn round the neck, a bead, beads.

Mungạ mala. Coral beads of a large size.
Baha mala. A garland of flowers.
Poṇḍ mala. White beads.
Arak mala. Red beads.
Pạulạ mala. } Coral beads, smaller than munga,
Pãola mala. } (q. v.)
Bel mala. Beads made from the shell of the Bel fruit.
Kaṭ mala. Beads made from some kind of hard wood.
Bilạti mala. Beads of English manufacture.
Udrạh mala. Praying beads, a rosary.
Dhiri hisir mala. Beads made from rock-crystal.
Tuṛi mala. Beads resembling mustard seed.
Jihu mala. Beads resembling the eggs of the Jihu bird (q. v.)
Buḍhi mala. The old woman's bead, a bead with a wide hole which an old woman who does not see well can thread.
Bhạuri mala. Beads made from a certain fruit about the size of round pepper.

Jurul mala. A kind of bead which flashes in the sunlight.
Muṭi mala. A pearl necklace.
Malako horok̓adea. They gave her a necklace to wear.
Sikṛi-mala. A chain worn round the neck.
Bar lar mala. Two strings of beads.

Malaċ muluċ. } To smile.
Muluċ muluċ. }
Malaċ muluċ baṛaekanae. He is smiling.

Malan. } To rub the body or limbs, massage.
Malao. }
Khub lekako malaokedea. The *massaged* him well.

Mạlchạ. Whitish, white colour a little soiled.
Kicriċ mạlchạgetaea. Her cloth is a little soiled.

Maldar. Owner, proprietor, wealthy.
Nui kanae maldar do. This is the owner of the goods.

Malgoṫ. } Not perfectly white, as a cloth.
Malgodok̓. }
Malgoṫ malgoṫ ńelok̓kana. It looks of a greyish white.
Ạḍi bes do baṅ saphalena, malgoṫ malgoṫ. It did not clean perfectly, there was a little colour.

Malgujạri. Rent.

Malhan. A leguminous plant of garden cultivation, *Dolichos Lablab, Linn.*
Bir malhan. A wild plant, *Atylosia mollis, Bth.*, having a resemblance to *Dolichos Lablab.*
Malhan suṛe. A dish prepared as follows; the immature pods of malhan(q. v.) are finely shred and boiled, rice is then added and the whole cooked together.

Malhan cẽṛẽ. A small Tailor-bird, *Orthotomus sutorius,* which frequents the stakes on which *Dolichos Lablab* is trained. Cf ghar-didi.

Mali. A gardener.

Mạli. A small earthenware cup in which oil is burned for lighting purposes.
Diuhe. Oil vessel (mạli), oil and wick.
Diuhe mạli. The earthenware vessel which holds the oil for a lamp.
Mạliye benaoeda. She pushes out her under lip like an oil vessel (she is pouting.)

Mạli. To cup; the surgical process of cupping.
Mạli ocoepe. Cause him to be cupped.

Mạli baha. A flower in high repute among Santal females, *Ocimum Basilicum, Linn.*, var. *thyrsiflorum.*

Malik. Master, owner, lord.
Jirạuk̓ din ren mạlik. Lord of the Sabbath.

Maliki. Authority.
Mạliki calao. To exercise authority.
Onko cetanreko mạlikia. They will exercise authority over them.

Mạli mambla. } A law suit, a matter that requires consideration and decision by some properly constituted authority.
Mạli mamla. }

Mạlin buḍhi. An old woman whose name is mentioned in a Santal tradition regarding the creation of the world.

Maljal. } Goods, chattels, merchandise, wealth.
Jalmal. }

Malkao. To flash, to go here and there shewing off.
Ceṫ baṅ am dom malkao baṛaekan? kam udạm bạnuk̓ leka. Why are you going about shewing off? as if there was no work to do.
Malkao baṛaekanae. He is shewing himself off.
Bijli malkaok̓kana. The lightning is flashing.

Malkar. Owner, proprietor, master.

Malkaṭa. A coal miner.

Malkaṭhi. An upright with a slit in it through which the driving band (mal) of a spinning wheel passes from the driving wheel to the spinning axle (ṭaku.)

Malmal. } Fine, thin cloth.
Malmaliạ. }

Maloṭ. Barren, unproductive, as soil; famine, want.
Din kalom noakore ạḍi maloṭlena. Last year there was great famine in these parts.
Maloṭ ot. Unproductive soil.

Maloti. A variety of the rice plant.

Malun. To cause to wonder, or be astonished, to wonder, to be astonished, to be bewitched; to fascinate.
Mạluṅkediṅae. He caused me to wonder.
Mạk̓luṅ katha. A statement which astonishes.

Mama. Maternal uncle.
Mạmi. Aunt, wife of maternal uncle.

Mama bhạgnạ. Uncle and nephew, uncle and niece.

Mama bhạgnạ. Not in the same state of forwardness, late and early, as the different plants in the same crop.

Mama bhạgnạena noa matkom do. This matkom (q. v.) is not all in the same state of forwardness.
Noa jondra mama bhạgnạena. Some of this Indian corn is late and some early (not all ripening at the same time.)

Mamạsi. } Cousins by the fe-
Mamạsi. boehako. } male side, the relation between children of sisters.

Mambla. } A law suit, any matter requi-
Mamla. } ring discussion and settlement by a panchayat or any other assembly.
Peṛa mambla. A social matter.
Nonḍe oeťpe mamblakana? What matter are you discussing here?

Mambṛa mạmbṛi. Taking by handfuls, pushing and pulling, pushing one another aside.
Mambṛa mạmbṛiko toda gạobi do. They pull up the seedlings by both hands in handfuls.
Mambṛa mạmbṛikin tapamkana. They are fighting and pulling and pushing each other.

Mambṛao. To push aside, to break down, to destroy, as by forcing one's way through growing crops.
Bana ạkko mambṛaoakaťa teheń ńindạ do. Last night bears broke down the sugarcane.

Mạmi. Aunt, wife of maternal uncle. Cf. mama.

Mạmkuṛ. Relatives of the mother's sept with whom marriage is not allowed.
Mạrnḍi hoṛ mạmkuṛ kantińa. My mother belonged to the Marnḍi sept, Mạrnḍi is my mother's sept.

Mamla. Cf. mambla.

Mamo. Maternal uncle.
Momotteť hohoaeme. Call the uncle (your uncle.)
Mamo bala. Cf. bala.
Mamo hońhar. Husband's or wife's uncle.

Mamoea. Uncle and nephew, uncle and niece.

Mamo salaka. A piece of cloth given by a bridegroom to his bride's maternal uncle.

Man. Manna.

Man. Respect, honour, reputation, meaning.
Ińaǩ manko kaṭaokeťtińa. They shewed disrespect to me.
Man bạisạume. Explain this, prove this.
Manre bạisạuǩ lekae roṛkeda. He spoke so that he carried conviction to the hearers.

Man. } A maund.
Mon. }

Man. To entertain, to honour.
Khubko mankedińa. They entertained me well.

Mạn. Land held by village officials rent free.
Mạńjhi mạn. Land held by the village chief rent free.
Naeke mạn, Land held rent free by the priest.
Kuḍạm naeke mạn. Land held rent free by the village under-priest.
Parạnik mạn. Land held rent free by the village chief's assistant. Cf. parạnik.
Goḍet mạn. Land held rent free by the village messenger. Cf. goḍet.
Susạriạ mạn. Land held rent free by the person who officiates at the Jatra (q. v.) festival.
Merom mạn. Land held at a quit rent of a goat annually.

Man baha. A plant with a reddish flower.

Man baha. A species of rock snake or python.

Man tuṛi. A variety of the Mustard plant.

Mana. To forbid, to warn, to remonstrate, to admonish, to reprove.
Manaledeań, bae ańjomleda. I warned him, but he did not take heed.
Mana bae ańjomleda. He paid no heed to the warning.
Mana manakadeań, menek bae ańjomleda. I warned him repeatedly, but he gave no heed.

Manadi. } To proclaim, to preach, pro-
Monadi. } clamation, preaching.
Manadi baṛaedae. He goes about preaching.

Manạhi. Forbidden, unlawful.
Noa pukhrire umoǩ do manạhigea. Bathing in this tank is forbidden.

Manan. To vow.
Manan doho. To make a vow.
Manan dohoakaťae, merom emoǩ hoyoǩtaea. He has made a vow, he must give a goat.
Mananakať pon hoṛ ale ṭhen menaǩkoa. There are with us four men who have a vow on them.

Manao. To pay respect to, to honour, to obey.
Mapanao. To pay respect to each other.
Gun manao. To thank, to praise, to shew gratitude.
Sedae leka netar do Mańjhi bako manaokoa. They do not respect the village chief now as they did in the olden time.

Manbir. The name of a forest mentioned in Santal traditions.

Manḍa. The quantity of grain spread out on the threshing floor at one time to be trodden out by cattle.
Miť dintege bar manḍale enkeda. We threshed twice in one day.

Manda. Cold in the head, coryza.

Manda sapakadea. } He has caught a cold in
Manda ńamakadea. } the head.
Mandaḱkanae. He has a cold.
Manda uthumte bohoḱ haḱsoa. The head aches owing to the cold in the head.
Khoḱ manda. Cough and cold.

Mandal. A hunting term, part of the carcase claimed by the killer of game.

The mandal is a hind quarter of an animal and the breast of a bird.

Mandanbheḍ. } A large trumpet.
Mandanbheṛ. }

Manḍao. } To occupy a new house, to
Mạnḍiạu. } take up one's residence.

Nesko mạnḍiạuena. They occupied the house this year.
Peṛa heckateko mạnḍiạuena. Friends (or visitors) have come and encamped.

Mandar. The head-man of a village.

Mandar buru. Cf. mandburu.

Mandargom. The Custard apple, *Anona squamosa, Linn.*

Mandaṛi. } A drummer, drum musici-
Mandaṛiạ. } ans.

Mandburu. } A sacred hilll about
Mandar buru. } thirty miles south of Bhagalpur.

Mande. A dung heap, a midden.

Guriċ mande. A heap of cattle dung.

Manḍer. In a long line, or wide circle, a wide area, a multitude.

Ạḍi manḍerteko duṛupakana. They are sitting in a wide circle.
Baṛe ḍạr manḍerte pasnaoakana. The branches of the Banyan tree radiate in a wide circle.
Pohoko manḍerteko calaḱkana. The locusts cover a large area in passing.

Manḍha. } A temporary shed or booth
Manḍhwa. } erected on the occasion
Manḍwa. } of a marriage.

Mandhak. Thick, fat, plump.

Mandhak ṭheṅga menaḱtaea. He has a thick stick.

Manḍhal. Not sloping sufficiently, as the roof of a house.

Oṛaḱ manḍhalko benaoakaṭa, onate joroḱkana. They have not made the roof with sufficient slope, for that reason it leaks.

Mandhas. } Fat, corpulent, wealthy, res-
Mȧdhas. } pectable, influential.

Niạ atore nuige mandhastalea. This (man) is our most influential man in this village.

Mandhe. }
Mondhe. } From among, among, middle.
Madhe. }

Noko ṛa there okakom kusiḱa? ona hataome. Take whichever of these pleases you.
Onạ modheregeń calaoena. I went away at that time.

Mạndhuạ. To decrease, slovenly, fusionless, sluggish; to become mildewed or go bad; sickly, blighted.

Mạndhuạ mạndhuạ janamakana.
Mạndhuạ hoṛ kanae. He is dull in wit and slow in movement.
Bes ṭhik bañ doholenkhan mạndhuạḱa. If it is not stored properly it will go bad.

Manḍhwạ. } A temporary shed or booth
Manḍwạ. } erected on the occasion of a marriage.

Baplareko manḍhwaea. They erect a temporary shed on the occasion of a marriage.

Mạnḍi. Cooked rice, food, the water in which rice has been cooked.

Daḱ mạnḍi. Rice water.
Laċ mạnḍi. Food.
Mạnḍialeme. Cook rice for yourself and us.
Daka mạnḍi. Rice water.

Mandiạu. } To occupy a new house, to
Manḍao. } take shelter, as a wild animal in a thicket, &c., when run to ground.

Onḍeye sen manḍiạnakana. He has gone there and taken up his residence.
Hạnḍi salre ḍhere mạnḍiạuḱa. He hangs about the liquor shop a great deal.

Mạndil. }
Mondil. } A temple.
Mundil. }

Mạndir. }
Mondir. } A temple.
Mundir. }

Manḍlạ. A present given to the head man of a bride's village by the bridegroom on the occasion of a marriage.

Manḍlạ caole. A return present of rice given by the head-man of a bride's village to the bridegroom's party.
Manḍlạ hạnḍi. A return present of liquor given by the head-man of a bride's village to the bridegroom's party.
Manḍlạ ṭaka. A rupee given to the headman of a bride's village by a bridegroom.

Mandmanḍe. To stand in the way of others.

Mandmande akanae. He is standing in the way, idling himself and obstructing others.

Mandoli. } A hollow ornament of various
Madoli. } metals, worn usually round the neck and often filled with something in the nature of a charm.

Manḍom. A raised platform or scaffold. Cf. maṛom.

Mando Siń. A traditional hero whose name appears in the oldest traditions of the Santals.

Manḍrao. To sweep round in circles, as a bird of prey; to spread with the hand, as grain in the sun to dry.

Coṭre gidi kuṛiƙko manḍraoƙkana. The vultures and kites are flying round in circles high in the sky.
Hanḍi daka manḍrao ńogme reaṛoƙ lagiƙ. Spread out the rice which has been cooked to make liquor with so that it may cool.

Manḍri. } **Marnḍi.** } A weed of rice cultivation. Cf. marnḍi.

Manḍria. A drummer, drum musicians. Cf. mandaṛia.

Manḍua. } **Manḍwa.** } Cf. manḍhwa.

Manḍwa daka. Boiled rice given to the young men who erect the *manḍhwa* (q. v.)

Manḍwa koṛa. The young men who erect the *manḍhwa*. Cf. manḍhwa.

Manḍwa hanḍi. Liquor given to the young men who erect the *manḍhwa* (q. v.)

Manḍwa khunṭi. A post fixed in the centre of the *manḍhwa* (q. v.)

Manḍwa sim. Three fowls, two white and one brown sacrificed on the day the *manḍhwa* (q. v.) is erected.

Manḍwa oƙtoṛ daka. Boiled rice given to the young men who remove the *manḍhwa* (q. v.) after a marriage.

Manḍwa manḍwi. } **Maṛwa maṛwi** } To throw down, or to one side. Scottice, to *toozle*.

Haṛup karmaṭaokateye manḍwa manḍwikedińa.

Manḍwari. } **Marwaṛi.** } The Marwari caste of Hindus.

Mane. Meaning.

Mane kitap. A dictionary.

Mań. } **Mańg.** } Cf. maƙ.

Bugite mańgoƙkan sahan. Much firewood is being cut.

Mańgal. To depreciate, to shew disrespect, to disgrace, used only in conjunction with other verbs.

Roṛ mańgalkedińako. They spoke disrespectfully to me.
Ńum mańgalkedińako ińge. The kept naming me disrespectfully.
Sanamko roṛ mańgalmea. All will reproach you with it.
Ruheƙ mańgalkedeako. They scolded him and ashamed him.
Sanamiće roṛ mańgalmea.

Mańgal. } **Khusal mańgal.** } **Kusal mańgal.** } News, welfare.

Mańgal. } **Mońgol.** } Tuesday.

Mańga muṛa. Dirty, slovenly, depressed, sad looking, miserable looking.

Mańga muṛae ńeloƙkana. He looks slovenly.

Mańgao. To send for, to acknowledge.

Nunaƙiń ghaṭkeda, adoń mańgao jońkana. I have committed so much of a fault, and I acknowledge it.
Aḍi baṛiciń kaiakaṭa, ghaṭiń mańgaoeda, ma dayawańpe. I have greatly sinned, I acknowledge my fault, have pity on me.
Uni hoṛ mańgaoem. Send for that man.

Mańgar. Plump, in good condition.

Pe pon mãhã khubko jom ocokedekhane mańgar goćena. They having fed him well for three or four days he got plump.

Mańgaṛ. An alligator.

Mańgaṛ gupi. To shepherd alligators.
Referring to the ashes of a funeral pyre being thrown into a tank, &c. in which alligators live.
Mańgaṛ gupie calaoena. He has gone to shepherd the alligators, i. e. he is dead and his ashes thrown to alligators into a tank.

Mańgar. } **Mońgor.** } Tuesday.

Mańgar mońgor. } **Mańgaṛ mońgoṛ.** } To mumble when eating as one without teeth.

Mańgaṛ mońgoṛe jomeda. He mumbles when he eats.

Mańgo. Another name for the Mahla, or Palm-cat, *Paradoxurus hemaphroditus,* var. *niger*. Cf. mahla.

Mańgri hako. A kind of fish so named.

Mańgri goco. A moustache twirled up at the ends like the beard of a *mańgri* (q. v.) fish.

Mańnite. For the asking, gratis.

Okoe mańniteko emama? Who will give you for the asking?

Mạni. A kind of precious stone.

Mạniaḍar. Cor. of the English word "money order."

Mạnik. A kind of gem said to be found in the heads of certain snakes, a pearl.

Mạnikjoṛ. A species of wading bird, *Ardea leucocephala.*

Mańj. The centre, heart-wood, core of of certain trees.
Terel mańj. Indian ebony the black heartwood of *Diospyros tomentosa, Roxb.*
Mańjteṭ. The heart-wood.
Mańj khunṭuṭ. Heart-wood of a tree stump left in the ground.

Mańja. Insufficiently cooked, as rice.
Mańjagea. It is insufficiently cooked.

Mańjal. Heart-wood, mature timber.
Bes mańjalakana noa kaṭ do. This log is good heart-wood, or this log is good mature timber.

Mańja mạńjhi. } In the centre, in the
Mańjha mạńjhi. } middle.
Mańjha mạńjhirekin ńapamena. They met in the centre.
Mańja mạńjhirekin duṛupakana. They are sitting in the centre.

Mańjan. Breakfast, to breakfast; mid-day meal, to partake of mid-day meal.
Aụrile mańjanoka. We have not yet breakfasted.
Mańjan jome calaoena. He has gone to get his breakfast.
Mańjan ber. Breakfast time, dinner time.
Mańjanokkanae. He is breakfasting, or having his dinner.
Upạr mańjan. Luncheon.

Mańjao. To scour, as a brass vessel, &c. with sand or ashes. Cf. gitil.
Thạri mańjao ạguipe. Scour and bring the plates.
Mańjaoak kangea. It has been scoured.

Mańjela. Heart-wood, mature timber.
Mańjela kaṭ. Heart-wood timber.

Mạńjgut. } Right, proper, well, strong,
Mạjgut. } substantial, efficiently.
Mạńjgutte kạmime. Do the work properly.
Khub mạńjgut sagaṛ kana. It is a good substantial cart.

Manjha mạńjhi. In the middle, in the centre. Cf. mańja mạńjhi.

Mańjhe. } After meal-time.
Sańjhe na mańjhe. }
Sańjhe na mańjherem hedena. You have come neither before nor during meal-time.

Mạńjhi. A village chief, a village headman, a Santal male.
Ato mạńjhi. The village chief.
Des Mạńjhi. An over-chief.
Jog Mạńjhi. The village censor of morals.
Hạnḍi Mạńjhi. The liquor-chief, the village social chief, when the head-man of the village is not a Santal.
Mapańji. } Village chiefs.
Mạpạńjhi. }
Mạńjhi era. The wife of a village chief.
Mạńjhi haṛam. The village chief.
Mạńjhi buḍhi. The wife of the village chief.
Mạńjhikedeale. We made him village chief.
Mạńjhi mạn. Rent free land held by a village chief.

Mạńjhi khil Kisku. A sub-sept of the Santal sept Kisku (q. v.)

Mạńjhi khil Murmu. A sub-sept of the Santal sept Murmu (q. v.)

Mạńjhi khil Hembrom. A sub-sept of the Santal sept Hembrom (q. v.)

Mạńjhi khil Mạrnḍi. A sub-sept of the Santal sept Mạrnḍi (q. v.)

Mạńjhi khil Soren. A sub-sept of the Santal sept Soren (q. v.)

Mạńjhi khil Ṭuḍu. A sub-sept of the Santal sept Ṭuḍu (q. v.)

Mạńjhi khil Baske. A sub-sept of the Santal sept Baske (q. v.)

Mạńjhi khil Besra. A sub-sept of the Santal sept Besra (q. v.)

Mạńjhi khil Cōṛē or Guạ Soren. A sub-sept of the Santal sept Cōṛē or Guạ Soren (q. v.)

Mạńjhi khil Pạuriạ or Pạuliạ. A sub-sept of the Santal sept Pạuriạ or Pạuliạ (q. v.)

Mạńjhian. A Santal female.
Gicho mạńjhian. A Santal female named Gicho.

Mạńjhlạ. } M. } The fourth of a family
Mạńjlạ. } } in point of birth or age.
Mạńjhli. } F. }
Mạńjli. }
Mạńjlạ koṛa. } The fourth son.
Mạńjhlạ koṛa. }
Mạńjli kuṛi. } The fourth daughter.
Mạńjhli kuṛi. }
Mạńjli bạhu. } Wife of the fourth son.
Mạńjhli bạhu. }
Mạńjlạ mamo. } Fourth oldest maternal uncle.
Mạńjhlạ mamo. }
Mạńjlạić. } The fourth male in point of birth.
Mạńjhlạić. }
Mạńjliić. } The fourth female in point of birth.
Mạńjhliić. }

Mańjla ra̤s. M. } **Mańjli ra̤s. F.** } Average or middle, intermediate.
Khub usul hõ bań, khub gi̤dri hõ bań ma̤ńjli ra̤sgeako. They are neither very tall nor very short (females) but middle sized.

Ma̤njur. } **Monjur.** } To approve of, to accept, to admit.
A̤pil bań ma̤ńjurlena. The appeal was dismissed.
Darkhas ma̤njurentińa. My complaint has been admitted.

Ma̤njur gṳda̤. To tie the hands together, then push them over the knees, and then put a stick under the knees and over the hands, to tie the hands behind the back.

Man kauda. A cultivated root plant.

Ma̤n marja̤d. } **Ma̤n marja̤t.** } **Man marja̤t.** } To treat hospitably, to entertain to a feast, to treat with distinction.
Cet́ lekako ma̤n ma̤rja̤t́keťpea? How did they entertain you?

Manoa. Cf. manwa.

Manot. To honour, to shew respect.
Bako manotledea. They did not honour him.
Manot lek hor̤ kanae. He is a man worthy of respect.
Manotan hor̤. A respected person, an honourable man.

Manot rar̤. An air to which certain songs are sung.

Manotan. Respectable, honorable.

Manotia̤. Honourable, respected.

Manoti manwa. Human beings.

Ma̤nsi. Each person, each one.
Ma̤nsi nina̤k̓ hapa̤tiń hoeena. Each person's share was so much.

Manta. } **Mantao.** } To soften, to reconcile, to persuade, to put off.
Bae mantaok̓kana. He will not be persuaded.

Mantar. An incantation.
Bińmantar. An incantation used for snake bite.
Bis mantar. An incantation used for poison.
Ato tol reak̓ mantar. An incantation used to shield a village from an epidemic, &c.
Mantar par̤hao. To recite an incantation.

Manwa. A human being.
Manwa ja̤t. Human beings.
Manwa janam. Human.
Manwa janam doe bań kana. He is not human.
Duk jokhenko ror̤a manwa janam bań besa. When afflicted they say it is not good to be human.
Manwa Hopon. Son of Man.
Hor̤ manwa. Human beings.
Manwalenae. He became a man.
Manoti manwa. Human beings.

Ma̤nus man. To become well-to-do, to become respectable.
Kurumuťu hor̤ onḍeko ma̤nus manok̓a. Industrious men become well-to-do there.

Mão. The mew or call of a cat (imitative.)
Nonḍem ror̤eda, menkhan mão ťhen ohom ror̤lea. You are saying that here, but you won't say it before the cat.
Mice once laid a plan to do away with the cat, but when it came to seizing her no one had the courage to approach her.

Maor̤a. } **Ma̤ur̤a̤.** } A strip of skin round the end of a drum to which the lacing is attached.

Map. } **Maph.** } To forgive, excuse, overlook.
Nia̤ dhao mapkatińme. Forgive my fault this time.

Map. } **Nap.** } To measure, a grain measure of about 2 maunds.

Mapak̓. Reciprocal form of mak̓ (q. v.)
Mapak̓kanako. The are slaughtering each other.

Ma̤pa̤ńjhiko. Head-men of villages, village chiefs.
Mapańjhikoko jaoraakana. The village chiefs are assembled.

Maph. To forgive, excuse, overlook. Cf. map.

Ma̤phik. Like, resembling. Cf. ma̤pik.

Ma̤pik. } **Ma̤pit.** } Like, resembling.
Noa ma̤pikem ka̤milekhan a̤sulok̓am. If you work like this you will earn a living.

Ma̤r. A chaplet sometimes worn by bridegrooms and brides at marriage.

Ma̤r. Game killed at a hunt, calamity.
A̤di ma̤r hoeena. Much game has been killed.
Ma̤rre mĩhimre, unrele ńamme, ńumme, dahinre̤m tahena. In calamity and affliction, when we seek thee and call upon thee, be at our right hand.

Mar. } **Marmar.** } Quickly, instantly, rapidly, hastily,
Marmare calak̓kana. He is going quickly.
Marge ka̤mipe. Work quickly.

Mar. } **Marpa̤sir.** } To finish, to complete.
Dakań ma̤r pa̤sirakaťa. I have eaten all the cooked rice.
Ka̤mińma̤rpa̤sirakaťa. I have finished the work.

Ma̤r̤ baha. A species of tree.

Mā̤r Soren. A sub-sept of the Santal sept Soren (q. v.)

Mar muhim. } Distress, suffering, affliction.
Mār mūhin. }

Mārā. On the point of, about to.
Gujuk mārāenae. He is almost dead.
Gujuk mārāe ruakkana. He is sick unto death

Mara. } To allow a corpse to remain in the house overnight when it might have been disposed of before sunset.
Basi mara. }

Nunak hor tahen tulué cedakpe basi marakedea? When there were so many people at hand why did you allow him (the corpse) to remain in the house overnight?

Mara. Loss, damage, to defraud, to oppress, to stint.
Nes adi mara hoeéntińa. I have suffered great loss this year.
Guti alom maraea. Do not stint your servant in his food.

Mara. A depreciatory term used mainly when finding fault, scolding or abusing, scoundrel, rascal, villain, miscreant, jade, witch, &c., in contempt or irony.
Kurbia mara hor. A lazy scoundrel.
Nui bodro mara hor oka bō bań bujhauktaea. This stammering fool is unintelligible.
Candal mara hor. A vicious scoundrel.
Dodhio mara budhi An old worn out hag.
Jōi mara gidra. A little imp of a child.
Juknué mara budhi. A shrivelled hag.
Kadua mara herel. A limping scoundrel.
Karbuh mara hor. A tall round-shouldered rascal.
Nui gojra mara hor. This consummate sluggard.
Boka mara hor. An ignorant fool.

Marae marae. Hungry.
Marae marae durupakanae.
Tinak marae marae rengeétem tahena?

Marak. A peacock, peafowl.
Pińcar marak. A peacock.
Matu marak. A peahen.
Dende pińcar marak. A species or variety of peacock with a short tail.
Marak rak. Peacock crow, about 2 a. m. when the peacock begins to call.
Marak tikli. The disk on the tail feathers of the peacock.

Marak bele. }
Marak eneć. } A children's game.
Marak gud. }

Marak morok. To stare wonderingly, to stare vacantly, as one half-witted when spoken to, to be sad, to be depressed, to be disappointed.
Marak moroke beńgeć tarąeda. He is staring in wonder.

Maramat. To mend, to repair

Marań. Great, large, big, huge, to become or cause to become great, large, big, huge; first born, principal, head, chief.
Adi marań sadom. A very big horse.
Marań kora hopon. } First born son.
Marańić kora hopon. }
Marań kuri hopon. First born daughter.
Marańić. First born.
Khad ren marań Saheb. The colliery manager.
Marań Babu. The head baboo.
Marań hor kanae. He is a great man.
Iń khone marańa. He is older than I am.
Marań utarić kanae. He is the head or chief.
Marańkedeań. I promoted him.

Marań. Before, first, in time or place.
Uni marańreń seterena. I arrived before him.
Am marańre menaka. It is in front of you.
Taeom marań. One after the other.
Taeom marańkin goćena. They died one after the other.
Iń geń ror marańa. I will speak first.
Uni geye dal marańkedea. He struck him first.
Uniko marańkedea. They put him forward.

Marań Buru. The great or chief Spirit. Cf. Buru.

Marań buru. The great mountain, Paresnath, which is the highest in the Santal country.

Marań kongat. A large woody twining plant, *Dregia volubilis, Benth.*

Marań ojo. Carbuncle.

Marań jhunka. A wild plant, *Crotalaria alata, Roxb.*

Marań duk. Cholera. Cf. hawa duk.

Marao. To become extinct, to be annihilated, to be exterminated, to die, to put an end to, to kill, when used with another verb it is intensive.
Goć maraoenako. They have been exterminated by death.
Marao udarenako. They are extinct, they have all died.
Sanam ghās maraoena. All the grass has been exterminated, all the grass has died.
Kathako maraokeda. They settled the matter, put an end to it.
Simko goć maraokećkoa. They killed and exterminated the fowls.
Maraokedeako sukri. They killed the pig (found trespassing.)
Maraokećkoako hon do. They exterminated the rats.
Sanam gustiko goć maraoena. The family has become extinct by death.
Mohnda marao. To close an aperture, in the mouth of a vessel, to finish off, as the top of a stack of hay &c., to put the finishing touches to.

Lapak marao. To hit with something soft, as clay, a snowball, &c.
Dhŏk marao. To rest.
Ona khun do goṭa disom cão marao goćena. That murder spread through the whole country.
Kul botorteye keṭel maraoena. He gave a great start through fear of the tiger.
Noa arăṛ reak mohnḍa marao gotkakme. Put the finishing touches to this yoke.
Dare khonin lapak marao goćena. I fell down flop from the tree.
Ona dhiri doe kuṛyuć marao gotkeda. He swallowed that stone right away.
Rạskạteń rumuń marao goćena. I gave a start from joy.
Borlomte banae gaj maraokedea. He transfixed the bear with a spear.
Pocorte dake phecreṭ maraoadea. He threw water at him swish with a squirt.
Mić bạṭi hạnḍiye bodoṛ maraokeda. He drank a cup of rice beer at one gulp.
Jaṅe raṭuk maraokeda. He crunched the bone right away.
Ma tho mić dhao hnduṛ marao gotkam. Come make it sound once.
Cẽṛẽ ṭuṭiteye bhuḍ maraokedea. He hit the bird plump with a blunt arrow.
Ạpạṛite kulạiye khac marao gotkedea. He transfixed the hare with an arrow.
Suitelaṅ cubuć maraomea nahak. I shall presently stick a needle in you.
Seta ạuri emaeregeye khabol marao gotkeda. The dog seized it before he gave it to him.
Ạpạṛi do kiṛbić maraoktama. Your arrow will pierce and stick.
Raj reak katha añjomteko luyuć maraoena. They trembled at the king's word.
Setań dalkedekhane kãć marao gotkeda. When I struck the dog he howled.
Gạruṛ do bạndukte diṛim maraokedeań. I let off the gun bang at the adjutant bird.
Nui sadom do calak calakte bidnạk marao goćenae. This horse when going stopped all at once.
Ma tho noa ṭuṭi do mić dhao roiyol marao gotkam. Come, let fly this arrow once.
Gidrạ do parkom khone ḍhui marao goćena. The child fell with a thud from the bed.
Noa pukhrire katla hakoe huḍrạk maraokeda. A katla fish gave a great splash in this tank.
Saram do ṭhukedeteye sanak marao goćena. When he hit the Saram (q. v.) deer with an arrow it fell down forthwith.
Bijli do bilić maraoena. There was a flash of lightning, the lightning flashed.
Tale do dare khon luṭhum marao goćena. The palmyra fruit fell thud from the tree.
Phokok marao gotkedeań nui kulại do. I swished an arrow at this hare.
Cuṭi khub ăṭe or gotkette dhũae podoe marao gotkada. Having pulled strongly at the cigar he blew out a cloud of smoke.
Hạrup gotkedekhanin humcạk marao goćenae. When I threw my arms round him he gave a start.

Marăṛ. A bhangy pole.

Marăṛ. } A small tree with gorgeous red flowers, *Erythrina indica, Lam.*
Maraṛ.
Marăṛ baha.
Buru marăṛ baha. A small tree found on the hills, *Erythrina arborescens, Roxb.*

Maraṛ tejo. A kind of insect.

Marca. To be exhausted, as soil, to become unproductive, unfertile; to lose vigour, deteriorate physically.
Noa ato marcaena. The soil of this village has become exhausted.
Noa dare marcaena, bań harakkana. This tree has become stunted, it is not growing

Mardao. To rub and knead the body or limbs, to perform massage.
Khub lekale mardaokedea. We rubbed and kneaded his body well.

Marde. Used by brothers-in-law when addressing each other.

Mardhar. Quickly, hastily, rapidly.
Mardharko kạmikana. They are working quickly.

Mare. Old, ancient, original, surplus over requirements for year, savings of year.
Mare hapṛamko. The ancients.
Mare purnạ. Old, over from previous years.
Mare purnạ kicrić menaktaea. Her clothes are old.
Mare purnạ jomak menaktakoa. They have grain from previous years.
Barpe mare menaktalea. We have savings from two or three years.
Kicrić mareĕna. The cloth is old.
Mare guti. An old servant, one who has served his master for a long period.
Noa ato ren mare hoṛkoko dạṛakaća. The original inhabitants of this village have left.

Maren. Old, applied only to animate objects.
Maren hoṛ kanae. He is an old man.
Marenak. Old, applied to inanimate objects.
Marenak kaṭ kana. It is a log of mature timber.

Mare ore. Old, applied mainly to cloth; stale, as cooked rice.
Mare oreko em baṛaadińa. They gave me some stale rice.
Mare ore menakkhan emańme, lańgaṭenań. If there is a piece of old cloth give it to me, I am naked.

Margạiṭhạ. }
Marghạiṭhạ. } Dirty, soiled.
Marghạṭh. }
Marghạṭ. }

Marge. Now, now and quickly, without delay.
Marge metakpe nitok do. Now you can begin to eat.
Marge sabepe, marge sabepe.

Margot. Cf. margaiṭha.

Marhaṭha. A Mahratta, to persist in spite of discomfort and difficulty.

Marhaṭha lekae kạmieda. He works like a Marhaṭha (takes no note of sun, cold, rain, &c.)

Marheṛ. Withered grass that has withered in the ground, as at the cessation of the rains.

Gaḍa seć idikom, onḍe khub marheṛ menaꞌa. Take them towards the river, there is much withered grass there.

Mạṛi. A corpse, a dead body.

Mạṛi murdạ. A corpse.

Mạri. Old.

Mạri katha nāwāetam. Rejuvenate your old stories.

Mạri.
Mạri bhoe. } Cholera.

Mạri.
Maha mạri. } The plague.

Mạri guṭi. Small pox.

Mạri meṭāhā. Face pock-pitted.

Mạri poda. Wandering, vagrant.

Mạri poda hoṛ kanae. He is a wanderer.

Mạriạu. To occupy a new house, to take up one's abode, to take refuge, as a wild animal in a thicket when hard pressed. Cf. mạnḍiạu.

Mạric. Pepper.

Gol mạric. Round pepper.

Ḍinḍi mạric.
Dare mạric. } Long pepper.

Caole mạric. A kind of pepper resembling grains of rice.

Mạrjad.
Mạrjat. } To entertain, to shew respect to by hospitality.

Peṛa khubko mạrjadkeꞌkoa. They entertained the visitors right hospitably.

Mạrjạdi.
Mạrjạti. } A present, mainly of a small piece of flesh meat.

Mạrjạtiye emaꞌmea. He gave you a piece of meat.

Mạrji.
Murji. } Will, assent, pleasure, taking favourably.

Amaꞌ mạrji leka hoyokma. Let it be according to your pleasure.

Maṛkao. Pain in the muscles.

Maṛkaoenae calaꞌ calaꞌte. He has pain in the muscles through continued travelling.

Maṛka mạṛki. Cf. maṛkao.

Maṛka mạṛkienae. He is suffering from muscular pain.

Markaṭ. To fight, to fight and slay each other, to persevere, to be assiduous, to be diligent.

Hulreko markaṭlena. In the rebellion they fought and killed each other.

Ạḍi markaṭkatele bañcaoena. We were saved with much difficulty.

Markha.
Cak markha. } Fine cotton twist.

Mạrkhu. The portion of rice broken small in husking, grain of different kinds found in the refuse from the husking machine.

Mạrkhu marao. To extract the broken grain from the refuse of the husking machine. Cf. mạrkhu.

Mạrkin. Cotton cloth of European manufacture.

Mạrkin sạṛi. A sạṛi (q. v.) of European manufacture.

Maṛkoca. The ridge of a roof.

Maṛkoca marao. To finish thatching the ridge of a roof.

Mar mar. Quickly.

Marmar.
Seṅgel marmar. } A species of large poisonous centipede.

Mar masala.
Mor mosola. } Spices of different kinds.

Mạrnḍi.
Mạrnḍi kipisāṛ. } One of the twelve septs into which the Santals are divided.

Mạrnḍi. A weed of rice cultivation, *Ischaemum rugosum, Salisb.*

Maṛom. A platform, used to keep straw on, or from which to watch crops.

Maṛomakaꞌale. We have erected a platform or scaffold (on which to store straw.)

Roṭe maṛom. The frog's platform, i. e. water.

Marot. To finish, to complete.

Goć marotenako. They are all dead.

Marotkedako kạmi. They finished the work.

Marpase. Denotes uncertainty, possibly.

Marpaseñ ñamkaꞌ.

Marpase ruheꞌkadiñge.

Mạrpạsir. To finish, to complete. Cf. mar.

Marpiṭ. To assault, assault and battery.

Khubko marpiṭkedea. They severely assaulted him.

Marsal. Light.

Siñ marsal. Day-time, daylight.

Siñ marsalre. In daylight, in day-time.

Marsalakome. Give them light.

Marsalena. It is light.

Beṅgeꞌ marsalkedae. He received sight.

Marte. Affixed to certain roots it forms adverbs implying sudden and single action. Cf. mente.

Chaṭ marte geꞌ gocena. It was cut at once.

Khap marte sapkedea. He caught him with one swift swoop.

Mạrtu marak̇. The peahen.
Piñoṛ marak̇. The peacock.

Mạrtul. A hammer.

Mạruk. Without doubt, certainly, obligatory, perforce, of necessity, *nolens volens*, compulsory.

Jhak mạruk.
Jhak mạrukh. } Cf. mạruk.
Jhak mạrukamgem calak̇a. You will certainly go.
Jhak̇ mạruk unigeye bạḍaea. Without doubt he knows.

Mạruk̇. To eat.
Karu hõe mạruk̇keda. Karu also ate.

Mạruṛ. To decay, to shew signs of decay, to be past the best.
Mạruṛ mạruṛge ñelok̇a. It looks much decayed.
Mạruṛkate baplaenae. She was past the flower of her age before she was married.
Cetlekan jawãepe ñamkedea? Mạruṛgeae. What kind of a bridegroom have you got? He is past full age.

Maṛwa mạṛwi. Cf. manḍwa mạnḍwi.

Mas. A month.
Din mas. The end of the agricultural year, season.
Mag mas. The month of Magh, the end of the agricultural year.
Mag mas munḍạre. At the end of the month of Magh, the close of the agricultural year.

Masać musuć. Silent, taciturn, seldom speaking.

Masar masar. Crunching sound, to gobble quickly.
Masar masare jomeda. He makes a crunching sound as he eats.

Masdar. Independent, well-to-do.

Mase. Cf. ma.

Mạsi. Christ.

Maskao. To subside, applied to swellings, rashes and pustules, as measles, smallpox, &c.
Guṭi do maskaoentaea. His smallpox pustules are drying up.

Maskuṛa. The gums, a gumboil.
Maskuṛạ janamakawadea. He has a gum boil.
Ḍaṭa ñur cabalenkhan eken maskuṛạ ge tahena. When all the teeth fall out only the gums remain.

Maskuṭạ. Soft, as iron that will not take an edge.
Pal do maskuṭạ mẽṛhẽćte hoyok̇a. Soft iron will do for a ploughshare.

Masmas.
Masmasao. } Indisposed, out-of-sorts, applied mainly to the premonitory symptoms of fever, pain in the stomach.
Masmasgeñ ṣikạueda. I feel indisposed.
Hoṛmo masmasaogeñ ṣikạueda. I feell pain in my body.
Hoṛmo masmasaok̇kantiña. I fed the premonitory symptoms of fever.

Masṛa. Monthly, monthly receipts or salary.
Masṛa mõṛẽ ṭakae ñameda. He receives a monthly salary of five rupees.

Masra mạsri. To eat quickly, to put more food into the mouth before it is empty.
Masra mạsriye jomeda. He keeps stuffing food into his mouth.

Masrao. To crunch, as a horse eating gram.

Masrao. To stuff food into the mouth.
Saname masrao cabakeda. He stuffed it all into his mouth.

Mạsri. A cultivated pulse, *Ervum lens, Linn.*
Mạsri dạl. The split pea of *masri.*

Mạsul. Cf. mạhsul.

Mạsuṛdañ. Exceedingly, excessively, applied to corpulency.
Mạsuṛdañe moṭaakana. He is excessively fat.

Mạsuṛdañ. A common plant during the rains, *Wedelia Wallichii, Less.*

Maswa. Indolent, lazy.

Maswar. Independent, well-to-do, to pay respect to.

Mać. A bamboo.
Buru mać. The hill bamboo, *Bambusa stricta.*
Bar lañga mać. A kind of bamboo having long spaces between the nodes. Flutes are made from this bamboo.
Kaṭañ mać.
Khaṭañ mać. } A species of bamboo having spikes on the nodes.
Ropa mać. A planted bamboo, a cultivated bamboo.
Des mać. A variety of very thick bamboo.
Mać catom. A bamboo umbrella.
Mać caole. Husked seed of the bamboo.
Khol mać. A hollow bamboo.
Mać dạndhi. A clump of bamboos.
Mać pạṭiạ. A bamboo mat.

Mać sakam hako. A species of river fish.

Mat.
Math. } A temple, a monastery.

Matal.
Matala. } Drunk, intoxicated, addicted to liquor.

Matao. Full grown, applied to bulls, he-goats, &c. rampant, lustful, ruttish.

Maṭar muṭur. Munching or crunching sound. Cf. muṭur muṭur.

Matbor. Well-to-do and honourable, independent, proud.
Bes matbor hoṛ kanae. He is a very well-to-do and honourable man.

Math. A temple, a monastery. Cf. mat.

Maṭha. Perverse, obstinate, lazy, indolent, false.
Alo katha do eṛeKme maṭhaKme.
Juṭhạ maṭha. To be falsified.

Matha. }
Matha matha. } The forehead, the head or principal, a leader.
Matha matha hoṛ lekhakope. Count the principal men, (the leading men.)

Maṭha muṭhu. Adult, grown up.
Eken maṭha muṭhu hoṛko heśakana. Only full-grown people have come.

Maṭhasuṛa. }
Suramuṭha. }
Suṛamaṭha. }
Suṛamaṭha. } A small bush. Cf. suramaṭha.

Maṭha aṛak. A small bush, *Antidesma diandrum, Tulas.*, the leaves of which are eaten as a pot-herb.

Maṭhao. To smooth.
Maṭhaö baṛakaKme. Smooth it (by patting it with the back of a kudali.)
Kaṭiń laKakaṭa, nitoKiń maṭhao baṛakaKa. I have roughly hewn the log, now I will smooth it.

Maṭia pathra. A kind of soft, slatey stone.

Matkom. A large, very branchy forest tree, *Bassia latifolia, Roxb*; the flower of *Bassia latifolia*, which is used as a food.
Matkom khõc. The calyx of the flower of *Bassia latifolia*.
Matkom sohoe. The stamens of the *Matkom* flower.
Miṭ phulạ matkom. One single *Matkom* flower.
Bhugạk matkom. A hollow *Matkom* flower.
Bhugạk matkom lạgiṭko repeḱkanạ. They are quarrelling over a hollow *Matkom* flower. (something not worth quarrelling over.)
Matkom pusi jaṅgaKkanạ. The flower buds of the Matkom tree are just beginning to form.
Teke matkom. The Matkom flower boiled for food.
Matkom lathe. A preparation of the flower of *Bassia latifolia* for food.

Matkom hako. A kind of fish.

Matkom aṛak. A wild pot-herb, *Hygrophilla salicifolia, Nees.*

Maṭku. }
Moṭka. }
Moṭko. } Fat and short, squab, squat.
Maṭku hoṛ kanae. He is a squat man.

Matla. Drunk, intoxicated, addicted to liquor.

Maṭmaṭ. }
Maṭmaṭao. } To gnash the teeth, to grind the teeth.
Maṭmaṭe togoḋ ḍaṭaeda. He is grinding his teeth.
Togoḋ maṭmaṭaokedae. He ground his teeth.
Maṭmaṭaoadińae. He gnashed his teeth at me.

Matṛań. Before, in time or place, in front of.
Iń matṛańteye heśena. He came before me.

Maṭri. }
Maṭri ojha. } A charm doctor, a master of incantations, a diviner.
Maṭri ojha ṭhenle senlena. We went to the diviner.

Maṭruk maṭruk. Crunching noise, as a dog eating a bone, cracking sound, as when one breaks a nut with his teeth.
MaṭruK maṭruKe togoḋeda. He is crunching.

Matuạ. Intoxicated, drunk.
Ńu teṅgar maṭuạ ńoKena menkhan hajar goṭeḋko ehoba mare disom reań. When they have drunk to slight intoxication they begin to tell a thousand things about the old country.

Maṭu maraK. A peahen. Cf. maraK.

Matwar. A kind of dance so called.

Matwar serem. Songs sung during the dancing of the *matwar* (q. v.) dance.

Matwar ru. The time beaten on the drums during the dancing of the *matwar* dance.

Matwar raṛ. The tune or air to which the *matwar* (q. v.) songs are sung.

Maurasi. Hereditary, applied to tenures.

Mauṭạ. To kill, slay, destroy, abolish, do away with.

Maya. Kindness, pity, sympathy, compassion, mercy, affection, feeling; to pity, to compassionate, to shew mercy, kindness, affection.
Maya daya. }
Daya maya. } Mercy and pity.
Maya jalate. By the force of pity, compassion, mercy or affection.
MayaKme. Have mercy or pity.
Mayawańme. Have pity on me.
MaKyaiḋ kanae. He is a compassionate (man.)
Maya iń khone chaḍaokeda. He lost sympathy with me, he ceased to have affection for me.
Maya alom chaḍaoa. Do not cease to pity.
Bae mayalena. He shewed no pity.

Maya. Used when addressing males.
Maya sabepe. Ho, seize him.
Maya maya, hante dạṛkedae. Ho, ho, he ran in that direction.

Mayaḱ moyoḱ. To stare wonderingly, to stare vacantly, as a half-witted person when spoken to, to be sad, to be depressed.
Mayaḱ moyoḱe beṅgeć baṛaeda. He is staring about vacantly.
Mayaḱ moyoḱenae. He is sad.
Mayaḱ moyogoḱkanae. He is sad.

Mayam. } Blood, to bleed.
Mãyãm. }

Mayam pańja. To track wounded game by blood stains, to take revenge for social or other injuries, to retaliate.
Mayam oḍokoḱ. Dysentery.
Mũ mayamentaea. His nose is bleeding, or bloody.
Bul mayam. Offering of human blood. Cf. bul mayam.
Dal mayamkedeako. They beat him to the effusion of blood.

Mayam pańja eneć. A children's game.

Mayaṅ muyuṅ. Silent, mute, taciturn.
Mayaṅ muyuṅe beṅgeć baṛaea. He looks about and remains speechless.

Mayo. A eunuch, one having a feminine appearance.

Mayo. Employed in addressing males. Cf. maya.

Me. The form taken by the 2nd personal pronoun in inflections.
Calaḱ *me*. Go thou.
Dal *meae*. He will strike thee.

Me. Cf. ma.
Me delabon. Come, let us go.
Me seń kạmi hoda. Let me now push on with my work.

Meaṅ. The day after tomorrow.

Mec. } A table, a chair.
Mej. }

Mecka mecki. To be restive, as a bullock, &c., to move the head conceitedly, to give oneself airs.

Mecka micki. To be sprained or strained. Cf. meckao.
Mecka mickikoḱaeem. You may get sprained.

Meckao. Bent and slightly broken, sprained, strained.
Noa ḍạr meckaoakana. This branch is bent and slightly broken.

Meckoḱ marte. } With a smile.
Meckoḱ mente, }
Meckoḱ marteye duṛuṕ goćena. He sat down with a smile.

Mecoṛ. To eat all.
Manjan dole mecoṛkeda. We have eaten all the breakfast.

Mehao. Damp, wettish, moist.
Diṡ salae mehaoḷenkhan do seṅgel baṅ lagaoḱa. If a match is damp it will not ignite.
Bạruj mehaoena, baṅ lagaoḱa. The powder is damp, it will not ignite.

Meh ḍaṅra. The bullock on the left side of a row of bullocks treading out grain, the pivot on which the others turn. Cf. mehkhunṭi.

Mehẽć mehẽć. Slowly, gently.
Mehẽć mehẽće roṛeda. He speaks gently.
Mehẽć mehẽće taṛameda. He steps slowly.

Mehkhunṭi. A post to which bullocks are tied and round which they turn as a pivot when treading out grain.

Mehndi dare. } A small bush, *Lawsonia*
Mihndi dare. } *alba, Lam.*, used largely for hedges.
This plant yields the *henna* dye which is used to give the nails, feet, hair, &c. an orange colour.
Gul mihndi dare. A bush so called.

Mehnot. Labour, trouble, exertion; to exert oneself.
Ạḍi mehnotkateń ńamkeda. I obtained with much labour.
Ạḍi mehnot lagaoḱa. It entails much labour.

Mehnotiạ. Industrious, hard-working, pains taking.
Ạḍi mehnotiạ hoṛ kanae. He is a very industious man, or he is a painstaking man.

Mej. } A table, a chair.
Mec. }

Mejaj. Temperament, disposition, temper.
Ạḍi kạṛa mejajtae. His temperament is stern.

Mejas. } To consult together, to take
Meńjas. } counsel together, to consider.
Mejas miṫkedako. They came to an agreement.
Puruliate calaḱ reaḱ ńapamkateko meńjas johkana. Having met they are consulting about going to Purulia.
Katha ạḍi mejasgetalińa. We are in harmony.

Mekeć. } Without care, without
Mekeć mekeć. } anxiety.
Mekeć mekeće jom johkana. He lives without anxiety.

Meḱ meḱ. An imitative word, to bleat as a goat.
Meḱ meḱko bebhaoḱa merom. Goats bleat *meḱ' meḱ'*.

Mel. Concord, affection, fondness, harmony, agreement.
Nukin ạdikin melena. These two have great affection for each other.
Melte baṛe tahenpe. Live in harmony.

Mela. A fair, a gathering on the occasion of a public religious observance, which also partakes of the nature of a fair.
Mela lagaoḱkana. A fair is being held.
Mela ṭạṇḍi. The place where a fair is held.

Mela. Without particularising, general.
Haṛam budhi ṣurikin gidrạ joh hẹbić melakin hoho joha. A husband and wife before they have a child call to each other without particularising. (It is not considered proper for a husband to mention his wife's name, or a wife that of her husband, so that in calling to or addressing each other they use general terms. On the birth of a child, however, this difficulty is overcome by the husband calling his wife, for instance John's mother, John being the child's name, and her calling him John's father.)
Eho, hijuḱme, mela hoho kana. I say, come, is a general call.

Mela bhag. A system of cultivation in which the cultivator receives one half of the produce in return for his labour, and the owner the other half.

Mela. } Wide, large in area.
Melan. }
Mela jaega. A wide place.
Melan ṭạṇḍi. A plain of large area.

Mela oṛaḱ. An empty house, used as a guest house, &c.

Melan. Cf. mela.

Melaṅ cetaṅ. Always eating, always ready for anything eatable.
Melaṅ cetaṅe jom baṛaeda. He eats anything he comes across.

Melao. To spread out, as anything to dry or cool.
Kicrić melaokam. Spread the cloth out (to dry.)

Melco. } Middling, tolerable, moderately good.
Melco melco. }
Ạdi do bae besa, melco melcogeye ṅeloḱa. He is not very good, he looks only moderately well.
Melco kạpi. A moderately good battleaxe.

Melećmecoṅ. }
Meloć mecoṅ. } Laughing and talking, laughing and joking, mirthful.
Meloṅ mecoṅ. }
Melo meco. }
Melećmecoṅ baṛaedako. They are laughing and talking.

Mele mele. Numerous, in crowds.
Mele meleko heċakana. They have come in crowds.

Mele mele. To look on wistfully while others are eating.

Meloṅ cetoṅ. Cf. melaṅ cetaṅ.

Meloť. } To protrude the tongue,
Meloť meloť. } to moisten the lips with the tongue, to lick the lips, to dart out the tongue.
Meloťedae. He is licking his lips.
Biṅko meloť baṛaea. Snakes dart out the tongue.
Ona joloḱ seṅgel meloť tioḱkedeae.
Meloť meloťedae. He keeps darting out his tongue (a snake.)

Meloť cetoť. Always eating, keeping the lips moving, as when eating.

Memeḱ. A goat in the language of children.

Men. An exclamation of warning, caution, admonition, or alarm; beware, take care, mind what you are about, look out.
Men ocoḱme. Clear out of the way.
Men men dạṛpe kul menaea. Look out, look out, flee, there is a tiger.
Menho. Look out.
Men baba. Beware, father! look out, father! &c., &c., respectful form used to elderly people.
Men go. Used when addressing a woman, look out, woman; woman, take care, &c.
Menya. } Look out.
Menea. }
Menna. Used to a female younger than the speaker.
Men ja. Look out! boy.
Men sontoroḱpe. Mind, be careful.
Men, okoe hõ alope lại baṛaea. Take care, let none of you tell it.

Men. } To say, to tell, to wish, to call.
Met. }
Menjoh. To wish, to purpose.
Calaḱiṅ menjohkana. I wish to go.
Ać hudiṅe menogoḱkana. He abases himself.
Menadeaṅ. } I told him, I said to him.
Metadeaṅ. }
Onkoṅ metaḱkoa. I said to them.
Noa cetem metaḱa? What do you call this?
Calaḱiṅ meneťkana. I purpose going.
Mepenkatekin kajakakaťa. They consulted and have settled it finally.
Menako. They say, it is said.

Mena. Probably, perhaps, belike, most likely.
Hijuḱkanae mena. He is probably coming.
Ṅamkedako mena. They most likely obtained.
Mena, menaḱkogea. They are probably there.

Mena. }
Menaǩ. } To exist, to be.

Menaea. He is.
Oṛaǩre menaǩkoa. They are in the house.
Hijuǩtege menaǩkoa. They continue to come.
Gujuǩtege menaǩkoa. They continue to die.
Jiweťge menaea. He is alive, he continues to live.

Mendoǩ. }
Meť. } To suffer from inflamation of the eye and appendages, conjunctivites. Cf. meť.

Mendoǩkanae. }
Meťakanae. } He is suffering from inflammation of the eye.
Medoǩkanae. }

Menea. Cf. men.

Menek. But.

Senlenań, menek bań ńamledea. I went, but I did not find him.

Meńjas. To consult together, to take counsel together, to consider, to conspire.

Uni goje reaǩko meńjaskeda. They conspired to kill him.
Uni reje reaǩko meńjaskeda. They conspired to deprive him of it.
Ceť coṅko meńjaseťkana. They are consulting about something or other.

Menkhan. A particle which, when standing at the beginning of its clause, is a co-ordinating conjunction, signifying "but," and, when occurring at the end, a subordinating conjunction or conjuuctive adverb, signifying "if" or "when."

Ńelledeań, menkhan bań galmaraodea. I saw him but I did not speak to him.
Sanamko jom baṛakeda menkhan tarasiń ńjokheć do oṛaǩteko ruạṛa. When they have all partaken of food they return home about three o'clock.
Naekeko aderkadea menkhan hạṇḍi ńuńukoḱdo hạṇḍiko ńuia, ar enećko do Bahako eneća. When they have taken the priest inside, the liquor drinkers drink, and the dancers dance the Baha dance. Cf. eneć.
Ńindạena menkhan arhõ koṛa kuṛi do enećte kulhiko daṛana. When it is night the young men and maidens again parade the street dancing.
E baba, hopon ren ạḍi marań sukri uni hotete bako goć ocoedekan tahẽkantaetama menkhan, enḍekhan phạsiara metańme. Hear, if they were not causing the very large pig of your son to be killed by him, then you may call me a deceiver.

Men na. Cf. men.

Mensikte. Cf. sikte.

Mente. An affix signifying for, for the purpose of; also a conjunctive particle which constitutes the sentence it subordinates an adverbial clause of purpose or a noun clause.

Nahel menteye maǩkeda. He cut it (a piece of timber) for a plough.
Rupạ menteko idikeda. They took it away thinking it silver.
Itạ hoṛo ạguia menteye senakana. He has gone for the purpose of bringing seed dhan, he has gone to bring seed dhan.
Jemon okoe hõ aloko lạiako, ać do Masi kanae mente. So that they should tell no one, that he is the Christ.
Oṛaǩ mente kaṭ ạgu johkanae. He is bringing timber to build his house with.

Mente. Affixed to certain roots to form adverbs implying sudden and single action. Cf. marte.

Dhạu mente jol goťena. It burned with a sudden blaze.
Jhap mente heć goťenae. He came at once.
Jaṛap mente bereť gotenae. He rose instantly.
Kalaǩ menteye roṛ goťkeda. He immediately replied.
Perel menteye don paromkeda. He bounded nimbly over.
Pehlań mente ebhen goťenae. He awoke with a sudden start.
Paṭ mente goć goťenae. }
Phaṭ mente goć goť enae } He died on the instant.
Paṭas menteye dalkedea. He struck him one sounding smack.

Menya. Cf. men.

Meoṅ. The mew of a cat (imitative.)

Meoṅ meoṅ pusiko raga. Cats mew.

Mepen. To speak together, to consult, the Reciprocal form of men (q. v.)

Mepenkanakin. They are talking to each other.

Mera. Malted grain before and after the liquor has been extracted.

Noa do ceť hạṇḍi? mera bale ńameť do. What liquor is this? (from what grain has it been made?) We do not see any of the grain.

Merahiť. Uselessly, unavailingly.

Meraić. An insignificant person. Cf. mera.

Uni meraić ạḍiye roṛa. That insignificant speaks a great deal.

Meral. A small tree, *Phyllanthus Emblica, Linn.*

Merao. To twist strands into a rope.

Baber uńkate barạhi benao lạṛićko meraoa. Having twisted the cords or strands, they twist the strands together to make rope.

Merayaǩ. In vain, groundlessly, of no importance. Cf. mera.

Merayaǩe roṛeda. What he says is of no importance.

Mereć. }
Mereć mereć. } Just appearing, just beginning.

Mereć mereć aṛaǩ sagenoǩkana. The pot-herbs are just beginning to sprout.
Tin marahae jãwãe do? nạ̃ťege mereć mereć moca goco janamoǩkantaea. How old is the bridegroom? His moustache is only now beginning to sprout.

Merel. } Eagerly, cravingly, hankeringly, wistfully.
Merel merel.
Merel merele ñeñelkana. He is watching eagerly.

Meṛha. M. } Twisted, crumpled, as a horn.
Miṛhi. F.
Meṛha dereñ. A crumpled horn.

Meṛhao. To wind into a ball, to roll up, as a roll of paper or cloth, to pass round, as twine round anything to fasten or tie it.
Meṛhao ṣcurkate tolme. Pass it round and tie it.

Mĕṛhĕt́. Iron.
Mĕṛhĕt́ idena. The iron is rusty.
Ispat mĕṛhĕt́. Steel.
Dul mĕṛhĕt́. Cast iron.
Mĕṛhĕt́ khanḍa. Iron implements.

Merleć. A small forest tree bearing an edible fruit, *Flacourtia Ramontchi, L' Herit.*

Mermer. Suddenly, without warning.
Mermertege dak̕ heḍena. The rain came suddenly,.
Mermertegeye eṛeketlea. He died suddenly.

Merom. A goat.
Merom boda. A he-goat.
Merom ehga. A she-goat.
Merom khaṣi. A castrated goat.
Paeda merom. Large flap-eared goat.
Paṭhi merom. A she-goat before it has a kid.
Boda merom. A he-goat.
Ram khaṣi merom. A hermaphrodite goat.
Merom jel. Goat's flesh.
Merom hopon. A kid.

Merom ghao. Sore at angle of mouth.

Merom jel. The hind of the Ravine-deer, *Gazella Bennettii.*

Merom met́. The goat's eye, the name given to two plants, one a small tree, *Ixora parviflora, Vahl.*, and the other a scandent bush, *Olax nana, Wall.*

Meṛsa. To kick backwards, or sideways, to move from side to side, as a snake its tail.

Meṛsa meṛsi. To move from side to side, as an elephant its trunk, a snake its tail, &c.
Haṭhi do sunḍte meṛsa meṛsiae.

Mersitur. } Unimportant, trivial, paltry.
Mersiturak̕.
Mersitur katha kana. It is a trivial matter.

Mesa. Of solitary habits, unsociable, quiet and reserved.
Mesageae. He is quiet and reserved.

Mesal. To mix, to adulterate.
Pal alope mesalkoa. Do not mix the herd (of cattle.)
Rupạ rañteko mesalakaṭa. They have mixed the silver with pewter.
Asol rupạ do bañ kana, mesalak̕kangea. It is not pure silver it is an alloy.
Mesal mesal ạgnime. Bring them mixed.
Bar jạt hoṛoko mesalakaṭa. They have mixed two kinds of dhan.
Mesalgea. It is a mixture.

Mesa misi. To mix, to mingle, to confuse.
Hoṛoko mesa misikeda. They mixed the dhan together.
Mesa misi mit́teko ṭtiñkana. They are mingled and grazing together (cattle belonging to two villages.)

Mesao. To mix.

Meset́ meset́. Slowly.
Meset́ mesete jomeda. He eats slowly.
Cetlekam jomeda meset́ meset́? How are you eating so slowly?

Meskoć. } To smile, applied also to a bunch of matkom (q. v.) flowers buds when fully formed.
Meskok̕.
Cerejekhan meskoć godae. If you chirrup to him (a baby) he will smile inmediately.
Matkom meskoćakana. The bunches of flower buds of the matkom tree are fully formed.

Met́. The eye.
Met́ kuṭi. The eye brows.
Met́ gaḍa. The eye cavity.
Met́ pipni. The eye lashes.
Met́ dak̕. Tears.
Met́ jolok̕ kantaea. He is envious.
Mete jomkeda. He was overcome with lust.
Met́ dak̕e jorokeda. He shed tears.
Met́ jhạpni. The eye lids.
Met́ ṣạrim. The eyelids.

Met́. } Inflammation of the eye and appendages.
Mendok̕.
Mendok̕kanae. } He is suffering from inflammation of the eye.
Metakanae.
Medok̕kanae.

Meťăhă. The face, countenance.
Metăhă ñelkate bae bioạreda. He is not a respecter of persons.

Metak̕me. That is to say.
Oṛag lạgit́ sanamak̕ko juṛạukeda, metak̕me, sener, pạṛ, khunṭi, mat́, baber, emantea̕k̕. They had all in readiness to build a house, that is to say, rafters, beams, posts, bamboos, twine, &c. &c.

Meṭao. To blot out, to wipe out, to settle.
Mohor meṭao. To blot or wipe out entirely.
Mohor meṭaokedale. We settled it finally.
Riniñ meṭaokeda. I wiped out my debt.
Meṭaok̕a nahak̕. It will be blotted out presently.

Meṭmaṭ. To settle, to decide. Cf. meṭao.

Meṭoć. To rob, to plunder.
Kombṛoko meṭoćkedea. Thieves plundered him.

Meṭreć. }
Meṭreć meṭreć. } To grind the teeth.
Meṭreć meṭreće togoćeda. He is grinding his teeth.
Meṭreć meṭrejoḱkanae. He is grinding his teeth.

Meṭreć jel. The buck of the Ravine deer, *Gazella Bennettii.*

Meya. }
Menea. } Used when addressing males.

Meyoṅ. }
Meyoṅ meyoṅ. } To mew, as a cat.
Pusiko meyoṅ meyoṅa. Cats mew.

Miạd. }
Mead. } Term, period.
Miṭ bochor miạdenae. He has got a term of one year (imprisoned for one year.)
Miạd purạuena. The term has expired.

Miạdi. }
Meadi. } Terminable.

Michạ. False, in vain, fruitlessly.
Michạgem heċena. You have come in vain.
Nui do michạ hoṛ kanae. He is a false person.
Michạ do alom roṛa. Do not speak falsely.

Michạ michi. In vain, trifling, without sufficient cause.
Michạ michigeko kaphạriạuḱkana. They are quarrelling over something trifling.
Michạ michigeṅ heċakana. I have come in vain.

Midoḱ. Cf. miṭ.

Mihĩ. }
Mihin. } Fine, thin.
Mihĩ sutạm. Fine thread.
Mihĩ gitil. Fine sand.
Mihĩ kicriċ. Fine, thin cloth.
Mihĩ mihĩ. Very fine, very thin.

Mihindi dare. A small bush, *Lawsonia alba, Lam.* Cf. mehndi dare.

Mihnot. Cf. mehnot.

Mihũ. A calf.
Bacha mihũ. A bull calf.
Bạchi mihũ. A female calf.
Mihũ merom. Cattle in general.
Mihũ jel. Veal.

Mil. Affection, regard, fondness, harmony, agreement, absence of friction, friendship.
Nukin do milgeakin. These two have a fondness for each other.
Nukin do ạdi mille bujhạueḱkina. We consider these two as having a great affection for each other.
Noko do ohoko millena. These will never agree.

Mil. A mile, cor. of the English word.

Milạn. }
Milon. } To unite, to join, to mix, to fit closely, as a joint in woodwork, to get, to receive.
Khubko milạnakaṭa. They have fitted it closely.
Begargea, baṅ milạnoḱa. They differ and will not unite or mix (as oil and water.)

Milạṗ. }
Milạp. } Concord, harmony, agreement, reconciliation.
Khub milạṗteko tahenkana. They live in great harmony.
Mel milapte menaḱkoa. They live in concord.

Milạṭ. }
Miloṭ. } To make a good joint, as in two pieces of wood, to piece together, to fit together.
Khub milạṭakadako. They have fitted them very closely together.

Milạu. To mix, to unite, to reconcile, to cause concord, to get, to receive.
Sipi milạume. Mix it by kneading.
Unkin doko milạukaṭkina. They reconciled them to each other.
Sunum ar daḱ oho milạulena. Oil and water will not mix.
Milạuaea. He will receive.

Mili guṭi. To arrange, to consult, to scheme.
Bes miliguṭie hạṭiṅa. He will divide equally.
Oeṭ ooṅ ondeko mili guṭieṭkan? What is it they are consulting about over there?

Milijili. }
Miljul. }
Miljol. } Agreement, concord, union, mixture; to reconcile, to bring about harmony or concord.
Milijulikaṭkoale. We reconciled them to each other.
Miljulte tahenpe. Live in harmony.

Mili misi. }
Mili misiạ. } Concord, harmony, agreement, to consult, to scheme.
Mili misiteko jomkeda. They lived in harmony.
Mili misiạ johkanako. They are consulting, or laying a scheme.
Mili misiteko tahenkana. They live in harmony.

Mil jol. }
Miljul. } Cf. mili jili.

Milmiliạ. Measles, chicken pox, any eruption or rash over the whole body.
Milmiliạ rakạpakawadea. Measles have broken out on him.

Milon. Cf. milạn.

Miloṭ. Cf. milạṭ.

Miluạ. }
Milwa. } Mixed, desire, affection, regard, fondness.
Ạdi miluạ menaḱkina. They have great affection for each other.

Miluk̃.
Miluk̃ miluk̃. } Cf. miluk̃ jiluk̃.

Miluk̃ jiluk̃. } Miserable, woebegone,
Jiluk̃ miluk̃. } wretched looking, poor and wasted.

Rehgeöte miluk̃ jiluk̃enako. They are woebegone through hunger.

Milwạ. Cf. miluạ.

Milwạ milwi. To form an illicit union.

Milwạ milwikin baplaena.

Mimańsa. } To settle, to set a question
Mimańso. } at rest.

Noa katha reak̃ do oho mimańsa daṛelena. This matter will not be settled.

Minạ. } To deduct, to substract, to
Minhạ. } remit, as revenue or rent, to credit.

Ninạk̃ doe minạadińa. He deducted so much from what I had to pay.

Inạk̃ minạm ńama. You will be credited with so much, a deduction of so much will be made to you.

Mindok̃. } Cf. mit̃.
Mit̃. }

Minhạ. Cf. minạ.

Mirgi. Epilepsy, the falling sickness.

Mirgi rog henak̃taea. He suffers from epilepsy.

Mirgik̃kanae. An epileptic fit is coming on him.

Mirgi jel. A species of deer.

The skin of this deer dried and reduced to powder is snuffed up the nostrils as a cure for epilepsy (mirgi, q. v.)

Miṛhi. F. } Twisted, crumpled, as a
Meṛha. M. } horn.

Miridos. Innocent, blameless, immaculate, guiltless, faultless.

Alom dosale, ale dole miridosgea. Do not blame us, we are blameless.

Mirju baha. } The tree and flower of
Mirńju baha. } the Indian Laburnum, *Cassia Fistula, Linn.* Cf. Ńuruc̃.

Miṛik hako. A fish so called.

Mirluń. Sad, dejected, pitiable, miserable looking.

Rehgeöte mirluńakanae. He is miserable looking through starvation.

Mirluńe duṛupakana. He is sitting dejected.

Mirńju bahạ. Cf. mirju baha.

Mirtikạ. Death, the world.

Mirtikạ tiok̃entaea, bae ṭikạk̃a. The time of his death has come, he will not pull through.

Miru. A parrakeet, or paroquet.

Bhonḍa miru. A large paroquet.
Bheladạgiạ miru. A species of paroquet.
Ḍoḍhạriạ miru. ***Palæornis Alexandri.***
Kuinḍi miru. ***Palæornis rosa.***
Doė miru. ***Palæornis torquatus.***
Miru kantińam. You are my parrakeet (dear one.)

Mirũ. Rimless, not having a rim.

Miṛũ bạṭi. A large cup without a rim.

Adom bạṭi do kańkhạgea, ar adom do miṛũgea. Some ***batis*** **(q. v.) have a rim and others are rimless.**

Miru baha. A wild plant which yields a good fibre, *Abutilon indicum, Don.*

Miruk̃ miruk̃. Wistfully, longingly, hungrily.

Miruk̃ miruk̃le ńel johkana. We are looking on wistfully.

Mis. To consult together, to plot, to scheme, to conspire.

Galmarao miskedako. They consulted together.
Noako misakat̃a. They have plotted this.
Misakawanako. They have hatched a plot.
Mimiskanako. They are plotting, or consulting.

Misera. A sister.

Miserako. Sisters.
Miserań. My sister.
Miserańko. My sisters.
Miseram. Thy sister.
Miserat. His sister.

Misi. A powder with which the teeth are tinged a black colour.

Ḍaṭako misia. They apply ***misi*** **to the teeth.** ***Misi*** **is prepared by mixing sulphate of copper, iron filings and myrabolams. It is said to keep the teeth firm in the gums.**

Misi. Hair on the upper lip.

Misi juạn. A youth or maiden.

Misil. The papers or records of a case, to act as a magistrate or judge, a court of justice.

Misil lagaoena. The court is sitting.
Misil sapakat̃ae. He has taken up the case, or has begun court.
Hakopako misile lagaoket̃talea. He took up our case without delay.

Misit̃.
Misit̃ misit̃. } Gently. Cf. hisit̃ hisit̃.

Misit̃ misit̃e hoeëda. It blows gently.

Misri. Sugar-candy.

Cini. Refined sugar.

Misri bạṭ. } To divide, a method of
Misri baṭa. } dividing village lands so that no person gets two contiguous fields, or too much of one quality of land. Cf. khiċṛi bạṭ.

Misriċ. } To be mixed, as two herds of
Misrit̃. } cattle, &c.

Misrijok̃ape. You will get mixed (as in a crowd.)
Misriạ adok̃ape, You will get mixed (with the crowd) and get lost.

Mistri. A tradesman, a mechanic.
Kaṭ mistri. } A carpenter.
Baṛhi mistri. }
Raj mistri. A mason, a bricklayer, a maker of clay images.
Kamar mistri. } A blacksmith.
Lohar mistri. }
Dhubi mistri. A washerman.

Miť. A (the indef. article), one, single, to unite, to join, to mix,
Miťkateko calaoena. } They went away together.
Miťteko calaoena. }
Mimiť mimiťteko boloena. They entered singly one after the other.
Miťke miťko calaoena. They have all gone.
Miť miťteko calaoena. All have gone.
Mimiť poesakate emakom. Give each one pice.
Miť daṛtegeye tioǩkeťkoa. He overtook them in one race, without once stopping to draw breath.
Miť maǩtege topaǩena. It broke through with one blow.
Miť dhao. Once.
Miť tur. } Of equal age.
Miť turiạ. }
Miť barabạri. Equal.
Miť sāo. Level, plane.
Miť machageako. They resemble each other.
Miť lekako juriǩa. They resemble each other in one aspect.
Miť lekageako. They are equal, they resemble each other.
Miť lekakom. Make them equal.
Miť bar hoṛaǩ mocareń añjomkeda. I heard it at the mouth of one or two people.
Miťgeako. They are equal, they resemble each other.
Miť sentege menaea. He has not returned once since he went.
Miť gidrạ khon. From childhood.
Miť laė boeha. Own brothers or sisters, children of the same parents.
Dul miť. The confluence of two rivers.
Dul midoǩ. To conflux, as two rivers; to flow into, as a river into the sea.
Nạị ar Baṛakar dul miť ṭhen. The place where the rivers Damudar and Barakar conflux.
Jalapurire dul miťakana. It flows into the sea.
Katha do bań miťlentakoa. Their statements did not agree.
Miť muṭhạngeako. They resemble each other.
Enga honkin miť muṭhạngea. The mother and child resemble each other.
Miť talao. Without intermission.
Miť talaogeye daǩeťkana. It rains without intermission.
Miť lagaogeye dạǩeda. It rains unceasingly.
Miť rogoṛ. Without intermission.
Miť rogoṛgeye kokoekana. He begs without intermission.
Miť monte. With one mind, with all one's mind.
Miť murukte. Perseveringly, with heart and soul.
Miť mohndate. Straight, in one direction.
Miť ṭuń botor hō bae botorlena. He was not in the least afraid.
Miť jomkao. } All together, in a body.
Miť jomok. }
Miť jomkaotegeko calaoena. } They left in a body.
Miť jomoktegeko calaoena. }
Miť ṭen. }
Miť ṭeė. }
Miť ṭań. } One individual or article.
Miť goṭeė. }
Miť gcṭań. }
Unkin miť ṭhenre menaǩkina. They are in the same place.
Miť senko calaoena. They have gone in the same direction.
Miť seėenako. They have taken the same side.
Ale do miťrege menaǩlea. We are united, a united family.
Miťregele kạmikana. We are working in partnership.
Bań midoǩkana. } They are not uniting or mixing; they do not agree, harmonise, correspond, tally, a similate.
Bań mindoǩkana. }
Miť goǩtegeye ańgakeda. He beat the drum all night, never had it once off his neck.
Miť lapeť mạṇḍiń ńamlekhange. If I get a mouthful (or handful) of cooked rice.
Gel miť. } Eleven.
Gel khon miť. }
Miť ṭań ba miť ṭań. One or another.
Miť hō bae lajaoǩa. He is never in the least ashamed.

Miť. } Each, singly.
Mimiť. }
Mimiť hoṛ. Each person.
Mimiť mimiťteko boloena. They entered singly.
Mimiť mimiťte roṛpe. Speak singly (not all at once.)
Mimiť poesakate emakom. Give each of them one pice.

Miť sae. One hundred.

Miť isi. Twenty, a score.
Miť isi miť. Twenty-one.
Miť isi barea. Twenty-two.
Miť isi pea. Twenty-three.
Miť isi ponea. Twenty-four.
Miť isi mōṛē. Twenty-five.
Miť isi turui. Twenty-six.
Miť isi eae. Twenty-seven.
Miť isi irạl. Twenty-eight.
Miť isi are. Twenty-nine.
Miť isi gel. Thirty.
Miť isi gelmiť. Thirty-one.
Miť isi gelbarea. Thirty-two.

Miť kaṛ goć. Hemiplegia.

Mitạr. } Cf. hit mitạr.
Mitor. }

Miṭhạ. } Sweet.
Miṭho. }
Miṭhạge aṭkaroǩkana. It tastes sweet.

Miṭhai. Sweetmeats.

Mithi. A kind of spice.
Mithi mithi so kana. It smells like the *mithi* spice.

Mitor. Cf. hit mitạr.

Miyuń miyuń. The mew of the cat, to mew, as a cat.

Mo. To swell, swollen.
Bebaṛiće moakana. He is very much swollen.
Dal mokedeae. He struck him and raised a swelling.
Moǩae. He will swell, or it will swell (hand, &c.)

Moao. To damp, to moisten.
Moaokateko joma. They moisten it and eat it.
Bąṅgąura moaokateko era. They damp the cotton seed and then sow it.

Mõc. A cultivated pulse, *Phaseolus aconitifolius, Jacq.*

Moca. The mouth.

Mocmoc. } To pout, to push out the lips
Mocmoco. } when sullen or displeased.
Mocae mocmocoakana. She is pouting her lips.

Moćmoć. Sad, dejected, distressed looking.
Uni do moćmoćgeye ńeloẞkana. He looks dejected.

Mocolka. } Personal recognizance, a bond,
Mucilka. } an agreement.
Gel ṭaka mocolkakateko aṛaẞkadea. They took his personal recognizance in ten rupees and liberated him.

Mocoń. Snout, mouth of an animal.

Mocṛa mucṛi. To writhe, to contort, twisting from side to side, to gripe; luxuriant, as a crop.
Nui ḍaṅra ądiye mocṛa mucṛi baṛaekana. This bullock is twisting from side to side (to free himself from the yoke.)
Nui hoṛ laḋ hasoedete ądi mocṛa mucṛi baṛaekanae. This man is writhing owing to colic.
Laḋ mocṛa mucṛi hasoedekana. He is suffering from griping (or pain in the intestines.)
Mocṛa mucṛi hor. A winding path.
Ąk khub mocṛa mucṛi hoeakanaa. The sugar cane has grown luxuriantly.

Mocṛao. To twist, to contort, to writhe, to gripe.
Mocṛaokateye peṭerkeda. He twisted it and broke it off.
Laḋ mocṛaoẞkantińa. I have a griping in the stomach.

Mocṛao. To eat.
Okatepe calaẞkana? Taben mocṛaole calaẞkana. Where are you going? We are going to eat parched rice. i. e. we are going to a betrothal (jawãe horoẞ q. v.)
Khube mocṛaokeda. He ate well.
Taben khube mocṛaoakaća, onate laḋ hasoedekana. He has eaten a large quantity of parched rice, for that reason he has stomach ache.

Mod. } Amidst, from amongst. Cf.
Modre. } motore, mudre.
Noko modre okaṭaẞem hataoea. From amongst these which one will you take?
Ape mudre miť hoṛe hataoakaća. One of you has taken it.

Mod. Distilled liquor mainly that distilled from the flower of the matkom tree (q. v.)

Modam. } Continually, always, every
Mondam. } day.
Modamgeye hijuẞkana. He comes every day.

Mõde. To become mildewed, or mouldy. Cf. monde.

Modet. To assist; assistant, ally, one appointed to assist another and look after his interests.
Ohoń senlena, nią kathareń modetakanań. I cannot go, I am helping in this matter.
Modete dohoakadińa. He has appointed me to assist and promote his interest.

Modhe. } From amongst. Cf. mod.
Modhere. }
Nią modhere uni hõ emaeme. Give him also out of this.

Modhom. Middle, intermediate, the middle.
Tin marańae bąhu do? Bes modhom. How big is the bride? Of nice middle size.

Modhu. Sluggish, slow, fusionless, guileless, artless, simple.
Ądi modhu hoṛ kanae. He is a sluggish man.

Modhubon. } A honey forest, a desirable
Modhuban. } place.
Salbonić modhubonkeda. I converted a sal (q. v.) forest into a desirable place of residence.

Modod. } To help, to assist; help, assis-
Modot. } tance.
Mododalepe. Help us.

Modor muli baha. } A flower in high
Mondor muli baha. } repute among Santal females, *Ocimum Basilicum, Linn*, var. *thyrsiflorum.* Cf. mąli baha.

Moela. Cf. mąilą.

Moera. A Hindu caste, large numbers of whom are traders or pedlers.

Mogoe mogoe. } Soft.
Moṅgoe moṅgoe. }
Ąlu mogoe mogoe sebela. Potatoes have a nice soft taste.

Mogoj. The brain.
Mogoj bąṛićentaea. His brain is injured, (he is angry, or insane.)

Mogol. A Mogul, a Cabulee.

Mogon. To be astonished, to be amazed, to be merry or careless, as one intoxicated. Cf. moṅgon.

Mogra. } A drain pipe, the ridge tiles
Moṅgra. } of a roof.

Mogra thamakhur. } A variety of the
Mongra thamakhur. } tobacco plant.

Moh. Pity, compassion.

Mohge ṣikṣuedae emoḱ do. } Giving distresses
Mohge aṭkaredae emoḱ do. } him, i. e. he is niggardly.

Ạli emoḱae moh bae dohoea. He gives freely, it does not distress him (to give.)

Ạdi mohgeń bujhṣueda. I feel much reluctance (to give.)

Mohan mala. A variety of the rice plant.

Mohan bạsi. A variety of the Plantain.

Mohẽ. To bud, as a flower.

Ul mohẽḱkana. The mangbe (tree) is in bud.

Mohipal. A variety of the rice plant.

Mohjut. } To prepare, to collect ne-
Mohńjam. } cessaries, to get in readiness.

Oṛaḱ lạgiḱ kaṭiń mohjutakaḱa. I have in readiness the timber required for a house.

Mohlao. To direct one's course, to steer. Scottice, to *airt.*

Okatem mohlaoakana? Where are you directing your course to?

Mohlaoge bae mohlaoḱkana.

Mohlon. } Medicine for external appli-
Mahlon. } cation mainly by rubbing, to apply medicine externally.

Mohlonkedeako. They rubbed ointment on him.

Mohnḍa. Direction, in front, like, resemblance, to direct one's course, to die. Scottice, to *airt.*

Abo mohnḍategeye hijuḱkana. He is coming towards us (in our direction.)

Okatem mohnḍaena? Where are you directing your course to? Where are you going?

Tebeńe mohnḍaena. He died to-day.

Miḱ mohnḍae jomkeda. He only ate once.

Miḱ mohnḍateye calaoena. He went straight ahead.

Moṛa mohnḍa lekage. As if dead.

Nui do Kolhe mohnḍageye ńeloḱa. This (person) resembles, or has the appearance, of a Kol.

Miḱ mohnḍa calaḱme. Go straight forward.

Mohnḍa marao. To close an aperture, as the mouth of a jar, &c. to put the finishing touches to.

Guṛ handha mohnḍa maraokam. Seal the mouth of the vessel in which the raw sugar is with clay.

Mohńjam. To have or be in readiness, to exist, to be present.

Sanam mohńjamena. All is prepared.

Goṛoako lạgiḱ mohńjam godoḱa. He will at once be in readiness to help them.

Sińre aṭare sen mohńjamenae. During the day he went and took his place in the ambush.

Mohńjor. Difficult.

Ạdi mohńjorteń tijakaḱa. I have with great difficulty acquired property.

Ạdi mohńjorgea. It is very difficult.

Mõhõk. Odour, sweet smell, pleasant odour.

Mõhõk mahkaoḱkana. There is a pleasant odour.

Mohokop. Cf. mạhkup.

Mohol. A large house.

Bhitri moholteye calaoena. He went into the house.

Raj mohol. A king's house, a zemindar's residence.

Mohoni. Cf. muhni.

Mohor. A seal, to seal.

Dolele mohorada. } He sealed, or put
Dolelre mohore lagaokeda. } his seal to the document.

Mohor. A large earthenware vessel.

Mohor. A gold coin, a gold mohr.

Mohor marao. } To obliterate, to settle,
Mohor meṭao. } to finish.

Noa kathale mohor meṭaokeda. We settled this matter.

Uniaḱ ńutumge mohor meṭaoena. His very name is obliterated.

Uni hoṛe mohor meṭaoena. That man is dead.

Mohrao. To refuse. Cf. mahrạu.

Emamkanań, adom mohraoḱkana. I am giving it to you and you are refusing it.

Moiḍoń. Having no hair on the upper lip, without a rim, as a vessel.

Mojlis. } Conference, assembly.
Mońjlis. }

Mojlisle duṛuṗakana. We are sitting in conference.

Mojra. Deduction, allowance, set off.

Noa reaḱ mojra ṣuriń ńama. I have not had this deduction made (in my account.)

Mojur. } A daily labourer, a workman
Mạjur. } paid by the day.

Mojuri. } Daily wages, wages.
Mạjuri. }

Din mạjuri. Daily wages, pay for the day's work.

Moka. The elbow, from the elbow to the tip of the middle finger, a cubit; to measure with the arm from the elbow to the tip of the middle finger.

Bar moka osar. Two cubits broad.

Ma mokaeme. Come, measure it (with the arm from the elbow to the tip of the middle finger.)

Kiorić mokaańme. Measure it for me.

Pe moka gan jeleń. About three cubits long.

Mokareń bajaoena. I have knocked my elbow.

Moka ghaṭi. The elbow joint, from which the cubit (moka) is measured.

Moka ḍaṭop. } **Moka raṭop.** } The exact measurement, neither more nor less.

Moka ḍaṭopgeye emadiña. He gave me the exact measurement (neither more nor less.)

Mokabilạ. To confront, bring face to face.

Mokabilạkeṭkinako. They brought the two face to face.

Mokam. Residence.

Mokmoko. To sulk.

Mokmoko baṛaekanae. } Mokmokoakanae. } She is sulking.

Mokmokor. To sulk, to be sullen, to scowl.

Mokodoma. } **Mokordoma.** } A suit, a law suit; to sue in a court of law.

Uni upạrreñ mokordomaakaṭa. I have brought a suit against him.

Mokodomareñ paṛaoakana. There is a suit, or case, against me.

Uni upạrre mokordomiañ calaoa. I will bring a suit against him.

Mokordoma mokordomategeñ lahgaena. I am reduced to poverty through continued law suits.

Mokoñ. To tire, to finish, to lose the relish for, to be done.

Duṛup mokoñenañ. I am tired sitting.

Boṛ mokoñenañ bae añjoma. I am tired speaking, he will not listen.

Jom mokoñenae. He has eaten sufficient.

Mokoñ geñ sikạueda. I feel as if I had had, or had done, enough.

Ạuri mokoñoṅae. He is not yet done, or he is not yet tired.

Mokordoma. Cf. mokodoma.

Mokoror. } **Mokorora.** } Perpetual.

Mokosto. } **Mukosto.** } By word of mouth, verbally, to commit to memory, to repeat from memory.

Mokostotegele epemakana. We gave to each other by word of mouth (nothing committed to paper.)

Mol. To price.

Ninạṅe molena. He is priced at so much.

Molam. Soft, yielding.

Molamge aṭkaroṅkana. It feels soft.

Molao. To give property or goods in payment of a debt.

Ḍañrañ molaoakaṭkina. I have given two bullocks in payment of a debt.

Molao. } **Malao.** } To polish, to burnish.

Kạpi khube molaoakaṭa. He has polished the battle axe well.

Molaṭ. To sharpen, to give an edge to, as a razor on a strop.

Holaṭ molaṭ ñogme. Sharpen the razor a little.

Molok. To appear for the first time.

Moloṅ cando. The new moon.

Bale moloṅ. Moon 2 or 3 days old.

Moloṅ tikin. The moon at the meridian at sunset.

Moloṅ candoko dinadiña. They fixed the next (or coming) month for me.

Pon dinte mologoṅae. It will appear in 4 days (the moon.)

Tisem moloṅena? When did you come?

Moloñ. The forehead, fortune, fate.

Bhage moloñanae. He is fortunate.

Molso. Greyish, of a greyish colour.

Momal. A clue, part or whole of stolen property. Cf. bomal.

Momal odokena. Part of the stolen property has been found.

Mombla. } **Momla.** } **Mamla.** } A law suit, any matter requiring discussion and settlement by a panchayat or any other assembly. Cf. mambla.

Momomoc. Worn out, feeble, as a very old or sick person.

Momomoce ñeloṅkana. He looks worn out.

Mõmõṛ. Cf. mõṛẽ.

Momoyoc. Sorrowful, sad, dejected looking.

Boṛ momoyockedeako. They saddened him by what they said to him.

Mon. Mind, spirit.

Mon khaṭoentiña. I am much hurt (as by an unkind remark, &c.)

Mon ṭuṭentiña. } Mon ṭuṭạuentiña. } My spirit is broken (I am disappointed or dispirited.)

Mon loṅkantaea. He is in great sorrow.

Miṭ monte. With heart and soul, with all one's mind.

Goṭa monte. With all one's heart, unreservedly.

Mon bạrieentaea. He is dispirited, or become crazed.

Mon col goṭentiña. } Mon coñcol goṭentiña. } I am disturbed in mind.

Mon dukakanae. He is sorrowing.

Mon. A weight and measure, liquid and dry, of 40 seers.

Monadi. To preach, to proclaim; proclamation, preaching. Cf. mạnạḍi.

Moncopuri. The passing world.

Monḍ. The tail of a serpent.

Jambṛo monḍ. The tail of the Rock snake.

Monda. To spoil, to go bad, to deteriorate, fall in price.

Caole mondaena. The rice has deteriorated.

Dor mondaena. The price has fallen (is against the seller.)

Ạgni mondaentaea. His digestion is impaired.

Mondam. Continually, always, every day.
Mondamgeye hijuřkana. He comes every day.

Monde. } To become mildewed, or
Mõnde. } mouldy.
Monde piṭhạ. Mouldy bread.
Kicrič mondeřa. The cloth will become mildewed.

Mondhaeni. The stirrer or stick moved in a churn.
Ghor arud mondhaeni. The stirrer for the purpose of churning milk, a churn stick.

Mondil. } A temple.
Mondir. }

Monḍoř monḍoř. To be perplexed, to smoulder.
Jiwi monḍoř monḍogořkantiňa. I am perplexed.
Monḍoř monḍoř loř. To smoulder.

Monḍol. The Headman of a village, a name of the Hindu caste Sunḍi.

Moňḍoň. } Having no hair on the upper
Moiḍoň. } lip, without a rim, as a vessel.
Moňḍoň hoṛ. A man with no hair on the upper lip.
Moňḍoň bạṭi. A brass cup without a rim.
Hoyo moňḍoňenam. You have shaved your upper lip.

Mone. Mind, spirit, to wish, to purpose, to think.
Mone joň. To wish for oneself.
Mone monete. Mentally.
Monere hečadiňa. I remembered, it suggested itself to me.
Monere khaṭikedaň. I made up my mind.
Onageň moneakaťa. I am pleased with that, I have set my heart on that, or I have thought that.
Calař reař mone tahěkantiňa. } I had a wish to
Calař mone tahěkantiňa. } go.
Moneanae. He wished.
Mone khentoentaea. He is relieved in mind.

Mone. } Five.
Mõṛẽ. }
Mone isi. Five score.
Mone sae. Five hundred.

Moneko turuiko. Cf. mõṛẽko turuiko.

Moňgoe moňgoe. Soft, soft to the mouth.
Ạlu moňgoe moňgoe sebela.

Moňgol. } Tuesday.
Moňgor. }

Moňgol. } News, welfare.
Kusạl moňgol, }
Mase lạitape, kusạl moňgol oeťleka. Come, tell us of your welfare.

Moňgon. To be astonished, to be amazed, to be merry or careless, as one intoxicated.
Moňgonenaň. I am amazed.
Bulkate moňgonakanae. He is drunk and merry.

Moňgor. Tuesday. Cf. moňgol.
Moňgor hiloř. Tuesday.
Moňgor ạyuṕ. Tuesday evening.

Moňgra. A drain pipe, the ridge tiles of a roof. Cf. mogra.

Moňj. Beautiful, pretty, beguiling, to ridicule.
Ạdi moňj baha. A very beautiful flower.
Baha do ạdi moňja. The flower is very beautiful.
Eṛe moňj. To deceive.
Kạmi moňj. To cause to work and withhold payment.
Ạcu moňj. To employ one in a trifling manner.
Roṛ moňj. To cause to speak of trifling matters.
Kuṛiko jawãe ạdiko moňjea. The maidens make fun of the bridegroom.

Moňjlis. Cf. majlis.

Monjolo. Worn out, as by sickness or age.
Monjologeye ňelořkana. He looks worn out.

Monjur. Cf. manjur.

Monsa. The Hindu Serpent-goddess.
Monsa porob. A festival in honour of the Hindu Serpent-goddess.

Monsuba. To contrive, to wish, to purpose.
Calař reařle monsubaakaťa. We have decided to go.

Munucạť. } The end.
Munuceť. }
Buru munucạť. The end of the hill.
Bir munuceť. The edge or termination of the jungle.

Mophosol. } Secret, private.
Moposol. }
Mophosolkedako. They kept it secret.
Mophosol katha kana. It is a private matter.

Mophot. } Gratis, free, without payment.
Muphut. }
Mophot reaň do baň kana. It is not gratis.

Moposol. Cf. mophosol.

Mopot. Cf. mophot.

Mor. An interjection of surprize, dear me!
Mor! cedař bako heělena? Dear me! Why have they not come?

Mora. Dead, weak and lean.
Uni ḍãhra moragea. This bullock is weak and lean.

Mõṛã. } A number of shoots to spring
Moṛa. } from one root, to become a tuft, as grass, grain. &c.

Moraba. The American aloe, *Agave americana, Linn.*

Mora muri. Weak and lean, half-dead, in a dying state.

Mora jora. Weak and lean.

Mora muhã. } The South, the direction
Mora muhãṛ. } of the Damuda river into which the Santals throw a bone of the dead.

Moramot. } To repair, to mend.
Maramat. }
Oṛak̓e moramoteda. He is repairing the house.

Moṛasi. } Hereditary.
Mauṛasi. }
Moṛasi paṭṭa. A hereditary lease.

Mordha. A depreciatory term, lean, feeble.
Nui mordha mara herel. This feeble rascal.

Mõṛẽ. Five.
Gel mõṛẽ. Fifteen.
Mõṛẽ gel. Fifty.
Mõṛẽ hoṛ. A council, a conference, a panchayat, a party whose duty it is to consider and decide any matter, arbitrators.
Mõmõṛkate. Five each, in fives.
Mõmõṛ ṭakakate emakom. Give them five rupees each.
Mõmõṛ gelkate. Fifty each, in fifties.

Mõṛẽko. } Certain Santal god-
Mõṛẽko turuiko. } lets so named.

Morgoć. A depreciatory term.

Moṛhao. Cf. meṛhao.

Morhak̓. An exclamation of surprize, dear me !
Morhak̓ ! bako hijuk̓kana. Dear me, they do not come.

Morjad. } To shew respect to, to honour,
Morjat. } mainly by entertaining to food.

Morjadi. } Cf. morjad.
Morjati. }

Morjha. Weak, feeble. Cf. marca.

Morji. } Wish, pleasure; to entertain,
Murji. } as a guest, to shew hospitality.
Bhage murjiadiñae, sime goćadiña. He received me well (or he entertained me well), he killed a fowl for me.
Amak̓ morjite jagem emok̓. Whatever it may be your pleasure to give.

Mormor. Quietly and meekly.
Mormore duṛuṕakana. He is sitting quietly and meekly.

Mormorao. } To detain, to keep in cus-
Moṛmoṛao. } tody.
Mormoraoket̓leako bańko em hoćat̓lea. They detained us, they did not give us at once.
Thanareko mormoraoket̓koa. They kept them in custody at the thana.

Morna. Death.
Harna morna jokheć. Time of death.
Harna morna reak̓ nuigeye ńama.

Mornaha. Weak and lean, feeble.
Nui mornaha cet̓e kạmia? What work will this weakling do.

Moroć. } Acid, acidulated.
Jojo moroć. }

Moroć. To dry before being ripe, as a fruit.
Bele morośena ul do.

Morol morol. Fixed stare, eyes rivetted on, intently.
Morol morole ńeńelkana. He is looking with a fixed stare, he is gazing intently.

Morom. Hidden meaning or purpose, method.
Noa reań morom bań badaea. I do not know the hidden meaning of this.

Moron. Death.

Moron aṛak̓. A wild plant the leaves of which are eaten as a potherb, *Gymnema hirsutus, W. & A.*, var *Decaisneanum, Wight.*

Moron soman. Like death, like to die.
Moron somanań ruạena. I am sick unto death.
Nonkae roṛkediña, moron somanań ạikạukeda. He spoke thus to me, I felt like to die.

Morot. Weak, lean and feeble.

Morot. Stinking, fetid, noxious smell of decaying flesh.
Jahanak̓ko roekhan morotge soa. If flies attack anything (dead animal) it smells offensively.

Morot bhũi. The dying world.

Morot sorot. Deteriorated, not fresh, as meat, &c.
Morot sorot peṛa menaetalea. We have a poor relative.
Morot sorot tạmakhur menak̓talea. We have some inferior tobacco.

Morṛao. Cf. moṛmoṛao.

Mortoman. A variety of the Plantain.

Morubi. } An elder, head of family,
Murubi. } old man.

Jom mosao. } To take money, as the price of a bride, and give no presents in return.

Bandi koṛa dehgue kuṛipe baplakin khan eyae ṭaka jom mosaope. If you give a spinster in marriage to a widower take seven rupees (the price of the bride) and give no return presents.

Mosmoso. Silent, silent and dejected.

Mosmoso ñeloḱkanae. He looks dejected.

Oka do onko usaḱ hoṛko mosmosokoḱa. Some times sulky people refuse to speak.

Mosodi. The person through whom the raja or Zemindar communicates with his amla.

If any question arises the amla send the mosodi to the raja for orders.

Mosokot. Difficult, difficulty.

Aḍi mosokotkatele ñamkeda. We got it with very great difficulty.

Mosokusi. To compel, to force, against one's will, to persuade, to coax.

Mosokusikateko idikedea. They compelled him to go, they took him away against his will.

Mosola. Spice.

Mosoḱ. To finish, to cease, leave off, give up, change one's mind, to fade.

Noa katha mosoḱena. This matter is finished (settled.)

Baha mosodoḱa. The flower will fade.

Eneḱko mosoḱkeda. They left off dancing.

Calaḱe mosoḱkeda. He gave up the idea of going.

Moste. }
Mostete. } Freely, gratis, for nothing, difficulty.

Mosteteko emoḱkana. They are giving gratis.

Moste reaḱ do bah kana. It is not gratis.

Aḍi mosteteñ ñamkeda. I obtained it with great difficulty.

Mosto. Big, fat, thick, wealthy, well-to-do.

Aḍ moto bes mosto menaea. He has amply sufficient for his own wants.

Mostoram. Independent, without anxiety, careless of what may happen, lordly, dignified.

Ho, nui doe mostoramena, bae kamikana. He has become independent (or dignified), he is not doing his work.

Mot. }
Moṭra. } A bundle, to tie or make up into a bundle.

Moṭ. Total, to total.

Jomae moṭkeda. He totalled up the rent.

Mot. }
Mat. } Purpose, wish, intent, opinion, method, way, mode.

Sanam hoṛ miḱ moṭge menaḱkoa. All the people are of one mind.

Moṭa. Stout, fat, thick, clumsy, coarse, rich, wealthy; low, as a note in music, hoarse, gruff.

Moṭa hoṛ. A fat man, or a wealthy man.

Uni do aḍi moṭae roṛa. He speaks very gruffly.

Noa hanam aḍi moṭa saḍekana. This fiddle has a very low tone.

Nese moṭaen do. He is well off this year.

Asul moṭakedeae. He fattened him, or fed him till he became fat.

Moṭalen tahěkanae. He was fat once.

Nui do khube moṭaḱa. This one will fatten well.

Moṭa gundli araḱ. A wild pot-herb, Cyanotis axillaris, R. S.

Moṭa hemca araḱ. }
Moṭa jubhi araḱ. } A wild pot-herb, Limnophila conferta, Benth.

Moṭa gundli. A cultivated millet Panicum Helopus, Trin, usually found growing along with gundli, Panicum miliare.

Moṭa bir jhunka. A common wild plant, Crotalaria calycina, Shrank.

Moṭa bhiḍi janaṭeḱ. A commmon plant in the vicinity of villages, Urena sinuata, Linn.

Moṭa uṛiḱ alaṅ. A small plant used as a pot herb, Portulacca oleracea, Linn.

Motaen. }
Motean. } To be appointed to, to fix, to be in readiness.

Moṭa muṭi. Stout, full grown, wealthy, substantial.

Moṭa muṭi hoṛ kanako. They are adults.

Moṭa muṭi hoṛko haṭiñ joha. The substantial people divide it among themselves.

Motam oḱ. A species of edible mushroom.

Moṭeam. To appropriate, to take.

Nonḍe tahěkana, saname moṭeamkeda. It was here, he appropriated it all.

Aḱ eskargeye moṭeamkeda. He has appropriated it all to himself.

Motean. Appointed to, fixed, in readiness. Cf. motaen.

Moth. Force, forcibly.

Mothgeye idikedea He took him away forcibly.

Mothe. }
Mothere. } In all, total.

Mothere poesa inaḱgetiña. In all I have so much money, (or copper money.)

Mothe miḱ arāḱgetiña. In all I have one yoke of oxen.

Moṭh maria. Forcibly, by force.
Moṭh mariṭe jom ocokediñ. He forced me to eat.

Moti. } A pearl.
Muti. }

Moticur. A variety of the rice plant.

Moṭ jhoṭ. Bundles, packages.
Moṭ jhoṭko idi ocokeṭkoe. They caused them to carry bundles.

Moṭkuri. } Gravel, small gravelly stones.
Muṭkuri. }

Motlob. } Purpose, wish, intention, method, way, mode, health, reason, meaning.
Matlab. }
Noa kạmi reak motlobakaṭa. He has purposed to do this work.
Noa hatao reaṅ motlobakaṭa. He intends to take this, has purposed in his own mind.
Motlobre bañ jut iñ ṣikạneda. I feel indisposed.

Moto. Only, like.
Niạ moto baṛe kạmime. Do only this, or do like this.
Ini moto hohoepe. Call him only.
Jom moto emaepe. Give him only as much as he can eat.
Idi motoe hataokeda. He took only what he could carry away.
Moka motoge emaepe. Give him only one cubit (of cloth.)
Aḋ motogeye calaoena. He went away alone.
Iñ do iñ motoñ sen joña. I will go alone, or by myself.

Motoṅ. Like. Cf. moto.
Niạ motoṅ calakme. Go like this.

Moṭor. } The pea, *Pisum arvense, Linn.*, and *Pisum sativum, Linn.*
Maṭor. }

Motore. From amongst, a midst. Cf. mudre.
Noko merom motore okoeṭakem kusiaekana? Which of these goats are you pleased with, or from among these goats which one do you choose?
Ape motorege miṭ hoṛe hataokeda. One of you took it.

Moṭra. A bundle, to make into a bundle. Cf. moṭ.
Sanamak moṭrakateye idikeda. He made all into a bundle and took it away.

Moṭra jhoṭra. Bundles, packages.
Moṭra jhoṭra menaktiña. I have a bundle or two.

Mowạsi. Cattle, live stock.
Ạdiye mowạsiana. He has many cattle.

Mū. The nose.
Mū geṭ. To cut off the nose, to disgrace, to humiliate, to put to shame.

Muć. An ant.
Mué daka. Ants' eggs, which have the appearance of grains of husked rice.
Muć dakako ṣtkireda, dag coe oeṭ ooñ. The ants are removing ther eggs, it may possibly rain. (This procedure on the part of ants is regarded as a sign of rain.)

The following are several species of ants:—
Sunum muć. The oil ant.
Cuṭuñ muć. A small black ant found in the hollows of trees.
Ḍonḍa muć. The large black ant of Santalia.
Lobok muć. The flour ant.
Arak muć. The red ant.
Kolhe muć. The Kolhe ant, named after the Kolarian tribe of Kols or Kolhe (q. v.)
So muć. The stinking ant. This species is said to smell offensively.
Saheb muć. The English ant. This ant, it is said, was introduced into India along with the Burma rice which was imported during the famine of 1874-75.
Hende muć. A black ant.
Khonṭa muć. A large red ant.
Hao muć. The large red ant.
Muć chatta. An ants' nest fixed in a tree.

Muć aṛak. A small, wild plant used as a pot-herb, *Polygonum plebejum, Br.*

Mucalkạ. } Personal recognizance or bond. Cf. macalka.
Mucilkạ. }
Macalka. }

Mucạṭ. } To end, finish, cease; end, termination.
Muceṭ. }
Kulhi mucạṭre. At the end of the village street.
Mucạṭenae. He is dead.
Ạuri mucạdoka. It is not yet finished.
Kạmi mucạṭkedae. He finished the work.

Muci. A Hindu caste of leather workers and shoemakers.

Muci oṭ. A kind of edible mushroom.

Mucu. A kind of basket used to catch fish with.
The mucu is like a wicker basket wider at one end than the other, with both ends open. It is plunged with the wider end down into the water over the the fish, and the hand put in through the smaller opening and the fish secured.
Hakoe mucueṭkoe. He is catching fish with a mucu.

Mucur. } Crunching sound, as when eating anything crisp.
Mucur mucur. }
Mucur mucure jojomkana. He crunches as he eats.
Mucur maraokedae. He crunched it up.

Mud. } From amongst, amongst, amidst.
Mudre. }
Noko mudre nuigeye sorosa. This one is the best of them.
Onko mudre nui hoṛ ḍhere arjaoakaṭa. From amongst them this man had the best crops.

Mudali. Defendant, accused.

Mudguć. A depreciatory term, dirty.

Mudi / Mahri. } A shopkeeper, a Hindu caste.

Mudoe. Plaintiff, suitor, claimant, enemy.

Mũga. Cf. munga.

Mugdi. A variety of the rice plant.

Muhã. The quantity of iron produced at one time in a native smelting furnace.

Mũhã. / Rokot mũhã. } To be incensed and attack, to ravage, as a man eating tiger, &c., to run amok, blood thirsty.

Ona birte alope calaka, kule rokot mũhãskanae. Do not go to that forest, a tiger is ravaging there.

Hoṛ goć goćte rokot mũhãenae, okoe hõ bae dayawatkoa. From continued killing of men he has become blood thirsty, he had pity on no one.

Muhã muhĩ. Over against, in front of, face to face.

Muhãr. Direction, to head towards. Scottice, to *airt*. Cf. mohnda.

Note muhãrakanae. He comes in this direction. (He is *airting* here.)

Uni muhãra ñelokkana. He resembles him.

Muhceba. Cf. mahla.

Muhim. / Muhĩn. } Danger, difficulty, affliction, suffering, distress.

Gar muhim. Difficulty and distress.

Adi muhimreñ paraoena. I am in great affliction.

Muhni. A philter, to administer a philter, to hypnotise, to wheedle, lure, cajole, decoy.

Muhniko ñu o'okedea. They caused her to drink a philter.

Muhni idiketkoako. They cajoled them into going.

Muhri. A clerk, a vernacular clerk.

Muhri. The Anise seed, *Pimpinella Anisum, Linn.*

Muhujut. Cf. mohjud.

Muhur muhur. Pleasant. applied mainly to the smell of certain kinds of rice.

Muhur muhur sokana. It smells sweetly.

Muhũt. / Muhũt muhũt. } Mildewed, mouldy, to become mouldy or mildewed, to become sour, as milk, cooked rice. &c.

Muhũt muhũt sokana. It smells of mildew.

Muhũtgea. It is mouldy.

Muiguć. A depreciatory term, dirty. Cf. mudguć.

Muisil. / Musil. } A mode of extorting payment of a debt or compliance with any demand by making the person sit by himself until he agrees to the terms offered to him. Cf. dharna.

Mukau. / Mukeṛ. } To strike, to hit.

Khubko mukaukedea. They beat him soundly.

Mukha. The mouth.

Unisk mukha khoniń añjomkeda. I heard it from his mouth.

Mukha mukhi. Face to face, to confront.

Mukha mukhiliń ñapamlena. We met face to face.

Mukhar. The cross stick to which the fish trap torodań or torodhoć (q. v.) is attached.

Mukharat. / Mukharot. } By word of mouth. without the intervention of a second person.

Iń mukharot noań añjomkeda. I heard this by word of mouth.

Mañjhi mukh rotte noań añjomkeda. I heard this from the head man himself.

Mukharottele ñel aguakata. We have been and seen for ourselves.

Mukhi. A variety of saru (q. v.)

Mukhia. Chief, principal, elder, leader.

Noa atoren mukhia hoṛ kanae. He is the chief man of this village.

Mukhia mukhia hoṛko senlena. The leaders went.

Mukhu. Ignorant. simple, illiterate.

Mukhu hoṛ kanae, cet hõ bae badaea. He is an ignorant man, he knows nothing.

Mukosto. / Mukosta. } By word of mouth, verbally, to commit to memory, to repeat from memory. Cf. mokosto.

Mukup. / Mukuph. } To be deferred, postponed, delayed, relinquished. Cf. makup.

Mukur mukur. Munching or crunching sound, as when a raw carrot, &c. is being eaten.

Mukur mukure jomeda. He is munching.

Mul. Chief, principal, original fundamental, real.

Mul rehet. The principal root, the tap root.
Mul dar. The principal branch, the trunk above the bole.
Mul oṛak. The original house, round which others have been built.
Mul katha. The real fact, the fundamental fact.
Mul ńutum. } Real name as opposed to a sobri-
Mun ńutum. } quet, or a nickname.

Mul. Principal.

Mulke mul ruaṛkatińme. Return me the principal.
Mule sude. } Principal and interest.
Sude mule. }
Sudiń emama, multeć tahentama. I will pay you the interest, the prinipal will remain.

Mula araḱ. } The Radish, *Raphanus*
Murai araḱ. } *sativus, Linn.*

Mulahan. To destroy, to lay waste, to make havoc.

Mulaiya. To fix the price of a thing without weighing.

Ceṫlekam hataokeda? Mulaiyaṫ ń hataokeda. How did you take it? I took it without having it weighed.

Mulapha. } Profit, advantage.
Munapha. }

Mulaᴗha bań ńamlaḱa. I received no profit.
Munapha bań hoelena. There was no profit.

Mulau. Cf. mulao.

Mulehabad. To destroy, to ruin.

Mulehabad goᴗ cabaena. It all died (dban) the seed was not even returned.
Mulehabadena. It is destroyed root and branch.

Mulin. Sad, dejected, to become sad, or dejected.

Mulinenae. He is dejected.
Mulingeye ńeloḱkana. He looks sad.

Muluć. } To smile, smiling.
Muluć muluć. }

Muluć muluće lauda joákana. He is smiling.
Muluć mentoye landakeda. He smiled.

Mun. A mythical semi-divine being.

De bbala maharaj, am hō munge, ala hō munge, de bhala, manoti manwa ceṫ lekatebo sirjaukoa.

Mun. Cf. mul.

Mun ńutum. Real name, as opposed to a sobriquet or a nickname.

Munai. Centre, or core, as of a boil; to begin.

Ojo reaḱ munaiteć. The centre of the boil.
Kathae munaikeda, menkhan bae puraᴗlaḱa. He began the statement, but did not finish it,

Mund. Head.

Pon muṇḍ dańra. Four head of oxen.

Munda. A Kolarian tribe inhabiting the Chota Nagpur plateau.

Kol munda. } Divisions of the Munda tribe.
Laṛka munda. }

Munda. The Paharias of the Raj mahal hills.

Munda. Head, end.

Kulhi munda. The head or end of the street.

Munda. } To close an opening, hole &c.
Mundau. }

Daḱ joroḱkana, bhugaḱ mundau goḱkaḱpe. Rain is coming through (the roof), cover the hole, stop up the hole.
Duare mundaukeda. He closed to the door.

Mundam. A finger ring.

Bapla mundam. The marriage ring.

Munda mundi. } In equal proportions,
Mundha mundhi. } head for head.

Mundha mandhiye utińkeṫkoa. He exchanged them head for head (cattle.)

Mundghos. A species of small deer.

This species of deer is said to receive its name from its holding down its head when running.

Mundguć. } Polled, having no
Mundguć mundguć. } horns.

Mihń mundguć mundugóeako. The horns of the calves have not yet grown, the calves are hornless.
Nui dańra doe mundguógea. This ox is polled.

Mundha. }
Mundhaṫ. } Stump of tree, a log.
Mundheṫ. }

Nit hō mundheṫ lekae giticakana. Even now he is lying like a log.

Mundhaḱ. Stump of a tree, a log.

Mundha mundhi. Head for head, in equal proportions. Cf. munda mundi.

Mundhan. } The ridge pole of a roof, the
Mundhna. } ridge of a roof.

Mundhan khunṭi. A post or posts which support the ridge pole of a roof.
Mundhna maraope. Finish the thatching over the ridge of the roof, or thatch over the ridge.

Mundhaṫ. Stump of tree, a log. Cf. mundha.

Mundhaṫ citri. The Black partridge, *Francalinus vulgaris.*

Mundheṫ. Stump of tree, a log. Cf. mundha.

Mundhni. } Peak, highest point, as of
Muthni. } a hill, &c.

Mundil. }
Moṇḍil. } A temple.

Mundir. }
Mondir. } A temple.

Munḍla. M. } Having the hair on the
Munḍli. F. } head shaved or closely cropped, to crop the hair.

Munḍla ḍaṅra. A polled or hornless ox, a tiger.

Munḍli gai. A polled or hornless cow.

Munḍlakeťmeako? Did they shave your head?

Munḍliakadeako. They have shaved her head.

Munḍlą panąhi. Shoes without the peculiar turn up at the toes which is usual in India.

Munḍrą. A measure, the distance between the elbow joint and the knuckle of the middle finger with the fist closed.

Munḍrą. M. } Having the hair on the
Munḍri. F. } head shaved or closely cropped, to shave the head, crop the hair.

Munḍrikedeako. They shaved off her hair, or cropped it closely.

Hoyo munḍrikedeako. They shaved her head.

Munḍrą munḍrigeako. They (boys and girls or males and females) have shaved heads.

Munḍrą panąhi. Cf. munḍlą panąhi.

Munḍrą badha. A kind of wooden sandal. Cf. badha.

Munḍruć. } Polled, having no
Munḍruć munḍruć. } horns, as an ox. Cf. munḍguć.

Munḍu. A jungle, a copse.

Munḍu pakaṛ. Bush and brake.
Gaḍa munḍu. River and forest.
Munḍu bapla. A forest marriage, a runaway match.

Munḍu Baske. A sub-sept of the Santal sept Baske (q. v.)

Munḍu lać. A certain portion of the entrails of a fowl.

Munḍu Pąuria. } A sub-sept of the San-
Munḍu Pąulia. } tal sept Pąuria or Pąulia.

Muṅ. A cultivated leguminous plant, *Phaseolus Mungo*, var. *Max*, *Linn*.

Muṅ dąl. The split pea of *Phaseolus Mungo*.

Mungą. } The Horse-radish or Ben
Mungą dare. } nut tree, *Moringa pterygosperma*, *Gaertn*., the leaves, flowers and fruit of which are used as food.

Mungą arak̕. The fresh leaves of the Mungą or Horse-radish tree, *Moringa pterygosperma*, *Gaertn*., which are used as a pot-herb.

Mungą suti. The fruit of the Horse-radish tree, mungą (q. v.) used as an article of food.

Mungą mutąk. A thick club or stick of some light wood such as that of *Mungą* (q. v.)

Muṅgą. } The cocoons of univol-
Muṅgą lumąm. } tine individuals of the Tassar silk worm.

Muṅgą mala. A kind of necklace.

Muṅgąr. A mallet.

Muṅgią pathra. A kind of soapstone.

Muṅreť. A log tied to the neck of a cow, &c. given to straying from the herd.

Munib. Employer, master.

Munis. A male farm servant.

Jon munis. Farm servants.

Muńjil. A day's journey.

Tinąk̕ muńjil hoyok̕a? Khubem calak̕khan bar muńjil. How many days' journey is it? If you walk well, two days' journey.

Muńjrą. To count up, to total.

Ąurile muńjrąia. We have not yet totalled it.

Munsąli. Belonging to a munis (q. v.) or agricultural servant.

Munsąli binḍą. A sheaf or sheaves given to a munis (q. v.) daily during harvest.

Munsąli khet. Land given to a munis as part of his wages.

Munsąli ṭaka. A sum of money given on loan to a munis.

This money bears no interest, but the munis cannot cancel his agreement to work for his master until this money is repaid.

Muńjlis. Conference, assembly.

Munucąt. }
Munuceť. } Cf. mucąť.

Muphut. }
Mophot. } Gratis, free, for nothing.

Mur. Cf. mul.

Murạd. } Respect, honour, wish, inten-
Murat. } tion.

Iñak murạd bae doholeda. He did not respect my honour.
Be-murạdkediñae. He insulted me.

Muṛãhạn. To destroy, to ruin, to lay waste, to make havoc.

Sạul do kạlisiạ renkoe muṛã'ạnkeťkoa. Saul made havoc of the church.

Murạị. A grain store.

Murạị aṛak. Cf. mulạ aṛak.

Murcạ. } To corrode, to rust, to wear
Murchạ. } or be eaten away gradually.

Murchạena. It is rusty, or it has rusted.

Murchạu. To cut off evenly and neatly, to dress by paring, as the end of stick, beam, &c.

Murchạuakať lekako jomkeda. They cropped it as if it had been cut off neatly close to the ground.
Giri murchạu. To cut the end neatly.

Murchi hoṛo. A kind of black rice.

Murculu. } Huddled up, drawn to-
Murculuṅ. } gether.

Murculuṅ duṛupạkanae. He sits huddled up.

Murdạr. A corpse.

Murdạr sahan. The unconsumed firewood of a funeral pyre.

Murgạ. A cock.

Murgạ. } A small forest tree,
Murgạ dare. } *Pterocarpus marsupium, Roxb.*

Murgạn. } Drugs or medicines in
Ran murgạn. } general.

Morgoť. } Dirty and ill-condi-
Morgoť morgoť. } tioned, slovenly and lean.

Murguć. } Dirty and ill-condi-
Murguć murguć. } tioned, applied
Muiguć. } mainly to children.
Muiguć muiguć. }

Muṛhạť. Cf. mundhạť.

Murhuć jom. Leprosy.

Murhuć jom hoṛ. A person suffering from leprosy.
Murhuć jom rog. The disease of leprosy.

Murhuć. } To devour, to strip, as
Jom murhuć. } locusts, caterpillers, &c.

Pohoko jom murhućkedako. The locusts stripped the trees.

Murhuť. An image, an idol.

Mūṛī. A measure about a maund.

Mūṛī khaclak. A basket which holds a *muri.*

Mūṛī. } A measure of land of varying
Muri. } quantity.

Miť mūṛī ot. A mūṛī of land.

Muri khunṭi. A short post fixed in a beam which rests or the side walls on which the ridge pole rests.

Murjạt. Cf. marjat.

Murji. Pleasure, assent, will, taking favourably, agreeable, acceptable.

Amem murjilekhan. If it please you, or if you so please.
Amak murji leka. According to your pleasure.

Murli. A whistle with six or seven finger holes.

Murmu. } One of the twelve
Murmu Ṭhạkur. } septs into which the Santals are divided.

Mursiṅ bạrsiṅ. } A day or two, a short
Musiṅ bạrsiṅ. } time.

Mursiṅ bạrsiṅ thir hataṛokme. Wait quietly a day or two.
Musiṅ bạrsiṅ dole bes baṛagea. We are well for the last day or two.

Murubi. Aṅ elder, head of family, an old man. Cf. morubi.

Muruk. Physical or mental energy, force, vigour, strength, determination, perseverance, constancy, tenacity of purpose; to energize, to be resolved, steadfast.

Murukakae tahenme. Continue steadfast.
Ạḍi murukkateye calakkana. He is going with great determination.
Mone murukakae tahenpe. Continue stedfast in purpose.
Ti baṅ murukokkantiña. My hand will not energize, I have no power in my hand.
Baṅ lebeť muruk daṛeakkana. I cannot step with vigour, I cannot put down my foot with force.
Ać murukteye dalkedea. He hit him with all his might.

Murum jel. The Nil gae, or Blue cow, *Portax pictu.*

The flesh of this deer is taboo to the Murmu sept of Santals.

Murum ot. A species of edible mushroom.

This mushroom is taboo to the Murmu sept of Santals.

Murum. } A species of snake.
Hawal murum. }

Murup̣. } A small gregarious forest
Murup̣ dare. } tree, *Butea frondosa*, *Roxb*.

Naṛi murup̣. A large forest climber, *Butea superba*.
Ot murup̣. A small plant *Flemingia nana Roxb.*, with leaves resembling *Butea frondosa* and *Butea superba*.

Murup̣ goḍo. A species of rat.

Mururi. A veiled name for cholera.

Murut. An image, an idol, a statue.
Murut lekae teṅgoakana. He is standing like a statue.

Muruť hende hasa. A kind of black stiff soil.

Murwạd. Respect, honour, wish, intention. Cf. murad.

Musạ. Moses.

Musạ. A rat.

Musaǩ. } Silent, listless, mel-
Gundur musaǩ. } ancholy. Cf. gundur musaǩ.

Musaphir. A traveller.

Mushar. A semi-Hinduized caste of aborigines.

Musil. Cf. muisil.

Musiń. } A day or two, a short
Musiń barsiń. } time. Cf. mursiń barsiń.

Musiń din hape thiroǩme. Have patience for a few days.

Muskil. } Difficulty, strait, distress; diffi-
Mạskil. } cult.

Muskilreń paṛaoena. I am in a strait.
Muskil kạmi. Difficult work.
Muskilgea. It is difficult.
Muskilkediñako. They put me in a difficulty.

Muslạ. A Musalman, a Mahomedan.
Muslạ era. A Musalman woman.

Musnạ. } Fine cloth.
Musnạ kicrić. }

Musrạ. The pestle of a ḍhiṅki (q. v.)

Musrạ. M. } Dusty, dirty, stout, fat.
Musri. F. }

Musrạ lekae ńeloǩkana.

Musur. A variety of the rice plant.

Muṭ. } The seed sown on the first aus-
Muṭh. } picious day of the season.

Muṭ tehoń iń hataokeda. I sowed the first handful of seed to-day.
The first three days of Rohini (q. v.) are considered lucky for rice cultivation, and most cultivators make it a point to sow at least a handful of rice on one or other of these days.

Muṭạk. } Thick, applied to clubs. sticks,
Muṭkạ. } &c. of light wood, a thick club or stick of some light wood.

Muṭh. The closed fist, a handle, as of a knife, sword, &c.

Tarwaṛe muṭh. A sword handle.

Muṭh. The first seed sown in the season.

Muthạ ghãs } A common garden weed
Bindi muthạ. } *Fimbrystylis monostachya, Hassk.*

Muṭhạn Form, likeness, resemblance.

Apat muṭhạne ńeloǩkana. He resembles his father.
Hoṛ muṭhạnanae. He has the form of a man, or the likeness of man.

Muṭhi. A handle.

Jonoǩ muṭhi. The handle of the broom.

Muṭhiạu. To seize and close the fist upon, to grasp tightly.

Ṭheṅgae muṭhiạukeda. He grasped the club tightly.
Hakoe muṭhiạukedea. He grasped the fish.

Muthni. Peak, point, as of a hill, spire, &c.

Buru reaǩ coṭ muthniteť. The highest peak of the mountain.

Muṭhu. } Big, stalwart, strong.
Muṭhu muṭhu. }

Muṭhu muṭhu hoṛ bachaokom. Select the stalwart men.

Muṭhu. A children's game.

Muṭkạ. Cf. muṭạk.

Muṭkuri. Gravel, small gravelly stones. Cf. moṭkuri.

Mutul. Gable of a house.

Mutul khunṭi. The post at the gable of a house which supports the ridge pole.
Mutul duạr oṛaǩ. A house with a door in one of the gable ends.

Mutul kạṭup̣. The middle finger.

Mutul ḍar. The main branch of a tree, the upper part of a tree.

Muṭur muṭur. Steadfastly, having the eyes fixed, staring.

Muṭur muṭure ńeńelkana. He is gazing steadfastly.

Muṭur muṭur. Sound produced when eating anything crisp, crunching sound.

Muṭur muṭure togoćeda. He is crunching.

N

N. In ballads, placed before a word beginning with a vowel to avoid a hiatus with the last letter of the preceding word, often also, when a line begins with a word the first letter of which is a vowel.
Buru jharna daḱ ho Baṛe *n*umul
*N*ạdi reaṛ ho *n*ạdi reaṛ.
Not ma lolo serma setoṅ guru ho
Not ma lolo serma setoṅ, guru
Celako dom lalaokeṫko
Guru ho, celako dom lalaokeṫko.

Na. Used by males addressing females younger than themselves, and by females unless the age is very disproportionate.
Henda na, okatem calaḱkana? Ho my girl, where are you going?
Añjomme na. Listen, girl.
E dại na, note hijuḱme. Oh, my elder sister, come this way.

Na. } This.
Nah. }
Na sa ma hijuḱme. Come to this side.

Na. A particle signifying doubt or uncertainty.
Jinis na jinis, oka jinis coṅem ṅamkan? There are various kinds of things, what thing is it you want?

Ṅā. Cf. ṅam.
Ṅāwaṫlese. He got it for us.

Nabab. A rich man.

Nabalok. Young, under age, immature.
Nabalok gidrạ. A minor.
Nabalokgeae. He is a child, or under age.

Nạbhuạ. } Funny, humorous, jocular,
Nạphuạ. } whimsical, waggish; buffoonery, tomfoolery.

Nạbi. A prophet, to prophesy.
Am ṅutumte bale nạbilaḱa? Did we not prophesy in thy name?
Nạbi era. A prophetess.

Nacao. To cause to dance, to cause to come and go fruitlessly.
Nui hoṛ do ạdiye nacaoediṅkana. This man is causing me to dance attendance on him fruitlessly.

Nacar. } Helpless, without resource.
Lacar. }
Nacargeaṅ. I am without resource.
Nacaroḱae. He will be without resource.

Nacaria. Helpless, resourceless.

Nạchim. Cf. ạchim.

Nạcnia. } A dancer.
Naconi. }
Bes nạcniạ kanae. She is a good dancer.

Nạcu. } A small bamboo basket.
Ạcu. }
Gelbar nạcu oṛeko goćkeṫkoa. They killed twelve baskets of quails.

Nạcu. To hire, to engage to perform a service. Cf. ạcu.

Nạcur. To turn, to return, to turn round, to revolve. Cf. ạcur.

Nạcu ṭuplaḱ. A kind of small basket.

Nadhao. Cf. nandhao.

Nạdi nala din. The rainy season when the rivers are full.

Nadoḱ. Cf. aṫ.

Naeke. The village priest of the Santals.
Kuḍạm naeke. The priest who conducts the worship of the lesser dieties of the village.
Naeke era. The priest's wife.
Naeke man. Rent free land cultivated by the priest.
Uniko naekekedea. They elected him to be priest.
Uni ren apatteṫ naekeăṫ tahĕkanae. His father was performing the duties of a priest.
Uni ren apatteṫe naekelena. His father was priest.

Naeke khil Hăsdaḱ. A sub-sept of the Santal sept Hăsdaḱ (q. v.)

Naeke khil Kisku. A sub-sept of the Santal sept Kisku (q. v.)

Naeke khil Murmu. A sub-sept of the Santal sept Murmu (q. v.)

Naeke khil Hembrom. A sub-sept of the Santal sept Hembrom (q. v.)

Naeke khil Mạrnḍi. A sub-sept of the Santal sept Mạrnḍi (q. v.)

Naeke khil Soren. A sub-sept of the Santal sept Soren (q. v.)

Naeke khil Ṭuḍu. A sub-sept of the Santal sept Ṭuḍu (q. v.)

Naeke khil Baske. A sub-sept of the Santal sept Baske (q. v.)

Naeke khil Besra. A sub-sept of the Santal sept Besra (q. v.)

Naeke khil Cŏṛĕ. A sub-sept of the Santal sept Cŏṛĕ or Guạ Soren (q. v.)

Naeke khil Pạuria. A sub-sept of the Santal sept Pạuria or Pạulia (q. v.)

Naenam. Remembrance.

Nae napae. Cf. napae.
Nae baṛe napae baṛe tahenmale.

Nagad. }
Nogod. } Cash, mainly silver.
Nagadtegeñ hataokeda. I paid cash for it.

Nagar. } A city, large town, the town
Naṅgar. } or village in which the raja or zemindar of a large estate resides.

Nagar bhuli. To go from house to house, applied to females.

Nager caker. }
Naṅger caker. } Area of village.
Phalna Mạñjhiak̕ naṅger caker age ḍige solo kos menak̕a.

Nạgi gando dak̕. } Reddish coloured
Nạṅgi gando dak̕. } scum found at times on stagnant water.

Nagnạgin. A species of snake.

Nagraha. } A city, large town, the town
Naṅgraha. } or village in which the raja or zemindar of a large estate resides.

Nạgu. Cf. ạgu.
Nạguạdar. Cf. ạguạdar.

Nahak̕. Present, in opposition to past or future, shortly, presently.
Nahak̕ jug. The present age.
Ne nahak̕e bijuk̕a. He will come presently.
Gujuk̕ae nahak̕. He will die in a very short time.
Nahak̕ renko. Those of the present day.

Nahak. Uselessly, causelessly, fruitlessly, vainly. Cf. benahak.
Nahakgem heċakana. You have come in vain.
Kạmi nahakentiña. My labour has been in vain.

Ńaham ńạhum. } Grey dawn, dim twi-
Ńaham ńuhum. } light, dusk.
Ńaham ńạhumiñ seṭerena. I arrived at dusk.
Matkom halaṅ lạgit̕ ńaham ńạhumko oḍokok̕a. They go out in the grey dawn to collect matkom (q. v.)

Nahan. } A ceremony observed five
Tel nahan. } days after a death.
Tel nahankedape? Is the ceremony of *tel nahan* over?
Mõṛẽ mãhãreko tel nahanok̕a. They observe the ceremony of *tel nahan* five days after (death.)

Nahar. A canal, a large open drain.

Ńahãṛ ńohõṛ. } Melodiously, sweetly,
Ńahãṛe ńohõṛe. } soft and clear.
Ńahãṛ ńohõṛko sek̕reńkana. They are singing softly and clearly.

Naharni. A small instrument containing tweesers, needle for extracting thorns, and knife for cutting nails, carried suspended to a string round the loins.

Nahas. } To waste, to squander.
Tahas nahas. } Cf. tahas nahas.

Nahel. A plough.
Nahel gaḍa. A furrow.
Nahel gaḍa dak̕. Rice beer.
Nahel aṛak̕ ber. Time to loose the cattle from the plough.
Nahel joṛao. To yoke the plough.
Tinạk̕ nahel ạcurok̕kantapea? } How many
Tinạk̕ nahelpe joṛaoeda? } ploughs have you in use?

Nạhī. } Sign of the Preliminary
Nạhī tho. } Expostulative tense, used
Nạhī thor. } when exposing the fallacy of an argument or the unreasonbleness of a demand.
Kombṛo cak̕ bape ạ̃guledea? Unile sạble nạhīle ạguea. Why did you not bring the thief? We must first catch him then we will bring him (we must catch him before we can bring him.)
Dak̕le nạhī ende nạhīm arjaoa. It must rain first, then you can raise crops.
Arjaole nạhī thom joma. You must raise the crop before you can eat.
Senlen nạhī thorem ńama. You must first go and then you will receive.

Nạhi nindhạn. About, thereabout, somewhere about.
Nạhi nindhạn nonḍe khon pon kos gan hoyok̕a. It will be about four *kos* from here.
Nạhi nindhạn dos baro bạnd hoṛo hoyok̕a. There will be somewhere about ten or twelve bạndis (q. v.) of dhan.

Ńạhum dạrum. Black and bulky.
Bitkilko ńạhum dạrum. Black, bulky buffaloe cows.

Ńạhum dạrum. } To eat greedily, to
Ńạhum tạgum. } devour food in large mouthfuls.
Ńạhum tạgume jomkeda. He ate greedily.

Nại. A river, the Damuda river
Nại as a common noun is obsolete in Northern Santali. It is used as a proper name and applied to the Damuda river.
Nại gạḍa. The Damuda river.
Nạiteko calaoena. They have gone to the Damuda river.

Nạ̃i. This (animate.)
Nạ̃iṭak̕. This particular one (animate.)

Naib. A deputy.

Naihar. Applied to parents' house after marriage.

Sasrar. Applied to the house of parents-in-law.

Naihar seā renko tulučiń ńepellena. I met some people from my father's house.

Nainu. Butter.

Nāiya. A semi-Hinduized caste of aborigines.

In many Hindu villages priests of this caste are employed to propitiate the aboriginal deities who are still supposed to occupy the place from which their original worshippers have been ousted.

Nāiyali man. A piece of rent free land given to the Nāiya priest of a village. Cf. nāiya.

Najar. }
Najer. } To see, to look; sight, vision.

Najer bond. Blind, to imprison.
Noteye najerkeda. He looked this way.
Najer bondkedeako. They put him in hajot.
Najer bondreko dohoakadea. They have put him in hajot.

Najhar. Busy, no time for anything else, filled full, fully occupied. Cf. lajhar.

Nak. A naik, a corporal.

Naka. Cf. aka.

Nak dandi. Where the nose joins the forehead, bridge of nose.

Nāk risa. Nasal polypus.

Nakabul. To deny, to refuse assent.

Nakarar. To deny.

Nakararkedae. He denied it.

Nakara. Offensive, polluted, defiled, dirty.

Adi nakara hor kanae. He is a very dirty man.
Nakarage ńelokkana, bape saphaeda. It looks offensive, you do not clean it.

Nakatia. }
Nakatio. } Rascal, scamp, scoundrel; rascally, mischievous, naughty.

Marań nakatia kanae. He is a great scoundrel.

Nakbadho. }
Kat bandho. } Said by a mother to a child when it sneezes.

The mother holds the child by the arms and stretches them out, and then folds them over its breast, and each time she does so she says *nak badho*.

Nakha. Direction, point of the compass.

Jojom ti nakha. The right hand side.
Etom nakha. The right side.
Kone nakha. The left side.
Purub nakha. The east.
Pachim nakha. The west.
Uttar nakha. The north.
Dakhin nakha. The south.
Oka nakha khon hijukkana? Purab nakha khon. From what direction is it coming? From the east.
Sojhe nakhategeye calaoena. He went straight ahead.

Nakhe mukhe. Of a good countenance, good looking, comely

Bes nakhe mukhe ńelokkanae. She is good looking.

Nakić. A comb, to comb the hair.

Nakijokkanae. She is combing her hair.
Roć nakić. To comb and tie up the hair.
Kat nakić. A wooden comb.
Dereń nakić. A comb made of horn.
Sar nakić. }
Kundar nakić. } A comb made of bamboo, or some other substance and carried tied to a cord round the loins.
Kundag nakić. A comb worn in the hair by men.
Kakri nakić. A small-toothed comb.

Nakić ghās. A common species of sedge, *Fimbristylis miliacea, Vahl.*

Nakkata. }
Mū geṭ. } To cut off the nose, to disgrace, to dishonour.

Ań doko nakkatakedińa. They disgraced me.

Nakra. }
Nakran. } To wash the hair.

Nakra hasa. }
Nakran hasa. } A kind of soapy earth used to wash the the hair with.

Naksa. A picture, a representation.

Nakta. M. }
Nakti. F. } Snub-nosed, having the bridge of the nose broken.

Nal. A horse shoe, a bullock shoe.

Sadom nal. A horse shoe.
Dańra nal. A bullock shoe.
Panhi nal. A toe or heelplate on a shoe.
Nalband. A horse-shoer.
Nal tol. To shoe a horse or bullock.
Nal tol ocoakadań. I have caused (the horse) to be shod.
Sadom nal tolko idiakadea kamar theć. They have taken the horse to the blacksmith to be shod.

Nal. }
Nol. } Land reclaimed and cultivated during a lengthened period.

Nal khet. A piece of rice land which has been under cultivation for a long time.

Nal. }
Nol. } A tube, a pipe.

Nala. A stream, a ditch, a ravine.

Buru nala. A mountain stream running in the bottom of a ravine of greater or lesser depth.

Nala. The pulse at the wrist.

Nalage banukantae. He is pulseless.
Nala bań hijukkantaea. His pulse is not beating, i. e. there is no pulsation.

Ńalaḱ.
Ṅalaḱ ńalaḱ. } Indistinctly, as anything very distant.

Buru ńalaḱ ńalaḱ ńeloḱkana. The hill is seen indistinctly.

Ńalaḱ marte.
Ṅalaḱ mente. } With an indistinct glimpse.

Naseaḱ ńalaḱ mente ńelledeań. I only caught a very indistinct glimpse of him.

Nalha. To work for wages either in money or kind.

Nalha joh hoŗ.
Nalhaié. } One who works for wages.

Nalha johkanań. I support myself by working for wages.

Nalhakatele ạsuloḱkana. We support ourselves by working for wages.

Nạli.
Noli. } Barrel of a gun

Miḱ nạli bạnduk. A single barrelled gun.
Bar nạli bạnduk. A double barrelled gun.

Nạli.
Noli. } A stream, a ditch, a ravine.

Nọli gạḍa.
Noli gạḍa. } A ditch.

Nạlis.
Lạlis. } To complain, to bring an accusation, a complaint.

Nạlisadińa. He complained against me, brought a suit against me in the court.
Nạlis menaḱtiña. I have a complaint to make.

Ńaloḱ ńaloḱ.
Ṅuloḱ ńuloḱ. } Indistinctly. Cf. ńalaḱ ńalaḱ.

Nalsa nạlsi
Lạlsa lạlsi. } To complain or bring an accusation against each other. Cf. nạlis.

Ńam.
Ńa. } To seek, to find, to obtain, to get, to wish for.

Ńam baŗa. To seek for, to search for.
Ńam ceḱ. To select, to choose.
Hudis ńam. To solve, think out to a solution.
Noa kathań hudis ńamakaḱa. I have thought out and understand the matter, I have solved the matter.
Ńam apat. Step-father.
Uniga ńam apat kantaea. He is his step-father.
Nam ńam aesankadako. They searched for it.
Ńam ńamteko ruạŗena. They have returned searching all the way.
Ạdi bes kioriciń ńam ceńgeḱakaḱa.
Ań jom ńam kedale. We received news, or intelligence.
Jiweḱrogeń sen ńamkedea. I found him alive when I went.
Bań sen ńamledea. I went but did not find him.
Onḍege ńamoḱa. It will be found or obtained there.
Ṭeḱa ńawanae. He has received money.
Bạhuko ńawadiña. They got me a wife.

Nama. Joined to another word implies written; written document, a deed.

Hukum nama. A written order or authority.

Karạŗ nama. A written agreement or undertaking.
Ikrạŗ nama. A written agreement, indenture, bond, contract, a deed of assent or acknowledgement in general.

Ńamba ńumbạ. Twilight.

Nam cintạ. Remembrance, knowledge, thought.

Ona reaḱ nam cintạ bạnuḱanaḣ. No thought is being taken of that.
Nui mĩhu reaḱ nam cintạ bạnuḱanaḣ. This calf has been forgotten (by the owner.)

Namḍak. To be famous, to be well known.

Ạdi namḍakakanae. He is very famous.
Namḍak hoŗ kanae. He is a famous man.

Ńamea. The wives of brothers.

Namhạni. Cholera.

Namhạni duk. Cholera.

Nạmi. Late, late in the season.

Cas nạmiena nes do. The crops are late this season.

Namjadi. Famous, notorious, well known. Cf. namḍak.

Ńam ńam.
Ńam ńamte. } All, all without exception.

Ńam ńamteko calaoena. They have all gone.

Namor.
Nomor. } Cor. of the English word "number," to bring a suit in court.

Miḱ namor calaḱme. Go once.
Namorakadeae. He has brought a suit against him in the court.

This peculiar use of the word has probably arisen from the suits being numbered, and the number appearing on all copies of judgments or decisions given by the courts.

Namunạ.
Nomona. } Example, pattern.

Noa mamla reaḱ nạmunạ bale ńam dạreaḱkana. We cannot make out the precedent of this suit.
Namunạe em oṭoaḱbona. Hé left us an example.
Niạ nạmunạ leka baŗe benaome. Make it like this pattern.

Nana. Father's elder sister, aunt.

Nana bond.
Nana bondhe.
Nana bondhej.
Nana bondhek. } With much contrivance, with much thought or care, scheming, in various ways or modes.

Nana bondhejkateye ạgukeda. He got it after much scheming.

Nana chutạr. Cf. nana hunạr.

Nana huṇar.
Nana parka.
Nana parkar.
Nana parkanḍ. } Of many kinds, of great variety, in many ways, in various ways or modes.

Nana huṇar baha menak'a. There are many kinds of flowers.

Nana parkare egerkeda. She gave many kinds of abuse. (She said many abusive things.)

Nana parkanḍkedeako. They did many things to him (they annoyed him in many ways.)

Nana parkan.
Nana porkon. } Cf. nana huṇar.

Nandan.
Nandhạn.
Nindhạn. } Meek, poor, destitute, humble; to despise, to slight.

Nandhạn oabaenako. They have become utterly destitute.

Nanḍe.
Hanḍe nanḍe. } Here and there.

Hanḍe nanḍeye lại baṛaeda. He is telling it here and there.

Nandhao. To begin, to engage in.

Ahar tole nandhaoak'awana. He has begun to dam up a stream to make rice fields.

Nạndi gạndi.
Nạndi gundi. } To consider, to ponder, to deliberate, to bestow much thought on, to reflect.

Noa katha ạḍiko nạndi gundiek'kana. They are deliberating this matter very thoroughly.

Nạndi nala.
Nạndi nala din.
Nạdi nala din. } The rains, the rainy season, when the rivers are difficult to cross.

Nạndi nala dinre ohoń sen daṛelenạ. I will not be able to go in the rains (when the streams and rivers are full.)

Nandoa. Cf. nandwa.

Nạnḍri.
Naṛri. } The windpipe.

Nandwa. A large earthenware pot, a stone trough.

Nańga. Naked.

Nańga jugi. A naked ascetic.

Ńańgal ńańgal.
Nańgal ńuńgal. } Very dirty, filthy.

Ńańgal ńiṭe.
Ńańgal ńuṭạ. } Dirty, black, swarthy.

Ńańgal ńuṭạko ńelledea. They saw that he was swarthy.

Nańgar. A city, a town, the town or village in which the raja or Zemindar of a large estate resides.

Nańgar bhulạ. M.
Nańgar bhuli. F. } Wandering, a wanderer, a vagabond.

Oka seć nańgar bhuliye calaoena? Where has the wanderer gone?

Nańgar jugi. A wandering ascetic.

Nańger caker. Cf. nager caker.

Nạńgi ganḍo. Reddish coloured scum found sometimes on the surface of stagnant water. Cf. nạgi ganḍo dak'.

Nańgle. The thong which binds the yoke to the plough beam.

Nańgos. To pretend, to sham, to malinger.

Nańgosiạ. Given to shamming or malingering.

Nańgosiạ hoṛ kanae. He is a malingerer.

Ńańgoyak'. Very black, extremely, applied to blackness.

Kuilạ khadre kạmikanko do ńańgoyak'geako. The workers in a coal mine are very black.

Ńańgoyak' hende geko ńelok'a. They appear extremely black.

Nańgraha. A city, a town. Cf nagraha.

Nạńrạta. A kind of reed.

Nanha. Thin, slim, slight; sharp, high, as a tone or note.

Ạḍi nanhagea. It is very thin.

Ạḍi nanhageae. He is very slim.

Alom laga, nanhak'a. Do not pare it, it will be too thin.

Nanha roṛ hõko roṛa. They also speak in a high tones.

Nanha lać. The lower portion of the entrails.

Nanha binḍi muthạ. A common species of sedge, *Fimbristylis monostachya, Hassk.*

Nanha bodhạri. A common fern during the rains, *Cheilanthus tenuifolia, Sw.*

Nanha ḍudhi ghãs. A common grass, *Andropogon schœnanthus, Linn.*

Nanha jhunkạ. A small wild plant, *Crotalaria prostrata, Linn.*

Nanha pusi toa. A common milky plant, *Euphorbia thymifolia, Burm.*

Nanha bir jhunjhuni. A small jungle plant.

Nanha hemca aṛak'.
Nanha jubhi aṛak'. } A wild plant the leaves of which are used as a pot-herb, *Limnophila gratioloides, R. Br.*

Nanha dudhi loṭa. } A common climbing plant, *Ichnocarpus frutescens, R. Br.*
Ghiu chimbṛi. }

Nanha bāṛia kaṇḍhum. A small gregarious bush, *Phyllanthus multilocularis, Mull. Arg.*

Nañjer. } To look, to gaze; sight, faculty of seeing. Cf. nojor.
Nojor. }

Nañjom. A witch.

Nañjom duk. Wasting of body, marasmus.

Nañjom rehet́. A wild plant so called.

Nanka. Thus. Cf. nonka.

Nankar. An allowance of money or land to Zemindars, &c. for subsistence, land granted to servants for their maintenance.

Naṇuaṛ. Beautiful, pretty.
Gidrạ ạḍi naṇuaṛe ńeloḱkana. The child looks very beautiful.

Nao. A boat, a ship.

Nãogão. Name and residence, address.
Adoko mena, okare nãogão?

Naokar. } A servant.
Naokor. }

Naokaṛi. } Service. Cf. naukaṛi.
Naokoṛi. }

Nao ṭhikaṇ. Residence, address, particulars of residence.
Nao ṭhikạṇ okaretam? Where is your place of residence?

Nap. To measure.
Nap jok. To measure.
Din kalom khetko napkeda. They measured the fields last year.

Napae. Absence of blemish, disfigurement, deformity, imperfection, flaw, injury, accident, mishap, detriment, discord, decay or disease.
Napaegeae. He is well, he is clean, he is without deformity, disfigurement, blemish, defect, &c. &c.
Napae napaeteye heḍena. He arrived all right.
Napae okoṭe tahenpe. Live in harmony.
Kaḍako ạruṕ napaekom. Wash the buffaloes well.
Ti ạbuk napaetam. Wash your hands carefully.
Napaetege menaea. He is in excellent health.
Naenapaege menaḱkoa. They are well in every respect.

Ńapam. To meet, to agree, to coincide. Reciprocal form of ńam (q. v.)
Hortegeliń ńapamlena. We met on the way.
Katha do bań ńapamoḱkantakina. Their statements do not agree, or are at variance with each other.

Naparok. } Perforce, *nolens volens*, willing or unwilling, unable to do better.
Naparokh. }
Noa atore do naparok menaḱlea. We remain in this village as we are unable to do better.
Naparokiń bataokeda. I took it of necessity, I had no choice.

Napha. } Profit.
Lapha. }
Bań naphalaḱa. I made no profit.

Naphua. Cf. naḅhua.

Naṗit. } A barber, the Hindu Barber caste.
Laṗit. }

Naṗit́. Like.
Inạ naṗit́ baṛe emaeme. Give him in that proportion.
Din naṗit́re. At the proper season.
Raj do din naṗit́reko asoḱgea. The Zemindars at the proper season expect (to receive their rents.)
Kheas naṗit́iń ńuieda. I drink with discretion.
Gidrạ khan gidrạ naṗit́ emaeme. If a child give him as befits a child.
Jạruṛ naṗit́. As much as is needful.

Napoṛ. } In comp. gives the idea of indifference, outright, there is an end of it, be done with it, in the end, eventually. Cf. dapoṛ.
Nepoṛ. }
Idi napoṛ ocoae. Allow him to take (why make any ado about it?)
Jom napoṛ ocoae. Allow him to eat it.
Em napoṛaeme. Give to her and be done with her.

Napoṛ sate. } Cf. napoṛ.
Napoṛ sote. }
Napoṛ sateń joanrege.

Napṛaḱ. Great, large, big, wealthy; to become great, &c. Cf. hapṛaḱ.
Napṛaḱgea. It is large.
Napṛaḱ napṛaḱgea. It is very large.
Napṛaḱ napṛaḱ hoṛ. Great men.

Napti. To measure.

Naṛ. The umbilical cord.
Naṛkaṭaoni. Fee paid to the person who cuts and ties the umbilical cord of a child at birth.

Naṛa. } To leave a few ears of grain when reaping for gleaners.
Nāṛā. }
Tuḱmạlkoko naṛa idiakoa. They leave a little for the gleaners.

Nara. } A kind of ear ornament.
Nāṛā. }

Ńāṛādaṅ.
Ńāṛādoṅ. } Black, dark, heavy, as clouds.
Ńāṛēdaṅ.

Rimil ńāṛādaṅ ńeleǩkana. The clouds look dark.
Ńāṛādaṅe ńeloǩkana. He is very black.

Nara dhura. Afflicted, bodily affliction, as leprosy, sores, &c.
Ale do nara dhuṛạ beste do bale tahenkana.

Nara piṛạ. Cf. nara dhuṛạ.

Naraj. To be displeased, to become poor, to be humble, to be ill-at-ease.
Narajenako. They have become poor.
Narajenae, ikạkaepe. He is humble, leave him alone.

Narak.
Norok. } Excrement, filth.
Ḍạn do narakko jom ocokoa. They cause witches to eat filth.

Narak kunḍ.
Norok kunḍ. } Pit of filth, hell.
Bam añjomlekhan narak kunḍtem calaǩa. If you do not obey you will go to the pit of filth.

Ńaraǩ ńaraǩ. Pitifully, sorrowfully, bitterly.
Ńaraǩ ńaraǩko raraǩkana, debon oḍokea. They are weeping pitifully, come let us take him out (a corpse for burial.)
Miť ńindạ doe raǩlaǩa ńaraǩ ńaraǩ. She passed the whole night weeping bitterly.

Naṛaǩ. Cf. aṛaǩ.

Naraǩ. Cf. araǩ.

Naram.
Norom. } Soft, pliable. Cf. norom.

Naran. An epithet of Vishnu.
Dos naran. Ten gods, applied to the members of a panchayat who are supposed not to err in their decisions.
Ado de bhala, dos bhạị dos naran kạhu leka hendeye tahẽkana, bāk lekae ponḍena.

Ńaraṅ ńuruṅ.
Ńuruṅ ńuruṅ. } To beg whiningly, to importune, to ask for querulously.
Naraṅ ńuruṅko kokoea. They beg whiningly.
Ńaraṅ ńuruṅoǩako. They importune.

Naraṅgi.
Naraṅgi. } An orange.

Narca. Unfertile, exhausted, barren.
Narcaena ot ḍo. The soil is exhausted.
Narcaenae gại do. The cow has become barren, past the age for breeding.

Narda. Cf. arda.

Narba kharba. To waste, to squander.
Sanam ọije narba kharbakeda. He squandered all his property, he wasted all his substance.

Narcạ. A cultivated fibre yielding plant.

Naṛgi.
Naṛngi. } A kind of malignant sore.

Nāṛgo. Cf. āṛgo.

Narhaḍa. The space between the knee and the ankle.

Narda. A kind of early rice.

Naṛe joṛe. By littles from different places and at different times.
Naṛe joṛe kateń jumạuakaťkoa: I have collected them gradually from one place and another.

Naṛgi ghao.
Naṛngi ghao. } A kind of abscess.

Naṛha joṛha. Relatives by marriage, a wife's or husband's relatives.
Noko naṛha joṛha seḍren kanako.

Naṛi. The pulse at the wrist.
Nạri dabṛaoentaea. His pulse is feeble.
Oka do dabṛao dabṛaoge hijuǩa. At times the pulse is fitful and weak.

Nāṛi. A creeping, trailing, twining or scandent plant.
Malhan nāṛi. The climbing plant known as malhan (q. v.)
Nāṛiǩa. It will throw out suckers.

Nạri. To wind thread on the tube which is placed inside the shuttle, thread wound to put in the shuttle.
Toń lạgiť sutạmko nạria. They wind the thread on small tubes to put into the shuttle for weaving.
Nạri sutạm mạknareko bhoraoa. They put the thread when wound on a small tube inside the shuttle

Nāṛi ghās.
Naṛi ghās. } A common kind of grass, *Panicum vestitum, Nees.*

Naṛi murup̣. A huge jungle climber bearing gorgeous yellow flowers, *Butea superba, Roxb.*
Murup̣. A gregarious small tree, *Butea frondosa, Linn.*

Naṛi siris. A large jungle scandent bush, *Dalbergia volubibilis, Roxb.*

Naṛi ṭhuri. Only, entirely.
Niǩiṅetiń nạri ṭhuri. This is my only one.
Nạri ṭhuri cabaena. It is all finished.
Nạri ṭhuri unige peṛa menaetińa. This is my only relative.

Naṛjoṛ. To marry, relationship by marriage.
Noa atore naṛjoṛiń lagaoakaťa. I have married my son (or daughter) into a family in this village.

Naṛka. } To wash the hair with a kind
Naṛkan. } of soapy earth.

Naṛka hasa. } A kind of soapy earth used to
Naṛkan hasa. } wash the hair with.
Um naṛkaɁpe. Bathe and wash your hair.
Um naṛkankanako. They are bathing and washing their hair.

Narkaṭaoni. } A perquisite received by
Naṛkaṭauni. } a midwife for tying the umbilical cord. Cf. nạr.

Nạr khunṭi. Part of a weaver's loom, the posts which support the roller on which the cloth is wound as woven.

Nạrkol. } A cocoanut, the cocoanut
Nạrkoṛ. } tree.

Narkol sunum. } Cocoanut oil. Cf. nạ-
Narkoṛ sunum. } riạl sunum.

Narma. } Soft, pliant. Cf. norom.
Narmi. }

Naṛṛi. The windpipe.

Narpa. Cf. arpa.

Narta. A ceremony observed three or five days after birth.

Nas. The underside of the leg from the knee to the ankle.

Nas sir. The tendons or the underside of the leg.

Nas. } To destroy, to ruin, to anni-
Nasao. } hilate.

Sanam nasena. All is destroyed.
Nasaokedape kicriċ do. You ruined the cloth.

Nase. } A little, very little.
Nase nase. }

NaseaɁ. } A little.
NasenaɁ. }
NasenaɁiń badaegea. I know a little.
Nase naseń añjomkeda. I heard very little.

Nase sạri. } A little, incompletely.
Nase situr. }

Nase siturẹ bạḍaea. He knows a little.

Ṇase. Untrue, false.

Sạri se nase kana? Is it true or untrue?
Nasegea. It is false.

Nạsib. } Fate, luck, fortune.
Noseb. }

Nạsiban. Fortunate, lucky.
Nạsiban hoṛ kanae. He is a fortunate man.
Uni nạsibre tahẽkana. It was his fate.

Nason. } To be afflicted with a certain
Nasoni. } kind of malady, to be crippled, to be maimed, to suffer from disease.

Nasonenako, gujuɁkanako. They have been attacked by disease and are dying.

Nasonienae. He is suffering from a disease, (leprosy, &c.)

Nasoṛ. Cf. asoṛ.

Nạsti. To render null and void, to deny, to annihilate.

Kathae nạstieda. He denies the statement.

Nat. } To bore a bullock's nose and
Nath. } put in a string with which to guide him, a nose-ring.

Ḍaṅrako nathkoa. They bore holes in the noses of bullocks.
Hoṛ do nathko horoga. People wear nose rings.

Naṭ. To inform against, to denounce from ill-feeling.

Nui hoṛ ạḍiye naṭeɁbona. This man tells tales about us.

Nata. Temporary relationship, to assume relationship for the purpose of addressing each other. Cf. sạgni.

Hopobo lạ riɁko nata joṅa. They assume relationship for the purpose of calling to each other.

Ạḍe ṭola renko nata suṭạ joṅako. Neighbours assume relationship towards each other. People who are in the habit of meeting each other often assume relationship towards each other to simplify social intercourse by avoiding having to name names which under certain circumtances would be improper or opposed to social customs. Thus a younger man addresses an older man as uncle, a younger girl, an older as elder sister, and so on through most of the relationships.

Kisạṛ tuluċ nata menaɁtaea, jawabaekhan ado nata cabaena. There is a relationship between him and his master, but if he is dismissed that relationship ceases.

Ńatat era. Wives of brothers.

Natea. } The relationship between
Ńatea. } wives of brothers or cousins.

Natań era. My husband's brother's wife, or my husband's cousin's wife.
Nateakin miɁtegekin daṛankana. The wives of the two brothers are going about together.

Ńaṭaķ ńuṭuķ. To make a noise with the mouth as one does when it is dry during illness, or when anything very acid has been eaten.

ŃaṭaɁ ńuṭuɁe sade ocoeda.
ŃaṭaɁ ńuṭuɁiń añjomledea.

Nata suṭạ. Relationshp. Cf. nata.

Am tuluċ ceṭ nata suṭạ kantińa? What relationship have I with you?

Ńatea gotoṗ. } Cf. natea.
Natea gotoṗ. }

Onko ńatea gotoṗ bako sapahoṗkana. The wives of the brothers do not agree.

Naṭer guru. A fomenter of strife, a tale bearer.
Nui do naṭer guru kanae. This (person) is the fomenter of the strife.

Nath. Cf. naṭ.

Naṭhi. A bundle of papers, records of a law suit, an account book.

Naṭhi. Habit, custom, usage.
Pạhilaḱ nạthi bạgikate noa nạthi leka kạmiben. Give up the old habit and practice this habit.

Nathni. A nose-ring, to pierce the nose of a bullock to insert a cord by which to guide it. Cf. naṭ.

Naṭhu. The snout of an animal, the septum of the nose.

Naṭi. A grandchild.
Nạti koṛa. A grandson.
Nạti kuṛi. A granddaughter.
Aja nạti. Grandfather and grandchild.

Naṭika. The pulse at the wrist.

Naṭi natkoṛ. Grandchildren.

Naṭi puti. Grandchildren.

Naṭka. The pulse at the wrist.

Naṭkaṛ. A granddaughter.
Nạti nạtkạṛ. Grandchildren.

Naṭkhaṭ. } Roguish, artful, trickish,
Naṭkhaṭi. } naughty or fretful, as a
Naṭkhaṭia. } child; a rogue, a cheat.
Alom naṭkhaṭa. Do not be naughty.
Marań naṭkhaṭię hoṛ kanae. He is a great rogue.

Naṭua. Dom dancers.
Ruạṛ heċkate nạṭuạko sajaoḱa.

Naṭum. Cf. laṭum.

Naṭwa. A winder on which the thread spun on the spindle of the spinning wheel is wound, to wind thread off the spindle on to a (naṭwa) winder.
Kukuṛhi sutạmko naṭwaea. They wind the thread accumulated on the spindle (or spinning axle) on to a (naṭwa) winder.

Nau. A barber.
Nạukeć dhubikećkoale.

Nau. } A green coloured Mantis be-
Kaṭrua. } longing to the species *Hierodula tectiformis, Sauss.*

Nauwăi. To offer the first fruits, to partake of a crop first time in the season.
Matkomle nạuwăiakaṭa. We have performed the ceremony of offering the first fruits of the matkom (q. v.), or we have partaken of matkom (q. v.) for the first time this season.
Hoṛo nạuwăi. To offer the first fruits of the rice crop.
Gundli nạuwăi. To offer the first fruits of the gundli (q. v.) crop.
Until the first fruits have been offered Santals do not, as a rule, eat rice, the grain of gundli, &c.
The Baha or Flower festival is the offering of the "first fruits" of the matkom and other jungle fruits and flowers. Matkom is never eaten, except under great pressure, before the observance of the Baha or Flower festival.

Naukri. }
Nokri. } Service.
Nukri. }
Nạukriedań. I am in service.
Nạukri oḍokakanae. He has gone out into service.

Năwă. New fresh, recent.
Năwă Niam. The New Testament.
Năwă ot khet. Newly reclaimed land.
Năwă pẹṛa. A newly born child.
Ot do năwăentalea. Our land is newly reclaimed.
Nes do năwăḱgea. This year it is newly broken up (land.)
Năwănaḱ lekaena. It has become like a new one.
Nui dahra do năwănię kanae. This bullock is a new one.
Năwănaḱ iń hataoa, marenaḱ do bań. I will take a new one, not an old one.

Nawab. }
Nabab. } A rich man, a great man.

Nawan. } Bent, curved, to bend, to
Newan. } curve.
Pạṛ bes ṭhikko nawanakaṭa. They have given an excellent curve to the beam.

Nawatur. Newly reached one's prime, fully developed, just full grown, in prime vigour.
Nawatur kanae. He is at his prime.

Nayaṛ. } To pass the night fasting and
Niyaṛ. } sleeping on the ground, applied only to the village priest (naeke) lying on the ground the night before he officiates at the Baha, or Flower festival.
Teheńge naekege jạṭiregeye nayaṛlen. The priest slept last night on a mat on the floor.

Ne. Presently, in no long time, very recently.
Ne nahaḱ. Presently.
Ne gujuḱae. He will die presently.
Ne ge bereć calaoenae. He has just risen and gone away.
Ne nege bereć calaoenae. He has just this moment risen and gone away.
Ne ńoḱre. Very recently, a very short time ago.

Ne. A particle which signifies that something inanimate is being offered for acceptance, to offer, to give.

Neadeań. I offered it to him, I said to him *ne*, or take.
Ne legawaeme. Offer it to him to see if he will take it.
Ne hataome. Here, take it.
Ni is the same particle used with animate objects.
Neya. } Said when offering anything to a male
Neja. } younger than the speaker.
Ne na. Said when offering anything to a female younger than the speaker.
Ne ho atahme. Here, take this.

Ne. To assent to.

Nekedae. He assented.
Bae nelaka. He did not assent.

Ne. A particle signifying like the speaker, like myself, like ourselves.

Ne hoṛko. Ordinary people, people like myself.
Ne hoṛ do ohoe puchạulema. He would take no notice of people like us.
Kolhe leka ne hoṛ do ohom bhạriạ daṛelea. People like us can't carry on the shoulder like the Kolhes.

Neae. } To be at variance with each
Neao. } other.

Neao jhogṛa. A quarrel.
Neaokkanako. They are at variance with each other.
Okoe sohge hõ neao alo jhogoṛ alo hoyokma. May there not be quarrel or dispute with any.

Neae. } To judge, to decide, to settle a
Neao. } dispute.

Cetleka noa kathako neaoket? How did they decide this matter?
Noa do ạdi ṭhikko neaoakata. They have judged this matter excellently.

Nebetar. At the present time, now-a-days.

Nebetar matkomko halaheda. Now-a-days they are gathering the matkom (q. v.)

Nebae. An anvil. Cf. nihại.

Nehal. To do, to accomplish, used most frequently in sarcasm.

Nehalkedam, tulkedam. You did it, you lifted it.
Cetem nehala? What will you do?
Cetem nehalkeda, onate jomakiń emama? What did you do for which I should give you food?

Nehạli. } Of no use, unable to work,
Nehạliạ. } not able to earn anything.

Am nehạliạ do. You useless.

Nehat. } To despise, to slight.
Nihạt. }

Nehatge ńamkedińae. He slighted me.

Nehor. } To entreat, to solicit, to crave,
Nĕhor. } to beseech, to plead, to implore.

Am ṭheniń nehorokkana. I implore you.
Nehoradeań. I entreated for him.
Nehorkateń metamkana, niạ dhao do ikạkańme. I imploringly say to you, pardon me this time.
Kāwārikateń nehorokkana. I am praying and beseeching.

Nehor sehor. Cf. nehor.

Ạdi bạṛiciń nehor sehorenteye ańjomketińa. He heard me owing to my having pleaded so earnestly.

Nehot. } To transgress.
Nĕhŏt. }

Kathań nehotkettama. I transgressed your command.

Nehra jehra. }
Ahra jahra. } To coax, to persuade.
Ahra jahre. }

Ikạkaeme, cet bam nehra jehraedekan? Leave him alone, why should you coax him?

Nejhāṛ. } To impede, to hinder, to ob-
Nejhaṛ. } struct, to hamper.

Nui gidrạ iṭteń nejhaṛgea. I am impeded owing to this child.
Nejhāṛ menakgea. There is an impediment.

Nekĕ. This particular (thing) here.

Nekĕ nonḍe menaka. Here it is.
Neke ńelme. Look, here it is.
Nekĕ tape ḍera, ma jaegakpe. This is you sleeping place, retire to rest.
Nekĕ niạ roroṛ doń men jońkana. I wish to say this particular thing.

Nekraha. Dirty, dirty and ill-conditioned.

Nekraha mara hoṛ. A dirty rascal.

Ńel. To see, to look, to appear, to seem.

Ńel orom. To recognize, to know.
Ńel oromkedeań. I recognized him.
Ńel goṭ. To convoy one a short distance.
Ńel goṭkaeme. See him off, convoy him a short distance on his way.
Ńel ạṛuime. Go and see and return.
Ńel eṭakkedeań, I mistook him for another.
Ńel ńamkedeań. I saw him, I looked and found him.
Ńel gockedeań. I saw him die.
Ńel atketkoań. I lost sight of them.
Nindạre sehgel ạdi sạṅgiń hạbić ńeloka. Fire is seen at a great distance at night.
Ńeńel ṭạndi. The place where a festival is observed.
Ńeńelko senakana. They have gone to see the festival.
Ńepel opromko. Acquaintances.
Ńel ńokledeań. I caught a glimpse of him.
Ohoń ńel ḍhilaumea. I will not neglect you, I will not cease to care for you.

Ńele. A species of large honey bee.
Ńele rasa. The honey of the *nele* bee.

Ńele ńele. To hang about in the hope of getting food.
Reṅgeċteko ńele ńelekhan tahẽkana. They were begging through hunger.

Ńel hezr. } Experienced, to gain experience.
Ńel herer. }
Ńel herer ojha. An experienced doctor.

Nemaj paṛhao. } To pray, of Musalmans.
Namaj paṛhao. }

Nemak dhoromak. Cf. neo dhorom.

Neman. About here, here about, here and there, in this direction.
Nemankore dohoeme. Put it down a little way off.
Neman ńok hijukme. Come a little nearer.
Nemanre teṅgon me. Stand you here.
Ale do nemankorele tãṛãka. We will lie in ambush about here.

Nembrot. } To become assuaged, as anger; to be appeased, to be allayed.
Nemrot. }
Edre khone nembroṫena. His anger has cooled.

Nem dhorom. Cf. neo dhorom.

Nemor. Weak, to despise, to slight, to delay, to put off; meek, good natured.
Noa katha do alom nemora. Do not delay this matter.
Alom nemorińa. Do not slight me.
Nemorgem ńamkedińa? Did you find me one to be despised?

Nemos. Cf. nembrot.

Nemrot. Cf. nembrot.

Ne nahak. Presently, in a very little.
Ne nahakko hijukkana. They will arrive presently.
Ne nahak isinokkana. It will be cooked presently.

Nenḍa. To appoint or fix a time or place.
Nenḍa din tiokena menkhan atorenkoko jaoraka. When the appointed day arrives the villagers come together.
Abo ma ṭhik tikinbo nenḍawan. We fixed the time of the sun's being in the meridian.
Pe mãhã taeome nenḍaatlea. He fixed three days hence for us (to meet him.)
Sohraeko nenḍa jońako. They fix the day on which they will observe the Sohrae (q. v.) festival.
Nenḍa gonḍa. To fix a time.

Nenḍe. Here, in this place.
Henḍe nenḍe. Here and there.
Nenḍege tahẽkan, okoe oonko idiket. It was here, some one has taken it away.

Nenḍenak. The one (inanimate) of here.

Nenḍenić. The one (animate) of here.

Nenḍenkin. The two (animate) of here.

Nenḍenko. Those (animate) of here.

Ne neroń. Presently, used mainly when scolding or fault finding.
Ne nerohem joma. You will presently eat.
Ne nerohem aṭkara. You will presently feel (what it is to be hungry.)

Neṅghao. To transgress, to disregard, to despise.
Katha doe neṅghaokeda. He disregarded the order.
Hapṛamkoak bioạrko neṅghaoketa. They transgressed the customs handed down from the ancients.

Ńeṅget. } Bright red, very bright red colour.
Ńeṅget ńeṅget. }

Nenhak. Presently. Cf. ne nahak.

Nenheć. } Slender, thin, as a stick, or a lath.
Nenheć nenheć. }
Nenhećgea. It is thin.
Nenheć nenheć ṭheṅga. A very thin stick.
Nenhejoka. It will become slender (as a stick pared away.)

Neńjhãṛ. } To impede, to hinder, to obstruct.
Neńjhaṛ. }
Kạmiye neńjhãṛena. His work is in arrears.
Nui gidrạ neńjhaṛko dohoakawadińa, bae kạmi ocoańkana.

Nenka. Like this, such as this.
Nenkage tahẽkana. It was like this.
Nenkaeme. Do like this.

Nenkan. Such, such like, like this, such as this.
Nenkanak. One (inanimate) such as this.
Nenkanić. One (animate) such as this.
Nenkanko. Those (animate) such as these.
Uni doe nenkangea. He is such as this.
Nenkangea. It is such as this.

Neo. A foundation.
Neo bạisạu. To lay a foundation.

Neo. To sanctify, as an officiating priest by fasting, bathing, &c., previous to offering sacrifice.
Neoakatae. He has sanctified himself by abstinence, &c.
Neo dhoromakatae. He has sanctified himself by abstinence, &c.

Neota. To invite, as to a marriage feast, &c., &c.
Jel daka jomko neotaakadińa. They have invited me to partake of meat and rice.
Neota heċakawadińa. I have received an invitation.

Ne parom. On this side.
Ne parom hoṛ kanae. He belongs to this side (of the river.)

Ńepel. The Reciprocal form of ńel (q. v.)

Ńepel heeenań. I have been to see them.
Balań ńepellena. We did not see each other.
Ńepel opromko. Acquaintances.
Ńepel opromiḱkanae. He is an acquaintance.
Ńepel umul baṛaekanae. He keeps looking at his image (in a mirror.)
Ńepel umule dãṛã baṛaekanae. She is going about giving herself airs.
Ńepel apaṭkin ńeloḱkana. They resemble each other very closely.
Ńel tapaṕ. To see through.
Ńel taboḱa. It can be seen through, it is transparent.
Ńepel ṭhipiḱ. To recognize each other.

Nepeota. The Reciprocal form of neota (q. v.)

Ńepeṫ. The Reciprocal form of ńeṫ (q. v.)

Nepoṛ. Cf. dapoṛ.

Nepṛa. To do, to accomplish, used sarcastically when one has been boasting.

Nepṛakedam? You did it?

Nepṛan. Odious, provoking, annoying, bothering, worrying, horrid.

Nepṛanić, sińi saṭuþe hijuḱa. The horrid thing, she comes every day.

Ńere ńere. To cry, as a petulant child, to whine.

Ńere ńere raḱedae. He is whining.
Ńere ńere dãṛã baṛaekanae. He goes about whining.
Ńere ńere pańja baṛaediñae. He follows me about whining.

Ńereḱ ńereḱ. } Whiningly, plaintively,
Ńere ńere. } pitifully, sorrowfully. Cf. ńaraḱ ńaraḱ.

Ńeṛẽ ńeṛẽ. Low, as applied to sound; in an undertone, scarcely audible.

Ńeṛẽ ńeṛẽ saḍekana, banam. The fiddle sounds faintly.
Bań ańjom ṭhikeda, ceṫ ooh ńeṛẽ ńeṛẽm roṛeda. I do not hear distinctly, what is it you are saying in an undertone.

Nes. } This year.
Nesoḱ. }

Nes ạcuroḱ din. Within the year.
Nesaḱ. Belonging to this year (inanimate.)
Nesgeye hoeena. He was born this year.
Nesoḱ geko begarena. They separated this year.

Net. Abstinence from forbidden foods, faith, fidelity loyalty.

Amaḱ netiń ńelkeṫtama. I observed your abstinence.
Nete dohoaṫa. He has taken a vow of abstinence.

Ńeṫ. To bewitch, to assault, to kill, to overcome.

Boṅgae ńeṫkedea. A spirit bewitched him.
Gunteko ńeṫkoa. They kill by sorcery.
Boṅga ńeṫ. A disease affecting human beings and cattle, always terminating fatally.

Ńeṫ. To dye red, or scarlet.

Suṭạmko ńeda. They dye thread scarlet.

Netar. Now-a-days.

Netar ạdi setohkana. It is very hot now-a-days.

Nete. Here, in this place, this way.

Nete ạguiem. Bring him here.
Nete ńogoḱme. Move this way a little.

Neten. Belonging to or of here, belonging to this place.

Neten hoṛ geko senlena. People of this place went.
Neten alom aṭkariña. Do not despise me (as one who has lived all his life here.)
Netenaḱ. This of here (inanimate.)
Netenić. This of here (animate.)
Netenko. These of here, these of this place or neighbourhood.
Netenaḱ hataome. Take this one here.

Newaj. Cf. namaj.

Nha. This.

Hana mucạṫ khon nha mucạṫ hạbić. From that end to this end.
Nha sa. This side.
Nhaṭaḱ. This one (inanimate.)
Nhaić. This one (animate.)
Hana nhae ńamkana. He wants this and that.

Nhãi. This one (animate.)

Nhãiṭaḱ. This one (animate.)

Nhanaḱ. This, so much, so many.

Nhanaḱ hạbić. } Up till this, hitherto.
Nhanaḱ dhạrić. }
Arel do nhanaḱ ńurlena, je enka do ona disomre tis hõ bań ńurlena. So much hail fell, as never before fell in that country.
Nhanaḱ se hanaḱ do bań menakawadea. I have not said this or that to him.

Nhanḍe. There, yonder.

Nhanḍen. Of or belonging to there, or yonder.

Nhanḍenaḱ. Yonder one (inanimate.)
Nhanḍenić. Yonder one (animate.)
Nhanḍenkin. Yonder two (animate.)
Nhanḍenko. Those yonder, those of yonder (animate.)

Nhanka. } Thus, in this way. Cf. nonka.
Nhańka. }

Hanka nhankaedae. He does this and the other.

Nhate. Here, in this place, by this way.

Nhatere. In this place.
Hante nhateye dãṛã baṛaekana. He is going about here and there.

Nhĕke. } This particular thing, this
Nheke. } particular thing here.
Nhĕkekedam? You did this? used sarcastically the speaker shewing his thumb at the same-time.
Nheke tam ṭhenga. Here is your stick.

Nhenḍe. Here.

Nhenḍen. Of or belonging to here.
Nhenḍenak. The one here, or of here (inanimate.)
Nhenḍenić. The one here, or of here (animate.)
Nhenḍenkin. The two here, or of here (animate.)
Nhenḍenko. These here, or of here (animate.)

Nhenka. } This way, thus.
Nheṅka. }
Nhenka dalme. Strike thus.
Nhenka leka. Thus.

Nhĭkĭ. This particular one (animate.)
Nhĭkĭye heć goṭena. There he is, he has just come.

Nhoa. This. Cf. noa.
Nhoaṭak. This one (inanimate.)

Nhoko. These, those, (animate.)
Nhokoko hećena. These (men) have come.

Nhokŏe. Cf. nokŏe.

Nhonḍe. Here. Cf. nonḍe.

Nhonḍen. Of or belonging to here.
Nhonḍenak. The one here, or that of here (inanimate.)
Nhonḍenak dak. The water of this place.
Nhonḍenić. The one here, or of here, (animate.)
Nhonḍenkin. The two here, or of here (animate.)
Nhonḍenko. Those here, or of here (animate.)
Nhonḍenkoko tahĕkana. They were (people) belonging to here, or to this neighbourhood.

Nhonka. } Cf. nonka.
Nhoṅka. }

Nhonkan. Cf. nonkan.

Nhote. Here. Cf. note.
Nhotere. In this place, here.

Nhui. This (animate.) Cf. nui.

Nhukin. These two (animate)

Nhukŭi. Cf. nukŭi.

Ni. A particle which signifies that something animate is being offered for acceptance, to offer, to give.
Ni, idiom. Here, take him away.

Ni. } This particular (one, of animate
Nĭ. } objects.)
Ni cando ńirkate. At the end of this moon.
Nĭ hoṛ idiepe. Take away this man.
Nĭ boṅga, nĭ buru.

Nia. This, used of inanimate objects.
Niaṭak. This particular one (inanimate.)
Nia dhao. This time.
Nia bochor. This year.
Nia dare. This tree.
Nia hoṛom idia. You will take away this dhan.
Gapa nia bela bijukme. Come to-morrow at this time.

Niam. Rule, covenant.
Mare niam. The Old Testament Scriptures.
Nāwā niam. The New Testament.
Onkagem niamakkoa. You thus gave them rules.

Nibasi. A dweller, inhabitant.
Noa atoren nibasi kanae. He is an inhabitant of this village.

Nic. Low, mean, small, humble.
Nic hoṛ kanae. He is a low fellow.
Nic jat. Low caste.
Aćtegeye nicokkana. He is bemeaning himself.

Nicak. A small bush, *Woodfordia floribunda, Salib.* Cf. icak.

Nicak. A prawn, a shrimp. Cf. icak.

Nicak bando. Cf. icak bando.

Nicak arak. Cf. icak arak.

Nicak saram. Cf. icak saram.

Nicak kakitteć. Cf. icak kakitteć.

Nichan. Bothersome, annoying, provoking, odious, horrid, used when annoyed.
Nichan kicrić! That horrid cloth! (is always flapping.)

Nichanaha. M. } Cf. nichnaha.
Nichanahi. F. }

Nichnaha. M. } Bothersome, annoying,
Nichnahi. F. } provoking, odious, used when annoyed.
Nichnaha gidra sić saṭupko umoka. These provoking boys are always bathing.

Nichok. Mean, low, base.
Adi nichokgem metalekana. You think us very low.

Nichora. } Unalloyed, faultless, un-
Nichura. } mixed, entirely, without admixture, pure.
Nichora hende. Perfectly black.
Nichora pond. Perfectly white, all white.
Nichora hoṛo kana. It is is all one kind of dhan.

Nicind. } Without care or anxiety,
Nicit. } heedless, thoughtless, unwary, unconscious.
Nicite gitićakana. He lies unconscious.
Nicindte tahenpe. Be without anxiety.

Nico. Low, as opposed to high, scandalous, discreditable, unbecoming.
Ondege nicogea. It is low there.
Adi nico kathae metadińa. He said a very unbecoming thing to me.

Nicol. } Empty, deserted, lonely.
Nisun. }

Nicol jaega. A lonely place, an uninhabited place.
Burute nicolreye deđena. He went up into a mountain alone.

Nidạndi. } Without care, without anxiety, secure, unsolicitous.
Nirdạndi. }

Nirdạndigeae. He is free from care.

Nidhạn. Cf. nịndhạn.

Nidhạruạ. Free from debt, owing nothing.

Nidhạruạgeae. He owes no man anything.

Nidrạ. } Drowziness.
Nindrạ. }

Mić ghạṛibon gitiđa nidrạ marao lạgić. We will lie down a little to drive away drowziness.

Nihại. An anvil. Cf. nehae.

Nihạ̃t. } To despise, to slight, to disparage, to make light of, to set at naught. Cf. nehot.
Nihạt. }

Nihạtkedeako. They set him at naught.

Nij. } One's own, oneself, special, original.
Nije. }
Niṅj. }

Ać nijegeye kạmieda. He is working himself.
Nij jot. One's own farm, cultivated by oneself.
Nij bhại. } One's own brother.
Nije bhại. }

Nij Soren. The original Santal sept Soren from which the sub-septs of Soren have been derived.

Nij Ṭuḍu. The original Santal sept Ṭuḍu from which the sub-septs of Ṭuḍu originated.

Nij Hãsdak'. The original Santal sept Hãsdak' from which the sub-septs of Hãsdak' originated.

Nij Kisku. The original Santal sept Kisku from which the sub-septs of Kisku originated.

Nij Murmu. The original Santal sept Murmu from which the sub-septs of Murmu originated.

Nij Hembrom. The original Santal sept Hembrom from which the sub-septs of Hembrom originated.

Nij Mạrnḍi. The original Santal sept Mạrnḍi from which the sub-septs of Mạrnḍi originated.

Nij Baske. The original Santal sept Baske from which the sub-septs of Baske originated.

Nij Besra. The original Santal sept Besra from which the sub-septs of Besra originated.

Nij Cõṛẽ. The original Santal sept Cõṛẽ from which the sub-septs of Cõṛẽ originated.

Nij Pạuriạ. } The original Santal sept Pạuriạ or Pạuliạ from which the sub-septs of Pạuriạ or Pạuliạ originated.
Nij Pạuliạ. }

Nijạt. Without any recognized caste, having been out-casted.

Nayạdihre nijạt hoṛ menak'koa. There are casteless people in Nayadih.

Nijạu. } To throw off the effects of fever, liquor, narcotics, &c., to recover one's senses.
Niṅjạu. }

Nitok' doe niṅjạukeda. Now he has recovered from the effects of intoxication.

Nijgut. For certain, by oneself, at first hand.

Nijgut noa kathaṅ badaea. I know this matter first hand.
Iṅ nijgutiṅ aṅjom ạguakać. I have been and heard for myself.

Nijhor. Heavy, pelting as rain without wind.

Nijhore dak'keda. The rain fell straight down (no wind to drive it.)

Nijhuliạ. Weak, feeble.

Nijhum. Quiet, dead calm, breezeless.

Teheṅ do nijhumgea. There is a dead calm to-day.

Nijojor. Weakness, infirmity. Cf. nijor.

Okoere gel irạl sermakhon mićṭoć nijojor jiu tahẽkantaea. Who had a spirit of infirmity eighteen years.

Nijor. Weak, feeble, to become weak, feeble or poor.

Ruạteye nijorena. He is enfeebled by fever.
Nijor hoṛ kanae. He is a feeble person.

Nijuạn. Pubescent.

Nijut. For certain, by oneself, at first hand. Cf. nijgut.

Nije. One's own, oneself, themselves, himself.

Ako nijete jojomko ceda. They will learn to eat by themselves.
Aćren nije hoṛko then. To his own people.

Nikarkhar. } Entirely, altogether, in
Nikhar. } full, recovered, as from illness.

Nikarkhare bes utarena. He is altogether well.
Nikarkharin kharakedea. I paid up in full.

Nikas. Outlet opening, to make up an account.

Nikas bań tahẽlenkhaé posagoka. If there is no outlet it (embankment) will burst.
Nikaskate tinakiń ńama emkatińme. Make up the account and give me what is due to me.

Nikas baki. To make up an account to see how much is owing.

Nikhar. Empty, destitute.

Nikharenae ceť hõ banuktaea. He is empty handed, he has nothing.
Seere nikharlenae. At length he became destitute.

Nikhora. Cf. nichora.

Nikí. This one, this particular one, applied only to animate objects.

Nikí nigeń emamkana. I am giving you this particular one (cow, &c.)

Niki badi. Good and evil, good and bad.

Niki ar badi, noa dhartire niakin hẽnaka. In this world there are only these two, good and evil.

Nikin. These two, applied only to animate objects.

Nikin bare hataokinme. Take these two.

Nikind. Cf. nicind.

Nikti tula. Small scales used to weigh precious articles, such as gold, silver, coral beads, &c.

Nil. Cf. lil.

Nilaj. } Shameless, immodest.
Nilajia. }

Nilam. To sell by auction, to auction. Cf. lilam.

Nilkathi. Cf. lilkathi.

Nim. A common small tree, *Melia Azadirachta, Linn.*

Nim dak mandi. Rice water in which pounded *nim* leaves have been mixed. This bitter mixture is drunk in small quantities at the naming of children.

Nimak haram. } Disloyal, wicked, per-
Nimok haram. } fidious, ungrateful,
Nimuk haram. } disobedient.

Adi barić nimak haram hor kanae. He is a very ungrateful person.

Nimak harami. }
Nimok harami. } Cf. nimak haram.
Nimuk harami. }

Adi nimak haramigeae. He is very ungrateful.

Nimak kharami. }
Nimok kharami. } Cf. nimak harami.
Nimuk kharami. }

Nimbha. } To bring through, as through
Nibha. } a severe illness, time of
Nirbha. } scarcity, helplessness, difficulty, infancy, childhood, &c. &c.

Nin din do nimbhau aguakatań. I have managed to pull (him) through for so long.
Ninak gidrań nibhaketkoa. I pulled through so many children.

Nimbhau. To finish, to complete, to pull or bring through. Cf. nimbha.

Saname nimbhauketkoa. He has finished them all (married all his children.)

Nimin. So much, so big.

Nimin tiritko emaťlea. They gave us so much.

Nimok haram. }
Nimok harami. } Cf. nimak haram.
Nimok kharami. }

Nimon. Sound, solid, without flaw.

Noa kaṭ do nimongea. This log is sound throughout.
Noa mẽrhẽť do nimongea. There is no flaw in this iron.

Nimuk harami. }
Nimuk haram. } Cf. nimak haram.
Nimuk kharami. }

Nin. So many.

Nin din. So many days.
Nin jug. So many ages, so long a time.
Nin tiriť. So much as this.
Nin horle tahẽkana. We were so many people.
Nin horgeale. We are so many men.
Ninte do honah adi utarlah galmaraokea. We might have conversed a great deal in this time.

Ninak. So much, so many, this much.

Ninak horle tahẽkana. There were so many of us.
Ninak bare emaeme. Give him so much.

Ninda. } To despise, to slight, to deny,
Nindau. } to revile.

Jomake nindaukeda. He denied having received food.
Jahãe bako nindaukoa. They do not despise anyone.

Ńinda. Night, to become night.

Teheń ńinda. Last night, to-night.
Noa ńinda ńut cakpe hijukkana? Why do you come after it is dark?
Babon taramlekhanbo ńindaka. If we do not step out night will overtake us.
Miť siń miť ńinda. All day and all night.
Siń lae ńinda lae. All day and all night.
Siń ńinda. Day and night.

Ńindạ cando. The moon.

Nindạn. Estimating roughly, by guess.
Nindạn ponro ser gan hoyoḱa. By guess it will be about 15 seers.
Nạhi nindạn bar isi hoṛko jarwalena. By a rough estimate forty people were assembled.

Nindara. Formerly, in the past.
Nindara do babon jaoraḱkan taḱekana, teheń oedaḱbon jaoraena? We have not been in the habit of assembling previously, why are we assembled today?
Nindara do babon kapharịạuḱkan taḱekana, nui heokatebo kạpharịạuḱkana. We did not quarrel in the past, since he came we are quarrelling.

Nindạu. Cf. nindạ.

Nindhạn. Meek, humble, poor, destitute, to despise, to slight.
Nindhạngeae. He is humble, or poor.
Nindhạnkedeako. They slighted him.
Nindhạnkatele nehoroḱkana. We humbly pray.

Ńindir. A species of termite or white ant.
Buku. The species of white ant which raises the ant hills.
Ńindir hasa. The earth with which white ants raise the covering over themselves when they venture above ground.
Ńindirko jomkeda. } White ants ate it, or destroyed it.
Ńindirkedako. }

Nindrạ. Cf. nidrạ.

Ninghạ. Axle of cart, &c.

Ninghạr. To finish, to complete, to exhaust.
Kạmile ninghạrkeda. We finished the work.

Ninghraoni. A present given to the weaver by the person for whom he is weaving on finishing the web.

Ninghrạu. To finish, to complete, to exhaust.
Hola Sohraele ninghrạukeda. We brought the Sohrae festival to an end yesterday.

Nińj Cf. nij.

Nińjam. Master, owner.

Nińjam. Genuine, pure, unalloyed, important.
Nińjam nińjam katha galmaraope. Discuss only the important points.

Nińjhau. } To decline, to become less.
Nijhạu. }
Matkom sạrdi khon nińjhạuakana. The *matkom* (q. v.) is less now than it was at mid-harvest.

Nipạt. To spend, to use up, to exhaust.

Nipạt. } Exactly.
Nipoṭ. }
Nipạṭ uni lekae ńeloḱkana. He looks exactly like him.
Nipạṭ nui ḍahra lekage. Exactly like this bullock.
Nipạṭ seta leka. Exactly like a dog.
Nipoṭ kul lekae ńeloḱkana. It looks exactly like a tiger.

Niphoṛ. Having only one stalk, not producing shoots from the roots.

Niphuṭ. Sound, flawless, without defect, without blemish.

Nipoṭ. Cf. nipạṭ.

Niptạu. To settle, to finish, to bring to a conclusion.
Niptạukedako bapla. They brought (all the ceremonies connected with) the marriage to a conclusion.

Nipun. Skilfull expert, clever, handy.
Sanamaḱre nipungeae. He is clever at everything.

Ńir. To run, to flee, to flit, to disappear, as the moon.
Ńir haparao. To run a race to see who will win.
Ńir boloḱ bạhu. A woman who has installed herself in a man's house as his wife.
Ńir cando. The moon just gone or disappeared.
Nirjao cando. The moon with 3 or 4 days still to run.
Cando tise ńira? When will the moon disappear?
Ńir bạgiaḱkoae. He went away and left them, he ran away from them.
Laga ńirkedeako. They drove him away.
Nirenae. He has fled.
Noa ato khonko ńirena. They have left this village.
Ńirateye heć goćena. He arrived at the run.

Nirạ. }
Nirạla. } Pure, unadulterated, unalloyed.
Nirola. }
Nirạ kuindi sunum. Pure mahua oil.
Nira sona. Pure gold.

Nirạị. Peace, without care or anxiety, secure.
Nirạite jom johme. Eat your food without anxiety.
Mạńjhi nirạigeae, khube arjaoakaḱa. The village chief is without anxiety, he has had good crops.
Nirạị mone. A heart or mind at peace.

Nirạla. Cf. nirạ.

Nirạs. To be disappointed, to be without hope.
Nirạsenań. I am disappointed.
Nirạs utạrkedińae. He made me utterly hopeless, he left me not a shadow of hope.

Nirbạh. Fare, daily fare.

Nirbạḱ. Foolish, ignorant.
Nirbạḱ gidrạ kanae. He is a foolish child.
Nirbạḱ mara gidrạ roṛaḱ dhej do bạnuḱtaea.

Nirbhạ. Cf. nimbhạ.

Nirbhoe. Fearless, intrepid.

Nirbhuj. Incomprehensible, unintelligent.

Nirbis. A spice resembling ginger.

Nirbis. Poisonless.

Nirbis. A small plant so named.

Nirbodh. ⎫
Nirbudh. ⎬ Foolish, ignorant, unintelligent.
Nirbudhi. ⎭

Nir budhigeae. He is ignorant, or he is foolish.

Nirbŏs. ⎫ Childless, without descen-
Nibŏs. ⎬ dants.

Nirbŏsoᵺam. You will be without a descendant.

Nirbos. Weak, without strength or vigour.

Nirdae. ⎫ Absolutely, altogether, to-
Nirdąi. ⎬ tally, completely, wholly, without doubt.

Nirdae cabaentalea. Our (supply of food) is altogether exhausted.

Nirdand. ⎫
Nirdandi.⎬ Without care or anxiety.

Nirdhok. Without restriction, without stint, intensifies the action to which it refers.

Nirdhokko dalkedea. They beat him unmercifully.
Nirdhokko emaᵵlea. They gave us without stint.

Nirdom. Breathless.

Nirdos. ⎫
Nirdosi. ⎬ Faultless, blameless, inno-
Nirdusi. ⎭ cent, not guilty.

Iń doń nirdosgea, oeᵵ hŏ bań menakawaᵵkoa. I am innocent, I have not said anything to them.

Ńire hojor. ⎫ Quickly, rapidly, without
Ńire hojore.⎬ delay.

Ńire hojore heᵭ goᵵenae. He came quickly.
Nire hojor calao hodoᵵme. Go quickly.

Niret. To substantiate.

Nirghin. Woe begone, depressed, dispirited, disfigured by grief, &c.

Nirghine ńeloᵺkana. She looks woe begone.

Nirhi. Cf. lindhi.

Nirik. ⎫ Rate, price current, tariff,
Nirikh. ⎬ allotted task, to fix rate,
Niruk. ⎬ price current, tariff or allot-
Nirukh. ⎭ ted task.

Dor ąuriᵺo nirika. They have not yet fixed the rate.
Aleaᵺ nirik do cąukęre bar anna. Our rate is two annas per chauka (100 cubic feet.)

Ńirjao. ⎫ The last three or four days
Ńirjąu. ⎬ of the fourth quarter of the moon.

Ńirjaokoteye hijuᵺa. He will come within the last 3 days or so of the moon.

Nirjhum. Cf. nijhum.

Nirmoli. A kind of fruit employed to clear water.

Nirogi. ⎫ Sound, healthy, untainted,
Nirugi. ⎬ without disease, infirmity, ailment or malady.

Nirugigeae. He is of sound constitution.

Nirola. Pure, unadulterated, without admixture, without obstruction.

Nirola hende. Pure black.
Nirolam beńgeda. You will see clearly.

Niron. ⎫
Niron din. ⎬ The hot weather.

Nironreko silaᵺa. They ploughed it during the hot weather.
Niron setoń. The hot weather.

Niropon. To ascertain, to determine; safely, well.

Tinąᵺ sąńgińgea, onąle niroponakaᵵa. We ascertained how far it is.
Niropone ńam ruęᵲkede teᵲoń. Because he received him again safe and sound.

Niros. ⎫ Inferior in degree or size, less,
Nirosa. ⎬ under.

Noa joᵲo khon noa do nirosgea. This share is smaller than this one.

Nirot. Breezeless, still, calm, windless.

Nirotrebon umoᵺa. We will bathe where there is a calm.
Nirot setoń. Breezeless heat.
Nirotkateye daᵺkeda. It rained without wind.

Ńirphor. To escape, to leave abruptly.

Motgeń ńirphoᵲena. I escaped with difficulty, I got away with difficulty.

Nirugi. Cf. nirogi.

Niruᵺ. ⎫ Cf. nirik. To settle, to decide,
Nirukh.⎬ to determine.

Hor bae niruᵺ daᵲeaᵵteye teńgo thirena. Not being able to decide which road (to take) he stood still.

Nisą. An intoxicant or narcotic, such as opium, ganja, alchohol, &c.

Nisą lagąoąkawadea. He is intoxicated, or is under the influence of a drug such as opium, ganja, &c.

Adom hoᵲ do ąphim nisąko kusiaᵺa, ar adom do pąurę nisą. Some men prefer intoxication by opium, and others that by alchohol.

Nisąn. A mark, as on a target, to make a mark.

Nisana Token, sign, proof.
Ceť nisanam aguakaťa? What token have you brought?

Nisand. Solid, sound, without flaw.
Nisandgea baṅ khola. It is solid, it is not hollow.

Nisarthi. False, untrue.

Nisarthi. } Without a protector or
Nisarti. } guardian.

Nisas. Breath.
Nisas bondentaea. His breathing has ceased.

Niscae. } Certainly, truly, without
Niscoe. } doubt.

Nised. To forbid.
Calakiṅ menlaka, uniye nisedkediṅa. I intended to go, but he forbad me.

Nisera. Cf. misera.

Niskapat. } Without deceit, sincere,
Niskopot. } without subterfuge.

Nisok. Weak, feeble.

Nisoń. Worn out, fatigued.

Nispetar, Cor. of the English word "inspector."

Nisrau. To chaff, to deride, ridicule, to banter, to upbraid, to chide.
Napae okoćteń galmaraoae kankhan uni doe nisrauktana.
Procarako jokheć adom adom bedin hoṛkoko nisrauka. Some heathen ridicule when being preached to.

Nisrauna. Reproof. Cf. nisrau.

Nista. To confirm, to prove, to make sure.
Cećem nistakeda? What did you find proved?
Kuli nistaem. Ask him to make certain.

Nistan. Token, sign, confirmation. Cf. nisana.
Nistanko uduga. They shew a token (as proof of their statement.)

Nisun. Empty, desolate, tenantless, solitary.
Nisunre senkateko galmaraoana. They went into a solitary place and conversed.
Nisun jaega. A solitary place.

Nit. } Now, at the present time.
Nitok. }
Nitge calakme. Go now.
Nitokgeye hećena. He has just come.
Nit ńokgeń ńelledea. I saw him a little while ago.
Nitenećte hijuka. He will come presently.

Niṭ. To fix, to decide, to settle, to determine.
Niṭ katha banuktaea. He can say nothing definitely.
Kathako niṭkeda. They settled the matter.
Niṭ okteko. Fixed times or seasons.

Nite. Dirty, filthy.
Nite gendṛak leka. Like filthy rags.

Niti. Absolutely none, not one (used only with negatives.)
Ona disomre Hoṛ nitige banukkoa. There are absolutely no Santals in that country.
Calak nitige banuktakoa. They have not the slightest intention of going.
Napṛak janwar nitige bako odoklena. Not one large animal emerged.

Nitsahi. Exact, truly.

Niuri. A small forest tree, *Elæodendron Roxburghii, W. & A.*

Niyar. } The pass the night lying on the
Niyar. } ground, applied to the village priest's sleeping on the ground the night precediug the Baha (q.v.) festival at which he officiates.
Naeke niyarlen.

Niyẽ. } By means of, owing to, along
Niyẽte. } with.
Am niyẽ noa kaj do hoyoka. By your instrumentality this business will be accomplished.
Am niyẽte hoeakana. It has been accomplished through you.
Am niyẽtegebo calaka. We will go along with you.

Niyõṛ niyõṛ. Applied to the cry of the peacock, (imitative.)
Marakko raga niyõṛ niyõṛ.

No. This.
No parom. This side (of a river, &c.)
No mohol. This region.

Noa. This (inanimate.)
Noako. These.
Noakin. These two.
Noa ṭhenre. In this place.
Noare. In this.

Noaṭak. This one (inanimate.)
Noaṭakiń hataea. I will take this one.

Nobab. } A great man, a prince.
Lobab. }

Nogda. } Cash, ready money.
Nogod. }

Nogda nogdi. Ready money.
Nogda nogdigele emapea. We will deal with you in ready money.

Nohẽ. } To disregard, to disobey.
Lohẽ. }
Kathae nohẽakaťa. He has disregarded the order.

Ńohõṛ ńohõṛ. } Sweetly, entrancingly,
Ńohoṛ ńohoṛ. } applied to sound; beautiful.
Tirioko oroha ńohõṛ ńohõṛ. They play the flute sweetly.
Ńohoṛ ńohoṛko sereńa. They sing sweetly.
Mõṛẽ dare munga naṛak ńõhõṛe ńõhõṛe. Five beautiful munga (q. v.) trees.

Ńohoť. To brush slightly against.
Ńohoťkedińae. He brushed slightly against me.

Nojor. Noṅjor. } To look, to gaze, sight, faculty of seeing.
Ceťem nojoreda? What are you looking at?
Ạdi sạṅgińte nojor calaǩa.
Nojor bạnuǩtaea. He is sightless.

Ńoǩ. A little, used only in composition.
Ṇete ńogoǩme. Come a little nearer.
Ńel ńoǩledeań. I saw him for a short time.
Ale ṭhen heć ńoǩlense. He came to us for a little, he was with us a short time.
Hante idi ńogeme. Remove him away a little.
Reaṛ ńoǩgea. It is a little cold.
Hende ńoǩgeae. He is a little black.
Esel ńoǩgeae. She is fairish.

Noklạhi. Malingering.
Noklạhi ạimại. A malingering woman.

Noǩõe. This, this particular one.
Noǩõetam bakhra. This is your share.
Noǩõe noako. These.

Noǩõeko. These, these particular.
Noǩõeko matkom daretam. These are your *matkom* (q. v.) trees.

Noǩõekin. These, these two particular.
Noǩõekin rukạ bạslatam. These two are your chisel and adze.

Nokol. A copy, to copy.
Rae reaǩ nokol ńama menteń darkhasakaťa. I have petitioned to get a copy of the decree.

Nokol. To sham illness, to malinger.
Nokoleťkanae. He is shamming illness.

Nokor. A servant.
Nokor cakor. Servants of all kinds.

Ńokor cẽṛẽ. Ńukur cẽṛẽ. } A small bird, whose tail continually shakes.

Ńokor. Ńukur. } St. Vitus' dance, paralysis agitans.
Adom hoṛko ńokoroǩa. Some people are afflicted with St. Vitus' dance.

Noksan. Nuksan. } To destroy, to injure, to waste. Cf. loksan.
Ạdi noksan hoeña. There is great injury, great injury has been done.
Noksankeťtińape. You injured my (house, crops, &c. &c.)

Nol. A pipe.
Hukạ reaǩ nol. The hollow stem of the hukạ.

Nolao. To investigate and decide upon, to select, to choose.
Ato lạgiť nolaoakaťale. We have fixed upon a place for a village after investigation.
Gaḍa aṛea menteko nolaoakaťa. They have after investigation fixed upon a place at which to dam the stream.
Bạhuko nolaoakadea. They have chosen a bride.
Bar dhao kaṭhiń nolaokeda, bako aṛaǩadińa. Twice I selected timber, but they did not let me have it.

Ńolhať. Soot, particularly soot deposited by a flame; very black, smirched with soot.
Ńolhaťkedińae. He smirched me with soot.
Ńolhať huriťkate sunumre milạukate aenomko benaoa.

Noljol. To select, to choose. Cf. nolao.
Nui miť din dom noljolkedea, cedaǩem bạgiedekana? You chose her once, wherefore are you forsaking her? (a wife.)

Noman. Neman. } A little way off, here about.
Nomankore giripe. Cut it off about here.

Nomona. Cf. nạmuna.

Noṇḍe. Here, this place.
Noṇḍe tahenme. Stay here.

Noṇḍen. Of or belonging to here or this place.
Noṇḍenko. Those (animate) of or belonging to this place.
Noṇḍenkin. Those two (animate) of or belonging to here or to this place.
Noṇḍenaǩ. The one (inanimate) of or belonging to here or this place.
Noṇḍen renko. Those of this place.
Noṇḍen hoṛko. People of this place or neighbourhood.
Noṇḍenaǩe idikeda. He took away the one that was here.

Ńoṅg. Cf. ńoǩ.
Idi ńoṅgeań. I will take him a little apart.

Nonhoť. Cf. ńolhoť.

Noṅjor. Cf. nojor.
Uniaǩ noṅjor do serma seć. His eyes towards heaven.

Nonka. Thus.
Nonka kạmime. Work thus.
Cedaǩem nonkakeda? Why did you do thus?
Nonka leka alom roṛa. Do not speak thus.
Nonkate calaǩme. Go this way.
Nonka calaǩme. Go thus.
Isin lahaente nonkaena. It has become thus by being over cooked.

Noparom. This side (of a river, &c.)
On parom. The other side, the far side (of a river, &c.)
Barakar noparomreko atoakaťa. They have made a village on this side of the Barakar river.

Nor. Cf. or.

Noraj. Cf. naraj.

Ńõṛāǩ. Loṛāǩ. } Past the meridian, of sun and moon.
Bere loṛāǩena. Bere ńoṛāǩena. } The sun is past the meridian.
Tikin loṛāǩ. Tikin ńoṛāǩ. } About 1 p. m.

Norma. } Soft, to become soft, to
Normao. } decline, to decrease, to become less. Cf. norom.

Dakte lohoťlenkhan normaoka. If it gets wetted with water it will soften.
Ruạ do pạhil khon normaoentaea. His fever is less than it was.
Narmaoakanae rehgeďte. He is weakened through hunger.

Ńor ńor. To be silent, to be taciturn.
Usạť hoṛ ńor ńor baṛaeae. A sulky man is taciturn.
Ńor ńorokkanae. He is silent.

Norok. Cf. narak.

Norom. Soft, to become soft, to decline, to decrease, to become less. Cf. norma.

Noromko dakaakaťa. They have cooked the rice too little.
Khub noromko dakaakaťa. They have cooked the rice nice and soft.
Daṛere noromgeae. He is deficient in strength.
Kisạṛre noromgeae. He is less wealthy.
Noromgeye kạmia. He is an inferior workman.
Dakakkhan noromoka. If water be applied to it it will become soft.
Am khone noromgea. He is inferior to you.

Ńoṛom ńoṛom. } Sweet and juicy, beauti-
Ńoṛoń ńoṛoń. } ful, pleasant to the sight, taste or hearing.

Ńoṛom ńoṛom sebela. It is deliciously good.
Ńoṛom ńoṛom heṛema. It is deliciously sweet.
Ńoṛoń ńoṛońko oroheda. They play the flute sweetly.
Ńoṛoń ńoṛoń sadekana. It sounds sweetly.

Nosib. Cf. nạsib.

Nosṭo. To destroy, to ruin, to waste, to injure, to depart this life.

Nosṭokedape. You ruined it.
Nosṭoenae. He is dead.
Nonosṭoić. The destroyer.

Noṭ. }
Loṭ. } A currency note.

Not. }
Nat. } A nose ring.
Nath. }

Note. Hither, this way.

Note hijukme. Come hither.
Notekme. Come this way, come hither.
Notekediñae. He put me to this way.
Onte note. This way and that, here and there, hither and thither.
Note añjomme. Listen here.

Noten. Of or belonging to this vicinity.

Notenak. Of or belonging to this vicinity, used of inanimate objects.
Notenić. The one of or belonging to this vicinity, used of animate objects.
Notenkin. The two of or belonging to this vicinity, used of animate objects.
Notenko. Those of or belonging to this vicinity, used of animate objects.
Notenko. Those of or belonging to this vicinity, used of animate objects.
Notenak haliń lạiamkana. I am telling you the news of this part of the country.
Notenko hoṛ. The people of this vicinity.
Notenko okoe hŏ bako senlena. No one belonging to this neighbourhood went.

Ńu. To drink.

Ańu. To cause or give to drink.
Jom ńuiak. Food and drink.
Ńu ṭuilạ. To drink to satiety.
Ńu ṭuilạenań. I have drunk to satiety.
Ńu bulenae. He has drunk till he is drunk.

Ńu tehgar. }
Ńu tehgar mạtua. } Slightly intoxicated.
Ńu laser. }

Nonḍenak dakle ńuieda. We drink the water of this place.
Mit́ dak gele jomeda. We use the water of the same place.
Dake ńuana. He has drunk water.

Ńuhum. Twilight, between sunset and darkness.

Ńuhumokkana. Twilight is falling.
Tinrepe seṭerena? ńuhum ńuhumle seṭerena. When did you arrive? We arrived as twilight was falling.

Nui. This, this one, applied to animate objects only.

Nui hoṛ. This man.
Nui ḍańra. This bullock.
Nuigeye hataokeda. This (person) took it.

Nuiṭak. This particular one, applied to animate objects only.

Nuiṭak ḍańrań hataoea. I will take this bullock.

Nukṅi. This one here, applied to animate objects only.

Nukṅi nonḍe ńelepe. This one here is he, look at him.
Nukṅitako ḍańra do. This one here is their bullock.

Nukin. These two, applied to animate objects only.

Nukinkin senlena. These two went.
Nukinak oṛak kana. It is the house of these two.

Nuli. }
Nạli. } Barrel of a gun, pistol, &c.

Bar nuli bạnduk. A double-barrelled gun.
Mit́ nuli bạnduk. }
Ek nuli bạnduk. } A single barrelled gun.

Ńu lolo. To be possessed of a bare sufficiency.

Uni do nalha tumạlkate ńu lolo ocoekan tahĕkana. By working and gleaning he provided him with a bare sufficiency.

Ńulok ńulok. Cf. ńalak ńalak.

Ńum. To name, to call by name, to praise.
Celepe ńumkedea? What name have you given him?
Alope ńum baṛaińa, peṛa doń bah kana.
Ạdiko ńumkedea. They praised him highly.
Ńutum ńumkate hohoaeme. Mention his name when calling to him.
Ma ńumtińpe kudum do. Come, tell me my guess, solve my riddle.

Ńumbạk'. } **Ạyuṕ ńumbạk'.** } After nightfall.
Ạyuṕ ńumbạk'ena.

Ńum ceṅgeť. To name a child after its grandfather.
The child thus named is supposed to inherit the qualities as well as the peculiarities of its grandfather.

Numin. } **Numinạk'.** } So many, so much.
Numinạk' hoṛre hõ bape cabaleda? Although there were so many people did you not finish it?
Numinạk'e hataokeda. He took so much.

Nun. So, so many.
Nun marań. So big.
Nun jeleń. So long.
Nun tiriť. So much.
Nun din. So many days.
Nun serma. So many years.
Nun hoṛ. So many people.

Nunạk'. So many, so much. so.
Nunạk' hoṛ. So many people.
Nunạk' jeleń. So long.
Nunạk' osar. So broad.
Nunạk' nunạk' emakom. Give each so much, so many.
Nunạk' jondra hoeakantaea, ohoe jom caba daṛelea. He had such a crop of Indian corn that he will not be able to consume it all.

Nunạń. So much, so many.
Nunạń hoṛ. So many people.
Nunạń dhon. So much wealth.
Nunạń nunạń dhon tahẽkana cekateko cabakeda? How did they get through so much wealth?

Nunchaha. Saline, as sea water.

Nundi. Cf. lundi.

Nundni. To tell tales, to asperse.
Nundniadińae. He told tales about me.

Nungun. Gratitude.
Nungun bam doholeťtaea. } Nungun bam manaoleťtaea. } You shewed him no gratitude.

Nunu. The female breast, to give the breast, to suckle, to suck.
Nunu gidrạ. An unweaned child, a child still being suckled.
Nunu bele. Mammary abscess.
Nunu ghao. A sore on the mammae.
Mihũe nunukana. The calf is sucking.
Nunuaekanae. She is suckling it.

Ńupum. The Reciprocal form of ńum (q. v.)

Ńur. } **Ńurhạ.** } To fall, to cause to fall, from a height.
Dare khone ńurena. He fell from a tree.
Dare doe mak' ńurkeda. He felled the tree.
Ḍhaka ńurkedeae. He pushed him and caused him to fall (from a height.)
Ul ńuraeme. Knock down a mango for him.
Daṛe do ńurentaea. He has become weak, he is failing (from old age.)

Ńuṛạk'. To hiccough.
Ńuṛạk'enae. He hiccoughed.
Ńuṛạgok'kanae. He is hiccoughing, or he has hiccough.
Jahãeko ńuṛạk'ena menkhanko metakoa, Mạńjhiak' dahem kombṛoakaťtaea. When any one hiccoughs they say to him, you have stolen the Mạńjhi's (q. v.) curds. (The child when accused of theft gets frightened and the hiccough ceases.)

Nursiń barsiń. } **Ursiń barsiń.** } Cf. ạrsiń bạrsiń

Ńũṛũć. A small forest tree, the Indian Laburnum, *Cassia Fistula Linn.*
The flowers of this tree are eaten as a pot-herb, and the fruit yields a valuable medicine.

Ńuruć. } **Ńuruć ńuruć.** } Lean, emaciated, applied to children in ill-condition.
Akalre ńuruć ńurućko asen baṛaetko tahẽkana. In the famine they were carrying about emaciated children.

Ńũṛũ ńũṛũ. } **Ńũṛũń ńũṛũń.** } **Ńuṛuń ńuṛuń.** } To burn feebly, to burn with very little flame, the opposite of burning brightly.
Ńuṛuń ńuṛuń sengel menak'a. There is a very feeble flame.
Ńũṛũ ńũṛũ jolok'kana. It burns feebly.

Ńuruń ńuruń. } **Ńarań ńuruń.** } To whine, to beg whiningly, to importune, to beg hard, importunately and whiningly.
Reṅgeć gidrạ ńuruń ńuruńko koea. Hungry children beg whiningly.
Jom lạgiť ńarań ńuruńok'kanae. He is whining for something to eat.
Ńuruń ńuruńok'ako. They importune.

Nuruť. Cf. uruť.

Nusib. Cf. nạsib.

Ńut. Dark, darkness, to become dark, to darken, to cause to become dark.
Ńutok'kana. It is getting dark.
Ńutgea. It is dark.
Ńutena. It has become dark.
Alom ńutea. Do not make it dark for him.
Kaṛań kaṛań ńut. Pitch darkness.
Ńindạ leka ńutena. It was dark as night.
Ńindạ ńut. The darkness of night.
Ńut ńindạ. The dark night.

Ńutạt. The time between nightfall and the rising of the moon, applied only to the wane of the moon.
Netar doe ńutạteda.

Ńuṭuk̇ ńuṭuk̇. Very sweet, delicious.
Ńuṭuk̇ ńuṭuk̇ sebela. It tastes delicious.
Ńuṭuk̇ ńuṭuk̇ heṛema. It is deliciously sweet.

Ńutum. Name.
Mul ńutum. Real name.
Cetan ńutum. A to-name, the upper name, the name one is known by to prevent the real name being used.
Latar ńutum. Real name.
Bahna ńutum. A nick name.
Ńutumte. For the sake of, for the purpose of, by name.
Itạ ńutumteko baekȧka. They store it for seed.
Ńutum tahentama. Your name will be remembered, or will continue.
Ńutumteće jomkeda. He only ate in name, he only ate every little.
Ńutum dohoe. To name, to give a name to.
Ńutum ńum. To mention the name.
Ńutum marańok̇tama. Your name will be great.

O

O. An exclamation of anger, or defiance.

O. A privative prefix, not, without.
Odhorom. Unrighteous, unholy, unjust.
Olekha. That cannot be counted.
Obicạr. Unjust.
Onese. Unjust.
Obiswas. Faithless, unbelieving.

Oar. To take or pull out of, as out of water, a pit, &c., to skim, as cream off milk or oil off water, to rescue, to deliver.
Nạinu oarme. Skim off the cream.
Gaḍakhonko oarkedea. They pulled him out of the river.
Nui do gạr khone oarkedińa. He rescued me from difficulty.
Ok̇warić. Rescuer, deliverer.
Dạlạhi khone oarkedea. He rescued him from the bog.

Oaṛa Murmu. A sub-sept of the Santal sept Murmu (q. v.)

Oạris. Helper, owner, heir, claimant.
Nui ren oạris bạnuk̇koa. He has no heiṛ.
Nui ḍańgra ren oạris bạnugićte lilạmok̇ae. As there is no one to claim this bullock it will be sold by auction.

Obhok̇ obhok̇. Excessively, extremely, applied to corpulency.
Obhok̇ obhok̇e moṭaakana. He is extremely fat.

Obidhạn. A dictionary.

Obidhan. Unaffected by adverse supernatural influence.

Obobo. Excessively fat, with folds of flesh, idle.
Oboboe moṭaakana. He is excessively fat.
Duṛuṗ obobok̇anae. He is sitting idle.

Obor. To lie down, to fall down, to collapse, to squat, as a hare; to sit on eggs or over chickens, as a hen.
Pusi oborakanae. The cat is crouching down (about to spring at something.)
Eto ḍańra oka doko obork̇a hamalte. Sometimes bullocks that are being broken in lie down owing to the weight (on their necks.)
Kulại obọrakanae. The hare is squatting.
Sim do beleye oboreda. The hen is sitting on eggs.
Hoste oṛak̇ oborena. The house has collapsed with the wind.
Uni hoṛ do pinḍạre oborakanae. That man is sitting in the verandah.
Obor sãoha. To lie down through fatigue.
Jaṛao ḍańra doko obor sãohạk̇gea.
Alań oborgetaea. He is tongue tied.
Alańge oborentaea bae roṛ daṛeak̇kana. His tongue is fixed, he cannot speak (indicating the point of death.)

Obor Kisku. A sub-sept of the Santal sept Kisku (q. v.)

Obor Hãsdak̇. A sub-sept of the Santal sept Hãsdak̇. (q. v.)

Obor Murmu. A sub-sept of the Santal sept Murmu (q. v.)

Obor Hembrom. A sub-sept of the Santal sept Hembrom (q. v.).

Obor Mạrnḍi. A sub-sept of the Santal sept Mạrnḍi (q. v.)

Obor Soren. A sub-sept of the Santal sept Soren (q. v.)

Obor Ṭuḍu. A sub-sept of the Santal sept Ṭuḍu (q. v.)

Obor Baske. A sub-sept of the Santal sept Baske (q. v.)

Obor Besra. A sub-sept of the Santal sept Besra (q. v.)

Obor Pạuriạ, or Pạuliạ. A sub-sept of the Santal sept Pạuriạ or Pạuliạ (q. v.)

Obos. Out of control.

Oboso. Certainly, necessarily.

Obosta. Condition, ill-conditioned, to impair, to ruin, to destroy, to deteriorate, to waste, to squander.
Ḍańra sanamko obostaena. All the bullocks are out of condition.
Cij sanamko obostakeda. They squandered all the property.

Obra. M.
Ubri. F. } Having a pendulous belly.

Õć õć. Grunt of buffaloe.
Õć õjedae kaḍa do.

Ocha. Straw from which the grain has been trodden out by cattle, and afterwards so drawn out as to lay it lengthwise. It is then tied up into small sheaves.

Oco. Causative inflection.
(1) With dative giving sense of "allow."
(2) With accusative giving sense of "cause."
Sen ocoadeań. I allowed him to go.
Goć ocokedeań. I caused him to be killed, or I caused him to die.
Uni ṭhene goć ocoǩkan tahẽkana. He was being killed by him.
Uni ṭhene dal ocolena. He was struck by him.
Kul ṭhene jom ocoǩa. He will be eaten by the tiger.

Ocoǩ. To remove.
Ocoǩ ocoenae. He is removed.
Ocoǩ ocokedeako. They caused him to remove.
Noa do ocogoǩa. This will be removed.
Ocoǩ ńohgoǩme. Remove a little.
Hor khon dareko ocoǩkeda. They removed the tree from off the road.

Ocoṭ. The hump of an Indian bull.

Oḍ.
Aḍ. } To shelter, to protect, to hide, to screen, to veil, to screen from sight.
Sisir oḍre gitićakanae. He is lying under shelter from the dew.
Dare oḍre menaea. He is behind the tree, hidden by the tree.
Meṭ khone oḍena. He is hidden from the sight, lost sight of.
Buru oḍre menaǩkoa. They are in the shelter of the hill.
Ńindạ cando rimilte oḍakanae. The moon is hidden by clouds.

Oda. Damp, moist, wet.
Odagea ot do. The floor is damp.
Odaǩa nahaǩ. It will become damp presently.

Odabạd.
Odabạdi. } To be at variance with each other, to contend, to compete, to strive.
Odabạdiakanakin.
Odabạd geakin. } They are at variance.
Kạmire hõko odabạdoǩgea. They also contend at work.
Odabạdiǩakin. They will be at variance.

Odam. The common Indian otter, *Lutra nair.*

Oda moda. Damp, moist, wet. Cf. oda.

Oḍi.
Uḍi. } Cf. ạḍi.

Odga.
Lodga. } Stout. Cf. lodga.
Odga aesane moṭaakana.

Oḍao. To set, as a snare, trap, net, &c., to lie in ambush, to lie in wait.
Kạti oḍaome. Set up the mark to play at.
Galmaraoae lạgiṭ oḍaoakanako. They are lying in wait to speak with him.
Kulại jhạliko oḍaoakaṭa. They have set a hare-net.
Jal oḍaokate hakoko [illegible] t a net and netted fish.
Lutur oḍao. To listen attentively.
Lutur oḍaope. Listen attentively.

Odhrao. To chip, to remove, to become detached, to carry away parts, as of the ridges of rice fields by water. Cf. odrao.

Odgaǩ bidgaǩ.
Odgaǩ bodgaǩ. } Heavy footmarks, displacing the soil, breaking the surface, as a heavy animal passing over soft soil.
Kul odgaǩ bidgạǩ calao paromakanae. The tiger has passed leaving deeply indented foot prints.
Odgaǩ bidgạǩ pańjạ calaǩkana. Deeply indented foot prints pass this way.

Odgel. Not to the full, short of, insufficient, used in comp. with verbs. Cf. hań.
Ńu odgelaṭań. I have not drunk sufficient.
Jom odgelaṭań. I did not eat to satiety.
Gitić odgelaṭań. I had to get up before I had sufficient sleep.

Oḍo.
Ata oḍo. } To roast, applied to the roasting of beans, gram, and other leguminous fruits, also to Indian corn. Cf. ata.
Jonḍra seńgelreko oḍoea. They roast Indian corn in the fire.
Ata oḍoaǩko emaṭlea. They gave us roasted food (a hasty preparation.)
Oḍo baṛaabonpe. Prepare food for ourselves by roasting (gram, Indian corn, &c.)

Odoe balbal. Very hot, hot and perspiring.
Odoe balbale kạmiǩana.

Odoe padoe. Blowing or puffing out smoke.
Aurige dhuạ̃ odoe padoe giḍiedae.
Rel reaǩ dhuạ̃ odoe padoe oḍokoǩkana. The engine smoke comes puffing out.

Oḍok.
Oḍoṅ. } To put out, to expel, to go out, to extract, to issue forth, to to come out,
Laćoḍoǩ.
Laćoḍoṅ. } To suffer from a bowel complaint.
Laće oḍokoǩkana. He has diarrhœa.
Ṭaka oḍokańme. Become surety for me for a loan of money.
Oḍoṅ calaoenae. He came out and went away, or he has gone away.
Dal oḍoǩkedeae. He beat him out, he beat him and so put him out.

Or oḍohkedeako. They pulled him out.
Ḍaṭa oḍokkatiñme. Pull out a tooth for me.
Oṛak khonko oḍok goḱkadea. They expelled him from the house
Setaḱkhon mit oḍoḥtege menaña. I have been out since morning.
Dhuã oḍokoḱkana. Smoke is issuing.
Oḍokok hor. Way of egress.
Oḍohoḱme. Go out.

Odoṛ odoṛ. Plump and fat, naked and fat, naked and ill-conditioned.
Sukri bạdhiạ odoṛ odoṛko ñir baṛaekana.
Odoṛ odoṛko moṭaakana.
Ekon hoṛmo nui do odoṛ odoṛe dãṛã baṛaekana.

Odor thopor. Dirty, owing to something such as mud, &c., adhering to the person.
Oṛaḱ sanam odor thoporakaṇa, oaḱ bape cikãṛã? The house is all dirty, why don't you clean it?
Sạkṛite gidrạe odor thoporakana, cedaḱ bape arupkaea? The child is dirty with the remains of food sticking to him, why don't you wash him?

Odrao. To chip, to remove, to become detached, to carry away as water the ridge of a rice field. Cf. odhrao.
Ot odraoena. The surface of the floor is broken.
Dare baklaḱ odraoena. The bark of the tree has been peeled off.
Dal odraomealaṅ. I will beat you and peel off your skin.
Bhit khon pilaster odraoena. The plaster has become detached from the wall.
Pilaster ódrao ñurakana. The plaster became detached and fell.

Odra udri. Chipped here and there, parts here and there peeled off, pieces here and there detached, broken in places.
Daḱte odra udrikedae. The water broke down (the ridge of the rice fields) in many places.

Odroḱ. Fat, corpulent.

Odṛoṅ. } Naked, uncovered.
Ondṛoṅ. }
Odṛoṅe gitiċakana. He is lying without a covering.
Ondṛoṅe ñeloḱkana. He is naked.

Oghe. } To ask, to demand dues,
Oghe oghe. } as a chaukidar, blacksmith, cowherd, &c., who are paid once a year.
Oghe baṛaeẽdae. He is collecting his dues.
Oghe oghe emoḱ hoyoḱtiṅa. I must give to all who have a right to demand dues in proportion to that right.
Oghe oghe ohoṅ emlema. I can't give to you by computation (as if you had a claim upon me.)

Ogher. Unconscious, insensible.
Ogher goćenae. He became insensible.

Ogor ogor. } To move as one out of
Ogur ogor. } breath and fatigued,
Agar ogor. } used mainly of ani-
Egor ogor. } mals run down at a hunt, to move as a very unwieldy person.
Ogor ogor baṛaekanae.
Ogor ogorenae. He is tired and out of breath.

Ogor. } To give liberally, or generously.
Ugur. }
Ogoroḱkantaea ti. His hand is becoming liberal, he is giving liberally.

Ogoroj. } Having no desire for, no
Ogorji. } appetite or relish for, not to be in need of, be indifferent.
Jojome ogorojoḱkana. He has no appetite for food.
Ogorjigeae. He has no desire for it.

Ograo. To wait, to lie in wait, to lie in ambush.
Gidrạ heokate tinkhon oċhe ograoakana.

Oh. } An exclamation of pain or
Uh. } sorrow.
Oh! noape bạṛiċkeda, rạpuḱkedape. Oh dear! you destroyed it, you broke it.
Ñindạre cedaḱem ohoheć tahẽkana? Ḍaṭa hasoḍiñ tahẽkanteṅ ohohlaḱa. Why were you calling out oh! oh! during the night? I called out oh! oh! because I had toothache.

Ohae. An exclamation of surprize, sorrow or pain.
Ohae! goċentaeae ḍaṅra do. Alas! his bullock is dead.
Ohae! nonka doṅ andhalena. Oh, dear me! I was so blind.
Ohae! ceṫiṅ cekaea? Oh dear! what shall I do?

Ohae hae. An exclamation of surprize, sorrow or pain.

Ohdar. Big and stout with a long stomach.

Ohdar. A Zemindary official who assists the ḍihdar in his work among the villages.

Ohjao. To prove, to explain, to drive home.
Ohjaoaleme. Explain it to us.
Noa reaḱem ohjaoa, endeñeċle chuṭimea. You will prove this, then we will set you at liberty.

Ohjar. Big-bellied.

Ohma. } To infer, to deduce, to derive
Ohman. } as a consequence.
Unkinaḱ kathateṅ ohmakeda unkin bõ onḍekin calaḱkan tahẽkana. I inferred from their words that they also were going there.
Ohmatele roṛeḱkana. We are speaking inferentially.

Oho. A negative employed in conditions, an assuring or emphatic negative, (generally used with the form in le or len.)

Ohowa, nonka oho hoelena.
Ohoteť. Emphatic negative.
Ohoteť geń senlena. I cannot possibly go.
Ohogeń em dareleа. I cannot give.
Ohoko dallema. They will not beat you.
Gel ṭaka dom emkeńa? Ohowa. Can you give me ten rupees? No.
Ohotoben gujuǩa. You shall not surely die.

Ohoć. A piece of broken earthen ware put to several uses.

Ata ohoć. } A piece of broken earthen ware in
Aǩta ohoć. } which grain, &c. is roasted.
Sehgel seć ohoć. A piece of broken earthen ware used to hold fire under a bed
Hako aǩreć ohoć. A piece of broken earthen ware used to bale out water to catch fish.
Kanḍa rạpuťlenkhan onageko sehgel eć ohoja. When a waterpot is broken they make it into a holder of fire to put under a bed.

Ohoe. To pass the hand over a waterpot that has been dipped in water to remove the water adhering to the outside.

Daǩko ohoe giḍia. They wipe off the water with the hand.
Ohoekateko dipila. They wipe off the water off the waterpot with the hand and then put it on the head.

Õhõǩ. } No, emphatic with a shake of
Ẽhẽǩ. } the head, an emphatic negative.

Ohomao. } Cf. ohma.
Ohman. }

Ohra. } To lessen, to decrease, to
Ohrao. } subside.
Ohṭao. }

Barakar daǩ ohraoǩkana. The water in the Barakar river is subsiding.
Ḍherge molena, ohrao ńoǩakana. It was greatly swollen, it has subsided a little.
Ạuri ohraoǩa. It has not yet begun to subside.
Ohraǩkana. It is decreasing.
Ohṭao din. The shortened day.

Oi. A reply to a call, yes, what is it?

Jahãepe hohoaekhane oi goḍa. If you call to any one he will at once say, what is it?
Onḍe khone oi oiyoǩkan, heḍge bae hijuǩa. He calls out from there yes, yes, but he does not come.

Oj. Reasonable amount, to prove, ascertain.

Oj leka emaeme. Give him like a reasonable amount.
Oj mạphik. } Reasonable, equitable, fair.
Oj mạphit. }
Noa katha iń do oj bạisạuańme. Prove this statement to me.
Noa reaǩ oj tinạǩ hoyoǩa, ona emańme. Give me what would be a reasonable amount for this.
Niạ khonge oj barakedale.

Oja. } Substitute, exchange.
Uji. }

Noa reaǩ ojań emama. I will give you an exchange for this.

Ojạt. } To put out of caste, put out of
Ojạtia. } caste.

Ojạtkedeako. They put him out of caste.
Ojạtią hoṛ kanae. He is a man who has been put out of caste.

Ojha. A medicine man, a charm doctor, an exorcist, a diviner.

Ojha. A piece of twine with a knot on it used to keep the net work of a bed in place while being woven, a piece of rope wound round the straw of a *bạndi* (q. v.) while being filled with rice.

As the weaving progresses and as the *bandi* is filled the ojha is moved forward or upward.

Ojhṛao. To lose flesh, to contract.

Lać ojhṛaoentaea. His stomach is contracted.
Ruạ ojhṛaoenae. He has lost flesh through fever.

Ojo. A boil.

Ojo reań dar. The inflamed surface round a boil.
Ojo posaǩentaea. His boil has burst.
Ojo baltaepe. Pierce his boil with a red hot iron.
Marań ojo. A carbuncle.
Ojoakanae. He is suffering from a boil or boils.

Ojoǩ. To anoint, to rub on, as oil, &c.

Ojoǩ sunum. Oil for anointing purposes.
Sunum ojoǩ jońkanae. He is anointing himself with oil.
Bohoǩre sunumko ojoga. They oil the hair, rub oil on the head.
Ranko ojoǩakawadea. They have applied healing ointment to him.

Ojoǩ jalať. } To incriminate, to blame.
Ojoǩ japaǩ. }

Ạuṛiaǩtegeko ojoǩ japaǩańkana, noa reaǩ ceť hõ bań badaea. They are falsely incriminating me, I know nothing of this.

Ojon. Medicine, medicinal ointment, to weigh.

Ojon lagaoeme. Give him medicine, internally or externally.
Ojon baṛe lagaoeǩpe. Put in a reasonable quantity (as salt in food, &c.)
Pạki ojon. 80 tolas to the seer.
Kạci ojon. 72 tolas to the seer.
Ojonadeań. I weighed it out to him.

Ojra. Carelessly dressed, cloth or string round waist too low down. Cf. bojra.

Ojra mare gidrạ.

Ok̀. To smoke, Scottice, to *smeak*; to be burned as food when being cooked by sticking to the pot.

Utupe ok̀ ocokeda. You allowed the relish to stick to the pot when cooking.
Bhugək̀ khon oḍok ocoko ləgit̀ honko ok̀koa. They smoke rats to make them leave their holes.
Culhə sehgelre khub utər mərice khañjoea ar babre khone tol poṭomkae, onkate khub lekae ogea.

Ok̀ Kisku. A sub-sept of the Santal sept Kisku (q. v.)

Ok̀ Murmu. A sub-sept of the Santal sept Murmu (q. v.)

Ok̀ Soren. A sub-sept of the Santal sept Soren (q. v.)

Ok̀ Ṭuḍu. A sub-sept of the Santal sept Ṭuḍu (q. v.)

Ok̀ Baske. A sub-sept of the Santal sept Baske (q. v.)

Ok̀ Besra. A sub-sept of the Santal sept Besra (q. v.)

Ok̀ Cõṛẽ. A sub-sept of the Santal sept Cõṛẽ (q. v.)

Ok̀ Pauriạ se Pauliạ. A sub-sept of the Santal sept Pauriạ or Pauliạ.

Oka. What, where.

Okaenae? Where is he?
Okañ metat̀mea, ona do alom ləi bəṛaea. Do not tell that which I told to you,
Okare tahẽkana? Where was it?
Okakhonko hećakana? Where have they come from?
Oka reak̀ kana? Where does it belong to?
Oka ren kanae? Where does he belong to?
Oka senteye hećena? How did he come? By which way did he come?
Ṭeṅgoć okakedam? Where did you put the axe?
Oka okatepe dạṛẫleda? To what places did you go?
Okako katha reak̀? About what matters?
Okage bań disə hoḍok̀kana. Nothing whatever is remembered.
Oka həbićpe taṛamlak̀a? How far did you go?
Oka ṭhenpe ńelledea? Where did you see him?
Oka okateye hećena? How did he come?

Oka bate. An exclamation of surprize, how is it!

Oka bate cohe kəmi cabaket̀? How is it that he finished the work?
Oka bate cohe sen heć goćena? How is it that he went and came so quickly?
Oka bate coe eṛekediña. How is it that he deceived me?
Oka bate cohem jomket̀? How is it that you ate it?

Oka bhạg. } What chance, by what
Oka bhạgte. } chance, fate or fortune, by chance.

Oka bhəge bańcaok̀a? What chance has he to get well?
Oka bhəgtelaṅ ńapamena? By what chance have we met?

Okaj. } Useless, worthless, unservice-
Okajuạ. } able.

Okajena. It is unserviceable.

Okako. Which.

Okako dare? Which trees?
Okako ṭakako emat̀mea, onako doho johme. Keep the money which they gave you.

Okakin. Which two.

Okakin oṛak̀? Which two houses?
Okakinem kusiak̀kana, onakin hataome. Take the two which you are pleased with.

Okaleka. } How, in what way, in what
Okalekate. } manner,

Oka lekakedae? How did he do it?
Oka lekate calaoenae? By what way did he go?
Oka leka hõ bań. In no way whatsoever.
Oka lekakatem ṭaulok̀kana? How do you earn a living?

Oka lekan. What kind, what manner, like what.

Oka lekan hoṛe tahẽkana? What manner of man was he?

Oka dhạbić. } Up to where, how far.
Oka dharić. }

Oka dhəbićem senlena? Up to where did you go?

Okare. Where, in what or which place.

Okaṭak̀. Which one, inanimate.

Okaṭak̀em hataoa? Which one will you take?

Oka ṭhen. } Which or what place, in
Oka ṭhenre. } which or what place.

Oka ṭhen tahẽkana? Where was it?
Oka ṭhenem ńelledea? In what place did you see him?

Oka seć. } Which direction, which side.
Oka sen. }

Oka sene calaoena? In which direction has he gone?

Oka dara. } Which direction, which
Oka ṭotha. } neighbourhood.

Ona ato oka darare menak̀a. In which direction is that village?

Oka tora. How, by which way.

Oka toram hećena? By which way did you come?
Oka toram senok̀a? By which way will you go?

Oka utaṛ. To what particular place, to what distance.

Oka utərem calak̀a? To what distance will you go?
Gobindpur tora Katras utəriń calak̀a. I will go by way of Gobindpur to Katras.

Okhulạn. Ugly, unprepossessing.

Oko. } To hide, to secrete.
Okon. }

Okote. } Privately, secretly.
Oko okote. }
Okoǩae. He will hide.
Okoǩkanae. He is hiding.
Okonkanae. He is hidden.
Okore menaea. } He is in hiding.
Okonre menaea. }
Okore lạiaeme. Tell it to him in private.
Okokedeako. They hid him.
Oko okoteye calaoenae. He left secretly.

Okoć. } In comp. with a limited
Okoćte. } number of adjectives and adverbs signifies very, in a high or eminent degree.

Bes okoće ńeloǩkana. He looks very well.
Bes okoćte dohoem. Look well after him.
Ḍher okoć emakom. Give them a large quantity.
Ạdi okoćko tahĕkana. There were a very large number of them.
Uḍi okoće lạiadińa. He told me a great deal.
Ạdi okoć alom joma. Do not eat a great quantity.
Napae okoćtele seṭerena. We reached without [the least mishap.
Aẹma okoćko tahĕkana. They were very many.
Gnṭeǩ okoćko goćena. A very large number have died.
Napae okoćte tahenpe. Live in harmony.
Marań okoć hạthin ńelledea. I saw an extremely large elephant.

Okoe. Whom, who, which.

Okoeko. Who, whom, (plural.)
Okoekin. Who, whom (dual.)
Okoekope hataokeda? Which of you took it?
Okoekinben jomlaǩa? Which of you ate it?
Okoe okoepe tahĕkana? Who of you were there? [those whom you saw.
Okoekom ńelkećkoa, onko hohoakome. Call
Okoeaǩ. Whose (singular) }
Okoekoaǩ. Whose (plural) }
Okoekinaǩ. Whose (dual.) }

Oko eneć. } A children's game,
Oko oko eneć. } hide and seek.

Okoeṭaǩ. Which person, which one (animate.)

Okoeṭaǩem hataoea? Which one will you take?
Okoeṭaǩ reaǩ kana? To which one does it belong?
Okoeṭaǩ ren kanae? To whom does he belong?
Okoeṭaǩben hataokeda? Which one did you take? [died.
Okoeṭaǩ sadome goćena? Which horse has

Oǩ koḍor. } To be smoked in cooking,
Oǩ koḍro. } so as to taste of smoke.

Cedaǩpe oǩ koḍroǩ ocokeda? Why did you allow (the food) to become smoked?

Oǩoǩ. Imitative of the sound produced when one is sick and about to vomit, to retch. Scottice, to *bouk.*

Oǩoǩkanae. } He is retching.
Oǩogoǩkanae. }

Okor. Where.

Okorana? Where is it?
Okorem senlena? How is it you did not go? or you went did you?
Okor okare menaǩa? Where is it?
Am ar alińre okor cet pharak? Where is the difference between you and us?

Okorić. } Where, used only with sin-
Okurić. } gular animates.

Okurić coń okare. Where may he be?
Okurić okare menaea? Where is it?

Okorko. Where, used only with plural animates.

Okorko okare menaǩkoa? Where are they?

Okorkin. } Where, used only with dual
Okurkin. } animates.

Okurkin okare menaǩkina? Where are they?

Okoṭ. } Hinder, to impede, to delay.
Oṭkao. }

Ceť karnetem okoṭlena? Bako em hoťadińa. What impeded you? They did not give to me at once.

Okoť. The crop, craw or first stomach of birds.

Hoṛ okoť. Adam's apple in cases where it is abnormally large.

Okroť. } Short-necked, bull-necked.
Kondo. }

Okroť mara hoṛ. A short-necked rascal.

Okta. To depreciate, to speak evil of.

Hoṛaǩ alom oktawạ. Do not speak evil of people.
Jahăe hoṛaǩ alope okta cintạ baṛaea. Do not speak evil of any person.

Okte. Time, season.

Niạ oktetele seṭerena. We arrived at this time.
Okte machare. At proper time or season.
Okte machare erpe. Sow at the proper time.
Okte okte emaepe. Give to him at proper times.
Okte ạuri seṭeroǩa. The time has not yet arrived.
Ạpuń oktere In my father's time.

Okulạn. Insufficient, inadequate, too little, not enough, not provided with, to want, lack, need.

Kicrićteń okulạngea. I am in want of clothing.

Ol. To mark, to make a mark, to write, to draw patterns, figures, &c.

Jańgateye olakada. He has made a mark with his foot.
Sohraere goṛa duạrreko ola. During the Sohrae (q. v.) festival they draw figures (or patterns) at the door of the cow shed.
Dal olkedeako. They struck and waled him.
Oloǩ paṛhaoǩ ceť johmo. Learn to read and write.
Oladińae. He wrote to me.
Oloǩkanae. He is writing.
Olećkoae. He is writing down their names.

Ol. The condition induced in moist vegetable matter when air is excluded.

Dare bele do baṅ kana, ol bele kana. It has not ripened on the tree, it has been kept in a place from which air has been excluded till it ripened.

Hoṛo cakerege olena. The dhan has heated in the rick.

Ol. To lie down.

Okarem ollena? Where did you lie (pass the night?)

Hoṛmo okarem ollaka? Where did you lay your body (pass the night)?

Ol. A plant cultivated for its root-stocks which are used as an article of food, *Amorphophallus campanulatus, Blume.*

Olahĕt. Damp, moist.

Olahĕt ṭhen tahena. It is found in moist situations.

Olaṅ mocaṅ. Given to eating anything and everything, greedy, covetous, faithless.

Nui do aḍi olaṅ mocaṅ hoṛ kanae. This is a very greedy man.

Olapạlite.
Orapạlite.
Oraparite. } Turn about, by turns, alternately.

Olat. Two small forest trees receive this name, *Grewia vestita, Wall.*, and *Grewia tiliæfolia, Vahl.*

Jaṅ olat. A small forest tree, *Grewia asiatica, Linn.*

Poska olat. A small forest tree erroniously regarded by Santals as of Grewia sp., *Kydia calycina, Roxb.*

Ol bạndhi.
Ol bạndki. } Mortgage, to mortgage.

Noa jaega doṅ ol bạndhiakaṭa. I have mortgaged this rice land.

Olḍhao. To lie down, as on the bare ground, to throw oneself down as when very tired, drunk, &c.

Otre olḍhaoenae. He is lying on the bare ground.

Usạṭenteye olḍhao gotena. Being sulky he threw himself down on the ground.

Olḍhao olḍhaoteye rakeṭkana. He is throwing himself down again and again on the ground and weeping.

Ol goroj. Cf. ogoroj.

Olhan. Damp, moist.

Olhan jaega. A damp place.

Olhanre alom tahena. Do not stay in this damp.

Band latar olhange tahena. It is always moist below a dam.

Oljol.
Onjol.
Onmuk. } Food and drink, to partake of food and drink.

Bae oljoloka. He will not partake of food.

Bam oljollenkhan koljol do tạnukan. If you do not take food, there is no respite for you.

Olkobaha. Foolish, ignorant, imbecile, unintelligent, simple.

Olkopolko.
Ulkhu pulkhu. } Close, oppressive, as a hot unventilated room.

Olkopolko aṭkaroḱkana. It feels very close (in this room.)

Olo. Ignorant, foolish. Cf. orlo.

Olocolo. Restless, moving about, doubting, wavering, fitful.

Alom olocolo baṛaea, nonḍe khonle lagamea. Do not keep moving about, we will drive you away from here.

Mone alom olocoloetama. Do not keep changing your mind.

Oloegotoe. Close after each other, following each other.

Miṭtegeko calaoena oloegotoe. They left in a body following one after the other (in Indian file.)

Bhugạk khonko oḍokena oloegotoe. They came out of the hole one after the other.

Olok. Cf. ol.

Olom jholom.
Oloṅ jholoṅ.
Oloṅ pholoṅ. } Swaggering, acting the gentleman, strutting, neglecting work, lounging.

Oloṅ jholoṅe dạṛã baṛaekana. He goes swaggering about.

Olom jholomkin dạṛãbaṛaekana. They are going about acting the gentleman.

Oloṅ. To be disconsolate, sad, depressed.

Alom oloṅoka. Do not be disconsolate.

Jiwi alom oloṅtama. Do not allow your spirits to fall. (Keep up your spirits.)

Oloṅ jholoṅ. Cf. olom jholom.

Oloṅ oloṅ. Fully employed, as opposed to out of work.

Joto oloṅ olohre menakloa. We are all in full employment.

Oloṅ pholoṅ. M.
Uliṅ phuliṅ. F. } Lounging idly, Cf. olom jholom.

Oloṅpholoṅe dạṛã baṛaekana. He is going about lounging.

Uliṅ phuliṅ baṛaekanae. She is lounging about idly.

Olpoṭaha. Cf. olkobaha.

Olsiť.
Olsiť aṭeť siť. } Fated, irreversible.
Inạǩ rege uniaǩ olsiť aṭeťsiť tabǒkana. He was fated only to get so much.
Hukum nama olsiťena. The order is irreversible.

Ombaǩ. To bend the body forwards from a kneeling position.
Ombaǩakanae. He has kneeled down and is bowing.
Ombagoǩako. They will kneel and bow.
Ombaǩ japaǩ gidrạ. A child beginning to use its legs or to crawl.
Ombaǩ ikṛumko kạmikana. They are kneeling and bowing as they work, for they are working very hard

Ombe.
Hombe. } Call of a calf.

Ome. A large forest tree, ***Miliusia velutina, Horask. fil. & Ths.***

Omon. To spring up, to sprout, to germinate.
Erakaťań, menek ạuri omonoǩa. I have sowed it, but it has not yet germinated.
Omonakana. It has germinated.

Omor. Undying, immortal, perennial, wealthy, always having a sufficiency of moisture so that crops do not die.
Khub omor hoṛ kanae. He is a very wealthy man.
Khub omor khet kana. It is a field the crop of which never dies (for want of moisture.)

On.
An. } Grain, food.
Onge bae pacao daṛeaǩkana. He is unable to digest his food.

On cun. Food.

On jol. Food and drink, to partake of food. Cf. ol jol.
Ạurile onjoloǩa. We have not yet broken our fast.

On muk.
On mukh. } Food. Cf. on cun.
On mukhenae. He has partaken of food.

Onpạni. Food and drink. Cf. on jol.

Ona. That.
Ona oṛaǩre menaea. He is in that house.
Okań dharaolaǩa, onań halakeda. What I owed, that I repaid.

Onako. Those.
Onako ạguime. Bring those.
Okakoń uduǩaťmea, onako emaeme.

Onakin. Those two.
Onakin idime. Take away those two.

Ona leka. Like that.
Ona lekagea. It is like that.
Ona lekaeme. Do like that.

Ona lekan. Like that.
Ona lekangeae. He is like that, he resembles that.
Ona lekanko kanako. They are like that.
Ona lekanaǩ iń ńelkeda. I saw one like that, the one I saw was like that.
Ona lekan katha alom roṛa. Do not say a thing like that.

Onaṭaǩ. That particular one.
Onaṭaǩ iń hataoa. I will take that one.

Oncol.
Ońcol.
Ancal. } Neighbourhood, vicinity.
Noa oncolre bạnuǩkoa. There is none in this neighbourhood.
Niạ oncol renko. Those of this neighbourhood.

Onḍe. There.
Onḍeko jarwaakana. They are assembled there.

Onḍen. Of or belonging to there, or that place.
Onḍenaǩ. That of or belonging to there.
Onḍenić. That one (animate) of there, or of that place.
Onḍenko. Those (animate) of that place.
Onḍenkin. Those two (animate) of that place.
Onḍenaǩko. Those (inanimate) of that place.
Onḍenren. Belonging to that place (animate.)

On dhon. Wealth, mainly of agricultural stock and grain.
On dhon menaǩtaea. He has wealth.

Onḍga.
Oṛnga. } One who kills human beings for the purpose of offering the blood to a malignant spirit, one who offers human sacrifices.
Oṛnga ṭhonga. A piece of hollow bamboo in which the blood of the victim is caught. The popular idea is that the *ondga* catches the blood of his victim in a piece of hollow bamboo and afterwards offers it up at the shrine of his deity.

Onḍioť.
Onḍo. } Foolish, ignorant, imbecile.
Onḍioť mara hoṛ oeťem oekakeda? You imbecile scoundrel what did you do?

Onḍoń. Cf. oḍoń.

Onḍroć. The grunt or low of a buffaloe.
Kaḍako onḍroja.

Onḍyoť. Cf. onḍioť.

One. That which, that, that there.
Onekin. Those two which, those two there.
Oneko. Those which.
One ńelme. Look, that there.
One onage. That one there.
One onḍege menaǩa. That, there it is.
One ona kathań metaťm.a. That thing which I told you.
One unilań ńellede. He whom we saw.
One uni reahiń lạiaťme. About whom I spoke to you.
One okaṭaǩ iń lạiaťme. That which I told you.

Oneao. Unjustly, unrighteously. Cf. neao.
Oneao alom kamia. Do not act unjustly.
Oneaoko bicarkeda. They decided unjustly.

One dhone. Wealthy.
Khub one dhone kisarge menaea. He is a very wealthy man.

Onsoṅ. To be on friendly terms with each other, to be fast friends, to be bosom friends, to be close companions.
Unkin aḍikin oṅsoṅa. These two are bosom friends.
Oṅsoṅte tahenpe. Be on friendly terms with each other.
Am tulué ohoṅ oṅsoṅlena. I will not be on friendly terms with you.

Oṅsa boṅsa. Cf. ạunsa bạunsa.

On jol. Cf. oljol.

Onka. Like that, as that.
Onka kamime. } Do like that, do thus.
Onkaeme. }
Cetlekae tahekana? Onkage menaea. In what condition was he? He is in the same condition.

Onkan. Like that.
Onkangeae uni do. He is like that.
Onkanak. A thing like that.
Onkanić. A (living) one like that.
Onkanko. (Living) beings like that.
Onkankin. Two (living) beings like that.
Onkanak iń koekedea. I asked him for one like that.
Onkanić hoṛ. A man like that.
Onkanko hoṛ. Men like those.
Onkanko ḍaṅra. Bullocks like those.
Onkankin merom. Two goats like those.
Onka leka. Like that, in the same way as that.
Onka lekań ńelledea. I saw him like that, I saw him in that condition.
Cet lekań hukumaṭmea onka lekaeme. Do as I ordered you.

On mahnder. The fourth day counting backwards, four days ago.

Onman. To consider, to deliberate, to estimate, to think about, to make up one's mind, to form an opinion.
Niṅre khet hoyoka onmanre. In my opinion after consideration a dhan field could be made here.
Uni bahuń onmanakadea. I have thought of this marriageable girl as a bride (for my son.)
Noa kathale onmankeda. We considered that matter.
Onmanre bhagegeliń metaca. After, or on consideration we think it good, or right.

Onnot. } Wattle and daub wall.
Onot. }

Onoḍoṅ. Place of emerging or egress.
Munḍu onoḍoṅ. The place of emergence from the jungle.

Onol. A stripe.
Onolanae toṛ do. The squirrel has stripes, the squirrel is striped.

Onol bonol. } Striped, as a tiger, &c.
Onol gonol. }

Onoli. Cf. anoli.

Onot. Wattle and daub wall.

Onparom. On the other side, beyond.
Noparom. On this side.
Naai onparomiń dukana. I went to the other side of the Damuda river.

Onte. Over there, beyond, in that way.
Ontere menaea. He is over that way.
Onteye calaoena. He went that way.
Ontekedako. They put it over there.
Ontekme. Go over there, go away a little in that direction.
Onte khone heċena. He came from that direction.

Onten. Of or belonging to that direction, yonder, that place, or over there.
Ontenak. The one (inanimate) belonging to that direction, &c.
Ontenić. The one (animate) belonging to that direction, &c.
Ontenko. Those (beings) belonging to that direction, &c.
Ontenkin. Those two (beings) belonging to that direction, &c.
Ontenko hoṛko calaoena. The people from over yonder have left.

Onte note. Hither and thither.
Onte note baṛaekanae. He goes hither and thither.

Ontor. Mind, heart.
Ontorre gaḍaoadińa. It impressed itself on my mind.
Ontorge loentińa, uniak kathate. My heart burned owing to what he said.
Ontorre rebet dohoeme. Keep it carefully in mind.

Opat. A small sapling tree or shoot.
Sener lekanak bań maklaka, opatiń maklaka. I did not cut (a tree) like a rafter, I cut a small sapling.

Ophsor. }
Opsor. } Opportunity, leisure.
Aphsor. }
Ohoń senlena, ophsor do bań ńameda? I cannot go, I have no leisure.
Ophsorokkhan iń calaka. If I have leisure I will go.

Opjos. } Bad repute, ill name.
Apjos. }
Uni do aḍi opjose harana. He has got himself a very bad name.
Jos baṛe hoyokma, opjos do alo hoyok.

Opoḍok. Reciprocal form of oḍok (q. v.)

Oponom. A plant of great repute as a medicine, and as a ferment in the manufacture of rice beer, *Angelica glauca, Edgew.*

Oponom. A shoot.
Ot oponom. A shoot springing from the ground.
Dare oponom. A straight shoot springing from a tree.

Opor. To pull against each other, the Reciprocal form of or (q. v.)
Alope opora. Do not pull against each other.

Opor jopor. } **Ora sora.** } Of equal size, of equal age, well matched as regards size or age.
Nukin do mit́ opor jopor hoṛ kanakin. These two are persons of equal age.
Opor joporgeakin. They are equal in size.

Opota. The Reciprocal form of ota (q. v.)

Opotoṅ. } **Optoṅ.** } The Reciprocal form of otoṅ (q. v.), used mainly of males following females when in heat.

Oprad. A fault, a crime.

Opṛadi. Guilty, criminal.

Oprom. Reciprocal form of orom (q. v.)
Ñepel opromko. Acquaintances.
Ñepel opromko kanako. They are acquaintances.

Opsor. } **Apsor.** } Opportunity, leisure. Cf. ophsor.
Opsorok̀ leka. According as opportunity may offer.
Baṅ opsorlena. I had no opportunity, or I had no leisure.

Or. To draw, to pull, to attract, to subside, to evaporate.
Orok̀ko. Plough cattle.
Sutạm or. The operation of setting the warp of a web.
Dak̀e orakaṭa. The water has subsided.
Edre or ruạṛtam. Restrain thine anger.
Sutạmle orakaṭa. We have prepared the warp of the web.
Or tap̣. To draw through, as a thread through the eye of a needle.

Oṛ. To bring into subjection, to punish, to chastise, to get the better of one.
Oṛ mealaṅ. I shall chastise, or punish you.

Oṛ. Beginning, inception.
Oṛ khon galmaraome. Recite from the beginning.
Noa reak̀ oṛ bạnuk̀an. This has not got a beginning, i. e. unintelligible.

Orad. To infer, to guess, to estimate.
Ape oradre tinạk̀ hoyok̀a? In your estimation how much will it be?
Begor oradtegem emok̀kana. You are giving without first estimating (whether there will be sufficient for all.)

Oṛak̀. A house, dwelling place, home, family, to erect a house.
Oṛak̀ hoṛ. } Oṛak̀ gomke. } Oṛak̀ boṅga. } Oṛak̀ ṣimạṛi. } Wife, a housewife.
Oṛak̀renko. Family, members of the household.
Oṛak̀ duạr. House and possessions.
Dak̀ka oṛak̀. A kitchen, a cook house.
Oṛak̀ oṛak̀ renko. Members of the several households.
Catom oṛak̀. } Guḍi oṛak̀. } A pavilion roofed house, a house without gables.
Baṅgla oṛak̀. A house with two gables.
Koṭha oṛak̀. A house with a ceiling of timber and earth.
Dolan oṛak̀. A brick and mortar house with a flat roof, a palace.
Khapra oṛak̀. A tiled house.
Girjạ oṛak̀. A church.
Ran oṛak̀. A dispensary.
Duạra oṛak̀. A roofed shed through which access is had to the street from the court-yard.
Goṛa oṛak̀. A cow house, a byre.
Kạd oṛak̀. A prison.
Kuṛiạ oṛak̀. A small hut.
Sạuṛi oṛak̀. A house thatched with grass.
Thana oṛak̀. A police out-post, a police station.
Nonḍe oṛagiṅ menek̀kana. I intend to erect a house here.
Oṛak̀te senakanae. He has gone home.

Oram. To begin, to set one's hand to.
Noa kạmiṅ oramakaṭa. I have set my hand to this work.

Orapạlite. } **Orapạrite.** } By turns, turn about, alternately.

Or ạsit́. To pull or draw in or together, as a noose, a running knot, a snare, &c. Cf. ạsit́.
Or ạsit́tebon tol goda. We will tie it with a running knot.
Or ạsit́te oḍaome adoe jhạli godok̀a. Set a noose and it will be snared at once.

Ora sora. } **Rod bodol.** } Equal, equally. Cf. opor jopor.
Ora sorakin kạmikana. They are working equally.
Maṅgat hopon ora sora gekin ñelok̀kana.

Oṛȧt́. Beginning, original.
Oṛȧt́ khonge menak̀koa. They have been from the beginning.
Oṛȧt́ren nui kanae. This is he who has been from the beginning.
Onko oṛȧt́ ren doko baṅ kana. They are not the original (settlers.)

Ora uri. Enticed, lured, beguiled, inveigled.
Hoṛ ñelte ora uriko calaoena. By seeing people (go) they were enticed into going.

Oṛe. A quail.

Ore.
Mare ore. } Old, worn out.

Topa ore. Long buried, as rupees, &c.
Giḍi ore. Unserviceable through being worn out, laid aside as being unserviceable.

Oṛeć. To tear, to rend, to cut cloth to sew into a garment.

Oṛećentaea sanam kicrić. His cloth is all torn.
Raboṛ oṛećkedeae. The (bear) rent him with its claws.
Sukri hoṭaḱ oṛećkedeae. The boar rent him with his tusks.
Oṛeć oṛeć kicrić omaṅme. Give me a piece of tattered cloth. (a piece of old cloth.)
Oṛejoḱa. It will tear.

Or daḱ. A method of snaring the Lapwing when sitting on her eggs.

A running noose is hidden in the sand round the nest and when the bird is sitting the noose is pulled by a long string and tightened round her legs.
Ṭeṭeṭeṅgoćko ordaḱkoa belere. They snare the Lapwing when sitting on her eggs.

Oṛe oṛ.
Oṛe oṛpać.
Oṛe ŏṛpać. } From the beginning, full details.

Oṛe ŏṛpaće lạiaṅlea. He related it to us in detail.

Ore ṭikur. Dragging and carrying, as a mother a number of small children.

Ore ṭikurko calaoena.
Sanam gidrạ ore ṭikurko calaoena.

Oṛgo poṛgo. Inefficiently, unsuccessfully, again again but unsuccessfully.

Oṛgo poṛgoko sikeda. They ploughed it inefficiently.
Oṛgo poṛgoe otakedea. He tried to hold him down but unsuccessfully.
Oṛgo poṛgoe haṛup baṛaećkana, noa kaṭ do bae goḱ daṛeaḱkana. He is trying unsuccessfully to encircle it with his arms, he cannot lift that piece of wood on to his shoulder (he can't shoulder the piece of wood.)

Oṛhẽ. To praise, to sing in praise of.

Oṛhẽedeako. They are praising him.
Baplare bạhu jawãeko oṛhẽkina ṅutum ṅumate. At a marriage they sing the praises of the bride and bridegroom by name.

Oriao. To repair a thatched roof without fastening down the thatch with bamboo laths.

Nes do oṛaḱle oriao baṛakeda. This year when we repaired our house we just laid the thatch on.

Or jal. A drag net.

Orjon.
Orjon birjon.
Arjon. } Crops, produce of the soil, wealth. Cf arjon.

Oṛjonịạ. Earner, supporter, as of a family. Cf. orjon.

Nui do orjonia kantiṅae, ohoṅ sen ocolea. This is he to whom I look for support I cannot allow him to go.

Orlo. A species of monkey.

Orlo.
Olo. } Foolish, ignorant.

Orlo mara hoṛ. An ignorant rascal.

Orloporlo. In dishabille, dusty, white with dust, disarranged, as garments, looking dejected, sad, ill, sleepy, downcast, out of countenance, as one ill, sad, sleepy, &c., &c., looking out of sorts.

Dal orloporlokedeako. They beat him and covered him with dust (by throwing him to the ground.)
Orloporlo bereć hijuḱkanae. He is coming but has not got rid of his sleepy look.
Dhuṛire orloporlokate ṅiraḙe uni ṭhene hećena. Having rolled in the dust he came running to him.

Oṛmoć. A bug.

Oṛna sạṭ. Unintelligible, muddled, confused, vague.

Oṛna sạṭe roṛeda oka hõ baṅ bujhạuḱkantaea.

Oṛna soṛ. Muddled, confused, as a statement, unintelligible, without beginning or end, vague.

Oṛna soṛ oećlekam roṛeda ?
Oṛna soṛe lại baṛaeda. He muddles what he has to say.

Oṛnga. Cf. onḍga.

Oṛ na pathan. Unintelligible, confused, mixed.

Oṛ na pathan noa katham galmaraoeda. You are mixing up what you are saying.

Oroc. Being without appetite for food, unable to retain food on the stomach.

Oroj. A petition, a representation, to petition, to make a representation.

Orojoḱ kanaṅ. I am petitioning.
Oroj menaḱtiṅa. I have a representation to make.

Orom. To recognize.

Ńel orom. To recognize by seeing.
Aṅjom orom. To recognize by hearing.
Baḍae orom. To know, to recognize.
Ńepel oprom. To recognize each other.
Oromkedeaṅ. I recognized him.

Oroṅ. To blow or play a wind instrument, as a horn, trumpet, flute, &c.

Tiryoko oroṅa. They play the flute.
Ramsiṅgae oroṅeda. He is blowing a rạm's horn.

Orop̣. To pile on fuel.
Khubko orop̣akaṭa. They have piled on the fuel.

Orop̣. A jungle plant, *Costus speciosa, Sm.*

Orop̣ koṭop̣. Nothing, not even the shakings of a bag.
Orop̣ koṭop̣ ceť hõ bạnuťtalea. We have nothing, not even the shakings of a bag.

Oṛpheḍ. Beginning, inception.
Oṛpheḍ khon lạime. Tell it from the beginning, begin at the beginning.

Oṛpher To exchange, to interchange.

Oṛososo. To be benumbed, to look unhealthy, or sickly.
Rabańte oṛososo baṛsekanae. Owing to the cold he is benumbed.

Oṛsa aṛaǩ. A wild plant used as a pot herb.

Oṛseć.
Õṛseć. } To draw in or contract the stomach, with all one's might.
Lać oṛsećkatem heđena.
Lać oṛsejme, bandekamań. Draw in your stomach and I will bind your cloth round your loins.

Orsõṛ. A kind of plant so named.

Orsoṛiń. A medicinal plant of *Curcuma sp.*

Ortho. Meaning.

Oṛtogoṛẽ. On the ground, in the dust.
Otrele gitićena ortogoṛẽ.
Otre ortogoṛẽpe tahenkana.
Kiorićem dhuṛiețtińa ortogoṛẽ.

Ortoť oť. A kind of edible mushroom which is much relished.

Orwal. To curtain, a curtain.
Khạṛkhạṛiko orwalakaṭa bạhu aloko ńelea mente. They have curtained the open palki that no one should see the bride.
Bale ńelledea, orwal esetakadeako. We did not see her, they have screened her with a curtain.

Oṛyo poṭyo. Quickly, getting quickly into position for running, &c.
Toyo do oṛyo poṭyo bereťkate bogeteye daṛkeda. The jackal sprang quickly to his feet and fled fast away.
Oṛyo poṭyoe ńir bereť goťena kulạị do. The hare sprang quickly to his feet and fled.
Hako pakoe ńir bereť goťena oṛyo poṭyo. He sprang quickly to his feet.

Osad.
Osadhi. } Weak, feeble, impracticable, impossible.
Osạdhi cekaeań? What can I do with a weakling?

Osar. Broad, wide, to make broad, to widen.
Osarteť. The breadth.
Kiorić khub osargea. They cloth is of a good breadth.
Osarteť do komgea. It is deficient in breadth.
Gaḍa bebạṛiḍ osara. The river is very wide.
Osaraǩme. Make it broader.
Ạḍiteťem osarkeda. You have made it very broad.

Osmao.
Ojmao. } To lose flesh, to become lean.
Noa karonteye osmao goťena. This disease has caused him to lose flesh.
Ạḍi moṭae tahẽkana, siadete osmaoenae. He was very fat, he has lost flesh by being ploughed with.

Osne. Inferior, not up to the mark.
Sạlisiko osnegetaea. His arbitrators are not up to the mark.

Osne osne. Excellent, good, superior, large.
Osne osne ḍańra menaǩkotaea. He possesses excellent bullocks.
Osne osne sạlisikoe jaoraakaťkoa. He has assembled excellent arbitrators.

Osoć osoć. Heavy, deep, as sleep.
Osoć osoće gitić jońkana.

Osoǩ. To become emaciated, to become lean, to waste away.
Osoǩenae. He has become emaciated.
Osoǩgeae. He is emaciated.
Osogoǩkanae. He is wasting away, or becoming emaciated.

Osombhag. Uncommon, inconsistent, unlikely, wonderful, unexpected.

Osor. To feel a call of nature.
Ṭạnḍi seć osorkedea. He felt a call to stool.
Daǩ seć osorkedea.
Raca seć osorkedea. } He felt a call to pass water.
Am do ceť osoreťmea? Alińdolińjãhãlekaǩgelińn.

Õsõs. Heavy, deep, as sleep.
Õsõse gitićakana.
Õsõse gitićjońa kạmi reaǩ do bae disạia.

Osot. False, untrue.
Oka do kacahạrire osotko roṛa. Sometimes they speak falsely in court.

Osrao. To begin, to take in hand.
Kame osraoakaṭa. He has taken the work in hand.
Baplako osrao lạgiť nes do. They are to take the marriage in hand this year.

Oste.
Oste oste. } Slowly, carefully, gradually.
Oste osteteń emkatama. I will give it to you gradually.

Osṭo ghuṛi.
Asṭo ghuṛi. } Always, continually.
Nui do osṭo ghuṛiye hijuǩkana. This (person) comes continually.

Osuk. Unwell, out of sorts, indisposed.
Osukgeń ṣikṣueda. I feel indisposed.

Oť. Applied to mushrooms almost without exception, and to several forms of fungi.
Motam oť. A form of edible mushroom.
Ortoť oť. Do
Kəṛwəpaṭka oť. Do
Sim oť. A form of edible mushroom of a red colouṛ.
Murum oť. A form of edible mushroom. It is taboo to the Murmu sept of Santals.
Kisni oť. A form of non-edible mushroom.
Biń oť. Do
Tormaṛ oť. A form of edible mushroom.
Piskə oť. Do
Muci oť. Do
Oṭeć oť Do
Gopha oť. Do
Hasa oť. Do.
Dak̕ məṇḍi oť. Do
Həthi oť. A form of mushroom seldom eaten.
Tumbə oť. A form of edible mushroom.
Sagak̕ oť. Do
Seta puṭkə. } Seta oť. } Do
Roṭe oť. } Roṭe puṭkə. } An edible form of puff ball.
Hoṛ puṭkə. } Erok̕ puṭkə. } Do
Ponḍ kaṭ oť. An edible form of fungus which grows on timber.
Hende kaṭ oť. A non edible black fungus which grows on timber.
Arak̕ kaṭ oť. A non-edible red fungus which grows on timber.
Mãť oť. } Mať oť. } An edible form of fungus which grows on the bamboo.
Huruť oť. A non-edible fungus which grows on the stumps of trees left in the ground.
Sisir oť. A form of edible fungus which grows on wood.

Ot. World, earth, soil, ground, floor of a house.
Ot serma. Earth and heaven, the earth and heavens.
Ot sermae ok̕gerkana, ipil hõe goťeť koa. She scolds the earth and heaven, she also plucks the stars.
Ot khet. A complete farm comprising all kinds of land.
Sebel ot. Fertile soil.
Bel ot. Level ground.
Roḍgo dhiri ot. Gravelly soil.
Hasawan ot. Good soil, land, with soil in it.
Khaṅgoṭ ot. Barren soil.
Gitil ot. Sandy soil.
Dhiri ot. Stony soil, stony ground.
Muṭkuri ot. Gravelly soil.
Hende ot. Black soil.
Koṭko ot. Soil on a knoll.
Buru ot. Hill soil.
Lipindić ot. Mica schist soil.
Ot laṛaolenre oṛak̕ ruṗentaea. His house collapsed when the earthquake occurred.
Ot odagea. The floor is damp.

Ot ḍhompo. A small perennial plant *Lepidagathis cristata, Willd.*, with inflorescence resembling a ball.

Ot kondro. A small leguminous plant, *Cassia mimosoides, Linn.*

Ot poraeni. A small acquatic fern, *Ophioglossum vulgare, Linn.*

Ot ṭipoć. A small bulbous plant so named.

Ot muruṗ. A small leguminous plant *Flemingia nana, Roxb.*

Ot kuṇami. Cf. kuṇami.

Ota. To press down, to pounce upon and press down, as a cat, tiger, &c. &c.
Ota tabere calak̕kana. He is moving on his hands and knees, or knees and elbows.
Ota gitićkedeae. He pressed him down into a recumbent position.

Otahole. } **Otahuli.** } With an interval of a day or two, one after another.
Otaholeko loena. They were burned out within a day or two of each other.
Otaholeko kombṛokeťkoa. Thefts occurred within a few days interval.
Peṛako hećadińa otahole. Visitors came within a day or two of each other.

Oṭak̕. To remove, to put out of the way, to uncover, to open, as a book, to remove a covering, lid, &c., to turn over.
Simpe oṭak̕ goťkadea. You removed the covering from off the hen.
Daka oṭak̕kateye jomkeda. He removed the covering and ate the boiled rice.
Parda oṭak̕leenećem paromok̕a. You must push aside the parda before you can pass.
Parda oṭak̕kateye paromena. He pushed aside the parda and passed through.
Hoete oṭak̕ oṭak̕ ṭanḍikedae. The wind carried away all the thatch off the house.
Kitab oṭak̕ baṛae oṭak̕ baṛae oṭak̕ ńamkedań. Turning over the pages I at last found the place.

Oṭań. To be carried by wind, to be blown, to be blown away.
Hoete oṭańena. It was blown away by the wind.
Sakam leka oṭańena. It was carried away by the wind like a leaf.
Peṭećko oṭań gidia. They blow or fan away the chaff.
Jiwi oṭań goťentińa botorte. My spirit was blown away by fear, I was appalled.
Oṭańanae. He has been carried off, (absconded.)
Il oṭańok̕a. A feather will be blown away, or a feather will blow away.
Oṭań hećena. It was blown hither.

Oṭaṅ polaṅ. Bare, empty, the feeling of emptiness after the dispersion of a crowd, the gathering in of the crops, &c., &c.,

Ote. } Listen, hear, people say, I hear,
Otea. } I am told, I am led to believe.

Seri ote haṭhi ɔapaṭ giḍiem menlaka? Is it true, as I have heard, that you said you would sling an elephant?
Ote ote, saḍekana. Listen, listen, it is making a noise.
Ote, añjomme. Listen.
Ote, ceṭ saḍekana? Hear, what is making a noise?
Sedaere do oteko mena, tumdak leka jonḍra, ṭamak leka piskạ, ḍeḍger leka kunạm. It is said that in the olden times Indian corn was like the tumdak (q. v.) drum, the piskạ (q. v.) root like the ṭamak (q. v.) drum, and the kunạm (q. v.) root like the ḍeḍger (q. v.) drum.
Ote, na. Listen girl, did you hear that, girl?
Oteya. } Listen, boy, did you hear that boy?
Oteja. }
Otea, oeleko sesreñkana? Hear, who are singing?

Ote torae. Listen.

Ote torae calaoena. Listen, he has left.

Oṭeć. To open, to gape, as a ripe pod, or as roasted grain, with or without a noise., to burst.

Seṅgel oṭeć pạsiroka. The fire will emit sparks.
Ohoere jonḍrako atae jokheć ạḍi oṭejoka.
Kaskom oṭećkana. The cotton pods have burst. [puff ball.
Puṭkạ lekam oṭejoka. You will burst like a

Oṭeć ot. A form of edible mushroom.

Oteṭ. The plain, as regarded from a higher elevation.

Oteṭre menakkoa. They are on the plain, (at the foot of the hill.)
Oteṭ hạbić ńelgoṭkam dele heckana. We are come to convoy you down to the plain.
Buru khon oteṭteko ạrgoena. They have descended from the hill to the plain.

Oṭhṅgao. } To prop, to lean to for sup-
Oṭṅgao. } port, to lean upon, to prop under.

Latarre ḍhiri oṭhṅgaoakme, baṅkhan ńindirko joma. Place a stone under it, or else the white ants well eat it. [the road.
Horre oṭhṅgaoakana. He is lying in wait on
Siṛhiko oṭhṅgaoa bhitre. They lean the ladder against the wall.
Saul aćtege tarwaṛe oṭhṅgaokeṭteye bhoṣa goćena. Saul threw himself upon his sword and was pierced and died.

Oṭhor poṭhor. Tired, uncomfortable, wearied, used mainly with *duṛup*, to sit. Cf. eṭher poṭher.

Oṭhor poṭhor tiṅakbon duṛupkoka?

Oṭkao. To hinder, to delay. Cf. aṭkao.

Oṭṅgao. Cf. oṭhṅgao.

Oṭo. Only used in conjunction with other verbs and conveys the idea of the actor departing after having performed the action.

Bạgi oṭoeme. Leave him and come away.
Doho oṭokam. Put it down and leave it.
Lại oṭokam. Tell it and come away.
Idi oṭokam. Take it there and come away.
Jom oṭokam. Eat and depart.
Ńel oṭokadeae. I saw him (and have come back.)
Em oṭoadeaṅ. I gave to him before I left.

Otoṅ. To follow, to be in heat, applied mainly to cattle.

Gại otoṅokkanae.
Optoṅ ḍaṅgra.

Otoṅ taenom. } One after the other, in
Otoṅ taeom. } Indian file.

Otoṛ. To pull down, to dismantle, to demolish.

Oṛakko otoṛkeda. They took off the old roof, (to put on a new one.) [fence of branches.
Jhạnṭiko otoṛkeda. They pulled down the
Bhitko otoṛkeda. They pulled down the wall.
Oṛak otoṛoka nes. The house will be pulled down this year.

Otor. The warp of a web.

Otor gotor. One after the other, in Indian file, in succession.

Otor gotorko calakkana. They are going in Indian file.

Otor ombak. To lie in wait, to hang about.

Otor ombak ṣour baṛaṇako. They are hanging about waiting for an opportunity.
Otor ombak menakkoa. They are waiting for an opportunity.

Owara. Cheap.

Bes owarae ńamkeda. He got it very cheap.

Owaris. Cf. oaris.

Oyo. } To put on, as a shawl, plaid,
Oyon. } &c., to cover, as with a sheet, blanket, &c.

Oyon kiorić bạnuktaea. He has no cloth to wear as a shawl. [children when sleeping.
Gidrạ gitić jokhećko oyokoa. They cover
Oyo poṭomkate gitićakanae. He is lying completely wrapped up (in a blanket.)
Oyo uṛhu buṛhukateye gitićakana. Having wrapped himself up (in a blanket) he is lying down.

Oyoṅ. To look down, to look into, to look out.

Kũiye oyoṅeda. He is looking into the well.
Oṛak khone okyoṅkana. He is looking out of the house.
Kulạiye oyoṅ ńamkedea. He peered into (the bush) and saw the hare. [in passing.
Ale hõ oyoṅ torakaleme. Look in also upon us
Uni oṛakte noako ạkgupe calak jokheć do buḍhi kumbạ okyoṅ delabon menkate calakpe. When you go to his house to bring these things say, come let us go to peep into the old woman's hut.

P

Pạbli.
Pạblikạ.
Pạblikar.
Pạblikor. } Public works cess, a cor. of the English "Public works."

Pac. To make an incision, to lance, in surgery ; to nick.

Packateko mạlikoako. They make an incision and then cup.
Posta jer oooe lạgiťko paca. They incise the poppy (head) to cause the opium to flow.

Păc. Five

Păc lae pacis lae celate cạţiạte duŗuþlen beţharlen.

Pạc.
Pạchlạ.
Pạclạ.
Pạchuạu.
Pạcuạu. } To recede, to draw back, to give way, to shrink, to abandon, to withdraw.

Miť taŗam pạcoǩme. Recede a step.
Uni hoŗ do ohoe heǿlena, pạclạenae. That man will not come, he has drawn back.
Pạcuạu baŗae kanae. He is wriggling out of it.
Pạcko. Renegades.

Pacaǩ.
Pacaǩ pacaǩ. } To spread out, as anything soft falling on the ground.

Pacaǩ pacaǩko thoeda.

Pacaǩ marte.
Pacaǩ mente. } With a spatch.

Pacaǩ menteye thokeda.

Pacan. A rough fence of branches made to guide hares to where the net is set, a narrow border of double thread on cloth.

Kulại jhạliko jokheǿko pacana. When netting hares they make a rough fence of branches to guide them to the net.
Noa kioriǿ besko pacanakaťa. They have made a good border to this cloth.

Pacao. To digest, to defraud.

Jom pacaokedań. I ate and digested it.
Jomaǩ bae pacao daŗeaǩkana. He is unable to digest food.
Ţakae pacaokeťtińa. He defrauded me of my money.

Pacar. A wedge driven into a wooden pin, wedge, &c. to tighten it.

Bań uriǿlena, pacar lagaoaǩme. It (a wooden pin) is not tight, drive a wedge into the middle of it.

Pacaţi. To make a beginning with rice planting.

Teheńko pacaţiakaťa. They have planted the first rice of the season to-day.

Pace. Cf. pase.

Pacek. Perhaps.

Pacha.
Pacha pacha. } To follow up, prosecute a search, to trace, to track, to put to the proof, to pursue an enquiry, to insist on a matter being brought to proof.

Pachaegeań. I shall insist on the matter being put to the proof.
Nui pacha pachategeń heǿakana. I came tracking him all the way, I followed him all the way.
Ona do okoe hŏ bako pachaeť tabǿkana. No one was prosecuting that matter, no one took any notice of it.

Pachan. To perceive, distinguish, to recognize.

Bạń pachanledea. I did not recognise him.

Pacha pache. One after the other, following each other.

Pacha pacheko heǿena. They came one after the other.

Pachen. Cf. pasen.

Pạchiạ. From the West, applied mainly to rain and wind.

Pạchiạ hoe. A West wind.
Pạchiạ daǩ.
Pạchiạ jạpuť. } Rain from the West.

Pạchiạri. A kind of sore, a pain affecting the side and chest, sores all over the body as in syphilis.

Pạchim. The West.

Pạchim nakha.
Pachim seǿ.
Pạchim sen. } The West.
Pạchim ren hoŗ. A West-country man.

Pạchil. The back part, the stern of a boat, to load too heavily on the back part, as a cart.

Bhạripe pạchilkoda. You have put the load too far back (on the cart.)
Lạukạ reaǩ pạchil. The stern of the boat.

Pạchlạ.
Pạclạ. } The part of a cart, &c, from the axle backwards, to move backwards, backwards.

Pạchlạ ńogoǩme. Move back a little.
Laukạ reaǩ pạchlạ. The stern of the boat.

Pạchlạ sener. Rafters put on a roof with the thick end on the ridge pole.

Pạchli. Cf. pạchlạ.

Pạchli sen. The hinder part, backwards.
Pạchli bela. The afternoon.

Pachmạhi. Belonging to or haling from the West.

Pachmạhi kanao. He is a West country man, or he belongs to the West country.

Pachnao. Cf. pacnao.

Pachoṛ. Cf. pacha.
Unạk' pachoṛ reak' amak' ceť kantama? What interest have you that you press it so much?
Ona katha cedak'em pachoṛeda? Why do you insist on that matter being gone into?

Pạcil. Cf. pạchil.

Pacnao.
Pachnao. } To recognize, to distinguish, to examine.
Noa rog pacnaome. Diagnose this disease.
Pacnaokeťmeañ. I recognized you.

Pacna pạcni. To recognize each other.
Pacna pạcnienakin. They have recognized each other.

Pacpacao. Used always in conjunction with other verbs and demotes sudden, abrupt, forcible action.
Pacpacao calaoenako. They went right away.
Pacpacao kũiḍi holoṅ icena. The kũiḍi (q. v.) flour burst out (through its wrapping in the oil press.)
Pacpacao toťena. It spurted out.
Sen pacpacaoenañ. I went right away.
Bolo pacpacaoenako. They went right in.
Birko pacpacao idikeda. They took the jungle right before them (in hunting.
Noa doṅ kạmi pacpacaokeda. I finished this work right away.
Si pacpacaokedako. They ploughed it right away.
Pacpacao oḍokena. It spurted out.

Pạcri. An enclosing wall, to enclose by a wall.
Pạcri ạcur. To circumvallate.
Pạcriakaťako. They have erected an enclosing [wall.
Ạcri pạcri. Cf. ạcir pạcir.

Padak'.
Padak' padak'. } To bound, to jump.
Padak' padak'e daṛ idikeda. He fled bounding away.

Padak' marte.
Padak' mente. } With a bound or jump.

Paḍạri. Cf. paḍer.

Paḍer. A large forest tree, *Stereospermum suaviolens, D. C.*

Pạḍga.
Pạḍgu. } Coarse, hard, mature, as leaves or herbs too old to be suitable for food.
Haṛam pạḍguena aṛak' do. The herbs are old and hard.

Pạḍgak'.
Pạḍgak' pạḍgak'. } Sudden jump or start as from a bite, prick, &c.
Pạḍgak' pạḍgak'e donkeda. He suddenly jumped several times.

Pạḍgak' marte.
Pạḍgak' mente. } With one sudden jump or start, as when bitten, spurred, &c.
Pạḍgak' marteye donkeda. He gave a sudden jump.

Pạḍgak'.
Pạḍgak' pạḍgak'. } Deep, deeply indented footmarks, displacing the soil, breaking the surface, as a heavy animal passing over soft soil. Cf. odgak' bidgạk'.

Padguṛae. M.
Pidguṛạe. F. } Extremely, applied to fatness of short people.
Padguṛaeye moṭaakana. He is extremely fat.
Pidguṛaeye moṭaakana. She is extremely fat.

Pạdhua.
Pạṛhuạ. } Educated, lazy.
Pạdhuạ hoṛ kanae. He is an educated man.

Pạdlạk. Cf. pạṛlạk.

Padna. M.
Pạdni. F. } Given to passing wind, suffering from flatulence, applied mainly to children.

Paḍra. A wooden cage with bars in front.
Gunḍri paḍra. A quail's cage.
Citri paḍra. A partridge's cage.

Paḍrak'.
Paḍrak' paḍrak'.
Poḍrok'.
Poḍrok' poḍrok'. } An imitative word, the sound produced when the hooka or hubble-bubble is being smoked.
Paḍrak' paḍrak' hukạe ñuñukana.

Pạdua. M.
Pạdwi. F. } Cf. padna.

Pae. A copper or bronze coin one twelfth of an anna.

Paeda. To give birth to.

Paeda merom. A large breed of goats with long, hanging ears.

Paek̃an. A piada or foot messenger.

Paemana.
Pạimana. } A measure.

Paenḍao.
Pạiḍau. } To shampoo, to rub and knead the body, to massage, to knead.
Lahga hecakanae, ma paenḍaokaeme. He has come in tired, massage him.

Paera. To swim.
Paera dak'. Water too deep to wade in, water deep enough to swim in.
Dak'reko paerak'a. They swim in water.
Paera paromok'me. Swim across.
Paera baṛaekanae. He is wandering about, going here and there to keep out of the way.

Pãeṛã. A wooden goad.
Arjan. A goad with an iron point.

Paeraha. M.
Paerahi F. } Expert in swimming.

Paeraha hor kanae. He is a good swimmer.
Paerahi hor kanae. She is a good swimmer.

Päerẽ. An overflow channel of a tank, &c.

Band päerẽ. The overflow channel of a tank or pond.
Oka do dene banar seć päerẽko dohoea. Sometimes they make an overflow channel at each end (of the tank.)
Arekate mit sene päerẽkeda. He dammed it up and made an overflow channel at one side.

Paesa.
Poesa. } A pice, one fourth of an anna.

Paetar. To foretell, or prognosticate by divination, or omens, to augur.

Paetarkate thikakatae nonde menaea mente. He has determined by divination that he is here.

Paetara. Auspicious, a good omen.

Tehen do din kana, paetara dohokakabo. Today is the fixed day we will maintain the auspiciousness (of the forecast of the journey by starting to-day.)

Paeṭhan. A Pathan.

Paeṭhani. Of or belonging to a Pathan.

Paeṭhani ror. The speech or language of a Pathan.

Paeṭhan.
Paeṭhani. } A sore which affects the soles of the feet.

Pagae pugui. To mumble when eating, as one having no teeth, imitative of the sound produced by the Kol iron smelter's bellows.

Pagae puguiko dhukaueda. They are blowing the bellows and producing a sound resembling "pagae pugui, pagae pugui."
Pagae puguiye jomeda.

Pagal.
Pagol.
Pagla. } Mad, demented, humorous, funny.

Pagolenae. He has gone mad.
Pagol hor kanae. He is a funny man.

Pagar. A water channel.

Paghaia ḍaṅra. A pack bullock.

Paghaia nurić, baba, darakokan,
Paghaia nurić, baba, dohoalahme.
Pack bullocks, father, are coming,
Pack bullocks, father, buy for us.
(Sohrae song)

Paghrao. To bring, as rain; to collect as rain in clouds ready to be discharged.

Dake paghraoakata. The clouds are ready to discharge their contents.

Paghraokedae nitok do, ma duhauem. She (cow) has now let down her milk, milk her.

Pagla. M.
Pagli. F. } Mad, demented.

Pagligeae. She is mad.

Pagol. Proficient, expert; mad, demented.

Khubin pagolakatkoa. I have made them very proficient.
Pagolenae. He has gone mad.

Pagra. An ear ring worn in the lobe of the ear.

Makri. An ear ring worn higher up in the ear.

Pagrao. To construct a water channel, to lead water by clearing a way for it. Cf. pagar.

Dakko pagrao idikeda. They led away the water.

Pagur. To chew the cud.

Ḍhekar oḍokkateko pagura.

Paha.
Paha tulạm. } The amount of cotton carded or cleaned at one time by the bow or carding implement.

The cotton having been cleaned is gathered into a ball (paha) and laid aside and a fresh quantity of cotton is then operated on.
Mit pahale pitetkeda. We cleaned one ball of cotton.
Bar paha tulạmle khorockeda. We used two balls of cleaned cotton.
Paha tulạmte lutur tubet esedpe. Stop your ears with cleaned cotton.

Pahalwan. A wrestler, a stout fellow.

Pahapoho. Day-break.

Pahapohon oḍoklena. I started at day-break.

Pahar.

Ḍanḍ okoć pahar okoć.

Pahara.
Pahra. } A guard, a watchman; to guard, to watch.

Paharaedako. They are on guard.
Pahra kanako. They are guards.

Pạhi.
Hora. } A line of the breadth one person can hoe, a tea garden term.

Mimit pạhile pokeda. We each hoed a line.

Pạhil. First, foremost, before, in time or place.

Pạhil porthomre. At the beginning, at the start.
Pạhil hilok.
Pạhil din. } The first day.
Jom pạhilkedae. He ate first.
Pạhilak. The first (inanimate.)
Pạhilić. The first (animate.)
Pạhilteak. The first (inanimte.)
Pạhilten. The first (animate.)
Pạhiltenko. The first ones (animate.)
Pạhil berelko ale kangeale. We are the first settlers.

Hijuk pạhilreń ńelledea. I saw him before I came.
Pạhilten berel hoṛ kanako. They are the first settlers.
Pạhiltenkoko ńamkeda. The first (comers) received.

Pạhilauṭhạ. First-born.
Pạhilauṭhạ hopon. First born child.

Pahlwan. } A wrestler. Cf. pahalwan.
Pahlon. }

Pạhnạ. To visit, to attend a feast.

Pạhnạ. } To make the first sale of the day for cash.
Pohna. }

Pahpahao. To break, as the morning.
Pahpahaokkana. The day is breaking.

Pahra. To guard, to watch; a guard, a watchman.
Pahradar. A guard, a watchman.
Kaṭ aloko maga mente birko pahraea. They watch the forest so that they may not cut timber.

Pahṭa. Side, strip, piece, direction.
Lenga ti pahṭa hasoedekana. His pain is in the left side.
Soṛok khon etom pahṭa. The right side of the road.
Mić pahṭa baṛgeko emadińa. They gave me a strip of garden land.
Purub pahṭare menaea. He is on the west side.

Pahṭao. To square roughly, to rough hew, as a round tree into a log. Cf. pahṭa.
Ṭeṅgoćte pạhilko pahṭaoa, khanko lak cikāṛa. They first rough hew it with an axe, then they smooth it with the adze.

Pạhuṛ. } An animal or fowl intended for a sacrifice.
Pạhur. }
Okatem calakkana? Pahuṛ ńanamiń calakkana. Where are you going? I am going for an animal for a sacrifice.

Pạhuṛ. To be beaten or conquered.

Pại. A measure equal to ½ pạila, or ½ ser.
4 paoa—1 pại.
2 pại—1 pạila, 1 seer.

Pāiḍạu. Cf. paenḍao.

Pạihạ. A disciple, a follower, one who tends Tusser silk worms.

Pạikạha One who knows the pạk (q v) dance.

Pạikạr. A trader, one who buys and sells; to trade.
Ạḍi pạikạre badaea. He knows well how to buy and sell.

Pạilạ. A measure=2 pạis.

Pại mana. A measure. Cf. paemana.

Paimara. To use a short measure.
Nui kisāṛ pai maraećleae. This employer gives us short measure.

Pạiṅgạn. A hollow anklet of bell metal having shot or small stones inside which rattle as the wearer moves.

Pạiṭhạni ghao. A sore which affects the soles of the feet.

Pajao. Cf. pagrao.
Dak ma pajao aderme. Lead the water in.

Pajhaṛ. A species of large vulture.
Buru pajhaṛ. A species of eagle which frequents hilly country.

Pajet. } To trouble, worry, bother, to cause to be wretched, to distress; trouble, worry, bother; wretchedness, distress, affliction.
Pajhet. }
Phajhet. }
Ạḍi sạuko pajhetkedińa. The money lenders troubled me greatly.
Kiorićteń pajhetena. I am in distress for want of cloth.
Oṛak jorokkantakote ạḍiko pajhetokkana. They are suffering much owing to their house leaking.

Pajhet. Cf. pajet.

Pajhrao. } To lose flesh, to become lean.
Pajhṛao. }
Ruạteye pajhraoena. He has become lean through fever.

Pạji. A scoundrel, scoundrelly, base, mean.
Pạji mara hoṛ. A mean rascal.

Pạk. } The sword and shield dance, to dance the sword and shield dance.
Pạk don. }
Pạk eneć. }
Pạkko enećkana. } They are dancing the sword and shield dance.
Pạkko doneda. }
Previous to the disarmament swords were always used, but since then a stout stick has taken the place of the sword.

Pāk. To twist, as when making a rope, to turn; a twist, a turn.
Baber khubko pākakaṭa. They have twisted the twine well (when making it.)
Thoṛako pākakaṭa. They have not twisted it sufficiently
Mić pāke ạcur ocokedińa. He caused me to go and come again before he attended to me.
Mić pāk nahel ạcurme. Plough once round.
Ghur pāk. To cause to turn round, to raise afresh a matter which has been settled.
Nui hoṛ do ghur pāke lagaoeda. This man is raising the matter afresh.

Pāk. } Silt.
Pāk hasa. }
Pāk bạisạuka. Silt will be deposited.

Paka. } **Paki.** } Ripe, efficient, thorough, full, complete, sure, certain, settled, incontrovertible.

Paka gupiió kanae. He is a first class herdsman.
Pạki ser. A seer of 80 tolas.
Paka oṛaḱ. A house built of stone or brick and lime.
Calaḱ reaḱ pakaentabona. Our going is settled.
Paka miḟ candoe tahōkana. } He was a full
Pạki miḟ candoe tahōkana. } month.

Paka paki. To establish an agreement or propositon so that no donbt or subject of dispute can remain; thoroughly, completely.

Khub paka pạkikin galmaraokeda. They settled, or discussed, the matter thoroughly.

Pakaṛ. } **Pakoṛ.** } To seize, to take hold of, to catch.

Iḟko pakaṛkediña. They apprehended me.
Pakoṛanae, se bań? Has he caught any or not?

Pakaṛ. Round about, a place.

Pakaṛ.
Bir pakaṛ. } Wood and brake, bush and brake.
Munḍu pakaṛ. }

Eskar bir pakaṛe daṛana.
Birpakaṛ, munḍu pakaṛ.

Pakaṛe dare. A species of large fig tree, *Ficus infectoria, Willd.*

Pakaṛe tejo. A kind of caterpillar.

Pakas pukus. To be restless, as an infant when hungry.

Pakas pukusoḱkanae. It is restless. (owing to hunger.)

Pake sake. At times, sometimes, now and then.

Pake sakeye hijuḱa. He comes at times.
Pake sakeko omaea. They give to him sometimes.

Pakha. A recess in a wall used as a shelf, &c.

Pakoṛ. Cf. pakaṛ.

Pakoṭ. Ripe, mature, hard.

Pakṛao. To seize, to take hold of, to catch.

Kisạṛem pakṛaoana, se bań? Have you engaged yourself to an employer, or not?
Cedaḱ umul bam pakṛao johkana? Why don't you get into a shade (have some one to protect you.)

Pakre. To hunt up, to search for.

Nonkatele pakre idia. We will search, or hunt in this direction.
Mabon pakre idia, panteḱpe. Come let us hunt, get into line.

Pakṛo. Mature, hard.

Netar do gọchi pakṛoena. At this time the dhan seọdlings are mature.

Pakṛo. Cf. pakṛao.

Pakṭa. } **Pokṛa.** } **Pokṭo.** } Mature, full grown, ripe, in good condition, strong, able bodied, lusty, skilled, efficient.

Pạk ṭanḍi. The place where the pạk (q. v.) dance is performed.

Pãkuạha. Silty, composed of silt.

Òna disom do ɽãkuạha hasa kana. The soil of that country is composed of silt.

Pạkursaḱ. Chubby cheeked, broad, fat faced.

Pạkursaḱe moṭaakana. He has very fat cheeks.
Khube pạkursaḱena. He has very chubby cheeks.

Pal. A ploughshare.

Nahel pal. A ploughshare.

Pal. A herd, a flock.

Gại pal. A herd of cows.
Bhiḍi pal. A flock of sheep.
Pal bhingao. To separate the cattle of different owners from the herd.
Gại doko palentama. Your cows are in calf.
Palakanae nes do. She is fecundated this year (cow.)

Pal bhiṅjan. Together, in a body, in a company, to combine, as herds of cattle; company, party.

Pal bhiñjanko calaoena. They went away in company.
Pal bhiñjanre menaea mente bujhạukeṭte miḟ din horkin calaoena. Supposing him to be in the company they went a day's journey.

Pala. Leaves of trees which cattle will eat.

Pala maḱ ñurakome. Cut down some branches with leaves for them.
Pala de emaṅme. Give me some leaves of the munga tree (used as a potherb.)
Pala dare. A tree the leaves of which cattle will eat.

Pala. Hoar frost, snow.

Pala ñurakana. Hoar frost has fallen, there is hoar frost on the ground.

Palak aṛaḱ. } **Palaṅ aṛaḱ.** } **Palon aṛaḱ.** } A kind of spinach, cultivated, *Beta vulgaris Moq.*

Palak parkom. A bed with a closely woven net-work, which takes the place of a mattress.

Palaḱ poloḱ. Indistinctly, blurred vision, dimly, the grey dawn before anything can be distinctly seen.

Palaḱ poloḱe ñeñelkana. He sees indistinctly
Palaḱ poloḱreñ oḍokena. I left at grey dawn.

Palan. A saddle of the native variety for a horse or a pack bullock, to put on a saddle.
Kicrið sadomreko palankeda. They spread cloth on the horse for a saddle.

Palaṅ aṛak. Cf. palak aṛak.

Palạnia ghao. An abscess on the back.

Palao. To nourish, to bring up, as a child.
Palaokedeañ. I brought him up.
Iñiñ palao haraakadea. I brought him up from childhood.

Palaṭ. A change of raiment, to change one garment for another.
Jarge palaṭ. A change of raiment for the rains.
Den palaṭ emañme. Give me a change of raiment.
Lohoc heckateko palaṭok'a. When they come in wet they change their clothes.

Pale. If, if ever, perhaps.

Palek. Almost, peradventure.

Palha. A leaf, leaves.
Dak're palha ñurhạente bạṛicena. The water has become bad through leaves having fallen into it.
Hoṛo do palhaena. The dhan is growing all to leaf.

Pạli. }
Pạri. } Turn, shift.
Pạli ruạ. } Intermittent fever of the tertian and
Pạri ruạ. } quartan types.
Apeak' pạli kantapea. It is your turn.
Pạli pạli. }
Pạli pạlite. } By turns.
Pạli pạliko kạmia. They work by turns.

Pạlike pasa. } To borrow and lend, to
Pạli pasa. } assist each other by lending.
Epem kanako pạlike pasa. They assist each other by lending.

Pạli pasạri. }
Pạli pasạrite. } By turns, in rotation.

Pạlki. A palankeen.

Pạlku. Mixed with grey, as hair.
Uṗ pạlkuentaea. His hair is mixed with grey.

Palo. To be too old or too mature and unsuitable for food, as leaves, herbs, &c. which are used as potherbs; to change colour from bright green to yellow, as grain, &c. when ripe.
Aṛak' palok'kana, dela sitabonpe. The potherbs are getting too mature, come and gather them.

Paloe. A rick, to make into a rick or cock.

Palon. }
Lukhi palon. } Famine, scarcity.

Palon. Forbidden.
Noa reak' cet' palon menak'a? Is anything forbidden along with this?

Palon aṛak'. Cf. palak aṛak'.
Sãṛi palon. }
Cukạk palon. } Varieties of palon aṛak'.

Palpal. } To go bad, applied mainly to
Palpalao. } flesh meat.
Palpalaok' kana jel do. The meat is going bad.

Palpal. Numerous.
Palpalko ñelok'kana. They appear to be very numerous.

Palpalao. To increase, as a sore.
Ghao palpalaoentaea.

Palṭon. } An army, a regiment, a sol-
Palṭon. } dier.
Palṭonreye bhạrtiena. He is enlisted in the army.

Paltuṛ. }
Kaptur. } Tradition, traditional lore.

Pạluạ. Individuals of a household, persons to be supported, numerous.
Tinak' pạluạ menak'pea? How many mouths are there of you to feed?

Pạlwạ. A spice prepared by pounding the young dried leaves of the tamarind.

Pan. The leaf of *Piper Betle, Linn.*, along with lime and certain spices which is chewed by the people of India.
Khili pan. A quid of pan.

Pana. } Water having raw sugar
Pana dak'. } dissolved in it. Cf guṛ pana.

Panạhi. A shoe, shoes, boots.
Mundrạ panạhi. The English shape of shoe.
Ṭontha panạhi. Shoes with turned up toes.
Dhạpi panạhi. A shoe with a lappet at the heel with which to pull it on.
Ṭopar panạhi. Half shoe and half boot, laced or tied in front.
Kicriċ panạhi. Shoes lined with cloth.
Mẽṛhẽt panạhi. Shoes shod with iron.
Disi panạhi. }
Desi panạhi. } Native shoes.
Bilạti panạhi. English shoes.
Panạhianae. He has on shoes, he is wearing shoes.

Panaska. The ball of the foot, under the big toe. Cf. paska.

Pańc. } A council, an assembly, a meet-
Pońc. } ing, applied generally to an assembly convened to act as arbitrators, or to settle matters of dispute in an informal manner.

Pańcko duṛupakana. The council of arbitrators are sitting.

Pańc. Five.

Pańc sikẹ. Five four anna pieces, 1 rupee 4 annas.

Pańca. To lend, to borrow.

Pańcateń ạguakaṭa. I have borrowed it.
Pańcateye ńamkana. He wants it on loan.
Pańcaakaṭań. I have borrowed it.
Pea ṭakań pańcamea. I will borrow from you three rupees.
Pańcateń hataokeda. I took it on loan.

Pancạhit. } Cf. pańc.
Poncạhit. }

Pancạhiteṭ kanako. They are sitting in panchayat.

Pạńci. A piece of cloth of less than the usual width.

Pạńci bande. A girl of from 8 to 9 years for whom a piece of cloth less than the usual width (1 yard) suffices.

Panḍa. A Brahman resident in a temple.

Panḍe. The region over the symphysis pubis.

Panḍet. A pandit, a learned man.

Pandol. To be set aside to be cast into the shade, to yield the palm, to miss, to lose.

Pandolkedeako. They left him out of their calculation.
Iń hecente pandolok lekae ạtkareda. By my coming he feels as if he were being set aside.
Uni geye suhuka, ar okoe pạhile kạmikan tahẽkana unigeye pandoloka. He will be praised, and he who was working before will be set aside.
Kạmiye pandolena. He missed getting work.
Aćak kạmi khone pandolena. He has lost his work.
Mit hoṛak darkhast mạńjurentaete bar hoṛ gebin pandolena. Owing to the petition of one man being granted two men were set aside.

Pandrạhi. Slovenly, slatternly, untidy.

Pandrạhigeae. She is slatternly.

Panḍra. M. } Having a white skin, grey-
Pạnḍri. F. } ish in colour.

Pạnḍri. F. } Greyish coloured, applied
Pạnḍuạ. M. } to buffaloes.

Pandrao. To whitewash.

Pond hasateko panḍraoakaṭa bhit do. They have whitewashed the wall with white earth.

Oṛak panḍrao ạcurakaṭako. They have whitewashed the house all round.

Panḍu. Grey, as hair; hoary, white, as hair, to become greyhaired, to become yellow, as leaves, in autumn or grain when ripe.

Panḍukkanae. He is becoming grey haired, his hair is getting grey.
Pạnḍuenae. He is grey haired, his hair is grey.
Jạṛi leka uṕ pạnḍuentaea. His hair is white as flax
Pạnḍuk ehobok kantaea. His hair is beginning to get grey.
Pạnḍu cabaenae. He has not got a dark hair.

Pạnḍu bih. A cobra snake, a sword.

Pạnḍuạ. M. } Greyish coloured, applied
Panḍri. F. } to buffaloes.

Panḍubạ. A coot.

Panḍuć. To flee, to run away.

Dạṛ pạnḍućkedae. He fled away.
Oka seć oce pạnḍućkeda. He has fled somewhere.
Pạnḍućlekhan cetẹ cekańa? If I run away what will you do to me?

Pańgao. To lop, as branches.

Hesak dare pańgaome kaḍa palako joma. Lop the Pipul tree, the buffaloes will eat the leaves.

Pańgas hako. } A species of fish.
Pańgas boaṛ. }

Pańgaṭ pańgaṭ. Insipid, not such as can be relished, unpalatable, as coarse, inferior food.

Tinạkem joma pańgaṭ pańgaṭ? How much will you force yourself to eat of this unpalatable food?
Jom jomteń pańgaṭ pańgaṭena. I have eaten till the food is unpalatable.
Ạdi eneć pańgaṭ pańgaṭe jom cabakeda. After a long time he forced himself to eat it all.

Pango nạṛi. } Cf. panjot nạṛi.
Pańgo nạṛi. }

Pańpanḍrań. } To tear, to make a big
Ponponḍroń. } rent, to become larger, as a tear in cloth.

Kicrić oṛeć pańpanḍrańentaea. There is a big tear in her cloth.
Oṛećte pańpanḍrańoka. The tear will become larger.

Panhạiyạ. A shoemaker. Cf. panạhi.

Panhao. To let down the milk, as a cow.

Gạiye panhaoakada, duhạuem. The cow has let down her milk, milk her.
Mihũ nunu panhaolege. Let the calf first suck to bring down the milk.
Panhao ocoae, adom orea. Allow her to let down the milk, then milk away.
Mihũ nunu panhaokedae. The calf sucked and brought down the milk.

Pạni. Water.
Pạni ke pạni, dudh ke dudh bicạrpe. Judge justly (call water water and milk milk.)

Paniḍubạ. A coot. Cf. panḍubạ.

Pạni kokha. } Pan kokha. } The side below the ribs. Pạni pokha. }

Paniạu. To annoy, to harass, to irritate.
Pạniạukedińae nui gidrạ do. This child irritated me.
Jao hiloṅ kạmi kạmiteń pạniạu cabaena. I am harassed by having to keep working every day.
Pạniạu ńamkedińae. I am harassed.

Pạnichạ.. A bamboo bowstring. Cf. pōṛcha.

Pańja. Foot mark, foot-print; to follow, to trace, to track.
Pańja tioṅ. To overtake.
Kombṛo pańjareń lebeṭena. I am accused of being a thief, or as a companion of thieves.
Pańja pańjatele hedena. We came tracking all the way.
Hapṛamkoaṅ pańjarele lebeṭakana. We are in the way our fathers trod.
Hoṛ pańja. A human foot-print.
Gại pańja. A cow's foot-print.
Kul pańja. A tiger's pug marks.
Pańja ńamkedeań. I tracked and found him.

Pańjar. A rib, the part of the body in which the ribs are.
Ibil pańjar. The fifth rib.
Pańjar bhorte gitić. To lie on the side.
Pańjarreye soboṅkedea. He stabbed him in the side.

Pańjar ḍahar. The Milky-way.

Pạńji. An almanack, a calendar.

Pańjon. A forest tree, *Polyalthia cerasoides, Benth.*

Pańjot. A small wild plant, *Clerodendron phlomoides, Linn, fil.*

Pańjot nạṛi. A climbing or twining bush, *Porana paniculata, Roxb.*

Pạńjri. A rib, ribs.
Catom pạńjri. The ribs of an umbrella.
Gạḍi pạńjri. } The cross bars uniting the shafts
Sagaṛ pạńjri. } (hudạṛ) of a cart.
Lạukạ reaṅ pạńjri. The ribs of a boat.

Pankokha. Cf. pạni kokha.

Panmuhri. The Anise seed, the seed of *Pimpinella Anisum, Linn.*

Panpanao. To feel a strong call to pass water.
Raca seć panpanaokedińa.
Kupnạu panpanaoakada.

Panserali. A species of waterfowl.

Pansińgha. A plant common on the edges of tanks, *Dysophilla verticillata, Bth.*

Panta. } A line, a row.
Pata. }
Hana pantare menaea. He is in that row.
Raj panta ren kanae. He can sit in the same row with the raja.
Panta panta tahenpe. Remain in rows, or remain in line.

Pante. } A line, a row, in rows,
Pante pante. } to arrange in rows, to agree together.
Katha do bań panteṅkantakina. Their statements do not agree, or they are at variance with each other.
Panteṅpe. Range yourselves in a row.
Oṛaṅ pantere. In a line with the house.
Pante pantete duṛuṗ ocokope. Make them sit in rows.

Pante bele. The testicles.

Panṭeć. } Miserly, stingy, crooked, wick-
Konṭeć. } ed.
Ạḍi panṭeć hoṛ kanae. He is a very stingy person.
Panṭeć geko roṛa. They speak so as to cause division.

Panwar gocho. Whiskers.

Pao. The foot, feet.
Tinạṅ sạṅgiń pao dom baṛhaoakaṭa? How far did you intend to go?
Ninạṅ hạbić paoiń baṛhaoakaṭa. I intend only to go so far.
Pao piṭhạ. } Bread made from dough kneaded
Pao ruṭi. } with the feet.

Pao. } One fourth, a quarter, a quar-
Paoa. } ter seer by weight or dry
Pawa. } measure, and one eighth seer by liquid measure.
Pao bhor. A full quarter.
Bhar paoam gunạkeda. There can be no extenuation of your fault

Pāola mala. Coral beads.

Pap. Sin.
Pap pholao. To receive the recompense of one's sin.
Pap pholaoakadea. He received the recompense of his sin.

Pap. To know carnally.

Papi. } Miserly, stingy, sinful.
Pạpiạ. }
Papiạhi. }
Pạpigeae. He is stingy.
Pạpi hoṛ kanae, jahānạṅ koeye bae emoṅa. He is a stingy man, if you ask him for anything he will not give.
Ạḍiye pạpiạgea. He is very niggardly.
Ạḍi pạpiạhi kanae. He is a very stingy man.

Papista. Bad, sinful, disobedient.

Papor. Cor. of the English word "pauper" introduced by the law courts.

Papuk. To be finished, to be exhausted, used by children.

Par. Relief, escape, refuge, across.
Pare ńamkeda. He escaped, he got relief.
Ojo posaḱentaete pare ńamkeda. He got relief by the bursting of his boil.
Sind mubąnire bae saplente pare ńamkeda. Owing to his not having been caught in the act of breaking into the house he escaped.

Pąr. The beam or beams supporting the roof of a house.
Satepąr. The beam or beams supporting the rafters on the long side of the house.
Mutal pąr. The ridge beam or pole of a house.
Kupi pąr. / Khupi pąr. } The beam or beams supporting the roof of the ends of a house.

Pąr. / Pąrląk. } A coloured border on cloth.
Dhuti pąr. The coloured border of a dhoti or loin cloth.
Sąri pąr. The coloured border of a sąri, the garment worn by women.
Pąrląkteć bań osara, kicriéteć osargea. The coloured border is not wide, the cloth itself is wide.
Pąrląk kicrić. A cloth with a coloured border.
Khubko pąrląḱakaća. They have given (the cloth) a good broad coloured border.
Pąrląk sohor. A coloured border on the width end of a cloth.

Para. Mercury, quicksilver.

Para. A part of a town or village, a near village, vicinity.
Iną parate senoḱme. Go to that near village.
Muci para. The part of a village inhabited by shoemakers.

Para. A cockpit, place where game cocks fight.

Parab. / Porob. } A festival, a mela or fair.

Par ądhin. / Por ądhin. } Dependent, subject to another.
Por ądhin ren dоń bań kana. I am not subject to another, I am independent.
Por ądhin renko apnar mone leka bako kąmi dareaḱa. Those who are dependent on others cannot do as they wish.

Paragare. / Paragarete. } Stealthily, unpremeditatedly, on some pretext, without disclosing real purpose.
Paragareteye calaoena. He went away stealthily.
Para garete ńel ąguiem. Have a look at her stealthily, do not let any one know that it is to see her that you go.

Para jara. / Para jare. } Very ill, seriously ill, applied to fever.
Ądi para jarae ruąḱkana. / Uni doe ruąḱkana para jare. } He is seriously ill, with fevver.

Paraḱ. To split, to crack.
Kaț paragme. Split the log.
Bhit paraḱena. The wall is cracked.
Ot paraḱena. The earth is fissured.
Bar paragme. Split it into two.
Miť paraḱ áćgeye hataoana, ar miť paraḱ ińe emadińa. He took one of the pieces into which it was split and gave me one.
Bhitre marań paraḱ menaḱa. There is a large crack in the wall.

Paraḱ. The first ploughing of a field for the season.
Deć. The second ploughing.
Uțhąu ruar. The third and last ploughing after which the seed is sown.
Bąrgele paraḱakaća. We have ploughed the garden the first time this season.

Paramąnik. / Parąnik. } Assistant to the mańjhi or headman of a village.

Parames. / Porames. / Poramos. } To consult, to take council.
Parames joḿkanako. They are consulting together.

Parąnik. Cf. paramąnik.

Parao. To be, to befall, to fall into or on.
Dukre paraoakanae. Affliction has befallen him.
Jahäkorem paraolena, se bań? Did you get food anywhere or not?
Dand paraoadea, onateye ocoḱena. He had great anxiety, therefore he has lost flesh.
Rohni ni candore paraoḱa. Rohni (q. v.) falls in this month.
Setoń paraoena netar do. The sun is hot now.
Rabań parąokateń calaḱ. I will go when the cold weather sets in.
Uni tireń paraoena. I have fallen into his hand.
Uni tireń paraoakante bań cekaḱa. Through my falling into his hand no harm will come to me.

Parao. Weak, feeble.

Parãoca. A large raised platform or scaffold with straw piled on it.
Marom. The platform on which the straw is placed.
Parãoca latarreko ḑeraḱma. Let them encamp under the platform with straw on it.

Para parite. / Pari parite. / Ola palite. / Ora parite. } By turns, by shifts.
Para pąrite kąmipe. Work by turns.

Parapạt. Advantage, benefit.
Okoe parapạtre hõ bañ hoelena. No one was benefited thereby.
Amaḱ parapạtre bañ hoelena. It did not benefit you.
Unạḱem arjaokeťrehõ amaḱ parapạtre bañ hoelena. Although you had such a good harvest it was not to your benefit (the money lender seized it all).

Paras. A helping to food.
Pe paras dakako jomkeda. They ate three helpings to food.
Pe parasko emaťkoa. They gave them three helpings to food.

Paṛas. } Sounding of a slap, succession of slapping sounds. Cf. paṭas.
Paṛas paṛas. }

Paṛas marte. } With a slap, with a slapping or smacking sound.
Paṛas mente. }

Paraṭ. } To thump, to thwack, to whack.
Paraṭ paraṭ. }
Paraṭadeako. They thwacked him.
Paraṭ paraṭko dalkedea. They beat him thwack, thwack.

Paraṭ marte. } With a thwack, with a thwacking sound.
Paraṭ mente. }
Paraṭ marteye dalkedea. He hit him one whack.

Paṛbhạ. } Relations.
Peṛa paṛbhạ. }
Cele hõ bạnuḱkotaea peṛa pạṛbhạ. He has no relatives.
Iń ren peṛa pạṛbhạ kantińako. They are my relations.

Parca. } Acquaintances, to be become acquainted, to become known to each other.
Cinhạ parca. }
Cinhạ parca menaḱkotama noakore? Have you any acquaintances about here?
Cinhạ parcaenakin. They have come to know who each other is.

Parcao. To increase, to spread.
Khubko parcaoakana. They have increased greatly.

Paṛchạ. } Clean, clear, to settle as a disputed matter, to clear up.
Phaṛchạ. }
Khub pạṛchạ pondena. It is very clean and white.
Meť pạṛchạentaea. His eyes are clear.
Paṛchạkatińpe. Clear up this matter for me.
Niạ do pạṛchạentaea. This of his is settled.

Paṛchạu. A ceremony observed when a bridegroom takes his bride home.
Thạri sudhạtege jãwãe koṛa ar bạhu kuṛitekin cumạuṛa seye pạṛchạukina.

Paṛchạu ader. Ceremonies connected with the introduction of a bride to her new home.
Bạhuko pạṛchạu aderkoa. They observe certain ceremonies on the entry of a bride to her new home.

Paṛdaḱ. } To bound, as a deer, to move by a succession of bounds or leaps.
Paṛdaḱ paṛdaḱ. }
Paṛdak. }
Paṛdak paṛdak. }
Paṛdaḱ paṛdaḱe dạṛkeda. He fled bounding away.

Parek. A nail.
Parek kuṭạm. To drive a nail.

Pare pore. } At the expense of or by the assistance of another or of others.
Pare porete. }
Pareporete kạmiye calaoeda. He does his work with the assistance (or at the expense) of others.
Pare poretegeye ạsuloḱkana. He lives at the expense of others.

Pargana. } A division of a country, or an estate, generally for fiscal purposes.
Porgon. }
Ragda Mạńjhi, Sakin Biswaḍih, pargana Ṭunḍi. Ragda Manjhi inhabitant of Biswaḍih, in the Pargana of Ṭunḍi.
Hana porgon ren kanako. They belong to yonder division or pargana.

Pargana. A Santal Over-chief, who has a varying area of country or number of villages in his jurisdiction.
The office of pargana is, as a general rule, hereditary.

Paṛhanḍ. A piece of cloth about three cubits long.

Paṛhao. To read, to study, to teach, to recite, to say an incantation.
Paṛhaoḱkanae. He is studying, or he attends school, or he is reading.
Oloḱ paṛhaoḱ hoṛ kanae. He is a person able to read and write.
Paṛhao ańjomatkoae. He read it out to them.
Iskulreye paṛhaoeťkoa. He teaches in school.
Sikhạu paṛhaokeťkoae. He tutored them, (told them what to say.)
Mantar paṛhao hoṛ. A person able to recit incantations, one versed in charms ore incantations.
Sunum paṛhao. A method of divination with oil.

Parhaṛ. } Clean, free.
Pharhaṛ. }
Moca parhaṛentaea. His month has become clean, as of a person recovering from illness.
Parhaṛiń ạikạueda nitoḱ. I feel my mouth clean, bad taste removed.
Khub parhaṛtaea moca do. His mouth is free, he is a good talker.
Parhaṛko dakaakaťa. They have cooked the rice so that each grain is free, or separate from another.

Paṛhuạ. } Educated.
Paḍhuạ. }
Pạṛhuạ hoṛ kanae. He is an educated man.

Paṛi. } Turn, by turns, turn about, alternately, by shifts.
Paṛi paṛi.
Paṛi paṛite.

Iñak' paṛi kana. It is my turn.

Paṛi paṛiteko lena sunum. They use the oil press by turns.

Paṛipạrite dãtteko laca. They dig turn about with the pick.

Paṛi ruạ. Intermittent fever, of the tertian and quartan types.

Paṛi ruạ menak'taeạ. He has fever one day, and is free the next, with a return of the fever on the third day.

Paṛiạ. Time.

Iñ paṛiạre. In my time.

Hapṛamko paṛiạre. In the time of our ancestors.

Budhi paṛiạre. } In the time of old age.
Haṛam paṛiạre.

Iñ paṛiạrenko. Those of my time, my contemporaries.

Noa paṛiạren hoṛko. People of the present day.

Paṛiaṛe. The four pieces of wood forming the framework of a bed, chair, &c.

Jeteleñ paṛiaṛe. The two pieces running the long way.

Ganaḍe paṛiaṛe. The two pieces running across each end.

Paṛiạu. } Meaning, explanation.
Poṛiạu.

Noa reak' paṛiạu ạguańme. Explain this to me.

Poṛiạu bah bạisạuk'kana. The explanation is not conclusive.

Pariba. } Acquaintances, relatives.
Parijan.

Noakorege parijan bạnuk'kotińa. I have no acquaintances about here.

Parikha. } To test, to prove, to examine.
Porikha.

Pari pasạri. Cf. pạli pasạri.

Paris. A sept, the name by which the septs into which the Santals are divided are known.

The Santals are divided into eleven septs, but originally, it is said, there were twelve one of which has been lost. Each sept is subdivided into sub-septs of which according to the popular belief among Santals there are twelve. In fact, however, the sub-septs of each sept vary in number as the following list will show.

SEPT KISKU. Sub-septs. *Nij Kisku, *Gaṛh Kisku, Ok' Kisku, Obor Kisku, Mạńjhi khil Kisku, *Naeke khil Kisku, Son Kisku, Aḍ Kisku, Badaṛ Kisku, Biṭol Kisku, *Sada Kisku, Pạṭi Kisku, *Jabe Kisku, *Ṭikạ Kisku and *Katwa Kisku.

SEPT HÃSDAK'. Sub-septs. *Nij Hãsdak', *Cil bindhạ Hãsdak', *Boḍoar or Bonḍwar Hãsdak', *Keḍwar Hãsdak', *Jihu Hãsdak', Kuhi Hãsdak', Sada Hãsdak', Obor Hãsdak', *Kãṛã Gujiạ Hãsdak', Kạhu Hãsdak', Sãk Hãsdak', *Naeke khil Hãsdak', *Rok' lutur Hãsdak', *Bedwar Hãsdak' and Kundạ Hãsdak'.

SEPT MURMU. Sub-septs. *Nij Murmu, *Sada Murmu, *Obor Murmu, Mạńjhikhil Murmu, *Naekekhil Murmu, *Biṭol Murmu, *Gaṛh Murmu, Badaṛ Murmu, Ok' Murmu, Laṭ Murmu, Jihu Murmu, *Ṭikạ or Tilok Murmu, Kuḍạm Murmu, Gajaṛ Murmu, *Copiạr Murmu, *Ponḍ Murmu, *Boara Murmu, *Hạnḍi Murmu, *Koṭha Murmu, *Ṭuṭi sarjom Murmu, *Samak'sah Murmu, Oara Murmu, *Munḍu Murmu, *Jugi Murmu, *Kaḍa Murmu, *Turku lumạm Murmu, Sạu Murmu, and Powar Murmu.

SEPT HEMBROM. Sub-septs. *Nij Hembrom, Mạńjhi khil Hembrom, *Naeke khil Hembrom, *Sada Hembrom, Biṭol Hembrom, *Guạ Hembrom, *Guạ Soren Hembrom, Obor Hembrom, Badaṛ Hembrom, Gaṛh Hembrom, *Laher Hembrom, *Casa Hembrom, *Hạnḍi Hembrom, *Sole Hembrom, *Ṭhạkur Hembrom, *Laṭ Hembrom, *Datela Hembrom and *Kuạri Hembrom.

SEPT MARNḌI. Sub-septs. *Nij Mạrnḍi, *Goda Mạrnḍi, *Mạńjhi khil Mạrnḍi, *Naeke khil Mạrnḍi, *Rot Mạrnḍi, *Rok' lutur Mạrnḍi, Obor Mạrnḍi, Biṭol Mạrnḍi, Siduṗ Mạrnḍi, Jugi Mạrnḍi, Kaḍa Mạrnḍi, Khara Mạrnḍi, Gaṛh Mạrnḍi, Kulkhi Mạrnḍi, *Turko lumạm Mạrnḍi, *Sada Mạrnḍi, *Khanda jagao Mạrnḍi, *Ṭikạ Mạrnḍi, *Ponḍ Mạrnḍi, *Keḍwar Mạrnḍi, *Buru bereṭ Mạrnḍi, *Khanḍa Mạrnḍi, *Babṛẽ Mạrnḍi, *Rupạ Mạrnḍi *Jonok' Mạrnḍi, *Miru Mạrnḍi and *Bhoso Mạrnḍi.

SEPT SOREN. Sup-septs. *Nij Soren, *Siduṗ Soren, *Sada Soren, *Jugi Soren, Mạńjhi khil Soren, *Naeke khil Soren, Biṭol Soren, Ok' Soren, Munḍu or Badaṛ Soren, Mal Soren, Jihu Soren, Sãk Soren, *Bạrchi Soren, *Sada siduṗ Soren, *Ponḍ Soren, *Khanḍa Soren, *Obor Soren, *Mãṛ Soren, *Cehel Soren, Dãtela Soren, *Rok' lutur Soren, *Guạ Soren and *Turku lumạm Soren

SEPT ṬUḌU. Sub-septs. *Nij Ṭuḍu, *Cigi Ṭuḍu, *Laṭ Ṭuḍu, *Mạńjhi khil Ṭuḍu, *Naeke khil Ṭuḍu, *Sada Ṭuḍu, *Gaṛh Ṭuḍu, Jugi Ṭuḍu, *Dãtela Ṭuḍu, *Ok' Ṭuḍu, Biṭol Ṭuḍu, Obor Ṭuḍu, Baske Ṭuḍu, Tilok Ṭuḍu, Babṛẽ Ṭuḍu, Curuė Ṭuḍu, *Kuḍam Ṭuḍu *Bhokta Ṭuḍu, and *Kharhara Ṭuḍu.

SEPT BASKE. Sub-septs. *Nij Baske. *Mạńjhi Khil Baske, Naeke Khil Baske, Biṭol Baske, Laṭ Baske, Kuhi Baske, Ok' Baske, Munḍu Baske, Obor Baske, Bindạṛ Baske, *Sada Baske, Keḍwar Baske, Jihu Baske, *Sạru Gaḍa Baske, *Bhiḍi Baske, *Suṛe Baske and *Hende Baske.

SEPT BESRA. Sub-septs. Nij Besra, Mạńjhi khil Besra, *Naeke khil Besra, Kuhi Besra, *Son Besra, *Bindạṛ Besra, Gaṛh Besra, Tilok Besra, Biṭol Besra, Laṭ Besra, Baske Besra, Ok' Besra, Obor Besra, and *Kạhu Besra.

SEPT CÕṚẼ or Gua Soren. Sub-septs. * Nij Cõṛẽ, Gua Cõṛẽ, Hembrom kuar Cõṛẽ, Gua Hembrom Cõṛẽ, Sada Cõṛẽ, Biṭol Cõṛẽ, Mañjhikhil Cõṛẽ, Oḱ Cõṛẽ, Gaṛh Cõṛẽ, Naekekhil Cõṛẽ. * Sindur Cõṛẽ, Bindar Cõṛẽ, Kahu Cõṛẽ, Lać Cõṛẽ, and * Ṭhakur Cõṛẽ.

SEPT PAURIA OR PAULIA. Sub-septs. Nij Pauria, Mañjhi khil Pauria, Naekekhil Pauria, Sada Pauria, Oḱ Pauria, Cauria Pauria, Bhitar Pauria, Obor Pauria, Sidup Pauria, Biṭol Pauria, Gaṛh Pauria, Mundu Pauria and Lać Pauria.

Note. An asterisk denotes the sub-septs with families of which the writer has come into contact. The names of the other Sub-septs have been gathered from well informed Santals.

Parjat. } Porjat. } Belonging to another caste.
Nui parjat sohge cedaḱem gateḱa? What should you make a friend of this man of another caste?

Parjat. Even.
Jomaḱ parjat bań ńameda, ceć lekateń tahena nui kisāṛ ṭheć? I do not even get food, how can I remain with this employer?
Daḱ parjat bań juṭauama. You will not even get enough water.
Jomaḱ parjatiń deaakaća. I have neglected even my food.

Parkar. } Nana parkar. } Of many kinds, all kinds, all sorts.
Nana parkare roṛ halaheć tahẽkana. He was saying all sorts of things.
Nana parkar jinis. Goods or articles of all kinds.

Parkau. To become accustomed, to become confident through non-interference, to become habituated, to become familiarized, to be at home in, to lose fear.
Parkauakana e, dinam biloḱe hijuḱ kana, nui toyo do. This jackal has become confident through non-interference, he comes every day.
Bana do ak jome parkauena. The bear has got accustomed to eat the sugar cane.
Am ṭhenko parkauakana. They have become familiarised with you (and take advantage.)
Parkau iate nonkako hijuḱkana. Through having lost fear they are coming thus.

Parkom. A bed.

Parkom bana. The Indian Badger, *Mellivora indica.*

Parlak. Cf. par.

Parlek. Whether......or.
Parlekiń gujuḱ, parlek jiweńiń tahen enhõń calaḱgea. Whether I die or I live, still I shall go.
Parlekiń ńam, parlek bań ńam kami ohoń bagilea. Whether I receive or not I will not forsake my work.

Paro. A plant so named.

Parok. } Na parok. } Nolens volens, per force, of necessity.
Na parokiń jomkeda. I ate of necessity.
Na paroke kamikana. He is working because he cannot help it.

Parom. Across, beyond, far side; to put across, to put or convey to the other side, to go across, to go over, to pass over, to go past.
Parom calaoenae. He has gone past.
Daḱ hante parom calaoena. The rain has passed over that way.
Gaḍa paromre. On the other side of the river.
Bar ato paromre. Two villages beyond.
Gaḍa paromkańme. Put me across the river.
Nenda din paromena. The fixed or appointed day has passed.

Sima alope lebeć paroma. Do not step over the boundary.
Alom roṛ paromea. Do not contradict him, do not shew disrespect to him.

Paromoḱme. Cross over, or pass.
Sen parom porob. The Jewish Passover.
On parom. The other side, the further side.
No parom. } Na parom. } Ne parom. } This side.
Gaḍa on paromre menaḱkoa. They are on the other side of the river.
Phanka phayaṛe roṛ paromkeda. He spoke out fearlessly.

Paron. Cf. ḍhula paron.

Paroṛ jhiṅga. A cultivated vegetable, *Luffa acutangula, Roxb.*

Parosi. } Arosi parosi. } Ar parosi. } Neighbours.
Ar parosi ren hoṛko kulikom. Enquire at the the neighbours.

Parpande. To be nearly ripe, more than half ripe.
Jondra parpandeakana. The Indian corn is nearly ripe.

Parpao. } Parpau. } To burn clearly and brightly, as a fire, to cause to burn brightly and clearly.
Ma ewer parpaupe bańkhan datrom oho dhipaulena. Fan the fire and make it burn clearly or else the sickle will not become red-hot.
Sehgel parpaupe jondrabon rapaga. Make the fire burn brightly, we will roast Indian corn.
Jol parpaupe joroḱabo. Stir up the fire, we will warm ourselves.

Parpaṛ. Imitative of the sound of rattling, as of hail on a roof.
Arel parpaṛ ńuroḱkana. The hail falls rattling.

Parparao. To smart, as the eyes with smoke, &c.
Meť parparaoǩkantaea sabun paraoadete. His eyes are smarting through soap getting into them.

Parpau. Cf. parpao.

Parpasind. } To select, to choose, to think
Parposind. } well of, to like, to approve, to prefer.
Par pasindkateko kiriňa. They buy after they have approved, or selected.

Parsadte. }
Parsatte. } By means of, through.
Nui parsadteň jomkeda. He was the means of my eating it.
Seta parsadte mandalbo ňamkeda. We got the leg of venison through the dog.

Parsao. To help to food, to distribute cooked food, as to a number of persons at a feast.
Daka parsaope. Distribute the cooked rice.

Parsao. To begin to take in hand, to set agoing.
Uni do adi kamiye parsaoakawana. He has much work in hand.
Kamile parsaoakaťa, ohole senlena. We have begun to work, we cannot go.
Nonde kami parsaoakana, sangiňte calaǩ baň jaruya. Work is begun here, there is no need to go to a distance.

Parsatte. Cf. parsadte.

Parsi. Language.
Aćaǩ parsiteye roreda. He is speaking his own language.
Diku Parsi. The language of the Hindus.
Aňgreji parsi. The English language.
Jonom parsi. Mother tongue.

Partap. Potency, splendour, courage, prosperity.
Amaǩ partapteň baňcaoena. I am delivered by your potency.

Parti. } Fallow, uncultivated, unfertil-
Porti. } ized, unemployed.
Nes do khet partige taheňena. This year the fields remained uncultivated.
Dahra parti menaetama, se baha? Hẽ, miťten menaetiňa. Have you an unemployed bullock? Yes, I have one.

Parwa. The Rock pigeon, *Columba intermedia*, the domestic pigeon.

Parwa cipcirip. } A common plant the
Parwa lata. } seed cases of which stick like a burr.

Parwa jhara. A small plant, *Crosophora pilcata, A. Juss.*

Parwana. A written order or notice.

Pas. Cor. of the English word "pass," a permit.
Pas menaǩtaea. He has a pass (for a gun, &c.)
Uni doe pasakana nes. He passed his examination this year.
Bae paslena. He did not pass (the exam.)

Pas. Side.
Ek pasre senkateye durupena. He went aside and sat down.

Pas. Near, connection, practice.
Iň do onako pasrege baň tahena. I will have no connection with these matters.
Ona mamla pasre baň tahena. I will take nothing to do with that suit.
Asamol reaǩ pas banuǩtaea. He has no connection with forbidden foods, he does not indulge in forbidden food.

Pas.
Aspas.
Pase. } Neighbourhood, vicinity.
Ase pase.
Nia aspasren hor sanamko badaea. All the people of this neighborhood know.

Basa. A variety of the rice plant.

Pasaǩ. } Without relish, as un-
Pasaǩ pasaǩ. } palatable food, unpalatable. Cf. pangat pangat.
Pasaǩ pasaǩ sikauǩkana. It feels unpalatable.
Noa caole reaǩ daka pasaǩgea. This rice when cooked is unpalatable.

Pasante. } To spread, to scatter, to
Pasanti. } begin, to take in hand.
Horo hõpe pasante baraeťkana. You are also spreading about the dhan.
Kamiko pasanteakaťa. They have taken the work in hand.

Pasar. } To open, to unfold, to spread,
Pasar. } out, to distend, to expand, to increase.
Catom pasarme. Put up the umbrella, open the umbrella.
Cupuť pasartam. Open your hand.
Cupuť thon baň pasaroǩtaea. He is stingy.
Kitape pasarakaťtaea. He has opened his book.
Pasarkateko ňela, besa se bariča. They unfold (cloth) and see whether it is good or bad.
Jaňga pasarkate durupakanae. He is sitting with his legs wide apart.

Pasar. } To be out of order, to
Pisar pasar. } be in disorder, to be disarranged, to be topsy turvy, to be dislocated.
Pisar pasarpe dohoakaťa. You have placed them topsy turvy.
Tonol raralenkhan pisar pasaroǩa. If the band is untied they will become disarranged.
Pisar pasarkedae. He disarranged them.

Pasar pusur. To whisper, to speak in a low tone.
Onteko pasar pusureda. They are whispering yonder.

Pasạri.
Pạli pasạri. } Cf. pạli pasạri.

Pasari.
Paseri. } Five seers in weight.

Pase.
Paseć.
Paseť. } Perhaps, mayhap.

Pase tehengeye dag. Perhaps it may rain to-day.
Paseń ced pase bań ced. Perhaps I may learn, and perhaps I may not learn.
Alom dejoǩa, pasem ńuroǩ. Do not climb, perhaps you may fall.

Pasere pase. Perhaps, it may possibly so happen.

Ma nonkate sendraepe, pasere pasebo ńamkadege. Hunt in this direction, it may possibly so happen that we may find him.

Paseri. Five seers weight. Cf. pasạri.

Paseť. Cf. pase.

Pạsi.
Phạsi. } A Hindu caste, a toddy drawer.

Pạsi. An iron staple fastening share to plough.

Pạsi.
Phạsi. } A running knot, a noose, to snare by a noose, to hang by a noose.

Cẽṛẽko pạsikoa. They snare birds.
Khuniạhikoko pạsikoa. They hang murderers.

Pạsiara. Cf. phạsiara.

Pạsind.
Posind. } To select, to choose, to think well of, to like, to approve, to prefer, to estimate.

Ińaǩ pạsindre bań lagaoǩa. In my judgment it will not have to be paid.
Pạsindkedape, se ṣuri? Have you selected it, or not yet?

Pạsir. To break up and spread as water falling on a hard surface, to fly off, as sparks, spray, to spatter, &c.

Dạl pạsir. To cause to fly off by beating or hammering.
Hoṭaǩ pasir. To overcome, to conquer.
Jom pạsir. To eat up.
Kolsa pạsir. To kick over.
Mạr pạsir. To eat all up.
Maǩ pạsir. To cut off, to hack through.
Daǩ pạsiramkana. The water is flying, or spattering, over you.
Sehgel oṭeć pạsiroǩkana. Sparks are flying from the fire.
Koṭeć pạsiredae. He is hammering and causing sparks to fly.

Pạsiri. Cf. pạsri.

Paska. To paw the earth, as an enraged animal; to turn over the soil, as a cultivator.

Paska uṭkaukedae hasa. He is pawing up the the soil.
Bam paskalekhan oeť lekatem ṣuloǩa? If you do not turn over the soil (cultivate) how can you live?
Sim leka ińtegeń paska ṣuloǩkana. I make a living for myself by turning over the soil like a hen (which scratches.)

Paskao.
Phaskao.
Pạskut.
Phạskuṛ. } To escape, to slip through, to let slip through.

Sanam oij bạsutiń paskaokeda. I have let all my property slip through my fingers, I have lost all my property.
Paskao oookedeale miť hoṛ. We allowed one man to escape, one man escaped us.
Ṭhengań paskaokeda. I have left my stick.
Kạmiń phaskaokeda teheń do. I have missed work to-day.
Ti khon paskao ńurena. It slipped from the hand and fell.
Moca reaǩ jeliń phaskaokeda. I missed flesh meat for my mouth, I missed catching a hare, deer, or bird, &c. which I might have eaten.

Pạskuť.
Phạskuť. } Cf. paskao.

Pasnao. To spread, to disperse, to strow.

Hoṛo pasnaokam. Spread out the dhan.
Kathae lại pasnaokeda. He published the matter, he blazed the matter abroad.
Goṭa dhạrtireko pasnaoena. They are dispersed over the whole earth.
Cedaǩem pasnao ocoakaťkoa? Why have you allowed them to disperse themselves?

Pasna pạsni. To spread here and there.

Gạiko pasna pạsniena. The cows are spread here and there.

Pasnga. Anything put in one scale to equalize it with the other.

Pasra. A smithy, place where a blacksmith works, to work as a blacksmith.

Kamar pasra. A smithy.
Pasrae lagaokaťa se bah? Has the blacksmith begun to work?
Pasraedae. The blacksmith is at his work.

Pasrao. Cf. parsao.

Pạsri. Day about, on alternate days.

Pạsriteliń sioǩkana. We plough on alternate days.
Mạńjhitelińliń pạsriakana. The village headman and I alternate (he ploughs with the bullocks one day and I the next.)

Pasu.
Posu. } An animal, cattle.

Ato posu. A domesticated animal.
Bir posu. A wild animal.

Pạsuṛ. To miss, to lose, to fail in purpose.

Dakae pạsuṛena. He missed his food (came late.)
Kạmiye pạsuṛkeda. He lost his employment.

Paṭ.
Paṭh. } A lesson.
Paṭiń hataotakoa. I hear them their lessons.

Paṭ. a leaf.
Paṭkar. A cess levied on the rearing of tusser silk worms.
Tejpat. An aromatic leaf used in curries, the leaf of *Cinnamonum obtusifolium, Nees.*

Paṭ. A sinew.

Paṭ son. Deccani hemp, the fibre of *Hibiscus cannabinus, Linn.*

Paṭ. To finish, to complete, to end.
Noa kạmile paṭkeda. We finished this work.
Jom paṭkedae. He ate it all.

Paṭ.
Jaṭ paṭ. } Caste and customs governed by it.
Jaṭ paṭ nui reaḱ ṭhik bạnuḱtaea.

Paṭsal. A school, a village school.

Paṭ. A wedge driven into anything to tighten it.
Kuḍi paṭ. A wedge driven into the handle of a kodali to keep it from coming off.
Nahel paṭ. A wedge tightening the plough beam into the plough.

Paṭ. Half-full of a bottle.
Mit́ paṭ pạurạe emadińa. He gave me half a bottle of liquor.
Mit́ paṭ sunum menaḱa. There is half a bottle of oil.

Paṭ marte.
Paṭ mente.
Phaṭ marte.
Phaṭ mente. } Suddenly, without warning.
Paṭ marte goć got́enae. He died on the instant.
Barahi paṭ mente topaḱ got́ena. The rope suddenly broke.

Paṭa. A lease, to give a lease.
Noa atoń paṭaakat́a. I have taken a written lease of this village.
Paṭa purạuentakoa. Their lease has expired.
Har paṭa. A cultivating lease.
Raj do paṭao emoḱa. The Zemindar will give a written lease.
Raje paṭaat́lea. The Zamindar gave us a written lease, or leases.

Paṭa. A primitive kind of oil press, a wooden slate.
The oil press consists of two planks which are pressed together by means of a lever.
Sunum lenoḱ paṭa.
Sunum lelen paṭa. } An oil press.

Pata. A festival in honour of Mahadeo.
This is the hook swinging festival of India.
Pata ṭanḍi. The place where the *pata* festival is observed.

Pata. A leaf, a very small piece of meat from the carcase of an animal killed in the chase wrapped in a leaf and sent to some one.
Patatet́ seṭerakome. Send them a small bit of meat in a leaf.
Patatet́ko emat́lea. They gave us a little bit of the meat in a leaf.

Paṭa.
Paṭo. } Coarse or thick, as hair or leaves.

Patahań.
Patohań.
Potohań. } Saliva or froth dried at the corners of the mouth, generally through thirst or fever.
Banae heć got́enteye potohańena.
Uniaḱ moca do pondge patohań rohoṛentaea.

Paṭaicaḱ. A small hairy caterpillar which stings when touched.

Patal. Deep, in the bowels of the earth.
Ạḍi bạṛić pataltoko lakat́a. They have dug down very deep.
Koela do ạḍi patalre menaḱa. Coal is found very deep down.

Patal puri. The nether world.

Patal roṭe. A frog which is found at considerable depth under the surface of the soil.

Patal kaṭkom. A species of crab.

Patal kohnda.
Tirṛa da. } The edible tuber of *Pueraria tuberosa, D. C.*

Paṭan.
Paṭnia. } Irrigated, that requires irrigating.
Paṭan ạk.
Paṭnia ạk. } Irrigated sugar cane, sugar cane that requires irrigation.

Patańget́. The bark of a very small sapling (of sarjom q. v.) when stripped off.
Patańget́te sakamko binḍạia. They tie up leaves in bundles with the bark of a sarjom (q. v.) sapling.
The dihri (q. v.) of a hunt has his hands and feet tied with patańget́, and is decorated with a turban of the same material before he offers the sacrifice required before a hunt can begin.

Paṭao. To irrigate.
Ạkko paṭaoa. They irrigate sugarcane.

Paṭao. To harden, to consolidate, as earth, gravel, &c., opposite of loose, as soil, &c.
Ḍańrako lebet́ paṭaokeda. The bullocks trampled it hard.
Paṭao ruạṛena. It has again become hard.
Daḱ paṭaokedae. The rain consolidated it.
Gitić paṭaoakanae. He is lying fast, as if he were asleep.
Duṛuṗ paṭaoakanae. He is sitting fast.

Patao. To exchange flowers in token of friendship.
Phulkin pataokeda. They exchanged flowers in token of friendship.

Paṭapaṭ. Sound of thumping or smacking.

Dal paṭapaṭkeḱkoe. He thumped them all round.

Paṭapuṭu. To sound, or crack as, grain when being roasted.

Jondra atae jokhed paṭa puṭu oṭejoḱa. Indian corn when being roasted cracks and jumps.

Laeho oḱa do sadea paṭa puṭu.

Paṭar. Paṭăr. } To close up, to close up or stop a hole.

Uni biń ma paṭarkaeme. Shut the snake in the hole.

Bhugeḱko paṭăr esetakaṭa dhirite. They have closed up the hole with a stone.

Patar. A sheet or piece of iron beaten out till it is thin.

Kuḍi patar. Iron beaten out to the thinness required to make a kodali.

Kara patar. Iron beaten out to the thinness required to make a pan for boiling sugar-cane juice.

Pataraḱ. A shoot from a tree, applied mainly to a shoot from a sarjom (q. v.) tree, split up the middle.

Sahan pataraḱ. A piece of a thin branch split for firewood.

Pataragoḱ. To spring or sprout, as a shoot.

Sarjom pataraḱ. A shoot from a sarjom (q. v.) tree.

Sahan pataraḱteye dal godkedea. He beat him to death with a piece of split firewood.

Pataraḱ aguime, goṭanaḱ do bah. Bring a split piece, not a whole one.

Pataraḱ. To be of full growth, just before ripening, as a mango fruit.

Ul pataraḱakana. The mango is full grown, and will now begin to ripen.

Pataraḱ jokheko amsia. When the mango has attained full size but while still green they make amsi (q. v.) of it.

Patar caṭa. Patar caṭia. Patar caṭua. } Going about in search of food, a licker of plates. Cf. patra.

Paṭarhań biń. A species of poisonous snake found on trees.

Patarohar. A girdle, a girth.

Patarphor. Fathomless, bottomless.

Pataṛ potoṛ. Scrubby, as a jungle in which are no large trees, having bare spaces or places, in patches.

Pataṛ potoṛ bir kana. This is a scrubby jungle.

Paṭar poṭor ghăsakana. The grass is sparse.

Patar satar. Thin, sparse.

Patar satar ḍher do bań jolena. There was not much fruit, it was sparse.

Paṭas. Paṭas puṭus. } Sounding of a slap, succession of slapping sounds.

Paṭas puṭusko dalkeḱkoa. They struck them slap, slap.

Paṭas marte. Paṭas mente. } With a slap, with a slapping or smacking sound.

Paṭas menteye dalkedea. He slapped him, gave him one smacking blow.

Paṭaulaḱ. Fallen leaves, a heap of fallen leaves.

Paṭaulaḱ radbadaoedae. He rustles the fallen leaves.

Paṭaulaḱreye boloakana. It has gone in among the fallen leaves (scorpion, &c.)

Paṭea. Crooked, disobliging.

Paṭea theńga. A crooked stick.

Paṭea hoṛ. A disobliging person.

Paṭeć. To dam or obstruct and cause to go another way, as water; to block a way, to lever.

Daḱko paṭeć giḍikada. They dammed the water and caused it flow away.

Kaṭkomko paṭeć oḍokkedea. They blocked the crab's way and levered him out of the hole.

Uni hoṛko paṭeć oḍokkedea. They turned that man out (by underhand means.)

Sahan bhari urija mente paṭećko lagaoa. They apply a lever to twist and tighten the load of firewood.

Paṭeć. To cross the legs, to interlace, to braid, to plait.

Nui gidra jańgae paṭećeḱtaea, puniḱae. This child is crossing his legs, he will become emaciated.

Paṭećakaṭae kioric ańcar. He has plaited the fringe of the cloth.

Paṭgando. To sit cross legged.

Paṭgandote duṛupakanae. He is sitting cross legged.

Paṭh. Paṭ. } A lesson.

Paṭh cela. The head scholar, the class leader.

Paṭh bhokta. Assistant to the bhokta who conducts the sacrifices at the pata (q. v.) festival.

Paṭh sal. A school. Cf. paṭsal.

Paṭha. A young he-goat.

Boda paṭha. A young he-goat.

Paṭhaona. To send.

Paṭhaonaadeale. We have sent to him.

Aṭhaona paṭhaona lagić mić hoṛle dohoakadea. We have engaged a man to go messages.

Paṭhauri. Andhe paṭhauri. } At random, carelessly, thoughtlessly, unintelligible, confused.

Andhe paṭhauriye dalkedea. He struck him at random.

Pathauri. } Groundlessly, in vain,
Auri pathauri, } inconsiderately, frivolously, serving no purpose.
Auri pathauri katha kana. It is a frivolous matter.

Pathe. } To one side, along the
Pathe pathe. } edge.
Patheteye calaoena. He passed along the edge.
Pathe patheteye dak idikeda. The rain passed over on one side.

Pathe, To bind round the loins.
Pathe denga. Wearing a piece of cloth round the loins.
Pathe ketecenae. He bound his loins tightly, he has girded his loins.
Cele, pathe ketecenam? Have you had your food?
Kicrić pathemé. Bind your cloth round your loins.

Pathi. A she kid.
Merom pathi. A she kid.
Patha pathikin busakakana. A male and female kid have been born.

Pathok. A colic or pain in the stomach.

Pathra. A stone plate.
Before the use of brass plates became so general stone plates were in common use.

Pathri. To bewitch and cause unconsciousness, to cast a spell on.
Ńeńel tandireko pathrikedea. They bewitched him at the place where the mela was being held. Cf. ńeńel tandi.
Jhinthiak alo, pathriak alo lagaok bajaokma. Let no spell or charm be thrown over us.

Pathor kala banduk. A flint and steel gun.

Pathor orot. } A small, rush like plant
Pathu orot. } having large elegant purple flowers, *Aeginetia indica, Linn.*

Pati. To prick, to bore, as the ears; to insert in the flesh, to draw blood by pricking to offer in sacrifice.
Janumte patienae. He has been pricked by a thorn.
Luturko patikoa jahanak horog lagić. They bore the ears to wear something in them.
Amem patiakana? Have your ears been bored?
Pati tapena. It is bored through.
Bhoktako patika. Those who swing at the swing festival have (hooks) inserted in the flesh.
Ganok horko patika. Those to whom it is allowable offer their own blood (to the deity).

Pati dhiri. A broad, flat stone on which spices are ground.

Pati. Each of the out-side planks of the solid wheel of a sagar (q. v.)

Pati. A line, a row, a strip.
Mić pati khetiń ńamkeda. I got a line, or strip of rice fields.

Pati Kisku. A sub-sept of the Santal sept Kisku (q. v.)

Pati eneć. The game of polo.

Patia. A mat.
Khijur patia. A mat made from the leaves of the khijur (q. v.) palm.
Sura patia. A reed mat.
Tale patia. A mat made from the leaves of the palmyra palm.
Mać patia. A bamboo mat.

Patiar. To believe, to trust, to credit; faithful, trustworthy.
Mahajon theniń senlena bae patiaradińa. I went to the moneylender but he would not trust me.
Patiar guti. A trustworthy servant.
Bae patiaradińa. He did not believe me.

Patiau. To believe, to trust, to credit.
Rengeć hor okoeye patiauama? A poor man who will trust you?
Nit utariń patiauena. Now at last I am convinced, or I believe.
Patiauae lek hor kanae. He is a trustworthy man.
Hor patiaue kamikana. He is making believe to work.
Uni theniń patiau erakana. I am working for him, I am his servant.

Patihar. To bewitch, to charm, to spell bind.

Patiol. A kind of tall reed.

Pat jhara. Autumn, when the leaves fall; a kind of diarrhoea which affects children in the autumn.

Patior. Expert, efficient.

Patit. Licentious, shameless, perverse, disobedient.
Patit hor kanae. He is a licentious man.

Patit. Fallow, uncultivated.
Adi ot patitena nes do. Much land is fallow this year.

Patka. A narrow strip of home-made cloth sixteen cubits long and one span broad worn as a turban.
The patka has gone out of fashion since the introduction of Manchester cotton cloth.

Patka. Tough, hard, mature, coarse.
Arak baram patkaena. The pot-herbs are old and coarse.

Patku naru. Unequally mixed or cut, applied to minced vegetables.
Patku naruko gerakata arak do. They have minced the vegetables unequally.

Patla. Thin.
Kicrić do patlako teńakada. They have woven the cloth thin.

Patloe. A small earthen vesssel used to cook in.

A meal of rice for four persons can be cooked in a *Patloe*.

Patna. A large round earthenware vessel two feet or more in diameter.

Patnại. A variety of the rice plant.

Pạtni. The female moth of certain silk producing caterpillers.

Lumạñ pạtni. The female of *Antheraea mylitta*, or the Tusser silk moth.

Bhạṛuạ pạtni. The female of *Attacus* Selene and *Attacus Atlas*.

Paṭo. Coarse or thick, as hair or leaves. Cf. paṭa.

Aṛak̇ haṛam paṭoena. The pot-herbs are old and coarse.

Uḃ paṭogetaea. His hair is coarse.

Paṭocak̇. Coarse and bristly, as hair.

Patohañ. } Saliva or froth dried at the
Potohañ. } corners of the mouth. Cf. patahañ.

Uniak̇ moća do pondge patohañentaea.

Patpala. } Leaves and branches.
Patpalha. }

Onte idikom patpalhako joma. Take them (cattle) over that way, they will eat the leaves.

Paṭpaṭ. } Suddenly, distressing, se-
Phaṭphaṭ. } vere, in close sucession.

Paṭpaṭk̇o gujuk̇kana. They are dying in close succession.

Rengeċte paṭpaṭle ạikạueda. We feel great distress owing to hunger.

Paṭpaṭ setoñkana. The heat is distressing.

Paṭpaṭ. } Cracking, pattering.
Paṭpuṭ. }

Paṭpaṭ rapudok̇kana. It is cracking and breaking, it is breaking and making a cracking sound.

Arel paṭpuṭ ñurok̇kana. The hail falls pattering.

Paṭpaṭao. To be distressed. Cf. paṭpaṭ.

Dak̇ tetañtele paṭpaṭaok̇kana. We are distressed with thirst.

Rengeċtele paṭpaṭaoena. We are distressed through hunger.

Paṭpaṭao. } To crack, to patter.
Paṭpuṭok̇. }

Rạpuṭ paṭpaṭaok̇kana. It is cracking and breaking

Setoñte rohoṛ paṭpaṭaoena.

Goć paṭpaṭaoena setoñte.

Paṭra. } A plate made of leaves pinned
Paṭri. } together with thorns, &c.

Paṭra rok̇ johme. Pin leaves together and make a plate for yourself.

Patra. } An almanack by which
Patra pạñji. } Brahmins foretell the
Pạtri pạñji. } future, to foretell the future by means of oil and incantations.

Patra pạñjiko ñela. They consult the almanack.

Dihri patra pạñjikatoyo lạiak̇koa, kulo jompoa mente. The master of the hunt having performed an incantation told them that a tiger would devour them.

Patrañga. M. }
Patrañgaha. M. }
Patrañgạhi. F. } Lean, never putting on flesh.
Patrañgea. M. }
Patrañgi. F. }

Patrañgahageae. He is lean.

Patrañgạhigeae. She is lean.

Paṭra poṭra. Big-bellied.

Paṭra poṭrageako. They have big bellies.

Paṭrat̉ poṭret̉. Big-bellied. Cf paṭra poṭra.

Pạṭri. A plate made of laaves pinned together.

Sae ṭaka sae pạtrile ạgumea. We will fine you a hundred rupees and a hundred plates (of food.)

Pạtri pạñji. Cf. patra pạñji.

Paṭrịạ. A disease so called.

Paṭsamle. A peg fixed into each end of a yoke to keep it in position on the bullocks' necks.

Paṭsir. A sinew. Cf. paṭ.

Patta. } A leaf.
Pạtti. }

Pạtti hećko ealaoena. They have gone to pluck leaves.

Pạttiwala. Tea leaf pluckers.

Paṭu. Mature, and so unsuitable for food, as pot herbs.

Paṭuć. } To force down from a per-
Paṭuḃ. } pendicular position anything fixed or rooted in the ground, to throw down by a lever.

Dare hoete rehet̉ sudha pạṭuḃena. The tree was uprooted by the wind.

Khunṭiko paṭuḃkeda. They pulled down the post.

At aser pạṭuḃle ealak̇kana. We are going to dig *at* and *aser* (q. v.]

Paṭuć. } Impetuously, violently.
Uṭuć paṭuć. }

Uṭuć pạṭuć holae dak̇keda. It rained heavily yesterday.

Uṭuć pạṭuće kạmikana. He is working impetuously.

Paṭwa. Intestinal worms, wanton, lecherous.

Paṭwako jomekana. He is suffering from intestinal worms.

Paṭwabo goćkoa. We will partake of food.

Paṭwa ghãs. A small plant, *Cassia mimosoides, Linn.*

Paṭweť. Stubborn, perverse, stingy, niggardly, deceitful, disobliging.

Nui do aḍiye paṭweťa. This person is very stingy.

Jahãnaǩem koyea bae emoǩa, aḍi paṭweť hoṛ. If you ask him for anything he will not give it, he is a very disobliging man.

Pãuchi. / Pạunchi. } A ridge of earth, to make a ridge.

Tạmbuko pãuchi ạcura, daǩ alo beloǩa mente. They make a ridge of earth round the tent to prevent water getting in.

Oṛaǩ berhaeteko pạunchiakaťa. They have raised a ridge of earth round the house.

Pạudạri. / Pạusdạri. } Cf. phạujdạri.

Pạunchi. Cf. pãuchi.

Pạuliạ. Cf. pạuriạ.

Pạurạ. Liquor distilled from the flower of *Basia latifolia.*

Pạurạ cuạ. To distil liquor.

Pạurạ gạdi. A grog shop.

Pạurạ ńuko senakana. They have gone to drink liquor.

Pạurạteye ńu bulena. He is drunk by drinking liquor.

Pạurạ bhạṭṭi. A liquor still.

Pạuriạ. One of the twelve septs into which the Santals are divided.

Pạusdạri. Cf. phạujdạri.

Pawa. One fourth of a pạilạ, or seer; a measure of that capacity.

2 pawa=1 pạị.
2 pạị=1 pạilạ or seer.

Pawetar. / Pawetar pawetar. } Said to bullocks when turning them in little space at the end of a furrow.

Paya. A deep and long pool in a river.

Paya. A very large earthenware pot or tub.

Payaǩ poyoǩ. Indistinctly. Cf. palaǩ poloǩ.

Payaǩ poyoǩ iń ńelledea. I remember having just seen him (said by one of an old man whom he could just remember.)

Payań. / Piạń payań. } Dawn, before sunrise.

Piạń payańrele oḍoklena. We started at dawn.

Payar. Time.

Ayuṕ payar. Even tide.

Setaǩ payar. Morning time.

Setaǩ payar reaǩ katha bah ṣuṛiạgoǩa. A matter taken in hand in the morning will not be in vain.

Payar. / Paera. } To lie down, mainly on the stomach, to swim, to float in water, to go backwards and forwards.

Payarakanae. He is lying on his stomach.

Daǩreko paera baṛaekana. They are swimming about in the water.

Kaḍa ḍherko payaroǩa daǩre. Buffaloes are greatly given to lying down in water.

Payar baṛaekanae. He is passing and repassing.

Pe. / Pea. / Peaṭa. / Pene. } The numeral three.

Pe hoṛiń ńelkeťkoa. I saw three people.

Pea poesa emańme. Give me three pice.

Pea ḍańra menaǩkotaea. He has three oxen.

Peaǩako. They are three, there are three of them.

Pepon hoṛko heeena. Three or four people came.

Pe goṭeć aguime. Bring three.

Pea goṭećiń hataokeda. I took three.

Peaṭageako. There are three of them.

Peaṭa khon jahãṭaǩgem hatao. Whichever of the three you may take.

Pe gel. Thirty.

Pe isi. Sixty.

Peada. A messenger who goes on foot, a peon, a court bailiff who serves summonses, &c.

Peadae heeakawadińa. A court peon has come to me.

Aćte do bae peadaadińa. He did not himself send the peon to me.

Mit́ din lạgiť iń peadalena. I was a foot messenger for one day.

Peaj. The onion, *Allium Cepa, Linn.*

Kaḍa peaj. / Ponḍ peaj. / Sạci peaj. } Varieties of the onion.

Peaṭa. Cf. pe.

Pĕc. A screw, strait, difficulty, pressure.

Pĕc lagao. To bring pressure to bear on one.

Pĕcko lagaoadińa. They brought pressure to bear on me, they put the screw on me.

Noare bae daṛeadińa, nhoa pĕce lagaoadińa. He was not able to subdue me in this, (so) brought this pressure to bear on me.

Pĕc paṛaoakawadea. He is in a strait or difficulty.

Peca. A species of owlet. Cf. kokor.

Pecha. } To follow up, to prosecute a
Picha. } search, as for one lost or strayed, to trace, to track, to prosecute an enquiry or claim, to prefer a claim.

Noa kathań pechaegea. I will follow up this matter, I shall have this matter thoroughly sifted.
Noa pecharen hoṛ kanae. He is the person who is pushing this enquiry, or pressing this claim.

Pĕckas. A screw driver.

Peco. The call of a certain species of owl.

Pedeć pedeć. } Small, applied to child-
Piḍić piḍić. } ren.

Peḍel peḍel. Quickly, rapidly, applied to females.

Peḍel peḍele daṛ idikeda. She ran on quickly.

Peḍgo. A plant the root of which is eaten.

Peḍgo. M. } Short, dwarfish.
Piḍgi. F. }

Pedgoṛ. M. } Fat, fat and big buttock-
Pidguṛ. F. } ed.

Khub pedgoṛ gidrạ kanae. He is a fine fat child.

Peḍle. M. } Short, dwarfish, low, dumpy.
Piḍli. F. }

Nui piḍli do ạḍiye ećgerkana. This dumpy is scolding awfully.
Peḍle dare. A low tree.
Peḍle peḍlege dareakana. The trees have not grown high.
Peḍle peḍlegeako. They are dwarfish.

Pedoṛae. M. } Fat, fat and big buttock-
Pidguṛae. F. } ed.

Pedeć pedećko ńir baṛaekana. The little ones are running about.

Pedoṛ pedoṛ. M. } Shaking as the flesh
Piduṛ piduṛ. F. } of a very fat person.

Pedoṛ pedoṛ moṭaakanae. He is so fat that his flesh shakes.
Piduṛ piduṛe moṭaakanae. She is so fat that her flesh shakes.

Pehlań. } To start, to move sud-
Pehlań pehlań. } denly, or quickly.

Pehlań pehlańe beńgeć baṛaeda. He keeps a sharp look out on all sides.
Pehlań pehlańe beńgeć idia. He goes looking furtively round about.
Pehlań pehlańe daṛ idikeda. He continued to run looking behind again and again.

Pehlań marte. } With a sudden start,
Pehlań mente. } with a sudden stare.

Ebhen goćenae pehlań mente. He awoke with a sudden start.

Pejleć. } Dirty, untidy. Cf.
Hejleć pejleć. } hejleć.

Peke poko. } Fat, chubby-cheeked.
Piko poko. }

Pela. A support under rafters.

Pela oṛaḱ. A house having supports under the rafters.

Pelao. To shove, to push, to throw, to trample over, to overcome.

Pelao giḍikedeae dosre. He threw (the responsibility) on the panchayat.
Sojhe pelaoḱkanae bae pạcoḱkana. He shoves straight ahead, he will not give way.

Pelka. M. } Short-sighted, having a
Pilki. F. } squint, oblique-eyed.

Pelpel. } To go bad, as cooked food,
Pelpelao. } flesh, &c.

Pelpelaoena jel do. The meat has begun to go bad.
Daka pelpelaoena. The boiled rice has soured.

Pĕnc. A screw, narrow, crowded, strait, difficulty, pressure brought to bear on one. Cf. pĕc.

Pĕnc oḍokenae. He was forced to leave.
Nonkan pĕnc jaegare ohoń tahĕlena. I will not remain in such a crowded place as this.

Pencoḱ. } To sulk.
Bencoḱ. }

Pencoḱ baṛaekanae. She is sulking.

Pend. A patch.

Pendko lagaoakaṭa. They have put on a patch.

Pend. } Deceitful, untrustworthy,
Endpend. } unreliable.

Katha reaḱ ṭhik bạnuḱtaea, endpendgeae. You cannot trust what he says, he is unreliable.
Pendgeae. He is unreliable.

Penda. The bottom, base, foot, underpart.

Band penda. The foot or base of the tank embankment (on the opposite side to that on which the water is.)
Buru penda. The base of the hill.
Kanḍa pendare bhugạḱgea. The waterpot has a hole in the bottom.
Bohoḱ do ḍạhguạ, penda rocoćgea.

Penda ḍopoć. Having a flaw or crack in the bottom, used also metaphorically for a widow or divorced woman.

Ale do eken penda ḍopoćaḱle ńamkana. We only want one with a flaw, (a widow or divorced woman.)

Penḍko. } Just beginning to ripen, as
Penḍkoć. } a fruit.
Penḍo. }
Penḍoḱ. }

Penḍoakana. } It is beginning to ripen.
Penḍkoćakana. }

Pendla.
Pendṛa. } Untrustworthy, unreliable, perverse, deceitful.
Pendṛaha.
Pendla hoṛ kanae. He is a deceitful person.

Penḍo.
Penḍok̕. } Cf. penḍko.

Penḍra. M.
Pinḍri. F. } Grey-eyed, white-eyed.
Penḍra kaḍa. A grey-eyed buffaloe.
Pinḍri ṣimṣi. A grey'-eyed woman.
Penḍra mara herel. A grey-eyed rascal.

Pindṛaha. Cf. pendla.

Peṅgha. To pretend ignorance.
Peṅghak̕kanae nui hoṛ do. This man is pretending he does not know.
Peṅghak̕tegeye tahena. He continues to feign ignorance.

Penḍra met̕. Chronic ophthalmia.

Pene. Three collectively.
Pene hoṛko calaoena. The three have left, all the three have left.
Pene eṅgahonko heċena. The mother and her two children have come.
Pene boehako benḍaoena. The three brothers are dead, all the three brothers are dead.

Pĕpĕ. Imitative of the sound produced by a bugle, trumpet, &c., more especially that produced by the pepṛĕt̕ (q. v.
Note torako calak̕kana pĕpĕ. They are passing this way making the sound of pĕpĕ (on their trumpet.)

Pepe. In threes, by threes.
Pepe goṭeċkateko calaoena. They left in threes.
Pepe goṭeċkate hapṭiń hoeĕna. In the division each got three.

Pephṛa.
Pephra. } Pretending not to understand, dogmatic, obstinate, mulish, stiff-necked, contumacious, wily and tenacious, unscrupulous, dissimulating. Cf. phepṛa.

Pepĕrkat̕. To brim with tears, to be suffused with tears, as the eyes.
Met̕ dak̕ pepĕrkat̕entaea. Her eyes were brimming with tears.
Met̕ dak̕ pepĕrkadok̕kantaea. Her eyes are being suffused with tears.

Pĕpŏ. Imitative of the sound produced by two trumpets (pepṛĕt̕) of a higher and lower tone, the pĕ being applied to the higher and pŏ to the lower toned instrument.
Pĕpŏko oroheda. They are blowing the trumpets pĕpŏ.

Pepreċ. To fill, to fill into, full. Cf. pereċ.
Pepreċ pepreċ dipilpe. Bring full baskets on your heads.
Pepreċkanako. They are filling (basket, &c.)

Pepṛĕt̕. A kind of trumpet, to roll up as a piece of parchment or paper, to make into a roll.
Pepṛĕt̕ ok̕rohkanae. He is blowing a trumpet.
Dolel pepṛĕt̕kateye dohoakat̕a. He has rolled up the document and laid it past.

Peṛa. A kinsman, a relative, to receive one as a kinsman, to show hospitality, to visit.
N̄epel oprom peṛa. Acquaintance.
Sor se saṅgiń peṛa kanae? N̄epel oprom peṛa kanae. Is he a near on a far off relative? He is an acquaintance.
Nij peṛa. Blood relative.
Peṛa paṛbhạ.
Peṛa paṛbhại. } Friends and relatives, acquaintances and relatives.
Ato saṅgai peṛa. Assumed relationship of those residing together or in the same village.
Deko peṛa. A Hindu acquaintance.
Jomloe peṛa. One who can partake of sacrificial flesh with a family at certain festivals.
Gutiạ peṛa. Of the same sept or sub-sept.
Bako peṛalediṅa. They did not treat me as a relative, they did not treat me hospitably.
Peṛa peṛale kuli n̄apamena. We asked and found that we were relatives.
Okoeko kanako? Ho, peṛa hoṛ kanako. Who are they? Oh, they are visitors.
Peṛaapeań hapen. I will pay you a visit in the future.

Peṛa. A kind of sweetmeat.

Peṛa hoṛ.
Peṛa horok̕. } A visitor, a relative, to become a visitor, to go on a visit.
Peṛa horok̕ko calaoena. They have gone on a visit to relatives.
Noko okoe kanako? Peṛa hoṛ kanako. Who are these? They are visitors.
Peṛa horok̕ lagitiń senapea. I will pay you a visit.

Pereċ. To fill, to fill in, full.
Kaṅkha habić perejpe. Fill to the brim.
Gaḍa pereċena. The river is full.
Pereċkate sareṛok̕kana. It is full and overflowing.
Pereċak̕ aguipe. Bring a full one.
Pereċ baṭi. A full cup.

Perek. A nail.

Perel.
Perel perel. } Nimbly, light footed, agile.
Perel perele don idikeda. He bounded away with great agility.

Perel marte.
Perel mente. } Nimbly, lightly, with agility, applied to a single action.
Perel menteye don paromkeda. He jumped lightly over it.

Perepere. Just beginning to throw out shoots, as a tree.

* Perepere sagenakana. It has begun to throw out shoots (a tree that has been lopped.)
Pereperelḱana mungɐ do. The mungɐ (q v) tree is just beginning to throw out shoots.

Peresań. A kind of musical instrument made from the shell of a pumpkin with one string.

Peresań. } To jump or bound, as crea-
Persań. } tures without feet; to fall, to roll, as one in a recumbent position.

Mić barea matkom persaholḱana. One or two flowers of the matkom (q. v.) are falling.
Persań calaḱkanako. They are moving by jumps (as certain insects that have no feet move by throwing themselves forward.)
Hakoko persaholḱana. The fish are jumping (live fish out of water.)
Gidrɐ parkom khon persań ńurenae. The child rolled over off the bed.
Persań gurenae. He slipped and fell.
Gend persań rakapḱana. The ball bounds upwards.

Perla. M. } Dim-sighted, half-blind,
Pirli. F. } squinting, applied to imperfect vision from whatever cause.

Persań. Cf. peresań.

Perta. Perverse, having a twist, at an angle, off the straight, unsociable.

Pertako lagaokeda. They placed it wrongly, off the straight
Perta pertako roṛa. They speak perversely.

Pes. To present, as a written petition or complaint, to prefer a complaint.

Kagoje peskeda. He presented the document.

Peseć peseć. } In small quantity, appli-
Peseń peseń. } ed to oozing, exuding, percolating, &c.

Peseń peseń setenolḱana. It is percolating in small quantity.
Peseń peseń jorolḱana mayam. It is bleeding a little.
Baṛe loṛe peseń peseń jorolḱana. The juice of the Banyan tree is dripping, or oozing out in small quantity.

Peseć peseć. Unpalatable, insipid, unappetizing, unrelishable.

Jomjomte peseć pesećenae. He has eaten till the food has become unpalatable.
Peseć pesećɐ jomkeda. He ate without relish.

Pesgi. }
Peski. } An advance of pay, &c.

Peska. The testicles.

Peskar. The official whose duty it is to lay petitions before the magistrate.

Peski. An advance of pay, &c.

Pesor. }
Phesor. } Cf. paskao.

Sanamiń pesorḱeda. I missed all.
Phesoṛenań. I have fallen short.

Pesṛao. } To overcome, to conquer, to
Phesṛao. } vanquish; to be unsuccessful, to weary. Cf. bhagao.

Nui horiń pesṛaokedea. I overcame this man.
Pesṛao ruɐṛenae. He was driven back.
Poesa lɐgić iń pesṛaolḱana. I am not succeeding in getting my money.
Pesṛao pɐairkedeako. They vanquished him.

Peṭ. The belly, the stomach.

Peṭ posa. A glutton.
Peṭlaha. Gluttonous, greedy, avaricious.
Peṭdɐndiɐ. A glutton, one whose god is his belly.

Peṭcamṛa. A small bush, Helicteres Isora, Linn.

Peṭcamṛa banda. A parasite found most frequently on Helicteres Isora, Linn., Viscum monoicum, Roxb.

Peṭara. } A kind of round bamboo basket
Peṭari. } with a lid used to hold clothes, or to carry on the end of a banghy pole.

Peṭari. } Widows and other poor
Ṛandi peṭari. } women.

Peṭeć. To snip off, to break off with the fingers, to nip off, as a twig or small branch.

Lumɐmko peṭećkedea, noa dare khon. They broke off the cocoon from this tree (nipped off the twig to which it was attached.)
Atnaḱ dar peṭeć ɐguime merom lɐgić. Break off a branch of the Atnaḱ tree (q. v.) for the goats.

Peṭeć. Light grain, blighted grain which has not filled, husk in which no grain has formed and which is winnowed out from among the good grain.

Koya horo ḋher do bań peṭejoḱa. There are few unfilled grains in koya rice.
Peṭećko te gidia. They winnow out the unfilled (or light) grain.

Peṭeć lipić. } The light grain separated
Peṭeć lipiḱ. } during the process of winnowing.

Peṭeć lipić joto samṭaope. Gather up all, the winnowings also.

Peṭe peṭe. Crammed, crowded together, cramped.
Peṭepeṭe daka isinena. The rice has been crammed in cooking (has not had space to swell.)
Tubeć peṭe peṭekedae. He crammed it in, pressing it closely together.
Peṭe peṭeko boloakana. They have crammed themselves in.

Peṭer. To twist, to screw, to writhe.
Hoṭoƙe peṭerkeda. He screwed round his head.
Hoṭoƙe peṭerkedea. He twisted his neck.
Bạti peṭer rakaḅme. Screw up the lamp.
Peṭer toćkedae. He screwed it out or off.
Peṭer totoćaƙ. A wrench, screw driver, &c.
Peṭer goć. To kill by wringing the neck.

Peṭer baṛe. A kind of Banyan tree so called.

Peṭer potam. A species of wild pigeon.

Peṭes. } **Peṭes peṭes.** } Applied to any short clicking or cracking sound.
Peṭes peṭes saḍekana. It is sounding click, click, click.

Peṭes marte. } **Peṭes mente.** } With a click.
Peṭes marte saḍeńa. It sounded click.

Peṭkhãokhão. Cry of fox at begining of the cold weather which is their pairing season.

Peṭdạndia. } **Peṭlaha.** } **Peṭposa.** } Cf. peṭ.

Petra da. A wild plant, *Jussioca suffruticosa, Linn.*

Phacak phucuk. To move about restlessly, to go here and there.
Phacak phucuk baṛaekanae. He is moving restlessly about.

Phac phuc. In all directions, singly, in twos or threes, in parties.
Phac phucko calaoena. They left in parties.

Phạd. A crowd, an army, a regiment, a legion, a host, a detachment, a band, a troop, a large party.
Noa phạdre menaea. He is in this band.
Ạdi phạd hoṛko jarwalena. A host of people were assembled.
Sendra phạd. A host of hunters, the hunter host.
Etom seć ren phạd ar koñyẽ seć ren phạd. The host on the right and the host on the left.

Phada. Open, unfenced, unenclosed, exposed, unprotected, unemployed, free, disengaged.
Ak baṛge phadagea. The sugarcane field is unfenced.
Dini nui ḍaṅgra emańme, phadagetamae. Give me this bullock, it is not employed.
Am dom phadagea. You are not employed.
Mại do phadagetapeae, se jahã seć reaƙ katha menaƙa? Is your daughter disengaged, or is there a purpose of marriage with any one?

Phadaphud, To flap the wings, to flutter (Imitative.)
Cele coe uḍauena phadaphud. Some one (bird) has flown away flappping.

Phada phodo. } **Phada phudu.** } To flutter or flap, as a young bird, to kick out as an infant unable to walk, to sprawl.
Potam hopon phada phudukin uḍạuena. The two young pigeons flew fluttering away.
Gidrạ ạdi phada phuduƙkanae. The child is sprawling and kicking.

Phaddạri. } **Phạudạri.** } **Phạujdạri.** } Criminal as opposed to civil courts, suits, &c.
Phạddạri mamla. } Phaddạri mokordoma. } A criminal case.
Phaddạri adalot. A criminal court.

Phadel. } **Phạdil.** } Over and above what is necessary, more than what is needed, overplus, surplus, in excess.
Nui ḍaṅra phadelgetińae. This bullock is in excess of my requirements.

Phadgal. To spurn, to kick, to drive back or away, as a cock using its spurs, to scratch, as a hen, to disarrange, to confuse, to disorder.
Phadgal goćkedae. The (cock) struck out.
Phadgal oḍokkedeako. They kicked him out.

Phadgao. To increase in size, as a sore.
Ghao phadgaoentaea. His sore has increased in size.

Phadphad. } **Phadphadao.** } To clap the wings, to flap the wings.
Sim sạṇḍiye phadphada. The cook claps his wings.
Parwa hopone phadphadaoƙkana. The young pigeon is flapping its wings.

Phadphadao. To break out or increase in size, as a sore.
Ghao phadphadaoƙkantaea. His sore is increasing in size.
The popular idea is that if a person suffering from a sore eats the beans of certain leguminous plants the sore will grow larger.

Phadphadao. To chatter, to gabble.
Sić sạṭuḅ phadphadaotegeye tahena. She is always chattering.

Phạdruk̔. } To move the limbs
Phạdruk̔ phạdruk̔. } spasmodically, as an animal on the point of death, or a person in an epileptic fit; a series of scratching or tapping sounds.

Phạdruk̔ phạdruk̔e phandaeda. It is kicking spasmodically.

Phaeda. } Profit, advantage, recompense,
Phaidạ. } benefit.

Noate cet̔ phaeda hoyok̔tiña? What will this profit me?

Phael. Broad, wide, ample, extensive, spacious, roomy, expansive.

Phaelte duṛuppe. Occupy a larger area in sitting.
Onkoak̔ ạdi phael jaega menak̔takoa. They own a very extensive farm.
Phaelgea. It is wide, or spacious.

Phaela. } To broaden, to widen, to
Phaelao. } extend, to spread; broad wide, ample, extensive, spacious, roomy, expansive.

Noa do khub phaelao jaega kana. This is a fine roomy place.
Hante phaelao idik̔pe. Spread yourselves over that way.
Mak̔ phaelaope. Hew and enlarge it (extend it by cutting down the jungle.)

Phạguạ. Of or belonging to the month of Phalgun (q. v.)

Phạguạ porob. A festival observed in the month of Phalgun.

Phạgun. The eleventh Hindu month Feb.-March.

Phạgun cando. } The month of Phalgun.
Phạgun bongo. }

Phahak. } To clear away, as mist.
Pahak. }

Phajhet. } To trouble, worry, annoy;
Pajet. } trouble, worry, annoyance.
Pajhet. }

Ạdi baṛiće phajhetkediña. He annoyed me greatly.
Ạdim phajhetok̔a. You will have much worry.

Phajil. Over and above what is necessary, overplus, surplus. Cf. phadel.

Phãk. Open space, free space, a blank, an opening, an interstice, an interval, an interspace, a gap, a rift, opportunity.

Birko mak̔ phãkkeda. They cut a clear space in the jungle.
Nia phãkte calak̔pe. Go by this clear space.
Phãk phãkteye laga idiket̔kina. He drove them away through the open space.
Rimil phãkena. There is a rift in the clouds.
Phãkiñ ñamlekhaniñ calak̔gea. If I get an opportunity I will go.
Phãk ñamlenkhan calak̔geañ. If an opportunity offers I will go.
Phãkreñ paṛaolena bañ ñapamlena. I was unsuccessful, I did not meet with him.
Boroṛ phãkge bañ ñamlak̔a. I did not get an opportunity to speak.
Uni tuluć galmarao reak̔ phãk bañ ñamlak̔a. I did not find an opportunity to speak to him.

Phakak̔ phukuk̔. To mumble when eating or speaking, as a very old person or one who has lost his teeth.

Phakak̔ phukuk̔e jomeda. He mumbles when eating.
Phakak̔ phukuk̔e hạṛamena. He is so old as only to be able to mumble.

Phakar phukur. To breathe heavily.

Phakar phukure sahet̔eda. He is breathing heavily.

Phakat. Only. Cf. phokot.

Phaki. } A medicine in powder, a
Phãki. } medicinal powder which is
Pạki. } taken in a dry state.

Phạki ran. Medicinal powder.

Phạki. To deceive, to trick, to diddle, to play one false, to victimize.

Phạkikediñae. He victimised me.

Phạkir. A Hindu fakeer or religious mendicant, poor, destitute.

Jugi phạkir menak̔koa. There are jugis (q. v.) and fakeers.
Phạkirenae. He has become a fakeer.

Phakphak. } To puff, to bubble when
Phakphakao. } boiling, an imitative
Phukphak. } word.

Phak phak sạdekana. It sounds puff, puff.
Phakphakaok̔kana jondra daka. The Indian corn porridge is bubbling (producing the sound phakphak.)
Rel gạḍi phakphakao calak̔kana. The railway train goes puffing (making a sound like phakphak.)

Phakphak. Extremely very, applied to hunger. Cf. phokphok.

Phakphak rengejiñkana. I am very hungry.

Phạkni. } A medicine in powder.
Phạkni ran. } Cf. phạki.

Phạkṛãk̔. A wing, wings, the shoulder blade. Cf. dạbi.

Phạkṛãk̔anko. Winged creatures, birds.
Phạkṛãgok̔ako. They will become winged.
Phạkṛãk̔ pasarkate udạuenae. It spread its wings and flew.

Phakuạ. Deceitful, tricky. Cf. phạki.

Phạkuṛạ. A wing. Cf. phạkṛãk̔.

Phal.
Phol. } Fruit, result, recompense.

Noa reak phalem ńama, purą. You will receive the fruit of this in full.

Phal ḍol.
Phol ḍol. } All kinds of fruit.
Phal phol.

Hąṛu phal ḍolko joma. Monkeys eat all kinds of fruit.

Netar phol ḍol din kana. The present time is the time of fruits.

Phalna. A certain, a particular, applied to inanimate objects.

Phalna jaegareń ńelleda. I saw him in a certain place.

Phalna ṭhen menaka. It is in a certain place.

Phalna. M.
Phạlni. F. } A certain or particular person, used when the speaker wishes to avoid particularising.

Phalna ṭhen menaka. A certain (male) person has it.

Phalna hoṛe ląiadińa. A certain man gave me the information.

Phalnage, bańmae roṛ ocokedińa. I said it of myself.

Phạlni ṭhen calakme. Go to a certain female.

Phalna tuską nite ląieṭkana, ar aḱ kangeae. He is now saying it was so and so, and it is himself.

Phalnateko ṭhen calakme. Go to a certain person and those with him.

Phạlti.
Phạltu. } Disengaged, extra, supernumerary, superfluous, irrelevant, overplus, surplus.

Phạltu ḍabra menaetama? Have you an extra bullock?

Phaltu jaega. A disengaged piece of land.

Noa do phạltu katha kana. This is an irrelevant remark.

Ale oṛakre miḱ hoṛ phạltu menaea. In our family one person is unemployed.

Phạlu. To joke, to make fun, humourous conversation, casual conversation before serious business begins.

Noa do phạlu katha kana, ceḱ bape sapeḱ? This is a joke, why do you seize upon it?

Nukin do phạlu hoṛ kanakin. These two can joke together.

Phạluteye ląi bujhąuaea. He explains it to him jokingly.

Ąuri ehobokreko phạluia. Before they begin (the work of the panchayat) they joke with each other.

Phand.
Phanda. } A noose, a net, a trap; to ensnare, to entrap, to falsely accuse.

Noa phandko lagaoakawadińa. They falsely accuse me of this.

Jal phande lagaoańkana. He is laying this trap for me.

Carale ńelkeda phanda do bale ńelleda. We saw the bait, but the trap we did not see. (we did not read the signs aright.)

Phãnḍ. Wide, broad.

Khub phąnḍko dohokeda. They made it very wide.

Noa oṛak do ạḍi phąnḍa. This house is very wide.

Phanda. To kick, to kick with the hind feet or a hind foot.

Ḍahra ṭhen alom calaka, ạḍiye phakndawa. Do not go near the bullock he is very much given to kicking.

Sadome phandamea. The horse will kick you.

Phanda. Cf. phand.

Phanḍao. To decide, to settle a dispute, to judge, to discuss with a view to settlement.

Noa katha phanḍaokatalepe. Decide this matter for us.

Jarwa male jarwalengea, menkhan phanḍao do bale phanḍao daṛeada. We did assemble, but we were not able to settle the matter.

Phanda phondo. Inefficiently, blunderingly, slowly.

Tin marańae? phanda phondoe siokkana. How big is he? He ploughs blunderingly.

Phạnḍgar. To become fat again, as one who has been reduced by illness or hunger.

Khube jom phạnḍgạrena. He has eaten himself fat.

Phanḍi. A thanna, a police out-post.

Alom lạṛhaia, bańkhan phạnḍitem calaka. Do not fight, or you will go to the thanna.

Phanḍo. Distress, perplexity, difficulty.

Ạḍi phanḍotale. Our distress is great.

Phanḍorele paṛaoakana. We have fallen into great distress.

De noa phanḍo kaṭaokatalepe. Relieve us from this distress (by incantations.)

Phandṛa.
Phandṛa phandṛa. } Wide apart, as the bars of a cage, having large interstices, with wide openings.

Phandṛa phandṛako eṭeḱakaṭa. They have not fenced closely (left gaps.)

Noa kicrić ạḍi phandṛagea. This cloth has wide spaces between the threads (not closely woven.)

Ḍaṭa phandṛagetaea. His teeth are wide apart.

Phańga. Deceitful, tricky, plausible, sophistical, jesuitical, exaggerated.

Phańgakedińae. He took me in.

Phańga hoṛ kanae. He is a plausible person.

Phańga reak katha kana, alope ańjomtaea. It is an exaggerated statement, do not listen to him.

Phańgwa. Cf. phańga.

Nui do phańgwa hoṛ kanae, alope patiąuataea. This man is a tricky fellow, do not believe his (story.)

Phaṅka phayaṛ. Freely, frankly, con, cealing or overlooking nothing-manifest, uncovered.

Iń baṅcaoiń leka bae roṛleda, phaṅka phayaṛe roṛ goṭkeda. He did not speak so as to screen me, he blabbed all out.

Phāṅk. Cf. phāk.

Phạṇṭil. To rebound, as a ball striking the ground perpendicularly, to move by bounds, as certain insects not provided with feet, to spring up, or back; to fly, as chips from an axe, to ricochet.

Ot khon phạṇṭil rakaboḱa. It rebounds up from the ground.

Aḿtege phạṇṭil toṭena. It came out itself with a spring.

Kuinḍi tejo phạṇṭil baṛaeako. The insect found in the kuinḍi (q. v.) moves by bounds or springs.

Phạṇṭil ruạṛena. It rebounded backwards.

Phaph. } **Phaphuḍạ.** } To boast, to blow, to yarn; a boaster, a yarner, an exaggerator. Cf phaṅga.

Phaphuḍạ kanae. He is a boaster.

Phaphuḍạedae. He is yarning.

Phaphu. Strongly, heavily, as breathing, blowing, &c.

Phaphue saheṭeda. He is breathing heavily.

Phaphue oṭoṅkana. He is blowing strongly. (with his mouth.)

Phaphu hoṛ. An exorcist, a diviner, who receives his name from his blowing upon his clients.

Phar. To increase, to become more, to abound.

Nitoḱ do phar goṭena. It has now become more.

Phaṛa. A piece, one, applied to wristlets or bracelets.

Miṭ phaṛa sakom. One piece bracelet (one bracelet.)

Bar phaṛa sakom. Two pieces bracelets (two bracelets.)

Pharak. Distance, separation. difference, distinction, absence; to put to a distance, to separate; distant, separate, different.

Noakinre ạḍi pharak menaḱa. There is great difference between these two.

Pharakte idikate giḍikam. Take it to a distance and throw it away.

Sen pharakoḱme. Go to a distance.

Kathako pharakkeda. Their statements did not agree.

Ạḍi pharak khon ńel ńamoḱkana. It is seen from a great distance.

Pharak pharak tahenpe. Keep at a distance from each other.

Pharakkom. Separate them, put them at a distance,

Pharcha. To clean, to finish, to clear up, as after rain; clear, as water.

Racako pharchakeda. They cleaned the court yard.

Kạmiko pharchakeda. They finished the work.

Khub pharcha daḱ kana. It is very clear water.

Teheń doe pharchakeda. It is clear to-day.

Pharchaena, me delabon. It has cleared up, let us go.

Phareb. To trick, to deceive, to calumniate, to make a false charge.

Pharebadińae. He calumniated me.

Pharebe lagaokeda. He brought a false charge

Pharhaṛ. Non-cohesive, detached, segregated, as grains of sand; incoherent, loose, not fixed to each other; glib, as the tongue.

Ạḍi pharhaṛko dakaakaṭa. They have cooked the rice so that the grains do not adhere one to another.

Hasa pharhaṛko sipiạkaṭa. They have mixed the clay so that it is non-cohesive (will not stick together.)

Ạḍi pharhaṛe roṛeda. He talks glibly.

Moca pharhaṛgetaea. He has a glib tongue.

Phạriạ. To recover from an illness.

Phalna ruạḱkanae phạriạkoḱmae. A certain one is ill, may he recover

Phạṛi. The shoulder, a shoulder of meat.

Phạṛi ṭhen hasoedekana. He is pained in the shoulder.

Phạṛi latarre hasoedekana. He is pained below the shoulder.

Phạṛi jaṅ. The shoulder blade.

Goė tora phạṛi goṭkedeae. Immediately it was killed he cut off the shoulder (of an animal.)

Jel phạṛi. A shoulder of venison.

Phạṛi jel. The meat or flesh of a shoulder of mutton, beef, venison, &c.

Phạriạ. To cure, to recover, clear, as water; clear, recovered, sincere.

Ruạ phạriạena. He has recovered from fever.

Ạuriye bereṭ phạriạḱa. He has not yet recovered from drowsiness after getting up.

Phạriạ daḱ. Clear water.

Hape, laṅgań phạriạ lenge. } Hape, laṅgań phạriạ lege. } Wait, let me first recover from my fatigue.

Laṅga phạriạko emadińa. } Laṅga phạriạwaḱko emadińa. } They gave me a cure for my fatigue (liquor.)

Phạriạ mon. A sincere heart.

Phạriạ. Cf. pharcha.

Phạriạ phạṭi. Clear, pure, as water, sincere, free from all anxiety, solicitude, fear, suspicion, &c., secure, to recover.

Phạriạ phạṭibon tahena. We will continue free from anxiety.

Ạḍi phạriạ phạṭi daḱ kana. It is very clear water.

Teheń khon doe phạriạkoḱ phạṭikoḱma, ruạḱ hoṛ do. May the sick person recover from to-day.

Phạriạu. Cf. phạriạ.

Phạriạu. To separate the threads of the warp which have stuck together by the starch which has been applied to them; to settle, to decide, to disentangle.

Ma niạ sutum phạriạukam. Separate these threads (in the warp.)

Ona kathale phạriạukeda. We settled that matter (We disentangled it.)

Pharkao. To fly, to flee.

Onte noteko pharkaoena. They have fled here and there.

Pạtniko pharkaoena. The silk moths have flown away.

Pharma. A mould. Cf. phorma.

Pharmao. } To recognize.
Phormao. }

Bań ńel pharmao daṛeadea. I could not recognize him.

Pharmaokedeań. I recognized him.

Pharmas. } To give an order for anything to be made.
Phormas. }

Mahle iń pharmasakawadea. I have ordered the Mahle (q. v.) basket maker to make it.

Pharnao. To be cured, to recover.

Ruạ khone pharnaoena. He has recovered from fever.

Bereć pharnaoakanae. He has risen and has recovered from his drowsiness.

Dal pharnaomealań nahak. I shall beat you and cure you of your drowsiness, or laziness (said when scolding.)

Eger pharnaokedeae. She cured him of his drowsiness by scolding him.

Ruheć pharnaokedeae. He cured him of his drowsiness, or laziness, by scolding him.

Pharphar. } Imitative of the sound of tearing, as cloth.
Phaṛphaṛ. }

Phaṛphaṛ kicriće oṛećeda. He is tearing cloth and making the sound phaṛphaṛ.

Pharphar. } To talk glibly, to talk volubly, to chatter, glibly, trippingly on the tongue.
Pharpharao. }

Pharphare roṛeda. He talks glibly.

Pharpharaokkanae. He is talking glibly.

Pharpharao. } To tear, to make a long tear, as in cloth.
Phaṛphaṛao. }

Phaṛphaṛao calaoena. It went tearing and sounding phaṛphaṛ.

Or phaṛphaṛaokedae. He pulled and made a long tear.

Phaṛphạriạ. } Non-cohesive, detached, loose, not fixed to each other, glib, distinctly, intelligible.
Pharphạriạ. }

Phạrphạriạ daka. Cooked rice the grains of which do not cohere.

Phạrphạriạ kathae roṛeda. He tells an intelligible story.

Phạrsi. Language. Cf. pạrsi.

Phasad. } Violence, crime, iniquity, mutiny, sedition, false accusation, difficulty.
Phesad. }

Aḍi phesadreń paṛaoena. I have become involved in great difficulty.

Phasal. } Crop, crops, harvest.
Phosol. }

Phasar phusur. To whisper, to speak in a low tone.

Phasar phusur bạị bạitekin galmaraokana. They are whispering together in low tones.

Akin akinrekin phasar phusur johkana. They are whispering.

Phạsi. A noose, a loop; to noose, to strangle, to snare, to kill by hanging, to be entangled; ensnared, involved.

Phạsi goć. To kill by hanging.

Phạsi gujuḱae. She will hang herself.

Phạsiko oḍaoakaṭa. They have set a snare.

Phạksiić. A hangman.

Phạsiaṛạ. Deceitful, tricky, hypocritical.

Alope phạsiaṛạka. Do not be deceitful.

Phạsiaṛạ hoṛ kanae. He is a deceiver.

Phasir. Cf. pasir.

Alom ewer phạsira. Do not fan so as to spread (the ashes) about.

Phaskao. Cf. paskao.

Phạskuć. Cf. pạskuć.

Phasphus. To speak in a low tone, to whisper.

Phasphus johkanakin. They are whispering together.

Ceć oohko phasphusana. They are whispering about something.

Phạsuṛ. To escape, to get loose, slip away, to pass over, to miss, to be overlooked.

Taeomenań, phạsuṛkedińako. I am late, they overlooked me.

Bań sạp ṭahraoledea, phạsuṛ ocokedeań. I could not hold him, I allowed him to escape.

Hijukko metadea, oka seć cohe phạsuṛena. They told him to come he has slipped away somewhere.

Agu daraepe, alope phạsuṛ ocoea. Bring him along with you, do not allow him to escape.

Phaṭak. Cf. phaṭok.

Phaṭakdar. Cf. phaṭokdar.

Phaṭak phuṭuk. } To go here and there, to be restless.
Phaṭań phuṭuń. }

Phaṭań phuṭuń baṛaekanae. He is going about here and there.

Phaṭao. To become sour, to go bad, to curdle, as milk.

Toa phaṭaoena. The milk has curdled, or become sour.

Phaṭar phaṭar. Imitative of a grating sound, to grate.
Phaṭar phaṭar saḍekana. It sounds gratingly.
Ṭoṭko phaṭar phaṭar saḍekana.
Hon phaṭar phaṭarko gereda.
Hutiye phaṭar phaṭareda.

Phaṭi. Cf. phaṛia phaṭi.
Suć dak, ḍaḍi dak leka phaṛiakok phaṭikokmae. May he recover and become as free from infirmity as spring water is free from impurity.

Phaṭiak. A small basket.

Phaṭkao. To sift with the haṭak (q. v.) to winnow, to dust, to shake or knock off anything slightly adhering, as dust, &c.
Phaṭkao pasirkedeako.
Phaṭkao giḍikedeako.
Garda tanak taben khanko phaṭkao giḍia.

Phaṭkar. To vomit.
Phakṭkarak. } An emetic.
Phaphaṭkarak. }
Ran bae jiṛau daṛeada phaṭkar giḍikedae. He could not retain the medicine, he threw it up

Phaṭ marte. } With a sound as of a tear, split, or crack.
Phaṭ mente. }
Phaṭ marteye dal jalaćadiña. It struck me with a crack.
Phaṭ marteye roṛ goćkediña. He at once chid me. [with a crack.
Baber topakena phaṭ mente. The string broke

Phatoe. A sleeveless waistcoat.

Phaṭok. } A gate, a large door, a prison; to shut in, to deprive one of his liberty.
Phaṭak. }
Phaṭokreko dohokediña. They kept me a prisoner.
Phaṭokreko aderkedea. They put him into jail.
Phaṭokakadeako. They have imprisoned him.

Phaṭphaṭ. To produce a sound resembling phaṭphaṭ; quickly one after the other, quickly.
Phaṭ phaṭe roṛeda. He talks glibly.
Phaṭ phaṭko gujukkana. They are dying quickly one after the other.
Phaṭ phaṭ saḍekana.
Phaṭ phaṭ topakena baber.

Phaṭ phuṭ. Imitative of the produced by anything cracking or falling with a sharp thud; to disperse, to separate.
Phaṭ phuṭenako. They are falling thud thud.
Phaṭ phuṭ topakena. It broke with a crack.

Phaud. Cf. phaḍ.

Phauti. Extra, unoccupied, ownerless, unemployed, not in use, over and above requirements, surplus, gratis, without giving anything in return.
Phauti khet. A rice field not leased to or owned by any one.
Phauti baṛge. A garden not leased to any one.
Phauti ḍanra. A bullock not in use, an extra bullock.
Phauti oṛak. An empty house, an unoccupied house. [ployed.
Phauti ge tahenkanae. He continues unem
Ñamam phautite? Will you get it for nothing?

Phec. } To drop, to drip, to fall in spray.
Phec phec. }
Phec phec pasirokkana. It is falling in spray.
Phec phec losoćakana. It is muddy on the surface.

Phec marte. } With a splash, with a splatch, with a spray.
Phec mente. }
Phec mente losoć pasiradiña. The mud flew spraying over me.

Pheca. The hip.
Pheca ghao. A sore on the hip.

Pheca cẽrẽ. A species of owl, so called from its note. Cf. dondor kokor.

Phecań. To backbite, to slander behind one's back,
Uni hoṛe phecańadiña. That man slandered me.
Eṭaktegeye roṛ phecańeda. He is introducing extraneous matter.

Phecań phecań. } Cry of the Tailor bird, *Orthotomus sutorius.*
Phecoń phecoń. }

Phecek phecek Cf. phec.

Phecek phecek. Imitative of the sound produced by dumping wet cloth on a stone when washing and the water spraying and swishing out.
Phecek phecek saḍekana.

Pheḍ. Near, close, low, the bottom or lowest part of anything, base, foot.
Coṭ pheḍ. High and low.
Pheḍ khoć coṭ babić. From bottom to top, from top to botton.
Pheḍren hoṛ. A neighbour.
Oṛ pheḍ khon. From the beginning, from the inception. [all about it.
Nui hoṛ do oṛ pheḍe badaea. This man knows
Khub pheḍre joakana. It has fruited very low down, on the low branches.
Buru pheḍ. The base, or foot of the hill.
Dare pheḍ. The tree root, where the tree enters the ground. [low.
Sate dope pheḍkeda. You made the eaves too
Iñ pheḍre duṛupakan tahẽkanae. He was sitting close to me.

Phedar phedar. } To chatter, to gabble, to prate, to mutter, to complain.
Phede phede. }
Pheder pheder. }
Phed pheder. }
Pheder phederokkanae. He is continually chattering.
Tinak bah phede phede aṛisakaćam? How long will you continue to annoy by your chatter?

Phedat. Root, base, birth-place. Cf. phed.

Am reah phedattet okare? Where is your birth place, where do you come from?

Ale do buru phedatre menaklea. We live at the base of the hill.

Phede phede. To chatter, to gabble, to flutter. Cf. phedar phedar.

Phede phede roredae. She is chattering.

Phedok. Cf. phet.

Phedrao. To speak, to speak, or say the same thing over and over again.

Tinakem phedraoka? bae añjoma. How long will you speak? he will not heed.

Pheke pheke. To bubble when boiling, imitative of the sound produced by anything thick boiling, such as Indian corn meal porridge, clothes, &c.

Jondra daka pheke pheke hedejokkana. The Indian corn porridge is boiling and producing a sound resembling pheke pheke.

Hape, tahgi ńogme pheke phekekkana. Stop, wait a little it is bubbling (and will soon be cooked.)

Pheknok. } Chubby-cheeked, fat-faced,
Pheknot. } applied to girls; to sigh as a child who has had a lengthened cry.

Pheknoke motaakana. She has fat chubby cheeks.

Alom pheknok pheknoga, thirokme. Do not sigh, be quiet (or give over.)

Phĕkphăk. To quibble, to employ subterfuge, to deceive.

Phĕk phăkte alom adeńa. Do not take the advantage of me by quibbling.

Phel. Cor. of the English word "fail."

Bae paslenkhanko mena phelenae. If he does not pass (an examination) they say he has failed.

Phel. Unmarried and of full or over full age, applied only to females.

Jahă atore jabăe ren hara hoponera bahko thăo hodokkhanko metakoa phelgeako. If in any village the grown up daughters of any one are not married quickly they call them phel or old maids.

Phen. A parable a metaphor,

Phente rorańkanae, bań bujhaueda. He is speaking to me in parables, I do not understand.

Phen. Cf. phĕr.

Pheńcor. To fly off in an oblique direction after having come into contact with something, to fly off at a tangent, to glance off, to be deflected.

Jahgare pheńcoradińa. (The axe) slipped obliquely (after having hit the wood) and hit me on the foot.

Guli dhiri khon pheńcorena etak secte. The bullet having hit the stone flew off in an oblique direction.

Kathae ror pheńcor gotkeda. He went off at a tangent and introduced another subject.

Phende. A parable, a metaphor.

Pheńkao. } To be lost, to stray, to
Phenkao. } conceal, to put out of the way.

Kombroko pheńkaokedea. They gave the thief a hint that he was wanted, (they concealed him.)

Gai okare cońe phenkaoentińa. My cow has strayed some where.

Gaiko phenkaokedea. They sent the cow out of the way (they hid her.)

Pheń pheń. To grumble or complain whiningly, to scold in a whining tone.

Pheń pheńokkana. She is grumbling.

Pheń pheńe egereda. She is scolding.

Pheń pheń. To twang, imitative of the sound produced by a string when pulled tight and suddenly let go.

Dhuniako piteda, pheń pheń sadea. The cotton carder twangs his bow.

Phente phere. } To writhe and twist,
Phente pere. } to struggle, as one trying to get free, to wriggle, to wriggle as an eel out of water, to dodge about.

Phente phere don. To jump as a fish out of water, to bound spasmodically as an animal when decapitated.

Chadaok lagit phente phere baraekanae., He is wriggling to free himself.

Phente pherekkanae, bań sap tahrao dareakana. It is struggling (a fish,) I cannot hold it.

Phente perentaea sar. His arrow wriggled.

Phentoć. To turn away the head when sulking.

Phentor. } To leap, to fly, as sparks, &c.,
Phantil. } to jump, as fleas, &c.

Phentor phasiroka.

Phĕ phĕ. } To pant.
Phĕs phĕs. }

Dar darte phĕ phĕ sahetkedae. He panted with continued running.

Phĕphĕedae. He is panting.

Phephra. } Pretending not to under-
Phephra. } stand, dogmatic, obstinate,
Phepra. } mulish, stiff-necked, con-
Phepra. } tumacious, wily and ten-
Pephra. } acious, unscrupulous, dissi-
Pephra. } mulating.

Phẽṛ. Foam, froth, to foam, to froth.
Moca hõ phẽṛoka dak tetańte. The mouth also foams through thirst.
Dak phẽṛakana. The water is frothy.
Dakre phẽṛ rakaḇena. There is froth on the water.

Pheṛ. Cf. pheḍ.

Pher. Again, change, turn, circumference.
Aḍi pherteń heċakana. I have come very round about.
Pher senok hoyoktińa. I will have to go again.
Pherke pher nonḍegeye heċena. He has come here again.
Pher dosi. To transgress a second time.

Pher bepar. To buy and sell again, to trade.
Aḍiye pher bepareda. He does much trade.

Pher endrae. Four days hence.
Gapań calaka, meań ar endrae onḍeń tahena, ar pher endrae oṛakteń ruṛa. I will go tomorrow, and stay the next two days there and return home on the fourth day.

Pher satom. Three years hence.
Nes. This year.
Kalom. Next year.
Satom. The year after next.
Pher satom. Three years hence.

Phera. } A strip of hair on the fore-
Phera up. } head kept shorter than the rest of the hair on the head.
Koca phera. The hair shaved in a little above the temples.

Pherao. To change, to turn,
Nia lugṛi pheraome. Change this cloth.
Dak pheraoe senakana. He has gone for a change of air.
Din pheraok jokheć. At the change of the season.
Pherao pheraotele idikeda. We carried it by turns.
Din pheraoena. The season has changed.

Pheṛao. Cf. phoṛao.

Phera phiri. To change, to alternate, to exchange.
Phera phirikate emańme. Give it to me in exchange.
Phera phiritele gok idikeda. We carried it on our shoulders by turns.

Phercoć phercoć. } Imitative of the
Phercoṭ phercoṭ. } hooting of a cer-
Pherkoć pherkoć. } tain species of owl.

Phere phere. To gush, to issue with violence and rapidity, as anything semi-liquid from confinement.

Pherkoć pherkoć. Cf. phercoć phercoć.

Pherkaṭite. Cunningly, craftily, by stratagem, by knavery.
Pherkaṭiteko saḇkedea. They caught him by guile.

Pherkoć. } To sulk.
Pherkoć pherkoć. }
Pherkoć pherkoć baṛaekanae. She is sulking.
Pherkoć pherkoće rakeda. She cries sulkily.

Pherphar. Cf. phera phiri.
Pherphar gogben. Carry it by turns.
Polisko pherpharkoa. They transfer the police (from one station to another.)

Pheṛsań. Cf. peṛesań.
Pharak pharakrege pheṛsań baṛaekanae. He is going about keeping out of the way.

Pherwek. } A seller, mainly applied
Pherwekia. } to traders in cattle and other live stock who traverse the country.
Pherwekia ṭheniń ńamkedea. I got it from an itinerant cattle dealer.
Pherweketkanae. He deals in cattle.
Pherwektegeye aṣulokkana. He earns a living by dealing in cattle.

Phesad. } Difficulty, violence, wicked-
Phasad. } ness, false accusation.
Aḍi phesadreń paṛaoena. I am in great difficulty.
Phesadadińako. They accused me falsely.

Phesoṛ. Cf. pesoṛ.

Phẽs phãs. } To no purpose, vainly,
Phes phas. } make believe.
Phesphastege dine kaṭaoeda. He spends his time to no purpose.
Mahajon doe phesphasedekana. The money lender keeps him in suspense.

Phẽs phẽs. To pant, to breathe heavily, as one fatigued, or suffering from asthma, &c., an imitative sound.
Phẽs phẽse saheteda. He breathes heavily.
Phẽsphẽsenae. He is panting.

Phesṛao. Cf. pesṛao.

Pheć. To let go anything pulled tight, as a bowstring, to play, as on a harp strings, &c., to vibrate, to jerk.
Phetaeme. Let go the arrow at him, twang the bow at him.
Tulame phețeda. He is teasing the cotton, by twanging a bow string in it.
Husiaṛokme, bańkhanem phedoka. Look out, or else you will be struck (as by a branch when released.)

Pheṭ. } To mix, to beat up, as an egg,
Pheṭao. } to shuffle, as cards.
Tasko pheṭaoa. They shuffle cards.
Khub pheṭme. Mix it well.

Pheṭãṛ. A heifer.

Pheṭe pheṭe. Imitative of the noise produced by fluttering or flapping, to writhe.
Note pheṭepheṭeń ańjomkeda. I heard a flapping here.

Seta dak̇teko lohoćlenkhaṅ dak̇ko koṭa giḍia pheṭe pheṭe. When dogs are wet with water, they shake it of with a flapping sound (their ears flap.)

Phi. To reject; unsuitable, defective, imperfect.

Nui hoṛ doe phiena. This man has been rejected.

Uni lekate phienae. He was unsuitable for his purpose.

Phickaṛi. } A syringe, to squirt liquid
Phocor. } with a syringe.

Phidi. Cf. phidli.

Phidgạl. Cf. phadgal.

Phidgạ phidgi. Perfunctorily, imperfectly, applied to sweeping.

Phidgạ phidgiye jok̇keda. She swept (the floor) perfunctorily.

Phidgil. To spurn with the hands, to spead with the hands.

Hoṛo phidgil baṛaakaćako. They have spread out the dhan (with the hand to dry.)

Phidil. } Cf. pidil.
Phidil phidil. }

Phidli. To tease, to card as wool, cotton, &c., to open out anything that adheres together, or is compact, to disarrange, to disorder, to jumble, to rumple, to towzle.

Jemṭheskan khaṅ tulạmko phidlia. If cotton sticks together they tease it.

Kiorić cak̇pe phidlikećtińa? Why have you disordered my cloth (which was folded neatly?)

Uḅ alope phidlitińa. Do not towzle my hair.

Phidrạk̇ phidrạk̇. A tapping or rapping sound, a succession of tapping or rapping or scratching sounds.

Sińi sạṭuḅ phidrak̇ phidrạk̇e egereda.
Phidrạk̇ phidrạk̇e phandaeda mihū do.
Phidrạk̇ phidrạteye roṛeda.
Note phidrạk̇ phidrạk̇ińi ańjomkeda.

Phikir. Thought, reflection, consideration, solicitude, contrivance, endeavour.

Ạḍi phikirkateń ńamkeda. I obtained it after much endeavour.

Phikirem lagaoa. tobekhanem ńama. You must do your endeavour, then you will obtain.

Ạḍi phikirreń paṛaoena. I am in great solicitude.

Phīk leka. Unsullied, pure white, as snow, as chalk, as a lily, as ivory, as driven-snow; milk-white, snow-white.

Phīk leka pondgea. It is as white as driven snow.

Phinạu. To become clear, as water the impurities in which have settled at the bottom; to rise to the surface, as the serum or watery part of milk.

Dak̇ do phinạuena. The water has cleared (the impurities have settled at the bottom.)

Dahe baṅ jamaolena, phinạuena. The curds did not congeal, water has risen to the surface.

Phini phik̇. Clear, pure, as water; bright, cloudless. Cf. phīṛīphīć.

Phin phiniạ. Fine, thin, semi-transparent, as cloth, paper, &c.

Phinphiniạ etaṅ dak̇. Saline water, water exuding from saline soil.

Ceńlekam teńkeda? phinphiniạgea. How did you weave it, what like did you weave it? it is thin.

Phinphiniạ etaṅgea. It is very thin.

Phirạu. To go to stool.

Jahālekate phirạu ocoem. Cause his bowels to move in some way or other.

Phirạu. To restore, to give back, to return.

Bape dohoekhan phirạu goćkataepe. If you do not buy it, return it to him at once.

Phiri. A shield of metal with a sharp projecting point used for stabbing

Ḍhal. A buckler of hide studded with nails, &c.

Phiri ar ḍhal. Shield and buckler.

Phiriạdi. } An accuser, a complainant,
Phuriạdi. } a plaintiff.

Phiṛipaṅ. } Clear, bright; to clear,
Phiṛiphaṅ. } as after rain, or by the dispersion of clouds, bright weather.

Phīṛīphīć. } Clear, pure, unsullied,
Phiniphik̇. } smooth, glassy, as a sheet of clear still water.

Nitok̇ do phīṛīphić ńelok̇kana, phākkedae. It is now bright, the clouds have vanished.

Hana band reak̇ dak̇ phīṛīphić phạriạwa. The water of that tank is brightly clear.

Phiṛiphaṅkedae, delabon calak̇a. It has cleared, come we will go.

Phiṛiphaṅkedako. They cleared it (the jungle) completely.

Phiṛi phoṅ. Cf. phirphoṅ.

Phirkạ. Stratagem.

Phirkạkateko sạpkedea. They caught him by stratagem.

Phiṛki. A door, a window opening.

Phiṛki bhugạk̇te oḍokkateń daṛkeda. I came out by a hole at the door and fled.

Tạṭi lagal, phiṛki lagal, soboe kichu gelre, Ghare binu, nạihạr gel, bạri namo hagalre.

Note. Song sung by Dasāe koṛa (q. v. in sup.) when the inmates of a house do not shew themselves.

Phirot. To return, to give back, what is returned after deductions.
Noa ṭaka khon pon anna phirotem ṅama. You will receive back four annas out of this rupee.
Phirot goṭkedae. He returned it at once.

Phirphir. } To be restless, skittish,
Phirphiraụ. } to start suddenly, to turn round, sullenly, restlessly.
Phirphir baṛaekanae. He is going here and there.
Eneòre phirphirko ṣourok̇a.
Bạhu kuṛi phirphirạu baṛaekanae. The bride is moving restlessly about (being dissatisfied with her new environment.)

Phirphoṅ. } Clear, clear, as the sky,
Phiṛiphoṅ. } having clear spaces, that admit of being seen through or into, a clear space with nothing to interrupt the vision.
Oṛak̇ge phiṛiphoṅgetama.

Phiṭ. To reject, defective, imperfect, spurious.
Sona menteye hataolak̇a, menkhan phiṭentaea.

Phitạ. Tape, braid, wick of lamp, a band of plaited hair used by women to tie up the hair.

Phiṭi. A skein of thread.

Phiṭkiri. Alum.

Phocor. A squirt, a syringe, to squirt with a squirt.

Phodle. M. } Fat, stout, applied to
Phudli. F. } little children.

Phodlo. To be frayed, to open or untwist, as the end of a rope, &c., not sufficiently twisted, as twine, thread rope, &c., pulverised, broken up, as soil by the plough.
Barạhi phod̄loena. The rope has opened out, untwisted.
Ot khub phodloena. The soil is well pulverised.

Phoḍophoḍo. Cf. poḍo.

Phogra. M. } Having lost the front teeth,
Phugri. F. } toothless.
Phogṛaeae. He has lost his front teeth.
Phugṛi mara ṣimṣi. A toothless jade.
Phogṛa haṛam. A toothless old man.
Pugṛi budhi. A toothless old woman.

Phohom. } To recognize, to see distinct-
Pohom. } ly, applied mainly to one suffering from an affection of the eyes.
Baṅ pohomlak̇a. I did not see distinctly.

Phŏk. The nock of an arrow, the notch on the end of an arrow where the string fits in.
Ghuṛã phŏk. The nock for a fibre bow string.
Poṛcha phŏk. The nock for a bamboo bow string.

Phoka. To blister, to rise in a blister.
Ti phokaentaea. His hand is blistered.
Lo phokaentaea jaṅga: His foot is burned and blistered.
Phokak̇a nahak̇. A blister will presently rise.
Dal phokakedeae. He struck him and raised a blister or swelling.

Phoka matkom. Mạtkom (q. v.) cooked in a certain way.
The matkom is washed in water and while still wet is put into an earthen vessel over the fire and roasted.

Phokot. Only. Cf. phakat.

Phokphok. To puff, imitative of the sound of puffing or bubbling.
Phokphok heḍejok̇kana jonḍra daka do. The Indian corn porridge is boiling and bubbling.

Phokphok. Extremely, very, applied to hunger.
Phokphok reṅgejiṅkana. I am extremely hungry.

Phokphoko. To puff. Cf. phokphok.

Phoksaha. Soft, flabby soft and insipid. Scottice, *fossy*.
Hoṛmo phoksahagetaea. His body is flabby.
Hoṛmo phoksahaenae. His body is flabby.
Noa matkom do phoksahagea, baṅ sebela. This matkom (q. v.) is soft, it is not palatable.

Phokṭi. } Humorous, joking, jocular.
Phukṭi. }

Phokṭiạ. } A humourist, a comical fellow,
Phukṭiạ. } a joker.
Phokṭiạ ṭkanae. He is a comical fellow.

Phol. Fruit, result.
Kạmi reak̇ pholem ṅamkedạ. You got the fruit of your labour.

Pholao. To bear fruit, to retribute, to suffer the pains and penalties of wrong doing, nemesis.
Duk pholaoadea. He suffered for his misdeeds.

Pholhar. Cf. polhar.

Pholok. To clear away, as mist.

Phond. To misrepresent, to calumniate, to malign, to falsely accuse or impute, to slander.
Phondadiṅae. He calumniated me.
Phonde joṛaoeda. He is getting up a false accusation.
Phonde lagaoeda. He accuses falsely.

Phoṅ. } Imitative of the sound produc-
Phuṅ. } ed by a tight string suddenly relaxed, to twang, to swish.

Phoṅ marte. } With a twang or swish.
Phoṅ mente. }
Phoṅ mente saḍe goṭena. It sounded twang.

Phoṅke. } That can be seen through,
Phoṅphoṅ. } as anything with a hole
in it, as a pipe, drain, culvert, &c.
Phoṅ phoṅ ñel taboḱkana. You can see right
through it.

Phoṅphoṅ. Broken in several places.
Phoṅphoṅ bhugeḱena. It is broken or holed
in many places.

Phophra. Rotten, decayed, particles
not cohesive, hollow through decay
or the action of insects, applied
mainly to timber.
Phophra kaṭ. A log rotten in the centre.
Baṅ nimona, phophragea- It is not sound, it
is decayed.
Ñindirko jom phophrakeda. The white ants
ate it hollow.

Phoṛ. To cut a dam to allow the water
to run out, to be breached, as an
embankment of a dam, &c.
Daḱko phoṛakaḱa. They have cut the dam
and let the water out.
Daḱte phoṛena. It (embankment) has been
breached by water (by a flood:)
Ñir phoṛenae. He has run away (like water
from a breached dam.)

Phora. Hollow in the centre, as some
bamboos, and the stalks of certain
plants; having a hard shell, but
soft inside, decayed in the centre,
applied mainly to certain fruits.
Kohnḍa phoragea. The kohnḍa is [q. v.] hollow
in the centre.
Phora maḱ kana. It is a hollow bamboo.

Phoṛao. } To transplant from where the
Pheṛao. } plants are thick to where
they are thin.
Jonḍra ḍherko phoṛaoe. They oftenest transplant Indian corn from where it has germinated thickly to where it is sparse.

Phoṛao. } To snort, to make a
Ṇaṭhu phoṛao. } noise through the
nose.
Sadom naṭhu phoṛaoedae. The horse is snorting.

Phorma. } A mould, as for bricks, &c.
Pharma. }

Phorman. } To bespeak, to give an or-
Phormas. } der for something to be
made or prepared.
Phormasiñ lagaoakaḱa. I have placed an order.
Phormasle nehiṁ ñama. You must first give
the order before you can get it, (you cannot
get till you order it.)

Phormao. To recognize.
Phormao goḱkedeañ, Biswaḍiḥ māñjhi kanae.
I recognized him at once, he is the head-
man of Biswaḍiḥ.

Phorme. Cf. phormao.

Phorophoro. Imitative of the sound
produced by flames, to flame, to
blaze.
Sehgel phorophoroḱkana. The fire is blazing.

Phorphond. } To misrepresent, to cal-
Phorponde. } umniate, to malign, to
falsely accuse or impute, to slander.

Phorphor. } Imitative of the sound
Phorphorao. } produced by a strong
flame, to blaze, to roar, as flames.
Sehgel phorphor saḍea.
Sehgel phorphoraoḱkana.

Phorphundi. Cf. phorphond.

Phoska. } Particles non-cohesive, rot-
Poska. } te, decayed, soft.
Baber phoskagea. The twine is decayed.
Poska kaṭ. Rotten wood.
Poska hasa. Crumbling earth.

Phoska olaṭ. } A small forest tree Ky-
Poska olaṭ. } dia calycina, Roxb.

Phosol. Crop, grain.
Nes phosol baṅ hoelena. The crops failed this
year.

Phosol. Spurious, counterfeit.
Asol do baṅ kana, phosol sona kana. It is
not genuine, it is spurious gold.

Phosol, } Cf. dhoṅgol phosol.
Dhoṅgol phosol. }

Phoṭ. A cob of Indian corn, to form
into a cob.
Bar pe phoṭe emadiña. He gave me two or
three cobs of Indian corn.
Jonḍra phoṭoḱkana. The cobs are forming on
the Indian corn.
Khub bhage phoṭakana. Very good cobs have
formed.

Phoṭ marte. } Cf. phaṭ marte.
Phoṭ mente. }

Phoṭ cerē. A wild bird so named from
its call.

Phoṭao. } To strike a ball, bit of stick,
Phaṭao. } &c. which has been raised
into the air by being hit when on
the ground.
Khube phoṭaoakaḱa. He has hit it and sent it
a long distance.

Phoṭao. To pass over, to conquer, to
diddle, to deceive.
Phoṭaokediñako, bako emadiña. They diddled
me, they did not give to me.

Photo.
Photo photo. } Froth, to froth.

Adi photo ạṛgonkana, hape alom paromoḱa. There is much froth coming down (on the river,) wait, do not cross.

Kumbiṛ chal koṭeċkate dak̃re hudgạrlekhan photoḱa. If the pounded bark of the kumbiṛ (q. v.) tree be stirred into water it will foam or lather.

Banako photophotoea, aṛ sukri hõ. Bears foam at the mouth, and pigs also.

Photophoto. Imitative of the sound produced by a ṭoṭko (q. v.) or wooden bell sometimes tied round the necks of cattle.

Gại ạtiń ǰokheć ṭoṭko photophoṭo sadea. When the cow is grazing the ṭoṭko q. v.) sounds photophoto.

Phũ.
Phu. } Imitative of the sound produced by blowing with the mouth, to blow with the mouth, to sigh or breathe through the mouth.

Ohkedae phũphũ. He blew and produced the sound phũphũ.

Phũ marte.
Phũ mente.
Phu marte.
Phu mente. } One long sound produced by breathing outwards through the mouth, with a long expiration.

Bir paromkate phũ marteń sahećkeda. Having crossed the jungle I gave one long sigh.

Neḱe utạr phu marteń sahećkeda. Not till then did I breathe freely.

Phuphuạu.
Phupuạu. } Cf. phu.

Phuci.
Phuci cẽṛẽ. } A small bird so named, applied also to small birds in general.

Phuci hõ bam goć daṛeadea. You could not kill even a small bird.

Phucią. Small, attenuated buttocks, narrow in the hind quarters, as a horse, bullock, &c.

Phucią ḍahra. A bullock narrow in the hind quarters.

Adi phuciạreye dhutiakana. His dhoti is bound low down (not round the waist which makes the buttocks appear small.)

Phuckạ. M.
Phucki. F. } Narrow from the waist downwards, dhuti or putli (q. v.) so bound as to give the appearance of small buttocks, applied to children.

Phuckạ.
Phuckuć. } Too low down, too short, projection too small, too small.

Sate do phuckạgea. The eaves are too small, do not project sufficiently.

Phuckućreko tolakata. They have tied it too low down.

Phuckućkedako. They have made it too low.

Sate phuckućena. The eaves are too short, or too small.

Phuckạ. Thicker at one end than the other.

Bindạ do phuckạgea. The sheaf is thicker at one end than at the other.

Phuckạ phucki. Large and small, big and little, applied mainly to children.

Iń sãote phuckạ phuckiko heċena. The (children) big and little have come with me.

Phuckuć,
Phuckuć phuckuć. } Cf. phuckạ.

Phuckuć phuckuće suṭakana. Her knot of hair (at the back of her head) is very small.

Phucuć.
Phucuć phucuć. } Quickly, without delay.

Phucuć marte.
Phucuć mente. } Suddenly, quickly, on the sudden, on the instant.

Phudnạ. An ornament of cotton or silk thread worn on the upper arm.

Phudphud.
Phudphudạu. } To flap, to bubble, an imitative word.

Sime phudphudạuḱkana, peṛako hijuḱa. The hen is clapping its wings, visitors will come.

Phudphudạuena daḱ do. The water is bubbling (boiling.)

Phugṛi. F.
Phogṛa. M. } Toothless, having lost the front teeth.

Phugṛi maṛa ạimai. A toothless hag.

Phuhi.
Puhi. } To rain gently, to drizzle. Cf. puhi.

Phujạu. To pay up, to repay or return, as a loan, to make up deficiency or arrears.

Ṭakale phujạuadea. We repaid him the money.

Phujkuć. Cf. phuckuć.

Phuk.
Phuk phuk. } To breathe quickly and heavily.

Phukphuk reṅgeje kana. He is panting with hunger.

Phukphuk sahećećkanae. He is panting.

Phuk marte.
Phuk mente. } With a swish, as of some sharp instrument piercing something soft.

Phuk marteń tuń ńamkedea.

Phukạr. An opening, an aperture, a hole through and through, as in a wall, a chimney opening.

Nią then phukạrpe dohoea, daḱ oḍok lạgić You will leave a hole here for the water to escape.

Phukạr.⎫ Summons, call, applied mainly
Pukạr. ⎭ to the calling on of cases
in a court.
Iṅ$k phukạr hoeĕna. My case or suit has been
called on, I have been called.
Thir hataṛoĺme, tinre phukạr hoyoĺtạma,
unrem hạjiroĺa. Wait in the meantime,
when your case is called then you will
appear.

Phukạr.   ⎫
Hăkar phukạr. ⎭ Cf. hăkar ṭokar.

Phuki. Empty, hollow, empty, applied
to cocoons, &c., from which the
insect has emerged.
Phuki lumạm. ⎫ An empty tassar cocoon from
Lumạm phuki. ⎭ which the moth has emerged.
Phuki lạhi. The rezinous encrustation from
which the lac insect has emerged.
Netar lạhiko phukiena. At this time of the
year the lac insect has emerged.
Huti jonḍrako jom phukikeda. The huti (q. v.)
ate the Indian corn hollow.

Phukni. A piece of hollow bamboo
used as a blowpipe, the Indian
substitute for bellows.

Phukrin. A witch.

Phukṭi. To jest, to joke; joking, jes-
ting, funny humorous.
Phukṭi katha kana. It is a jest.
Phukṭi johkanako. They are jesting with each
other.
Phukṭiaekanae. He is joking him.
Ado Mạñjhi phukṭi kathae roṛa. Then the
Mạñjhi cracks jokes.

Pukṭiạ. A humorist, a joker.
Phukṭiạ kanae. He is a humorist.

Phukur.   ⎫ To breathe quickly
Phukur phukur.⎭ and heavily. Cf.
phuk.
Phukur phukure sahetetkana. He is breathing heavily.
Phukur phukur reṅgeốediṅkana. I am panting
through hunger.

Phukur marte. ⎫ With one long breath,
Phukur mente. ⎭ with a heavy sigh.
Phukur mente sahet goťkedae. He gave a
great sigh, he sighed heavily.

Phul. A flower.

Phul.   ⎫ To perform a ceremony
Phul patao. ⎬ wherein two young
Phul poran. ⎭ persons of the same
sex engage themselves to life long
friendship.
The ceremony consists mainly in an interchange of presents of cloth and the fixing
of a flower (phul) in the hair of each other.
The two who thus engage themselves to
life long friendship always address each
other as phul (flower), never employing
the real name. It is more common among
females than among males.

Nuiteĺiúliń phuloĺa. This girl and I will engage our selves to life long friendship by
observing the phul (flower) ceremony.
Iń phul kanae. She is my phul (flower), she
and I have gone through the phul ceremony.
Phulkin pataoakaťa. They have gone through
the phul ceremony (whereby they have
engaged themselves to life long friendship.)
Phul poranoĺaliń. We two will go through
the phul ceremony
Phul poranko heĕena. My phul (the person
with whom I have gone through the phul
ceremony) and her friends have come.

Phulạ. The Matkom (q. v.) flower, the
fresh flower of the Matkom (q. v.)
Miť bar phulẹ ńuroĺkana. A few flowers of
the matkom are falling.
Phulẹ matkomko teke joma. They cook and
eat the fresh flowers of the matkom q. v.)

Phulại. To jest, joke, make fun.
Phulạiedae. He is making fun.
Ceťem phulạiediń kana? Why are you making
fun of me?
Phulạiea mente. For the purpose of making
fun of him.

Phulạniạ. A humorist, a funny fellow
one given to making fun; funny
humorous.
Phulạniạ kanae. He is a humorist.
Phulạniạ hoṛ kanae. He is a funny fellow.

Phulạu. To swell, to distend, to be
proud, vain, overweening. vain-
glorious.
Jaḣga phulạuentaea. His foot is swollen.
Phulạuĺkanae. He is vain.

Phulbạriạ. A flower garden.

Phul dhạriạ. Assistant to a witch-
finder. The phuldhạriạ attends the
jan (q. v.) when engaged and
gives him whatever is required at
the proper time. He is also said
to ferret out information from
those who have come to consult
his principal and privately convey
it to him.

Phulgad. The second scum which
forms on sugar cane juice when
being boiled.

Phuli.   ⎫
Ḍali phuli. ⎭ Cf. ḍali phuli.

Phuli pạurạ. The pure spirit distilled
from matkom (q. v.)

Phundi.   ⎫
Phorphundi. ⎭ Cf. phond.
Phundiadiñae. He is bringing a false charge
against me.

Phuṅ. } To twang, as a bowstring,
Phuṅ phuṅ. } to swish, as a stone flying through the air, an imitative word.

Phuṅ marte. } With a twang, with a
Phuṅ mente. } swish.
Phuṅ mente saḍeëna. It sounded swish.

Phuphuạu. } To blow, to hiss, as a
Phupuạu. } snake; to snort; (an imitative word.)
Biṅko phuphuạuk̕a. Snakes hiss.
Adom ḍaṅra joṛaoko jokhečko phuphuạuk̕a. Some oxen snort when being yoked.

Phuphunḍạ. To become mouldy, or mildewed.
Panạhi phuphunḍạena. The shoes are mouldy.
Phuphunḍạk̕a. It will become mouldy.

Phur. To eject from the mouth, as the stone of a fruit, &c., to blow out of the mouth, to snort.
Jaṅteč phur giḍikam. Eject the stone from your mouth
Ado togoč caoleko phurana.
Sadome phurečk̕ana. The horse is snorting.

Phuran. To fine, to mulct.
Phurạnkedeako. They fined him.

Phurkạu. To spout up or out, to rise up.
Lumạm ṭolkate cunko phurkạua. When the tusser silk moth has spun its cocoon it spouts out lime (a substance which hardens the cocoon.)
Basaṅ dak̕ phurkạu toṭena. The water boiled [over.

Phursạt. } Leisure, opportunity.
Phursut. }
Ạuriṅ phursutok̕a. I have not yet had leisure.
Baṅ phursutlena. I had no leisure.

Phurti. } Quickly, rapidly, to be quick.
Phuṛti. }
Ạḍi phurtiye kạmikeda. He worked very quickly.
Phurtitalaṅme. Be quick.

Phuṛuk̕. A leaf cup.
Hạnḍi phuṛuk̕. A liquor cup, made of one leaf.
Utu phuṛuk̕. A cup for holding relish, made of two or three leaves, according as the supply is large or small. [is served.
Jel phuṛuk̕. A leaf cup in which cooked meat.
Aṭal phuṛuk̕. A cup made of double leaves.
Bhạutič. A four-cornered leaf cup.

Phus. Trivial.
Noa phus k̕atha hõpe lạliskeda, atorege cabak̕ok̕a. You complained about this trivial matter, it could be settled in the village.

Phus marte. } Quickly, within a short
Phus mente. } time, immediately.
Phus menteye lại goček̕eda. He at once blabbed it out.

Phus caṭao. To do one out of anything, not to give, not to receive.
Phus caṭaoenaṅ. I am done out of it.

Phusalạu. } To cajole, to coax, to whee-
Phuslạu. } dle, to flatter.
Phuslạu idikedeae. He cajoled him away.

Phuski. To privately inform, to whisper.
Phuski ṅok̕aeme. Tell it to him privately, whisper it to him. [tell him only.
Uni moto phuskiaeme. Whisper it only to him,

Phuskuč. To slip out.
Hoṛo binḍạ khoč phuskučena. The dhan has slipped out of the sheaf.

Phuskuč. } To slip, to let slip.
Phaskuč. }
Phuskučkedaṅ. I let it slip.

Phuslạu. Cf. phusalạu.

Phusphas. } Slightly, very slightly, tri-
Phasphus. } vially, very small in quantity.
Phusphase dak̕ak̕lea. There was very slight rain with us.

Phusuč phusuč. } Well, quietly, comfor-
Pusuč pusuč. } tably.
Phusuč phusuče gitič joṅkana. He is sleeping quietly.
Nui do phusuč phusuče gitičtalea, ḍher do bae raga. This (child) of ours sleeps well, he does not cry much.

Phusur phusur. } Gently, softly, whis-
Pusur pusur. } peringly.
Lusur phusur. }
Phusur phusurkiṅ galmarao joṅkana. They are conversing in low tones.
Phusur phusure dak̕ečkana. It is raining gently.

Phuṭ. To separate, to break off from, to be unpaired, to become odd, as one of a pair, the other having died.
Phuṭenako. They have become separated.
Ḍaṅrae phuṭentiṅa. My bullock is odd (the other which made the pair having died.)

Phuṭ. A kind of melon, *Cucumis Melo, Linn.*, var. *Memordica.*

Phuṭ marte. } Suddenly, without warn-
Phuṭ mente. } ing.
Phuṭ marteye goč goṭena. He suddenly died.

Phuṭạ phuṭi. To separate, to disperse, each to go his own way.
Phuṭạ phuṭienako. They have dispersed, and each gone his own way.

Phuṭạu. To spring, to burst, to arise, as a smell; to make public, to begin, to start.
Ghao phuṭạuadea. A sore has broken out on him. [sins.
Pap phuṭạuaekana. He is suffering for his
Ado kathae phuṭạuačkoa. Then he spoke to them plainly, or then he revealed the matter to them.
Dak̕ phuṭạuena. Water burst out.

Phuṭiạ. Coppers.
Phuṭiạ bạnuktiña, goṭa ṭaka menaka. I have no coppers, I have a whole rupee.

Phuṭiạ kạuḍi. The small shell used in India as money.

Phuṭ phaṭ. } To separate, to disperse,
Phaṭ phuṭ. } each to go his own way, to break up, as a crowd.
Phaṭ phaṭenako. They have dispersed.

Piạ. } To fit closely, as a joint in wood
Piạu. } work; to be in close friendship.
Khub piạu hoṛ kanakin, unkin bẽkak hũkak. They are close friends, they say yes to what each other says.
Piạka, inạkge lagme. Cut off so much as will make it fit.
Gotao lagaeme, piạka se bań. Insert it to see if it will fit or not.
Ạdi jute piạuakaṭa. He has fitted it very nicely.

Piaj. The onion.
Kạli piaj. Onions raised from roots.
Kaṭh piaj. Onions raised from seed.

Piạk. } Bibacious, greatly addicted
Piạkạṛ. } to liquor, a drunkard, a drunken sot.
Tisren piạk kanam? Since when have you been a drunkard?
Nui do ạdi piạk hoṛ kanae. He is a person greatly addicted to liquor.
Ạdi piạkạṛe tahẽkana. He was a great drunkard.

Piạń payań. The first blush of morning, break of day.
Nitok do piạń payań marsalena. It is now grey dawn.
Piạń payańrele oḍokena. We left as the dawn was breaking.

Piạń piań. The cry of the bird Ghardidi, *Orthotomus sutorius.*

Piạu. Cf. piạ
Noko do kathako piạuakaṭa. These (men) have agreed as to what to say, they have agreed to tell the same story.

Picạ. The buttock.

Pichạ. Cf. pecha.

Pichạ. } Each, severally, as often as,
Piche. } every time.
Oṛak pichạ ṭaka lagaokkana. Each house has to pay money, money is levied on each house.

Pichạr. Too far back, as a load on a cart.
Pichạrokkana. It is getting too heavy behind.
Bape jutiaka, pichạrena. You did not do it rightly, it is too far back (load on a cart.)

Pichạri baha. A small flowering shrub, *Wendlandia exserta, D. C.*

Pichạuṛi. A large cotton shawl or plaid, generally made by sewing two or more widths of cloth together.

Piche. Each, severally, as often as, every time.
Ńapam piche noae ṭhokraoańkana. As often as we meet he brings up this matter.
Ṛoṛ picheko bengeṭańa. Every time I speak they stare at me.
Oṛak picheko nomborakaṭa. They have numbered each house.

Picom poḍroć. To turn tail, to take to one's heels, applied to running away after defeat.
Dạṛkedae picom poḍroć. He turned tail and fled.

Pichlạu. To slip, to take a false step.

Pichol. To slip, to slide, to ignore, to take no note of, to make a slip of the tongue.
Onḍe alom calaka picholgea. Do not go there it is slippery.
Picholenae. He has slipped.

Pichrạu. Cf. piclạu.

Picir. } To fly off, as small chips
Picir picir. } from an axe, or water falling on a hard surface, to splash, to sprinkle.
Picir picir pạsirokkana. It is flying off in spray.
Picirena. It has flown off (spark.)
Picir pạsirena. It has broken up and spread (a drop of water having fallen on a hard surface.)

Picir marte. } With a spray, with a
Picir mente. } flight. Cf. picir.
Picir marte ńurena.

Pickạri. Cf. phickạri.

Picki. A species of *Colocasia* the norms of which are eaten.
This differs from *Colocasia antiquorum.*

Piclạu. } To slip, to take a false step.
Picrạu. }
Lebeṭ picṛạuenae. He stepped and slipped.

Picor pocor. Applied to slight diarrhoea through indigestion.
Picor pocore oḍokokkana.

Picopoco. Weak, inferior, below par, not up to the mark.
Ḍahra doko picopocogetińa. My bullocks are inferior.

Picpic. } Very, applied to fear; to
Picpicạu. } hide through fear, as one dodging here and there behind any shelter.
Picpiciń botorokkana. I am very much afraid.
Botorte picpicạu bạṛaekanae. He is hiding here and there through fear.

Picpicạu. Cf. pacpacaó.
Dhaka piepicạukediñako..
Picrạu. Cf. piclạu.

Pidgạk.] To frisk, to gambol, as lambs,
Pidgạu. ʃ kids, &c; to gallop, as a
runaway horse, to twitch, as the
eyelids, &c., to throb,, as an artery.
Ñeñelko calaḲkhanko mena, pidgạuenako.
Pidgạḱae.. He will gambol..

Piḍil piḍil.] Quickly,, rapidly,. used
Peḍel peḍel. ʃ only of small beings.
Piḍil piḍilko calaḲkana. They are going along
quickly.

Piḍil piḍil.] To flap the wings while
Phiḍil phiḍil. ʃ sitting.

Piḍga piḍgi. Bounding, trippingly,
frisking, trooping.
Piḍga piḍgiko calaoena ñeñel. They have
gone tripping to the fair.

Piḍić piḍić.] Restless, neglecting work
Piḍić piḍić. ʃ and going here and
there, used by women when scolding girls.
Piḍió piḍió barạakanae. She is going here and
there neglecting her work.

Piḍir piḍir. Cf. piḍić piḍić.

Piḍgić.] Applied to the raising
Piḍgić piḍgić. ʃ of the body or a part
thereof in starting, jumping
straight up, kicking, &c.
Piḍgió piḍgiée doneda. He is jumping.
Sadom piḍgió piḍgiéko phandaeda.

Piḍgić marte.] With a start, or jump,
Piḍgić mente. ʃ or raising of the
body or part thereof.

Pikopoko. Fat-faced, fat-cheeked,
chubby, stout and fat.
Pikopoko moṭaenae. He is chubby-cheeked.

Pidgụr. F.] Fat, stout, applied to
Pedgọr. M. ʃ children.
Pidgụre moṭaakana. She is very stout.
Pidgụre ñeloḲkana. She looks fat, or she is fat.

Pilạ. The spleen, to suffer from enlarg-
ed spleen.
Pilạakanae.] He is suffering from
Pilạ harạakantaea. ʃ enlarged spleen.
Pilạ ruạ. Fever with enlarged spleen.

Pilcu. Little, small.
Sakam pilcuɡea. The leaf or leaves are small.
Oeṭ lekanaḲem ạgukeda. pilcu pilcu? What
kind did you bring, very small? or you
brought very very small ones.

Pilcu harạm. The name given by
Santals to the first man.

Pilcu budhi. The name given by Santals
to the first woman.

Pilcuṅ. Little, small.
Pilcuṅɡeako hako do. The fish are small.

Pilhoe. A disturber of the peace.
Nuige pilhoeɡetabonae. . This is our disturber
of the peace.
Nui do pilhoe kanae. This is a disturber of the
peace.

Pilhoe. High, higher than the remainder of the plot, applied to a portion
or portions of a rice field which
are too high to be submerged.
Nonḍe pilhoeɡetama. It is too high here (it
will not be submerged.)
Nonḍe pilhoe menaḲa. There is an eminence
here which will not be submerged.

Pilhoe. A disease which affects cattle.
Pilhoeteko gujuḲkana. They are dying from
pilhoe.
PilhoeoḲkanako. They are becoming affected
with pilhoe.

Piliń.] Fine, thin, very fine,
Piliń piliń. ʃ very thin, as a thread,
or thread spun by a spider.
Piliń piliń autạmko takoea. They. spin very
fine thread.
Piliń piliń suhɡạwana. It has very fine awns.

Pilsin.] Pension, a pencil.
Pinsin. ʃ

Pinc. The disk on the end of the
tail feathers of a peacock, the tail
of a peacock.
MaraḲ pinc. A peacock's tail.

Pińcar maraḲ. A peacock, a peafowl
having disks on its tail feathers.

Pinḍ. An altar, a small raised platform for the purpose of an altar.

Pinḍa. A raised platform round a house
occupying the space between the
wall and the drip of the eaves.
Atah pinḍạ. A verandah made by lengthening
the roof by the addition of other rafters.
Jorạ pinḍạ. A pinḍa (q. v.) having a step up
to it.
Ạurile pinḍạia. We have not yet made the
platform round the house.

Pinḍe. A small forest tree the fruit of
which is eaten, Randia uliginosa,
D. C.

Pinḍe.] A cultivated plant the
Ato pinḍe. ʃ corms or solid bulbs
of which are eaten, Amorphophallus campanulatus, Blume.

Pindha. } A ridge, as of a rice field ; an
Pindhe. } embankment, as of a tank, dam, &c.

Khet pindhe.　The ridge of a rice field.
Ahar pindhe.　The embankment of an ahar (q. v.)
Band pindhe.　The embankment of a dam.
Pindheakaṭako.　They have made a dam.
Pindhe latarre gitiḍakanae.　He is lying at the base of the embankment.

Pio. } The Golden Oriole, *Oriolus*
Pio córě. } *melanocephalus.*

Pioṅ poyoṅ. Holed, having holes in it.

Nui do pioṅ poyoṅ oraḱṭae, okoe unireye rebena?　His house has holes in it, who would agree to haveṡhim for a husband?

Piopoyo. Emerging from a number of holes, as water from the rose of a watering pot, &c., spraying.

Piopoyo daḱ oḍokoḱkana.　The water is spouting out from a number of holes.

Pipa. A barrel.

Pipni.
Meṭ pipni. } The eye lash.

Pipol. } A small fruit sold in the ba-
Pipor. } zaars and employed as a febrifuge.

Pippriaṅ. A butterfly.

Pirga.
Pirgau. } Cf. pidga.

Meṭ pirgaḱa.　The eye (lids) will twitch.

Piṛhi. A generation.

Piṛhi cetan piṛhi.　From generation to generation.
Ape do nonḍe tin piṛhi menaḱpea? Iṅ lagaete pon piṛhi.

Piṛhi. A cushion of wood on which a beam rests.

Saṅga piṛhi.　The cushion on which a saṅga (q. v.) rests.

Piri. A small round basket for keeping snakes.

Piriaḱ. } To move the limbs
Piriaḱ piriaḱ. } spasmodically as an animal when dying.

Piriaḱ piriagoḱkanae, baṅcaoḱ ooe baṅ ooṅ.

Piriaṅ piriaṅ. Call of the Sauri bird.

Piriapaṭe. To wriggle, wriggling.

Biṅko piriapaṭeko calaḱa.　Snakes progress by wriggling.
Cele ooe tahěkan, piriapaṭeṅ ạiḱạuledea.　It was something or other; I felt it wriggling.

Piriċ piriċ. To run slightly, as a sore, to nip as the eyes owing to glare, &c.

Pirioṅ. To clear up, as after rain, clouds to disperse, as after rain.

Nitoḱe pirioṅkeda.　Now it has cleared up.

Pirit. Affectionate, friendly.

Ạdi piritliṅ tahěkana.　We were very friendly.
Ạdi pirit henaḱkina.　They are very friendly. they have great affection for each other.

Pirit. To be ill, or indisposed.

Pit rua. Fever resulting from taking meals irregularly.

Pit mara. To lose appetite through having fasted, or passed the regular meal time.

Pit marakedeape.　You made him lose his appetite by not giving him his food at the proper time.
Pit marakateye jomkeda.　He ate without appetite (having fasted for some time.)

Piriċ. } Glistening, resplendent,
Piriċ piriċ. } dazzling, shining.

Piriċ piriċ ponḍa.　It is shining white.
Gaḍa gitil ṅeloḱkana piriċ piriċ.　The sand of the river glistens.

Pirthi.
Pirthimi. } The world.

Pirthi córě. A small bird about the size of a blackbird.

Pirtŭs. Biestings, or the first milk given by a cow after calving.

Pisaṛ pasaṛ. Loose, loosely, non-cohesive, slack.

Pisaṛ pasaṛko tolakaḱa.　They have tied it slackly.
Piṭhe sanam pisaṛ pasaṛena.　The bread is not cohesive.

Pisiṅ pisiṅ. Cf. peseṅ peseṅ.

Pisiṛ. To turn back the foreskin, self-abuse.

Piska. A common climbing plant, *Dioscorea oppositifolia, Linn.*, the root and aerial tubers of which are eaten.

Piskiċ. To part with the tips of the fingers of one or both hands, as the hair; to remove with the thumbs.

Piskiċ ṭenḍiako, ṅela mente jowaoakana se baṅ. They open out a part of the covering (of a cob of Indian corn) with the thumb nails to see if it is ripe or not.

Pit. The gall, anger, wrath.

Pit bae sambraolaḱa.　He could not restrain his wrath.
Pit caṛhaoentaea.　He has become angry or enraged.

Pitạl. } Brass.
Pitạr. }

Pitạl reak. Made of brass, brazen.

Piṭạu. To beat with the hand or any implement, to hammer.

Piṭạukedeako. They beat him.
Mẽṛhẽćko piṭạua. They hammer iron.
Gidrạ hoetora calke piṭạua. On the instant a child is born they beat the roof (of the house.)

Piteć. To card or tease cotton with a bow.

Tulạmko piteda. They card cotton.

Piṭhạ. Bread, to make bread.

Pikṭhạić. A baker.
Ḍombok piṭhạ. Bread baked in little balls.
Ạrsạ piṭhạ. Flour and guṛ or raw sugar, boiled together and then fried in oil.
Dalpiṭhạ. Batter bread, fried in oil.
Khapra piṭhạ. Bread baked in a piece of broken earthenware.
Sim piṭhạ. Dough mixed with minced meat and baked.
Patrạ piṭhạ. Dough wrapped in a leaf and baked in hot ashes.
Oć piṭhạ. Dough in which minced mushrooms are mixed and baked in ashes.
Jọṇḍra piṭhạ. Bread made from the flour of Indian corn.
Kode piṭhạ. Bread made from the flour of Kode (*Eleusine coracana.*)

Piṭhạu. Cf. piṭạu.

Piṭhiạ. A market.

Piṭhiạ lagaokkana. The market is being held.

Piṭi. To curl up, to coil.

Biṅko piṭika. Snakes coil themselves up.
Kạṇḍhumko piṭia. They coil pads for the head (as a cushion on which to carry.)
Piṭi up. Curly hair.
Setae piṭiakana. The dog is (lying) curled up.

Piṭić. Cf. liṛić piṭić.

Piṭiri. A swelling of the glands as in mumps.

Pitol. Brass.

Pitoṅj. A forest tree, *Putranjiva Roxburghii, Wall.*

Pitoṅj malla. A necklace made of the stones of the fruit of the *Pitoṅj* tree.

Piṭu. Without ornament, as the ears; small, as the ears.

Piṭu lutur geae. She has no rings in her ears.
Adom bhiḍi reak lutur piṭugetakoa. Some sheep have very small ears.

Piṭuạ ghãs. } An exceedingly common
Piṭuạ aṛak. } wild plant, *Spermacoce hispida, Linn.*, eaten in times of famine.

Piṭuạ paṭwe. Crooked, serpentine, winding.

Noa hor do piṭuạ paṭwegea. This road is winding.
Noa kaṭ do piṭuạ paṭwegea. This log is crooked.
Biṅ piṭuạ paṭweạnae. The serpent is serpentine.

Piṭuk. A glutton.

Piṭuk kanae. He is a glutton.

Piṭukiạ. Gluttonous.

Piṭukiạ hoṛ kanae nuige. He is a gluttonous man this.

Piũri. To make little hollow rolls of cotton to be spun into thread.

Piũrikateko takoea.

Piyol poyol. } To pass through a hole
Piyoṛ poyoṛ. } or opening, as a fish through a hole in a net; or water, through a hole in the roof, &c.

Piyoṛ poyoṛ jorokkana. It is dripping through.
Noa jhạlire piyoṛ poyoṛ hakoko paromokkana. The fish are escaping through this net.

Po. To hoe, to dig with the Indian digging implement, the kudali.

Jonḍrako poea. They hoe Indian corn.
Poak. That which has been hoed.

Poạti. To be with young, applied to animals.

Poạti gai. A cow in calf.
Poạtiakanae. She is in calf.

Poć. }
Pŏć. } Imitative of a creaking, or
Poćpoć. } nipping sound.
Pŏćpŏć. }

Poć poć saḍekana. It is creaking.

Poć marte. }
Pŏć marte. } With a cracking, creak-
Poć mente. } ing or nipping sound.
Pŏć mente. }

Poć marteye gạsićkeda.

Poca. Rotten, decayed, unserviceable, feckless, fusionless.

Nui poca ceće cekaṅa? What will this feckless (fellow) do to me?

Poca nạrgi. A sore inside the nose.

Poca pilhoe. A disease which affects cattle.

Pochim. The West.

Pocla. Weak, rotten, decayed.

Pocla mara hoṛ. A rascally weakling.
Pocla ḍahra. A weak bullock.
Pocla kaṭ. Weak, or rotten timber.

Pocla gam. An old wife's fable.

Pocoe hạṇḍi. Pacwae, liquor made from rice.

Pocol.
Pocor. } Cf. phocor.

Pocoṅ haṇḍi. Cf. pocoe haṇḍi.

Pocra. M. } Cowardly, timid, faint heart-
Pucri. F. } ed.

Pocra pucrigeakin. They are a timid pair.

Pod. A title.

Pod. To build a second house at a distance from the first and to occupy both. Cf. ḍohta.

Podakaćako. They have built a second house, they occupy two houses.

Podartho. A creature, a thing.

Podgoe. Rufous, of a brownish red colour, applied mainly to thread.

Podgoe. Cf. pidguṛae.

Podina. Mint.

Poḍo. Two fig trees receive this name Hoṛ poḍo, *Ficus Cunia, Buch.*, and Seta poḍo, *Ficus sp.*

Poḍo daka. The seeds of *Ficus Cunia* boiled as rice.

Poḍo.
Phoḍo phoḍo. } Imitative of the sound produced when the
Poḍo poḍo. } hubble bubble is being smoked.

Poḍo poḍo saḍekana.

Podoe.
Podoe podoe. } Fine, as dust, rain, &c., to fly off, as dust, or anything small or light, carried by the wind.

Capaṫ podoe goṫkedeaṅ kulṣi do. I hit the hare and caused (the hair) to fly.
Daṫedae podoe podoe. It is drizzling.

Podoe.
Podoe podoe. } In puffs, puffing.

Podoe podoe ṅuṅuksnae thamakur.

Podoe marte.
Podoe mente. } With a puff.

Podoe marteye dalkedea. He struck him and caused (something) to fly.
Podoe mente oṭahena. It was blown away lightly.

Podor.
Podor podor. } To reduce to a fine powder or dust, to become powder or dust.

Jom podorkedako huti. The *hutis* (q v) have eaten it into dust.

Podra.
Podraha. } Decayed, rotten.

Nui podra mara hoṛ. A farting scoundrel rotten inside.
Podra ganḍke. A rotten log.

Poḍroć.
Poḍroć poḍroć. } Applied to forceful issuing of semi-liquid matter from the bowels.

Poḍroć poḍroće ciḍireṫkana.

Poḍroć marte.
Poḍroć mente. } With a rush. Cf. poḍroć.

Poḍroḱ.
Poḍroḱ poḍroḱ. } Imitative of the sound produced when bubbling, as a hubble bubble.

Poḍroḱ poḍroḱ hukạko ṅuieda.

Poe. The consequences attending on an evil action, nemesis.

Poeye ṅama. He will reap the consequences of his evil doing.

Poesa. A pice, one fourth of an anna.

Poeta. The sacred thread of the twice born Hindu.

Poeta boć hiloḱ. The fifth and last day of the pata or hook swinging festival when the swingers take off the thread with which they have been invested for the occasion.

Pogaṛ.
Pogar. } A surface drain, to surface drain

Daṫko pogaṛ idikeda. They drained away the water.

Pogoe.
Pogoe pogoe. } To enter or rush in as a current of air or wind.

Pogoe pogoe hoe boloḱkana.

Pogoe marte.
Pogoe mente. } With a rush, as air or wind.

Hoe pogoe mente boloena. The wind came in with a rush.

Poha. A shoot springing from the ground, a seedling of a tree.

Pohale rohoeakaṫa. We have planted tree seedlings.

Pohaḱ. To bite, to bite off a piece from a lump, to devour as a tiger a carcase.

Miṫ dhaoe pohaḱlaḱa. He took one bite.
Ulko pohaga. They bite mangoes (do not cut or break off a piece.)
Onte alope calaḱa, kule pohaḱkepea. Do not go there, the tiger may devour you.

Pohaṅ. To break, applied to earthen ware vessels.

Kanḍa pohaṅena. The water pot is broken.
Celaṅ dom pohaṅkeṫtiṅa. You broke my cooking pot.

Pŏhcao. Cf. pohncao.

Pohlan. Healthy, vigorous.

Bes pohlane ṅeloḱkana. He looks fine and healthy.
Khub pohlan dareḱkana. It is growing very vigorously.

Pohncao. } To arrive, to take to.
Poncao. }
Niạ do pohncaokatiñme Mạñjhi then. Cause this to reach the Mạñjhi, i. e. take this to the Mạñjhi (q. v.)
Tinrem pohncaoena? At what time of the day did you arrive?

Poho. A locust.

Poho sosroć. A kind of grasshopper.

Poho. Not fully cooked, hard in the centre, as half-cooked rice, potatoes, &c.
Daka pohoakana. The rice is not fully cooked.

Pohol. To square, as a log, &c.
Niạ dom pohola. You will square this.
Tin pohol. Three sided.
Cạr pohol. Four sided.

Pohom. To recognize, to discern, to see distinctly.
Bạń pohomledea. I did not recognise him.
Bạń pohomlaka. I did not see distinctly.

Pohor. Time, a division of the day of three hours.
Niạ pohor. At this time of day.
Ayup pohor. Eventide.
Setak pohor. Morning time.
Tikin pohor. Mid-day.
Daka jom pohor. Meal time.
Gitić pohor. Bed time.

Pohoṭ. } Dilatory, protracted, in-
Rohoṭ pohoṭ. } terminable.
Ạdi ghạrićkedale rohoṭ pohoṭ. We were an interminable time.
Tinrem sapṛaoka rohoṭ pohoṭ.

Pohoṭ. } Direction, out-lying country.
Pahaṭ. } Cf. pahṭa.
Niạ pohoṭ bań senakana. I have not gone in this direction.

Pohrek pohrek. } From time to time.
Pohre pohre. }
Pohre pohre dakae khojkana. He asks for boiled rice from time to time.
Pohre pohreye hirikoa. He visits them from time to time.

Pojhaṛ. A sprout from the root.
Bar pe pojhạṛ menaka. There are two or three sprouts from the root.
Khub pojhaṛakana. Many shoots have come up from the root, it has become a big tussock.

Pojhot. Cf. phajet.

Pojo. A large forest tree, *Tetranthera monopetala, Roxb.*

Pokha. } The part of the body
Pạni pokha. } under the ribs.

Pokhao. To rear, to bring up, to nourish.
Pokhaokeťmeale, ar nitok dom dạṛkana? We brought you up, and now you are running away?

Pokhao. To cause to fast, to withhold food.
Pokhaomealań nahak. I shall make you fast presently.

Pokhor. } A tank with the earth
Pokhori. } thrown up on all sides.

Pokhori } A tank mentioned in
Tuṛi pokhori. } Santal traditions.

Pokhoria khad. A quarry, a quarry-mine.

Pokhri. Cf. pokhor.

Pokneť. Full-cheeked, chubby-cheeked, applied only to girls.

Pokos. } Soft, puffy.
Pokos pokos. }
Pokos pokos ṣikạukkana. It feels very soft.

Pokoť. Cf. pokto.

Pokoť pokoť. To scold, to chatter, to gabble.
Pokoť pokodokkana. She is scolding.

Pokoť roṭe. A frog of the species which appears on the arrival of the rains.
Pokoť roṭe sege peṭeko oḍokakana. The frogs have emerged in swarms.

Pokpoko. } To swell, to be blown or
Pukpuku. } puffed out, to be swollen, to be sulky.
Roṭe pokpokokako. Frogs puff themselves out.
Cedakem pokpoko baṛaekana? Why are you sullen?

Pokroť. Full-cheeked, chubby-faced. Cf. pokneť.

Poksa. Cf. phoksa.

Pokta. } Strong, hard, substantial, well
Pokto. } seasoned.
Pokto hoṛ kanae. He is a strong man.
Pokto ḍaṅra. A strong bullock.
Pokto kaṭ. A strong piece of timber.
Pokto oṛake benaoakaťa. He has built a substantial house,

Polhar. } The second day of the pata
Pholhar. } (q. v.) festival on which no boiled rice is partaken of, fruit by preference being eaten.
Tehen doko polharokkana. They are observing the *polhar* to-day.

Poloć. } To issue in small quan-
Poloć poloć. } tity, to flee.
Polockedae. He fled away.
Poloć poloće cidiretkanae.

Poloć marte. } With a gush or spurt.
Poloć mente.

Poloc. } To issue, to gush, as semi-
Polocok. liquid from a small aperture.

Poloc poloc oḍokoḱkana. It is gushing out.
Polocoḱkana. It is gushing out.

Poloc marte. } With a gush, or a
Poloc mente. rush.

Poloc marte oḍok goćena. It came out with a gush.

Poloḱ. } Indistinctly. Cf. palaḱ
Poloḱ poloḱ. poloḱ.

Poloḱ poloḱ ńeloḱkana. It appears indistinctly, it is indistinctly seen.

Poloḱ marte. } Indistinctly, applied to
Poloḱ mente. a single action.

Poloḱ marteń ńel goćkedea. I just caught a glimpse of him, I only saw him for an instant.

Polok. } An instant.
Polokh.

Mić polokh hŏ bae sahaoleda. He did not suffer it even for an instant.

Polom. To delay. Cf. bilom.

Cećrem polomena? What delayed you?
Alom polomlea. Do not delay us.

Polpol daḱ. Cf. nagi ganḍo daḱ.

Polso. Small degree of, applied to the colours red and white.

Polso ponḍ. Not pure white, whitish.
Polso araḱ. Not pure red, reddish.

Pon. } The numeral four.
Ponea.

Pon gel. Forty.
Pon isi. Four score,
Pon hoṛako. They are four people.
Poneaḱako. There are four (animates.)
Poneaḱa. There are four (inanimates.)
Pon oṛaḱale. We are four households.
Ponaḱ. The fourth.

Pon. Cf. gonoń.

Pon. } An aggregate number consisting
Pan. of 20 gandas (q. v.), that is 80.

Bar pon gachi. 160 bundles of rice seedlings.
Mić pon lumam. 80 tusser cocoons.

Pon. Price paid for land for which rent is payable, price paid for the transfer of cultivating rights in land.

Tinaḱ ponem emkeda? Bar isi ṭaka. What price did you pay for the transfer of cultivating rights to yourself? Forty rupees.

Poncao. Cf. pohncao.

Ponḍ. White, to become white, to whiten.

Ponḍ bhit. A white wall.
Ponḍ poesa. A white pice, a rupee.
Ponḍ merom. A white goat.
Ponḍoḱa. It will become white.
Ponḍaćako. They have whitened it.
Kahu leka hendeko tahĕkana, ado bak lekako ponḍena. They were black as a crow, now they are white as the paddy bird.

Ponḍ Murmu. A sub-sept of the Santal sept Murmu (q. v.)

Ponḍ Marnḍi. A sub-sept of the Santal sept Marnḍi.

Ponḍ Soren. A sub-sept of the Santal sept Soren.

Ponḍ jhar. White or milky urine.

Ponḍ sul. Dysentery with mucous discharge.

Ponḍ disom horeć. The white variety of *Glycine Soja, Sieb. & Zinn.*

Ponḍ gandhari araḱ. A cultivated pot herb, *Amarantus tristis, Linn.*

Ponḍ kaweć. The white variety of *Abrus precatorius, Linn.* Cf. kaweć.

Ponḍ raj baha. The white variety of the sweet scented Oleander, *Nerium odorum, Solan.*

Ponḍ sosroć. A kind of grasshopper.

Pond risa. Passing of blood, as in case of piles, &c.

Ponda. Rotten inside.

Ponda kaṭ. A log rotten inside.

Ponḍe. Used in playing a certain game, to be put out of the game.

Ponḍekedea. He put him out of the game.

Pondhaṛ potam. A species of wild pigeon.

Poneaṭaḱ. Four.

Poneaṭaḱ baṛe magme. Hew down four (trees.)

Poneaṭaḱ. The fourth.

Poneaṭaḱ baṛe magme. Hew down the fourth one (tree.)

Ponpoń. Immodestly.

Duṛupakanae pohpoń.

Ponkonḍ. } In all directions, four cor-
Ponkŏṛ. ners, four square.

Ponon. Four taken collectively, all the four.
Ponon koṇḍ. } All the four corners or directions.
Ponon kõṛ. }
Ponon kõṛ ren hoṛ. The people of the four corners, all the people on the earth.
Ponon boehako goćena. All the four brothers are dead.

Pontha. To devise, to arrange, to contrive, to scheme, to intend, to meditate.
Nonka babon ponthalekhan oho ṭhikłena. If we do not contrive it thus it will not be right.

Popolhoť. Almost, used always with ńut (dark.)
Popolhoť ńut. Almost dark, applied to the evening.

Popolheť. } Imperfect, as vision; dim-sighted.
Popolhoť. }
Popolhoťgeñ beṅgeťeda. I see dimly, my eyes are not good.

Popon. By fours.
Popon hoṛkateko calaoena. They have gone by fours.
Popon goṭeǒkate emakom. Give four to each.
Popon goṭeǒkate jhomblepe. Tie them up in bunches of four each.

Popṛo. } A large forest tree, *Gardenia latifolia, Ait.*
Popṛo dare. }

Por. A low bush, low bushes.
Por gajaṛ. A thicket of low bushes.

Por sendra. A one day hunt.
A hunt of this kind is conducted without the presence of the dihri (q. v.) or hunt master. No sacrifices are offered and all return home in the evening. *Gitic' sendra* is one of the annual tribal hunts when the hunters spend one night in the open air.

Por. Long.
Noa mať do khub porana. This bamboo has long spaces between the nodes.
Hoṛo khub por geleakana. The ears of this dhan are long.

Poraeni. The White Lotus of the Nile, *Nymphoea Lotus, Linn.*
The roots of this species of lotus, which is very common, are eaten.

Porames. } To consult, to take council together, to advise.
Poramors. }
Poramos. }
Onḍeko poramoseda. They are consulting together there.

Poran. Life.
Poran uḍauťkantińa. I am frightened to death, my life is flying away.
Jiwilae porantele daṛkeda. We fled taking only our life with us (left all behind.)

Poran. Cf. phul poran.

Porani. A living creature.

Porao. To cremate.
Poraokedeale. We cremated him.

Porbas. } A festival. Cf. porob.
Porob. }

Porbhaha. } Cf. porob porbhaha.
Porob porbhaha. }

Porbhae. Anxiety, care, thought, fear, solicitude.
Ni porbhae. Without anxiety, without care.

Porbosti. Cherishing, care, protection, nourishing, necessaries of life.
Porbosti hoyoťkantaea uni iṭṭe. His wants are being supplied through him.
Porbosti bań calaťkantińa. My wants are not being met.

Porcar. To preach.
Porcaraťokanae. He is preaching to them.

Porcarok. A preacher.
Porcarok kanae. He is a preacher.

Por caṭa. } Living at the expense of others, throwing the expense on others.
Por caṭia. }
Por caṭua. }
Por caṭia kanae. He lives at the expense of others.

Põṛcha. A bow string made of a thin slip of bamboo.

Porchaṭi. } Living on others, throwing the expense on others. Cf. porcaṭi.
Porchaṭia. }
Porchaṭua. }

Porda. } A curtain.
Parda. }
Porda bạnuťtaea. She is in want of clothes.
Be-pordageae. She is in need of clothes.
Pordako lagaoeťkaťa. They have put up a curtain.

Pordapos. Cf. porbosti.
Ińať pordapos ińiń calaoeda. I earn my own living.

Pordesi. Foreign, belonging to another country or district.

Pordesia. A foreigner, a person from another country or district, a stranger.

Pordhan. Chief, principal, respectable, first.
Pordhan iń manaoketmea. I regard you as a respectable man.

Pordhol. } A female menstrual disorder
Pordol. }
Ponḍ pordhol. } Leucorrhoea.
Ponḍ pordol. }

Porek. Another, another person.
Porekak dhonteye dhonokkanae. He is becoming wealthy with other people's wealth.
Porekakre ceć lagaoaekana? What does he feel for another, what care has he for another's?
Porek reakem ńamakać, coj bań lagaoamkana. You have received what belonged to another, you can afford not to be stingy.

Porepare. Gratuitously, for nothing, at no expense to oneself.
Porcẹṭię do poreparete [illegible]miye calaoa.

Poret. To become stained, as with oil or grease, oily, greasy, as cloth.
Sunum kicriére poretakawadea. There are stains of oil on his cloth.

Porgol. To increase, to become more intense.
Ghao porgolentaea. His sore is enlarging.
Ruą porgolentaea. His fever is increasing.

Poṛha daka. } Boiled rice offered at the
Porha daka. } Bhandan (q. v. ceremony.

Poṛha dăṛĕ. } Sacrifice offered to the
Porha dăṛĕ. } dead person at the Bhandan (q. v) ceremony.

Porhao. } To put on, as clothes, orna-
Pahṛau. } ments, rings, &c.
Malako porhaoadea. They put a necklace on her.
Hãsliko pạhrạuadea. They put a hãsli (q. v.) on her neck.

Por hĕsạlią. Spiteful, vengeful, vindictive.
Nui do por hĕsạliạgeae. This (person) is spiteful.

Porho. Profit, advantage.
Ceć porhom ńamkeda. What profit did you get? what were you advantaged?
Ṛorhoanak kạmi. Profitable work.

Poriskar. Clear, to become clear. to clear off, as a debt.
Riniń poriskarkeda. I cleared off my debt.
Khajnań poriskarkeda. I paid up all my rent

Porja. A tenant, a ryot, a subject.
Uni ṭheniń porjaakana. I have become a ryot of his.

Porja pạni. } Tenants, ryots, subjects.
Porja pạti. }
Porja pạniko jaoraakana. The ryots are assembled.

Porjạt. } Belonging to another caste.
Parjẹt. }

Por jạtią. } One of another caste.
Par jạtią. }

Porjont. }
Porjot. } Up to, also, even.
Parjat. }
Jomak hŏ porjote bạgiakaća. He has left off taking even food.

Porkan. } Cf. nana porkar.
Nana porkan. }

Porkar. Stratagem, wile, craft, cunning, kinds, sorts.
Porkarteko sapkedea. They caught him by stratagem.
Porkartegeye jojomkan. He lives by his wits.
Sabe reake porkarakaća. He is trying to catch him by craft.

Porkar. Cf. nana porkar.

Pormae. Lease of life.
Pormae tiokentaea. His lease of life has been reached.
Pormae menaktaea. He has still some time to live.

Porman. Witness, evidence, to depose, to prove, to substantiate.
Porman daṛeakam? Can you prove it?
Pormanko emoka. They give proof.

Por monda. } To harm, to injure, to
Por mundạ. } belittle through spite or malevolence.
Pormonda hoṛ kanae. He is a spiteful man.
Jahãe alom pormondaea. Do not spite any one.

Porob. } A feast, a festival, an anniver-
Porbas. } sary, to observe a festival or an anniversary.
Sohrae porob. The Sohrae (q. v.) festival.
Porobokkanako. } They are observing a festi-
Porobedako. } val.
Porobre pihạre. At all festival times.
Jomlekhange porob, umlen khange sakrat. A festival is a feast, the Sakrat (q. v.) is a bath.

Porodhol. The ghost, shade, or soul of a deceased father, the manes of a father.
Haṛam porodhol. The manes of a grand-father.

Porodhol. Cf. pordhol.

Poroe. } Fine, as rain, drizzling.
Poroe poroe. }
Poroeada. It drizzled.
Poroe poroeye dakeda. It is drizzling.

Porok. }
Porokh. } To recognize, to distinguish, to make out.
Parok. }
Porok ṭhikkedeań. I recognized him perfectly.
Rogem porokkettaea? Did you diagnose his disease?

Porol jhiṅga. } Cf. parol jhiṅgạ.
Paroṛ jhiṅgạ. }

Poroporo. } Sound as of semi-liquid
Phorophoro. } bursting out.

Poroć. } Sound of breaking wind.
Poroć porot. }
Poroć poroće gạsićeda.

Porpor. Cf. phorphor.

Porsad. A small piece of flesh meat sent by the person who has killed the animal to his neighbours, food that has been offered to the deities, leavings of a spiritual guide.

Porsadteć seṭerakawadiña. I have received a small piece of meat.

Porsạti. Pregnant, *enciente.*

Porthom. First.

Porthom ren kanae. He is the first.
Porthom cas. The first cultivation.
Porthomre. In the beginning, at the outset, in the first place.
Pạhil porthomre. In the beginning, at the first.

Porti. Cf. pạrti.

Porti. Cf. proti.

Porton. To begin, to set oneself to.

Rorore portonena. He began to speak.
Seřreñe portonkeda. He began to sing.
Ařhare portonakaťa. He has begun to make an ahar (q. v.)

Pos. Nourishing, cherishing, a domesticated animal.

Pose manaokeda. He became domesticated, he became tame.
Pos bae manaolaťa. He did not acknowledge nourishing, he would not tame (tiger, lion, &c.)
Uniren bhage pos menaťkotaea. He has good cattle.

Posak'. To break, to smash, to burst.

Kanḍa posaťena. The water pot is broken.
Kanḍa posagoťa. The water pot will break.
Ojo posaťentaea. His boil has burst.
Bele ñur posaťena. The egg fell and was broken.
Dal posaťkedae. He struck and smashed it.
Bohoť posaťentaea. His head is split.
Bohoťe dal posaťkeťtaea. He struck and split his head.
Bohoť posagoť leka hasoiñkana. My head aches like to split.

Posan. To profit, to pay, to yield a return, to draw profit, to obtain a return.

Inạťte posanoťae. He will be profited by so much, he will be no loser at this price.

Posao. To nourish, to rear, to supply the necessaries of life, to fatten.

Uni gidrạñ posaoakadea. I have reared that child.

Poseť. To break, to smash, to burst. Cf. posak'.

Posind. Cf. pasind.

Poska. Cf. phoska.

Poska olať. A small forest tree, *Kydia calycina, Roxb.*

Poskoť. Cf. paskao.

Posoṅ. To leak, as bellows; applied also to the blowing of a person who has lost his front teeth.

Bae oṅ daṛeaťkana, posoṅ oťoedae. He cannot blow, he allows the wind to escape.

Posṛa. To despise, to contemn, to feel contempt for, to look down upon.

Posṛakedeako. They despised him.
Ṭuạr posṛako ñamkedea. They regarded him as a despised orphan.

Posta. The opium poppy plant.

Posta dana. The seed of the opium poppy.

Posta. The hind of the spotted deer, *Axis maculatus.*

Posta. Red thread employed to make the borders of cloth.

Posta pạḍlạť. } **Posta pạṛiạť.** } Cloth with red borders.

Posṭo. Distinctly, clearly.

Khub posṭoe roṛ daṛeaťa. He can speak very distinctly.
Posṭote baṅ ñel daṛeaťa. I cannot see distinctly.

Posu. A beast, an animal, applied mainly to domesticated graminivorous animals.

Ato posu. A domesticated graminivorous animal.
Bir posu. A wild animal.

Poṭa. Stomach.

Poṭa. First stomach, paunch of ruminating animals.
Remeť. Second stomach of ruminating animals.

Poṭak'. To strip off or remove the outer covering, as the bark of a tree; to rub off, peel off or remove a portion, as of the skin; to break or injure a smooth surface, as a floor, &c; to bare, as a field of its crop, grass, &c.

Dare mať bindạṛkate baklaťko poṭaťkeda. They cut down the tree and removed the bark.
Dal poṭaťkedeako. They struck him and removed a portion of his skin.
Ir poṭaťakaťako, ma gạiko ontebon idikoa. They have reaped all the crops, let us take the cows over there.
Gạiko jom poṭaťkeda. The cows grazed it bare.
Lebeť poṭaťkedako ot do. They tramped on and removed the smooth surface of the floor, (they wore holes in the floor with their feet.)
Sadome ghasao poṭaťena. A portion of the horse's skin is rubbed off.
Jom poṭaťkedeako. They ate him bare (ate up all he had.)

Potam. A wild wood-pigeon.
Varieties of wild wood-pigeons.
Barge potam. } Turtur Cambayensis, the little
Thikri potam. } brown dove.
Pondhar potam.
Mala potam. }
Kudbar potam. } The Ring dove.
Tilạị potam. }
Kẽndrõ potam. The spotted dove, *Turtur Surattensis.*
Bhosko potam.
Kisar potam. } The Imperial pigeon, *Carpophaga sylvatica.*
Gudru gum. }
Toyo dedger potam. } Cf. barge potam.
Sendi kakar potam. }
Note. The Green pigeon (huhar), *Crocopus chlorigaster*, and the Blue Rock pigeon, (parwa) *Columba intermedia*, are not included among the pigeons by Santals.

Potam bele. *Epsilon Lyrae*, two small stars very close to each other, near *Vega*, in the constellation *Lyra.*

Potam cupi tengoć. A shape of battle axe so named.

Potao. To white wash, with lime or white earth.
Bhitko potaoa. They white wash walls.

Pote. Cf. lede pote.

Pote. Cf. potea.

Potea. } Having a large protuberant
Potma. } stomach.
Potea hor. A man with a large protuberant stomach.

Potea garai. A species of fish.

Potea tarup. The smaller species of leopard, *Felis leopardus, Hodgson.*
Tarup. The larger species of leopard or panther, *Felis pardus.* Cf. sona cita tarup.

Potea jondra. A stunted variety of Indian corn.

Potha hako. A species of fish.
The fry of this fish are known as puthi hako.

Potkoć. To germinate.
Ańkurkate potkojoka, khan suioka.

Potma. M. } Big-bellied, having a pro-
Putmi. F. } tuberant stomach.
Potmageae. He is big-bellied.
Putmigeae. She is big-bellied.
Potma mara gidra, ańjom hõ bae ańjoma.

Potoć. To dislocate, out of joint.
Ti potoćentaea. His wrist is dislocated.
Katup potojoktaea. His finger will be dislocated.

Potohań. Cf. patohań.
Moca do pondge potohań rohorentaea.

Potol. A kind of vegetable.
Gend potol. The plant raised from root tubers.
Palta potol ,, ,, ,, cuttings.

Potolia. A species of snake.

Potom. To wrap up, to wrap round as a parcel in paper, &c., to cover, as a book.
Sim potom. To shut up, or in.
Orakreko siń potomkedea. They shut him up in the house.
Oyo potom. To cover up, as with a shawl, sheet, blanket, &c.
Kamrateye oyo potomakana. He is wrapped up in a blanket.
Tiye oyo potom esećakattaea. He has covered up his hand.
Tol potom. To close way of egress by tying, as a door, &c.
Dal potom. To strike heavy blows.
Dal potomkedeako. They beat him severely.
Matkomko potoma. They wrap up matkom (q. v.) in leaves.
Matkom potom. A parcel of matkom.
Kitapiń potoma. I will cover my book.

Potom dundu. A species of owl.

Potom bardũrũć. A species of bat.

Potor. To strip off, to pluck off, to denude.
Kicrićko potorkedea. They stripped off his clothes.
Lo potorenae. He is burnt out, he is stripped by fire (house, &c. burned.)
Ti lo potorenae. The skin has been scalded off his hand.
Simko potorkoa. They pluck fowls.
Dal potorkedeako. They beat and stripped him.
Sukriko ro potorkoa. They scald the bristles off pigs. Scottice, they *plot* them.
Onkoko oyoakana, onageye or potoretkoa. He pulls off their covering.

Potor potor. } Denuded, patches or
Putur putur. } portions denuded, patchy.
Potor potor up menaktakoa. There are places on his skin without hair, there are hairless places on his body.

Potor. } A document, documents,
Kagoj potor. } papers.

Potoť. } Uncomfortable through
Potoť potoť. } thirst.
Potoť potot aikauedań. I feel uncomfortably thirsty.
Oka do rubre potoť potoť aikauka. Sometimes in fever one feels uncomfortable owing to thirst.

Potpoto. } Prominent, swollen as the
Putputu. } belly when full, satisfied, full stomach.
Lać potpotoentaea. His stomach is swollen.
Jom potpotoenae. He has eaten to repletion.
Potpotogeń aikaueda. I feel satisfied.
Potpoto matkom. The flowers of certain matkom (q. v.) which do not become flat when cooked but retain their rotundity.

Potra. M. } Big-bellied, paunchy.
Putri. F. }

Potreć. } Protuberant stomach and
Potret. } neglected, as a child.

Potret jel. Cf. ghotret jel.

Potyot. Small, applied to children.

Powa. Cf. pawa.

Powar Murmu. A sub-sept of the Santal sept Murmu (q. v.)

Poyor. } Continued progression,
Poyor poyor. } as of running water; without halting.

Poyor poyorko paromokkana. They are streaming past.

Poyor marte. } Continued progression,
Poyor mente. } as of running water, without a halt.

Poyor marte parom goćenae. He went past without a halt.

Atu calaoena poyor marte. It floated right away.

Poyot. } Applied to the move-
Poyot poyot. } ment of the lips when smoking a cigar, a pipe or the hubble bubble.

Poyot poyot thamakhure ńuieda.

Pracar. To preach.

Pracarak. A preacher.

Praja. A tenant, a ryot, a subject.

Prajapati. Tenants, subjects.

Prerit. An apostle, one sent.

Prithimi. } The world. Cf. pirthimi.
Pritivi. }

Procar. To preach.

Procarok. A preacher.

Prokar. Kind, sort, stratagem, wile, craft.

Adi prokar kicriće agurkata. He has brought many kinds of cloth.

Nana prokar. Of many kinds or sorts.

Proti. }
Porti. } Each, severally.
Parti. }

Hor proti. Each person in succession.

Puc marte. } On the sudden, suddenly,
Puc mente. } applied to fear.

Puc mente botor goćenae. He was instantly seized with fear.

Pucau. } To ask, to shew respect, to
Puchar. } consult, to take notice of.
Puchau. }

Iń do bape puchauledińa. You did not consult me.

Puche. To enquire, to ask.

Bako khoj puchekedea, bankhane laikegea. They did not enquire of him, else he would have told.

Iń do khoj na puche cele bae bengetam.

Iń do khoje na puche cele bae bengetam.

Puchia. A gratuity, generally one pice, given by the purchaser of an animal to the herd or shepherd.

Gupiić puchia poesae ńama. The herd will receive a gratuity of one pice (when an animal of which he has had charge is sold.)

Puchla puchli. To seize the tail of a bullock as if about to twist it, to give a fillip to an ox by twisting its tail.

Puchla puchli baraem. Twist his tail.

Puchlau. To twist the tail of a lazy bullock to urge it on, to stimulate, to inspirit, to stir up, to give a fillip.

Puchlauem. Twist his tail.

Pueki. Cf. phueki.

Puckuć. } Cf. phuckuć.
Puckuć puckuć. }

Pucpuc. } To quail, to be in a funk,
Pucpucau. } terror stricken.

Pucpuce botorokkana. He is terror stricken.

Pucri. F. } Cf. pocra.
Pocra. M. }

Pucuć. } Quickly, without
Pucuć pucuć. } delay.
Phucuć phucuć. }

Pucuć pucuće hijuk senokkana. He comes and goes without delay.

Pucuć marte. } Suddenly, quickly, on
Pucuć mente. } the sudden, on the instant.

Pucuć menteye calaoena. He left on the instant.

Pucuć marteń tuńkedea. I shot him suddenly.

Pudina. } Mint.
Pudina arak. }

Pudruk. } To breathe heavily
Pudruk pudruk. } as a bear, &c.

Bana do pudruk pudruke darkeda. The bear ran away breathing heavily.

Pugui. } To mumble when eating
Pugui pugui. } or speaking, as a person who has lost his teeth.

Pugui maraokedae. He mumbled it all up.

Pugui puguiye jomeda. He eats mumblingly.

Puhi. } To rain gently, slight rain.
Phuhi. }

Puhiadae. It rained a little.

Puhi ńokakkhan beskoka. If it rain a little it will be well.

Puhi. A float for a fishing line.

Puhna. The day on which certain agricultural operations are begun, as sowing, planting, &c.; to begin sowing, planting, &c.

Tehenle puhnakeda. We began operations to-day.

Puipui. To bulge, protrude, swell, as the stomach, a water mussuck, &c.

Puipuiakanae. His stomach is swollen, or bulges out.

Puipuiko bhorao peredakata dalte. They have filled and caused (the mussuck) to swell out with water.

Puja. } Worship, to offer sacrifice
Puja agha. } and worship.

Puja aghaedako. They are engaged in sacrificing.

Puja aghaenako. They have performed sacrificial worship.

Okoeak tite puja agham kusiaka? At whose hand will you accept sacrificial worship?

Pujhar. A sacrificing priest, the title given to the family of a sacrificing priest.

Pukar. Cf. phukar.

Pukar. Cf. phukar.

Pukhri. Cf. pokhri, pokhor.

Pukni. Cf. phukni.

Pukpuku. Cf. pokpoko.

Pukri. Cf. pokhri.

Pukus. } To breathe, the only
Pukuspukus. } sign of which is the heaving of the stomach.

Pukus pukusokkanae. His stomach is heaving.

Pukus marte. } With a long sigh, or
Pukus mente. } breath.

Pukus menten sahetkeda. I drew a long sigh (of relief.)

Pul. A bridge.

Nondeko pula. They will bridge here.

Adiko pulakata. They have erected many bridges, they have bridged many places.

Puli. Cf. pali.

Puluć. } Cf. poloć.
Puluć puluć. }

Pun. Virtue, merit, religious merit.

Nuiye punakata. This (person) has acquired merit.

Pundit. Cf. pandet.

Pungi. To twist into a point, to make into a cone, compressed into a point, as a flower bud.

Baha pungiakana, guri saroka. The flower bud is pointed, it has not yet opened.

Sakam pungikate botolko eseda. They twist a leaf into the shape of a cone and cork a bottle with it.

Puni. Infantile mirasus or wasting.

Nui gidra puniakanae. This child is suffering from infantile miramus or wasting.

Puńji. Capital, stock.

Puńjiakatae. He has accumulated stock.

Mõrẽ taka reak puńji menaktaea. He has five rupees of capital.

Puńji. A heap, to make a heap.

Hasako puńjiakata. They have heaped the earth, or made a heap of earth.

Puńji pata. Capital, stock.

Puńji pata oet hõ banuktińa. I have not got any capital whatever.

Pupulhet. Cf. popolhot.

Pura. Entire, complete, exact, full, perfect, total, the whole.

Pura kathań badaea. I know the whole story.

Pura dom ghatiakata. You are wholly guilty.

Purageye kamikeda. He worked full time.

Candoe puraka. The moon will be full.

Purab. }
Purub. } The east, easterly.
Purua. }

Purua hoe. An east wind.

Purua dak. Rain from the east.

Purub nakha. }
Purub sen. } The east.
Purub mohnda. }

Purai nari. A succulent climbing plant cultivated as a vegetable *Basella alba, Linn.*

Katić purai arak. A variety of *Basella alba*, with small leaves.

Puran. } Sufficient, plenty, to satisfy.
Purun. }

Jomakte doko purungea. They have sufficient food.

Kathateko purunkedea, menkhan oet bõ bako emadea. They filled hin with words, but gave him nothing.

Puranti. To discharge an obligation, to complete, to satisfy a demand.

Purantiadińako. They satisfied my demands, paid or gave in full.

Purapura. } The whole, in full, complete-
Purapuri. } ly, to finish, to complete, to fulfill.

Pura puriye emadińa. He gave me the full (amount, quantity, &c.)

Pura puriakatań. I have completed it, I have fulfilled it.

Purapurin emkeda. I gave, or paid, in full.

Purau. To complete, to fulfill, to perfect, to accomplish, entire, full, complete, exact, perfect, total.

Candoe puraunena. The moon is full.

Kami purauk ateye calaoena. He finished the work and went away.

Purạuni. } Cf. cạk purạuni.
Cạk purạuni. }

Purbi. } Belonging to the east.
Purbiạ. }
Purbiạ hoṛ kanae. He is an east countryman.

Puṛchạ. Clear, distinctly.
Puṛchạ do bań ńellaǩa. I did not see distinctly.

Puṛchạ. } Clear, distinctly, intelligibly.
Puṛchạu. }
Puṛcho. }
Puṛchoteye lạikeda. He told it intelligibly.
Lại puṛchạuaṫleae. He explained it to us, he made it clear to us.
Khub puṛchạue roṛ daṛeaǩa. He can speak very distinctly.
Bes puṛcho daǩ kana. It is good clear water.

Purhut. } A spiritual preceptor, a
Purohit. } caste of Brahmins who sometimes visit Santals professionally and drink water from their hands.

Puri. The world, the sea.
Jalapuri. The sea.
Hana puri. The other world.
Noa puri. This world.
Monco puri. The passing world.
Patạl puri. The nether world.

Puri. A kind of very thin cake.

Puri. } A contribution given to-
Net puri. } wards the expenses of a funeral, marriage and certain festivals by relatives whose relationship requires their presence at such function.
Net puri lagaoakoa. They have to contribute to the expenses.

Puriạ. A small packet.
Miṫ puriạ sindur. A small packet of sindur.
Miṫ puriạ ran. A medicine powder.

Purkhạ. An elder, an ancestor, a patriarch.
Bapa purkhạ. Ancestors.
Nuige purkhạ kantaleae, bańkhan sanamko lahaena. This is our patriarch, all the rest have gone on before.

Purmu. Damp, wet, to damp, to moisten, to wet.
Daǩte purmuena. It is wetted with the rain.
Daǩte purmukedae. The rain wetted it.

Purnạ. } Cf. mare purnạ.
Mare purnạ. }

Purohit. Cf. purhut.

Pursạ pạil. } A measure larger than the
Bursạ pạil. } standard.

Puṛthạ. Clear, distinctly.
Khub puṛthạge ńeloǩkana. It is seen very distinctly, it appears very distinctly.
Puṛthạgeń bohgeṫeda. I see distinctly.

Purthi. The earth.

Puṛti Cf. parti.

Puruạ. } Cf. purạb.
Purub. }

Puruchun. To perform a religious rite, to propitiate, to remove ceremonial uncleanness by sacrifices or offerings, to fulfill a religious duty, as a vow, obsequies of the dead, &c.
Puruchunkedae. He fulfilled his religious duty, vow, &c.
Puruchunakaṫtaeań. I performed his rites (of a deceased person.)
Ạuri puruchunko emoǩ hạbić bhonḍgeko tahena. They remain unclean until they give the propitiatory offering.

Purun. Sufficient, plenty.
Mone purunentaea. His mind is at ease.
Sanamaǩ puruntegebo ńamkeda. We received a sufficiency of all.

Purus. A generation.
Noa atore tin purus khon menaǩpea? How many generations of you have occupied this village?

Purus. Husband.

Purus. The height of a man with his arms and fingers extended above his head, a fathom.
Miṫ purus daǩ menaǩa. There is a fathom of water.
Miṫ purusko gạḍaakaṫa. They have dug down one fathom.
Puruskate tiogme. Stretch your arms to the full height and reach it.

Pus. The ninth Hindu solar month.

Pus caṭao. Cf. phus caṭao.

Pusi. A cat.
Pusi hopon. A kitten.
Deko pusi. A Hindu cat, a moneylender, a [mahajan.

Pusi toa. A small, wild, milky plant, *Euphorbia pilulifera, Linn.*

Pusi pan. A moderately sized forest tree, *Ehretia laevis, Roxb.*

Pusi jaṅga. Applied to the bunches of flower buds of the matkom (q. v.) tree which resemble the sole of a cat's foot.
Matkom pusi jaṅgaakana.

Pusić. } A shout to drive away
Pusić pusić. } a cat.
Pusiǩ. }
Pusiǩ pusiǩ. }

Pusind. Cf. pạsind.

Pusi pusi. A children's game.
Pusi pusiko eneća gitilre. They play the game of *pusi pusi* in the sand.

Puski. To teach, to tutor, to put up to.
Puskiadeae. He tutored him, he privately put him up to it.

Puslạu. Cf. phuslạu.

Puspus. }
Pusuć pusuć. } Cf. phusuć phusuć.
Puspuse gitić johkana. He is sleeping quietly.

Pusri. A pimple.
Pusri janamakawadea. He is suffering from pimples.
Mit́ pusri hõ bań. Not at all, not in the least.
Mit́ pusri hõ bae jiwi daṛeada. He could not bear it in the least.

Pustạk. }
Pustok. } A book.

Pusṭạu. Distinctly, clearly, to speak distinctly.
Bes okoćte bae pusṭạu daṛeak̕kana. He cannot speak very distinctly, he cannot pronounce very correctly.

Pusṭi. }
Pusṭia. } A generation.
Ạdi pusṭi hoeena. } Many generations have
Ạdi pusṭi calaoena. } passed.

Pusṭi. }
Pusṭia. } Addicted to smoking tobacco.
Khadkiạ. Addicted to chewing tobacco.
Uni do ạdi pusṭiạ hoṛ kanae. He is a slave to tobacco.

Pusuć pusuć. Cf. phusuć phusuć.

Pusur pusur. To whisper. Cf. phusur phusur.
Pusur pusurkin galmaraokana. They are talking whisperingly.

Puṭ marte. }
Puṭ mente. } Cf. phuṭ marte.

Puṭạ. Cf. dbiạ puṭạ.

Puṭak̕. To rise to the surface at a distance from where one dived.
Pạni ḍubạko puṭạgok̕a. Coots come to the surface at a distance from where they dive.
Puṭạk̕enae. He rose to the surface at a distance from where he dived.

Puṭhi. A book.

Puṭhi hako. The small fry of the poṭha fish. Cf. poṭha hako.

Puṭhiạ. The wooden rim of a cart wheel.
Hal. The iron tyre of a wheel.

Puṭhuć. To boil leguminous fruits whole, such as beans, peas, gram, &c.
Raheṛ puṭhuć. Boiled raher (q. v.)
Buṭ puṭhuć. Boiled gram.
Malhan puṭhuć. Boiled malhan (q. v.)
Hoṛeć puṭhuć. Boiled hoṛeć (q. v.)
Ghańgra puṭhuć. Boiled ghańgra (q. v.)
Ramṛa puṭhuć. Boiled ramṛa (q. v.)
Oka do hoṛećko puṭhuja. They sometimes cook *horec'* (q. v.) by boiling it whole.

Puṭi. To swell, as the stomach, stomach swollen.
Puṭi diṛidahenae. His stomach is swollen very much.

Puṭiạ kạuḍi. Cf. phuṭiạ kạuḍi.

Puṭkạ. A puff-ball, a genus of fungi (*Lycoperdon.*)
Seta puṭkạ. }
Roṭe puṭkạ. }
Hoṛ puṭkạ. } Edible forms of puff-balls.
Erok̕ puṭkạ. }
Puṭkạ suṛe. Any of the edible forms of puff balls cooked along with rice.

Puṭki. A nose ornament worn by women.

Puṭki malla. A common hedge climber, *Cardiospermum Halicacabum.*

Puṭki. A variety of the rice plant.

Putlạ. } The centre piece of a solid
Putṛạ. } cart wheel. Cf. pạṭi.

Putli. A piece of cloth of from one cubit to one cubit and a half in length and one cubit in breadth, as a garment for a little girl, the first dress of a girl.
Putli bande. A girl of from two to six years of age for whom a putli (q. v.) suffices.
Tin marańae? Putli bande. How big is she? She wears a *Putli.*

Putli. }
Kaṭputli. } A puppet, *marionette.*

Puṭmi. F. }
Poṭma. M. } Cf. poṭma.

Puṭpuṭu. Cf. poṭpoṭo.

Putṛa. Cf. putlạ.

Putri. Cf. pạtri.

Puṭri. F. } Big-bellied, paunchy. Cf.
Poṭra. M. } poṭra.

Putri. }
Kaṭ putri. } A puppet, *marionette.*
Kaṭ putriko eneć̕koa. They make the puppets perform.

Puṭu. } To chafe or fret at being
Uṭu puṭu. } delayed.
Uṭu puṭu baṛaekanae. He is chafing at being delayed.

Puṭuć. To abstract or take anything out otherwise than by the proper opening, or by the proper method, as taking something out of a bundle without undoing it, or out of a house other than by the door.
Kombṛoko puṭućkedea. The thieves robbed him (by making a hole in the wall.)
Puṭuć oḍokkedae. He abstracted it (without opening the wrapping.)
Okare coṅ puṭuć oḍokena. It has slipped out and fallen some where.
Ḍanḍa khone puṭućkedea poesa. He abstracted money from his waist (cloth.)

Puturạ. A puppet, an image.

Puṭur puṭur. } Having bare patches, in
Poṭor poṭor. } patches.
Puṭur puṭur ghãsakana. The grass has grown in patches.

Puyul. } Very greatly, extreme-
Puyul puyul. } ly, applied to fear.
Bogetele botorok'kana puyul puyul.

Puyul marte. } With a start through
Puyul mente. } fear.
Puyul marte botor goćenae. He started with fear, he was frightened and gave a start.

Puyul. } To escape through an
Puyul puyul. } opening, to escape one after the other, or with a series of rushes.

Puyul marte. } With a rush, or dart
Puyul mente. } out.
Puyul marte parom goćenae, jhạli bhugạk're. It darted out through a hole in the net.
Dak' puyul mente oḍokena. The water came out with a gush.

Puyu puyu. To issue steadily from a small opening.
Dak' puyu puyu tabok'kana. The water is running out. [in a stream.
Puyu puyu dhũa todok'kana. Smoke is issuing

Puyuṛ. } Cf. puyul.
Puyuṛ puyuṛ. }
Puyuṛ puyuṛko paromok'kana. They are escaping through (a hole in the net) one after the other.

Puyuṛ marte. } With a rush, or a dart
Puyuṛ mente. } out. Cf. puyul marte.

R

Rabać rubuć. } Slowly, leisurely, gent-
Rabae rubui. } ly, heavily, without elasticity, without spring, as a heavy creature walking.
Rabać rubućko hijuk'kana. They are coming slowly.
Rabać rubuće dak'eda. It is raining gently.
Rabae rubuiye dak'eda. It is drizzling.
Rabać rubuće taṛamet'kana. He walks heavily, without elasticity in his step.

Rabak' rubuk'. Moving, as anything seen indistinctly in the distance.
Rabak' rubuk'ko ńelok'kana. They appear to move.

Rabaṅ. Cold, to feel cold.
Rabaṅ kana. It is cold.
Rabaṅ din. The cold weather.
Rabaṅge ṣikạuk'a. It feels cold.
Rabaṅediṅkana. I am cold.
Rabaṅ disom. A cold country.
Ạdi rabaṅok'kanae. He is very cold, he is very fearful of cold.
Rabaṅe kurumuṭuieda. He is taking care of himself by reason of the cold.
Rabaṅ iạte oyo poṭomakanae. He is wrapped up owing to the cold.

Rạbhuạ. Ugly and lumpish, ugly and inactive, used by women when scolding men.
Rạbhuạ mara hoṛ. An ugly lumpish rascal.

Rạbi. } Cold weather crops culti-
Rạbi cas. } vated after the cessation of the rains.

Rabon raj. } King Ravan or Ravani,
Rabona raj. } king of Ceylon, used metaphorically for cold.
Rabon rajae sapạkadea. King Ravan has seized him, i. e. he is very cold.
The Santals have a tradition that as Kherwars they accompanied the Hindu king Ram on his expedition to Ceylon to punish king Ravan for having carried off his wife Sita.

Raboṛ. To claw, to scratch with nails or claws.
Banako rak'boṛa. Bears claw.
Tạrupe raboṛkedea. The leopard clawed him.
Rapaboṛkanakin. The (children) are scratching each other.

Raboskak'. Big, protuberant, applied to the belly.
Raboskak'getaea lać do. His belly is big.
Marań utạrtaea lać raboskak'. His belly is tremendously large.

Rabraba. Over salted, salty taste, saline.
Ạdi rabrabagea. It is very salty.
Rabrabage ṣikạuk'a. It tastes salty.
Rabraba sebela. It has a nice salty taste.

Rac. The comb of a weaver's loom.

Raca. Courtyard of a house. [or out.

Racak'. To clutch, to tear or pull up
Ceće racak'keda? Kicrić. What did he clutch at? His cloth.
Ceć reye racak'edea? Upre. What did she clutch at? Her hair. [the hair.
Upre racak'akadeae. He has clutched him by
Rapacak'kanakin. They are clutching each other's (hair or clothing.)

Racaṕ rucuṕ. ⎫ Rustling, as of dry lea-
Racuṕ racuṕ, ⎬ ves, &c, sound as of
Rucuṕ rucuṕ. ⎭ anything crisp being
crushed, crackling, as of any thing
dry or brittle being crushed.

Racaṕ rucuṕ saḍekana. It rustles.

Racaṕ rucupe jomeda. He is crunching as he eats.

Racaṕ rucupko saḍe ooceda. They are causing a rustling.

Racaseć. ⎫ To urinate, used only of
Racate. ⎭ adult human beings.

Racateḱkanae.

Raca seće senakana.

Mayamge raca seḍećkanae. He passes bloody urine.

Race bacete. Carefully, discriminatingly.

Race bacete ḱạmipe. Work carefully.

Teheñ khon do bes okoćte sikhạu pạrhaoeben race bacete. From to-day teach her in a proper way and with discrimination.

Rad. ⎫ Scoundrelly, base, disobe-
Raḍa. ⎬ dient, wicked.
Raḍaha. ⎭

Rạdaha mara hoṛ. A base scoundrel.

Raḍ coaṛ. A low scoundrel.

Raḍ. M. ⎫ Scoundrelly, base, disobe-
Raḍin. F. ⎭ dient, wicked.

Raḍa. A row, a line, a course, as of
bricks on a wall, &c.

Mić rada bhitko rakaṕakaća. They have raised the wall one course. [line.

Niạ radate ubpe. Throw it down along this

Radabada. Sound of rustling as of
dry leaves, or the like. Cf. radobado.

Radbad. ⎫ Sound of rustling, an
Radbadao. ⎭ imitative word.

Radbadedae cole coh. Some thing is making a rustling sound.

Radbadaoedako. They are making a rustling.

Raḍga.roḍgo. Stony, gravelly.

Baṛge raḍga roḍgogeṭiña. My garden is stony.

Raḍgo baḍgo. Sound of rustling, as
of dry leaves, &c.

Tinạḱem daṛana raḍga roḍgo mundu pakaṛ? How long will you tramp the jungles rustling (the leaves ?)

Raḍgo paḍgo. Under-cooked, inefficiently, mainly applied to pot-
herbs.

Radgo paḍgope isinakaća. You have under cooked them.

Radha corok. A contrivance by means
of which Hindu devotees, and at
times also Santals, swing as a religious observance.

Raḍhuạ Sapless, dry.

Raḍhuạ dare. A sapless tree.

Raḍi. ⎫ Used up, waste, as paper, reject-
Rudi. ⎭ ed.

Raḍi kagoj. Waste paper.

Raḍin. ⎫ Scoundrel, jade, bad, disobed-
Raḍ. ⎭ ient female.

Nui raḍin do katha bae añjoma. This jade will not do as she is bid.

Radobado. Sound of rustling as of dry
leaves, &c.

Sakamteć radobado saḍe goćena. The leaf rustled.

Radrad. ⎫ Sound, as of anything dry
Radradao. ⎭ being crushed or shaken,
marks as of anything having been
dragged along the ground.

Radrade or idikeda.

Or radradao idikedae.

Rae. Wisdom, opinion, counsel, order,
custom.

Raekedako. They made a rule, or they came to an agreement.

Raere bae hijuḱkana. He has not given in his adhesion to the agreement.

Disom rae. The custom of the country.

Rae nokolle oḍokakaća adalot khon. We have taken a copy of the order of the court.

Raebar. To act as a go-between,
applied mainly to the arranging
of marriages.

Raebarió. A go-between, a person who negotiates a marriage.

Raebar buḍhi. A female marriage negotiator.

Raebarióe raebara. The marriage negotiator negotiates the marriage.

Raebundi. A variety of the rice plant.

Rae dohae. To cry out for justice, an
appeal for justice.

Nunạḱ iñ rae dohaekeda dos ṭhen. I appealed so much to the panchayat for justice.

Seḅgel ar daḱ rae dohae bae añjoma. Fire and flood heed not an appeal for justice.

Noa reaḱ rae dohae bạnuḱanah. There is no one who can lay claim to this.

Raeka. High, long, big.

Raeka dare. A high tree.

Raeka dereñ. A long or big horn.

Raekakaṛbaḱ. The chameleon.

Raela. ⎫ Tall, high.
Roela. ⎭

Raemundi. A variety of the rice
plant.

Raeot. A ryot, a cultivating tenant.

Rag. Anger, excitement, energy, spirit.
Rag baṅ cabaakantaea. His anger has not passed off.
Alo, ragoḱae nahaḱ. Don't, he will get excited presently.
Rag maraoentaea. His energy is exhausted.

Ragabaga. Leisurely, applied mainly to crabs, scorpions, &c., to produce a rustling sound, or a sensation of something creeping.
Delabon baibaite ragabagabon sen jarwaḱa. Come along, let us creep leisurely on our way.

Ragae. }
Ragae ragae. } Gritty, rough.
Meť ragae ragaeoḱkana. There is a gritty feeling in my eye.

Ragae ragae. }
Ragae rugui. } Gritty, rough.
Medoḱre ragae ragae haḱsoa.
Hoṛmo ragae ragae aṭkaroḱa. My (body) feels rough.

Ragam cagam. Sound produced by anything dry, as leaves, &c. when disturbed.
Ragam cagame hijuḱkana. He is coming making a rustling noise.

Ragam ragam. }
Ragam rugum. }
Rugum rugum. } Sensation as of something creeping on the skin, smarting sensation.
Ńindạre ragam ragam hasoea. He feels it smarting at night.
Ragam rugum cele coe ṭundạhediña. Something is creeping over me.

Raga rạgi. Quarrelling, disputing angrily.
Khubkin raga rạgiena. They disputed angrily.

Ragaṛ cagaṛ. Loquacious, glib.
Ragaṛ cagaṛ ạdiye roṛa. He is very glib.

Ragaṛ jhagaṛ. Quarrel, wrangle, dispute.
Okoe tuluć hõ ragaṛ jhagaṛ alom lagaoa. Do not quarrel with any one.
Khub ragaṛ jhagaṛkin kạphariạuena. They had an angry wrangle.

Ragaṛ rogoṛ. }
Rogoṛ rogoṛ. } Stony, gravelly, rough and stony.

Ragać. }
Ragać ragać. } Rough.
Dhar ạdi ragaća. The edge is very rough.

Ragać cogać. }
Ragać ragać. } Rough, rough or stinging, as speech.
Ragać cogać ạikạuḱkana. It feels rough.
Ạdi ragać ragać noa hor do. This road is very rough.
Ragać cogaće roṛeda. He speaks roughly.
Ona hor do ragać cogaćgea. That road is rough.

Ragać rogoć. To produce a slight noise when doing anything stealthily.
Ragać rogoće ńam baṛaeda. He is seeking it stealthily and making a slight noise.

Ragạu ragạu. Din, tumult.
Ạrisakaćako ragạu ragạu, meć hõ baṅ jạpidoḱa.

Ragbag. }
Ragbagao. } To move, to respond, movement, response.
Ragbag oeć hõ baṅ. No movement of any kind.
Ragbag bae laṛaoḱkana. He is a fixture.
Bae ragbagaoḱkana. He moves not.
Ragbagaoḱkanae, se baṅ? Bae ragbagaoḱkana. Is he moving or not? He is not moving.

Ragda rạgdi. }
Rigdạ rigdi. } Closely, at the heels of.
Ragda rạgdi khube lagakedea. He gave it a good chase keeping at its heels.
Ạdi khudạukediñako ragda rạgdi. They pursued me very closely.

Ragda rogdo. Rough.
Ragda rogdogea cikāṛ do baṅ. It is rough, not smooth.

Ragda rạgdi. Scrubbing.
Ragda rạgdi kaḍako ạrupkom. Scrubbing wash the buffaloes.

Ragdao. To rub, to scour, to scrub with the hand or hands.
Ragdao poṭaḱenae. His skin is rubbed off.
Kaḍa ạrupko jokheć khub lekako ragdaokoa. When they wash buffaloes they scrub them well with the hands.
Ragdao ghao. A sore produced by rubbing or chafing.

Ragdao. }
Rigdạu. } To chase or pursue at the heels of.
Ragdao idikedeako. They kept up the chase at his very heels.

Ragha rogho. Rough.
Onḍe khonge hor hõ ạdi ragha rogho tahẽḱkana. From there the road was very rough.

Ragho boaṛ hako. }
Raghoṗ boaṛ hako. } A species of fish.

Rạgi. Spirited, active.
Rạgi daṅgra kanae. It is a spirited ox.
Rạgi sadom kanae. It is a spirited horse.

Ragoṛ pagoṛ. Clambering, climbing with hands and feet, to scramble, to scrape with the feet, using hand and feet.
Ragoṛ pagoṛe geleṡeda. He is scraping it out with his feet (rat.)
Ragoṛ pagoṛe dejoḱkana darere. He is scrambling up the tree, he is climbing the tree by means of his hands and feet.
Kuḍi do ragoṛ pagoṛoḱkana. The kudali is scrambling over them (stones.)

Ragraga. In position, undetached, applied mainly to the teeth and to the flowers of the matkom (q. v.) which do not become detached.
Ragraga coṭrege menak̕a. It is high up undetached.
Eken ḍaṭa ragraga ṅelok̕kantaea. Only the teeth appear all in position, (as in a skull.)

Ragragia. Spirited, active. Cf. ragi.
Khub ragragia sadom kanae. He is a very spirited horse.

Ragṛao. To rub, to chafe, to apply friction, to come and go, to hang about in hope of getting something.
Ạdi din khone ragṛaok̕kana, enhõ bae ṅameda. He has been hanging around many days, still he has not got.
Ragṛao saphaedako. They are cleaning by attrition (as water and sand shaken in a bottle to clean it.)

Ragṛa ragṛi. Persistently, unceasingly, fiercely, applied to quarrels or disputes.
Ragṛa ragṛikin ropoṛena. They wrangled fiercely.

Raguisak̕. Rough as hair, shaggy, dishevelled.
Bana do raguisak̕ko upana. Bears have rough hides.
Bana up do raguisak̕gea. The hair of a bear is rough.

Ragumcak̕. } Rough, applied to hair,
Ragum cagum. } hairy, hirsute, bristly.
Icak̕ hako ragumcak̕ geako. Shrimps are bristly.
Ragumcak̕ko upana bana. Bears have rough hair.
Noko eskargepe goćkećkoa ragum cagum. You only killed these bristly things (shrimps.)

Rah. } Road, way.
Raha. }
Rahadeale. We made a way for him, we pointed out the way to him.

Rahai sahai. To shew pity, to forgive, to deliver, to settle.
Noa mamblako rahai sahaia. They will settle this suit.

Raham. Having the quality or taste of salt, saline.
Buluṅ do rahamgea.
Buluṅ leka rahamge cikak̕a. It tastes saline like salt.
Rahamge sebela. It tastes good as salt.

Raham rohom. Slowly, leisurely.
Raham rohome taṛama. He walks slowly.

Rahan rohon. Slowly, dilatory.
Rahan rohon bape laṛao hodok̕kana. Dilatory, you do not move quickly.

Rahao. To become numbed or stiff, to sleep, as a hand or foot.
Duṛup duṛupteṅ rahaoena. I am numbed with continued sitting.
Duṛup rahaoenaṅ. I have sat till I am numbed.

Rahap ruhup. Slowly, leisurely, heavily.

Rahaṛ. A large drum beaten by the fingers.
Rahaṛ dhaca. Bunches of feathers with which the rahaṛ is adorned.

Rahaṭ pahaṭ. The sound produced by rubbing the person with the hands; dilatory.
Rahaṭ pahaṭ abukok̕kanae.
Rahaṭ pahaṭe isirok̕kana.
Rahaṭ pahaṭ bae odok hodok̕kana. He is dilatory, he does not come out quickly.

Rahau. To save, to deliver, to rescue, to extricate from danger.
Ạdi rahau hoeena, baṅcaoenae. It is a great deliverance, he is saved.
Rahauketkoae. He delivered them.

Rahdani. Giving charity to travellers.
Rahdani kanae. He gives charity to travellers.

Raheṛ. A cultivated crop, *Cajanus indicus, Spreng.*
Caitali raheṛ. Raheṛ ripening in the month of Chaṭ, March-April.
Aghạṛ raheṛ. } Raheṛ ripening in the month
Aghanua raheṛ. } of Aghạṛ, November-December.
Magbi raheṛ. Raheṛ which ripens in the month of Magh, January- February.
Raheṛ dal. The split pea of raheṛ.

Raheṛ. } A cultivated leguminous
Buru raheṛ. } plant, *Cyamopsis psoralioides, D. C.*

Rahi. A traveller.

Rahi. } A kind of palki or
Rahi ḍanḍi. } doolie.
Rahire Man rani menaea. Queen Man is in the palki.

Rahi rahite. } Gradually.
Rahi sahite. }
Rahi sahiteṅ emama. I will give it to you gradually.

Rahṛuk̕. } Crashing, thunder-
Rahṛuk̕ rahṛuk̕. } ing, applied to any very loud noise or sound.
Rahṛuk̕ rahṛuk̕ bindaṛena dare. The tree fell crashing, the tree came crashing down.
Ḍhol adi sadekantakoa rahṛuk̕ rahṛuk̕. Their drum has a thundering sound.

Rahṛuk̕ marte. } With a crash, with a
Rahṛuk̕ mente. } loud noise.
Dare rahṛuk̕ marte bindaṛena. The tree fell with a crash.

Rại. } A variety of the Mustard
Rại tuṛi. } plant, *Brassica campestris.*

Rại. } Rule, order, opinion. Cf. rae.
Rae. }

Rạilạ gidi. The female of *Ologyps calvus*, the Indian King vulture.

Rạilạ baha. A jungle flowering plant of *Barleria* sp.

Rạimạl lenḍoṅ. A kind of very large centipede.

Raj. } A king, a title borne by certain
Raja. } Indian landholders, to reign, to become a king; a kingdom.

Maharaj. } A great king, a title superior to
Moharaj. } raj (q. v.), an emperor.
Raj rapajko. Kings, kings and their attendants.
Raj rapajko darakokana. The kings and their retinue are coming.
Raj kaj. Business, matters of business.
Unigeye raj kajeḱtalea. He transacts our business for us.
Raj kaj caḱlaoić. A manager.
Raj bheja. A cess paid to a zemindar.
Raj bhasa. The royal language, English.
Raj paṭ. The work of government.
Rajpaṭe calaoeda. He carries on the work of government.
Raj ḍahar. } The king's highway.
Raj rasta. }
Raje calaoeda. He carries on the work of government.
Iṅaḱ rajre baṅ dohoea. I will not keep him in my kingdom.
Serma raj. The kingdom of heaven.
Raj rapajko ren raj. King of kings.
Raj kumạr. A king's son, a title borne by the second son of a Ghatwal raja.
Raj pataren kanako. They are of the king's lineage, they can sit with the king, they can sit at the king's table.
Raj tilok. } The mark on the forehead given to a
Raj ṭika. } king on accession.

Raj rog. Phthisis, consumption.

Raj baha. The Sweet-scented Oleander, *Nerium odorum, Soland.*

Araḱ raj baha. The red variety of the Sweet-scented oleander.
Ponḍ raj baha. The white variety of the Sweet-scented oleander.

Raja. A king, a title borne by certain Indian landholders.

Moharaja. } A great king, a title superior to
Maharaja. } that of raja (q. v.), an emperor.

Raja muni. A variety of rice.

Raja paṭa. A children's game.

Rajaḱ rajaḱ. Moderately heavy, as rain.

Rajaḱ rajaḱe daḱeda. The rain is moderately heavy.

Rajan bajan. } Pomp and music.
Rajon bajon. }

Rajan bajanteko idikedea bahu do. They carried away the bride with pomp and music.

Rajas. } Pupil of eye.
Rajos. }

Rajon bajon. Cf. rajan bajan.

Rajos. Cf. rajas.

Rạji. To be satisfied, contented, pleased, willing.

Bae rạjilena. He did not agree.
Unireṅ rạjiakana. I am pleased with him.

Rạji nama. An acknowledgment of a cause being finally settled given by plaintiff, a compromise.

Rạji namaenako. They have come to a compromise.
Rạji nama olkate cabakedako mokordoma do. Having written a *rajinama* (q. v.) they put an end to the case.

Rajmohal. A variety of rice.

Rajoe. } A kingdom.
Rajosti. }

Rajoe hataokedae. He took the kingdom.

Rajpol. A variety of rice.

Raḱ. To weep, to beseech, the call, cry or note of a beast, bird or insect.

Ạdiko raḱeda. They are weeping bitterly.
Mạṅjhiṅ raḱadea. I laid my complaint before the Mạṅjhi (q. v.), I appealed to the Mạṅjhi (q. v.)
Raḱ gidrạ. A little child.
Cele ceṛẽ raḱedae? What bird is calling, or what bird is singing?
Rici ceṛẽ dayage ragae. The Rici bird calls plaintively.
Simko raḱkeda, aṅgaena. The cocks crew, it is dawn.
Toyoko raḱkeda. The jackals uttered their cry, the jackals howled.
Sim raḱ. Cock crow.
Maraḱ raḱ. Peacock crow, which is earlier than cock crow.
Raḱateye calaoena. She went away weeping.
Setae raḱeda. The dog is uttering his cry, the dog is howling.
Gadha ạdiko raga. Asses are much given to braying, asses bray much.
Hathi ạdi ạṭko raga. Elephants trumpet very loudly, elephants utter a very loud call.
Roṭe hõ ạdiko raga. Frogs also croak much.

Rakạp̣. To rise, to ascend, to appear, to fall, as rates.

Bere rakap̣ena. The sun is risen.
Ber rakap̣. Sunrise.
Ber rakap̣ seć. The east.
Caole reaḱ dor rakap̣ena. The price of rice has fallen.
Nãwã caole ạuri rakap̣a. New rice is not yet in the market.
Ale ṭhẽć doe rakap̣lena. He appeared at our place.

Ạḍi oṭṭeko rakaṗena. They have ascended very high.
Or rakaṗkedeaṅ. I pulled him up.
Oṛaǩre senerko rakaṗakaťa. They have raised the rafters on to the house.

Rakaṛ rokoṛ. To rattle inside, an imitative word.
Rakaṛ rokoṛ saḍekana. It is rattling.

Rakas. A demon, a glutton.
Rakas hoṛko jomkoa. Demons eat men.
Nui do rakasgeye taṗena. He has become a regular glutton.

Rakạsiạ. Demoniacal.

Rakḍaṅ. } High, tall, very, exceedingly, applied to height.
Rạkuḍaṅ.
Rakḍahe usula nui hoṛ do. This man is exceedingly tall.
Rakḍaṅ dare. A high tree.

Rạkḍuṅ. High, tall, tall and slim.
Ekenpe rạkḍuṅ ocokeťkoa. You have only allowed them to become tall and slim.

Rakha. To lay an embargo on, to preserve, as a forest, game, &c. &c.
Rakha bir. A preserved forest, a reserved forest, the timber of which it is forbidden to cut.
Noa sạuṛiko rakhaakaťa. They have laid an embargo on this grass, grazing has been forbidden.

Rạkhiạ. } Relief, deliverance, to relieve, to extricate, to deliver, to save.
Rukhiạ.
Ạḍi rạkhiạ hoeña. It is a great deliverance.
Rạkhiạkeťbonae. He delivered us.

Rạkhi jogao. To economise, to be frugal, to be thrifty, to save.
Rạkhi jogaokate jompe. Eat frugally.
Rạkhi jogaote dohoepe. Save it.
Rạkhi jogaote khoroepe. Spend it, or use it, thriftily.

Rakhsa. A piece of wood from 6 to 8 feet long and 6 inches broad, used in levelling rice fields.

Rakhwal. } A watchman, one who guards or watches.
Rakhwar.

Rakjak. Securely, tightly.
Rakjake siṅ poṭomakana. He is securely shut in.
Rakjake duṛuṗakana. He is sitting tightly.
Phaṭoǩ duạr rakjakko siṅ eseťkeda. They shut and closed the gate securely.

Rakraka. Sticking out, projecting, straggling, as the branches of a tree, &c.
Pusi rakrakae gitiċakana. The cat is lying sticking out, i. e. lying on its back with its feet in the air.
Rakraka hoṛreko doho eseťakaťa sahan do. They have laid the firewood so that it sticks out and blocks the pathway.

Rakṛiċ. Lean, skinny, lanky, slim.
Ṅui kuṛi doe rakṛiċgea, bae moṭaǩa. This girl is lanky, she won't get fat.

Rakṛoǩ. } To rattle, an imitative word.
Rakṛoǩ rakṛoǩ.
Dhiriko giḍieda rakṛoǩ rakṛoǩ. They throw down the stones rattle, rattle.

Rakṛoǩ marte. } With a rattle.
Rakṛoǩ mente.
Kulạiko jhạlilenkhan ḍaṅ rakṛoǩ mente ṅuroǩa. When hares are caught in the net the prop falls down with a rattle.

Rạksi. A machine for expressing the juice from sugar cane.

Raktao. To be engrossed in, to be absorbed in, to have the mind taken up or occupied with.
Kạmi raktaoakana. He is engrossed in his work.
Jom raktaoakanae. He is engrossed in eating.

Rakṭaṅ. } High, tall, lanky.
Rakḍaṅ.

Rạkuḍaṅ. Cf. rakḍaṅ.

Ralaǩ. } Clean, to make clean.
Ralaǩ ralaǩ.
Joǩ ralaǩakaťae. She has swept it clean.
Ralaǩ ralaǩ ṭạnḍi. To make a clean sweep.

Ralaǩ masaǩ. Clean, every particle.
Ralaǩ masaǩe jom cabakeda. He ate it up clean.

Rạli. A common wild plant, *Piper longa, Linn.*

Ram. } To fence, or block with thorns.
Rampha.
Caǩe hijuǩa ramakaťkhan? Why should he come if the way is blocked with thorns?
Duạrko ramakaťtiṅa. They have blocked my door with thorns.

Rama. A nail, a claw.
Ti rama. Finger nails.
Jaṅga rama. Toe nails.
Pusikọ, setako, banako, kulko, emantenkoko ramaana. Cats, dogs, bears, tigers, etc. have claws.

Rama kuṛiť. } A common jungle scandent bush, *Zizyphus oxyphylla, Edgw.*
Kuṛiť rama.

Rambaṛ romboṛ. Whole, unbroken, whole and hard, lumpy.
Rambaṛ romboṛ ạṭkaroǩkana. It feels whole.
Rambaṛ romboṛ noa caole reaǩ daka ạṭkaroǩ kana. This rice when boiled feels hard and whole.
Rambaṛ romboṛge tahẽena hasa. The clay is in lumps (not properly mixed.)

Rambaṛ rukhaṛ. Cf. rambaṛ rombaṛ.
Rạmbhuạ. Cf. rạbhuạ.

Rambṛa. A cultivated leguminous crop, *Phaseolus Mungo, var, Radiatus, Linn.*
Rambṛa ḍal. The split pea of *rambra.*

Ramcam. Bristly, rough, as hair.
Ramcam uptae. His hair is bristly, or like a mop.
Icạk hako eken ramcam. The shrimp is only bristles.

Rạmdhu. Stout, burly, big and fat.
Tin marañpe ñelledea? marañ rạmdhu kanae. How big is he? He is a big burly (fellow.)

Rạmjạu. To persuade, to talk over, to beguile.
Rạmjạukedeako. They talked him over.

Ram jhiṅgạ. A cultivated plant, *Hibiscus esculentus, Linn.*

Ramkhạsi. A hemaphrodite goat.

Ramo ramo. } Carefully, frugally, econ-
Ramo ratiṅ. } omically.
Ramo ramoteye khoroceda. She expends it economically.

Rampaṛ. } Long, high, large.
Rampeṛ. }
Rampaṛ dereñ. Long horns.
Rampaṛ dare. A high tree.
Rampaṛ herel. A tall man.

Ramṛa. Cf. rambṛa.

Ram roṛ. } To scold, to rebuke, to re-
Ram roṛe. } monstrate, to expostulate, to reprimand.
Ram roṛekedeañ. I reprimanded him.

Ram sạl. A variety of rice.

Ramsiṅgạ. A ram's horn, a musical instrument shaped like a buffaloe's horn.
Baplare ramsiṅgạko oroḥa. They blow the ram's horn at marriages.

Ran. Medicine, a drug, to treat medically.
Ranadeako. They gave him medicine.
Ṭakateñ rankedea. I bribed him.
Ran rehet. Medicinal roots.
Ran rehetadeae. He doctored him with medicinal roots.
Ran rehete badaea. He knows the properties of medicinal roots.
Raranić. One who gives medicines, a doctor.
Ran oṛak. A dispensary.
Setae gerakadiña, ran tanakem badaekhan ranañme. A dog has bitten me, if you know a medicine treat me medically.

Rana. A variety of plantain.

Ranakap. An incline, an ascent, steep, steep ascent.
Ranakap hako. Fish coming up a stream when in flood.
Hoe ranakap aṛak. The leaves of *Bauhinia purpurea, L.* used as a pot-herb. Cf. siñ aṛak.
Gaḍa ranakap, Ascent from the bed of a river.
Noa hor do ạdi ranakapa. There are many steep ascents on this road.
Note khon calak ranakap bujhạukkana, ar onte khon hijuk anạṛgo bujhạukkana. Going from here it is felt to be an ascent, and coming from there it is felt to be a descent.

Randhoni. A female cook.

Rạṇḍi. To become a widow or widower, a widow, a widower.
Rạṇḍi herel. A widower.
Rạṇḍi maejiu. } A widow, a widow woman.
Rạṇḍi ṣimạ. }
Rạṇḍi dukhi. } Poor widows.
Rạṇḍi peṭari. }
Rạṇḍi era. A widow.
Rạṇḍi era, heme era. Widows and poor women.
Rạṇḍienae. She has become a widow, or he has become a widower.

Ranḍo icak. A species of prawn or shrimp.

Ranebane. Plenty, profusion, abundance, *Scottice*, routh.
Nuiak oṛak ranebane ṣikạuka. This (man's) house appears well provided for.
Ranebane cij menaktaea. He has an abundance of goods.

Rañ. } Colour, dye, to colour, to dye,
Roñ. } to stain.
Rañakatae. He has dyed it.
Rañ baha. A flower possessing colouring, staining or dying properties.

Rañ. Pewter.
Rañ ṭoḍor. A wristlet of pewter.

Rañ bi rañ. } Of various colours.
Rañ bo rañ. }
Rañ bi rañ kicrić. Cloth of many colours.

Rañga. Coloured, dyed.
Rañga suṭạm. Dyed thread or yarn.

Raṅga. Pewter. Cf. rañ.

Raṅga coṅga. } Thorny, spikey, armed
Raṅga roṅga, } with spikes or thorns.
Edel dare raṅga coṅga dareka. The cotton tree grows with spikes on it.
Raṅga coṅga jạnumana. It is armed with thorns.

Raṅga hari. The name of a Santal godlet.

Raṅga rạṅgi. Fiercely, furiously, quarrelling or disputing fiercely.
Ạḍi raṅga rạṅgikin roporena. They disputed very fiercely.

Raṅgạini. } A common prickly
Raṅgạini jạnum. } plant, *Solanum xanthocarpum, Schrad et Wendl.*

Raṅgao. To be angry, displeased, offended, to be absorbed in any thing.

Jom rahgaoenae. He is in the middle of his repast, he is absorbed in eating.

Kami rahgaoenae nitok do oet bŏ bae añjoma. He is at present absorbed in his work, he will listen to nothing.

Dadalteye rahgaoakana. He is hardened by inflicting corporal punishment.

Kisar doe rahgaoena. The master is angry.

Rahgaokae nahak. He will become angry presently.

Raṅgaṗ.
Raṅgaṗ raṅgaṗ. } Thin, slim.

Adi bae motawa, rahgaṗ rahgaṗgeae.

Raṅgha roṅgho. } Rough, thorny, spikey,
Raṅgha roṅgha. } armed with spikes.

Cikar do baṅ rahgha roṅgho. Not smooth but rough.

Adi rahgha ronghogea hor do. The road is very rough.

Raṅgi. A variety of rice.

Raṅgia. Red, fair, as a person.

Rahgia hor. A fair man.

Rahgia daṅra. A reddish coloured bullock, fire, a tiger.

Rahgia daṅra rokkatkoae. The red bullock gored them, i. e. they were burnt out.

Raṅkar. }
Raṅkur. } High, tall.

Raṅraṅ. Reddish, of the colour of good haṅḍi (q. v.), having the taste of over boiled guṛ (q. v.)

Rahrah ñelokkana. It looks reddish.

Rahrah guṛ. Guṛ (q. v.) having the taste of having been over boiled.

Raṅruṅ Empty, as a vessel; to sound empty.

Rahruh caba utarena. It is completely exhausted.

Rahruh saḍekana. It sounds empty, it has an empty sound.

Raṇi. A queen, the wife of a raja(q. v.), a female Zemindar, to become a queen.

Nes doe reniena. She succeeded to the throne this year.

Moharani. A great queen, an empress.

Raṇiphul. A common flowering plant, *Polygonum indicum, L.*

Raṅjao. To twist a rope backwards to prevent its opening out.

Baber khub rañjaoko uñakafa.

Uñ jokheé do rañjao do bako rañjaolaka. When twisting (the rope) they did not also twist it the opposite way.

Kathako rañjao thikkeda. They settled the matter in such a way as it cannot be again revived.

Raṅjao. To boil down sugar cane juice.

Rañjao ghatao idikakako. They boil it down into less bulk.

Raṇki hoṛo. A variety of rice.

Ranran. } To produce a trilling or
Ranranao. } humming sound, a shrill sound as produced by certain insects.

Banran saḍekana. It sounds ranran.

Ranran. } To tingle, as from pain, to
Ranranao. } be numb.

Durup rahaolenkhan jahga ranranaoka. If one sits till he is numb his legs tingle.

Kidiñ katkome toṛkediñte katuṗ ranranaokkana. My finger tingles through a scorpion having stung me.

Banran eikeukkana. It feels numbed.

Ranu. } The ferment used in the
Ranu ran. } manufacture of rice beer.

Ranu capaĉ. To collect and prepare the materials of the ferment for rice beer.

Ranu capaĉe oeĉaĉkina. He instructed them in the preparation of the ferment for rice beer.

Rāoḍāo. The sound produced by a flawless vessel when struck, &c, reverberent, long drawn, as sound.

Bati rāoḍoakkana.

Tumdak khub rāoḍokkana.

Raocao. Too much, over, applied to salting.

Raocao buluhtepe adakeda. You put too much salt in it.

Rāoḍāo. To traverse, to go.

Noa bir goṭagele rāoḍāo acurkeda. We traversed this whole jungle through.

Noa bir goṭale rāoḍāokeda. We traversed the whole of this jungle.

Raona jhaona. Weeping, crying.

Raona jhaonako calaka.

Raona jhaonako rak idieda.

Iñ akote raona jhaonako hijukkana.

Raona jhaonako calakkana ehga hopon.

Rāoṛāo. To hum, as a crowd, the hum produced by a large crowd of people, imitative.

Adi utar rāoṛāo horko añjomokkana.

Rapak. To roast in fire or ashes, to cremate, to burn in a kiln, as bricks, earthenware, &c.

Jondrako rapaga. They roast Indian corn.

Hoṛkoko rapakkoa. They cremate people.

Iteko rapage. They burn bricks (in a kiln.)

Rapak ita. Burnt bricks.

Rapak jel. Flesh meat roasted in the fire.

Rapakkateko jomkeda. They roasted and ate it.

Rapaṅ rupuṅ. Emaciated and weak.

Rua beretakanae, rapah rupuhe dāṛā baraekana. He is just recovering from fever and is going about emaciated and weak.

Rapareć. The Reciprocal form of rareć. (q. v.)

Rapa ropo. Low, as fever.
Rapa ropoe ruạkkana. He has low fever.

Rap dhap. } To settle privately, to
Rop dhop. } effect a compromise privately, to reconcile without publicity, to come to an agreement without invoking the aid of a court of justice.
Atore bare rap dhapkakpe. Settle (the dispute) privately (in the village.)

Rape. } Rough, standing up, brist-
Rape rape. } ly, straggling, as branches.
Up do rapegetaea. His hair is standing up.
Bhage do bań dareakana rape rapegea. It has not grown well (a tree) it is straggling.

Rapet. Diligently, heartily.
Khub rapetko kạmikana. They are working very diligently.

Rap kotap. The shakings, as of a bag which held grain, &c.
Rap kotaple jom cabakeda. We ate all even the shakings of the bags.
Rap kotap ceć hõ bạnuktalea. We have not even the shakings of a bag.

Raprapa. } Sticking out, protruding, as
Rokroko. } horns, branches, &c., straggling, as the branches of a tree.
Pusi raprapae gitićakana. The cat is lying (on its back) with its legs in the air.
Raprapa horreko doho esetakata. They have placed them sticking out and have obstructed the way.

Raprup. To collapse, to fall down.
Raprup orak bindarena. The house collapsed and fell down.
Orak raprubokа. The house will collapse.

Rapta rapti. To strive together, to argue hotly, to wrangle, to dispute.
Ạdi rapta rạptikin roporena. They argued very hotly with each other.
Ako motogeko rapta rạptikkan tahẽkana. They were arguing hotly amongst themselves.

Raput. To break.
Dare rạputentaea. His strength is broken, his resources are exhausted, he is ruined financially.
Dạr rapuṭena. The branch is broken.
Rạpudoka nahak. It will break presently.

Rar. A tune, an air.

Rara. To loose, to unbind.
Rarakedeako. They unbound him.
Sadomko rarakedea. They loosed the horse.

Raraṅ. } To clang, as a bell; the
Raraṅ raraṅ. } the sound produced when a hollow metal object is struck, to sound shrilly.
Ghanta raraṅ raraṅ sadekana. The bell is sounding clang, clang.

Raraṅ marte. } With a clang, with a
Raraṅ mente. } shrill sound.
Raraṅ marte sade goćena. It sounded clang.

Raraṅ ruruṅ. Cf. raraṅ.

Rareć. To cool.
Jiwi rareć. To comfort, to console.
Jiwiko rarećkeṭiṅa. They comforted me, they cooled my spirit.
Usạt rarećе senakana. She has gone to get over her sulk.
Edre rarećentaea. His anger has cooled.
Dohokakkhan rarejoka. If it is kept it will cool.

Raro. A cluster of rocks in the bed of a river.
Hana dhiri rarore hako menakkoa. There are fish among yonder rocks.
Raro latarre idikom. Take them below the rocks in the river bed.

Raru. } A volume of sound, loudly.
Raru raru. }
Raruko bohoećkana seko roreckana. They are calling loudly, or they are making much sound by speaking.
Raru raru tirioko orońeda. They are producing a great volume of sound by flute playing.

Rạs. Luck success, return.
Rạs bań ńamleda, bań jahlena. I got no return, (the crop) did not fill.
Ạdi rạsoktaea. He will get a good return.
Ạdiye rạs ocо darеaka. He can command a good return.

Ras. Juice, moisture, sap.
Ạkle lenkeda, menkhan bań raslena. We pressed the sugar cane but it yielded little juice.
Bań goćakana dare do ras menaka. The tree is not dead, there is sap (in it.)

Ras. } The name of a Hindu
Ras porob. } festival, including songs and dances.

Ras. } A kind of sore on the
Ras phutau. } feet, to break into a sore on the feet.
Ras phutạuakantaea. He is suffering from a sore on the foot.

Ras. } Bridle, reins.
Ras jhin. }

Ras dharia. A dancing boy.

Rasa. Honey, juice, sweet juice.
Ńele rasa. } The honey produced by the different kinds of bees.
Dumur rasa. }
Terom rasa. }
Luti rasa. }
Icak rasa. The honey in the icak (q. v.) flower.
Ul adomak do ạdi rasaana. Some mangoes contain much sweet juice.
Rasaanak. Juicy.

Rasak. } Sound of wrenching,
Rasak rasak, } as that produced by a cow when grazing.

Rasak rasake jom idikeda. It grazed on producing a sound of wrenching.

Rasak marte. } With a wrenching
Rasak mente. } sound, as of a cow grazing.

Rasak marteye jomkeda. He (bullock) bit it off with a wrenching sound and ate it.

Rasao. To solder.

Baṭiko rasaoa. They solder brass basins.
Rasao esetkakako. They solder and stop (a hole.)

Rase. Soup, to prepare soup.

Hako rase. Fish soup.
Sim rase. Chicken soup.
Jel rase. Soup made from flesh meat.
Jań rase. Soup prepared from bones.

Rase rase. Leisurely, slowly, gently.

Rase rasete lagaeme. Drive him gently.
Rase rasete jomme. Eat leisurely.
Rase raseko dạṛ ocokoa. They make them run slowly.

Rạsi. Populous.

Rạsi ato kana. It is a populous village.
Rạsi bạsti. Very populous.
Rạsi bạsti ato kana. It is a very populous village.

Rạsiạ. Partner, sharer, parnership.

Rạsiạte ḍahraliń kirińkedea. We bought a bullock in partnership.
Rạsiạ kanakin. They are partners, they are in partnership.
Rạsiạtele caseda. We cultivate in partnership.

Rạsiạu. Lusty, applied to bulls kept for breeding purposes, rich, wealthy.

Rạsiạu ḍahra. A bull kept for breeding purposes.
Khub rạsiạu menakkoa ona store. There are very wealthy people in that village.

Rạsid. } Cor. of the English word re-
Rạsit. } ceipt.

Rạsid kaṭao. To write or give a receipt.
Rạsid kaṭaoańme. Give me a receipt.
Rạsidiń kaṭao ocokeda. I took a receipt.

Rạsik. } Happiness, mirth, rejoicing; to
Rạskạ. } be happy, to be mirthful, to be pleased.

Nui do ạḍi rạskạ hoṛ kanae. He is a mirthful man.
Sawãe dagkhane casako rạskạka If the rain is plentiful the cultivators rejoice.
Iń hõ calakiń rạskạakana. I also am pleased to go, I also am happy to go.
Kusi rạskạtem emańkhaniń hataogea. If you give it to me with pleasure I will take it.

Rạsi puṅji. Full return, as in a crop.

Rạsi puṅji bań ńamleda. I did not obtain a full return (for my labour and seed.)

Rạskạ. Cf. rạsik.

Rạskạ capeadea. } He rejoiced exceedingly.
Rạskạ bhijạuadea. }

Rasok. } Cf. rasak.
Rasok rasok. }

Rasok marte. } Cf. rasok marte.
Rasok mente. }

Rasras. } The feeling of indisposi-
Rasrasao. } tion at the beginning of an attack of fever.

Hoṛmo rasrasaokkantińa.
Rasrasiń aṭkareda. I feel a premonition of fever.

Rasta. A cart track, a road.

Rastateye hijukkana, se suṛuċte? Is he coming by the cart track, or by the foot path? i. e. is a large marriage party coming so that they require to come by the cart track, or a small party which can come by the foot-path?

Rạsṭana. Attracting all the luck to oneself, lucky.

Rạsṭanageae. He has always all the luck.

Raste. } Quietly, gently.
Raste raste. }

Ạḍi ajgargem roṛ goṭkeda, alo se onka dom roṛa, raste do bam roṛa? You spoke up roughly, do not speak so, will you not speak quietly?

Rạsuk. } Crunching of anything
Rạsuk rạsuk. } crisp and juicy.

Rạsuk rạsuk ạke jomeda.

Rạsuk marte. } With a crunch, applied
Rạsuk mente } to crisp and juicy things, as sugarcane, &c.

Rạsun. Garlic.

Rạsuniạ. } A kind of wristlet
Rạsuniạ sakom. } worn by women.

Rãt. Rays of the sun, glare.

Cando reak rãt. The sun's rays.
Setoń rãt. Glare, glare of the sun.

Rãt. A car, a four-wheeled carriage.

Rãt gạḍi. A chariot.

Rãt. } The Car festival of the
Rãt porob. } Hindus at which there is a procession of cars.

Raṭ. } To creak, creaking, an imi-
Raṭraṭ. } tative word.
Raṭraṭao. }

Raṭraṭ saḍe. To sound creak.
Ona duạr do jhijok jokheć ạḍi ãṭ raṭraṭ saḍe goṭena. When that door was being opened it creaked very loudly.
Raṭraṭaokkana. It is creaking.

Rata. } Full grown.
Hara rata. }

Rata kuṛi. A grown damsel.
Rata koṛa. A grown man.

Rata sukri. A boar.
Ratama dare. A kind of tree.
Ratañ. Hoar frost.
Ratañ ñuroẞkana. Hoar frost is being deposited. [frost.
Ratañ ñurakana. There is a deposit of hoar
Ratãode. Night-blind.
Ratãodeakanañ ohoñ senlena. I am night blind, I cannot go.
Ratãodegeae. He is night-blind.
Raṭa paṭa. } Rubbish, such as leaves,
Raṭu paṭu. } twigs, stubble, &c. on the surface; hard, as half boiled or too mature potherbs.
Gajaṛre alope boloẞa raṭupaṭugea. Do not enter the thicket there is much rubbish (leaves, grass, twigs, &c. or the ground.)
Aṛaẞpe tekeakaṭa raṭu paṭu. You have not boiled the vegetables soft.
Niṇkoge raṭupaṭugele emapekana. We are giving you these hard vegetables, we are giving you the best we have.
Raṭa ruṭu. Swelled, rotund, as the stomach.
Raṭa ruṭuko jom biena noko sukri do. These pigs have eaten till their sides bulge.
Raṭbañ. } Very tall, high, lofty.
Raṭbuñ. }
Khub raṭbañ hoṛ kanae. He is a very tall man.
Marañ raṭbañ dare. A very big, high tree.
Raṭ biraṭ. During the night.
Raṭ biraṭko calaoena. They left during the night.
Raṭcora. A species of grasshopper.
Raṭcora. Feeding at night, nocturnal.
Raṭcorako jomkeṭkoa lumañ do. Night feeding creatures devoured the tassar silk worms.
Raṭi kuṭi. Everything, stone and all, applied to the eating of fruit.
Raṭi kuṭi saname jomkeda. He ate it up stone and all.
Raṭkana. Night-blind. Cf. ratãode.
Raṭkanageae. He is night-blind.
Raṭko. Stout, hard, coarse.
Raṭko hoṛ. A stout man.
Raṭko uḅ. Coarse hair.
Raṭko paṭko. } Hard, as half-cooked, or
Raṭku paṭku. } too mature pot-herbs, or vegetables.
Raṭku paṭkuko isinaẞlea. They half cooked (the vegetables) for us.
Raṭpaṭ. } Securely, to make secure.
Raṭpaṭao. }
Raṭ paṭko siñakaṭa duar do. They have fastened the door securely.
Raṭpaṭ. } To crack, or snap, as dry
Raṭpaṭao. } twigs, &c.
Raṭ paṭ nondeñ añjomkeda. I heard a cracking here.
Raṭpaṭko abukoẞa. They make a cracking sound when washing the hands.
Raṭ raṭao. Tightly, tight.
Tol raṭraṭaokedeako. They bound him tightly.
Jom raṭraṭaoenae. He has eaten himself tight.
Raṭruṭ. To crack, cracking.
Raṭruṭ raputena. It cracked and broke.
Raṭruṭ sadeãna. It emitted a sound of cracking.
Raṭuẞ. } To crunch, crunching.
Raṭuẞ raṭuẞ. }
Raṭuẞ maraokedae. He crunched it up.
Jañko togója raṭuẞ raṭuẞ. They grind the fruit stones with the teeth crunch, crunch.
Saname raṭuẞkeda. He crunched all (stone and fruit.)
Raṭuẞ marte. } With a crunch.
Raṭuẞ mente. }
Raṭuẞ marteye jomkeda. He ate it with a crunch.
Raṭua kanḍa. A variety of rice.
Raṭupaṭu Cf. raṭapaṭa.
Raudaṛi. } The hot weather.
Raudaṛi din. }
Raunḍa. A carpenter's plane.
Raunḍau. To traverse, to go.
Raunḍau agukedale. We went over it all.
Goṭa birle raunḍau agukeda. We traversed the whole forest.
Rauka ḍañra. A bullock with long horns sticking out in front.
Raunḍa raunḍi. To trample upon.
Raunḍa raundikedako. They trampled it down.
Rãwã. Temperament, disposition.
Uniaẞ rãwãte tenkeṭbonae. We were delivered by his bravery.
Uniaẞ rãwã hamalgetaea. His temperament is brave or fearless.
Uniaẞ rãwã rawalgetaea. His temperament is fearful, he is easily startled or frightened.
Rawal. To lighten, to make light, light.
Rawal bojha. A light load.
Ceṭ lekanako? rawalgeako. What are they like? they are light, i. e. poor.
Aḍi rawalge bujhauẞkana. It feels lonesome.
Aḍi rawalge bujhauẞkana. It feels very light.
Rawana. To despatch, to send, to set out, to go.
Ciṭhiye rawanakeda. He despatched the letter.
Rawanaenako teheñ. They set out on their journey to-day.
Rayal ruyul. Not uniform, big and little, long and short, swaying gently from side to side.
Noa hoṛo do rayal ruyulge geleãna. The ears of this rice are not uniform.

Netare dalkette ghas do rayal ruyul sagenoḱkana. Owing to it having recently rained grass is springing up here and there.
Kạsi baha do hoete rayal ruyul hilạu baṛaekana. The kasi (q. v.) flowers are shaking gently with the wind.

Rayam rayum. } Sparse and not well
Rayam ruyum. } grown, unproductive.

Rayam rayum bań hoelena hoṛo.

Raya royo. Indifferently, below par, deficient, imperfectly, not up to the mark.

Sahan odagete sengel do raya royoge jolokkana. The fire burns feebly owing to the wood being damp.
Sarjom jore sengeliń lagaoakkhan raya royo lo baṛaena. I set fire to the sarjom (q. v.) fruit but they were only burned here and there.

Rạyul. } To move lightly and rapid-
Rạyul rayul. } ly, to bound, to bob up and down or backwards and forwards. Cf. royol.

Gidi do tukạilạgit rayul rạyul tale sakame ger idieda. The vulture is carrying a palm leaf, which keeps bobbing up and down to build its nest.
Kạsi baha hoete rayul rạyul hilạukkana. The kạsi (q. v.) are waving backwards and forwards with the wind.

Rạyul marte. } With one rapid move-
Rạyul mente. } ment.

Pusi do rạyul marte dareteye don deć goṭena. The cat with one swift bound got up on the tree.

Re. In, on, after.

Oṛakre. In the house.
Gạḍire. On the cart.
Atote calakreń ńelledea. I saw him in going to the village.
Galmaraokatere arhõe nonkakeda. After having spoken he again did this.

Reak. } Sign of genitive when the noun
Reań. } following designates an inanimate object; about, regarding, concerning.

Oṛak reak saṛim. The roof of the house.
Mạńjhi reań hukum. The order of the Mạńjhi (q. v.)
Noa katha reak cetpe meneda? What do you say about this matter?
Calak reańle galmaraokeda. We talked about going.
Oṛak reakak. The thing of the house,
Oṛak reakakko. The things of the house.

Reaṛ. To cool, to become cold, cool, cold.

Reaṛre duṛupakanae. He is sitting in the cold.
Reaṛ botorte. Through fear of the cold.
Daka reaṛoka. The boiled rice will cool.
Ạdi reaṛge bujhạukkana. It feels very cold.
Reaṛ ocoakme. Allow it to cool.
Ạdi reaṛa. It is very cold.

Reben. To consent, to comply with, to acquiesce, to agree to, to fall in with, to accede to.

Calak bae rebenlena. He did not agree to go.
Unire bań rebenlena. I will not acquiesce to him, I do not consent to him, I will not consent to marry him.
Reben ocokedeako. They caused him to agree.
Reben geae. He will fall in with it.

Reberebe. Slowly, leisurely.

Reberebeye calakkana. He is moving slowly.

Rebeṛ rebeṛ. Applied to the sound produced when the ḍeḍger (b. v.) drum is beaten.

Rebeṛ rebeṛko ruią.

Rebeť. To stick in, as a knife in the belt, &c, to insert, as anything in the thatch of the roof, a flower, in the hair, &c. &c.

Rebeť baekedae. He laid it past by sticking it in something, (in thatch, &c.)
Luturre rebeť dohoeme noa katha. Keep this matter in mind.
Calreń rebeť aťkeda. I stuck it into the roof and lost it.
Rebeť tubeť menaktaea. } He has it laid past
Tubeť rebeť menaktaea. } somewhere.

Rebrebe. Distended, as the stomach.

Jom rebrebeakanae. He has eaten and his stomach is distended.

Reć. To take by force or fraud.

Kicrićko rećkedea. They forcibly took his cloth from him.
Gidrạko rećkedea. They forcibly took away the child from her.
Baṛge rejogoka. The baṛge (q. v.) will be forcibly taken.
Reć ocokae. He will be forcibly dispossessed.

Rec. } Imitative of the sound of
Rec rec. } squeaking, creaking, cracking, &c.

Recrec saḍekana. It is sounding rec rec.

Rec marte. } With a squeak, creak,
Rec mente. } crack, &c. Cf. rec.

Receć. } Imitative of a sound of
Receć receć. } squeaking, creaking, cracking, &c.

Receć receć saḍekana. It sounds receć receć.

Receć marte. } With a squeak, creak,
Receć mente. } crack, &c. Cf. receć.

Reḍeń. } Imitative of the sound
Reḍeń reḍeń. } produced when the
Reḍheń. } ḍhak (q. v.) drum
Reḍheń reḍheń. } is beaten.

Reḍheń reḍheńko baplạ idikedea. They married her and took her away to the sound of the drum.
Reḍeń reḍeń ḍhakko ruia. They beat the ḍhak drum reḍeń reḍeń.
Reḍeń reḍeń saḍekana. It sounds reḍeń reḍeń.

Redgeć. } Gravel, small stones,
Redgeć redgeć. } gravelly.
Noa hor do ąḍi redgećgea. This road is very gravelly, or is covered with small stones.

Redhen. } Cf. redeń.
Redheń redheń. }

Rega. Dwarfed, stunted, little.
Rega hoṛ. A little man.
Rega ḍahra. An ox stunted in growth.
Regageae, bae haraka. He is dwarfed, he will not grow.

Regaṭhią. Dwarfed, stunted, small, undersized.
Regaṭhiągeae, bae haraka. He is dwarfed, he will not grow.

Rege cege. } Sound of crunching, as of
Rege coge. } sand in food, gritty, gravelly, rough, as a gravelled road, stony.
Rege coge dhiri menaka. It is gravelly.
Noa hor do rege coge dhiri menaka. This road is very stony.

Regeń regeń. Angrily roughly, naggingly, snappingly, applied to women.
Regeń regeńe roṛa. She keeps nagging.
Onka regeń regeń bako roṛa. It is not proper to speak angrily like that.

Regeń tegeń. To quarrel, to dispute, to altercate, to squabble, to wrangle, to bicker.
Regeń tegeń menaḱkogea. They are continually squabbling.
Regeń tegeńoḱkanako. They are wrangling.

Regeć. } Importunately, persis-
Regeć regeć. } tently, to importune.
Regeć regeće kokoekana. She is begging importunately.
Tinaḱe regeć regedoḱkan? How long will he continue to importune.

Regha. } To sing, to lilt, used sarcas-
Reghao. } tically.
Jom moṭaenae reghaoḱkanae. He has eaten himself fat, he is singing.
Reghaoḱkanae. She is singing.

Regha righi. Singing, lilting, used sarcastically.
Regha righiko calaḱkana. They are lilting as they go.

Rego peto. To quarrel, dispute, wrangle, bicker.
Rego peṭoko ropoṛkana. They are wrangling.
Chuṭki bąṭki dokin regopetoḱgea. The two co-wives bicker (each other.)

Regoṭhią. Cf. regaṭhią.

Regṛa. Toothed, notched, denticulated, jagged.
Regṛa ịṭe ạṛgo rakapkana. It descends and ascends owing to its being toothed (screw, &c.)

Regṛa sakom. A kind of notched wristlet worn by women.

Regrege. In position, undetached, applied mainly to the teeth and to the flowers of the matkom (q. v.) which do not fal from the tree.
Regrege coṭrege menaka. They are in position (flowers of matkom (q. v.) at the top (of the tree.)
Regrege ḍaṭa menaḱtaea. His teeth are in position.
Eken ḍaṭa regrege ńeloḱtaea. Only his teeth appeared in position (as in a skull.)

Rehąṛ. Without anxiety, without solicitude, without apprehension of evil.
Jom rehąṛenae. He has eaten and is relieved, has no further anxiety.

Rehḍa. Saline, applied to a certain kind of clayish soil.
Rehḍa hasa. Saline clayish soil.

Rẽhẽ. } Weak, feeble, emaciated.
Rẽhẽ rẽhẽ. }
Ruạteye rẽhẽena. He is feeble through fever.

Reheć. A root, foundation, to root.
Ran reheć baṛaaepe. Give him medicinal roots, i. e. give him medicine.
Rehećakana. It has taken root.
Rehedoḱa. It will take root.
Cele, reheć janamaćmea? Have you grown a root? you are staying too long.
Katha reaḱ reheć. The root of the matter.

Reheć sindheć. Medicinal roots, medicine.
Ma nui do reheć sindhećaepe. Give him medicine.

Rehlam sehlam. Healthy, robust, hale.
Rehlam sehlamko ńeloḱkana. They appear hale.

Rehõ. Although, though.
Dalerehõ bae raga. Although he be beaten he will not weep.
Rubederehõ bań hasoea. Although he be scolded he will not feel it.

Rejisṭari. } To register, cor. of the
Rejosṭori. } English word.
Doleliń rejosṭoriakaća. I have registered the document.
Rejosṭori bąbu. The native registrar.

Rejki. Small silver coin.
Goṭa ṭaka bąnuḱtińa, rejkiko menaka. I have no whole rupees, there are small silver coins.

Rek. } A measure of land.
Rekh. }

Rek bąndhi. To fix the rent per rek (q. v.)
Rek bąndhiakaćae raj do. The landlord has fixed the rate per rek (q. v.)

Rẽkh. A glutton.
Jel ren rẽkh kanae. He is a glutton for flesh.
Hako ren rẽkh kanae. He is a glutton for fish.

Rekhja. } To divide rice land into reks
Rekja. } (q. v.
Rekjaakat̀ale. We have divided the rice land into reks.

Rekṛeć. } To rattle. Cf. rakṛok̀.
Rekṛeć rekṛeć. }

Rekṛeć marte. } With a rattle, Cf. rakṛok̀ marte.
Rekṛeć mente. }

Rel. A method of winnowing with the haṭak̀ (q. v.)
Rel oḍokakat̀ale. We have winnowed it out.

Rel. A rail, a railroad, cor. of the English word rail.
Rel gaḍi. A railway train.
Rel soṛok̀. A railroad.

Rem. } To lift, to raise. (Kol.)
Rim. }

Rem. To take hold.

Rema. If, if so be, in case it be.
Ńamremae aguige, bae ńamkhan ekenak̀e ruaṛenge. If so be that he get it he will bring it, if he does not get he will return empty.
Hijuk̀remae agu darakedege, bae hijuk̀khan bagi otoadege. If so be that he come he will bring her with him, if he does not come he will leave her.
Sebelre maem jomket̀ge, bankhanem giḍikat̀ge. If so be that it is good you will eat it, if not you will throw it away.
Do na jãwãe sãote calak̀me, sebelamremae tahẽengem, bae sebelamkhan dole aguket̀mege. Come girl, go with your husband, if so be that he takes to you you wiill remain, if he does not take to you we will bring you home.
Hohoamre mako calaoengem, ar bankhan suriak̀ do oetem ńama. If so be that they call you, you may go, and if not what will you get by going vainly (when not summoned.)

Rembre. Small.
Ul adom do rembregea. Some mangoes are small.

Reme regot̀. Cf. remhe regot̀.

Remet̀. The *Manyplies* or third stomach of a ruminating animal.

Remet̀ remet̀. In divisions, in layers, in plies, as the third stomach of a ruminating animal. Cf. remet̀.
Remet̀ remet̀ menak̀a. There are many divisions.

Reme ṭele. } Short, stunted, little, diminutive, undersized.
Reme ṭhele. }
Uni reme ṭele bae harak̀a. That stunted one will not grow.
Reme ṭhelegeae. She is undersized.

Remhe regot̀. } As much as possible, a great quantity, quickly.
Reme regot̀. }
Remhe regot̀e boloena. He entered quickly.
Remhe regot̀e idi johkana. He is carrying off as much as he possibly can.

Ren. Sign of the genitive when the following noun designates an animate object.
Renić. The one (animate) belonging to, the one of.
Renkin. The two (animate) belonging to, the two of.
Renko. Those (animate) belonging to, those of.
Ińren seta. My dog.
Oṛak̀ renkinkin tahẽkana. They were belonging to the house, they belonged to the house.
Bir reniće tahẽkana. He was one belonging to the jungle, *i. e.* wild.
Palṭonrenko kanako. They belong to the regiment.

Rẽńca. A post to which a bullock is tied to break it in.

Rend bend. Completely, entirely.
Rendbendko eṭet̀akat̀a. They have fenced it completely.
Rendbendko esetakat̀a. They have closed it entirely.

Reṅgeć. Hungry, poor, to have need of.
Reṅgećedekana. He is hungry.
Reṅgećgeae. He is poor.
Reṅgejok̀ako hapen. They will become poor.
Noa katha reṅgećakawadea onateye hećena. This matter is of importance to him, therefore he has come.
Reṅgeć oreć. Abjectly poor.
Teheń bań calak̀a nondeń gitić reṅgeća. I will not go to-day, I must pass the night here.

Reṅget̀. } Cf. reget̀.
Reṅget̀ reṅget̀. }

Reṅgleć. Shapely, graceful, elegant, comeiy, handsome, neatly, beautifully, well.
Reṅgleć kuṛi. A handsome girl.
Reṅgleć koṛa. A shapely young man.
Reṅglećko uńakat̀a barahi do. They have spun the rope beautifully.

Reṅgos. } Groaning, continuously, a long time.
Reṅgos reṅgos. }
Reṅgos reṅgose ruak̀kana. He has been a long time ill with fever.
Reṅgos reṅgose kokoekana. He is begging whiningly.

Reṅgot̀. Worm in the tooth which causes toothache.
Reṅgot̀ko jomekana. Reṅgot̀s are eating him, he is suffering from tooth ache.

Reṅka. One addicted to liquor whose hand shakes when raising the first glass of liquor to his lips.
Uni reṅka kanae.

Reṅkao. To be impatient, to be anxious.
Jom lagiće reṅkaoḱkana. He is impatient to eat.

Reṇṭa. M.
Riṇṭi. F. } Lanky, skinny, lean, slim.
Reṇṭageae. He is lanky.
Riṇṭigeae. She is slim.

Reńjeć. To exhaust, to drain.
Duhạu reńjećkedeako. They milked her dry, they sucked him dry.

Reṇṭe peṇṭe.
Reṭe peṭe. } Packed closely, crowded, pressed together.
Reṇṭe peṇṭele duṛupakana. We are sitting closely packed.
Reṇṭe peṇṭeye boloḱkana. He is squeezing in.
Reṇṭe peṇṭeko dohoakaća. They have packed closely.
Kaskom reṇṭe peṇṭe ṭukućreko bhoraoakaća. They have squeezed the cotton into the ṭukuć (q. v.)

Reõreõ.
Reõreõ reõreõ. } To whirr, imitative of the sound produced by the charkha or spinning wheel.

Repeć. To quarrel, to dispute, to altercate, to bandy words.
Repećkanako. They are altercating.

Repeć ipicaḱ. Struggling, clutching.
Repeć ipicaḱko jojomkana.

Repe cirić.
Repeć cirić. } Closely packed, close together.
Repeć cirićko duṛupakana. They are sitting closely packed.

Reprep. Feeling of tightness over the stomach.
Jom reprepakanae. He has eaten till his stomach feels tight.

Rerad. To be at variance, to be at enmity.
Nokoko reradakana. These (people) are at variance with each other.

Reṛeć peṭeć. A children's game so called.

Rereń. A very common Cicada belonging to the species *Platypleura octoguttata, Fab.*

Rereć hako. A small river fish so named. [nant.

Res. *Residuum,* dregs, residue, remnant.
Noa karon reaḱ resteć tahẽena. The dregs of this disease remain.
Noa katha reaḱ resteć tahẽena. The dregs of (this matter remain.

Resạ risi. To be at variance with each other.
Resạ risigeakin. They are at variance with each other.

Reseć.
Sereć. } To crush, to squash.
Lebeć resećkedako.
Lebeć serećkedako. } They trampled on it and squashed it.

Reseć. Cf. nahi.
Dipil reseć hamal dom ṭikạua. You must put it on your head before you can feel it is heavy.
Calaḱ resećko emama. You must go before they can give to you.

Reseć.
Ende reseć. } Then. Cf. ende reseć.
Kạmime ende resećem joma. Work, then you will eat.

Reseć.
Tãhã reseć. } On the contrary.
Iń doń menkeda cele mundhạćge ṭtu hijuḱkana, ńelkede doń tãhã reseć mić goṭen hoṛe ṭtu hijuḱkan. I said it must be a log that is coming floating, I saw that on the contrary it was a man coming floating.

Reseć.
Reseć reseć. } Juicy, tender, applied to flesh meat.
Reseć resećle jomkeda.
Ạḍi bhage khẹsiye tahẽkana reseć resećko jomkedea.

Reṭ.
Rẽṭ. } To come to an agreement, to conspire, to concert, to collude.
Kathako reṭakaća nuibon ńuregea. They have conspired to bring him into difficulty.

Reć. To wrap up, as a small packet, a packet.
Ceć hõ bań ńellećtaea, reć hõ bań ńellaḱa. I saw nothing of his, not even a packet.
Sakamre cunko reda. They wrap up lime in a leaf.
Lumạhe redoḱkana. The silk worm is wrapping himself (in a leaf.)

Ret. A file.

Ret. The deep part of a river, the true course or channel of a river where it flows deepest.
Retem paromlekhan gem jitạuena. When you have crossed the deep part of the river you have won.
Onte doe retkeda, note do bah hoyoḱa. (The rain) has gone over that way, it does not come this way.

Reta. To saw, as when cutting with knife, sword, &c., to draw backwards and push forwards, as a fiddle bow.
Sim hoṭoḱko retaea. They saw the fowl's neck (with a knife.)
Banam retaleneć sadea. You must scrape the fiddle (with the bow) before 't will sound.

Reć ciput.
Reć cupuć. } To lay past, to store, to have in store.
Reć cupuće baeakawana. He has put it by him in store.

Reṭeć reṭeć. Crunching, grinding.
Reṭeć reṭeće togoć daṭaeda. He is grinding his teeth.
Reṭeć reṭeć pusi hone jomekana. The cat is crunching the rat.

Retekote. Plentiful, very stony, full of stones.
Retekoteẽna. It is very stony.
Baṛge dhiri retekote neko kuṛi gote.
Retekote dhiritege perećakana. It is full of stones.

Reṭe peṭe. To dispute, to altercate, to bandy words, to disagree.
Reṭepeṭeẽnale. We have had words together.

Reṭepeṭe. Packed closely, crowded, pressed together, compact.
Reṭepeṭeko duṛupakana. They are sitting closely packed.
Reṭepeṭeko doboakaṭa. They have placed them close together, they have packed it.

Reṭeť. To crush, to jam, to squeeze.
Kul hõ ńir tabok̀e menwana, menkhan atraregeye reṭeť tabẽena. The tiger also wished to rush out, but he stuck halfway.

Reṭha riṭhi. To be at variance, to be hostile, to strive, to dispute, to altercate.
Reṭha riṭhienako. They are hostile to each other.

Reṭha. } Reṭhea. } Small, stunted, undersized.
Reṭheagea. It is small.
Reṭhegeae bae haṛaka. He is stunted, he will (not grow.

Reṭhe kaṭkom. A species of small crab.

Reṭhma. M. } Reṭhmi. F. } Small, short in stature.
Reṭhma riṭhmi khubkin juriakana. The little man and the little woman are well matched.

Reto reto. Imitative of the sound produced when sawing wood, &c.
Reto reto saḍekana. It is sounding *reto reto*.

Ret rete. In line, in a row.
Ret reteko teṅgoakana. They are standing in line.
Ret rete lagṛẽko saṗakana. They are engaged dancing the lagṛẽ dance in a row.

Reť tepeť. Chock full, crammed, compact, packed closely.
Reť tepeṭe aderakaṭa. His has filled (his store) full.

Rewaj. Season, usage, custom, fashion.
Khub rewajiń ñamakaṭa kạmi reak̀. I have got seasonable weather for my work.

Riạ. } Riạu. } Riạu rajoṭ. } To compact, to come to a mutual agreement.
Riạukateko calaoena. They made an appointment to go and went.
Riạu calaoenako. They came to a mutual agreement and went.
Miť riạute. With one consent.
Ripiạukanakin. They are making an appointment.
Riạk̀iń añjomlećkoa. I heard them compacting.

Riại khiại. To squander, to fritter away, to waste.
Begaren khanko riại khiạikedako dhon do. After they set up house for themselves they frittered away their substance.

Riạť riạť. Quickly, rapidly, with difficulty.
Riạť riạṭe daṛ idikeda. He ran away very quickly.
Riạť riạṭe siok̀kana. He is ploughing with difficulty.

Riạu. Cf. riạ.

Riạu rajoṭ. Cf. riạ.

Ribić, } Ribić ribić. } Gently, as rain; drizzlingly, slowly, leisurely, heavily, Cf. rabać rubuć.
Ribić ribiće dak̀eda. It is raining drizzlingly, it is drizzling.

Ribi ribi. To wriggle, to shake as one shivering.
Hako ribi ribik̀kanako. The fish are wriggling
Ribi ribiko dạra tejoko. Caterpillars move by wriggling
Nitok̀ doko ribi ribiena. Now they are (tired out and are) wriggling.

Rihiṛ bidiṛ. With much noise.
Ona atoren rihiṛ bidiṛko calaoena. Those of that village went away with much noise.

Ribiṛ ribiṛ. Quickly, fast, with long strides.
Ribiṛ ribiṛko calak̀kana. They are going fast.

Riboć roboć. } Rabać rubuć. } Slowly, heavily, tardily.
Riboć roboće calak̀kana. He is going slowly.

Riboṅ koboṅ. Slowly, tardily, as a weak person, emaciated.
Riboṅ koboṅe daṛã baṛaekana. He is walking about slowly.

Ribribạu. To wriggle, to shake as one shivering, to be slightly intoxicated.
Ribribạu ńok̀lenae. He wriggled a little.

Ricaṅ picaṅ. Without appetite.
Ricạṅ picạṅe jomkeda. He ate without appetite.

Ricaṗ. To pick, to nibble, as a kid, lamb, &c., learning to graze.
Ricaṗ baṛaeẽdae mihũ do. The calf is nibbling grass.

Rici. } Rici cẽṛẽ. } The Pale Harrier, *Circus Swainsonii*.
Rici cẽṛẽ dayage ragae. The Pale Harrier calls plaintively.

Riciť. } Riciť riciť. } Imitative of the sound produced by the vibration of any long and flexible body.
Riciť riciť saḍekana. It sounds *ricit ricit*.

Ricoť. } To break, to snip off. Cf. rocoť.
Rocoť. }
Kanḍa reaǩ penda ricoťena. The bottom of the waterpot is broken off.

Ricoť rocoť. Imitative of a slightly rustling sound, creaking, as of boots, crackling, as of dry leaves.
Panạhi saḍekana ricoť rocoť. The shoes make a sound resembling ricoť rocoť.

Riḍe. A common small forest tree, *Casearia tomentosa, Roxb.*

Riḍeť. To crush, to jam, to squeeze.
Hoṛ talare riḍeť paromenae. He squeezed his way through among the people.
Kolre ti riḍeťentaea. His hand was crushed in the machine.

Riḍeť ciriť. Squeezing, crushing.
Riḍeť ciriťko paromoǩkana. They are squeezing themselves through.

Ridkhid. To discuss, to debate, to talk over. Cf. rond khond.

Rigạm cagam. Stealthily, quietly, slowly.
Rigạm cagam bạibạiteko hijuǩkana. They are coming quietly and slowly.

Rigdạu. To accustom, habituate, to train, to keep at it, to repeat.
Bạm rigdạulekhan ohom sojhe daṛelea. If you do not habituate him you will not perfect, or thoroughly train, him.
Khub leka rigdạuem bae bujhạueťkana. Train her well, she does not understand.

Righi. } Like the thread of a
Righi righi. } screw, toothed.
Righi righiko benaoakaťa. They have made it like the thread of a screw.

Rigiṛ. To persist, to persevere, again and again, over and over again.
Ạḍi rigiṛkateko kạmikana. They are working very perseveringly.
Ṭaka lạgiťe rigiṛeťkana. He is importuning for money.

Rigoṛ rogoṛ. } Stony, gravelly, rough
Ragaṛ rogoṛ } and stony.

Rihại. Liberation, escape, relief, deliverance acquittal, freedom, release.
Neskar din rihại hoeẽntaea. There is relief for this year.
20 ṭakạteye rihạiadea. He got a release for him for 20 rupees.
5 ṭaka reaǩ rihại hoeẽna. There was a relief of five rupees.

Rihạt. Cf. rihại.

Rihiṛ. } Sound as of crashing,
Rihiṛ rihiṛ. } banging, loud reverberating sound.
Rihiṛ rihiṛ bạnduk saḍekana. The gun sounds bang.

Rihiṛ marte. } With a crash, bang, or
Rihiṛ mente. } loud flop.
Dare gur goťena rihiṛ marte. The tree fell with a crash.
Bạnduk rihiṛ marte saḍeena. The gun sounded bang.

Rihṛạǩ. } Thudding, banging.
Rihṛạǩ rihṛạǩ. }
Rihṛạǩ rihṛạǩko ruieda. They beat the drum thud thud.

Rihṛạǩ marte. } With a thud or bang.
Rihṛạǩ mente. }
Rihṛạǩ marteye gurena. He fell with a thud.

Rij. } Choice, approbation, love,
Rij roṅ. } desire, wish, wanton plea-
Rijh. } sure; pleasing, satisfying.
Ạḍi rijko lagaoakaťa.
Ạḍi rij lagaoadea.
Rijge ṣikauedae.
Hajar rij menaǩa monere.

Rijhạu. To persuade, to win over, to overcome displeasure, to cause to be pleased, satisfied, delighted.
Baṅ rijhạu daṛeadea. I could not persuad. him, I could not over come his displeasuree

Rijhua. To be pleased, gratified, delighted.

Rijhwạr. } Merry, lighthearted.
Rijwạr. }
Bejãe rijwạre tahẽkana. He was very light hearted.

Rijhwạriạ. Merry, lighthearted.
Ạḍi rijhwạriạ kanae. He is very lighthearted.

Rijki. Small silver coins.

Rijwạr. Cf. rijhwạr.

Rijwạriạ. Cf. rijhwạriạ.

Rikạ. To do, to arrange, to attempt, to endeavour, to seek to do.
Noa ịạte bulạuiṅ lạgiť alom rikạia. Therefore do not endeavour to lead me astray.
Ceťkope rikạ aguạťbona? What arrangement have you come to for us?

Rikiṛ, Zealously, diligently, continuously.
Ạḍi rikiṛkateko kạmikana. They are working very diligently.
Ạḍi rikiṛteko kạmikana. They are working with great diligence.
Khub rikiṛko paṛhaoǩkana. They are studying very diligently.

Rikit. To settle, to fix, to come to an agreement, to contract.
Noae rikitakawadiṅa. He agreed with me to give me this.
Miť sikạte iṅ tuluć bam rikitlaǩa? Did you not agree with me for one sika? (q. v.)
Miť sikạ rikitkate adaǩ bagwanteye kolkeťkoa. He contracted to give one sikạ (q. v.) and sent them to the vineyard.

Rikoć rokoć. Singly, irregularly, unevenly, not at one time, not simultaneous.

Rikoć rokoćko janamoḱkana. They are not hatching simultaneously.
Rikoć rokoćko hijuḱkana. They are coming singly, not in a body.

Rikṛić. Lean, slim, lanky, applied to females. Cf. rạkṛić.

Nui kuṛi rikṛićgeae bae moṭaḱa. This girl is slim she will not get stout.

Rilạ mala. Clear, as water or the atmosphere, clearly, distinctly.

Rilạ mala daḱ. Clear, pure water.
Buru rilạ mala ńeloḱkana. The hills appear clearly.

Rili phili. Clean, clear, without impurity.

Rili philiko joḱ ṭạnḍiakaťa. They have swept it clean.
Rili phili sapha ńeloḱkana daḱ do. The water is clean and pure.

Rim. To raise the lever of the dhiṅki by pressing the foot in it.

Rimbạ rambe. Slowly.

Rimbạ rambeń daṛankana. I am walking about slowly.

Rimi. To find or pick up anything that is ownerless, applied mainly to things found in the jungle.

Rimi ạguaḱ. Some thing that has been found and brought (home.)
Munḍureń rimikeda. I found it in the jungle.

Rimil. A cloud, to cloud over.

Rimilakaťae. It has become cloudy.
Rimil rakaṭena. A cloud has, or clouds have, arisen.
Rimile ḍopḍopkeda. It became clouded over.

Rimil saḍe. To thunder.

Rimil saḍekana. It is thundering.

Rimsić. Small, little.

Rimsić ul. A small mangoe.
Rimsićgeae. She is small.

Rin. Debt, to incur debt, to borrow.

Rin cal anaj. Grain borrowed on interest.
Rin gaḍenale. We are swamped in debt.
Rin thokṛeakanae. He is swamped in debt.
Rin ṭheḱomenae. He is helpless through debt.
Rin ṭhubeońae. He is over head and ears in debt.
Aḍi utạrle rinakaťa. We have incurred much debt.
Rin reaḥ hopon. Interest, the offspring of debt.
Rin dharkate dinle calaoa. We live by incurring debt.
Rinle topaḱkeda. We cleared off our debt.

Rinḍiol. Satisfied, fat.

Jom rinḍiolenae. He has eaten to satiety.
Rinḍiole ńeloḱa. He looks fat.

Rindiṛ. / Rindiṛ rindiṛ. A ridge, saddle of hill, &c.

Rindiṛ rindiṛko siakaťa. They have ploughed it in ridges.
Buru reaḱ mit́ senaḱ rindiṛre. On a ridge of (one side of the hill.

Rinḍo ronḍo. Large, applied to certain kinds of fish.

Riṅgạm ciṅgạm. Stealthily, quietly, slowly. Cf. rigạm cigạm.

Riṅgạu. To move quickly or rapidly, with force.

Coṭte riṅgạuena. It has mounted up.
Okạtem riṅgạuena? Where are you going?
Riṅgạute sereńpe. Sing with force, sing loudly.
Sadom riṅgạuem. Make the horse move rapidly, make him gallop.

Riṅgi ṭiṅgi. To be delighted, to be very pleased, to exult.

Aḍiye riṅgi ṭiṅgi baṛaekana. He is greatly delighted.

Riṅgoṛ roṅgoṛ. At intervals, now and again, to suffer from disease.

Riṅgoṛ roṅgoṛe ruạḱkana. He has fever at intervals.
Mihũko riṅgoṛ roṅgoṛoḱkantalea. Our cattle are suffering from disease.

Rimkạ ṭamke. Slowly.

Rinić. Wife.

Mạńjhi rinić. The mańjhi's wife.
Rinićteť. The wife.

Rińjạ eneć. A certain kind of dance.

Rińjạrạṛ. The time beaten on the drums and the air sung when the *Rińjạ* (q. v.) dance is being danced.

Rińjạ sereń. The songs sung during the dancing of the *Rińjạ* (q. v.) dance.

Rińji. / Rińji rińji. Slowly, gently, in small quantity.

Rińji rińji daḱ atuḱkana. The water is flowing gently.
Daḱ rińjiena. The water has become less, it is now flowing in small quantity.

Riṛiń. / Riṛiń riṛiń. Ringing sound as when a metallic substance is struck.

Riṛiń saḍekana. It emits a ringing sound.

Riot. Cf. riạ and ṛiạu.

Rioť royoť. Cf. royoť royoť.

Ripi ripi. To flap the wings as a bird of prey hovering over its prey, to be seized with a fit, to shake as in a fit, to wink, to flutter, to whirl like a shuttlecock falling.

Ripiripilenae. She was seized with a fit.
Ceṛẹye ripiripiḱkana. The bird is flapping its wings to enable it to hover.

Gajuḱ lekae ripiripiḱkana. He is shaking as if he were about to die.
Dudṛumte meṫ ripi ripiḱkana. The eyes are winking through drowsiness.

Ripiṫ. To wink with both eyes.
Miṫ ripiṫte. In a twinkling.
Ripiṫ baṛaeẽdae. He is moving the eyelids.
Ripiṫadiṅae. He winked (with both eyes) at me.
Ripiṫ jhpiṫe beṅgeṫedae. He is blinking.

Ripripi. To stare, eyes wide open, staring.
Ripripi beṅgeṫ uriḱedae. He stared with eyes wide open.
Ripripienae. He is staring.

Riṛ. A ridge.
Bisi riṛ. The ridge formed by the backbone.
Sakam riṛ. The mid-rib of a leaf.
Hako riṛ. The ridge on the back of a fish.
Baru riṛ. The ridge of the hill.

Riṛaṅ raṛaṅ. To clang, as a bell, the sound produced by a hollow metallic vessel when struck, to sound shrilly. Cf. raṛaṅ.

Riṛiń. / Riṛiń riṛiń. } To sound, as a bell, or any hollow metallic vessel which produces a high or shrill note when struck.

Riṛiń marte. / Riṛiń mente. } With a shrill sound. Cf. riṛiń.

Riri riri. Joyfully, gleefully, in high spirits, good humouredly.
Sendrateko calaoena riri riri. They have gone to the hunt in high spirits.
Riri riri baṛaekanae calaḱ lagiṫ. He is in high spirits at going.
Riri riri hanko torako calaoena. Look, there they go gleefully.

Risa̤. Dysentery.
Risa̤ sap̣akadeae. He has dysentery.

Risa̤ sim. A fowl having feathers reversed.

Risbod. / Risbot. } To be friendly, to be on friendly terms.
Risbodkaṫkinale. We reconciled them.

Risbod. A bribe.
Risbode jomkeda. He took a bribe.

Risbot. Cf. risbod.

Riskiṫ. Rough headed, hair standing up.
Riskiṫ mara gidra̤. A rough headed rascally boy.

Risrisi. Standing up, ruffled.
Uḅ risrisientaea. / Risrisienae. } His hair is standing up.

Riṫ. To grind, to separate the seeds from the cotton.
Kaskomko rida̤. They put cotton through a machine to separate the seeds from it.
Riṫ lemeńkedakó. They ground it fine.

Rit. / Ritu. } Season, custom, habit, to be pleased.
Rit caṛhaoentaea. He has attained puberty.
Ritutećreko samṭaokeda. They garnered (the crop) in season.
Ritakanae. It is in season or in heat.
Calaḱe ritakanae. He is pleased to go.

Riṭha. Dirty, soiled.
Ạdiń riṭha̤kana. I am very dirty.
Riṭha̤ mara gidra̤. A dirty rascal of a child.
Riṭha̤ dapaṫ. Extremely dirty.

Riṭha riṭhi. Cf. reṭha riṭhi.

Ritia̤ ritii. Joyfully, gleefully, in high spirits.
Ritia̤ ritiiko calaoena. They went away in high spirits.

Ritia̤u. To be pleased, to be in high spirits.
Sendrako ritia̤uena. They are in high spirits at the prospect of going to hunt.
Koela khadte calaḱko ritia̤uakana. They are delighted to go to the coal mines.

Ritia̤u. To be in season, to be in heat, to be sexually mature.

Ritiṫ ritiṫ. Very, applied to cold.
Ritiṫ ritiṫ reaṛa. It is very cold.

Riṭo roṭo. Large and full, applied to the ears of Indian corn.
Jonḍra phoṭakana riṭo roṭo.
Riṭo roṭo phoṭakana.

Ritu. Season. Cf. rit.
Ka̤mi ritua̤kana. The work is in season.

Riya̤i khiya̤i. To squander, to fritter away, to waste.
Sanam cij ba̤sute riya̤i khiya̤ikeda. He squandered all his substance.

Riya̤ṫ riya̤ṫ. Cf. ria̤ṫ ria̤ṫ.
Riya̤ṫ riya̤ṫe lagaedekana. He is driving him fast.

Riyol royol. / Royol royol. } Long, tall, high.
Koṛako riyol royolko haraakana. The boys have grown tall.
Maṫ riyol royol dareakana. The bamboos have grown very long.

Ro. A fly.

Ro. To singe.
Simko roakadea. They have singed the fowl.
Meromko rokoa. They singe (the hides of) goats (before cooking.)

Robea. Pot-bellied, big-bellied.
Ruạ robeakanae. He has become potbellied through fever.

Roboć. } Juicy, luscious.
Roboć roboć.

Robojholo. } To appear out of sorts,
Romojholo. } indisposed, ill, poorly, ailing.

Robojholoe ńeloḱkana. He looks out of sorts.
Romojholoenae. He has the appearance of being ill.

Robo ropo. Cf. ropo ropo.

Robrobo. Inert, sluggish, heavy as one after having gorged himself with food.

Jom robroboenae. He has eaten till he has become sluggish.

Roboskaḱ. Big-bellied, big, applied to the stomach of a very fat person.

Laċ khub roboskaḱgetaea, His belly is very big.

Roc. } Desire of or pleasure in
Rocao. } eating.

Baṅ rocekana. He has no desire for food.
Baṅ rocaoediṅkana. I have no appetite.

Roco. To seize the top with the tips of the fingers, to pinch off the top.

Buluṅe rocokeda. He took a pinch of salt.
Cha sakam coṭ coṭko rocoeṫkana. They are pinching off the tea leaves from the tips (of the bushes.)

Rocoṫ. To break, to crush to pieces.

Kanḍa rocoṫena. The water pot has a piece broken out of it.
Sakam rocoṫena. The leaf is crushed.
Thamakhur rocodme. Break (or crush) up the tobacco.
Tiṅ rocoṫkedeaṅ. I hit him with a stone and broke (a bone.), I shied a stone at him and broke (a bone, leg, &c.)
Hoṛmo do rapuṫ rocoṫ hasoede tahẽkana. His body pained as if it were broken and crushed.

Rocroco. Sticking up, pointed, protruding.

Dəhṛiakanae rocroco. His turban is pointed.
Niṭaḱ rocrocogea, maḱ goṫkam. This one is sticking up, cut it off.

Rod. To infringe, to violate, to ignore, to transgress, to disobey.

Noa kathae rodkeda. He violated the agreement.
Hukum alom rodtaea. Do not disobey his command.

Rodbodol. Equally, neck and neck, tie, dead heat.

Rodbol dokin kəmikana. They are working neck and neck.
Rodbodolkin dəṛkana. They are running neck and neck.

Rodea. Pot-bellied, big-bellied. Cf. robea.

Roḍga. Rough, sharp edged as stones or gravel.

Eken dhiri roḍga. It is all stony.

Roḍga roḍgo. Coarse, as rice, gravelly, stony.

Noa caole roḍga roḍgogea. This rice is coarse, or there is gravel mixed with this rice.

Roḍgo. Rough, gravelly, stony.

Nonḍe alom khəṛaia dhiri roḍgogea. Do not make a threshing floor here it is stony.
Noa baṛge eken dhiri roḍgogea, coṫ hõ baṅ hoyoḱa. This garden is nothing but stones, nothing will grow in it.
Roḍgogea. It is stony.
Roḍgo ot kana. It is stony soil

Rodo bodo. Sound of rustling, as of dry leaves, &c. Cf. radobado.

Roḍoć. To squeeze out, to wring out or strain by squeezing.

Ranko roḍoća. They strain out medicine by squeezing (it through a cloth.)
Lemboko roḍoća. They squeeze lemons.

Rodoe. } Rustling, rattling, app-
Rodoe rodoe. } lied mainly to the sound produced by dry leaves, &c. when disturbed or crushed, an imitative word. Cf. rogoe rogoe.

Saḍe ocoedae rodoe rodoe. He is causing a rustling sound, or producing a sound resembling rodoe rodoe.

Rodoe marte. } With a rustle or a
Rodoe mente. } rattle. Cf. rodoe.

Don paromenae jhənṭi rodoe menteye saḍe ocokeda. He bounded over, he caused the fence to rustle.

Roḍoḱ. } Hill and dale, all kinds
Sopoḱ roḍoḱ. } of country.

Sopoḱ roḍoḱko dāṛākeda. They travelled over hill and dale.

Roḍoḱ roḍoḱ. Continuously, unceasingly, the whole night.

Roḍoḱ roḍoḱko enećkana. They are dancing without ceasing, i. e. the whole night.
Roḍoḱ roḍoḱe daḱeda. It rains continuously.

Rodoṫ. } Rough.
Rodoṫ rodoṫ.

Rodoṫ rodoṫ aṭkaroḱkana. It feels rough.

Roeda. Lanky, lean, skinny.

Roedageae. He is lanky.

Roela. M. } Tall.
Ruili. F.

Aobako juriakaṫkina roela ruili. They have matched them well, a tall man and a tall woman.
Ruili ruiliko haraakana neko kuṛi do. These girls have grown tall.

Roela. }
Roela roela. } High, tall, long.

Roela dareakana. It has grown into a tall tree, or it has grown high.
Roela roelako haraakana noko koṛa do. These lads have grown tall.

Rog. Disease, illness, defect, infirmity, disorder, malady.

Rog bighin cet hõ bạnuḱantaea. He has no infirmity whatever.
Rog menaḱtaea. He is diseased.
Ona atoko rogakana. There is disease among the people of that village.
Rog boloakana. Disease (cholera, &c.) has broken out.

Roga. }
Rugi } Diseased, afflicted with a disease, malady or disorder, having a defect or infirmity.

Roga hoṛ. A person afflicted with a disease or malady.
Rogageae. He is afflicted with a disease or malady.
Noa kaṭ do rogagea. This log is defective.

Rogaha. M. }
Rogahi. F. } Cf. roga.

Nui do rogahageae. He is diseased.
Nui do rogahigeae. She is diseased.

Rogda. }
Rogdaha. } Rough.

Rogdahagea. It is rough.

Rogdao. To scrub, to rub.

Rogdao poṭaḱkedeae. He scrubbed his skin off.

Rogda rogdo. Rough.

Rogda rugdi. Closely, at the heels of.

Rogda rugdi. To scrub, scrubbing.

Rogi. }
Rugi. } Cf. roga.

Rogoe. }
Rogoe rogoe. } Rustling, rattling. Cf. rodoe.

Rogoe rogoe saḍekana. It is rustling.

Rogoe marte. }
Rogoe mente. } With a rustle, with a rattle.

Rogoṛ. Stony, rocky, as the bed of a river.

Rogoṛ latarre paromoḱpe. Cross (the river) below the rocky (place.)

Rogoṛ. Strong desire or wish, exigency, eagerness, cupidity.

Aćaḱ rogoṛge tahenkantaea. His own exigency must be attended to, he only thinks of himself.

Rogoṛ. }
Miṭ rogoṛ. } Persistently, continuously.

Miṭ rogoṛte kokoekanae. He begs persistently.
Miṭ rogoṛgeye kokoekana. He begs continuously.

Rogoṛia. A cupidinous or persistent person.

Rogoṛia kanae. He is a persistent person.

Rogos. }
Rogos rogos. } To rustle, as dry leaves, &c.

Nonḍe cele coe rogos rogosoḱkana. Some thing is causing a rustling here.
Rogoseṭkanae. He is rustling (the leaves), or causing a rustle.

Rogos marte. }
Rogos mente. } With a rustle.

Rogos marte oḍok goṭenae. It emerged with a rustle.

Rogoṭ cogoṭ. Sound of rustling, as of leaves, paper, &c.

Rogoṭ cogoṭe hijuḱkana. He is coming making a rustling noise.

Rogoṭ pogoṭ. Cf. rogoṭ cogoṭ.

Rogoṭ pogoṭe saḍe ocoeda. He is making a rustling noise.

Rogoṭ rogoṭ. Persistently, continuously.

Rogoṭ rogoṭe kokoekana. He is begging persistently.

Rogoṭ rogoṭ. Sound of rustling, as of dry leaves, paper, &c.

Rogoṭ rogoṭ matkome oḍoka. He took out the makom (q. v.) causing (the dry leaf in which it was wrapped) to rustle.
Hone rogoṭ rogoṭeda. The rat is rustling (the straw.)

Rogṛaha. M. }
Rogṛahi. E. } A persistent quarreller, a causer of strife, quarrelsome.

Rogṛahageae. He is quarrelsome.
Rogṛahigeae. She is quarrelsome.

Rogṛa rugṛi. Fiercely, persistently, applied to quarrels or disputes.

Aḍi rogṛa rugṛikin ropoṛena. They disputed very fiercely.

Rogṛo. Stony, gravelly, rough with small stones.

Rogṛo dhiri. Gravel.
Rogṛo ot kana. It is gravelly soil.
Rogṛo dhiri menaḱte bah hoyoḱkana. Owing to the presence of gravel there is no yield (of crops.)

Rohḍa. }
Rohḍo. }
Rohḍoć. } Lanky, lean, remaining always lean although well fed.

Rohḍoć cabaenako daḱ tetahte. They (cattle) are completely emaciated through thirst.
Nunạḱe jomeṭrehõ rohḍojoḱkanae. Although he eats so much he is becoming emaciated.

Rohni. }
Ruhni. } A period of 13 days beginning on the 13th Jeṭh (q. v.)

According to the Hindus Rohni is the name of the fourth mansion of the moon, figured by a wheeled carriage, comprising *Aldebaran* and four other stars in *Taurus*. (Forbes.) Ruhni is considered a lucky period in which to sow the first seed dhan of the season.

Rohoć rohoć. Very, exceedingly, extremely, applied to weight.
Rohoć rohoć hamala. It is extremely weighty, or heavy.

Rohoe. To plant, to bury.
Rohoe dare kana. It is a planted tree.
Mõṛẽ hoṛtepe rohoekediñ. You five people planted me, i. e. I was lawfully married.
Rohoe boloakako. They fill up vacancies by planting other plants.
Ạdi utạr dareko rohoeakata. They have planted very many trees.

Rohom. Regard, restraint, subjection.
Rohom dohoe. } To be docile, to be obedient
Rohom manao. } to be amenable to discipline.
Rohomre menaea. He is under control, or he is law-abiding.
Hạthi ạdiko daṛea, enhõ rohomko manaoa. Elephants are very strong, still they are obedient.
Sadom do rohome dohoea. The horse is docile.
Kuṛi do bes rohome dohoakata. The girl is very docile.
Rohom do bae dohoeda. He is not amenable to discipline.

Rohoṛ. To dry, to become emaciated.
Tase rohoṛ. To spread out to dry.
Rohoṛ sakam. A dry leaf.
Rohoṛokkana. It is drying.
Gaḍa rohoṛena. The river is dried up.
Kicrić rohoṛpe. Dry the cloth.
Kakṛa lekam rohoṛena. You are lean like a lizard.
Rusạteye rohoṛ cabaena. He is completely emaciated through fever.
Jugre do jạtire hoṛo heṛeko rohoṛa, ado nui mạñjhige peṛako rohoṛetkoa.

Rohoṛ nañjom. Lean, emaciated owing to bad digestion, &c.
Rohoṛ nañjomakanae. He is emaciated owing to illness.

Rohoṭ pohoṭ. The sound produced by rubbing the person with the hands, dilatory. Cf. rahaṭ pahaṭ.

Rohpoṭ. } Much frequented, as a high-
Ropoṭ. } way, busy, as a thoroughfare.
Noa hor do ạdi rohpoṭ hor kana. This road is a busy thoroughfare.

Rohṛa. Cf. rohḍa.

Rohṛa. M. } Lanky, lean, remaining lean
Ruhṛi. F. } although well fed.
Nui do rohṛageae. He is lanky.
Nui do ruhṛigeae. She is lanky.

Roj. A day, daily.
Roje hijukkana. He comes daily.

Rojgar. To earn, to earn daily bread, livelihood.
Bese rojgar johkana. He earns good wages.
Din rojgar beege calakkantakoa. They have a sufficient supply of daily bread.

Rojgariạ. An earner, earning.
Mit hoṛ do rojgariạ aema hoṛ jojomko. One is earner and many eaters.

Rojha. A small earthenware dish.

Rok. To prevent, to prohibit, to hinder.
Rokkedae. He prohibited it.

Rok. To pierce, to perforate, to sew, to pin, to butt, to gore.
Kurtạe rokkeda. She sewed a jacket.
Senerko rokakata. They have perforated the rafters.
Kaḍae rokkedea. The buffaloe gored him.
Jạnumiñ rokena. A thorn has pierced me.
Rok mitkedae. She sewed them together, she sewed them into one.
Patṛa rogtabonme. Pin leaf plates for us.
Patṛae rorokkana. She is pinning leaf plates, she is making plates by pinning leaves together.

Rok lutur Hãsdak. A sub-sept of the Santal sept Hãsdak (q. v.)

Rok lutur Mạrnḍi. A sub-sept of the Santal sept Mạrnḍi (q. v.)

Rok lutur Soren. A sub-sept of the Santal sept Soren (q. v.)

Roka. Ready money, cash.
Rokategele hataokeda. We bought for cash.

Roka. An acknowledgment, as of money paid.
Rokae emadiña. He gave me an acknowledgment (of money paid.)

Roka. The same day, to-day.
Rokageñ ruạṛa. I will return the same day.
Roka dak kana. It is to-day's water (it is fresh having been brought from the well to-day.)

Rokao. To stop, to prevent, to detain, to interrupt, to prohibit, to lay an embargo on.
Iñko rokaokettiña khet. They laid an embargo on my field.

Roka ruki. On the same day, not deferred till another day.
Roka ruki galmarao hoeena. The discussion took place the same day, or the matter was settled the same day.

Rokme rokme. Gently, leisurely.
Rokme rokme lagaem. Drive him leisurely.

Rokoć. A snail, a snail and its shell, a snail's shell.
Jom rokoć. A species of snail which is eaten.
Seta rokoć. A species of water snail.
Ṭạnḍi rokoć. A species of land snail.
Rokoć jel. The snail.

Rokoć ghao. A kind of sore.

Rokom. Manner, kind, method, sort.
Sanamak reaṅ rokome baḍaea. He knows all methods.
Bar rokom. Two kinds, two sorts.
Nitoke rokomakaṭa. Now he has caught the method.

Rokoṛ. }
Rokoṛ rokoṛ. } To rattle.
Rokoṛ rokoṛ saḍekana. It is rattling.

Rokoṛ marte. }
Rokoṛ mente. } With a rattle. Cf. rokoṛ.

Rokoṛ. To hurt, as anything touching the skin, without any protection to the skin.
Rokoṛedekana. It is hurting him.
Rokoṛre gitiċakanae. He is lying on the bare (ground, &c.)

Rokot. Blood.

Rokot condon. A variety of sandal wood in colour resembling blood, a variety of rice.

Rokot muhạ̃. Ravening, to be inflamed, to become ferocious, to be frenzied, frantic, blood thirsty.
Kule rokot muhạ̃akana ona birte gại alom idikoa. The tiger is ravenous, do not take the cows to that jungle.
Hoṛ goċ goċte rokot muhạ̃akanae. He has become ferocious or blood thirsty, through continued slaying of man.

Rokṛoċ. }
Rokṛoċ rokṛoċ. } To rattle, to thud, an imitative word. Cf. rakṛok.

Rokṛoċ marte. }
Rokṛoċ mente. } With a rattle, with a thud. Cf. rakṛok marte.

Rokroko. Sticking up or out.
Rokrokoe gitiċakana. He is lying (with his knees) sticking up.
Rokrokoe teṅgoakana. He is standing sticking up (mainly used when fault finding.)
Dereṅ rokroko ṅelokkantaea. His horns are sticking out.

Rokṭok. Obstruction, impediment, to obstruct, to raise objections or difficulties.
Okoe hõ bako rokṭoklaka. No one offered any obstruction.
Rokṭoklediṅako. They obstructed me.

Rol. }
Rol dare. } A large forest tree, *Terminalia Chebula, Retz.*
This tree yields the myrabolams of commerce.

Rol. To exercise, as a horse.
Sadomko rolkoa. They exercise horses, take them out for an airing.

Rol. To take out of, as out of fire, or out of heated sand.
Seṅgel khon rol oḍokakat lo sareċ ṭhuṭkuṭ doe baṅ kana? Is he not a brand plucked from the fire?
Elaṅ iṭṭe ḍaṅteko rola. They take it out of the fire with a long stick owing to the heat.

Rol muċ. A species of ant.

Rola. A sapling used as a rafter.

Rolo. }
Rolo rolo. } To look steadfastly, to peer.
Rolo roloe baṅgeṭakaṭa. He is looking steadfastly, he has fixed his gaze.

Rombṛo. }
Rombṛo rombṛo. } Whole, unbroken, whole and hard, lumpy.
Rombṛo jondra. Whole Indian corn.
Rombṛo rombṛoge tahẽena hasa do. The clay is lumpy (has not been properly mixed.)

Romcolok. Drawn together, huddled up, applied to sitting.
Rom coloke duṛupakana. He is sitting huddled up.

Romcom. Silent.
Duṛup thirakanae romcom. He is sitting still and silent.

Romoċ koṭoċ. To spin out, to use sparingly, to cause to last by using sparingly.
Jomedako romoċ koṭoċ. They are eating sparingly.
Romoċ koṭoċko khoroceda. They are spinning it out.

Romrom. Steadfastly, without moving, still.
Duṛup romromakanae. He is sitting quite still.

Ron. The call of the night watchman or village chaukidar.
Ron. To call out when going his rounds at night as a chaukidar.
Rone emeda, se baṅa? Does he call out when going his rounds at night, or not?

Ron. Haze.
Ron rakapakana. A haze has arisen, it has become hazy.

Ron kubṛạ. A thick haze, a fog.

Rondar. A night watchman, a chaukidar.

Rondho. Fat, corpulent.
Khube moṭaakana rondho. He is very corpulent.

Rond khond. }
Ron khon. } To discuss, to debate, to talk over.
Khuble rond khondkeda. We discussed it thoroughly.

Rondoć. A common weed, *Blumea Wightiana, D. C.*

Roṅ. A method of applying spices to certain cooked foods, spices cooked in a certain way.

Onions, pepper, garlic, &c, are cooked in oil and then mixed with the food to be spiced.

Roṅ choṅkateko joma. They fizzle the spices and then eat (the food), they pour the boiling spices on the food and cause a fizzle.

Roṅ. Colour, to dye, to colour, to paint, to varnish.

Roṅanaḱ kana. It is dyed stuff.
Kicriċko roṅa. They dye cloth.
Dibiko roṅkoa. They paint images.

Roṅgo. To be burnt, to be burnt in cooking.

Roṅgoaḱ jom lek do baṅ kana. Burnt (food) is not fit to eat.

Roṅgo mundhet lekae ńeloḱa. He looks like a burnt log, i. e. is very black.

Matkompe teke roṅgokeda. You burnt the matkom (q. v.) in cooking.

Dakape roṅgo cookeda. You allowed the rice to be burnt (in cooking.)

Roṅgoć. Cf. roṅgo.

Roṅgo coṅgo. Burnt, as food in cooking.

Roṅgo coṅgo emańpe. Give me burnt food, (I shall be glad to get anything.)

Roṅgo era. }
Roṅgo budhi. } A Santal female godlet, supposed to be the wife of Roṅgo ruji (q. v.)

Roṅgo era is worshipped along with Roṅgo ruji (q. v.) and in the same manner.

Roṅgo ruji. The Santals' god of the chase.

This deity is supposed to reside in a tree of the species *Diospyros tomentosa, Roxb.* Before proceeding to one of the tribal annual hunts the men dance naked round the tree in which the deity is supposed to reside. Urine is also offered, and the worshippers freely urinate upon the stone which is the visible representation of Roṅgo ruji.

Roṅkhoṅ. Hoarse, rough-voiced.

Roṅkhoṅiń aṭkareda. I feel hoarse.

Roṅ rij. Amusement, merriment, pleasure.

Rońjo. Emaciated.

Buṛ rońjoenae. He is emaciated through fever.

Rońjok. The priming pan of a flint and steel gun.

Ronkhon. To discuss, to debate, to talk over. Cf. rondkhond.

Roń khoń. To be irritated, to be displeased, to take offence, to take umbrage, to complain.

Ropa. Planted, opposed to self propagated.

Ropa maḱ. A planted bamboo, a cultivated bamboo.

Ropam. To season, as wood, &c., to mature as cooked rice which is allowed to remain a short time in the pot after being taken off the fire to perfect the cooking.

Daka ãṛgokate ropam ocoam. Take the boiled rice off the fire and allow it to mature.

Rop dhop. To settle a dispute privately, to effect a compromise privately.

Noa mamblale rop dhopakaća. We have settled this case privately.

Ropha. }
Rapha. } To settle, to quiet, to pacify, to reconcile, to effect a compromise, to be contented.

Disom do rophaena. The country is at peace.
Mokordomale rophakeda. We settled the case.
Bahu rophaenae. The bride is contented.

Ropoḱ. The reciprocal form of roḱ (q. v.), conterminous, touching, contiguous.

Kaḍakin ropoḱkana. The buffaloes are horning each other.

Simạ ropoḱakana. The boundaries are conterminous.

Oṛaḱ oṛaḱ ropoḱ kana. The houses are contiguous.

Ropoḱ gopoćenakin. Their horning each other has terminated fatally, they are horning and killing each other.

Balaeako ropoḱa. The fathers-in-law butt each other, said of fathers-in-law, &c, (balaea q. v.) when saluting each other.

Roporopo. }
Rupurupu. } Slightly and at short intervals, applied to fever.

Roporopoń ruạḱkana. I have slight fever now and again.

Ropoṛ. The reciprocal form of roṛ (q. v.), to quarrel, to altercate, to have words with each other, to wrangle.

Roporenakin. They had words with each other.

Ropoṛ ropoḱ. }
Ropoṛ dapram. } To altercate, to quarrel, to dispute.

Ropoṭ. }
Ropoṭ ropoṭ. } To creak, as shoes.

Ropoṭedae. He is (causing) creaking.

Ropoṭ marte. }
Ropoṭ mente. } With a creak. Cf. ropoṭ.

Ropoć. }
Ropoć ropoć. } To creak, as shoes, an imitative word.

Panahi sades ropoć ropoć. The shoes sound *ropot' ropot'*.

Ropoť marte } With a creak. Cf. ropoť.
Ropoť mente. }

Roprop. Creaking as shoes, an imitative word.
Roprope taṛameťkana. He produces the sound of *rop rop* as he walks.
Panahi roprop saḍekana. The shoes sound *roprop*.

Ropropo. Lethargic, languid, indisposed, the feeling of indisposition experienced at the beginning of an attack of fever.
Nitoḱ do ropropoediñkana.

Roṛ. To speak, speech, language, word.
Hoṛ roṛ. The Santali language.
Ropoṛ. To dispute, to wrangle, to altercate, to have words together.
Ropoṛkanakin. They are disputing.
Miť dinliñ ropoṛlena. We had words one day.
Roṛ sohoť. To assist by speaking.
Roṛ sohoťadiñae. He spoke for me.
Roṛ parom. To contradict.
Roṛ paromkediñae. He contradicted me.
Roṛ land. To joke, to laugh and speak.
Roṛ landkanako. They are speaking and laughing.
Koṛa kuṛi ñeñelko calaḱkhan roṛ landtegeko tahena. The young men and maidens when on the way to the fair continue to talk and laugh.
Roṛ endeḱ. To speak when another is speaking and to prevent him finishing what he had to say.
Uni doñ roṛkedea. I reproved him.
Roṛ ocolenae. He was rebuked or reproved.
Roṛ siṭhạ. } To insult by speaking.
Roṛ siṛié. }
Roṛ ḍhiñku. To harm one's cause by what one says, judged out of one's own mouth.

Roṛa. A common jungle bush, *Mallotus philippinensis, Mull.*
This bush yields a valuable dye.

Roroć. Dry, sapless, emaciated.
Rohoṛ rorocenako. They are as dry as bone.

Roroť. To peel off, or become rough, as the skin, scaly. Cf. roť.
Rabah dinre bam umoḱkana, rodoḱkanam. You are not bathing in the cold weather, your skin is becoming rough.
Kakṛa hoṛmo hõ rorota. The body of the lizard is also rough or scaly.

Roṛ ses. A cess levied for the making and repairing of roads, cor. of the English *Road Cess.*

Ros. Sap, juice, the humours of the body.
Noa ạk do khub rosana. This sugar cane is very juicy.

Rosa. Time, season.
Rosa calaḱkana. The season is passing.
Kạmi reaḱ rosa. The time for the work of cultivation.

Ros amol. Derangement of the humours of the body.
Nui doe ros amolakana.

Rosao. To be absorbed in, to be engrossed in, to have the mind taken up with.
Jom rosaoenae. He is engrossed in eating.
Kạmi rosaoakanae. He is engrossed in his work.

Rosaṛ. Damp, moist, sappy.
Rosaṛ ot. Moist soil.
Noa khet do rosaṛgea. This field is moist.

Rosbot. } To be friendly, to be on friendly terms. Cf. risbot.
Rosbod. }

Rose rose. Leisurely, slowly, gently.
Rose roseteye calaḱkana. He is going leisurely.

Rosgar. } Damp, moist, sappy.
Rasgar. }

Rosgaria. } Juicy, sappy, moist.
Rasgaria. }

Roskar. } Damp, moist, sappy.
Raskar. }

Roskoť. To rustle.
Cele coe roskoteťkana. Some thing is causing a rustling.
Roskoť roskoťe calaḱkana. He goes rustling, he is causing a rustling as he goes.

Roskoť marte. } With a rustle.
Roskoť mente. }

Rosme. } Gently, leisurely, slowly, gradually.
Rosme rosme. }
Rosmeteye taṛameda. He is moving gently.
Rosmegeye roṛeťkana. He is speaking slowly.

Rosod. } Provision for travellers.
Rasad. }
Palṭon rosodko uṭhạueda. They are collecting provisions, &c. for the troops.

Rosod. Frequented, as a highway.
Rosod hor. A road on which there is much traffic.

Rosom. } Slightly, applied to fever, slowly, gently, leisurely.
Rosom rosom. }
Rosom rosome ruạḱkana. He has slight fever.

Rosoposo. } Slightly and at intervals, applied to fever.
Rosoroso. }
Roso posoe ruạḱ kana. He has a little fever now and again, or he is slightly feverish.

Roť. To peel off, to come off in flakes, as the skin.
Rabah dinre rorota. The skin peels off in the cold weather.
Rodoḱkanae. His skin is peeling off.

Roť. To tie up the hair and fix it with a pin or band, applied to females.
Rodeñ mese ayo, nạkijiñme. Tie up my hair, mother, comb my hair.
Roť nạkić. To comb and tie up the hair.

Rot Mạrndi. A sub-sept of the Santal sept Mạrndi (q. v.)

Rot. / Rot dare. A common forest tree, *Ougenia dalbergioides, Bl.*

Rot pạndu. Very old, applied to males.
Rot pạndu hesel pạndu ạdharo budharokateye goćena. He died having attained an extreme old age.

Roṭboṅ. Very tall, high, lofty.
Roṭboṅ mara herel. A tall rascal of a man.

Roṭe. A frog, a toad.
Roṭe maṛom. The frog's platform, i. e. water.
Roṭe maṛomko menlekhan daṅko ạguakoa. If they say the frog's platform, they bring them water.
Patal roṭe. A species of frog which is found deeply buried in the soil.
Pokoť roṭe. A species of frog.
Tuṭuriạ roṭe. The Indian frog which makes its appearance at the beginning of the rains, so called from its croak.
Bạrudaṅ. The Bull frog.
Hạrdiạ bạrudaṅ. The yellow Bull frog.
Both species of the Bull frog are eaten by Santals.
Bebebeć roṭe. A species of frog so called from its croak.
Kakṛa roṭe. A species of very small frog.
Ceṭer roṭe. / Ceṭe roṭe. The tree frog.

Roṭe puṭkạ. A form of edible puff-ball.

Roṭha. / Roṭha roṭha. Black and dirty, very black.
Roṭha mara hoṛ. A dirty, black rascal.

Roṭhaha. Black, black and dirty.

Rotho. Stout, burly, brawny.
Nui do rotho juạn kanae. He is a burly youth.

Roṭi. / Ruṭi. Bread, means of subsistence.
Roṭi uṭhạuentaea. He has lost his means of subsistence.
Pao roṭi. Bread the dough of which is mixed by tramping with the feet.

Rotoǩ. A seam. Cf. roǩ.
Rotoǩ raṛaena. The seam has opened.

Royo. / Royo royo. Small, not thick.
Royogea. It is not thick.
Royo royo joloǩkana. It is burning feebly.

Royol. / Royol royol. To move lightly and rapidly, to bound, to bob up and down or backwards and forwards.
Royol royole doṅ idikeda. He moved by a series of rapid bounds, he bounded lightly and rapidly away.

Royol marte. / Royol mente. With one light and rapid movement.
Royol menteye donkeda. He made a light and rapid bound.

Royo ropo. Small, not thick.
Royo ropoko ñam ạgukeda. They found only small ones.

Royoť. / Royoť royoť. Emaciated, only bones.
Royoť royoťe ñeloǩkana. He appears to be only bones.

Ru. To beat, to tap, to cause to sound, as a drum, &c.
Ṭamakko ruia. They beat the ṭamak (q. v.) drum.
Thạri kiriñ jokhećko ru aṭkara. When buying a brass plate they sound it to test it.
Kanḍa kiriñ jokhećko ruia. When they buy a water pot they tap it (to see if it is sound.)

Ruạ. Fever, to have an attack of fever.
Ruạǩkanae. He has fever.
Nui doe ruạ bereťakana. He is just recovering from an attack of fever.
Ruạ ehoṗkediñа. Fever has attacked me.
Ạdi̇le ruạ basoǩkana. We suffer much from fever.
Ruạ ohuṭạuentaea. His fever has left him.
Pạri ruạ. Intermittent fever of the tertian, and quartan types.

Ruạṛ. To return, to cause to return.
Ruạṛenako. They have returned.
Hatao ruạṛ. To take or receive back.
Beṅgeť ruạṛ. To look back.
Jiweť ruạṛ. To come to life again, to revive.
Roṛ ruạṛ. To reply.
Ṭakae ruạṛadiñа. He returned to me the money.
Ruạṛkeťkoae. He returned them, he caused them to return.

Rubdại rubdại. Tumultuously, noisily, uproriously.

Rubrubu. / Ruburubu. Lethargic, languid, the sensation one experiences when suffering from fever and enlarged spleen.
Jom rubrubuanae. He has eaten himself lethargic.

Rubuć rubuć. / Rubui rubui. Cf. rabać rubuć.
Rubuć rubuće calaǩkana. He is walking leisurely.

Rućruć. Securely, tightly.
Tol rućrućkedeako. They bound him securely.
Saṗ rućrućkediñako. They seized and held me securely.

Rucuṗ. / Rucuṗ rucuṗ. Crisp, brittle, sound of crunching or crushing anything crisp or brittle.
Rucuṗ rucuṗe jomeda. He is crunching.
Rohoṛ rucuṗena. It has dried brittle.
Rucuṗ marạokedae. He crunched it up.

Rudi. To be pained, in hand, arm, or leg.
Rudiakanae. He is pained.

Rudi. Waste, rejected.
Uniak katha rudientaea. His order was upset.

Rudhin. A variety of dhan.

Rudrudu. } Standing erect, as hair,
Rusrusu. } rough, as hair.
Bana reak up rudrudugea. The bear's hair is standing erect.

Rugi. Diseased, ill, unsound, afflicted with a disease, disorder or malady, having a defect. Cf. roga.

Rugubugu. Cf. ragabaga.

Rugum rugum. To creep gently.
Cele co hormore rugum rugumediñkanae.

Ruhen. A large forest tree, *Soymida febrifuga Adr. Juss.*

Ruhet. To scold, to rebuke, to speak angrily or sharply. Used mainly by males of males. Women use eger (q. v.)
Ruhet ñirketkoae. He scolded and drove them away, he caused them to run away by scolding them.
Adiye rukheta. He is greatly given to scolding.

Ruhi hako. } The name of a fish, *Cy-*
Rui hako. } *prinus denticulatus, Buch.*

Ruhini. } Cf. rohni.
Ruhni. }

Ruhri. F. } Lanky, lean, remaining
Rohra. M. } lean although well fed.
Nui doe ruhrigea. She is lanky.

Ruhuñ rupuñ. Emaciated, very skinny.
Ruhuñ rupuñ dārā baraekanae. He is going about in an emaciated condition.

Ruhur. } Sound of crashing,
Ruhur ruhur. } covered with fresh green leaves, as a tree.
Ruhur ruhur bindarena. It fell crashing.

Ruhur marte. } With a crash.
Ruhur mente. }
Ruhur marte bindarena. It fell with a crash.

Ruhutuhu. To exert oneself, to ardently desire, to take care of.
Calak lagite ruhutuhukkana. He ardently desires to go.
Uni khon amgeñ ruhutuhumea? Shall I prefer you to him?
Suhuk lagite ruhutuhu baraekana. He is fishing for compliments.
Kami bagikate nuigeye ruhutuhueda. He has left his work and is amusing himself.

Rui. The cotton of the Indian cotton tree, *Bombax malabaricum, D. C.* and also of *Cochlospermum Gossypium, D. C.*

Rui. A kind of fish, *Cyprinus denticulatus, Buch.* Cf. ruhi.

Ruiā. } Very small, weak.
Ruiā ruiā. }
Ruiā ruiāgeako. They are very small.
Ruiāgeae dare banuktaea. He is weak, he has no strength.
Rua ruateye ruiāena. He is weak owing to continued fever.

Ruila. M. } Tall, tall and lanky.
Ruili. F. }
Ruila ruilikin ñapamena. The tall man and the tall woman are mated.

Ruili. Gently, as wind.
Seke seke hoe do ruili ruili.

Rui rui. Very tall, applied to females.
Jawãe khon bahu do rui ruiye usula. The bride is much taller than her husband.

Rui rui. } Bobbing up and down,
Ruyu ruyu. } moving from side to
Ruyul ruyul. } side.
Sakam rui rui atukkana. The leaf floats bobbing up and down.
Kanda bhugaklenkhan ruyu ruyu dak todoka.

Rui rui cẽrẽ. A small bird so called from its note.

Ruka. A carpenter's chisel.
Kund ruka. A chisel for cutting out round holes, mainly the axle holes in wheels. Cf. kund.
Chimni ruka. A small chisel.

Rukar. } Dry.
Rukhar. }
Hormo rukharentaea. His body is dry.
Rukhar daka. Dry boiled rice (not pasty.)

Ruk birik. } Trees.
Ruk birit. }
Ruk birit ñelte bam berellena? Did you not take notice of the trees before you settled down?

Rukhi. An atom, a grain, a shred, a particle.
Sanam lo cabaena, mit rukhi hõ bañ sareclena. All was burnt up, not even one particle remained.
Jom cabakedeae, mit rukhi hõ bae sareclaka. He ate him all, he did not leave even a shred.
Rukhi pañja. To enquire into in detail.
Rukhi jogao. To economise, to be thrifty, to be frugal.
Rukhi jogaokate jompe. Eat frugally.

Rukhiạ. Relief, deliverance, to relieve, to extricate, to deliver, to save.
Rukhiạenale. We are delivered.
Isore rukhiạkediṅte uniṅ sarhaoedekana. I am praising God, because He delivered me.

Rukrạbon. Completely, entirely, not a scrap.
Oṛakre cet hõ bạnuktaea rukrạbon.
Rukrạbone ạtu idikeda. (The flood) carried away every vestige.
Rukrạbon ṅur cabaena matkom do. The matkom (q. v.) has all fallen.
Uniak cet cij hõ baṅ tahẽkantaea rukrạbon, nonḍeye cijlaka. He had not a shred of property, he became possessed of property here.

Ruku. To shake.
Ulko rukuia. They shake down mangoes (from the tree.)
Bohoke rukukeda. He shook the head.

Rukum rukum. To shiver, to shake, as in a paroxysm of fever.
Ruạ ehobe jokheć rukum rukumokae. When the fever is beginning he shivers.

Rukum tukum. } To shake, to shiver.
Rukun tukun. }
Haṛam rukum tukumenae. He is old and shaking.
Rabaṅte hõ rukum tukumko hilạuka. They also shiver with cold.

Ruli. A sapling used as a rafter. Cf. rola.
Ruli suli. Small saplings.

Rum. } To be possessed with a spirit
Rumok. } which is evidenced mainly by shaking of the head.
Hạṛũ boṅgae rumakana. He is possessed with the deity named Hạṛũ.
Landa boṅgako rumlenkhan gutlu baṛakoako. If they become possessed by the laughing deity they tickle them.

Rumbuć cumbuć. Heartily, rejoicingly, willingly, eagerly, fervently.
Ṅeṅel rumbuć cumbućko calaoena. They have gone to the fair rejoicingly.
Jahãn kạmim ạculekhan ạḍi cuṭạukae rumbuć cumbuć. If you engage him for any work he will set to it heartily.

Rumjhum. To enquire at an oracle, to enquire at one who is possessed with some deity or other, generally as to the recovery or otherwise of a sick person.
Boṅgako rumjhumketkoa.
Ruạk jokheć ko rumjhum ocokoa.
Ruạkić reak ṅutumko rumjhum ocokoa.

Rumuć. } To become willing, to be
Rumuj. } pleased, to be persuaded.
Nukinkin rumućena.
Rumuć godokkanako onkoak kathate.
Rumujenteye calaoena.

Rumuṅ rumuṅ. Creeping of the flesh, a tingling sensation, a sensation as of trembling in the flesh.
Am botorte iṅak jel do rumuṅ rumuṅokkana. My flesh is creeping through fear of you.
Ruạk ghuṛi rumuṅ rumuṅ ṣikạuka. During fever one feels a sensation of creeping in the flesh.

Run. A method used to keep flesh meat from going bad by half-roasting, during which process its bulk is reduced, to shrink.
Jel runlekhan baṅ ṣhnạuka. If flesh meat be half-roasted it will not go bad.
Uniak hoṛmo runentaea. His body has shrunk, or become reduced in bulk (as half roasted flesh meat.)

Run. To crease, to be creased, to shrivel.

Runḍạ. A species of wild cat.
Boak runḍạ. } Wild cats differentiated by
Sagak runḍạ. } Santals.
Silạ runḍạ. }
Kubrạ runḍạ. }

Ruṅku juḍuṅ. Weak, feeble.
Ruạ ruṅku juḍuṅakanaṅ. I am feeble through fever.

Ruṅruṅ. Clear, transparent, thin.
Ruṅruṅ phạriạ dak. Clear, transparent water.
Ruṅruṅ moakanae. It is swollen to thinness (skin.)
Ruṅruṅ harteko ṭanaoakaṭa. They have stretched the skin until it has become thin.

Runrunạu. To be numb, to tremble.
Runrunạukkanae rabaṅte. He is shivering with cold.

Run tukun. To shrivel, flesh to become rough or corrugated.

Rup. Form, appearance.
Uniak rupteṅ jomkeda. I obtained through him.
Manwa rupte. In human form.

Rup. To fall down, to collapse.
Oṛak rupena. They house has fallen down.
Dare rupena hoete. The tree was blown down, the tree was uprooted by the wind.

Rup. To poison fish.
Hakoko rupkoa. They poison fish.
Okarepe rubạ? Where will you poison fish?

Rupạ. Silver.
Rupạ reak. Made of silver.

Rupạ Mạrnḍi. A sub-sept of the Santal sept Mạrnḍi (q. v.)

Rupuṭ rupuṭ. Slowly, applied to eating.
Rupuṭ rupuṭe jojomkana. He is eating slowly.

Ruṛuṅ ruṛuṅ. Clear, transparent.
Ruṛuṅ ruṛuṅ dak phạriạwa. The water is clear to transparency.

Ruṛu ruṛu. Small and round, as a hole.
Ruṛu ruṛuko bhugạk̕akat̕a. They have made small round holes.
Ruṛu ruṛu bhugạk̕ khon lutiko bolo oḍokok̕a. The *Luti* (q. v.) bees go in and come out at a small round hole.

Ruru ruru. Inefficiently, as the music of one who is learning to play.
Rururuṛu tirioko orońeda.

Rusạ rusi. To be sullen towards each other, not to be on speaking terms.
Nukin dokin rusạ rusiakana. These two are not on speaking terms with each other.

Rusạu. To sulk, to be sullen.
Rusạuakanae. He is sullen.

Rusrusu. To be sullen, to sulk.
Rusrusuakanae. He is sulky and sullen.
Rusrusue beṅgeteda. He has a sullen look, or he looks sullenly.

Rusrusu. Standing up, as hair. Cf. rudrudu.
Rusrusu ap̕ teṅgoena.
Bana reak̕ uṭ rusrusugea.

Rusuk̕ rusuk̕. } Diligently.
Rasak̕ rusuk̕. }
Rusuk̕ rusuk̕e kạmi jońkana. He is working diligently.

Rusuk̕ rusuk̕. } Sound of cutting, crop-
Rasak̕ rusuk̕. } ping, or grazing, imitative.
Rusuk̕rusuk̕e ạtiń jońkana. It is grasing and producing a sound of cropping.
Rusuk̕ rusuk̕ ạsuṛiko ireda. They are cutting the grass and producing a sound of cutting.

Ruṭi. Bread. Cf. roṭi.

Ruṭruṭu. Puffed out, swollen.
Ruṭruṭu piṭhạ. Puffed out bread.
Jom ruṭruṭuenae. He has eaten till he is swollen (stomach.)

Ruṭuk̕ ruṭuk̕. To crack, to crunch.
Ruṭuk̕ ruṭuk̕e togoćeda. He is crunching with his teeth.

Ruṭyut̕. To satiety, to repletion, applied to children.
Jom ruṭyut̕enae. He has eaten to repletion.

Ruyu. } Without cessation, con-
Ruyu ruyu. } tinuous, bobing up and down, moving from side to side.
Ruyu ruyu ạtuk̕kana sakam. The leaf is floating and bobbing up and down.
Kanḍa bhugạk̕lenkhan ruyu ruyu dak̕ todok̕a. If a water pot be punctured the water issues in a stream.
Ruyu ruyu hilạuk̕kana suṛạ. The reed shakes from side to side.

Ruyul. } To move lightly and
Ruyul ruyul. } rapidly, to bob up and down, to move from side to side.
Ruyul ruyul ạtuk̕kana sakam. The leaf floats bobbing up and down.
Ruyul ruyul mat̕ko gok̕ idieda. As they carry the bamboo it bobs up and down.
Hoṛo gele hoete hilạuk̕kana ruyul ruyul. The ears of dhan are shaking from side to side by the wind.

Ruyul marte. } With one light and
Ruyul mente. } rapid movement.
Ruyul marteye donkeda. He bounded lightly and rapidly.

Ruyu ruyu. Gently, quietly easily, lightly.
Ruyu ruyu oṭańok̕kana Edel rui. The cotton of the cotton tree is being carried lightly by the wind.
Ruyu ruyu ṭunṭik̕kana. It is issuing gently.

S

Sa. Side, edge, to go or put aside.
Hana sa. The other side.
Noa sa. } This side.
Nha sa. }
Gaḍa hana sare. On the other side of the river.
Gaḍa nha sare. On this side of the river.
Hana sa renkoko hećakana. Those belonging to the other side are come.
Hana sateko calaoena. They have gone to the other side.
Sa ńogok̕me. Move a little away.
Mit̕ sa aṛere duṛupme. Sit to one side.
Sa ńogeme. Put him a little to the side, or to a little distance.
Sa got̕enae. He moved to the side at once.
Mit̕ satege calaoena dak̕ do. The rain passed to one side.
Mit̕ sa ren ḍańrae lohot̕lena ar mit̕ sa ren do bań. The bullock on one side was wetted and not that on the other side.
Mit̕ sa kaṛ hasoedińkana, banar kaṛ do bań. I am pained on one side, not on both sides.

Saba. A small tributary of a river in which the water is dammed back when the river is full.

Saba. Spur, as of a fowl; a dew claw on the hind legs of a dog.

Sabab. Reason, cause, motive, accusation, on account of, by reason of.
Cet̕ sababteko lagakedea? For what reason did they drive her away? Ḍạn sababte. On account of being a witch.
Sababe lagaokeda. He made an accusation.
Sababe lagaoadińa. He accused me.
Jahan sabab do menak̕a. There is a reason of some kind.

Sabad. Sound, noise, voice.
Cele reań sabad ańjomok̕kana. The noise of some creature is heard.

Sabak'. Insipid, owing to the absence of salt or sweetness. *Scottice*, wersh.
Noa utu do sabak'gea, buluń bań adalena. This relish is insipid, it is not sufficiently salted.
Roṛ sabak'kedeako. They talked him down.

Sabaṛ. To finish, to complete, to put the finishing touches to.
Kạmiko sabaṛkeda. They completed the work.

Sabạsi. Distinction, celebrity, fame, glory, praise.
Sabạsiye hạrkeda. He gained praise, or distinction.
Ạdiko sabạsiadea. They praised him highly.

Sabha. Council, an assembly convened for consultation, deliberation and settlement of disputed matters.
Sabhare duṛuṕ hoṛ kanae. He is a man who sits in the council.

Sạbik. Original, former, preceding, formerly, of yore, time past.
Onko eae sạbik khũṭ ohaḍa arhõko mõṛẽ khũṭkeda. They added five more septs to the seven original septs.

Sạbit. To be perfect, to be complete, perfect, complete, excellent.
Ạuri sạbitok'a. It is not yet perfect.
Bań bele sạbitakana. It is not perfectly ripe.
Bae phạriạ sạbitakana. He has not completely recovered.
Nui do sạbit hoṛ kanae. This is an excellent man.

Sabja. } To become moist by attrac-
Sabjao. } ting moisture.
Buluń do sabjaok'a dak' dinre. Salt becomes moist in the rains.
Ot hõ sabjak'a, buluń hõ sabjak'a. Soil also becomes moist by attracting moisture, salt also becomes moist by attracting moisture.
Sabjao godok'a. It will become moist immediately.

Sabod. } Noise, sound, voice. Cf. sabad.
Sobod. }

Sabok'. Cf. saṗ.

Sabol. An iron crowbar.

Sabori. Cf. sạburi.

Sạbrạ. } Insipid, tasteless, applied to
Sạbrạha. } those things which should generally taste sweet.
Baṛe bele sạbragea. The ripe fruit of the Banyan is insipid.
Sạbrạhage aṭkarok'kana. It tastes insipid.
Sạbrạhaena. It has become insipid.

Sạbṛi. A pole on which anything is slung and carried on the shoulders of two or more men.

Sạbri. A variety of plantain.

Sabsab. } Infiltrated moisture, satu-
Sabsabao. } rated, to liquify or dissolve, as salt, &c., the oozing out of infiltrated moisture, or water held in such substances as salt, &c.
Hoṛmo sabsabaok'kana. The body is dissolving.
Sabsab dak' menak'a. There is infiltrated water.
Buluńre hõ sabsab dak' oḍokok'kana. Water is also oozing out of the salt.
Buluń sabsabaok'kana. The salt is becoming watery.

Sạbud. To prove.
Sạbud daṛeak'am? Are you able to prove it?
Sạbudadeań. I proved it to him.
Sạbudena. It is proved.

Sạbur. To wait, to have patience, to endure.
Mit' ghạṛi hõ bae sạbur daṛeada. He could not have patience even for a little.
Mit' ghạṛi sạbur hataṛme. Wait for a little, have patience for a little.

Sạburi. Patient, enduring.

Săc. A mould.

Saca. True, faithful, truthful.
Saca hoṛ kanae. He is a truthful man.

Sạcại. Truthfulness, faithfulness.

Saċ suċ. } Without a sound being heard,
Săċ sŭċ. } in silence, silent as the grave.
Saċ suċko gitiċena. They are asleep and all is silent as the grave.

Sặci maric. A kind of pepper.

Sặci son. A fibre yielding plant, a variety of *Crotalaria juncea.*

Sad. } Wish, desire, inclination.
Sadh. }
Sad lagaoakawat'mea chuṭki ńame reah? You felt a desire to get a second wife?
Sadh maraoentama nitok' do? Has your desire perished, has the desire left you?
Bạṅki horog lạgit' sadhok'kanae. She has a desire to wear bạṅkis (q. v.)
Sad meṭaoentaea. His desire has been obliterated, i. e. has left him.
Sadre aċge gooo menak'tae leka.

Saḍ. } Sound, to sound.
Saḍe. }
Cele reak' saḍiń ańjomkeda. I heard the sound of something.
Saḍkedae. He made a sound.
Saḍe oookedae. He caused it to sound.
Bań saḍek'a. It will not emit a sound.
Bań saḍe ooo daṛeat'a. I could not cause it to sound.

Sạd. Authority, power, to train, break in, reduce to subjection.
Cet' sạd menak'tama? What authority, or power have you?
Nui ḍaṛań sạdakadea. I have broken in this bullock.

Sada. White, plain, clean, without admixture.

Sada kicriċ. White cloth, without a coloured border.

Sada kagoj. Clean paper, on which nothing has been written or printed.

Sada bohi. A blank book.

Sadawak̃iñ joma. I will eat plain, (or unsalted food.)

Sada. A kind of tobacco.

Sada Murmu. A sub-sept of the Santal sept Murmu. (q. v.)

Sada Hãsdak̃. A sub-sept of the Santal sept Hãsdak̃ (q. v.)

Sada Kisku. A sub-sept of the Santal sept Kisku (q. v.)

Sada Hembrom. A sub-sept of the Santal sept Hembrom (q. v.)

Sada Mạrnḍi. A sub-sept of the Santal sept Mạrnḍi (q. v.)

Sada Soren. A sub-sept of the Santal sept Soren (q. v.)

Sada Sidup̣ Soren. A sub-sept of the Santal sept Soren (q. v.)

Sada Ṭuḍu. A sub-sept of the Santal sept Ṭuḍu (q. v.)

Sada Baske. A sub-sept of the Santal sept Baske (q. v.)

Sada Pạuria or Pạulia. A sub-sept of the Santal sept Pạuria or Pạulia.

Sada Cõṛẽ. A sub-sept of the Santal sept Cõṛẽ (q. v.)

Sadae. / Sadại. } Continually, daily, always.

Sadaege hijuk̃ae. He comes continually.

Sadamạd. Continuously, without a break.

Sadamạd nui kisãṛ ṭheniñ kạmikana. I have been working for this master continuously.

Sạḍar suḍur. / Sạḍur bạḍur. / Sạḍur sạḍur. } Thin owing to the presence of liquid, too much liquid or moisture. Cf. suḍur suḍur.

Sạḍur sạḍurko utuakaṭa. They have cooked the relish too thin, too much water in it.

Sạddi. Strength, ability, power.

Besạddi. Impracticable.

Roroṛ daṛe se galmarao sạddi eken manwa reak̃ ge. Only human beings have the power to speak or the ability to converse.

Sadasuk. Super-abundant, lavish, excessive, too much, over much.

Sadasukem emadea. You gave to him lavishly.

Sadasuke jomkeda. He ate too much.

Sạḍe. Cf. sạḍ.

Sadga badga. / Sadga bạdgi. } Rough, surface uneven, pitted, to make rough or pitted.

Simko jereṛ cikãṛak̃ko sadga badgakedako. The fowls broke the surface of what had been plastered smooth.

Khạṛại pạliạure pạhil do sadga badgako losoda.

Sadga bidiṛ. Lying about, disarranged, out of place, anyway, in disorder, disorderly.

Sadga bidiṛ inkạgeko bạgiada. They have left the things in disorder.

Sadga bidiṛko dohoakaṭ. The have put them down anyway (in disorder)

Sadgaeak̃. / Sadgalak̃. } In disorder, disorderly, out of order, out of its proper place.

Sadgaeak̃em bạgiakaṭa kagoj potor do. You have left the papers in disorder.

Sadgaeak̃pe bạgiak̃kana katha do. You are leaving the matter unsettled.

Sadgal. A moneylender.

Tobe nitok̃ do sạure sadgalre hala dok̃ raṛa dok̃ ocolem.

Sadgalak̃. Cf. sadgaeak̃.

Sadgayak̃. Disarranged, in disorder, out of place, untidy, unfinished.

Sadgayak̃ ñelok̃kana. It looks untidy.

Sadgayak̃ko bạgiada. They left it in disorder.

Sạḍge. / Sạḍgea. } The relationship between the husbands of sisters.

Sạḍgea kanako. They are the husbands of sisters.

Sạḍgeñ kanae. He is the husband of my wife's sister.

Pon sạḍgea menak̃koa. There are the husbands of four sisters.

Sạḍgum bạḍgum. Bristly, rough owing to the presence of things sticking up.

Sạḍgum bạḍgum upanae. He is bristly haired.

Sạḍgum bạḍgumko losoṭakaṭa. They have mixed up the soil and left it bristly.

Sạḍgum bạḍgumko siakaṭa. They have ploughed and left it bristly, have not covered up the grass, &c.

Sạḍgur bạḍgur. Thin, owing to the presence of liquid, too much liquid or moisture.

Sạḍgur bạḍgurko dakaakaṭa. They have cooked the rice with too much water in it.

Sạḍgur bạḍgur ghoraokate bhitko potaoa. They stir (the lime) with water and make it thin and whitewash the wall.

Sadh. Wish, desire, inclination.
Ona sadhoᶄem horoᶄleda, nitoᶄ doe meneda hasoediñ. You desired to put (them, anklets) on, and now you say they hurt you.

Sadhao. To train, to discipline, to habituate or accustom to, to bring into unison with one's desire, to revenge.
Nui sadom do bañ sadhao daṛeaekana. I cannot discipline, this horse, I can't make him as I wish him to be.
Bạiri hõko sadhaokoa. They also wreak their vengeance on enemies.

Sadharon. Common, commonplace.

Sadher. Only, single, solitary.
Mić goṭeć sadher hopon tiñ. My only son, I have only one son.
Oh, aćaᶄge sadher menaᶄ lekae lạṭić baṛaeda, ale ṭhen hõ aema menaᶄa. He goes about telling as if he only had it, we have also a large number.

Sạdhi. Strength, ability, power.
Ado nitoᶄ do sạdhi bạnuᶄtaea. He has no strength now.
Chaḍaoᶄ reaᶄ sạdhi menaᶄtaea? Has he the power to release himself?

Sạdhin. Independent, free, one's own master.
Sạdhinre tahen do ạḍi besa. It is very good to remain independent.

Sạdhu. A certain class of Hindu mendicants.

Sạḍhu. }
Sạṛhu. } The relationship between the husbands of sisters. Cf. saḍge.

Sadom. A horse.
Anḍiạ sadom. A horse, a stallion.
Ehga sadom. A mare.
Sadom hopon. A foal.
Bandhar sadom. A horse that is kept in stable when not in use.
Sạdhin sadom. A mare that is kept tied up and kept from stallions.
Sadom oṛaᶄ. A stable.

Sadom mući. A kind of large red ant.

Saḍsaḍ. }
Saḍsaḍao. } Noise produced by water falling, or coming in contact with anything.
Saḍsaḍ daᶄ joroᶄkana.
Saḍsaḍaoćkanae daᶄ.

Sạḍur bạḍur. }
Sạḍur sạḍur. } Cf. saḍar suḍur.

Sae. A hundred.
Mić sae. One hundred.
Bar sae. Two hundred.
Sae saeko tahẽkana. There were hundreds of them.
Sae ṭaka sae patriko ạgukoa. They fine them a hundred rupees and a hundred plates of food.

Sae. Utterly, completely, entirely, the full hundred.
Hiṛiñ saekediñae. He utterly forgot me.
Giḍi saekećlese. He threw us off entirely.
Jom saekedale. We ate all up.
Saeenae. He is dead.

Saedañ. Sandy.
Saedañ hasare jonḍra bañ hoyoᶄa. Indian corn will not grow in sandy soil.
Noa hạsa do saedañgea. This soil is sandy.

Saegać. Rough, harsh.
Saegaćgea, bañ cikạṇa. It is rough, not smooth.
Saegaćgeye roṛkediña. He spoke harshly to me, he found fault with me harshly.

Saekaṛa. Per hundred, per cent.
Saekaṛare 10 ṭaka lagaoᶄa. It is ten per cent.

Saela boela. }
Soela boela. } Long, tall.
Saela boela koṛa kuṛiko haraakana. The boys and girls have grown tall.
Soela boela sahanko maᶄakaṭa. They have cut long pieces of fire wood.

Saera. }
Saeṛa. } A kind of fish trap which allows the water to pass through but not the fish.

Sãe sãe. Imitative of the sound produced by water about the boiling point, by a large snake moving quickly, by the breathing of a person suffering from asthma.
Daᶄ basaḥena sãe sãe saḍekana. The water is heated, it is sounding sãe sãe.
Jambṛo biñ ạḍi ãṭteko calaᶄ jokheć sãe sãeko saḍe oooea. When pythons move quickly they produce the sound of sãe sãe.

Sãe sũi. Imitative of the sound produced by expiration and inspiration of breath.
Sãe sũiye saheċeda. When breathing he produces the sound of sãe sũi, sãe sũi.

Sãe sũi dare. The Casuarina, *Casuarina equisetifolia, Forster.*
When the wind blows this tree produces a sighing sound.

Sagae. }
Sagae sagae. } To blow a breeze.
Sagae sagae duạr khon hoe boloᶄkana. A breeze of wind is coming in by the door.
Sagae sagaeye hoeeda. It is blowing a breeze.

Sagae daṛae. Loudly

Sagae sagae. Cf. sege sege.

Sạgại. Relationship, kinship.
Janam sạgại. Kinship by birth.
Bapla topol sạgại. Relationship by marriage.
Ato sạgại. Assumed relationship by those who meet together frequently.
Landa sạgại. Applied to the freer terms of relationship which exist between certain members of a family. Cf. landa sạgại.

Sagak̃. The awns of certain grasses which prick when they come in contact with the person, spear grass; to prick, as the awns of certain grasses.

Sạuṛi sagak̃. The awns of sạuṛi grass (q. v.) Ạḍiń sagak̃akana. Many grass awns are sticking in my clothes and pricking me.

Sagak̃ ruṇḍạ. A species of wild cat.

Sagak̃ oṭ. A form of edible mushroom.

Sagak̃ ruạ. A kind of fever recognized by Santal *ojhas* (q. v.), which they say is the result of a hair, grain of sand, a piece of bone, &c. in the body. The *ojha* having located the extraneous substance, whatever it may be, extracts it by sucking with his mouth.

Sagal sagal. Numerous.

Kạṭić kạṭić sim sukri, sagal sagal peṛa. Dakạeń, utuiań, niń do ayo ohoń hạṭińlea. A small fowl or pig, numerous visitors, I'll cook the rice, prepare the relish, but I will not divide.

Sagam sugum. } Stealthily, noiselessly.
Sugum sugum. }

Sagam sugum ńindạ cedak̃pe daṛankans? Why are you going about stealthily at night?

Sagaṛ. A solid cart wheel, a cart having solid wheels without iron tyres, to cart.

Ḍeṛh paṭa sagaṛ. A wheel made in two solid pieces. Tin paṭa sagaṛ. A wheel made in three solid pieces. Sagaṛ gẹḍi. A cart with wheels of two spokes each, and the rim in two pieces. Sagaṛreko ladekeda. They loaded it on a cart with two solid wheels. Sahanko sagaṛkeda. They carted the firewood (on a cart with solid wheels.)

Sagaṛiạ. The driver of a cart or sagaṛ.

Sagaṛ jhagaṛ. Driving a cart, carting.

Sagaṛ jhagaṛre mić hoṛ tala hoṛ alope calak̃a, bạrpe hoṛ calak̃pe, bạṛićlenkthanpe jut goda. When carting let not one man or a boy go alone, two or three persons go, so that in case of a breakdown you may quickly make repairs.

Saga roṛe. } Numerous small bodies,
Sege roṛe. } rough owing to the presence of numerous small bodies, gritty.

Gitić bań jutok̃kana, oeć coh menak̃ sege roṛe. Lying down is not comfortable, there are some rough things (underneath me.)

Soṛokre sege roṛegea. The road is rough owing to the presence of numerous small bodies (gravel.)
Pạpitạ jore saga roṛe jạh menak̃a. In the papita fruit there are numerous small seeds.
Sege roṛe jạhana. It has numerous small seeds.

Sagen. To bud, as a leaf.

Dare sagenok̃kana. The tree is budding. Matkom sagen. Of a bright reddish colour, the colour of the young leaves of the *Matkom* tree (q. v.) Gạndhạri aṛak̃ siflekhan arhŏ sagen bolok̃a. If the *gandhari* (q. v.) pot-herb is plucked it will bud again.

Sagor. } All, the full.
Sagorre. }

Din sagorre inạk̃gem emańa? Will you give me so much for the full day?

Sagra. Cf. saṅgra.

Sagué baguć. } In disorder, disorderly,
Sagui bagui. } out of order, disarranged, without order, confusedly.

Sagué baguéko duṛupạkana. They are sitting without order. Sagué baguéem roṛeda. You are speaking confusedly. Sagué baguékedape. You did some parts well and others ill. Sagué baguéko dohoạkaẗa. They have placed the things without order. Noa kathako sagué baguéakaẗa. They have confused this matter.

Sagudana. Sago, from the Sago palm.

Sagun. Omen, applied to both good and bad, but mainly to a good omen.

Sagun bah hoelena. The omen was not good. Saguniń ńamkeda. I got a good omen. Sar sagun. A good omen. Sagun ṭhili. A water pot with which an omen is sought. Sagun kanḍa. A water pot by means of which fortunes are told. On the occasion of the *Jom sim* (q. v.) festival an unmarried girl carries a pot full of water into the house. The next morning it is examined and if it is found still full it is considered a good omen.

Sagun. } The Teak tree, *Tectonis*
Saguna. } *grandis, Linn.*
Sagwan. }

Sah. } Side, edge, to go or put aside, or
Sa. } to a distance.

Ma noa duk sahke sindirkeam. Keep this suffering at a distance. Sahre teḥgonme. Stand at a distance.

Sạhại. To favour, to aid, to help, to be friendly, to be gracious; grace, favour, aid.

Bese sạbạiadińa. He favoured me well. Amak̃ sạhạiteń ńamkeda. I received by your aid.

Sạhaita. To favour, to aid; help, assistance, aid.
Uni sạhạitaadiṅteṅ daṛeõna. I won through his aiding me.

Sahaj. } **Sahoj.** } **Sohoj.** } Easy, light.
Noa kạmi do sahaj kana. This work is easy.
Sahajteṅ ṅamkeda. I got it easily.

Sãhãk. } **Sãhããk.** } **Sạhạk.** } Used at funeral ceremonies and some other religious observances. It is probably the same as the Sanscrit *swáhá*, an exclamation on offering to the gods.
Iṅ do inạk dinge cele ṡer tahẽkana, sãhãk. My pound of food was probably only for so many days, sãhãk.

Sahan. Firewood.
Gok sahan. To assist at a cremation.
Gok sahane senakana. He has gone to assist at a cremation.
Hela sahan. An abundance of firewood.
Laṛga sahan. Long pieces of firewood.
Niạtele sahanoka. We will use this as firewood.
Sahaniṅ paṛaga. I will split firewood.

Sahao. To suffer, to bear, to endure, to put up with, to be patient, to bear hunger.
Sahao khon bahregea. It is beyond bearing, insufferable.
Sahao hatạṛpe. Bear it for the present, suffer it (for the present.
Mit dhao doko sahaokaka. They endure it once, it is wrong to take offence on the first occasion.
Niạ do Gosãe sahaokak lahaokakme.
Sahaole eneõem lahaoka. You must first put up with it then you will succeed, to succeed you must be patient.
Bae sahao daṛeakkana. He cannot bear hunger.

Sahar. } **Sahar dare.** } A large forest tree, *Dillenia pentagyna, Roxb.*
The fruit of this tree is eaten.

Sahar. } **Sạhạr.** } Increase, as of crops, good luck, fortunate.
Nonḍe khon khạṛạibon pheraoa, ente nonḍe do sahar baṅ hoyokkana. We will remove our threshing floor from here because here we have not good luck. (crops.
Sạhạraleme. Give us good luck, or give us good
Jaega jaega gunte hõ sạhạr hoyoka. Increase also depends on the kind of land.
Khet khon hoṛo dele rakạpletgea, menkhan khạṛạire sạhạr baṅle ṅamleda.

Sahar. Dung, to void dung, applied mainly to cattle while on the threshing floor, or when being purchased.
The voiding of dung by a cow or bullock when being examined with a view to purchase is considered a good omen.

Sahar. } **Sohor.** } A town.
Sahar bajar. } Bajar sahar. } A bazaar or market place in a town, a market town.

Sahaṛ. To go or put to a distance.
Sahaṛakan tahenme sengel khon. Remain at a distance from the fire.
Biṅ menaea, sahaṛokpe. There is a snake, get to a distance.
Nonḍe khon sahaṛkakope. Put them to a distance from here.
Sahaṛ gotkadeae. He immedialety put him away to a distance.

Sahar lunḍạ. } **Sahar lunḍạl.** } A festival so named.
No sacrifices are offered at this festival. Bread is baked and eaten.

Sahas. } **Sahos.** } To aid, help, encourage; brave, fearless, courageous; courage.
Sahas ṅokaṅme. Aid me a little.
Sahos hoṛ kanae. He is a brave man.

Sahạsiạ. } **Sahosia.** } Fearless, brave, courageous.
Khub sahosia hoṛ kanae. He is a very brave man.

Sahasae. } **Sahosae.** } Openly, freely, boldly, fearlessly.
Sahosaeye galmaraoeda. He is speaking out freely.

Sạhbit. } **Suk sạhbit.** } At ease, without disturbance.
Suk sạhbittele galmaraoa. We will converse at our ease.

Saheb. A European, used by fathers-in-law when saluting each other.

Saher. A town. Cf. sahar.

Sahet. To breathe.
Sahet ader. To inspire.
Sahet oḍok. } Sahet giḍi. } To expire.
Rengec hoṛ sahetakome. Breathe on the poor, help the poor.
Sahet bondentaea. His breathing has ceased.
Ãṭte sahedme. Breathe heavily, take a long breath.

Sạhi. } **Sohi.** } To sign, to pledge, to agree, to promise; signature.
Raebariċle sạhiadea. We agreed to the proposal of the go-between.
Rạsidre hõko sạhiaka. They also sign receipts.
Uniak sạhi do baṅ kana. It is not his signature.

Sạhi juhi. To betroth, to negotiate a marriage.
Sạhi juhi hoeõntakina. They are betrothed.
Uni kuṛi reak bapla reaṅ sạhi juhi hoeõna. All the negotiations for the girl's marriage are complete.

Sạhit. } **Sohit.** } Including, along with, also.
Sud sạhit iṅ emkeda. I paid with interest.
Am sạhitle idimea. We will also take you.

Sahitte. | Bhage sahitte. | Boge sahitte. } Carefully, vigilantly, diligently, after a proper manner.

Bhage sahitte ńelepe. Look at him carefully, scrutinise him.

Bhage sahitte tolasepe. Enquire for him diligently.

Sahja. Cf. sajha.

Sahnas. Pleasure, rejoicing.

Sakwa do Bahare ar sendrare begor enećle oroha sahnas lagit. We blow the horn without dancing at the Baha (q.v.) festival and at a hunt for pleasure.

Sahop. To be contained, to be accommodated, to hold.

Duar then bako sahoplena. They could not be contained at the door

Phaelaoteko sahopena. They are all accommodated without crowding.

Adi repe ciritko durupa, bako sahopte. They sit close together, because there is no room.

Sahobokа, ma bhoraope. It will hold it, come, fill it in.

Iń do hor metre bań sahoplena. There was no room for me in the eye of a certain person. (A witch had compassed his death through envy.)

Sahra. | Sahra dare. } A small forest tree, *Streblus asper, Lour.*

Sahraj. | Sahraj cẽrẽ. } A bird so named.

Sahrak. | Sahrak sahrak. } To clink, to chink, a small sharp sound produced by the collision of little pieces of money or other sonorous bodies. Cf. sekreć sekreć,

Sahrak sahrakko lekhaeda taka do. They clink the rupees as they count them.

Sahrak sahrak sadekana. It sounds clink clink, clink clink.

Sahrak marte. | Sahrak mente. } With a clink or light metallic sound.

Sahrak marte ńurena. It fell (to the ground) with a clink.

Sahta. | Sasta. } Cheap, low, as a rate or price, abundant.

Sahta bhaole ńamkeda. We got it at a low rate.

Aghanre horo caole kiriń akriń sahtaka. In the month of Aghan dhan and rice are bought and sold cheaply.

Sai. To search for, to look for.

Niakorege amem sai bara jońkana? Are you looking for it about here?

Saika. A swearing of eternal friendship. Cf. phul.

This is a form of friendship between two women the mothers of an equal number of children. Presents are exchanged and the occasion is marked by a feast given by each woman at her own home.

Sãitau. | Saintau. } To store away, to lay by, to hoard.

Gitić saintauenako babon bolaokoa. They are fast asleep, we will not disturb them

Saintau hatarkakme. Lay it by for the present.

Saj. Dress, ornament, framework, game, to be decked out, to embellish, decorate, adorn, ornament.

Orak saj. The timber required for the framework of a house.

Cele saj hõ banukkoa. There is no game of any kind.

Etak horak kiriѓteye sajakana. He is decked out in another man's clothes.

Marak ilte sajena. It is ornamented with peacocks' feathers.

Osok cabaenae eken sajtet menaktaea. He is utterly emaciated, he has only the framework (bones.)

Sadom saj. Harness for a horse.

Saja. | Sajao. } To be seemly, befitting, proper, becoming.

Boror do bań sajaoktama. It is unseemly for you to speak.

Boror sajaolentaea. It was befitting for him to speak.

Sajai. To punish, to deal retributive justice.

Sajaikedeako. They punished him.

Sajaiye ńamkeda. He received punishment.

Sajan. | Sajon. } Watered, as liquor, mixed, as oil.

Sajan. Cf. saj, sajao.

Sajao. To put in, fill in, to deck, to adorn, to clothe, to harness.

Orakreko sajaokeda. They put it into the house.

Khaolakreko sajaokeda. They put it into a basket.

Sadomko sajaoakadea. They have harnessed the horse.

Sajao hodokpe. Get ready quickly (yourself and what things you require.)

Nui do etakko leka bae sajaolena. This one was not adorned like the others.

Sajbaj. Equipment, implements, harness, tools, materials, machinery.

Teńok reak sajbaj adi utara. The equipment required to weave is large.

Orak reak sajbajko jurauеda. They are collecting the materials for a house.

Sajha. | Sajhia. } Together, in common, in partnership.

Sajhateko casa. They cultivate in partnership.

Nui darha do sajhakantalińae. We have this bullock in partnership, this bullock is common to us both.

Marań buruteko ma sajha bonga, menkhan Abge bonga do apan apin ren. Marań buru (q. v.) and those with him are objects of worship common to all, but each has his own Abge bonga, or family deity.

Saji hasa. A kind of fuller's earth.

Sajok. Partial, prejudiced, tutored, partisan.

Sajok sakhi kanako. They are tutored or partisan witnesses.

Sajon. Cf. **sajan.**

Sajontar. Free from imperfection, without defect, beautiful.

Sajontare ńeloḱkana. She looks beautiful.
Oraḱ bes sajontarko benaoakaṭa. They have built a grand house.

Sãk. A system of borrowing money under which the borrower himself or some one in his name works for the lender in lieu of paying interest.

Sãke khaṭaoḱkana. He is paying the interest of borrowed money by working for the lender.

Sãk ṭakale hataoakaṭtaea. We have borrowed money from him and have agreed that one of us should pay the interest by working for him.

Sãkkatele hataoakaṭa. We have borrowed it on the **sãk** system.

Sãk. A conch.

Sãkko oroña. They blow the conch.

Sãk. A goose.

Sãk. One who sells coral beads.

Sãk. A division of threads in the woven mattress of a bed.

Sãk ghoṅga. A shell used as a conch.

Sãk alu. A kind of vegetable.

Sãk mala. Coral beads.

Sãk Hãsdaḱ. A sub-sept of the Santal sept Hãsdaḱ (q. v.)

Sãk Soren. A sub-sept of the Santal sept Soren (q. v.)

Sãk rokoć. A shell used as a conch.

Saka. } The relationship between
Bala saka. } the respective parents, uncles and aunts of a married couple. Cf. **bala.**

Sakaea. Cf. **saka.**

Sakam. A leaf of a tree, book, &c.

Bar pe sakamiń parhaokeda. I read two or three leaves.
Sarjom sakam. A leaf of the **sarjom** tree.
Ne nahaḱ sakamoḱa. It will burst into leaf presently.
Unre dareko sakamakan tahẽkana. At that time the trees were in leaf.

Sakam oreć. To go through the ceremony of a divorce.

A part of the ceremony observed at a divorce is the tearing of a leaf in two, which act gives the name to the whole function.
Nukin bahu jawãe tekin sakam orećkeṭtakina. This couple have been divorced.

Sakam reṭ biń. A species of tree snake.

Sakam okrećić. A leaf tearer, a veiled name for a goat.

Sakam okrećićem jomea, se ot uḱṭaićem jomea. Will you eat goat's flesh or pork.

Sakar. Partially refined sugar.

Sakardom. }
Sokordom. } Breathless, out of breath.
Sukardom. }
Sukurdum. }

Daldalteko sukurdumkedea. They made him breathless by beating him.
Ńir ńirte sukurdumenań. I am out of breath with running.

Sakarkenda. The Sweet Potatoe, *Ipomœa Batatas, Lamk.*

Sake. }
Sakete. } Certainly surely, doubtless.

Sakegeye ruheṭ oooḱa. He will certainly be scolded.
Sake bam ruhedea? You will doubtless scold him.
Sakete bam dalea, roraḱ hõ bae añjoma. You will doubtless beat him, he does not listen to what is said.
Nui gidra do sińsaṭup halbal baraekanae, sakete bam dal sereṭ gotkaea? This child is working mischief all day, you will doubless beat him to a jelly.

Saket. } The patron divinity of
Saket boṅga. } the Santal ojhas (q v) or doctors, the name of the offering made after restoration to health by one who has been treated by an ojha.

Saket merom. A goat devoted to **Saket.** (q. v.)

Sakewa. Cf. **sakwa.**

Sakhi. A witness, a token, in earthwork a "benchmark."

Sakhi em. }
Sakhi gujrau. } To bear witness, to testify, to give evidence, to depone,
Sakhi purau. } to depose.
Sakhi menaḱkotińa. I have witnesses.
Sakhiko gujrauakaṭa. They have given evidence.
Sakhi sabha. }
Sakhi sobha. } To see and hear.
Sakhiaḱ sobhawaḱpe. Be witnesses (as to the agreement come to and pledges given.)
Okoe calao calaoko do soroḱpe, ar okoe baṅ calaoko do pharak khon bare sakhiaḱ sobhawaḱpe. Let those who have a right come near, and those to whom it is not allowed look on from a distance.

Sąkhiyąt. } **Sakhyat.** } Manifestation, evidence, *data*, assurance of reliability.

Boṅga reaǩ sąkhiyąt baṅ ńeloǩkana. No manifestation of the *bonga* (q. v.) appears.

Uniaǩ kathare biswasoǩ lągić sakhyat hõ baṅ ńameda. I do not find any assurance of his reliability to believe in his word.

Sakho. A bridge.

Sąkhṛi. } **Sąkṛi.** } Dirty, used, as a plate, cup, &c.; bits of food, grains of rice, &c. that have fallen during a meal.

Sąkhṛi patṛa. A used leaf plate, a leaf plate from off which food has been eaten.

Sąkhṛi phuṛuǩ. A cup that has been used, a cup that has not been washed after being in use.

Sąkhṛi joǩ giḍipe. Sweep up and throw away the crumbs or grains of rice, &c. that have fallen during the meal.

Sąkiąt. Cf. sąkhiąt.

Sąkildar. A knife grinder.

Sąkim. To finish, to complete.

Noa dole sąkimkeda. We finished or settled this.

Sąkić. To congeal, to become dense, to coagulate, to clot, to change from a fluid into a more or less solid body, to dry, to evaporate.

Nąriąl sunum rabaṅ dinre sąkidoǩa. Cocoanut oil congeals in the cold weather.

Mayam sąkićena. The blood is clotted.

Daka sąkić ocoam. Allow the boiled rice to dry a little.

Sako. A bridge.

Sakoć. To shake.

Sakom. An ornament worn on the lower arms by women, a wristlet.

Piṭną sakom.	Different kinds of ornaments which go under the name of *sakom.*
Bąihã sakom.	
Amchola sakom.	
Kątri sakom.	
Regṛa sakom.	
Khilą sakom.	
Rąsunią sakom.	

Sakomanae. She is wearing the ornaments known by the name of *sakom.*

Sakor. } **Sakor sokor.** } **Sokor.** } **Sokor sokor.** } Sound produced by an obstruction in the wind pipe or nostrils, to gurgle, rattle in throat, an imitative word.

Sakor sakorko sąḍe ocoea. They make a sound in the throat like sakor sakor.

Sakor maraokedae. He gave one gurgle (in his throat.)

Sakor marte. } **Sakor mente.** } With a gurgle or sound resembling sakor. Cf. sakor.

Sakor menteye sahećkeda. He breathed with a gurgling sound.

Sakṛa. Narrow, strait, not being room enough.

Sakṛa hor. A narrow way.

Duąrpe sakṛakeda. You made the door narrow.

Sakṛa sąkṛi. Crowded, narrow. strait, to be crowded, to be in a strait or difficulty, to deprive of necessary room.

Sakṛa sąkṛienabon. We are crowded.

Peṛako heċenteko sakṛa sąkṛikediṅa. I am put into a strait by the coming of visitors.

Sakrat. } **Sakrat porob.** } A festival observed on the last three days of the Hindu year.

Sakrat biloǩ. The last day of the Sakrat festival and the last day of the year.

Sąkṛi. Cf. sąkhṛi.

Sąkṛi phol. A tree and its fruit so called.

Saksak. } **Saksakao.** } Quiveringly, tremblingly, to quake, to quiver, to tremble, to shake.

Ruą ehoboǩ jokheć saksak ąikąuǩa. At the beginning of fever one feels a quivering sensation.

Rabaṅte hoṛmo saksaksoǩa. The body shivers or shakes with cold.

Sąkti. } **Sokti.** } **Sukti.** } Strength, power, ability, to warn, to strictly charge.

Sukti hoṛ kanae. He is a man of strength, he is well-to-do.

Sąkti bąnuǩtiṅa. I have no strength, or I am unable to bear the expense.

Enhiloǩ dole sąktikeťpea. We warned you that day.

Sąkuć. To bring into subjection, to subjucate.

Sąkućkedeako. They subjucated him.

Ḍanḍom sąkućkedeako. They fined him and brought him into subjection.

Sakwa. A trumpet made of a horn.

Sakwa. The end of a yoke, the part projecting beyond the bullock's neck.

Sakwa suć. The Purple Sun-bird, *Arachnechthra asiatica.*

Sal. Wedges joining the parts of a solid cart wheel. Cf. sagaṛ.

Sal. A gregarious forest tree, *Shorea robusta, Gœrtn.*

Sal bonkhon modhubonakaṭań. From a forest of sal trees I have made a forest of honey, i. e. I have reclaimed the land from jungle and made it productive.

Sal. House, as in school house; shop, as in workshop; place, as in dancing place.

Kamar sal. A smithy.
Hạnḍi sal. } A liquor shop.
Pạurạ sal. }
Paṭhsal. A school house.
Ạk sal. A place where sugarcane is pressed.
Kaṭ sal. A carpenter's or joiner's workshop.
Lagṛẽ sal. A place where the Lagṛẽ (q. v.) dance is danced.
Piarsalare kamarko salakaṭa. Blacksmiths have opened a smithy in Piarsala.
Dare buṭạreko salakaṭa. Thy have set up a forge under a tree.

Sạl. The Indian Gaur, *Gavœus Gaurus.*

Sạl sakwa. A horn made from a horn of the *Gaur.*

Sal. A year.

Salbhor, The whole year.
Darakan sal. The next year
Ghuri sal. } The coming year, next year.
Ghuriạ sal. }
Hana sal. } Last year.
Calaoen sal. }
Niạ sal. This year.
Salsal. }
Salke sal. } Year after year, yearly, annually.
Salba sal. }
Salbe sal. }

Sal. A shawl, cor. of the English word shawl.

Sala. To pick out impurities, to remove the outer covering, as of peas, Indian corn, &c., to strip, as fibre, &c.

Jonḍra sala. To remove the sheath of Indian corn.
Kaskom sala. To pick impurities out of raw [cotton.
Tulạm sala. To pick impurities out of ginned cotton.
Maṭor sala. To shell peas.
Aṛak sala. To pick mature leaves out from [pot-herbs.
Kạirạ sala. To remove the skin from a plantain.
Ceṭem salaeda? From what are you picking out impurities? i. e. what are you doing?
Kaskomko salaeṭ tahẽkana. They were picking the impurities out of cotton.

Salak. With, along with, together with, to include.

Okoe salakem senlena? Uni salak. With whom did you go? With him.
Buluń salakko joma. They eat it with salt.
Ghãs heṛbedre hoṛo alope salaga. When pulling up the grass do not include the dhan, do not pull up the dhan along with the weeds.
Uni tuluć alom salagińa. Do not couple me with him.
Iń do alope salagińa. Do not include me.

Salaka. A present of cloth given to certain relations of a bride by the bridegroom.

Mamo salaka. A present of cloth given to a bride's maternal aunt. [uncle.
Goṅgo salaka. Given to a bride's paternal
Kaki salaka. Given to a bride's maternal aunt.
Hatom salaka. Given to a bride's paternal aunt.
Salaka gại. A cow given as a return present to the bridegroom by the bride's relatives who receive *salaka* cloth.

Salạmi. A present given to a landlord for granting a lease or bestowing a favour, a present given to a superior.

Gel ṭạka salạmi lagaoadińa. I had to pay ten rupees of salami.
Gel ṭaka salami iń emkeda. I gave ten rupees of salami.

Salas. The first time, unusual, unwonted, rare, new.

Salasreye hećakana. He has come for the first time.
Salas peṛako hećakawadińa. Friends who have never previously visited me have come.

Salaṭ. }
Galaṭ salaṭ. } Stupid, dull-witted, dull heavy looking.
Galaṭ solaṭ. }

Salesal. Yearly, annually.

Salesal khajna emok hoyoka. Rent must be paid annually.

Sale sale. In season, at the proper time.

Ńelpe sale sale matkom ar kuinḍiń emapekana. Behold, I give you matkom (q. v.) and kuinḍi (q. v.) at the proper season.
Sale sale iń boṅgakkana. I offer sacrifices at the proper seasons.

Salga. A large deciduous forest tree, *Boswellia serrata, Wall.*

Salgam. A turnip.

Salgao. To kindle, to light, to cause to burn, to inflame, to be at its height, as harvest or fruit season.

Seṅgel salgaome. Kindle the fire.
Matkom salgaoena. The matkom (q. v.) harvest is at its height.

Salgaṭ. Cf. solgaṭ.

Salha. } To advise, to consult, to be in harmony.
Solho. }

Salha joh kanako. They are consulting together.
Salhaenako. They are in harmony.
Salhateko tahenkana. They are living in harmony.
Mokordoma calao lạgiṭko salhaadea. They advised him to bring a suit in court.

Sạlis. } To mediate, to arbitrate. med-
Sạlisi. } iators, arbitrators.
Noa kathako sạlisiakaṭa. The have arbitrated on this matter.
Sạlisiko hoho jaoraakaṭkoa. } They have call-
Sạlisko hoho jaoraakaṭkoa. } ed together arbitrators.
Noape sạlis jahanlaka? Have you at any time arbitrated on this matter?

Sạlisdar. An arbitrator.

Sal mesal. Mixed, confused.

Salmuṅgạr. A heavy mallet used to put the pieces of a cart wheel together.

Sal muṅgạr. A kind of rice.

Salpoṭ. Small.
Alom āṛgoea salpoṭgeae, tahẽ ocoaeme. Do not bring it down (a pigeon from the nest) it is small, let it remain.
Nui salpoṭ mara gidrạ. This little imp of a child.

Salsal. } Fat, in prime condition, appli-
Salsạliạ. } ed mainly to cattle.
Acha salsạliạ meromem ṅamakadea. You have got a very fine, fat goat.
Sạlsạliạ meromko ṅeloḱkana. The goats appear to be in prime condition.
Salsalko ṅeloḱkana. They are in prime condition.

Salsãt. } Complete absence of any
Saltant. } disturbing or disquieting
Saltãt. } element, relief, deliverance, easement, alleviation, concord, harmony, safety, security, danger past, freedom from fear, or anxiety.
Nitoḱ do saltãtenako. Now they are at peace, now they are free from anxiety.
Noa bir do bes saltãtgea. This jungle is very safe.
Disom saltantgea. The country is at peace, is at rest, is pacified.
Hoṛo beleẽnteko saltantena. They are free from anxiety owing to the rice being ripe.
Nonḍenko do bako ruạ baṛaḱkana saltãtgeako. Those of this place are not now suffering from fever, they are now relieved.

Sạluć bạkuć. } Confused, disorderly, in
Sạluć bạguć. } disorder.
Kathako sạluć bạkućkeda. They confused the matter.
Sạluć bạkućko dohoakada. They have put them down in disorder.

Sama. A cess levied in kind by Zemindars at the Dạsại (q. v.) festival.
Sama lagaoaṅkana. I have to pay the *sama* cess.
Sama daka jome senakantalea. He has gone to eat *sama* rice, i. e. gone to pay the *sama* cess.

Sama cakor. Cf. cama.

Sama ghãs. An excellent fodder grass, *Panicum colonum, Linn.*

Samagiri. } Materials, elements.
Samagri. }
Boṅga samagiri. The materials for an offering to a deity.
Bapla samagiri. The materials required for the proper celebration of a marriage.

Samaḱ. To chop, to hack, to chop off or up.
Kạṭupe samaḱkeṭtaea. He chopped off his finger.

Samaḱ. To go away, used only by women.
Okate samaḱ kedetale? Where has our (or my husband) gone to?
Ceṭ ṅam samaḱ idileṭmea? What did you go to [get?

Samaḱ saṅ Murmu. A sub-sept of the Santal sept Murmu (q. v.)

Saman. } Cor. of the English words
Somon. } summon, and summons.
Saman jạri. To serve a summons.
Samanadeako. They summoned him.
Saman jạri lạgiṭe heċakana. He has come to serve a summons.

Saman. }
Miṭ saman. } Equal, similar, alike, akin,
Soman. } one, uniform, the same.
Miṭ soman. }
Dene banar samangea. Both extremities are alike.
Miṭ samanoḱako. They will become uniform.
Miṭ samangeako. They are equal.

Samaṅ. Front, to front or face.
Samaṅ seć. } The front.
Samaṅ sen. }
Samaṅre. Before, in front, in presence of.
Samaṅ ḍạṭa. The front teeth.
Purub seće samaṅkeda. He faced the east.
Bhit sene samaṅkeda. He faced the wall, he turned round fronting the wall.
Iṅ samaṅreye teṅgoakan tahẽkana. He was standing in front of me.
Maṅjhi samaṅreye roṛkeda. He spoke in the presence of the Maṅjhi (q. v.)

Samaṅ. To offer an offering or sacrifice, to place in front of.
Dāṛẽko samaṅkeṭkoa. They offered sacrifices.
Hoṛoko samaṅkeda. They offered dhan, they made an offering of dhan.
Baha porobre matkom ar sarjom bahako samaṅa. At the flower festival they offer matkom (q. v.) and sarjom (q. v.) flowers.
Dāṛẽko boṅgako samaṅakoa. They offer sacrifices to the boṅgas (q. v.)
Dakae samaṅadea. He placed boiled rice before him. [him.
Sandesko samaṅadea. They made presents to
Samaṅaḱ. An offering that has been offered.
Samaṅoḱaḱ. An offering not yet offered.
Samaṅić. A sacrifice that has been offered.
Samaṅoḱić. A sacrifice that has not yet been offered.

Samani. } Many, much, great, an ad-
Somani. } jective or an adverb possessing intensifying force.

Somani gharicem taheena. You stayed a very long time.

Samaniko dukkedea. They caused him very much sorrow.

Somani horko heć jarwalena. Very many people were assembled.

Somani takako agukedea. They fined him heavily.

Samaniko dalkedea. They beat him severely.

Samaniye dukena. He is in very great sorrow.

Samanom. A obsolete name for gold.

Samao. To be contained in. Cf. sahop.

Samar. Cf. sambar.

Sambao. To put into, to fill into, as anything into a jar, box, &c.

Tukuereye sambaokeda. He put it into a pot.

Sambar. } Provision for a short
Satu sambar. } journey or outing, generally roasted grain or meal which does not require cooking.

Cet sambarem aguakata? What food have you brought as provision for the journey?

Satu sambaranteko calaoena. They have gone taking with them provision for the way.

Sambhaora. Rubbish, grass, stubble, &c. adhering to a plough or harrow when at work.

Sambhaora ocokkam. Knock off the stubble, &c. sticking on your plough.

Nahelre sambhaora lagaoakana. Rubbish is sticking on the plough.

Sambhe. A ferule put on the end of a piece of wood to prevent it splitting.

Dhinki sambhe. The ferule on the end of the pestle of a dhinki (q. v.)

Tok sambhe. The ferule on the end of a *tok* (q. v.)

Sambhrao. Cf. sambrao.

Sambir. The back, on the back.

Sambirkam. Lay it on its back, i. e. the broadest side.

Sambirteye gitićakana. He is lying on his back.

Sambirkaeme. Lay him on his back.

Sambirteye bindarlena. He fell backwards.

Sambrao. } To hold or keep together.
Sambhrao. } to sustain, to assist, to help, to protect, to restrain, to check.

Bae sap sambrao dareadea. He could not restrain him, could not prevent him falling.

Sambrao sumuń hataome. Take only as much as you can manage or are able to hold, repay, carry, &c.

Edre bae sambrao dareada. He could not restrain his anger.

Mone bae sambrao dareattaea. He could not restrain his grief.

Mone sambraokettaeae, bae aral gidilaka. He controlled his spirit (grief), he did not give it rein, he did not relax his control of it.

Samdhi. Used by the fathers of a married couple when addressing each other.

Same game. Quietly, peaceably, in a friendly way.

Same gamete jom ńuitabonpe, alope ragar cagartabona. Eat and drink quietly, do not wrangle.

Same gamete endege sanam kathale sutrauket-te apan apin orakle ruarena. We enquired there into the matter in a friendly way and then returned each to his own home.

Same game bale badaea, cet coń hoeena, cet coń bań hoeen. We are oblivious of what may have taken place, and of what may not have taken place.

Same gamete kamime, onte note alom cahap catur baraea. Work quietly, do not keep looking about.

Samek. A vision, representation of some person seen in a dream.

Sameke ńelkette botor gotenae. He was frightened through seeing a vision.

Kukmute samekiń ńelkeda. In a dream I saw a vision.

Samek iń ńelkeda ayah bińe gerkediń, okoe pera cońko hećabona. In a vision I saw a snake bite me, some friends will visit us.

Samet. } With, along with, together
Samit. } with.

Sud samet. } Together with interest.
Sod samit. }

Samge. To reconcile, to make up a quarrel, to be reconciled, to become friendly.

Samgeenakin. They are reconciled.

Bujhantar hor do sanamko tuluć samgeakan-geko tabena. Men of understanding remain on friendly terms with all.

Nui do ale samge hor kanae. This is a friend of ours, he is not our enemy.

Samit. With, along with, together with.

Sod samit. } Together with interest.
Sud samit. }

Samjhao. To comprehend, to understand, to explain, convince, undeceive, warn, admonish, instruct, pacify, persuade, reason with, reconcile.

Bale samjhao dareadea. We could not make him understand, we could not get him to accede to our wishes.

Samjhaoem. Admonish him.

Samkasati. Face to face, to confront.

Samkasatiketkinale. We brought them face to face.

Samkasatikin kapharianena. They quarrelled face to face.

Samkhol. A kind of large wading bird.

Samna sạmni. In front, face to face, confronting.
Samna sạmnikaťkinale. We confronted them with each other.
Samna sạmnikin roporena. They wrangled face to face.

Sampak.
Sompok. } Relationship.
Ceť sampak kantapea? What is your relationship?

Samphola. The whole crop, the whole, a full crop no part of which suffered from blight, insects, drought, &c. &c.
Samphola oṛaktele aderkeda. We housed a full crop.
Samphola hoṛo beleakana. The whole of the dhan is ripe.

Sạmṭi umṭi. Bag and baggage, all one's worldly possessions.
Sạmṭi umṭiko calaoena. They have left taking all their worldly possessions with them.
Sạmṭi umṭi jotoko idikeťtakoa. They took away all that they possessed.

Samṛao. Cf. sambṛao.

Samsao. To dare, to venture.
Nonḍe bako samsao daṛeaľkana. They cannot venture here.
Bagạhi birre bako samsao daṛeaka. They cannot venture into a forest infested with wild beasts.
Gaḍa unạk peredakante hoṛ do bako samsao daṛeaka paromoľ lạgiť. People cannot venture to cross the river when it is so full.
Boloľ do bako samsaoka. They will not dare to enter.

Samṭao. To constringe, to compress, to collect together, to amass, to fold up, as a garment, &c., to garner.
Joľ samṭaokedae. She swept it all together.
Samṭaote duṛuppe. Sit together, sit close to each other.
Ir samṭaokedako. They reaped and garnered (the crops.)
Samṭao cabakedako. They garnered all (the crop.)

Sạmud.
Sạmut } A sea, the sea.
Soṛa sạmudte buhelen Siń sadom do. The Day horse has floated away to the Sora sea.

Sạmudar.
Sạmundar. } The sea.

Sạmuk.
Sạmukre. } In front of, in presence of, before one's face.
Iń sạmukrekin epemena. They gave in my presence.

Sạmundar phen. A variety of rice.

Sạmuń. The end, the finish, just sufficient, completely,
Ńel sạmuńkedeale. We saw the last of him, i. e. saw him die.
Er sạmuńge tahẽkana. There was just sufficient for sowing.
Mahajon reaľ em sạmuńge tahẽkana. There was just sufficient to pay the Mahajon his due.
Sạmuńkateko dohoakaťa. They have laid the heads or ends one way.
Soloľ bokoľ do alope dohoea sạmuńte baṛe dohoepe. Do not place them in disorder, place all the heads or ends one way.

Sạmut. Cf. sạmud.

San. A revolving whetstone, used for sharpening razors, knives, &c., to grind on a whetstone, to sharpen, to whet.
San lạgiťe kolakaťa. He has sent it to be whetted.
Holaťe sankeda. He ground the razor.
Sasanić. A grinder, a whetter.

San.
San boṅga. } The fourth Hindu month, July-August.

San.
Son. } The fibre yielding plant, *Crotalaria juncea, Linn.*
San jạṛĩ.
Son jạṛĩ. } The fibre of *Crotalaria juncea.*

Sana. Wish, desire, lust, to wish, to desire, to lust.
Calaľ sanaedińkana. I have a desire to go.
Bhabnaṛe sanaedińkana. I have a feeling of sorrow.
Lajao hõ bań sanaea. He has no feeling of shame.

Sanaľ. Instantly, at once.
Saram do ṭhukedeteye sanaľ marao goťena. The Sambar deer through being shot fell down at once.

Sanaľ marte.
Sanaľ mente. } On the instant, instantly.
Sanaľ marteye bindạṛena. He fell down on the instant.

Sanam. All.
Sanam ṭhen.
Sanam ṭạnḍi.
Sanam pạṛa. } Every where.
Sanamko calạoena. All have gone.
Sanamaľko. All things.
Sanamkoko idikeťkoa. They took them (animates) all away.
Sanamaľkoko idikeda. They took away all the things.

Sanaphana. Equipment, furniture, apparatus, materials, tools, arms.
Lạṛhại sanaphana. Arms, military equipment.
Sanaphanaante menaea. He is armed.
Oṛaľ sanaphana. Materials for the erection of a house.

Sãnc. A mould, a matrix. Cf. sãc.

Sańcao. } To lay past, to save.
Sońcao. }

Miṭ hajar ṭakae sańcao oṭolaḱa. He left savings to the amount of a thousand rupees.
Ḍher ṭakae sańcao dohoakaṭa. He has saved and laid past much money.
Gidrḁ lḁgiṭe sańcao oṭoakada. He left savings for the children.

Sanchep. Abridged, concisely, shortly, with brevity.

Sanchep kḁtha. An abridged statement.
Sanchepteye lḁiadińa. He told me concisely.

Sanḍ. A bull.

Sanḍ ḍahra. A bull.

Sanḍaṅ. } To lie down, to fall backwards,
Sãḍaṅ. } used by women only when fault finding.

Nonḍe sanḍaṅenae. He is lying here.
Okare coe sanḍaṅen, nonḍe do bae sanḍaṅlena. He lay down somewhere he did not lie here.
Sanḍaṅ goṭenae. He fell backwards.

Sanḍaṗ. To move as the jaws, to open or shut.

Moca baṅ sanḍaboḱkantaea. His mouth is not opening, he does not speak.
Ontere do aḍi sanḍaṗentaea, nonḍe do baṅ sanḍaboḱkantaea. She spoke plenty there, here she will not open her mouth.
Gojako chaḍaolekhan sanḍaṗ midoḱa. If they remove the wedge the edges will come together, or close. [a spring.)
Sanḍaṗena. It has closed, (with a snap as by

Sanḍasi. Tongs, pincers.

Sanḍe. Cor. of the English word Sunday.

Sandes. A present generally consisting of eatables or liquor given by a visitor to the person visited.

Sandes bajna. Music supplied by drummers hired by a guest to play at a marriage.
Sandes hḁnḍi. Liquor brought by a visitor and presented to his entertainer.

Sanḍgar. M. } A shameless, lustful
Sanḍgur. M. } person, having the
Chandgar. F. } propensities of a bull.

Sanḍgar kanae. }
Sanḍgḁr hoṛ kanae. } He is a shameless person.

Sanḍgaria. M. }
Chandgaria. F. } A shameless, lustful person. Cf. sanḍgar.
Chandgoria. F. }

Sanḍgariḁ kanae He is a shameless person.

Sandhaoṛe. } To enter, to force oneself
Sandhaṛe. } in, used by women and generally of a second wife.

Ńeńel tulućem sandhaoṛeakana. You went in with your eyes open.

Sanḍharu. A female buffaloe up till she has her first calf.

Sḁnḍhin. A quey, a heifer.

Sḁnḍi. A cock.

Sim sḁnḍi. }
Sḁnḍi sim. } A cock.

Sḁnḍi karkar potam. The little Brown Dove, *Turtur Cambayensis.*

Sanḍ manḍ. } Ugly, unsymmetric, ill
Sonḍ monḍ. } proportioned, irregular, shapeless.

Sonḍ monḍe moṭaakana. She is fat to shapelessness.

Sandṛa sondṛe. } Feeling every where, as
Sondṛa sundṛi. } when searching for something, putting in the hands, or the nose, as a dog.

Sandṛa sondṛeye ńam baṛaeda. He is inserting his nose every where in his search for it.

Sandoṛaṅ. }
Sanduṛaṅ. } Open, uncovered, naked.

Sandoṛaṅe gitićakana. He is lying uncovered, or naked. [left it open.
Sandoṛaṅe oṭaḱ oṭoakada. He opened it and

Sanegumane. } Quietly, stealthily, calm-
Senegumane. } ly, passively.

Sane gumaneko thirena. They became perfectly silent.
Nui herelma sane gumane ńele ńeleńkana se. This man keeps stealthily watching me.
Noa katha reaḱ do sane gumane ceṭ orge baṅ badaea. I am completely oblivious of the beginning of this matter.

Saṅ bhai. }
Soṅ bhai. } A companion.

Ṭheṅga reaḱko mena, niḁ kantińa saṅ bhai. They say of a club this is my companion.

Saṅga. A beam laid breadthwise supporting the roof of a house.

Saṅga. A friend, a companion, a comrade.

Saṅgańrege satahedińae. I am encourged by my companion.

Saṅgat. Used by brothers-in-law when addressing each other.

Saṅgat okare menama? Menańgea ho saṅgat.

Saṅgar. To go, to walk.

Oka bḁbiḁpe dḁṛẽakaṭ saṅgarakaṭ? To what distance, or to what point have you travelled?
Duk muhim ḁuri parom saṅgaroḱre do caḱ baṅ gitićen. Why did I sleep before my difficulties had passed?

Saṅgaṛhe. To support, aid, assist by taking hold of.

Saṅgaṛhekate ruḁḱko daḱko ańuakoa. They support sick people when they give them water to drink.
Saṅgaṛhekate dakale jom ocokedea. We supported him while he ate.
Saṅgaṛhe idikedeako, aćte do bae sen daṛelena. They took him away supporting him, he could not walk by himself.

Saṅge. Numerous, many, very many, thick, as trees, hair, &c.

Saṅge hoṛko heéena. Many people have come.
Saṅgeēnale. We have become numerous.
Uṗ saṅge ar jeleṅge tahẽkantaea. His hair was thick and long.

Saṅgha. To marry a second time, of a widower, widow or divorcee of either sex.

Saṅghaenaṅ. I (who have been previously married) have married (one who has also been previously married.)
Saṅghakedeae. He (a widower or a divorcee) married her (a widow or divorcee.)
Saṅghaanaṅ. I have taken a second wife, (both parties having been previously married.)

Sạṅgil. To look up, to raise or throw back the head.

Saṅgil ṅogoǩme. Look up a little.
Sạṅgilkate daǩo ṅukeda. He threw back his head and drank the water.
Sim sạṅgilkate daǩko ṅuia. Fowls raise the head to drink water.

Sạṅgiṅ. Distant, far, a long way off, long.

Sạṅgiṅ hor kana. It is a long way.
Sạṅgiṅ ren kanaṅ. I am from a distance.
Alom edre sạṅgiṅaṅa. Do not put yourself at a distance from me in anger.
Onkate ma ạdi sạṅgiṅoǩa. By that way it will be very distant.
Sạṅgiṅkedeako. They put him to a distance.
Sạṅgiṅediṅa. It is far for me (to go.)

Saṅgin. A bayonet.

Saṅgṛa. } Saṅgṛi. } A pole carried on the shoulders of two men from which things to be carried are slung, to carry slung on a pole. Cf. ṭaḍa.

Saṅgṛa kaṭ. A pole for carrying.
Saṅgṛakateko idikeda. They slung it on a pole and took it away.

Sạṅgṛạu. To collect, to amass, to lay past.

Poesa thoṛae sạṅgṛạuakaťteye uṡkana. He is bumptious through having amassed a little money.
Aė motoe sạṅgṛạuakawana. He has laid past for himself.

Saṅgri. Cf. saṅgra.

Saṅsar. } Soṅsar. } The world.

Sạṅti. A companion.

Hape, sạṅti iṅ ṅamlege. Wait, let me first get a companion.

Saṅwar. A companion.

Saṅwar menaetiṅa. I have a companion.

Sạni. Again, over again, re.

Sạni saman. A re-summons.
Sạni samanadeako. They resummoned him.
Sạǩni lạlis hoyoǩa. Must petition again, prefer another complaint.

Sạniạu. To be determined, to have made up one's mind, to be prepared for, to be angry, to be excited, to rouse anger.

Lại sạniạukedeae. He told him and roused his anger.
Sạniạu calaǩkanako. They are going excited with anger.

Saṅj. A meal.

Miť saṅj. One meal.
Bar saṅj. Two meals.
Caole miť saṅj hoyoǩtalea. The rice will be one meal for us.
Miť saṅj iṅ peṛakeťkoa. I entertained them to one meal. [of this.
Niạ do bar saṅjae. He will make two meals

Saṅjhe maṅjhe. } Saṅjhe na maṅjhe. } Between meals.

Saṅjhe na maṅjhem heéena, tinrele isinama? You have come between meals, when will we cook for you?

Saṅjholi. Evening, beginning at evening and lasting long.

Saṅjholi daǩe lagaokeda, bae asoṛ hoda. The rain has set in at evening, it will not soon cease.
Saṅjholireko lagaokaťa, bako eneć mokoṅoǩkana. They began in the evening they are not tired of dancing.

Sạṅjlạ. M. } Sạṅjli. F. } The third, applied to sons, daughters, sons-in-law and daughters-in-law.

Sạṅjlạ koṛa. The third son.
Sạṅjli kuṛi. The third daughter.
Sạṅjlạ jãwãe. Husband of third daughter, third son-in-law.
Sạṅjli jãwãe. Third daughter's husband.
Sạṅjli bạhu. Wife of third son.
Sạṅjlạić. The third son.
Sạṅjliić. The third daughter.
Huḍiṅ sạṅjlạ. The fourth son, where there are five or more.

Saṅjok. } Solo saṅjok. } The full complement of requirements for a marriage celebration, requirements in the form of food for an emergency; at times, now and again.

Solo saṅjokbo jumạulege atmabon boda.
Solo saṅjok utuko emalea. At times they give us relish (to our food.)

Saṅjok. Opportunity, proper time, timely.

Saṅjok paṛao. } Saṅjok lagao. } To be opportune.
Saṅjok lagaoena nonḍegeṅ ṅamkedea. It was opportune, I got it here.
Saṅjoke heć gotena. He came opportunely.
Saṅjokreye heéena. He came at the proper time.
Saṅjok paṛaoena, iṅ ṅamkeda. It was opportune, I got it.

Sańjot. } The ceremonies performed on
Sońjot. } the first day of certain festivals, shaving, washing clothes, cleaning houses, &c., &c., and partaking of the evening meal.

Sońjotedale teheń. We are observing the ceremonies proper to this the first day of the (Karma) festival, (or the Dasãe festival, &c. &c.)

Sãnk. A conch. Cf. sãk.

San karla. A wild plant, *Hiptage madablota, Gaertn.*

Sankha. A wrist ornament made of shell worn by women.

Sạnmuk. } Opposite, confronting, to
Sonmuk. } confront, without the interposition of a second person.

Iń sạnmukiń ńelkeda. I myself saw it.

Sansan. Rustling, an imitative word.

Jambro biń dạṛ jokheć sansanko saḍe ocoea. When pythons move rapidly they produce a rustling noise.

Daḱ baṛaṅoḱ deladili sansan saḍea. When water is about to boil it produces a sound resembling *sansan sansan*.

Gạruṛko uḍạu calaḱre sansanko saḍe ocoea. When the adjutant birds are flying past they produce a rustling sound, a sound resembling sansan produced by the flapping of their wings.

Sansan daḱ hijuḱkana. A storm (rain) producing a sound resembling sansan is coming.

Sansanao. To be excited or frenzied, to move rapidly as when excited or in a frenzy.

Edrete sansanao calaoenae. He rushed away in anger.

Sansanaoakanae edrete. He is inspired by anger.

Jom sansanaoakanae. He has eaten his fill.

Aphor sansanao dareẽna. The dhan seedlings grew rapidly.

Sansanaoḱ kanae dadal lạgiť. He is taken possession of by a desire to strike.

Sansar. The world.

Sansun. } Silent, hushed, no sound aud-
Sunsạn. } ible.

Sanam hoṛko gitićlenkhan sansun ṣikạuḱa. When all the people are asleep there is silence.

Santal.
Santar.
Sãotal.
Sãotar. } A Santal.

Santalni.
Sãotarni. } A Santal female.

Sansunia. A kind of beetle, *sternocera corysis.* Cf. sunsunia.

Santao. To afflict, to cause sorrow, suffering or distress, to persecute.

Alope santaoea. Do not afflict him, do not cause him suffering.

Santap. } Affliction, distress, to cause
Satap. } sorrow or suffering.

Ạdi santap menaea. He is greatly afflicted.

Ạdiko santapediña. They cause me much suffering.

Iñaḱ santapgea. It is my affliction.

Sanṭhao. } To be strong, to be strength-
Saṭhao. } ened, to recover strength.

Hoṛo sanṭhaoakana. The dhan seedlings have recovered themselves (recovered the erect position after having been transplanted.)

Neḱege sanṭhao ńoḱakanae. Only now has he got a little strength.

Jeḍer sanṭhaolenge. Let the sunshine first be strong.

Joroḱ sanṭhaoenae. He has warmed himself and got strength.

Jom sanṭhaoenae. He has eaten and is strengthened.

Reṅgećge tahẽkanae, netarge sanṭhao ńoḱakanae. He was poor, but recently he has become a little strong.

Sạnthi maric. A kind of pepper.

Sạnti. Peace.

São. } Together, with, along with,
São são. } in company with.

Sãogele tahẽkana. We were together.

Am sãore menaḱa? Is it with you?

Am sãote senlenae? Did he go with you?

Ạliń do são sãoliń hećena. We two came together.

Miť são. Level, plain.

Aṛgom miť sãokedako. They harrowed it level.

Sãotenić. A companion.

Sãotenko. Companions.

Am sãotenko okoekoko tahẽkana? Who were your companions?

Ać sãokeťkoae. He took them with him, he got them on his side.

Sãoãr. Straight and of uniform thickness, straight grained.

Saoda. } Trade, traffic, marketing, wares,
Soeda. } merchandise, goods; to trade, to traffic, to buy, to purchase goods.

Cedaḱem polomlaḱa? Ạdi okoćiń saodaeť tahẽkana. Why did you delay? I was buying many things.

Saoda bań ṣkrińakantalea. Our wares are not sold.

Sãohã. } To marry, applied to the
Baha sãohã. } marriage of a person who has been previously married.

Baha sãohãkeťkinale. We married them.

The ceremony observed at a marriage of this kind is that the man sticks a flower in the back hair of the woman with his left hand.

Sãohã. Well, befitting, proper, seemly, effectively.
Oyo sãohãkadeae. He covered him up properly.
Doho sãohãkedeako. They kept him and took care of him.
Kicriće sãohãkeda. He arranged his clothes properly.
Goras sãohã. To keep and provide for, as for one who is unable to provide for himself.
Goras sãohãkedeae. He took charge of him.
Duṛup̠ sãohãk̠me. Sit properly.

Sãoṛa. M } **Sãuṛi.** F } Dark grey colour.
Sãoṛa ḍanṛa. A dark grey bullock.
Sãuṛi gại. A dark grey cow.

Sãoraj. A small wild plant, *Vernonia anthelmintica, Willd.*

Sãorao. To bring round, to bring to one's senses, to win over, to talk over, to persuade.
Usạt̠lenae, adoko sãoraokedea. She was sulking and they brought her round.
Ado apatteć oḍokkate sãoraokedeae. Then the father went out and persuaded him.

Sãore. Cf. são.

Sãotal. } **Sãotar.** } A Santal.
Sãotalni. } Sãotarni. } A Santal female.

Sãote. Cf. são.

Sãoten. Cf. são.

Sap̠. To seize, to take hold of, to hold, to catch.
Sap̠kedeako. They caught him.
Kitape sap̠akat̠ tahẽkana. He was holding a book.
Khajna reaṅko sap̠ duṛup̠akadea. They compelled him to sit on account of rent.
Ceť sap̠kateń calak̠a? What shall I take in my hand?
Jo do baṅ sap̠lena. It did not fruit.
Jo do sabok̠ coṅ baṅ coṅ, menkhan khub bahaakana. I can't say if it will fruit or not, but it has flowered well.
Katharegeye sap̠ena. He was caught by his words.
Uni hõ enećreye sap̠lena. She also was engaged in the dance, she also joined hands in the dance
Sabok̠ae nahak̠. He will be caught presently.

Sapaharia. A snake charmer, one who performs with snakes.

Sapap̠. The Reciprocal form of sap̠ (q. v.)
Ḍạn reak̠ko sapap̠kana. They are accusing each other of being witches.
Eneć jokhećko sapap̠a. When dancing they hold each other (by the hand.)
Ako akoko sapap̠ena. They caused each other to be caught.
Sapap̠katekin calaena. They went away holding each other by the hand.

Sapap̠. Arms, tools, implements, instruments, gear.
Sendra reak̠ sapap̠. Gear for hunting.
Raj mistri reak̠ sapap̠. The tools of a mason.
Baḍhoe reak̠ sapap̠. The tools of a carpenter.
Kurta rorok̠ reak̠ sapap̠. The tools with which to sew a coat.
Lạṛhại reak̠ sapap̠. Arms.

Sapaonja. To be harmonious, to live in peace, harmony, peace.
Jaejug baṅgeko sapaonjak̠a. They will never live in peace.
Sapaonjate bako tahena. They will not live in harmony.

Saparom. A small tree, *Nyctanthus arbor-tristis, Linn.*

Sap̠dap̠. Serving at a feast, to serve, to assist.
Sap̠dap̠ hoṛ kanako. They are the servers at the feast.
Sap̠ dap̠ko disạkope. Remember the servers (to give them food.)

Sapha. Clean, clear, distinct, to clean.
Sapha dak̠. Clean or clear water.
Ạrup̠ sapha. To wash clean.
Jok̠ sapha. To sweep clean, to clean by sweeping.
Irci sapha. To clean (the inside of the thatch and rafters) by throwing white wash (on them.)
Urisu sapha. To clean out (a house.)
Um sapha. To clean by bathing.
Oṛak̠ko saphaakat̠a. They have cleaned the house.
Noa katha reak̠le saphakeda. We settled, or cleared up this matter.
Noa buru ạdi saphage ńelok̠kana. This hill appears very distinctly.
Nitok̠ saphaena, rimile oṭaṅakat̠a. Now it is clear, the clouds have been carried or blown away.
Kunạmi jokheć khub saphae terdeja. At full moon the moonlight is very bright.

Saphại. To settle a dispute, to clear up a disputed matter.
Noa kathale saphạikoda. We settled this matter.

Saphar. } **Saphor.** } **Sophor.** } A journey, a tour, to journey, to tour.
Saphorko hećakana.

Saphri am. The guava. Cf. ạmrud.

Sapin dare. The Prickly Pear, *Opuntia Dillenii, How.*

Sapo. Harmony, peace, amity.
Sapote bae tahen dareak̠kana. He cannot live in peace.
Ạdi sapote menak̠koa. They are very harmonious.

Sapoť. } Gentle, quiet, peaceable, pacific.
Sopot. }
Uni sadom do ạliye sapoťa. This horse is very quiet.
Sapoť hoṛ. A peaceable man.

Sapotia. Cf. sapoť.

Sapṛao. To get ready, to prepare.
Calaǩle sapṛaoakana. We are ready to go.
Sanamaǩ sapṛao hoeena. All is ready.

Saprot. } To make over to, to give in custody, to entrust, to deliver.
Soprot. }
Sạprud. }
Suprud. }
Sạprudadeako. They gave into his custody.
Polis sạprud hoeena. It is in the custody of the police.

Sạprum. Completely, fully, entirely, full.
Il sạprumenae. It is full fledged.
Hara sạprumenako sim hoponko do. The chickens are full grown.
Gele sạprumena. It is in full ear.
Hoṛo bele sạprumena. The rice is fully ripe.

Sapsor. To provide, to bring together the materials required for a festival, feast, &c.
Sanamaǩ sapsorena, eken daǩka. All is ready only the cooking (is to do.)
Neǩe sanam sapsorena. Only just now has all been provided.

Sapṭa. To put close together, to stick together, to join closely.
Baṅ sapṭaǩkana up do. The hair is not close together, is not smooth.

Sạr. Level, smooth.
Sạr ot. Level ground.

Sạr. A pad for an elephant's back.
Hạti sạr. An elephant pad.

Sar. } Cf. sạgun.
Sar sạgun. }
Sar sạgun besge ńamakana. The omen is good.

Sar. An arrow, to pierce with an arrow.
Aǩ sar. A bow and arrow.
Apạri sar. An arrow with an iron head.
Ṭuṭi sar. A blunt arrow.
Laṅṭa sar. A naked arrow, an unfeathered [arrow.
Ṭhoṅga sar. A magazine for arrows.
Sar ṭhoṅga. The arrow tube of a cross bow.
Sar mayam. A hunting term, blood drawn by an arrow.
Jahanko sar mayamleko eneć uni doe jom ńam joṅa. He is not allowed to partake of food until an animal has been wounded to the effusion of blood by an arrow.

Saṛ. To open, as a flower, the eyes of a kitten, puppy, &c., the hood of a snake, an umbrella, a mushroom, &c., &c.
Baha saṛena. The flower has opened.
Jhiṅga baha saṛena, nitoǩ do ạyuṗena. The Jhiṅga (q. v.) flowers have opened, now it is evening.
Ayaṅ biṅko saṛoǩa. Cobras also open out, i. e., raise their hood.
Pusi hoponko reaǩ meť saṛentakoa. The eyes of the kittens are open.
Catom mase saṛtam. Come, put up your umbrella.
Koṛako ńamkedea menkhan tolkateko dal saṛoa, eken jiwi geko dohoetaea. If the young men find him they bind him and beat him severely, they leave him only his life.

Sāṛ. A bull. Cf. saṇḍ.
Sāṛ ḍahra. A bull.

Sar. A tall grass, *Saccharum Sara, Roxb.*, from the culms of which arrow shafts are made.

Sara. A funeral pyre.

Sara daḥri. A cloth given to the bride's youngest brother by the bridegroom.

Sara. To turn over on the back, to tumble about like a horse on the ground, to bend the body as an Indian athlete practicing.
Pạk donkoko saraǩa. The dancers of the sword and shield dance tumble about.
Kulại nonḍeko saralena. Hares have been tumbling here, rolling over and over.

Sara. The whole, all.
Sara din. The whole day.
Sara rạt. The whole night.
Sara din sara rạte daǩkeda. It rained the whole day and the whole night.

Sarać soroć. } To cry as children with snuffling or snivelling.
Sarać suruć. }
Netar mandateko sarać sorojoǩkana Now-a-days people are suffering from slight colds.
Sarać surućko raǩeda. They are crying and snuffling.

Saṛae. A series of sticks fixed in the ground upon which a weaver sets his warp.

Saragbạti. A rocket.

Sarại. A caravanserai, a native inn.

Sarajan. } Materials, elements, used mainly with regard to marriages, offerings and sacrifices.
Saraṅjan. }
Sorojon. }
Soromjom. }
Bapla sarajan. The materials required for the proper celebration of a marriage.
Boṅga sarajan. The materials required for an offering or sacrifice to a deity.

Saraǩ saraǩ. Crushing, crunching, rasping, wrenching sound, imitative.
Saraǩ saraǩ babere uǩuṅkana. He is twisting the twine and causing a rasping sound.
Saraǩ saraǩe jomeda. He is crunching.

Sarak sarak añjomokkana. A sound of crunching is heard.
Sarak sarakko hoda hoṛo do. They strip the ears of dhan with the hand and produce a sound of wrenching.

Sarak marte. } With a sound of crushing, crunching, rasping or wrenching.
Sarak mente. }

Saram. The Sambar stag, *Rusa aristotelis.*

Saram babea. A species of Mongoose or Ichneumon, *Herpestes moticolus.*

Saram lutur. A small flowering plant, *Clerodendron serratum, Spreng.*
The leaves of this plant in shape resemble the ears of the Saram (q. v.) stag, hence the name.

Saraṅga. A kind of fiddle.

Sãṛaṅgom. Cf. sãṛgom.

Sarao. To surmount, to get over, to recover, to throw off the effects of liquor, narcotics, &c., to complete.
Kạmim saraoket khan, me delaṅ laṅ calaka. If you have surmounted, or completed your work, come, let us go.
Mitṭen doe saraokeda, ar mitṭen doe goćena. One recovered, surmounted his illness, and one died.

Sarañjan. Cf. sarajan.

Sarap. A curse, to curse.
Sarapadeako. They cursed him.

Sarapiạ. A curser, one given to cursing.
Ạḍi sarapiạ hoṛ kanae. He is a person much given to cursing.

Sarasar. Equally, not inferior or superior to each other, neck and neck.
Sarasarkin ropoṛena. They wrangled equally, one did not exceed the other.
Sarasarkin dạṛ idikeda. They ran neck and neck.

Saṛasi. } Tongs, pincers. Cf. ṣanḍasi.
Saṛsi. }

Sarbat. } Sherbet.
Sorbot. }

Sarbharao. } To have presence of mind, to occur to one on the spur of the moment, to feel an impulse to, to suggest itself to, to compass.
Sorbhorao. }
Sarbharao oco. To give an impulse to, to stimulate, to inspire, to put up to, to prompt, to encourage.
Bana tuluć ńapamlenre oeć hõ baṅ sarbharaolentaea. When he met with the bear he lost all presence of mind.
Roṛ lạgiće sarbharaoena. He felt impelled to speak, or had presence of mind to speak.
Roroṛ baṅ sarbharaokkantaea. He has not the presence of mind or power to speak, it does not occur to him what to say.
Sarbharao ocokedeae. He encouraged, or inspired him (to speak.)
Ṭakaṅ sarbharaokeda. I compassed the payment of the money.

Sardar. } A foreman.
Sordar. }
Odga sardar. Odga the foreman.
Sardarenae. He has become a foreman.

Sạrdi. To be at the maximum, utmost height, highest pitch or culminating point, to be in full swing.
Hoṛo rohoeko sạrdiakaṭa. They are in the height of dhan planting.
Matkom ạuri sạrdika. The matkom (q. v.) season is not yet at its height.
Ruạsạrdiakantaea. His fever has increased, or is at its height.

Sạrdum bạrdum. Rough on the surface, grass, weeds, &c. not covered by the plough.
Sạrdum bạrdumko siakaṭa. They have not covered the weeds when they ploughed.
Pạhil dhaoko silekhan sạrdum bạrdum ńeloka. After the first ploughing weeds, grass, &c. appear above the soil.

Sareć. To remain, to be left, to exceed, to survive, to be in excess.
Ale lạgiṭko sareć dohoakaṭa. They have left and put aside a part for us.
Ceṭ hõ baṅ sarećlena. Nothing was left over.
Jom sarećkedae. He ate and left a part, he did not eat all.
Itạ ńutumteye sareć dohoakaṭa. He has reserved some for seed.
Sareć kaṭ sagaṛ ạguipe. Bring the remaining timber on a cart.

Sareć bareć. What is remaining or left over, the remainder, balance, remnant, remains.
Sareć bareć tinạk menaka, ona ạguipe. Bring all that has been left.

Sareṛ. To overflow, to be full and run over.
Perećć sareṛena. It is full and running over.
Gaḍa sareṛ perećena. The river is full and overflowing.
Dul sareṛkedae. He poured and made it run over, he poured till it ran over.
Ạuri sareṛoka. It is not yet running over.

Sãrgao. Cf. sarngao.

Sargat. Rich, as soil, fertile, well manured.
Ạḍi sargat ot kana. It is very rich soil.
Gurić calaolekhan sargatoka ot do. If manured soil will become rich.

Sarghaṛiạ. } Expert, clever, handy, adroit.
Sarghaṛiạ. }
Sarghạriạ hoṛ kanae. He is a handy man.

Sãṛgom. To prostrate, to cause to lose the perpendicular, to disobey, to disregard, to transgress.
Kul do sãṛgom bindạṛgoťkedeae. The tiger knocked him down.
Dare sãṛgom ocokedae. He caused the tree to become prostrate.
Hoṛoko sãṛgoma kombṛo aloko ira mente. They prostrate the dhan so that thieves may not reap it.
Cekate uniaǩ katha sãṛgomkate am sãotele ruạṛa? How can we transgress his order and go back with you?

Sarhad. / Sorhod. } A boundary.
Iñaǩ sarhad. My boundary.
Noa reaǩ sarhad bạnuǩan. There is no limit to this.

Sarhao. To praise, to thank.
Ạḍiko sarhaokedea. They praised him greatly.

Sarhaṛ. / Sarhaṛ sarhaṛ. } Long, straight, and with few knots, as timber.
Sarhaṛ sarhaṛ kaṭko maǩakaťa. They have cut down long straight trees.
Ạḍi sarhaṛgea noa kaṭ do. This log is long and straight.
Okarepe ñamlaǩa noa sarhaṛ sahan do? Where did you find this long firewood?

Sarhe. To bud, used mainly of those trees the leaves of which are used as pot-herbs; to increase, to become wealthy, to get into good condition physically.
Hesaǩ aṛaǩ sarheǩkana. The Hesaǩ (q. v.) tree is budding.
Sarheǩkanako mihũ do. The cattle are increasing in number.
Uni hoṛe sarheǩkana. That man is becoming wealthy.

Saṛhe. One half more.
Saṛhe cạr. Four and a half.

Sạri. True, to take in earnest.
Sạri katha. A true statement.
Landa landateñ menkeda adoe sạrikeda. I spoke in fun and he took it in earnest.
Sạrige. Certainly, truly, of a truth.
Sạri utạr. / Sạri utạrge. } Perfectly true.
Sạri se nasepe roṛeťkana? Sạrige. Are you speaking truthfully or falsely? Truthfully.

Sạṛi. A dress for a woman, consisting of a piece of cloth from 8 to 12 cubits in length and two in breadth.
Dos moka sạṛi kana. It is a dress piece 10 cubits in length.

Sạṛi. The sheath-like leaves of certain plants.
Jondra sạṛi. The sheathing leaves of a cob of Indian corn.
Bajṛa sạṛi. The top leaves of bajra (q. v.)
Hoṛo sạṛi. The top leaves of the dhan plant.
Ạk sạṛi. The leaves of sugarcane.
Ạk sạṛite oṛaǩko daba. They thatch houses with the leaves of sugarcane.

Sạri. A form of address used between brothers-in-law and sisters-in-law.
E sạri! Oh, brother-in-law, or Oh, Sister-in-law.

Sạri sar. A tall grass, *Saccharum Sara, Roxb.*, from the culms of which arrow shafts are sometimes made. Cf. sar.

Sạri sarjom. A species of tree so named.

Sạri cạṇḍi boṅga. A godlet of the Santals.

Sạriạt. / Sạriạti. } The males of a bride's village who go out to meet the bridegroom's party.
Bạriạt. / Bạriạti. } The bridegroom's party.

Sạriạtko. Those who go to meet a bridegroom. Cf. sạriạt.

Sạriạu. To level, to make surface smooth, to finish.
Noa khetle sạriạukeda. We levelled this field.
Niạ kạmile sạriạukeda. We finished this work.
Nui hoṛle sạriạukedea. We put this man straight.

Sạrik. / Sạrikdar. } A partner, a shareholder.
Noa ren sạrik kanae. He is a partner in this.
Iñ hõ onare sạrik menaña. I also am a partner in that.
Bandre ale 17 jon sạrikdarte hakokole dohokeťkoa. We 17 people put fish in the tank in partnership.

Sạrim. A roof, to roof.
Sạrimle dạpakaťa. We have thatched the roof.
Miť sạrimle dạpakaťa, ar miť sạrim do bań. We have thatched one side of the roof and not the other.

Sạrinaǩ. True, truly, certainly.
Sạrinaǩ katha kana. It is a true statement.
Sạrinaǩgeń metamkana. I tell you truly.

Sarishta. / Sarista. } Applied mainly to the office in which the records of a court are kept, the records of a court.

Sạrishtadar. / Sạristadar. } The person in charge of the records of a court.

Sarjạmin. / Sorjomin. } On the spot, local, locality
Sarjạminle ñelkeda. We visited the locality.
Sarjạminle todarotkeda. We held a local investigation.

Sarjom. A gregarious timber tree *Shorea robusta, Gaertn.*, common in the Santal country.

This is the sacred tree of the Santals. Their principal deities are supposed to reside in sacred groves of this tree. Cf. jaherthan.

Sarjom. }
Boṅga sarjom. } A scandent bush, *Ventilago calyculata, Tullasne.*

Sarjom. }
Ule sarjom. } A tree so named.

Sarjom. }
Sạri sarjom. } A tree so named.

Sarkao. To move rapidly.

Sarkao rakap̣ goťena. It came up with a rush.

Sarkar. }
Sorkar. } The government, teacher of a village school.

Sarkạri. }
Sorkạri. } Belonging to the state or government, belonging to the master, institution, estate, &c., common to all partners in the estate.

Sarkạri jaega kana. It is land belonging to the Zemindar.

Ạuri hạṭiňoǩre sarkạri menaǩa. It is common to all till it is divided.

Sarlaha. Rotten, soft, used sometimes in abuse.

Sarlaha kaṭ. Rotten wood.

Sarlaǩ. A splinter of wood.

Tiye sarlaǩena. A splinter of wood has run into his hand.

Sarnga hon. A large species of rat.

Sarngao. To be excited as with anger, to be inflamed, to be in a frenzy.

Edrete hõko sarngaoǩa. They also become excited with anger.

Hape se alom sarngaoǩa. Stop, do not get excited with anger.

Ạdiye sarngao goťena. He became very excited with anger.

Sarnga sạrngi. To be excited with anger, to be inflamed, to be frenzied.

Sarnga sạrngikin ropoṛena. They argued angrily.

Sarnga sạrngienakin. They are excited with anger.

Saron. Cf. sara.

Sarngi. A kind of fiddle.

Sarota. A knife used to cut the areca nut.

Saṛpa. Two pieces of hard wood struck together to beat time to music.

Saparatiń. A common plant, *Globba orixensis, Roxb.*

Sarpaṭ. }
Sarpaṭ sarpaṭ. }
Sorpoṭ. }
Sorpoṭ sorpoṭ. } Sound of gulping, guzzling, thudding.

Sarpaṭ sarpaṭe jomeda. He is guzzling.

Kombṛoko dalkoa sarpaṭ sarpaṭ. They beat thieves thud, thud.

Sarpaṭ marte. }
Sarpaṭ mente. } With a thud thump, gulp or guzzle.

Sarpaṭ marteko dalkedea. They hit him with a thud.

Sạrpaṭ. To finish.

Jom sạrpạṭkedae. He ate it all.

Ńu sạrpạṭkedae. He drank it all.

Sạrpha. }
Surphạ. } A fruit tree, *Anona squamosa, Linn.*

Saṛphạṛiạ. Clever, quick-witted, handy, adroit, applied to young persons.

Ạdi saṛphạṛiạ gidrạ kanae. He is a very quick-witted child.

Sarsa. }
Sarsao. } To ooze out, to become moist.

Lalekhan daǩ sarsaǩa. If you dig water will ooze out.

Uli daǩ sarsaoǩkana. Saliva is flowing.

Sarsadle. Disarranged, in disorder, out of place, public, to spread as news.

Sarsadleko bạgiada. They left them in disorder.

Kathako sarsadlekeda. They made the matter public.

Sar sạgun. An omen.

Sarsạgunre bań jutlena. The omen was not propitious.

Sarsạgun bhagegele ńamkeda. We got a good omen.

Sarsar. Cf. sarsa.

Sarsar. }
Sarsarao. } Loud deep sound, booming sound, bubbling sound.

Daǩre sarsare paeraǩkana. He is swimming in the water and producing a loud, deep sound.

Daǩ sarsarao hijuǩkana. The storm comes booming.

Hukạ sarsare ńuieda. He is smoking the huka and making a bubbling sound.

Saṛasạtiń. }
Gitić saṛasạtiń. } All asleep, the time of night when all are asleep.

Gitić saṛasạtiń pohorle hedena. We came at the time of night when all are asleep.

Sāṛsi. Tongs, pincers.

Sarsor. To make preparatory arrangements, to make the preparations necessary for the beginning of a work.

Notarko sarsor bayaeda hoṛo roᵏhoe. They are making the preparations necessary to begin planting (dhan.)

Saṛsoṛ. To rustle as the leaves of surgarcane, Indian corn, &c., to cause to rustle.

Jonḍra baṛgere gaiye saṛsoṛeda. The cow is causing a rustling in the Indian corn garden.

Biñ saṛsoṛe calaᵏkana. The snake is causing a rustling as he goes.

Sartal. A small leaf plate.

Miť sartale jela. It will give one plate of meat.

Sartal jońkanako. They are making leaf plates for themselves.

Sartalaᵏ. To spread out flat on the surface of the ground, as some plants, to be like a flat plate. Cf. sartal.

Kantha aṛaᵏ sartalaᵏakana. The *Kantha* (q. v.) pot-herb has spread out on the surface of the ground.

Sạrthi. To become of necessity acceptable or desirable after having been refused or rejected.

Onkoko menkeda, Chạḍwigeae uni bạhu do bale ạguea, menkhan etaᵏ bạhu bańko ńamlente seere do uni bạhugeye sạrthiena. They said, this person eligible as a bride is a divorcee we will not take her, but as no others eligible as brides were found in the end that eligible bride became of necessity acceptable.

Sạru. The Taro plant cultivated for its farinacious corms which are eaten, *Celocasia antiquorum, Schott.*

Picki sạru. }
Kanda sạru. } Different kinds of Taro plants
Mukhi sạru. } distinguished by Santals.
Bhonḍa sạru. }

Sạru. } A plant much valued for
Kanṭa sạru. } its medicinal properties, *Lasia heterophylla, Schott.*

Sạru gaḍa Baske. A sub-sept of the Santal sept Baske (q. v.)

Sạruᵏ. } To produce a sucking
Sạruᵏ sạruᵏ. } sound when eating anything juicy, such as sugarcane, water melon, &c.

Sạruᵏ sạruᵏe jomeda. He is eating and producing a sucking sound.

Sạruᵏ maraoᵏedae. He ate it up with a sucking sound.

Sạruᵏ marte. } With a sucking sound.
Sạruᵏ mente. } Cf. sạruᵏ.

Sạruᵏ marteye jomkeda.

Sasań. Turmeric, and the plant, *Curcuma longa, Roxb.*, which yields it.

Baplare sunum sasańko ojoᵏ joha. At a marriage they anoint themselves with oil and turmeric.

Sasań beḍa. A place mentioned in Santal traditions.

Sasań pio. The golden Oriole. Cf. pio.

Sasań cẽṛẽ. The Grey-headed fly-catcher, *Cryptolopha cinereocapilla.*

Sasań daᵏ. Yellow, the colour of turmeric.

Sasań ḍora. A cord fastened round the loins of a child at narta (q. v.) It is dyed yellow with turmeric.

Sasań riť dhiri. A stone for grinding turmeric.

Saset. Trouble, pain, suffering, anxiety, distress; to cause, or be in trouble, pain, &c.

Ạḍi sasetre menaña. I am in great distress.

Ạḍiko sasetediñkana. They are causing me much suffering.

Harkhet saset. Trouble and suffering.

Sạs ghaṭi. Cry of a certain pigeon.

Sasla. Cf. sala.

Jāṛiko saslakana. They are stripping fibre.

Ceť saslam senlena? What did you go to pick, what business had you there?

Sasna. Cf. sana.

Jojom sasnakana. There is, or he has, a desire to eat.

Sason. Cf. sasot.

Disomko sasonkeda. They subdued the country.

Sasot. Entire absence of any disturbing or disquieting elements.

Sạsraṛ. Father-in-law's house.

Sasta. Cheap, low as prices; plentiful.

Sasta bhao. }
Sasta dor. } Cheap or low rate.

Sasta bhao ńamoᵏkana. A low rate prevails.

Sastor. Sacred books, scriptures.

Sãsõ. To breathe heavily.

Sãsõe sahećeᵏkana. He is breathing heavily.

Sat. Seven.

Sãt disom. A country mentioned in Santal traditions.

Saṭ. Time.

Noa saṭ do bań calaḱa. I shall not go this time.

Tisem calaḱa? Ińaḱ saṭ hoelen nạhi. When will you go? Not before my time.

Sat. True, truth, evidence, assurance of reliability.

Satge bale ńellekhan oećlo kuṭạmama? If we do not see some evidence of your reliability what will we sacrifice to you?

Sãṭ. }
Saṭ. } Together, of one mind, of one determination.
Saṭoṕ. }

Miť saṭakanako. They are of one mind.
Miť saṭoṕakanako. They are agreed.
Sãṭakanako. They are agreed.
Sãṭakaťako. They have agreed.

Saṭ. To finish, to complete.

Rohoe saṭkedako. They completed planting.
Saṭena. It is finished.

Sat. }
Sot. } Claim, legal right.

Sat bạnuḱtama. You have no legal right.

Saṭ marte. }
Saṭ mente. } Immediately, on the instant, forthwith.

Saṭ marte calao goćenae. He left on the instant.

Sat sokha. }
Sạri sokha. } A true prophet a true witch finder. Cf. sokha.

Sata. }
Satate. } On account of, in lieu of.

Am satate tahẽena. It remains with you, at your risk.

Sud satate jaegaeń ema. I will give the field in lieu of interest.

Haṛam satate bes besaḱgeko emakokana. They are feeding them well on the old man's account.

Satahet́. Breath.

Miť satahet́teń ńu gotkeda. I drank it with one breath, I drank it without stopping to take breath.

Miť satahet́te uni ahaakan hoṛ pe dhaoe bulạnea. He makes passes three times without taking breath over the man upon whom the evil eye has been cast.

Saṭhi. Seven days' rain, heavy continuous rain.

Saṭhiye lagaoakaťa. It has set in for a seven days' rain.

Saṭaḱ suṭuk. Sound of dripping, dropping, ripping or nibbling.

Saṭaḱ suṭuḱe daḱeda. It rains drip, drip.
Saṭaḱ suṭuḱ bae thiroḱkana. It does not cease dripping (continues to rain.)

Dare reaḱ sakamkhon daḱ do saṭaḱ suṭuḱ ńuroḱkana. The water (or rain) falls from the leaves of the tree drip drip.

Satalaḱ. Along with, together with, accompaniment. Cf. salaḱ.

Edre satalaḱe dalkedea. He struck him with anger, or angrily.

Satalaḱ bạnuḱtińa. I have no accompaniment, i. e. no relish to eat or give along with the rice.

Botor satalaḱe daṛkeda. He fled with fear.

Saṭao. To put close together, to stick together.

Kaṭ beako saṭaoakaťa. They have joined the wood very closely.

Leteko saṭaoakaťa. They have joined it with paste.

Bań saṭaoakana. It is not closely fitted.
Saṭaokate dohoeme. Place them close together.
Sen saṭaoakanae. He has gone and stuck there.

Idi saṭaoakaťae. He has taken it away and stuck to it, i. e. did not return it.

Sataṕ. Cf. santao.

Saṭapaṭa. Slight sound, as made by a rat or other small animal.

Saṭapaṭako ńam babṛakana. They are searching and making a slight noise.

Satar gatar. }
Sotor gotor. } Family.

Onko satar gatar kanako. They are of their family.

Satar patar. Sparsely, thinly.

Satarpatar joskana ul do. The mango tree has fruited sparsely.

Satareć. Remainder, excess. Cf. sareć.

Er satareć. Remaining after sowing.
Jom satareć. Remaining after eating.

Saṭar suṭur. Sound of nibbling.

Saṭar suṭure jomeda. It (rat) is causing a sound of nibbling.

Saṭasaṭ. }
Saṭasaṭi. } Close together, packed closely.

Saṭasaṭko duṛupa. They sit close together.

Satasoń. }
Sotasoń. } Companion, confederates.

Noko satasoń kanako. They are confederates, or companions.

Saṭasuṭu. To squeak, as a musk rat.

Saṭasuṭueťtem ańjom ńamkedea. You found him by hearing him squeak.

Sate. Eaves, the extent of roof projecting over the walls.

Kuḍam sate. The eaves of the back of a house.

Mutul sate. The eaves on the two ends of a house.

Sate khunṭi. The posts supporting the roof of the front and back of a house.

Sate kaṛkạṛi. Fastenings with which the roof is fastened down to the *satepar* (q. v.)

Sate paṛ. A beam, supported on posts, which is carried all round a house and which runs at the level of the side walls.

Satekate bengeťkedae. He shaded his eyes with his hand and looked.

Sate.
Soba sate. } Heads in opposite, or alternately in opposite directions.
Soba satete dohoepe. Lay the heads alternately in opposite directions.

Sate sote. Rice land that is dependent on rainfall.
Sate sote jaega kantales paṭan do bah. Our land depends on the rainfall, it is not irrigated.

Saṭhdag kul. A panther.

Saṭhi hoṛo. A variety of the rice plant.

Saṭhao. Cf. sanṭhao.

Saṭi. To be burned alive, as a moth in a candle, &c. &c., or as a Hindu widow with the corpse of her husband.
Saṭi gocenae pipṛiah do. The moth was burnt to death.

Saṭkao. To become stiff, as clay, food, &c., when exposed to the atmosphere.
Leher leherko lolekhan raṛeć saṭkaoka. If it (rice) is moist when taken from the pot it will stiffen when cool.

Saṭka suṭku. To make preparations preparatory to cooking food.
Nĕkele saṭka suṭku baṛaeda. We are just making preparations to begin to cook.

Saṭki saṛi. A saṛi (q. v.) with narrow white and red stripes.

Satok. To bite, to snap.
Alahiń saṭokena. I have bitten my tongue.
Seta roko saṭokkoa. Dogs snap at flies.
Binḍuć saṭok. To make a wry mouth when mocking.

Satom. The year after next coming, three years hence.
Pher satom. Four years hence.

Saṭop. Together, of one mind, of one determination.
Mić saṭopakanako. They are of one mind, they are acting together.

Saṭ paṭ. Quickly.
Saṭpaṭ jom hodme. Eat quickly.

Saṭpaṭ.
Saṭpaṭao. } To make a slight noise, imitative.
Honko saṭpaṭaoeda. The rats are making a noise.
Saṭpaṭko saḍe ocoeda. They are making a noise resembling saṭpaṭ, saṭpaṭ.

Satral.
Satraḷia. } A swimmer.
Khub satral kanae. He is a good swimmer.
Khub satraḷia hoṛ kanae. He is a very expert swimmer.

Saṭru. An enemy.

Satsayar.
Satsayar dare. } A forest tree, *Dalbergia latifolia, Roxb.*

Saṭsuṭ. Restless and touching things, as a child, mischievous.
Alom saṭsuṭ baṛaea. Do not be mischievous.

Saṭsuṭ. To complete, to finish, to do quickly.
Jăhănak bape saṭakaćkhan saṭsuṭ hodpe. If there is anything that you have not got ready do it quickly.

Saṭu. Meal, flour.
Saṭu is prepared by roasting certain grains and grinding into meal or flour. It is not re-cooked before being eaten.

Saṭu sambar. Provision for a journey or an outing, which is eaten without cooking. Cf. saṭu.

Saụ. A money lender, a mahajan.
This is probably the same as the Hindu caste whose patronymic is *Sao*, many of whom are money lenders.

Saụsaụ. Blazing, blazingly.
Saụsaụ sengel jolokkana. The fire is burning blazingly.
Lokkana saụsaụ. It is blazing.
Saụsaụe loena. He burned blazingly (on the funeral pyre.)
It is considered a happy omen if a corpse burns freely on the funeral pyre.

Sãuṛĩ. F.
Sãoṛă. M. } Dark, grey colour.

Saụṛi.
Saụṛi ghăs. } A tall grass, *Heteropogon contortus, R. & S.*, used largely for thatching purposes.

Saụṛi arak. A small plant used as a pot-herb, *Polygonum glabrum, Willd.*

Sawa. One fourth more,
Sawa ser. A seer and a quarter.
Sawa goj. A yard and a quarter.
Sawa ṭaka. One rupee four annas.

Sãwãe. A full supply of rain, a good harvest.
Nese sãwãekećte aḍi hoṛko baplaena. Owing to there having been a good supply of rain, or a good harvest, this year many people are marrying.
Sãwãe serma. A year in which there has been a full supply of rain and good crops.
Matkome sãwãeakawaćbona. There has been a good matkom (q. v.) harvest.
Dake sãwãeakawaćbona. There has been a full supply of rain.
Akal sãwãerelah ńapamakana. We have met after a very long time.
Sãwãeakokanae. He is throwing water on them (a custom observed at the Baha (q. v.) festival.)

Sawal. A question, to question, to address, as a pleader the court, or any one a panchayat or other gathering.

Bese sawalkeda. He made a good address to the court, he argued the case well, or he cross examined well.

Miť goṭeć sawal menaǩtińa. I have one question to put, or I have one argument to place before you.

Sawalia. A speaker, one able to address a court or a panchayat.

Sāwār. Straight and of uniform width or thickness, straight grained.

Sāwār kaṭ. A straight log of uniform thickness.

Sawasin. Elder sister.

Sawasin peṛako heċakawadea. His elder sister and her family (or some members of her family) have come to him.

Sayaṅ.
Sayaṅ sayaṅ. } Rushing, as a stiff breeze.
Sayaṅ soyoṅ.

Sayaṅ sayaṅ hoe boloǩkana. Wind is rushing in (at an open door, &c.)

Sayaṅ marte.
Sayaṅ mente. } With a rush.

Sayaṅ marte hoe bolo goťena. The wind came in with a rush.

Sayaṛ. To lie down, lying down.

Sayaṛakanae. He is lying down.

Sayaṛ.
Sayaṛ sayaṛ. } To blow hard, strong, as wind.

Sayaṛ sayaṛe hoeẽda. It is blowing hard.

Sayaṛ marte.
Sayaṛ mente. } With a rush.

Sayaṛ marte hoe heċ goťena. The wind came with a rush.

Se. Or.

Ińiń calaǩa, se uniń kolkaea? Shall I go or will I send him?

Calaǩa, sem baṅa? Will you go or not?

Se. Used to encourage or incite.

Ma se roṛme. Come, speak.

Alo sem raga. Do not weep.

Orme se. Come, pull.

Se. A louse, of the species *Pediculus capitis*.

Se tele. Young lice.

Se bele. A nit, nits.

Se menaǩkotaea. He is lousy.

Seakadeako. Lice are in his head.

Se. That, that same.

Se hoṛge. That same man.

Se. To boil over, to well up.

Seǩkana. It is boiling over.

Seẽna. It has boiled over.

Buru khon daǩ do gel mõṛẽ moka cetante se rakap̌ena. The water welled up fifteen cubits above the mountains.

Se. In like manner,

Se ke se.
Sei ke sei. } As formerly, as it was, in like manner.

Onkom aṛaǩkakokhan, ńelkoam, seike sei arhõko kombṛoea. If you let them go, you will se that they will again steal as formerly.

Se bhal. Rather than, in preference to.

Unạǩ iń kạmia ar beṛhon do thoṛagem emańa, se bhal bạń kamia. I work so much and the wages you give me are small, rather than that I will not work.

Se samta.
Se samtao. } Rather than that, preferably.
Se santa.

Eṭaǩ hoṛ ạcurem ạcukeťkoa, se samta oṛaǩren hoṛem ạculekokhan baṅ beskoǩa? You engaged other people (to do your work), rather than do that would it not be better to engage those of your own household?

Se bickom. Rather than that.

Onka do cedaǩem ruheťediṅkana? Se bickom miť ṭheṅga daleńme. Why are you scolding me like this? rather than that hit me one blow with a stick.

Kạmi tuluċ onkam roṛkhan do kạmige ohole kạmilea, se bickom berhonge alom emalea, enhõ alom roṛalea. If you find fault with us like this when we are are working, we will not work, rather than do that give us no wages, but do not find fault with us.

Se borom.
Se boromco. } Rather than that, preferably.

Nonka do alope egerińa, ohoń kạmi daṛelea, se boromco ḍakage alope emańa. Do not scold me thus, I cannot work, rather than that do not give me food.

Kaḍa do ńindạre aṛagem ar ńindạkate aderem, se boromco daṅrage besa, onko do setaǩ aṛagem ar ayup̌ torage aderkaeme. You let out buffaloes early in the morning and house them late at night, rather than these bullocks are better, you let them out in the morning and house them at evening.

Nunạǩ koolõn do okoe sahaoa? Se boromco herel reaǩ do daka hõ bań joma ar bań khaṭaoǩa. Who could bear so much ill treatment? rather than that I will not eat the food of a husband and neither will I work for him.

Se bhạtiċ.
Se bhatkoċ. } Of course, to be sure, now that I remember.

Se bhạtiċ onḍe ma am hõm tahẽkangea. To be sure, you also were there.

Sẽ phõ. To pant, to breathe heavily, an imitative word.

Sẽ phõe saheťeda. He is breathing and producing the sound sẽ phõ, sẽ phõ.

Sẽ phõeťkanae. He is panting, producing the sound sẽ phõ sẽ phõ.

Sẽ phõko khudạukedińa. They pursued me [panting.

Sẽ phõ ńiraǩkanko ńelkedea. They saw him running and panting.

Se getho. That at any rate.

Se getho baṅ hoyoǩa. That at any rate it will not be.

Se ge thor. Thus, (emphatic) certainly thus.

Se gethor oho hoelena. It shall certainly not be thus.

Sẽ marte.
Sẽ mente. } A sigh, with a sigh, produced by breathing outwards.

Paromenkhan sẽ marteñ sahećkeda. When I passed, or had passed, I breathed a sigh (of relief.)

Sea. To rot, to decompose, rotten, decomposed.

Seaena kaṭ do. The log is rotten.
Sim bele seaena. The hen's egg is rotten.
Seage sokana. It smells rotten.
Noa katha do laćre baṛe seaeme. Rot this matter in the belly, i. e. speak of it to no one, let the remembrance of it die.

Sean. Adult, well grown, cunning, crafty, sharp. artful.

Gidrąko tin tiriťa? Seangeako. How big are the children? They are well grown.
Nui do ạdi sean hoṛ kanae. This is a very cunning man.
Nui ḍaṅra doe seanena netar do. This ox has become crafty now-a-days.

Sebeć.
Sebeć sebeć } Humid, flind in small quantity.

Hakoko utukoa, sebeć sebećko raseakoa. They cook fish as a relish with a small quantity of fluid.

Sebeć sebeć daǩ todoǩkana. Water is issuing in small quantity.

Sebel. Palatable, savoury, well tasted, sweet, good, to take to, to appreciąte.

Sebel hasa. Good soil.
Daka utu do bań sebela, ǩathage sebela. Cooked rice and relish are not savoury, the words (spoken) are savoury.
Sebelam khanko tahẽengem, bako sebelam khanem heċenge. If they take to you you will stay, if they do not take to you you will come (return.)
Bań sebeledińkana. It is not palatable to me, I do not find it palatable.
Sebelań kana katha do. The matter commends itself to me.
Bań sebelań kana noa katha. This matter does not please me.
Ạdi sebela. It is very good, very palatable.

Sebok. To perform worship, a servant.

Teheń doko sebokeda. They are performing worship to-day.

Seć. Direction. side, quarter, towards.

Iń seć beṅgedme. Look in my direction, look towards me.

Ać sećkedeae. He made him to side with himself, he made him a partisan of his own.
Alope uni sejoǩa. Do not go over to his side.
Uni sećrenko. Partisans of his.
Uni seć alom roṛa, iń seć baṛe roṛme. Do not speak on his side, but speak on my side.

Lobhiạ hoṛ jom sećgeko calaǩa. Covetous or greedy people go on the side of food, or greedy people side with those who can pay them best.
Uni hõe sećada. He also went in with it.
Ape sećte jel dakań joma. I will partake of meat and rice with you.
Oṛaǩ seće senakana. He has gone towards his house, [self.
Daǩ seće senakana. He has gone to ease him-
Noa sećteye paromena. He passed in this direction.
Ape oṛaǩ sećteń calaǩa. I will go by way of your house.

Seć soć. Cf. sić soć.

Sedae. Olden times, long ago, ancient time, formerly.

Sedae kathań lạiamkana. I am telling you a story of long ago.
Sedae ren hoṛko. The ancients.
Sedae ạri. Ancient laws.
Sedae hiloǩko galmaraoakaťa. They have talked about the olden days.
Sedae sãwãe ado bạnuǩan. There are no longer harvests like the bumper harvests of the olden time.

Seḍe beḍe. Sound produced by anything moving, floundering or squirming in a small quantity of water.

Roṭeko seḍe beḍećǩkana. Frogs are making a noise by squirming (in the water.)
Noa darhare seḍe beḍe hako menaǩkoa. In this pool the fish are making a noise by squirming.

Sede bede. Roughly, carelessy, as a piece of work.

Sede bede patṛae roǩakaťa. He has pinned the leaf plates carelessy.
Sede bede Mahle haṭaǩe benaokeda. The mahle (bamboo worker) made the haṭaǩ (q. v.) roughly.

Seḍe beḍe. Dirty, muddy, as water; to dirty, to muddy.

Daǩko seḍe beḍećǩkana. They are dirtying the water.

Seder beder. Rough on the surface, as anything made of or plastered with clay.

Seder bederko jereṛakaťa. The have roughly plastered (the wall.)
Seder beder bań cikạṛa. It is rough not smooth.
Seder bederko benaoakaťa culhạ do. They have made the stove (of clay) roughly.
Seder beder bhitko rakapakaťa. They have built up the wall roughly.

Seḍer beḍer. Dirty, muddy, applied to water.

Seḍer beḍer daǩko ńuieda. They are drinking dirty water.

Sedge bedge. Rough, carelessly executed, as a piece of work.

Sedge bedge patṛae roǩakaťa. She has pinned the leaf plates roughly.

Seḍge beḍge. To dirty by stirring, to muddy, muddy, dirty.
Gidrạ sanam daťko seḍge beḍgeakaťa. The children have muddied all the water.

Sega. A species of squirrel.

Sega jạnum. A thorny bush, *Mimosa rubicaulis, Lamk.*

Segebege. / Segepeṭe. / Sagabaga. } Crammed together, closely packed, numerous.
Segepeṭeko boloakana. They have crammed themselves in.
Segepeṭe aema utạr gidrạ menaťkotaea. He has a very large family.

Sege roṛe. Applied to an aggregation of small roundish bodies, rough owing to the presence of small roundish bodies.
Soṛokre sege roṛegea. On the road there is an aggregation of small roundish bodies (gravel.)
Sege roṛe jahana. It has a mass of small round seeds.

Sege sege. / Sagae sagae. } Coarse, as meal.
Noa aṭa sagae sagaege ạikạuťkana. This meal feels coarse.

Segeć peṭeć. Big and little, irregularly, disorderly.

Sehoe. The same, the like.
Uni hõe sehoegea. He is also the same.

Sehor. / Nehor sehor. } Cf. nehor.

Sei ke sei. Cf. se ke se.

Sekao. To apply heat, to foment.
Hapele sekaomea nahaľ. Wait, I will warm you presently.
Bale gidrạko sekaokoa. They apply heat to infants.
Sengelreko sekao roboṛa. They dry it at a fire.
Ạdi rabaṅkana, sekao ṅoťlenme. It is very cold, warm yourself a little first.
Gadar jonḍrako sekao isina. They cook half-ripe Indian corn by roasting.

Sekeć. / Sekeć sekeć. } To clink, applied to the sound produced by metallic objects coming into contact.
Sakom sekeć sekeć saḍekantaea. Her wristlets are sounding clink, clink.

Seke doke. Covered with ornaments, as the neck.
Sekedoke horoťakaťae hoṭoľ pereć. Her neck is completely covered with ornaments.

Seke meke. Coverd with ornaments, as arms, &c.

Seke seke. To rage, to fume.
Seke seke baṛaekanae. He is raging about.

Sekeseke. Cf. sekseke.

Sekra. A Hindu caste who work in brass and bell metal.

Sekra sakom. A kind of armlet of bell metal.

Sekra. / Sekra dare. } A small tree, *Zizyphus rugosa, Lamk.*

Sekreć. / Sekreć dare. } A large forest tree *Lagerstroemia parviflora, Roxb.*

Sekṛeć. / Sekṛeć sekṛeć. } To clink, applied to the sound produced by metallic objects coming into contact with each other.
Sekṛeć sekṛeć saḍekana sakom do. The sakoms (q. v.) are sounding clink, or the sakoms are clinking.

Sekṛeć marte. / Sekṛeć mente. } With a clink.

Sekreć. / Heseć sekreć. } To be merry, to enjoy oneself; merrily, gleefully, with pleasure. Cf. heseć sekreć.

Sekseke. / Seke seke. } Covered, as the arms with ornaments, full.
Sekseke sakome horoťakaťa. She has covered her arms with ornaments.
Gaṅ nạị do seke seke. The Gaṅ river is full.

Sekseke. / Soksoko. } Sticking out, projecting.
Sekseke ḍaṭa menaťtaea. He has sticking out teeth, his teeth stick out.

Selep̣. / Kuṛmbi selep̣. / Selep. / Kuṛmbi selep. } The buck of the Ravine deer of sportsmen in Bengal, *Gazella Bennettii.*

Selep̣ samanom. A gorgeous flowering climbing plant, *Gloriosa superba, Linn.*

Seleť. Along with, together with, to include, to couple, to unite, to company.
Uni hõ onko tuluće seleťlena. He also was with them, he also was of their company, he also was united with them.
Ale do alom seleťlea. Do not include us.
Miť din ganle seleťlengea. We companied (with them) for one day or so.
Kombṛoko tuluć seledoľ do bah ṭhika. It is not right to keep company with thieves.
Dharaoaľ sud seleťiń em oabakeda. I paid all I owed with interest.

Sele ṭoke. Big and little, or little and less, applied to children.
Sele ṭoke gidrạ menaḱkotaea. He has a large small family.
Cele, noko sele ṭokem ạguakaćkoa? What, have you brought these children?

Selsel. Very fair, exceedingly, applied to fairness of complexion.
Selsel esela‍e. She is exceedingly fair.
Selsele ńeloḱkana. She appears exceedingly fair.

Sem. The abbreviated form of se am.
Calaḱa sem bań? Will you go or not?

Sembe suruć. To slabber, to slaver, slabberingly, slaveringand perspiring, blubbering, soaky, soggy.
Sembe suruć raḱ joń iń ńelkedea. I saw him crying and blubbering.
Gidrạ sembe suruće jom jońkanae. The child is eating slabberingly.
Sembe surujoḱkanae. He is slabbering.

Semeć. Small.
Semeć dhiri. A small stone.

Sen. Direction, side, quarter, towards.
Oṛaḱ sene senakana. He has gone in the direction of his house.
Ape senaḱ lạipe ceťleka hal cal. Tell about that of your direction, what is the news like.

Sen. To go, to pass.
Sen parom porob. The Passover.
Oṛaḱte senakanae. He has gone home.
Senoḱ senoḱteń lańgaena. I am tired with continued walking.
Sen hećenae. He has gone and come.
Am gem sen hamaloḱa. You must bear the responsibility.
Onḍele sen dohoḱa. We will pass the night there on our way.
Senoḱ hoyoḱtama. You must go.

Sen ạṛti. To go a little further.
Sen ạṛtime. Go a little further.

Sendra. A hunt, to hunt, to follow the chase, to search for.
Por sendra. } An informal one day's hunt.
Hakwa sendra. }
Disom sendra. } The annual tribal hunt. Cf.
Gipitić sendra. } dihri.
Sendrare karkare nui do niạ ńutum hohoaepe. At the chase and hunt call this (one) by this name.
Sendra ạgukedeale, bale ńamledea. We searched for him coming but did not find him.
Sendra herel. A hunter.
Sendratele senlena. We went to the hunt.

Sene dever. } Yearning hankering, solicitude.
Sene dewer. }
Siń sạṭupe hijuḱkana sene dewer. He is always comin hankering.
Ińaḱ jiwi do gujuḱ leka sene deweroḱkantińa. My soul is exceeding sorrowful even unto [death.

Sene gumạn. } Cf. sane gumane.
Sene gumane. }
Sene gumạn ceť hō bań baḍaea.

Sener. A sapling used as a rafter.
Terel hōko senera. They also use the terel (q. v) tree sapling for rafters.
Seneriń maḱakaťa. I have cut saplings for rafters.
Eńga sener. Thick rafters on which a frame work is laid to support the lighter rafters above.

Sener lekha haṇḍi. Liquor drunk inside the house at a marriage.
From the inside of the house the rafters can be counted, hence the name. To be taken into the house to drink is a mark of respect.

Seńgel. Fire.
Seńgel bugli. The fire bag, i. e. the stomach.
Seńgel jol. To light a fire, burn as a fire.
Seńgel lagao. To set fire to, to take fire.
Seńgel ịṛić. To put out a fire, to go out, as fire.
Seńgel saṗ. To catch fire.
Seńgel dhandkaoena. The fire is burning brightly, or if a big fire, raging.
Seńgel joloḱkana. The fire is burning.
Seńgel salgao. To kindle up a fire from embers.
Seńgeladeale. We cremated him.

Seńgel daḱ. Fire rain.
Eyae siń eyae ńindạ seńgel daḱe daḱlaḱa, Okareben tahẽkana manwa? Okareben soro ańgalen? Seven days and seven nights it rained fire rain, Human beings where were you? Where did you weather the storm?
The Santals have a tradition that fire rain once fell from the skies and that a man and a woman saved themselves by taking refuge in a cave. Another version has it that the two who were saved had a stone house with a stone door.

Seńgel ṭiṭi. The Guinea fowl.

Seńgel siń. A stinging plant, *Tragia, involucrata, Jacq.*

Ṣeńgel ere. A small species of Woodpecker.

Seńgel gidi. The male of The Indian King-Vulture, *Ologyps calvus.*

Seńgel marmar. A species of centipede, *Scolopendra versicolor.*

Seńgeť. To be breathless, to be out of breath.
Ńu seńgeťenae. He has drunk himself out of breath.
Ńir seńgeťenae. He has run himself out of breath.
Jom seńgeťkedeale. We ate him out of breath, we ate all he had.
Ńu seńgeťkedako. They drank up all.
Kul ńelte botorte seńgeť goťenae. He became breathless through fear on seeing the tiger.

Sepeń. To bear up, or carry on the hand or hands held flat without taking hold of.
Sepeń rakaṗkedeako. They raised him up on their hands.
Bale gidrạko sepeńkoa. They hold infants on the hands.

Ser. A weight of about 2lbs., a measure liquid and dry.

Paki ser. A seer of 20 gandas or 80 tolas.
Kaci ser. A seer of 12 gandas or 48 tolas, or 18 gandas or 72 tolas.
Kaṭ ser. A seer measure made of wood.
Pitar ser. A seer measure made of brass.
Ser dhiri. A stone used as a seer weight.
Ser ạuri puraụktaea. His measure of life is not yet complete.

Ser sidhạ. Provision for one meal or so.

Ser sidhạ. } ńamkateko calaoena. They got
Sidhạ ser. } food for one meal and left.
Raj ren sipạhiko heċlenkhan atoren ser sidhạ lagaoakoa. When the Zemindar's peon comes provision for one meal has to be supplied by the villagers.

Sĕṛă. Grown up, adolescent, of age, adult, large, big.

Sĕṛă hoṛ. An adult.
Uni khon do sĕṛă ńoṅgeye tahĕkana. He was a little older than him.
Sĕṛăgeae, bae gidrạwa. He is grown up, he is not a child.
Seṛă ńoṅaṅ ạguime. Bring one a little larger, bring a little larger one.
Sĕṛă sĕṛă taṛamme. Take long steps.
Sĕṛă hako saṗkope. Catch big fish.
Sĕṛăkateye goċena. He died after he had grown up, he was grown up when he died.
Sĕṛăenae. He is grown up.

Serali. A species of waterfowl.

Ser baṭa. Having located a quail the hunters go round and round it saying ser baṭa, ser baṭa, and the quail squats and is easily killed by a stick:

Sĕṛĕ. A kind of bamboo basket used to raise water for irrigating purposes.

Sere. } To exude, to ooze out, to
Sere sere. } distil, to discharge, as pus.

Ghao sere sereṅkantaea. Fluid is exuding from his sore.
Sere sere seteńoṅkana daṅ do. Water is exuding
Daṅ daṅteye sereked̩a. The continued rain injured it by keeping it too moist.
Jom sereĕnae He has injured himself by eating, has made himself uncomfortable.

Sere sere. } Fizzing sound, as that pro-
Soro soro. } duced by damp or fresh firewood when burning.

Berel sạhan ṭhekaoaṅ khan sere sereṅa. If green firewood be put on the fire it will make a fizzing sound when burning.

Sere sibuć. } Snotty, slavering, slob-
Sere simbuć. } bering, dirty.

Sereć. } To snivel, to have a dis-
Sereć sereć. } charge from the nose,
Suruć suruć } eyes or mouth, to cry as a child with snuffling or snivelling.

Mandate suruć surujoṅkanae. He is snivelling owing to his suffering from a cold.
Sereć bah caba hodoṅtakoa. They do not at once cease snuffling.
Surućkedae. He sniveled.

Sere gore. Applied to the evil effects of over-eating whatever they may be, anything and everything.

Sere goreko jomkeda. They injured themselves by eating too much, or they ate anything and every thing.

Sereń. A song, to sing.

Sereń joṛao. To compose a song.
Sereń joṅṛaoić. A composer of songs, a poet.
Dhorom sereń. A Hymn.

Different kinds of Santal Songs.

Lăgṛe sereń.	Loboe sereń.
Doń sereń	Duṅgeṛ sereń.
Golwari sereń.	Bir sereń.
Ḍahar sereń.	Bapla sereń.
Baha sereń.	Binti sereń.
Riṅjạ sereń.	Gam sereń.
Bhinsạr sereń.	Hoṛo rohoe sereń.
Jhikạ sereń	Morna sereń.
Humṭi sereń.	Mantar sereń.
Guńjạr sereń.	Jhạṛni sereń.
Sohrae sereń.	

Sereńedako. They are singing.
Sereńalepe. Sing to us.

Sereṛ. } To feel as if one were
Sereṛ sereṛ. } about to be sick, to feel the premonition of sickness.

Sereṛ sereṛiń ạikạueda. I feel as if I were about to be sick.
Sereṛ sereṛiń ạṭkareda bhaṛ bhaṛ daṅ todoṅkana. I feel sick, there is a large flow of saliva.

Sereṛ marte } Sudden turning of the
Sereṛ mente. } stomach.

Sereṛ marte ạikạukedae. He felt a sudden turning of the stomach.

Sereṫ. } To squash, to be squashed,
Sereṫ sereṫ. } as by treading on or by a weight.

Lebeṫ sereṫkedeae. He trod on and squashed it.
Ten sereṫkedeae. He pressed it (under something) and squashed it (animate.)
Oṭa sereṫakadeae. He has pressed it (animate) down and squashed it.
Roṭe lebeṫ lekhane seredoṅa. If (you) tread on a frog it will be squashed.

Sereṫ. } Applied to the noise pro-
Sereṫ sereṫ. } duced by passing wind.

Sereṫ sereṫe ghạsiċeda.

Sereṫ marte. } With a noise, as that
Sereṫ mente. } produced by passing wind.

Sereṫ marteye ghạsiċkeda.

Sereć bereć. } Fat, savoury and tender
Sirạt barat. } as good flesh meat. Cf. sirạt barat.

Serma. The sky, the firmament, the upper atmosphere, heaven.
Serma daḱ. Rain, rain water.
Serma ooṭ khon ńurena. It fell from the sky.

Serma. A year.
Mić sermaren. A yearling.
Bar serma ren gidrị. A child of two years.
Sermake serma. Yearly, annually, every year.
Sermake sermae hijuḱkana. He comes every year.

Serom. The neck.

Serom. } To assist, to help.
Sopo serom. }
Sopo serom ńoḱadeań. I assisted him a little.

Seṛwań. A climbing plant, *Vigna vexillata, Benth,* the root of which is eaten.

Ses. The end, to come to an end, to finish, to bring to an end, last.
Sesaḱ. The last one (inanimate.)
Sesić. The last one (animate.)
Sesaḱreń paṛaoena. It fell to me to get the last.
Ses kal. The end.
Seskalrem rohoekeda, ado hoṛo do hoyoḱtama? You planted at the end of the season, and will you have a crop of dhan?
Seskalre oeć leka hoyoḱa, babon baḍaea. We do not know what it will be, or how it will be at the end of time.
Kạmi seseekanako. They are finishing, or ending the work.
Din sesentaea gujuḱae. His days are ended, he will die.
Sesoḱa nahaḱ. It will come to an end presently.

Sesanti. To finish, to come or bring to an end.
Sesantire. In the end, at length.
Sesantire uni hõe goeena. In the end he also died.
Sesantienae. He is dead, or he is ended.

Sesao. To finish, to come or bring to an end.
Kạmiko sesaoeda. They are finishing the work.
Nele sesaowa. We are just about to finish, or end.
Din sesaokate hoṛo rohoelekhan bań hoyoḱa. If you plant dhan after the season is over there will not be a good crop.

Sesa sisi. About the end, about to come or bring to an end.
Aghāṛ sesa sisi. About the end of Aghāṛ.

Sẽ sẽ. } To produce the sound of sẽ sẽ
Sẽ sẽ. } or sẽ sẽ when breathing, as one suffering from bronchitis, an imitative word.

Seć. Said to a cow when milking it to keep it quiet.
Gạiko sećkoa. They say *seć* to cows.

Seta. A dog.
Seta hopon. A puppy.
Hopon seta. A little dog.
Aṇḍiạ seta. } A dog.
Seta aṇḍiạ. }
Eṅga seta. } A slut, a bitch.
Seta eṅga. }
Jarna seta. A dog that will seize anything in the shape of game.

Seta oć. } A form of edible mush-
Seta puṭkạ. } room.

Seta rokoć. A kind of snail.

Seta poḍo. A species of fig tree, *Ficus hispida, Linn.*

Seta sagaḱ. A common grass, *Andropogon aciculatus, Retz.*

Seta aṇḍir. } A small bush, *Grewia*
Seta ãṛga. } *polygama, Roxb.*
Seta kaṭa. }

Seta kaṭa aṛaḱ. A small plant, *Gynandropsis pentaphylla, Linn.*

Seta pan. } A small plant, *Mono-*
Seta pan dare. } *choria plantaginea, Kunth.*

Setaḱ. The morning.
Setaḱre. In the morning.
Aṅga setaḱre. In the dawn, at dawn.
Gitić setaḱkedako. They slept till morning.
Enka enka tegekin setaḱkeda. In that way they passed the night till morning.
Setaḱ ạyub̃e hijuḱa. He comes morning and evening.
Setagoḱa nahaḱ. It will presently be morning.

Seṭe. } Imitative of a suppressed
Seṭe seṭe. } bubbling sound, also that produced by crabs.
Kaṭkomko seṭe seṭeḱa. } The crabs are pro-
Kaṭkomko seṭe seṭea. } ducing a bubbling sound.
Daka seṭe seṭeḱkana. The rice is bubbling.
Daḱ thoṛaente seṭe seṭeḱkana. Owing to there being little water it does not bubble freely.

Seṭe sosroć. A kind of grasshopper.

Seṭeć. To husk dhan the first time.
Hoṛoko seṭeḍakaḱa. They have put the dhan through the first process of husking.

Seṭeć. To pierce, to penetrate.
Churite bań seṭeḍlena. The knife did not penetrate.
Nahelte hõ bań seṭejoḱkana. The plough is not even piercing (the soil.)
Jel tuńledeań, bahiń seṭeḍledea. I shot a deer (with an arrow,) I did not pierce it.
Noa katha bań seṭeć daṛeaḱa. I could not pierce this matter, could not understand it.

Seṭeć. To be able, to succeed, to overcome. Cf. leṭeć.
Nitok̄le seṭećakat̄a. Now we have succeeded.

Setolak̄. } With, along with, accompani-
Setelet̄. } ment.
Setelet̄ bạnuk̄antalea. We have no accompaniment, i. e. we have nothing to eat along with it as a relish.
Botor setelet̄e dạṛkeda. } He fled with fear.
Botor setelak̄e dạṛkeda. }

Seteṅ. To ooze out.
Gitil khon dak̄ seteṅok̄kana. Water is oozing from the sand.
Uli dak̄ baṅ seteṅok̄kantaea. He has not got a flow of saliva.
Toa baṅ seteṅok̄kantaea. Her milk is not flowing.

Seṭe peṭe. Noise produced by anything squirming in shallow water, or as a fish floundering in little water.
Seṭe peṭe hako menak̄koa. Fish are floundering.
Seṭe peṭeko sade ocoeda. They are making a slight splashing sound.
Seṭe peṭeko ạbukok̄kana. They are washing their hands with a noise.

Seṭer. To arrive.
Dak̄ seṭerena. The rain has arrived.
Idi seṭer oṭoaeme. Take it to him.
Seṭerkaeme. Arrive him, take him there.
Heć seṭerenako. They have come, or they have arrived.
Setoṅ din seṭerena. The hot weather has arrived.

Setoṅ. Direct rays of the sun.
Setoṅ din. The hot weather.
Ạdi ạṭ setoṅ. Very fierce sunshine.
Setoṅ lagaoakawadea. } The sun has affected
Setoṅ kharaoakawadea. } him, produced in-
Setoṅ bhijạuakawadea. } disposition.
Ạdi setoṅediṅkana. I feel the heat very much.
Uṛuć puṭuć setoṅkana. It is blazing hot.

Sewa. }
Sewa dewa. } To perform an act or acts of worship, to serve.
Sewa ṭewa. }
Boṅgako sewaakoa. They worship the boṅgas (q. v.)
Sek̄waić. A worshipper.

Sewal. Cf. sawal.

Seyaṛ. } Stiff, as a breeze blowing
Seyaṛ seyaṛ. } through an opening, gorge, &c.
Seyaṛ seyaṛe hoeda. It is blowing a stiff breeze.

Seyaṛ marte. } With a gust.
Seyaṛ mente. }
Seyaṛ marte hoe heć goṭena. The wind came with a gust, it blew a gust.

Si. To plough.
Siok̄kanae. He is ploughing.
Nes noa baṛge siogok̄a. This garden will be ploughed this year.
Siok̄ gupi kanae. He is able to plough and take care of cattle, i. e. he is about 12 years old.
Si ot. Ploughed land.
Siok̄ić. A ploughman.
Si lạhut̄. To plough land the second last time previous to sowing or planting.
Si lạhut̄akat̄ako. They have ploughed (the land) the second last time.
Siok̄ joṛaome. } Yoke the plough.
Nahel joṛaome. }
Ḍaṅrako siakoa. They plough with oxen.
Nukin ḍaṅraṅ si goćkina, baṅ ạkriṅkina. I will plough with those bullocks till they die, I will not sell them.
Si tukunkedeae. He ploughed with him (ox) till he was past feeling (the goad made no impression on him.)

Siạhi. Ink.

Siạṅ sayaṅ. Gentle, as a breeze.
Siạṅ sayaṅ hoe paromok̄kana. A gentle breeze is blowing through, or over.

Siạra. A grating, used mainly as an adjunct to a fish trap; anything made like a grating, such as a stretcher, &c.

Siboṛ. To strip, to take off or out, to take away.
Bạhu sanamak̄ko siboṛkedea. They stripped the wife of everything (ornaments, &c. when they sent her back to her parents.)
Siboṛkediṅako. They stripped me, (took away what I was unwilling to give.)
Kicrićko siboṛkedea. They stripped him of his clothes.
Catomko siboṛkedea. They took away his umbrella.

Sićkạṭup. The little finger, or little toe.

Sić soć. } Upstarts or persons of little
Seć soć. } importance.
Noko seć soć cetko cekaeda? What will, or can, these upstarts do?
Noko eken seć soć. These are only people of little importance.

Sić soć. Whistling produced through the teeth.
Sić soć gol baṛaedae. He is whistling through the teeth.

Sid. Effected, accomplished, perfected.
Sid ataṅ. To be accomplished, as a pupil.
Sid em. To perfect, to complete, to finish.
Sid emako lạgit̄ko metakoa. To make them accomplished they say to them.
Uni do ojhak̄ ar janok̄ reak̄ side emat̄koa. He made them accomplished charm doctors and witch finders.
Side atạṅkeda. He became accomplished.

Sidbid. Accomplished, finished, settled.
Oka hõ baṅ sidbidlena. Nothing whatever was settled.

Siḍgir. To remove, as earth, &c., by falling water, to wash or carry away by falling water.
Dakte siḍgirkedae. It was washed away by water.

Sidhạ. } Uncooked victuals, provi-
Ser sidhạ. } sions given according to allowance.
Sidhạko atankeda. They took their allowance of uncooked food.
Ser sidhạ purạuentaea. His allowance of food is exhausted, i. e. his end has come.

Sidhạ. Straight.

Sidhi. A preparation of opium.

Sidho. To become a statue, to be fixed, as an image.
Bengeć ruạṛkateye sidhoena. She looked back and became a statue.

Sidho. Clean, perfect, accomplished.

Sidi. To collect or demand payment of dues other than rents.
Binko sidia. They collect debts.
Ṭaka sidiye senakana. He has gone to collect money due to him.

Sidi bidi. Roughly, carelessly, inefficiently, as a piece of work.
Cećlekam jokkeć sidi bidi? How have you swept it,? it is carelessly done.

Siḍić. } Smarting sensation as that
Siḍić siḍić. } produced by the bite of a mosquito, &c.
Hasoedekana siḍić siḍić. It pains him smartingly.
Siḍić siḍićko gegerkana sikṛić do. The mosquitoes are biting and causing smarting.

Siḍić marte. }
Siḍić mente. } With a smart.
Siḍić marte sikṛiće gerkediña. The mosquito bit me with a smart.

Siḍik. }
Siḍik siḍik. } Cf. siḍić.

Siḍik marte. }
Siḍik mente. } Cf. siḍić marte.

Siḍor soḍor. Trickling, a little, applied to leaking.
Cećlekape phuṛukakaća? Siḍor soḍor jorokkana. How have you made the leaf cup? it is leaking tricklingly.
Siḍor soḍor goṭa oṛak jorokkantalea. Our whole house is leaking tricklingly.

Siḍo soḍo. A little, applied to leaking.
Siḍo soḍo jorokkana. It is leaking a little.
Khapra oṛak siḍo soḍo joroka. Tiled houses leak a little.

Siḍṛak baḍṛak. To waste, to use lavishly, to lavish, abusively.
Siḍṛak baḍṛak dakko areńeda. They are baling out the water lavishly.
Dak alope siḍṛak baḍṛaga. Do not waste the water.
Siḍṛak baḍṛak dakko duleda. They are pouring out the water lavishly.

Siḍrić biḍrić. } Very small, applied
Sirṛić birṛić. } mainly to leaves.
Siḍrić biḍrić sakam. A very small leaf.

Sidup̆. Perpendicular, erect.
Bohoke sidup̆kettaea gidrạ do. The child has raised his head erect, the child has arrived at the stage at which it can hold its head up.
Sidup̆teye ńurena. He fell head foremost.
Sidup̆ keṭeć gidrạ. A child of 2 months or more that can be held up erect.
Sidup̆teko doho idiakaća binḍạ do. They have set up the sheaves erect.
De bhala, ḍili leka hoṛmo dobon siduba doṛoma bisi mucạt do.

Sidup̆ Soren. A sub sept of the Santal sept Soren (q. v.)

Sidup̆ Mạrnḍi. A sub-sept of the Santal sept Mạrnḍi (q. v.)

Sidup̆ Pạuriạ. A sub-sept of the Santal sept Pạuriạ (q. v.)

Siḍwak baḍwak. Harshly, angrily.
Siḍwak baḍwake roṛkediña. He scolded or reprimanded me angrily.

Sigi. To make a deep incision with an axe on each side of a log previous to splitting it
Kaṭko sigia paṛag lagić. They make a deep incision on each side of a log to split it.
Sigi maṛańako, khanko paṛaga. They first make a deep incision on each side (of a log), then they split it.

Sigić bigić. Without order, confused, disorderly, disarranged.
Noa katha sanamko sigić bigićkeda. They confused this whole matter.
Sigić bigićkedako. They disordered it.
Sanamko sigić bigićakaća. They have disordered everything.

Sihại. Ink.
Kolom sihại. Pen and ink.

Sihạn. Prank, frolic, practical joke, given to pranks, frolicsome.
Nui ma sihạn lekageń ạikạuea siń sạṭup̆ dake buḍrućańkana
Iń do hor horteń calakkana, am do sihạn leka jaṅgam lebećkediña. I am going on the road, you like one given to pranks trod on my foot.
Henda na, am dom itić baṛaediña, sihạngem ńamkankhanlań udukama nahak. Listen girl, you are nipping me, if you wish to see a frolic I will shew you one presently.
Sahan hubạkiń metadekhan sihạn leka barea peageye hubạkleda. When I told him to chop fire wood he chopped only two or three pieces as if he were doing it for a frolic.

Sihạnia. Given to pranks, frolicsome.

Sij. A shrub with three angled prickly branches, *Euphorbia antiquorum*, *Linn*. Cf. ẹtkeć.

Sik. }
Sikte. } Mode, way, method.

Nuiáḱ sik kantaea. It is an imitation of him, it was learned from him.
Ona sikte. Analogously.
Ran jomkateye besena, ona sikte am hǒ jomlekhanem beskoḱa. He took medicine and was cured, analogously if you take medicine you will be cured.

Sikạ. }
Siki. } A small silver coin, a four or a two anna bit.

Sikạr. To confess, to acknowledge, to consent, to acquiesce, to assent.

Bae sikạrlena. He did not assent.

Sikạri. }
Sikạria. } A hunter, a trapper of game.

Sikạri kanae. He is a hunter.

Sikat. }
Sikhạt. } Teaching.

Uniạḱ sikhạtte sikhạtoḱkana.

Sikạu. To teach, to tutor, to suborn, to advise.

Sipikạu. The reciprocal form of sikạu.

Sikhạ. Three or five marks burned on the lower left arm by all Santal males.

This seems to be a mere custom without any religious or tribal signification.

Sikhạt. Teaching.

Uniạḱ sikhạtte sikhạtoḱkanae.

Sikhạu. }
Sikhlạu. } To teach, to tutor, to suborn, to advise,

Amte baṛe kạmime alom sikhạu ocoḱa. Do the work yourself, do not be told how to do it.
Sikhạu paṛhao goḱkadeako. They tutored him as to what he should say.

Sikhạuna. Teaching.

Sikhlạu. Cf. sikhạu.

Siknạt. }
Sikhnot. } To teach, to learn, teaching.

Bese sikhnạtakawana. He has learnt well.
Sikhnot joṅkanae. He is learning.
Sikhnotaekana. He is teaching him.

Siki. A small silver coin. Cf. sikạ.

Sikil. To polish, to burnish, to make bright as iron on a grindstone.

San sikilkedae. He ground and polished it.
Sikilakać leka ńeloḱkana. It looks as if it had been ground bright.

Sikim. }
Sạkim. } To finish, to complete.

Kạmile sikimkeda. We completed the work.
Oḱolle sikimakaća. We have finished writing.

Sikiom baha. A large lily (*Crinum*, nov. sp. *Watt*), found as yet only in the Santal country.

Sikiṛ. Itching, burning itchy sensation, dislike, antipathy, hate.

Hirom era etka sikiṛ bań sahaoḱa. A co-wife and the itching produced by the *etka* (q. v. in sup.) cannot be borne.
Sikiṛgekin ńeleńkana. They regard me with dislike.

Siki siki. }
Seke seke. } To rage, to be in a passion, to be restless through anger.

Siki siki baṛaekanae dadal lạgić.

Sikih. Cf. sikiṛ.

Siknạt. To teach, to learn, teaching.

Dekoko ṭhen phạsiạrako siknạtakaćte. By having learned deceit from the Hindus.

Sikol. A chain.

Sikol. }
Sikol baber. } Thin straw ropes with which *bandis* (q. v.) are bound.

Sikṛi. A chain.

Sikṛi mala. A chain worn on the neck.

Sikriạ. A hunter.

Ḍhal sikriạ. A hunter's henchman, an armour bearer.

Sikṛić. A mosquito.

Sikṛić. }
Sikṛić sikṛić. } To clink. Cf. sekṛeć.

Okoeaḱ sakom sikṛić sikṛić sadẹkana? Whose bangles are clinking?

Sikṛić marte. }
Sikṛić mente. } With a clink.

Sikṛić marte sade goćena. It sounded clink.

Sikṛić sikṛić. A children's game.

Sikuạr. A sling slung to each end of a pole in which things are carried.

Sikuṕ. To shut up, to close.

Bugliye or sikuṕkeda. He pulled (the string of) the bag and closed it up.
Kiorić catomko sikuba. They shut up cloth umbrellas.
Moca doe sikuṕkeda. He shut his mouth.
Adom baha setaḱ sikuboḱa, ar adom do ayuṕ sikuboḱa. Some flowers close in the morning and others at evening.
Roṛ sikuṕkedeale. We spoke to him and shut him up (shut his mouth.)

Sil. }
Sil dhiri. } A hone, to rub and sharpen on a hone.

Holaćko sila. They rub and sharpen razors on a hone.

Sil. Nature, quality, civility, benevolence, humanity, politeness, generosity.

Sil sorom. Shame, sense of decency, gravity,

Sil sorome jomkeda. He ate his sense of decency, he has no sense of decency.
Sil sorom bạnuktaea. He has no sense of decency.

Silạt. } A slate, a school slate
Siloṭ. }

Silạu. To sharpen, to put an edge on.
Ṭeṅgoe silạuakata. He has sharpened the axe.

Silgạć. Cf. sirgạć.

Sili. A rope made of hair.
Sili baber. A hair rope about ¼ in. in diameter and 3 or 4 feet long.
Sili mala. Beads threaded on twisted hair and worn on the neck.

Silmoć. Small and dirty, dirty.
Silmoć mara gidrạ. A small dirty rascal of a boy.
Sap silmoćkedeako. They took hold of it and dirtied it.

Silodha. Huge.
Marań silodha kul kanae. It is a great huge tiger

Siloṭ. A school slate.

Silpạṭ. } A railway sleeper.
Silpoṭ. }

Silpạṭ. A slipper without a heel.

Silpher. } To change from civility to
Silpherao. } impertinence, or the use of force.
Nui hoṛ do ạdi bạrice silpherao daṛeaka. This man can easily change his tone.
Silpher goćenae. He has changed his tone.

Silpiń. A door.
Duạr silpiń. A door.
Silpiń sińkakpe. Shut the door.
Ạurile silpińaka. We have not yet put on a door.
Silpiń jhijme. Open the door.
Silpiń hurkạrkakme. Bolt the door.
Silpiń lạdakkam. Draw to the door.

Siluń piṭuń. Slabberingly, slobberingly, defiled, dirty. *Scottice* slaistered.
Siluń piṭuńe jomeda. He is eating slabberingly.
Siluń piṭuń akanae. He is slabbered.
Siluń piṭuń dakko ạguieda. They are bringing dirty water.
Pạurạ godam reak ṭhik do bạnukanań, ondenak do siluń piṭuńgea. There is nothing right about a liquor shop, it is all dirty.

Sim. The Barn door fowl.
Bir sim. Wild jungle fowl.
Bisạ sim. A fowl with feathers turned the wrong way.
Sạṇḍi sim. } A cock.
Sim sạṇḍi. }
Sim eńga. A hen.
Kaloṭ sim. A pullet.
Sim hopon. A chicken.
Hopon sim. A small fowl
Sim jel. Flesh of fowl.
Sim bele. A hen's egg.
Cin sim. A Guinea fowl.
Sim pakha. A hen's nesting place.

Sim rak. Cock crow.
Simrakakana. It is cock crow.
Sim rakrele calaoena. We went at cock crow.

Sim jel. Goose flesh, flesh rough or corrugated with cold or fear.
Rabańteye simjelenae. Through cold his flesh has become goose flesh

Sim lać. A method of making by a series of loops a three strand thread with a single thread, to make a three strand thread with a single thread.
Sutạme sim laćakata. He has made a three strand thread with a single thread.

Sim oć. A form of edible mushroom of a red colour.

Sim gaṛ. A traditional fort said to have belonged to the Ṭuḍu (q. v.) sept of the Santals.

Sim gaṛ. } A corner of the house set
Sim kole. } apart for fowls.

Sim. } A festival observed after
Hạriạṛ sim. } the rice has been planted. Cf. hạriạṛ sim.

Sim. } A village festival observed
Erok sim. } after seed sowing has begun. Fowls are sacrificed and an oblation of milk offered to the village deities.

Sim } Fowls given by the villagers
Goṭ sim. } to be sacrificed at the Goṭ or Sohrae (q. v.) festival.

Sim. } A festival observed in the
Mag sim. } month of Mag (q. v.) after the reaping of the thatching grass.

Sim. } A festival observed in
Jom sim. } honour of the sun. Cf. jom sim.

Sim goyor. A game so called.

Simạ. Boundary, to set a boundary or limit.
Ato simạ. } The village boundary,
Ato reak simạ. }
Noa senteko simạkeda. They laid down the boundary in this direction.
Uniak daya reak simạ bạnukanań. There is no limit to his grace.

Sima̜ boṅga. The boundary godlet of the Santals.

Sima̜ sim. A fowl sacrificed to the boundary godlet sima̜ boṅga (q. v.)

Sima̜ d̜and̜i. A boundary.

Sima̜na. A boundary. Cf. sima̜.

Sima̜tbar̥. The limit boundary.

Simbr̥a̜. } Polypus of the nose, a disease
Simr̥a̜. } of cattle in which the septum of the nose is injured.

Simić simić. A children's game.

Simpasar̥e. To be at variance, to clink. Cf. sekr̥eć.

Simpasar̥e geakin. They are at variance.
Simpasar̥eakanakin. They are at variance.
Sakom do simpasar̥e sa̜d̜ekantaea. Her bangles are clinking.

Simr̥a̜. Cf. simbr̥a̜.

Siń. To shut, as a door, lid of box, &c.

Siń bahre. To shut out.
Siń pot̥om. To shut in or up.
Bhir̥a̜uk̓ leka bań sińakana. It is not shut close.
Siń bhir̥a̜ukam. Shut it close.
Siń bahrekedeako. They shut him out.
Or̥ak̓re siń pot̥omakanae. He is shut up in the house.

Siń. A day from sunrise to sunset.

Mit̓ siń mit̓ ńinda̜. All day and all night.
Siń sa̜t̥up̓. Often, continually, all day.
Siń marsal. Day light.
Siń lae ńinda̜ lae. All day and all night.
Siń sa̜t̥upe hijuk̓kana. He comes always.
Mit̓ siń mit̓ ńinda̜e dak̓keda. It rained all day and all night.
Sińge siń sińge ńinda̜. All day and all night.
Sińge siń ar sińge ńinda̜e rak̓eda. She weeps all day and all night.
Siń lae ńinda̜ lae bae ba̜giińa. He leaves me neither by day nor by night.
Sińke ńinda̜. Day and night.
Sińke ńinda̜ń rak̓amkana. I call to thee day and night.
Siń marsalre do bań, menkhan ńinda̜e hećena. He did not come in day light, but at night.
Ba̜rsiń pe mãhã. Two or three days.
A̜rsiń ba̜rsiń. A few days.

Siń dua̜r. A ceremony observed at a marriage.

Siń arak̓. A small tree, *Bauhinia purpurea, Linn.*, the leaves of which are eaten as a pot herb.

Siń boṅga. } The sun.
Siń cando. }

Siń candoe rakap̓kana. The sun is rising.
Siń candoe ha̜surena. The sun has set.
Siń candoe gahnak̓kana. There is an eclipse of the sun in process.

Siń sadom. The Day-horse, mentioned in the Santal tradition of the creation of the world.

Siń sadom ho, Siń sadom, buru d̜a̜nd̜it ho, buru d̜a̜nd̜it.
Torae calaoen ho, siń sadom ho, Gań ˊna̜ite Siń sadom.
Torae buhelen ho, Sor̥a sa̜mutte ho, Siń sadom.

Siń sa̜t̥up̓. Often, continually, all day.

Sina̜m. Exactly, precisely.

Sina̜m uni lekae ńelok̓kana. He looks exactly like him.
Sina̜m uni lekangeae. He is precisely like him.

Sind. } To break into a house by
Sindh. } ma̜king a hole in the wall.

Sindkateko kombr̥o idikeda. They broke through the wall and stole.

Sind ka̜t̥hi. The implement by which thieves make a hole in the wall of a house.

Sind muhã̜ni. The act of cutting a hole in the wall of a house or of abstracting goods.

Sind muhã̜nireń sap̓kedea. I caught him in the act of making a hole in the wall of the house.

Sinda̜ń. Mischief making.

Uni do sinda̜ńe jowaok̓a. He is a habituated mischief maker.
Sinda̜ńe ńam bar̥aeda. He is seeking mischief making.

Sindhet̓. Cf. rehet̓ sindhet̓.

Sindir. Edge, ridge.

Sindirkedae. He left ridges (in ploughing.)
Sindir sindirko ba̜giakawada. They left ridges (did not turn over all the soil with the plough.)
Sindir sindirte calak̓me. Go along the edge.
Sa̜khi sindirkeam? Can you prove it?

Sindra̜ dhan. The applying of red lead (sindur) to a bride at marriage.

A small quantity of red lead in a leaf is given to the bridegroom, who with the little finger of the right hand applies the *sindur* five times to the bride's forehead on the parting of the hair. This act is known as *sindra dhan*.

Sinduk. A chest, a box. Cf. sa̜nduk.

Sindur. Red lead.

Sindur bundi. Marked with sindur (q. v.), married, applied to females Cf. sindra̜ dhan.

Sindur bundiakanae. She is married.
Sindur bundiakadeae. He has married her marked her with red lead.

Sindur Cōr̥ē. A sub-sept of the Santal sept Cōr̥ē (q. v.)

Sindwạri dare. A common bush, *Vitex Negundo, Linn.*

Siṅgạ. } A ram's horn, a musical
Ram siṅgạ. } instrument shaped like a buffaloe's horn.

Siṅgạdar. A player on the ramsiṅgạ (q. v.)

Siṅgạṛ. Nightfall, the period succeeding twilight.
Siṅgạṛ jokha hoeña. It is nightfall.
Ạyuṗ siṅgạṛena. It is nightfall.
Pạhil siṅgạṛ. The first part of the night.
Pạhil siṅgạṛe goĉena. He died just after nightfall.

Siṅgạṛ. To develop and become rigid as the wings of an insect after emersion from the pupa-case or cocoon, applied mainly to Tasar silk moths.
Pạtniko siṅgạṛena. The wings of the moths have developed and become rigid.

Siṅgạr. To bathe and tidy oneself.
Tinạkem siṅgạroḱkana? How much will you tidivate yourself?

Siṅghaoṭi. To tie the horns of a buffaloe to each side to keep it still when being castrated.
Siṅghaoṭikaepe. Tie his horns to each side.

Siṅghin. Having horns projecting in front, applied to goats, spiny.

Siṅghin. Envious.
Nui siṅghin mara hoṛ. This envious rascal.

Siṅghin bhạruạ. Spiny caterpillars, applied mainly to the larvæ of *Attacus atlas*, and *A. selene.*

Siṅghin hako. A species of fish.

Siṅghason. A throne.

Siṅgh jạpuṫ. The rain which falls when the sun is in the sign Leo.

Siṅkoṛ soṅkoṛ. Loosely, not fitting tightly, as a bolt, &c. in a hole; sound of rattling as of anything loose.
Siṅkoṛ soṅkoṛena. It fits loosely.
Siṅkoṛ soṅkoṛ ḍhilgea. It is loose and rattling.

Siniĉ. } Opportunity, chance, excuse,
Siniṫ. } pretence.
Siniĉe ńam bạṛaeda. He is on the look out for an opportunity, (to do some one an injury.)

Siniĉ samanom baha. A gorgeous flowering wild plant, *Gloriosa superba, Linn.*

Siniń. A door, a small breathing hole or way of escape which can be quickly enlarged, a small opening made by rats from their holes to the air.
These openings serve as breathing holes and having only a slight covering of earth can be quickly enlarged and form a way of escape when the regular way of egress is closed.
Siniṅko jhiĉkeda. They opened the door.
Okare siniṅtako? Where is their breathing hole?

Siniṫ. Narrow, strait, as a place, road, defile, &c., difficulty, strait, at a disadvantage. Cf. siniĉ.
Jhạḱ siniṫreń ńammea. I shall find you in a difficulty, or I shall find you in such circumstance as I shall be able to take you at a disadvantage.

Siṅjo. The Bael fruit and tree, *Ægle Marmelos, Correa.*

Sio soyo. } Tricklingly, to exude or leak
Siro soro. } in small quantity.
Sio soyo joroḱkana. It is leaking tricklingly.

Sio soyo. Inefficiently, blunderingly.
Sio soyo tirioko oroheda. They are playing the flute inefficiently (as learners.)

Sipạhi. A peon, a messenger, a soldier.

Sipi. To knead, to knead while moist.
Sạtuko sipikeda. They moistened and kneaded the sạtu (q. v.)
Sipikedeako. They hammered him.

Sipi. To consult, to conspire, to agree, to elope.

Sipir sipir. Applied to drizzling rain.
Sipir sipire daḱeda. It is drizzling.

Sipoṫ. To squeeze in the hand.
Sipoṫ gejerkedako. They squeezed it in the hand and broke it up.
Daḱko sipoṫ giḍikeda. They squeezed the water out of it.

Sir. A nerve, a vein.
Daḱsir. Vein of a leaf, water bearing strata, a vein of water.
Daḱ sire la ńamakada. He has dug and found water bearing strata.

Sir. Superior, better.
Uni khon kạmire sirgeae. He is superior to him in working.
Uni khon unigeye sirena. This (person) is superior to him.

Sir. Edge.

Sir ṭaṭao. To sympathize with, to feel compassion for, to compassionate, to commiserate, to become stiff, as the muscles.
Boeha dukoḱ khan sir ṭaṭaoḱgetaea. If his brother is suffering, he sympathises with him.
Laṅgalenkhan sir ṭaṭaoḱa. When one is tired the muscles become stiff.

Siṛa. In the front rank, principal, leading, foremost, first.
Siṛa gai. A cow in the first rank of excellence.
Siṛa khet. The principal field.
Siṛa koṛa. The leading youth.
Siṛa kuṛi. The leading girl.

Siṛa. A strip.
Nia siṛateye calaoena. He went along this strip of jungle.
Mić siṛa jel emaṅme. Give me a strip of flesh meat.
Siṛa siṛa bir menak̇a. There is a jungle in strips.
Aka rohoṛ lagić jelko siṛaia. To be hung up and dried they cut fish meat into strips.

Siṛa. Edge, corner.
Pon siṛa. Four cornered, four square.

Siṛa. } Hydrocele, or any other
Eka siṛa. } swelling of the scrotum, having only one testicle.

Siṛa soro. } To flow as blood from a
Siro siro. } wound, or water from a small opening.
Siṛa soro jorok̇kana mayam. The blood is flowing or trickling.
Dal siṛa soroakadeako. They have beaten him and made him bloody (made blood to flow.)

Siṛak̇ barak̇. } Fat, savoury, tender, as
Siṛat barat. } cooked good flesh meat.
Itilanae siṛat barat. It is fat and savoury.
Siṛat baratko jomkedea. They eat it with great relish.

Sirba. } To have a splinter run into
Siṛba. } the hand, &c., to be torn into the quick, as a finger nail.
Rama sirbaena. The nail is torn into the quick.
Sirbaenaṅ. A splinter has run into my hand.

Sirgat. The wrong way, against the hair, backwards, rough.
Sirgatteye orkedea. He pulled him backwards, he pulled him by the heels.
Sirgatge aṭkarok̇kana. It feels rough.

Sirgiṭ aṛak̇. } A small plant, *Celocia*
Sirkiṭ aṛak̇. } *argenta, Moq.*, the leaves of which are eaten as a pot-herb.

Siṛhi. A ladder, a stair.

Sirhi. Branches laid on rafters underneath thatch.

Sirhoć hako. A species of fish.

Sirhoć cẽṛẽ. Cf. sirloć cẽṛẽ.

Siṛi. To enquire, to search for; to look out for.
Ḍahra siṛi aguiem. Look out for a bullock and bring information about it.
Bahule siṛi baṛaećkoa. We are looking out for brides.

Siri. Luck.
Sirianić hoṛe tabẽkana. He was a lucky man.
Bes siri uṭhaunakantabona. We are having good luck.

Siṛić. } To smell badly, to stink.
Siṛić. }
Siṛiċge sokana. It is smelling badly.
Thariko, baṭiko siṛijok̇a. The plates and cups will smell badly.

Siṛić soboć. Empty, without a sound.
Cele hõ bako aṭkarok̇kana siṛić soboć. No one is stirring, there is dead silence.

Sirijala. }
Sirijol. } Cf. sirjon.
Sirijon. }

Siṛik taham. Empty, without a sound, dead silence.

Siṛiṅ hako. A kind of fish.

Sirip. Only.
Sirip inage aguime. Bring that only.

Siṛip. } To clink, as small metallic
Siṛip siṛip. } sonorous objects coming into contact with each other.
Baṭri sadek̇a siṛip siṛip. The toe rings sound clink, clink.

Siṛip marte. } With a clink. Cf. siṛip.
Siṛip mente. }
Siṛip marte sade goćena. It sounded with a clink.

Siris. } A large forest tree, *Albiz-*
Siris dare. } *zia Lebbek, Benth.*

Sirishtadar. } The official in charge of
Siristadar. } the records of a court of justice.

Sirjau. To create, to begin, to prepare, to make.
Baplae sirjaunakawana. He has begun preparations for a marriage.
Haṇḍi sirjaunakawanae. He has made rice beer for himself.
Jel dakako sirjaunakaṭa. They have made a feast of rice and flesh meat.
Rua sirjaunakawadea. His fever has begun.
Cedak̇em polomlena? Ho, bohok̇ haso sirjauadiṅa. Why did you delay? Oh, I had a headache.

Sirjon. To make, to begin, to create, a creature.
Sirjon johkana. He is making for himself.
Okoeak̇ sirjon kana? Whose creature is it? to whom does it owe its existence?
Isorak̇ sirjon kana. It is God's creation or creature.

Sirkiṭ aṛak̇. Cf. sirgiṭ aṛak̇.

Sirloć cẽṛẽ. } The Ashy-crowned Finch
Sirhoć cẽṛẽ. } lark, *Pyrrhulauda grisea*, so called from its note. Cf. gõeṭha lipi.

Siṛo. To split, to tear.
Siṛo luṭi. A hair-lip.
Or siṛokedeae. He pulled and tore it (as a beast of prey tearing a carcase.)

Siro soro. Flowing, as blood, or as water from a small opening, trickling.
Dal siro sorokedeako. They beat him to the effusion of blood.
Kanḍa siro soro joroḱkana. The water pot is leaking tricklingly.

Siroć soroć. } Slight and frequent,
Sirot sorot. } applied to diarrhœa.
Siroć soroć oḍokoḱkanae nui gidrạ. This child has slight but frequent diarrhœa.

Siṛog. To mock, to taunt, to speak harshly.
Ạḍi siṛoge roroṛa. He speaks very mockingly.
Siṛogadiñae. He mocked me, he taunted me.

Sirom. } A tall grass, *Andropogon*
Sirom ghãs. } *muricatus, Retz.*
This is the grass from the roots of which the *khas khas tatties* are made.

Siropa. A piece of cloth, generally suitable for a turban, given as a sign of office or authority or as a token of respect.
Siropako tolkedea. They bound the turban on his head.
Raj ṭhen khon Pargana reaḱ siropae ńamkeda. He received a turban from the king as a sign that he had been appointed to the chiefship.

Siripạ. A cloth given as a present. Cf. siropa.

Sirpạ. Two sticks tied together used to prop up a cart when the bullocks are unyoked.

Sirpiṭiạk. Wet, damp, moist.
Ghãs sisirte sirpiṭiạḱakana. The grass is wet with dew.
Daḱ sirpiṭiạḱkedeae. The water wetted him (passing through wet bushes.)

Sirpuć. A piece of male attire. Cf. bhagwa.
Nonka sirpuć ḍeṅgatege ḍheriń ńelakaḱkoa. I have seen many of the class who wear the sirpuć.

Sirpuṭ. } Sound produced by
Sirpuṭ sirpuṭ. } sucking up liquid
Sirpuṭ. } or semi-liquid.
Sirpuṭ sirpuṭ. }
Siṛpuṭ siṛpuṭe siṛupeḱkana. He is sucking it up.

Siṛput marte. }
Sirpuṭ marte. } With a sucking sound.
Siṛpuṭ mente. }
Sirpuṭ mente. }
Siṛput marteye jom goćkeda. He ate it up with a sucking sound.

Sirṛi. To persist, to importune, persistent, importunate.
Sirṛigeae. He is persistent.

Sirṛi. } Cf. eksirṛi.
Eksirṛi. }

Sirṛić birṛić. Numerous, as the leaflets on the leaf of a Tamarind tree.
Sirṛić birṛić sakamakana. The leaves have numerous leaflets.

Sirsirạu. To start, to quake with fear. Cf. sisirạu.

Sirtạl. } Cf. eksirtạl.
Eksirtạl. }

Siruṗ. To sup, to suck in.
Bele ul jom jokhećko siṛuba. They suck when eating a ripe mangoe.
Rasateḱ joroḱkante siṛuṗ godae. As the juice is flowing he sucks it up.
Ṭheṅgate haṛhaćaḱko siṛuṗaekan. They are giving him a bitter thing on a stick to suck.

Sis. An ear of dhan.
Sis upạr sis, lar upạr lar, guti upạr guti, jemon pạihạ ạlom hạsi hanaokoa.

Sisạ. Lead.
Sisạ reaḱ. Leaden.
Sisạ reaḱ guli. A leaden bullet.

Sisgạr. Heart-wood.
Noa kaṭ do ạḍi sisgạra. There is much heart-wood in this log.

Sisi. A phial, a small bottle.

Sisiạr. } Thin, slim, as a stick.
Sisiạri. }
Noa sisiạri ṭheṅgate celem daleaᵽ What, or who, can you strike with this thin stick?

Sisiạrić. A species of large squirrel.

Sisiń hako. A species of small fish or minnow.

Sisir. } Dew.
Sisir daḱ. }
Sisir ńuroḱkana. } Dew is falling.
Sisir daḱ ńuroḱkana. }

Sisir daka. Boiled rice given to the dancers at the Sohrae festival who have been out dancing in the dew all night.

Sisir hạṇḍi. Liquor given at the Sohrae festival to those who have been out in the dew all night beating the drums for the dancers.

Sisir cas. Crops which depend mainly on the dew for moisture.

Sisir jạli. Applied to fruit forming after the rains have ceased, the only moisture being dew.
Sisir jạli jo kana. It is fruit that has formed after the rains had ceased.

Sisirạu. To start, to shiver, to quake with fear.
Sisirạu got́enae. He gave a start.

Sisi sisi. To whistle through the teeth, an imitative word.
Sisi sisi goledae. He is whistling through his teeth.

Siso soso. Imitative of the sound produced by whistling, to whistle.
Siso soso gol baṛaedae. He is whistling and making a sound resembling *siso soso*.

Sisu juạn. A lad of from 13 to 15 years of age.

Siswạ bajṛa. A kind of cultivated grain.

Sit́. To be exhausted, finished, nothing remaining.
Jokha sit́akat́ tahĕkana. It had been accurately measured, or made accurately to measurement.
Ninạk̕ge ol sit́ at̕et́ sit́ tahĕkantaea.
Sit́ cabaakantalea jomak̕. Our (stock of) food is completely exhausted.
Dak̕ phoṛ sit́ idikedae. He cut the ridge and took away all the water.
Añjet́ sit́ena dak̕ do. The water is all dried up.
Dak̕ sit́ utạrena. The water is entirely exhausted.
Jom sit́kedako. They ate up all.

Sit́. To pluck, as flowers, to gather, as pot-herbs or leaves used as pot-herbs.
Aṛak̕ko sida. They pluck or gather pot-herbs or leaves used as pot-herbs.
Sanam bahako sit́akat́a. They have plucked all the flowers.

Siṭ na sawad. Unpalatable.

Sitạ. A grain, applied to rice when boiled.
Mit́ sitạ hõ bae lagaoada dak̕ mạṇḍire. She did not put even one grain of rice in the rice water.

Sitạṅ. A kind of grass.

Sitạṅ. To be cold, as the body just before death, &c.
Hoṛmo sitạṅentaea. His body has become cold.
Sitạṅ sap̣akadea. Cold has taken him, he has become cold.

Siṭạp̣. To shut or close suddenly, as anything worked by a spring, to be caught in anything worked by a spring.
Ona laṛaolekhane siṭạp̣ godok̕a. If he moves that (spring of trap) he is caught at once.
Siṭạp̣kok̕am. You may be caught, you may be snapped (as in a trap.)

Sitạr A kind of guitar, to play on the sitạr.

Siṭạr paṭar. Having ornaments on all available places on the person, covered with ornaments.
Siṭạr paṭar horok̕akat́ae. She has covered herself with ornaments or jewelry.

Siṭạr paṭar. Not closely fitted, having spaces between.
Siṭạr paṭarko rok̕akat́a paṭṛa do. They have not pinned the leaves of the plate closely together.
Siṭạr paṭarko teñakat́a. They have not woven it closely.

Sitạsạl. A variety of rice.

Siṭbạsaṛe. } Sitpasãṛe. } Roughly, not fitting closely, inharmonious.
Siṭbasaṛegeakin. They are at variance.
Ạḍi din hạbić siṭpasaṛegekin tahĕkana. For many days they did not hit it off together.
Catom siṭbasaṛeko teñakat́a. They have woven the umbrella roughly.

Siṭ bhãṇḍ. } Siṭh bhãṇḍ. } Foul, vile, as abuse.
Uni ṣimạì do siṭ bhãṇḍe egera. That woman gives foul abuse when scolding.

Siṭhạ. Tasteless, weak, pithless, dry, juiceless, exhausted, as soil.
Ul copoć siṭhạkedae. He sucked the mangoe dry.
Ot do siṭhạena. The soil is exhausted.
Roṛ siṭhạkedeako. They spoke him pithless, or they cowed him by what they said to him.
Dal siṭhạkedeako. They beat the pith out of him.

Siṭhạl miṭhạl. Disappointed, unsuccessful, hopeless.
Siṭhạl miṭhạle ruạṛena. He returned disappointed.
Sesre siṭhạl miṭhạl inạgeye jomkeda. At length being hopeless (of getting anything else) he ate that same.

Sihạt́. Bee's wax.

Siṭhạu. To disappoint, to defeat.
Siṭhạukateye ruạṛena. He returned defeated.

Siṭhbhãṇḍ. Foul, vile, as abuse.
Siṭh bhãṇḍe roṛkediñ. He gave me foul abuse.

Sithet́. Bee's wax.

Siṭhwao. To disappoint, to defeat.

Siṭić siṭić, Siṭir siṭir. } Gently, as rain.
Siṭir siṭire daṙeda. It is raining gently.

Sitiḱ sabaḱ. Unpalatable.
Siṭ na sawad, sitiḱ sabaḱ.

Siṭir siṭir. Cf. siṭić siṭić.

Siṭkạ. Small.
Siṭkạ hako. A small fish.
Siṭkạ dare. A small tree.

Siṭkạ. Leucorrhoea or Whites, a female complaint.
Siṭkạ ruạ. Puerperal fever.

Siṭkạ. A small iron rod for cleaning the hooka.

Siṭkạ bowaṛ. A kind of fish.

Siṭkoć. Rohoṛ siṭkoć. } To be over dry.
Rohoṛ siṭkoćena. It is over dry.

Siṭkoć. Isiṛ siṭkoć. } Cf. isiṛ siṭkoć.

Siṭkoć. Unprepossessing.
Siṭkoće ńeloḱkana. He looks unprepossessing.

Sitlạu. To become cold.
Sitlạuena daka do. The boiled rice has become cold.

Sitlo. To become cold, to be affected by cold, a kind of numbness produced by cold.
Sitloenae. He has become affected by cold.

Sitoć sotoć. Sito soto. } Anyhow, carelessly, slowly, lazily, languidly.
Sitoć sotoć dhutiakanae. He is wearing his dhoti carelessly.
Sitoć sotoće ḍeṅgaakana. He is carelessly dressed.
Sitoć sotoće bereť calaoena. He lazily rose and went away.

Sitol. Cold.
Sitol pạni. Cold water.

Sitoṛ. Toothache.

Siṭo soṭo. Not close, having spaces.
Siṭo soṭo catome benaoakaťa. He has not woven the (bamboo) umbrella closely.

Sito soto. Cf. sitoć sotoć.
Sito sotoe deṅgaakana. He is carelessly clad.
Kạmi sito soto baṛaekanae. He is going about his work lazily.

Siṭ siṭi. Hard and insipid, as some kinds of cooked rice.
Noa caole reaḱ daka siṭ siṭigea. This rice when cooked is hard and insipid.

Situr. Mersitur. Nase situr. } Unimportant, trivial, paltry, vainly, in vain.
Nase siturem senlena. You went vainly.

Siu. To whistle, (imitative,) to whistle through the teeth.
Siuadińae. He whistled to me.
Siu siue goladińa. He whistled to me through his teeth.

Siu marte. Siu mente. } With a whistle.
Siu marteye goladińa. He gave me a whistle.

Siuṛ. Siuṛ siuṛ. Siyuṛ. Siyuṛ siyuṛ. } Whistlingly, as wind, &c. imitative of whistling with the fingers in the mouth.
Duạr horte hoe boloḱkana siuṛ siuṛ, siń goćkam. The wind is coming whistling in by way of the door, shut it. [fingers.
Siuṛ siuṛ goledae. He is whistling on his

Siuṛ marte. Siuṛ mente. } With a whistle on his fingers.
Siuṛ marteye golkeda. He gave a whistle on his fingers.

Siwiń siwiń. Thin, slender.
Siwiń siwiń nanhageae. He is thin as a lath.
Siwińgeae, bae moṭawa. He is slender, he is not stout.
Siwiń siwińgeae. He is very slender.

Siyahi. Ink.

Siyaṅ. Siyaṅ siyaṅ. } Thin, slim, slender, narrow.
Siyaṅ siyaṅhaḱteye ḍoraakana. His waist string is very thin.
Siyaṅ siyaṅgeae. He is very slim.

Siyoṛ siyoṛ. Siyoṛ soyoṛ. } Inefficiently, applied to the first ploughing of a field when it has not been well done.
Siyoṛ soyoṛko sioḱkana. They are ploughing inefficiently.

Siyuṛ. To whistle on the fingers, to whistle, as wind. Cf. siuṛ.

Siyuṛ marte. Siyuṛ mente. } With a whistle on the fingers. Cf. siuṛ marte.

So. Smell, odour, scent, effluvium, exhalation, to smell.
Bạṛić so. A bad or offensive smell.
Bes so. A good or pleasant smell.
Sea so. A rotten smell, the smell emanating from any vegetable or animal substance in a state of decomposition.
Seage soeńkana. I smell a rotten smell.
So aṭkar reaḱ daṛe bạnuḱtaea. He has no sense of smell.
So do bae aṭkar daṛeaḱkana. He cannot smell.
Ạḍi bes so kana. It is a very pleasant smell.
Ạḍi ạṭ sea so kana. It is a very strong rotten smell.

So. To pierce, to prick.
Ojo so posagme. Prick and break the boil.

So. A hundred.
So ṭaka so pạtrile ạgumea, enḍeenedle talamea. We will fine you a hundred rupees and a hundred plates (of food), then we will reinstate you (in your place in the caste.)
So so. In or by hundreds.

So sunum. Ghee, clarified butter, sweet smelling oil.

So johar. The common method of salutation among Santals.

So. } **So dare.** } A small tree, *Eugenia Jambolana, Lamk.*, which yields an edible fruit. Cf. soh.
So bele. The ripe fruit of the So tree which is of a deep glossy black colour
So bele lekae unḍuakaṭa dak. The clouds are black as the so fruit.

So kod. Cf. so dare.

Soań. Strength.
Soań bạnuktaea. He has no strength.
Uni khon bạṛti soańanide hijuka. One possessed of greater strength than he will come.

Soạṛiń. A species of cricket, *Gryllodes berthellus, Sauss.*

Soba. A handful, as much as can be lifted with the fingers spread.
Miť soba jelko emadińa. They gave me a handful of flesh meat.

Soba. To pierce by something thicker than a needle or thorn.
Hape, ceťte coń sobaen. Wait, something has run into (my foot.)

Sobasate. } **Sobasater.** } Heads and tails.
Sobasatete dohoepe. Put them down thick end and thin end alternately, or the grain and root alternately as sheaves.
Sobasatekin gitićakana. They are sleeping head and tail.
Sener sobasateko lagaoakaṭa. They have put on the rafters alternately thick end up.

Sobbo. All, every.

Sobbo kal. Any time, all times.

Sobha. To adorn, pleasant, beautiful.
Ạḍi sobha ạtkarokkana. It is charming.
Ạḍi jutko sobhaakaṭa. They have adorned it very prettily.
Gidrạko tahonkhan oṛak ạḍi sobhaka. If there are children the home is very much adorned.

Sobha. A council, a panchayat. Cf. sabha.
Sobhareko duṛupakana. They are sitting in council.
Sobhare duṛup hoṛ kanae. He is a person who sits in the council, he is a member of the council.
Niťko sobhaakaṭa. They are now sitting in [council.

Sobhab. } **Sobhaw.** } Nature, disposition, temperament.
Sobhab onkangetaea. His disposition is such.

Sobok. To stab, to push or thrust the end or point of anything with force, to be struck or pierced with the end or point of anything thrust, or driven with force, to jab.
Ḍhiṅkire sobokakanae. The pestle of the ḍhiṅki (q. v.) has struck her with force.
Ṭheṅgateye sobokkedea. He rammed him with a stick.
Meťreye sobokkedea. He thrust (the end of a stick) into his eye.
Bogdateye sobokkedea laɛre. He stabbed him in the stomach with a stabbing knife.
Khunṭi beṛhaete hasa sobok urijme. Ram the earth tightly round the post, or fix the post firmly by ramming the earth round it.
Kanḍa sobok posakkedae. He thrust (the end of a stick) at the water pot and broke it.
Ṭheṅgae sobok bitkeda. He struck and fixed his stick upright in the ground.

Sobok koyok. Heaving, stumbling, staggering.
Sobok koyok noa dak ạtukkana. This water heaves as it flows.
Khube hoeť tahẽkante lạuka do sobok koyogokkan tahẽkana. Owing to there being a strong wind the boat was heaving.
Saṗle botorte sobok koyok bogetele dạṛ idikeda. Through fear of being caught we fled away stumblingly.

Sobori. Patient, enduring. Cf. sạburi.

Soboť. To wash cloth by dumping it down on a board or a stone, applied mainly to cloth that has been boiled with ashes, to wash fibre by striking it on water.
Kiorić sobodtam. Wash your cloth.
Jạṛi soboťeťkana. He is washing fibre.

Soboť soboť. To swarm, swarming, numerous.
Mućsoboť soboťko oḍokena. The ants swarmed out.

Sobsob. } **Sobsobao.** } Infiltrated moisture, saturated, to liquify or dissolve, as salt, &c., the oozing out of infiltrated moisture, or water held in such substances as salt, &c. Cf. sabsab.

Soć. A call to drive away fowls.
Onko soćakokhanko bujhạua ar bako soroka. If they say soć to them (hens) they understand and do not come near.

Soć gaḍa biń. A species of snake.

Soć. To die,
Iń do soćen bindạṛen, inak dinge cele ser tahẽkana. I am dead and fallen, my lease of life was probably only for so many days.

Sŏc. } Place, to lay past, to store.
Soc.

Sŏc regele tahĕena. We remained in our places.
Sŏc bale ńam daṛeada, dare buṭarele gitić-lena. We could not find a place (to pass the night in) we slept under a tree.
Ape hŏ sŏcre baṛe tahenpe. You also remain in your places (houses.)
Murṛire bako sŏc joṅe. They do not store up for themselves in a granary.

Sŏc. } To consider, to think over, thought,
Soc. } anxiety.

Sŏcre menańa. I am in anxiety.

Soć soć. To go out, as a fire; to burn feebly without flame.

Sengel soć soć ṛṛijok̇kana. The fire is gradually dying out.
Sengel soć soćena. The fire has gone out.

Sod. } To pay off, to clear, to liquidate,
Sodh. } as a debt.

Jahãtinṅk̇le em enhŏ bań sodok̇kana. Let us pay ever so much still it is not paid up.

Sod. Interest. Cf. sud.

Soḍa. To cut a trench, to make a deep incision, to scold, to find fault with.

Dak̇ko soḍa aderakaṭa bandre. They have cut a trench and led the water into the tank.
Kaṭko soḍaea pareg lạgić. They make a deep incision in a log for the purpose of splitting it.
Okoe soḍaketmea? Who scolded you?

Sodae. Every day, always.

Sodamod. } Continuously, without a
Sadamaḍ. } break.

Sodamod nui kisạṛ then iń kamikana. I have been working continuously for this master.

Sodaram. Relatives, used mainly when scolding and in sarcasm.

Jojomre do, ńuńure do neko toram peṛako, neko toram sodaramko.
Dukre do dukhuṛre do tokorkotam peṛako, okorkotam sodaramko?
In eating and in drinking these are your friends, these are your relatives.
In sorrow and in suffering where are your friends, where are your relatives?

Soḍgok̇. A nala, a ravine, a deep trench worn away by running water.

Sanam soḍgok̇ idikedae dak̇ do. The water carried it (soil) away and made a deep trench.

Sodgoṛo. Disarranged, in disorder, out of place, unfinished, confused, in confusion, on the top, in the open, visible.

Noa katha sodgoṛogepe bạgiada. You left this matter in disorder, unsettled.
Noa kạmi sodgoṛogepe bạgiada. You left this work unfinished.
Bań sabaṛakana sodgoṛoge menak̇a. It has not yet got the finishing touches put to it, it is incomplete.

Sodh. Cf. sod.

Sodo sodo. } Rough, shaggy, hairy,
Sodo bodo. } hirsute.
Sodro bodro. }

Sodo bodo upanae. It has shaggy hair.
Merom do adomko sodo bodogea. Some goats are shaggy.
Cikạṛ do bań sodo bodogea. It is not smooth it is rough.

Soḍo. } Sound produced by water
Soḍo soḍo. } falling into water.

Dak̇ soḍo soḍo ạtak̇kana. The water is running and producing a sound resembling soḍo soḍo by falling into water.

Soḍok̇. A nala, a ravine, a trench hollowed out by running water.

Ạtu soḍok̇kedae. It washed away the earth and made it a trench.
Soḍok̇reko topakadea. They buried him in a ravine.
Soḍok̇ soḍok̇teye calaoenae kul do. The tiger went by way of the ravine.

Soḍok̇ roḍok̇. } Straight across country,
Sopok̇ roḍok̇. } over hill and dale, over rough ground and ravines.

Sopok̇ roḍok̇le dạṛkeda celehŏ bale ńamleḍea. We went over rough ground and ravines, but we found nothing (no game.)

Sodor. To make manifest, to make public, to publish, to become known, to bring, or be brought to light, to expose.

Sodorre. Openly, in public.
Lại sodor. To proclaim, to publish.
Alom sodorok̇a. Do not allow yourself to be seen, do not expose yourself.
Katha do sodorena. The matter has become known.

Soḍor soḍor. } Sound produced by pour-
Soḍor boḍor. } ing water, water which has been stirred up and muddied, muddy. Cf. seḍer beḍer.

Soḍor boḍor dak̇ko duleda. They are pouring out water and making a sound resembling soḍor boḍor.
Sanam dak̇ko boḍekeda soḍor boḍor. They dirtied and muddied all the water by stirring it up.
Soḍor boḍor boḍe dak̇le ńukeda. We drank water which had been stirred up and muddied.

Sodor ḅodor. Dirty, as face and hands after eating.

Sodor bodor bae abukakana. He has not washed his hands after eating.
Sodor bodore jojom kana. He is dirtying himself in eating.

Sodo rodo. Hairy, shaggy, rough. Cf. sodo bodo.

Sodo rodo baborko uńakaṭa. They have spun the rope roughly.

Sodre. Cf. sodor.
Sodreteye emadea. He gave to him openly.

Sodṛe. To enter, to enter without being invited, applied mainly to a woman's entering a man's house to live with him as his wife.
Amtegem sodṛeakana nui haṛam ṭhen. You yourself entered this old man's house without being invited to be his wife.

Sodro. A beard, a man with a beard.
Nui sodro daraekana. This bearded man is coming.

Sodro bodro. Hairy, shaggy, rough.
Sodro bodroe upana. He has shaggy hair.

Soḍsoḍao. To fall as water into water with a sound.
Dak soḍsoḍaok kana. Water is falling into water and making a sound.

Soebot. Without doubt, certainly.
Soebot kangeae kombṛo do. He is without doubt the thief.

Soeda. Cf. sauḍa.

Soedom. For the present, at present, in the meantime.
Soedom pea ṭaka bataome. Take three rupees in the meantime.

Soela. } M. } Long and sharp-pointed
Suila. } } tall.
Suili. F.
Soela soela haraakana. They (bamboos) have grown very tall.
Soela ḍaṅgra. A bullock with long sharp pointed horns.
Kāṛwāt jānum soelagea. The kāṛwāt (q. v.) thorns are long and sharp.

Soela boela. Tall.
Soela boelako haraakana. They have grown tall.
Soela boela menakkoa. There are very tall [ones.

Soetan. Satan, the devil.

Sogak. To peck, as a bird, to bite, as a snake.
Biṅ sogak goṭkadeae. The snake bit him right away.
Kahu sogak jomkoako roṭe do. Crows peck up [and eat frogs.

Soge. To insert, to push in between or among.
Kitapre soge goṭkadae. He put it in between the leaves of the book.
Satere sogekakme. Push it into (the thatch of) the eaves.

Soghoṛ. } Beautiful, well-behaved, do-
Sughoṛ. } cile, well-trained.
Ạḍi soghoṛiċem ṅamakadea. You have got a very well trained one.
Matkom ạḍi sughoṛe tekeakaṭa. She has cooked the matkom (q. v.) beautifully.
Sughoṛkedeae ḍaṅra do. He made the bullock docile.

Sogoe. A rude musical instrument made of bamboo, to play on the *sogoe*, a noise resembling that produced on the *sogoe*.
The *sogoe* is made by slitting a piece of bamboo into as many thin slips as possible leaving sufficient space unsplit by which to hold it. A notched stick is then inserted between the slips and worked backwards and forwards like a fiddle bow. Each slip into which the bamboo is split producing a note.
Another method of making a *sogoe* is to hold a number of dry leaves together and pierce a hole in the middle of them. In this hole a small stick is worked backwards and forwards like a fiddle bow.
Maṭ reak sogoeko benaoa. They make the *sogoe* of bamboo.
Lagṛẽ eneċ jokheċko sogoea. They play the *sogoe* when the Lagṛẽ (q. v.) dance is being danced.
Hoe sogoe sogoe saḍekana. The wind is sounding like the *sogoe*.

Sogor. To eat in large mouthfuls, to eat greedily.
Sogor maraokedae. He took it in one mouthful.
Sogor menteye jomkeda. He ate it in one mouthful.

Sogor bogor. In equal parts, half and half.
Sogor bogor daka tuluċ daheye jomkeda. He ate rice and curds in equal parts.
Sogor bogore sipiakaṭa. He has mixed equal parts.

Sogoṭ. The small Indian Civet, *Viverricula malaccensis*.

Sogoṭ baha. A kind of plant the flower of which is said to smell like the sogoṭ, or Indian civet.

Sogoṭ lutur apaṛi. An arrowhead in shape resembling the ear of the sogoṭ or small Indian civet.

Soh. } A small wild and also semi-
Soh dare. } cultivated fruit tree, *Eugenia jambolana, Lamk.* Cf. so dare.

Sohag. Deference, affability, love, dear.
Balaeakin sohag johkana. The two *balaeas* (q. v.) are treating each other with deference, or are conversing affably.

Sograo. To eat in large mouthfuls, to eat greedily.
Jom sograokedae. He ate it greedly.
Sograokedae daka do. He ate up the rice in large mouthfuls.

Sogra sugri. To eat by large mouthfuls, to eat greedily.

Sogra sugrikedako. They ate it up greedily, in large mouthfuls.

Sohaga. } Borax.
Sohga.

Sohạgi. } Dear, beloved, applied to
Sohagiạ. } females.

Sohan. } Susceptible to injury, easily
Sohna. } killed, lacking vitality, applied to plants requiring extra care in transplanting.

Backom ạḍi sohna jạt kana. *Backom* (q. v.) is of a nature very susceptible to injury (when being transplanted.)

Backom ạḍi sohana. *Backom* is easily killed.

Sohan. } Pleasing, charming, pleasant,
Sohāṛ. } beautiful.
Sohāṛa.

Aḍi sohan añjomokkana. It sounds very pleasant.

Aḍi sohan ńelokkana. It looks very beautiful.

Sohange ạikạukkana. It gives one a feeling of charm, it is charming.

Sohbod. Pleasant, cheerful.

Nonḍe ạḍi sohbod aṭkarokkana. It feels very pleasant here.

Sohela. } Long and straight.
Sohela sohela. }

Nia kaṭ do sohelagea. This log is long and straight.

Sohela sohela jhạnṭiko makkata. They have cut long and straight branches.

Sohga. To assist, to help, to be one of, to accompany.

Sohgawạńme noa mamlare. Help me in this suit.

Sohga ńokạńme baṛe. Do help me a little.

Sohga. Borax.

Sohij. Easy, light.

Sohna. } Susceptible to injury, easily
Sohan. } killed, lacking vitality, applied to plants requiring extra care in transplanting.

Backom ạḍi sohna jạt kana. *Backom* (q. v.) is of a nature very susceptible to injury (when being transplanted.)

Backom aḍi sohana. *Backom* (q. v.) is very susceptible to injury (when being transplanted.)

Soho. Cf. suhu.

Sohoda. A helper, an assistant, a succourer.

Soho doho. A traditional name said to be that of the Edel or Cotton tree, *Bombax malabaricum, D. C.*

Sohoe. The stamens of the matkom (q. v.) flower.

Matkom sohoe dak. Rain coming about the end of the matkom (q. v.) season.

Sohoe sohoe. Sound produced by a large body of running water, as a river in flood.

Tinạk dak menaka gaḍare? Añjomlakań sohoe sohoe. How much water is there in the river? I heard it rushing.

Sohoj. Easy, light. Cf. sahaj.

Sohoka. } Freely, openly, fearlessly.
Sohokar. }

Sohokaeye roṛkeda. He spoke openly.

Sohor. To thrust forward, to throw, as a javelin; to hurl, as a dart; to throw, as a shuttle; to move forward rapidly, to dart, to rush headlong.

Thạri dakae sohor goćadea. He pushed the plate of rice towards him.

Uniak bohok sohor lahaakantaea. His head projects (over the bed.)

Sohor lahakme. Push yourself forward (when in a recumbent position.)

Borlome sohorkeda. He threw the spear.

Sohor. Border of cloth, generally of coloured thread.

Halań sohor. A kind of border with an elaborate pattern in red.

Sohor. } A city, a large town.
Sahar. }

Sohor bajar. A large market town.

Sohor. To advance, to move forwards with difficulty.

Uni do noa ńelkate sohor ńokkateye menkeda. When he saw this he advanced a short distance and said.

Sohor seṭerenako. They have arrived.

Sohosae. Freely, openly, fearlessly.

Sohosi. } Cf. sahosi.
Sahosi. }

Sohoć. To help, to assist.

Roṛ sohoć. To help by speaking.

Kạmi sohoć. To help in work.

Em sohoć. To help by giving.

Roṛ sohoćkedińae. He spoke for me.

Em sohoćkedeako. They assisted him by giving to him.

Sohrae. The chief festival of the Santals.

The Sohrae festival is observed after the rice harvest has been gathered in. It is the harvest festival and is observed by all classes of the community.

Sohrae eneć. The dance danced during the Sohrae festival.

Sohrae seréń. Songs sung when dancing the Sohrae dance.

Sohrae raŗ. The air to which the Sohrae songs are sung.

Sohŗoć.
Sohŗoć sohŗoć. } To clink, to chink, applied to the sound produced by sonorous metallic objects coming into contact with each other.

Sohŗoć sohŗoć ṭakae lekhaeťkoa. He counted out the money to them clink clink.

Sohŗoć marte.
Sohŗoć mente. } With a clink, or chink.

Ṭakae uṗkeda sohŗoć marte. He poured out the money with a clink.

Sojha.
Sojhe. } Straight, upright, without duplicity, simple.

Sojhe hor. A straight road.
Sojhe hoŗ kanae. He is an upright man.
Niạ nakhatege sojhegeye calaoena. He went straight away in this direction.
Nui do bań sojhe daŗeaea. I cannot break in this (animal), or I cannot make this person behave well.
Ạuriń sojhea. I have not yet made it straight.

Sojhe mojhe. Straight, direct, straight away.

Ceť bań ṭaka sojhe mojheń ńamkana. I want the money straight away.

Sojontar. Cf. sajontar.

Sŏk. Fancy, desire, pleasure, gratification.

Sŏk menaťtińa. I have taken a fancy (to something.)
Kaḍa reaľ sŏkadińa. I have taken a fancy to buffaloes.
Nui sadom sŏk iạteń dohoakadea. I have bought this horse owing to a fancy.

Soľ. To carry a plough suspended on the yoke while still on the cattle's necks.

Nahelko soľ idia. They carry the plough suspended on the yoke.

Soľ. To clean grain by pounding in a ḍhińki (q. v.) or ukhuŗ (q. v.) before cooking.

Soľ caole. Rice that has been cleaned for cooking.
Tokte caoleko soga. They clean rice with a tok (q. v.)

Soľ. To thrust in, as the hand into a bag, a hole, a pot, &c. &c.

Soľ cabakedako ṭaka do. They put in their hands and took out all the money.
Kombŗo hoŗ bugliko sogtakoa. Thieves put their hands into other people's pockets.

Soľ sutruć. Searching everywhere, turning over everything, seeking out each one.

Soľ sutrućle ńam baŗakedea.
Soľ sutruće daŗaukana.
Soľ sutruć sanamgeye hirikeťlea. He visited us all.

Soka suki.
Sokha sukhi. } On the same level, equal, even, on a par, neck and neck, on an equality.

Soka sukikin kạmikana. They are working evenly.
Soka suki hoŗko lạŗhạilenkhan mokordoma do ạdi din tahẽna. If people on an equality with each other fight the case will last many days.

Soke. To take a fancy, to indulge a fancy or desire.

Jahãege sokea unigeye hataoa. Whoever takes a fancy to it he will take it, or buy it.
Uni do pạurạe sokeakawana, ado ạdiye roŗeda. He has been indulging in liquor, and is loquacious.

Sokha. A witch-finder.

Sokha ṭhećle calaľkana. We are going to the witch-finder.
Sokhako bhaoa. Witch-finders reveal.

Sokhao.
Sokhaṭ. } To dry up, to become parched, to make empty of liquid.

Daľ tetańte hõ hoŗe sokhaṭena. The person also became parched, through thirst.
Khet reaľ daľ ańjeć sokhaoena. The water of the fields has all dried up.

Sokha sukhi. Cf. soka suki.

Sokhaṭ. Cf. sokhao.

Sokoć. To shog, to shake up, to toss, to heave, to hitch up.

Haṭaľko sokoja. They toss up the haṭaľ (q. v.)
Gidrạe sokoćede kana. She is giving the child a hitch up (on her hip.)
Sadomre deċlenteye sokoćena. He shogged because he was mounted on a horse.
Sokoć ulṭạume. Toss it upside down.

Sokol.
Seńgel sokol. } Fire.

Men, seńgel sokol bes okoćte kạmitabonpe. Now work carefully with the fire.

Sokor.
Sokor sokor. } Applied to a gurgling sound in the throat.

Sokor marsokedae. He gurgled.
Sokor sokore saheťeda. He breathes gurgingly.
Mirgi hoŗ do ḍhergeko sokor sokora. Epileptics gurgle much (when in a fit.)

Sokor marte.
Sokor mente. } With a gurgle or rattle in the throat.

Sokor menteye saheť goťkeda.

Sokoŗ.
Sokoŗ sokoŗ. } Gulping, sound of gulping.

Sokoŗ sokoŗe ńuieda. He is gulping.

Sokoṛ marte. } With a gulp.
Sokoṛ mente. }
Sokoṛ menteye ñu goćkeda. He drank it with a gulp.

Sokordom. Breathless, out of breath. Cf. sakardom.

Sokot. Hard, tight.
Khub sokotko tolakaťa. They have tied it very tightly.
Khub sokotgea. It is very tight.

Sokṛa. A narrow sloping valley of rice fields, generally of second class quality.

Sokṛa sendeḱ. Fertile.

Sokṛoć. } To clink, to chink,
Sokṛoć sokṛoć. } applied to the sound produced by sonorous metallic objects coming into contact with each other. Cf. sohṛoć.

Sokṛoć marte. } With a clink or a
Sokṛoć mente. } chink. Cf. sohṛoć marte.

Soksoko. Long, projecting far out.
Soksokoe dereńana. It has long horns.
Soksokoe gocoana. He has long moustaches.
Soksoko jạnum kana. It is a long thorn.

Sokto. Hard, tight. Cf. sokot.

Sol. A small bush frequenting marshes, *Æschynomene aspera, Linn.*
This plant is valuable for its pith which is put to many uses, not the least of which is the manufacture of sun hats for Europeans.

Sol suluk. } Peace, harmony.
Sola suluk. }
Sola sulukte tahenpe. Live in harmony.

Sole icạḱ. A large species of shrimp.

Sole Hembrom. A sub-sept of the the Santal sept Hembrom (q. v.)

Solgať. }
Solgeť. } To hide the head by pushing
Solgoť. } it into grass, &c., to unite
Salgať. } with.
Aleṭhene solgoćena. He united with us.
Okare coń solgeť aćkeť. It has joined another herd somewhere and I lost it.
Bul solgoćenae. He is drunk and fallen head foremost.
Ghãsreko salgadoḱa. They hide their heads in the grass.
Solgoť senenae. It has gone along with the others.

Sol gol. Together, in company.
Solgolbo tahena. We will stay together.

Solgoť. Cf. solgať.

Solha. } To advise, to consult, to be in
Solho. } harmony.
Solho jońkanako. They are taking counsel together.
Solhaadeako. They advised him.

Solo. } Sixteen.
Sulo. }

Solo saṅjok. } The full complement of
Sulo saṅjok. } requirements for a
Solo sonjok. } marriage celebration,
Sulo soṅjok } requirements in the form of food for an emergency; at times, now and again.
Solo soṅjokbo jumạulege atmabon boda.
Solo saṅjok utuko emalea. At times they give us relish (to our boiled rice.)

Soloḱ bokoḱ. Confused, in disorder, disorderly, disarranged, untidy.
Soloḱ bokoḱkedako. They disarranged (the things.)
Alope soloḱ bokoga. Do not disorder (the things.)
Goṭa sohor ren hoṛko soloḱ bokoḱkeťkoa. They threw the whole city into disorder.

Soloman. } Fairly, equally, even hand-
Suloman. } ed, impartially, justly, affably.
Solomante hapaṭińpe jotoko. Divide it fairly amongst you all.
Solomanoḱpe. Be just to each other, live in peace.
Solomankaťkoale. We reconciled them, we settled their differences and made peace between them.

Solom loṭom. To pass off a stolen thing as another resembling it.
Onte do alope idikoa, boṅgaḱkanako solom loṭom oookoape merom do. Do not take them (goats) over that way, they are sacrificing (goats) and you may allow them to pass off your goat or goats as their own. (They may seize a goat belonging to you and kill it and if any enquiry is made they will say what we are cooking is our own.)

Soloṅ. To put into, as into a strait mouthed vessel or the mouth.
Ṭukućreko soloṅkeda. They put it into the pot.
Soloṅ baekedae. He laid it past in a strait mouthed receptacle.
Mocare jom cijko soloṅa. They put eatables into the mouth.
Sunḍtegeko soloṅ joṅa hạthi do. Elephants put (food) in their mouths by the trunk.

Solo soṅjoḱ. } Fairly, justly, equitably,
Solo soṅjok. } even handedly, to divide justly, to apportion fairly.
Solosoṅjokte jompe. Divide fairly and eat.
Solo soṅjokte tahenpe. Live in peace, treat each other fairly.
Solo soṅjokte jomaḱe emạṅkana. He gives me a just amount of food.

Solthonok. To be cleansed, to be purified.
Senparom porob ṣurire, jemonko solthonok. Before the passover so that they might be purified.

Som.
Sum. } Hard, niggardly, miserly.

Som.
Som hilok. } Monday.

Somae sokṛa. A traditional name.
Lemeń gitil, Somae sokṛateye calaoena. He has gone to the fine sand and the Somae sokṛa. i. e. he is dead.

Soman. Level, equal, alike, similar.
Mit somange haṭińpe. Divide equally.
Mit soman ot. Level ground.
Soman somangeye emaṭkoa. He gave them all alike.
Nitokko somanena. Now they are equal.
Mit somanko daṛ idikoda. They ran level.

Somasom. Equal, alike, similar.
Somasom hoṛkin ńapamakana. Two similar people have been mated.

Sombad.
Sombat. } News of the day, information, intelligence.
Boge sombat.
Bhage sombat. } Good news, the Gospel.
Calakkanam, noa sombat aguańme. You are going, bring me this information.

Sombhob. Possible, probable fit, right, possibility probability.
Noa katha sombhobgeń bujhạueda. I regard this matter as probable.
Hijuk reak sombhob bạnuktaea. There is no probability of his coming.

Sombhori.
Sombhuri. } To be forbearing, to be long suffering, to bear with, to have patience.
Sombhorite baṛe tahenpe. Live together in forbearance, bear and forbear.
Iń reak baṛe sombhurime. Have patience with me.

Sombhrao.
Sumbhrạu. } To suffer, to bear.
Aḍi duke sumbhrạuakaṭa. He has suffered much affliction.

Sombhuri. Cf. sombhori.

Sombol. Cf. somol.

Sombond. Connection, affinity, relation.
Sombondre. In regard to, in connection with.

Sombot. To fall forward, to fall on the knees, as a horse, bullock, &c.
Sombotenae. He has fallen on his knees.
Sombot torot iń heḍena. I came floundering.

Somoe Time.

Somojos. Equally, justly, in equal parts.
Somojos haṭiń jońpe. Divide it equally.
Somojosko jomkeda. They appropriated it in equal parts.

Somol. To prepare, to get in readiness, to prepare and take on a journey.
Dahe taben hõ khubko somolkaṭa. They prepare a good supply of curds and parched rice.
Hape, ṣuriń somolokṭa. Stay, I have not yet got (the food I am to take with me) ready.

Sompao. To entrust to, to deliver over to, to give in charge.
Boṅgae sompaoadińa. The boṅga (q. v.) gave this to me, caused me to be ill.
Amak tireń sompaokokkana. I entrust myself to thy hands.
Sipạhiye sompaoadińạ. The peon made it over to me.

Somphola. Cf. samphala.

Sompok. Relationship, kinship.
Ato sompok. Assumed relationship by people of the village.

Sompot. Goods, moveable property.
Cij sompot. Goods and chattels.
Sompotan hoṛ kanae. He is a man with property.

Somsom. Strait, embarrassment, pinch, critical situation, emergency.
Somsom kalreń emadea. I gave to him at a time of emergency.
Somsomreń emadea. I gave him at a pinch (when he was in a pinch.)

Somuk. Cf. sạnmuk.

Son. A cultivated fibre yielding plant, *Crotalaria juncea, D. C.*
Son jạṛī. The fibre of *Crotalaria juncea.*
Sạci son. A variety of *Crotalaria juncea.*

Son Kisku. A sub-sept of the Santal sept Kisku (q. v.)

Son Besra. A sub-sept of the Santal sept Besra (q. v.)

Sona. Gold.
Sona reak. Golden, of gold.
Sona murhut.
Sona ren murhut. } A golden image.
Sona dakteko ạńuakaṭa. He has gilded it with gold.
Asol sona. Genuine gold.
Phosol sona. Spurious gold, counterfeit gold.

Son jhunkạ. A wild plant, *Crotalaria striata, D. C.*

Sona citạ.
Sona citạ tarup. } The leopard, *Felis leopardus, Hodgson.*

Sonat. Circumcision.

Sońcao. To lay past, to save. Cf. sańcao.

Miṭ bajar ṭakae soncao oṭolaka. He left savings to the amount of one thousand rupees.

Soṇḍa. A tusk, as of wild boar, elephant, &c., to scold, to abuse, to injure.

Soṇḍaanić sukri. A pig (boar) with tusks.
Okoe amko soṇḍaeṭmea? Who is speaking ill of you?
Soṇḍa bań sahoḱkantapea? Is there not room for your tusks? (said to children when quarrelling.)

Sonde. To enter for the purpose of hiding.

Noṇḍe sonde baṛaekanae. He is hiding about in here.
Noṇḍe sondeakanae. He is hiding in here.
Sonde bolokkanae. He is forcing his way in to hide.

Sondgond. Strong, sweet, fragrant, as a smell, perfume, aroma; strong and savoury.

Utu do sondgond sokana. The relish smells savoury, the relish has a savoury smell.

Sondhaeni. A small plant *Tylophora longifolia, Wight.,* used as a medicine by Santals.

This plant is found in Chota Nagpur, but so far has not been met with in any other part of Bengal.

Sondhao, To heat an earthenware pot on the fire after it has been cleaned to complete the operation.

Ṭukuć sondhaome. Heat the pot on the fire to complete its cleansing.
Toa cukakko sondhaoa. After having washed milk vessels they heat them on the fire.

Sondhaṛ. Pleasant, pleasantly, applied mainly to the smell or taste of certain grains when roasted.

Sondhaṛ ge sokana. It has a pleasant smell.
Sondhaṛ ge sebela. It has a pleasant smell.
Hasa sondhaṛ ge soka daḱ paṛaoaḱ khan. The soil smells pleasantly when rain falls on it.

Sondhe. Difficulty, trouble, endeavour.

Aḍi sondheteń heena. I came with great difficulty.
Aḍi sondheteń ńamkeda. I got it with great difficulty, or after much endeavour.

Sondho. To doubt, to suspect, to be uncertain.

Sondhoḱ kanań. I am doubting, or suspecting.
Sondhoamkanako. They are suspecting you.

Sonḍmonḍ. Of equal thickness throughout length, of equal rotundity, uncomely in shape.

Sonḍmonḍe moṭaakana. She is so fat that her body is of equal thickness.

Soṇḍor. A scab.

Sondṛa sundṛi. To poke in the hand or snout when searching for anything.

Sondṛa sundṛi baṛae kanae ńut oṛakre. He is searching in the dark house by poking in his hand here and there.
Jomaḱ lagiṭ sondṛa sundṛi baṛae kanae seta do. The dog is poking in his nose here and there in search of food.

Sondṛe. Cf. sodṛe.

Sondro. A scab.

Ghao sondroka. A scab forms on a sore.

Sone sod. / **Sone sot.** / **Sone sud.** / **Sone sut.** } Uninjured, innocent. safe and sound.

Bań bedhoromeṭkhan sone sod oṛakteń ruaṛ calakma. If I am not forswearing myself may I return to my home safe and sound.

Soneson. / **Son ke son.** } Every year, annually, yearly.

Sonesonle emaekana. We give to him every year.

Soṅ. To measure.

Otko soṅga. They measure land.
Caoleko soṅa. They measure rice.
Sosoṅaḱ. A measure.
Sosoṅić. A measurer.

Soṅ. / **Soṅge.** } In the company of, along with, a companion, a partisan.

Nui soṅ kanae. He is with this man, or he is a partisan of this man.
Pargana soṅ kanae Des Manjhi. The Des Manjhi (q. v.) is the attendant of the Pargana (q. v.)

Soṅgaṛ. Uninitiated, applied mainly to the mysteries connected with the work of an ojha (q. v.), veiled expression, fasting.

Iń doń soṅgaṛgea. I am uninitiated, I know nothing of the mysteries connected with the work of an ojha.
Soṅgaṛgeale. We are fasting.

Soṅge. Along with, in company of, to accompany.

Soṅgetora johme. Take it along with you.
Soṅgetoraem. Take him along with you.
Soṅgeyem. Take him with you, make him one of you.
Soṅgete asen baṛaem. Take him about with you.
Soṅge soṅgetekin calaoena. They went in company.
Uni soṅgere menańa. I am along with him, or I am on his side.
Soṅgere dohoem. Keep him with you.
Soṅgentenić. Companion.
Soṅgetenko. Accompaniers.
Uni soṅgetenić. The one with him.

Soṅge loṅge. Together, in company.
Miťte soṅge loṅgebon calaǩa. We will go together in company.
Delabon soṅge loṅge. Come, let us go all together.

Soṅgha. A strip of rice fields in a valley.
Edel latar soṅghateye senakana. He has gone to the strip of rice fields below the Cotton tree.

Soṅkoṛ. } Loosely, not fitting
Soṅkoṛ soṅkoṛ. } tightly, as a bolt, &c. in a hole, sound of rattling produced by a loose bolt, &c, when shaken. Cf. siṅkoṛ soṅkoṛ.

Soṅkoṛ marte. }
Soṅkoṛ mente. } With a loose rattle.

Soṅkoṭ. Misfortune, difficulty, strait.
Soṅkoṭreń paṛaoena, jomaǩ hõ bạnuǩ tińa.

Soṅsar. }
Saṅsar. } The world.
Goṭa soṅsar renko. The people of the whole world.

Sonhar. A goldsmith, a silversmith, a maker and seller of personal ornaments.

Sońjok. Opportunity, proper time timely. Cf. saṅjok.
Sońjok lagaoena, nonḍeń ńamkedea. It was opportune I got it (goat, &c.) here.

Sonjok. } The full complement
Solo sonjok. } of requirements for a marriage celebration, requirements in the form of food for an emergency, at times, now and again. Cf. solo sonjok.

Sonk. Fancy, desire, pleasure, gratification. Cf. sõk.

Sonmot. Harmony, peace, good will.
Sonmotte menaǩkoa. They are in harmony.
Sonmotkeťkinale. We harmonised them.

Sonmuk. Opposite, confronting, to confront, without the interposition of a third person. Cf. sanmuk.

Sonoḍor. }
Sunuḍur. } A waterfall.

Sonot. Harmonious, holy.
Bes sonot henaǩkoa. They are very harmonius.
Sonot Jiu. Holy Spirit.

Sonotoǩ. } Two with no birth interven-
Soptoǩ. } ing.
Sonotoǩkin kanakin. These two precede and follow each other in point of birth.

Sonpat. } Fistula due to a decayed
Sonpat ghao. } tooth or teeth, any swelling of the lower jaw due to cancer, &c.

Sonsar. The world. Cf. soṅsar.

Sontor. To be careful, vigilant, cautious, alert, prudent, watchful, heedful.
Sontoroǩme. Have a care, be cautious.
Sontorte tahenme. Continue vigilant, or alert.

Sontori. } A military guard,
Sontori palṭon. } applied mainly to the local force raised to preserve the peace of the district after the Santal rebellion.
Sontoriteye senakana. He has joined the guards.
Sontoriireye bhạrtilena. He had been enlisted in the guards.
Okoe kanae? Sontori kanae. Who is he? He is a guard.
Sontori dolren miťṭạn palṭone kolkedea. He sent a soldier of the regiment of the guards.

Soṗ. To be breathless, to breathe heavily as one out of breath through continued exertion.
Dạṛ dạṛteye soṗena. He is out of breath through continued running.

Sop. Length of the arm from the shoulder to the finger ends, an arm's length.
Miť sopge ṭheṅgatae. His stick is the length of from shoulder to the finger ends, an arm's length.
Miť sopgeye la gaḍaakạťa. He has dug down an arm's length.

Sopo. The upper arm, between the shoulder and the elbow.

Sopohoť. Reciprocal form of sohoť (q. v.)
Roṛ sopohoťkanakin. They are speaking for each other.

Sopoǩ roḍoǩ. Straight across country, over hill and dale, over rough ground and ravines.
Sopoǩ roḍoǩle dạṛãkeda cele hõ bale ńamledea. We went over rough ground and ravines, we found nothing (no game.)

Sopor. } Near or close to each
Sopor sopor. } other, very near or close to each other. Cf. sor.
Sopor sopor ato menaǩa. The villages are very near to each other, there are villages very near to each other.
Soporgeale. We are near to each other.
Sor soporgeale. We are near to each other.

Sopoć. } To be in great fear, to
Leṅgeć sopoć. } be put out of breath and heart beating through fear.

Leṅgeć sopoćlenale. We were in great fear.

Sopoć. Gentle, mild, peaceable, pacific. Cf. sapoć.

Soproć. To entrust to, to deliver over to, to give in charge, to give in custody.

Noa kạmiye soproćadiñá. He entrusted this work to me.

Soptok̀. } Immediately preceding
Soptok̀ sotok̀. } and following each other in birth.

Soptok̀kin kanakin. They are next to each in age, there is no one between them.

Sor. Near, nigh, close, in time or space; to make near, nigh, close; to come near, nigh, close.

Sorok̀pe. Come near.
Sorakanako. They are near.
Bapla dole sorkeda. We have made the marriage near, we have fixed a near date for the marriage.
Sen sorok̀kanae. He is going near.
Heć sorok̀pe. Come nigh.
Sor dinre. Lately, recently.
Oṛak̀ do sorgetaea. His home is near.
Sor sor. Very near.
Sorsor renkoko ñir jaorak̀a. Those who are near run and assemble together.

Sor marte. } With one rapid impetuous
Sor mente. } movement.

Sor marte ok̀a bate coe calaoena. He has gone somewhere with an impetuous rush.

Sora. Saltpetre.

Soṛa. Artless, simple, unsophisticated, sincere, guileless, honest, upright, gentle.

Soṛageae. He is unsophisticated.

Soṛa. To divide, to split, to halve.

Soṛa nạị. Name of a river mentioned in Santal traditions.

Soṛa sạmud. The name of a sea mentioned in Santal traditions.

Soṛa sạmudte buhelen Siñ sadom do. The Day horse had been floated away to the Soṛa sea.

Sorabon. The fourth Hindu month, July-August.

Sorad. To chastise, to punish.

Soradmealaṅ nahak̀. I shall chastise you presently.

Soran. A cart track, an unmade cart road.

Sorañjon. Cf. sarajan.

Sorbharao. Cf. sarbharao.

Sorbonas. To destroy, to utterly ruin; ruin, destruction.

Saname sorbonaskeda. He ruined all.
Sorbonas hoeña. It is ruined.

Sorbot. Sherbet.

Sõrboć. To go or come near.

Kulạị heć sõrboć goćenae. The hare came up close.
Sõrbot goćenae. He came close.
Ñir sõrboćenae. He ran close up.
Sen sõrboćenae. He went near.

Sõrmboć. To be worn out, to be enfeebled, to go or come close or near.

Phaṭkar sõrmboćenae. He is worn out with vomiting.
Unạk̀ alom sõrmbodok̀a. Do not go so near.

Sordar. A foreman. Cf. sardar.

Sordol. A piece of timber laid along the top of a wall on which rest the beams which support a ceiling, or the floor of an upper story, a wallplate.

Sordor. Equal in value as two animals exchanged.

Soren. } One of the twelve
Soren sipạhi. } septs into which the Santals are divided.

Note. For sub-septs see *paris*.

Sorenko. The Pleiades, or seven stars in Taurus.

The Pleiad is the totem of the Soren sept of Santals.
Netar Sorenko do okare aṅgaakokana? Just now where (in what part of the heavens) are the Pleiades at dawn?

Sores. Superior. Cf. soros.

Ondenak̀ kãsã reak̀ jinis ạḍi soresa. The articles of bell metal (or bronze) of that place are very superior.

Sõṛga. } Big but slim, without rotund-
Sõrnga } ity of body, applied main-
Soroṅga. } ly to goats and swine.

Nui bạdhiṭ doe soroṅgagea. This hog is big but without rotundity of body.

Soṛha. A leaf cup.

Ponea sakamteko soṛhaea. They make a soṛha of four leaves.

Sorkoṭ. } Imitative of the sound
Sorkoṭ sorkoṭ. } produced by an animal sucking up liquid.

Sorkoṭ sorkoṭe ñuieda dak̀ do.

Sorkoṭ. } Imitative of the cry of
Sorkoṭ sorkoṭ. } a certain species of small owl.

Kokor doko raga sorkoṭ sorkoṭ. The *Kokor* (q. v.) owl calls sorkoṭ sorkoṭ.

Sorlok̕. To run into, to pierce, as a thorn or any other sharp pointed object, to enter craftily.

Moṭh maṛiạ sorlok̕ boloenae uni Deko do. That Hindu forced himself in (to a village.)

Sorma surmi. To put to shame.

Sorma surmikediñako ñindạko seṭerente. They put me to shame by arriving at night (when I could get no food to give them.)

Sormi. } Shameless.
Be-sormi. }

Soro. } To institute, to ordain, to originate.
Sorwa. }

Soroakat̕ako niạ rae do. They have institued this custom.

Ato ato cet̕ leka cope soroakawana.

Soṛo. To soak through, to follow interstices, as water.

Soṛo paromena. It has soaked through.

Soṛo bolok̕kana dak̕ do. The water is soaking through (a roof.)

Soṛo boloakana dak̕ do. The water, or rain, has soaked into (the hay stack.)

Soro. To take shelter.

Onḍeń sorolena. I took shelter there.

Onḍeń soro aṅgaena. I took shelter there till the dawn.

Soro soro. Hissing and spluttering, as when wet firewood is burning.

Seṅgel soro soro saḍekana. The fire hisses and splutters.

Soroboro. Half and half, well moistened, as food.

Haṛam hoṛ do soroboro utu ada enećko jom daṛeak̕a beste do. Not until they have well mixed half rice and half relish can old people eat well.

Soroboroko dula dak̕ do. They pour on plenty water.

Soroć. Fat, rotund. Cf. soroć hako.

Soroć lekan ḍahra kanae. He is a fat bullock (like the soroć fish.)

Soroć hako. A species of fish very thick when compared with its length.

Soroć poṭoć. Badly cooked.

Soroć poṭoćpe isinakat̕. You have cooked badly.

Emadiñae soroć poṭoćge. He gave me inferior food.

Sorojan. Cf. sarañjan.

Soṛok. } A road, a made road the opposite of a cart track.
Soṛop. }

Rel soṛok. A railway.

Pạki soṛok. A macadamised road.

Kạci soṛok. An un-macadamised road.

Soṛok soṛokteye calaoena. He followed the road

Sorom. Shame, modesty, diffidence, shameful.

Sorome jomkeda. He ate his shame, he is shameless.

Sorom reak̕ katha kana. It is a shameful matter.

Soṛom. Delicious, good, savoury

Soṛomteć. Flavour.

Ạḍi soṛoma. It is very delicious.

Ụḍi soṛomkediña. I found it very savoury.

Soromiạ. Modest, bashful, unobtrusive, shamefaced, diffident, unassuming.

Soromia hoṛ kanae. He is a bashful man.

Soromjan. Cf. sarañjam.

Soṛoṅ soṛoṅ. In the same key or tone, in unison.

Tirioko oroheda soṛoṅ soṛoṅ. They are playing the flutes in unison.

Tirio saḍekana soṛoṅ soṛoṅ. The flutes sound harmoniously.

Soroṅ soroṅ. Applied to the condition of a person suffering from a bad cold, who is snuffling, blowing his nose, &c.

Soroṅ sorohiń mandak̕kana.

Soroṅ potoṅ. Plaistered.

Soroṅ potoṅ moca sạkṛiakanae. His mouth is plaistered with food.

Soroñjam. Cf. sarañjam.

Soroṛ. To shoot forward, to go straight on as one unable to stop short owing to impetus.

Kulḍi doe ạcur goćena ar seta doe ñir soroṛ goćena. The hare turned quickly and the dog shot past it.

Dalahi losot̕ seć jaṅga soroṛok̕ reak̕ botor tahẽkana. There was a fear lest their feet should slip into the quagmire.

Soros. To be superior to, in size, skill, wisdom, strength, speed, &c. &c., with negative, to be inferior to.

Nui khone sorosena. He has conquered him.

Sanamko khone sorosgea. He is superior to all.

Noa khon sorosak̕ ạguime. Bring one bigger or better than this.

Imtihanre bae soroslena. He did not pass the examination.

Sorpha. Cheap, abundant.

Jomak̕ hõ ạḍi bes ar sorphages. The food also is very good and cheap.

Bes sorpha onte ñamok̕kana. It is good and cheap there.

Sorpoṭ. } Sound produced by sucking up liquid or semi-liquid.
Sorpoṭ sorpoṭ. }
Soṛpoṭ. }
Soṛpoṭ soṛpoṭ. }

Soṛpoṭ soṛpoṭe jojom kana. He is guzzling it up.

Soṛpoṭ maraokedae. He guzzled it up.

Sorpoṭ marte. ⎫
Sorpoṭ marte. ⎬ With a guzzle.
Sorpoṭ mente. ⎮
Sorpoṭ mente. ⎭
Sorpoṭ marteye jom goḱkeda. He ate it at one guzzle.

Sorr.   ⎫ Moving rapidly, moving
Sorr sorr.   ⎬ impetuously.
Sorr sorr sohoroḱ kanae. He is rushing impetuously forward.

Sorr marte. ⎫ With one rapid move-
Sorr mente. ⎬ ment.

Sorsoṛ.   ⎫ To rustle, as the leaves of
Sorsoṛao.   ⎬ sugarcane, Indian corn,
&c., to cause to rustle.
Biń sorsoṛe caḷaḱkana. The serpent goes rustling.

Sorṭa. The side, the side of the body.
Sorṭate gitiákanae. He is lying or his side.

Sorwa. Cf. soro.
Miḱ ṭaṅ hajotió aṛaḱako sorwa tahōkana. It was the custom to liberate an undertrial prisoner at their request.

Sorwa. A large leaf cup. Cf. sorha.

Sosa goṛa. The whole.
Sosa goṛa pirthimire miḱgetạbona rae do. The whole world over we have only one custom.

Sosam.   ⎫ The hind of the Nilgai
Sosam jel. ⎬ *Portax pictus.*

Sŏsŏ. Snoring, breathing heavily.
Sŏsŏe gitiákana nit hạbió.

Soso.   ⎫ The Marking-nut tree,
Soso dare. ⎬ *Semicarpus anacardium, Linn., var, cuneifolia,* to blister with the juice of this tree.
The acrid juice of the seeds of this tree is employed as a vesicant by the Santals.
Soso sunum. Oil obtained by distilling the seeds of *Semicarpus anacardium.*

Soso dereń bheḍa. A ram whose horns are just sprouting and resemble the nut protruding from the fleshy portion of the fruit of the *Soso* (q. v.) tree.
Tin marahae? Soso dereñakanae. How big is it? Its horns are just sprouting.

Sosroć khoda. The grasshopper's tattooing, a black blotch on the skin. It is said that when a certain species of grasshopper alights on the unprotected surface of the body it spits out an acrid fluid which causes a black blotch.

Sosroć. A grasshopper.
Boṅga sosroć. ⎫
Dhiṅki sosroć. ⎮
Buḍhi sosroć. ⎮ Different kinds of grass-
Guṇḍri sosroć. ⎬ hoppers known to Santals.
Poho sosroć. ⎮
Seṭe sosroć. ⎮
Poṇḍ sosroć ⎮
Guli sosroć. ⎭

Sosṭok. ⎫ Savoury, delicious, tasty,
Susṭop. ⎬ good, sweet, excellently well.
Khub sosṭokko daka utuakaṭa. They have cooked the rice and relish excellently.

Sosṭop. To nurse, to cherish, to shew kindness.

Sosṭor. Scriptures, sacred books.

Sot. True, truth, evidence or assurance of reliability.
Sot baṛe roṛme. Speak the truth.
Sot do bạń ńelleḱtakoa. I did not see that they were true, I saw no evidence of their being what they pretended to be.

Soṭ. Low, moist place.
Gaḍa soṭ. Streams and low moist places.

Soṭa.   ⎫ Sticking out, as the front
Soṭmal. ⎬ teeth.

Soṭa. A rafter placed alongside of another to strengthen it, a supporter, an assistant.
Liceṛgea soṭa lagaoaḱme. It is weak (a rafter), put another alongside of it.

Soṭasoń. A companion, a bosom friend, a comrade, a mate, a chum.
Soṭasoń hoṛ do mạr mūhīmre dopoḱte jiwi hŏko alaea. Comrades in times of distress give even their lives in defence of each other. **Noa iñaḱ soṭasoń do.** This (stick) is my comrade.

Sote. Sober, watchful.
Soṭegeae, bae bulakana. He is sober, he is not drunk.

Sotea. Worthy to be trusted, honest, true, just.
Khub sotea boṅga kantaeae. His bonga (q. v.) is very trustworthy.
Sotea biċạr. Just judgment.

Soṭel.   ⎫ Level, plane. even surface.
Soṭhel. ⎬
Bes noṇḍe soṭhel ot kana. Here is good level ground.
Soṭel jaega. A level place.

Soṭik. To enquire. Cf. suṭik.

Soṭmal. Sticking out as the front teeth.

Sotoḱ. Following, or next in order of birth.
Iń sotoḱ kanae. He is next to me in birth.
Uni sotoḱ doe baṅ kana, talare miḱṭene goóena. He is not next to him, one died between them.

Sotok. To follow another so that assistance may be rendered when necessary, to take care of, to help when following.

Nui leḍha ḍahra oraḱte sotoḱ idiema. Drive this lame bullock carefully home.

Gidrạ ma sotoḱ idikom hoedaḱ darakana. Take the children (home, making them go in front) a storm is coming.

Sotok sumuṅ. The last of all, the only one remaining of a family.

Sotoḱ sumuṅ jiwitiñ. I am the only soul remaining of our family.

Soto poto. Anyhow; quickly and inefficiently, as a piece of work.

Sotopoto goćkedae. He did it anyhow.

Nahel sotopotoe benao goćkeda. He made the plough anyhow.

Sotra. The catamenia, the menses.

Sotraḱ mosoćentaea.

Soṭsoṭo. Not lying close, sticking up above the level, jagged, as a stick half broken through.

Soṭsoṭoge henaḱa. There are places not close.

Soṭsoṭo ñeloḱkana. It is not lying closely.

Soṭsoṭoe duṛupakana. She is sitting indecently.

Sotyoć. Feckless, fusionless, weak, slow.

Sotyoć mara hoṛ. A feckless rascal.

Sowal. Sawal. A question, to cross-question, to argue or plead in a law suit.

Sowal reaḱ jobab emme. Give an answer to the question.

Mićṭeć sowal menaḱtiñ. I have a question (to put), or I have an argument or plea to lay before you.

Nui muktiạr do ạḍi sowal daṛeaḱae. This pleader is an adept at cross-questioning.

Sowar. Sawar. A rider, a palki

Sowarteye senakana. He has gone riding.

Sowari. Sawari. A rider, a palki.

Ćeĉte senakanae? Sowarite. How has he gone? By palki.

Soyoṅ. Soyoṅ soyoṅ. Sound as of wind rushing in to or out of an opening.

Soyoṅ soyoṅ hoe boloḱkana. The wind is whistling in.

Cạpuṣe soyoṅkeda. He caused the bellows to produce a sound as of wind rushing, he blew the bellows.

Ma ja soyoṅmeja. Come boy, blow the bellows.

Tirio soyoṅ ocoedae, bae saḍe ocoeda. He makes a sound of rushing wind on the flute, but he does not play it.

Soyoṅ marte. Soyoṅ mente. With a whistle.

Soyoṅ marte hoe bolo goćena. The wind entered with a whistle.

Sposṭo. Clearly, distinctly.

Sũ. Sũ sũ. To snort, as a bull when excited.

Sũadiñae. He (bull) snorted at me.

Sũ hako. A species of fish.

Suạni. A cricket.

Suạpukạ. A kind of hairy caterpillar.

Subạ. A leader, a military leader, applied mainly to the leaders of the Santal rebellion.

Sido Kanhu subạkin tahẽkana. Sido and Kanhu were rebel leaders.

Hanteko subạlena, note do baṅ. There were rebel leaders over there, there were none here, the people over yonder rebelled but not here.

Subha Subhab. Suspicion, to suspect, to blame.

Subhạbte sabekanae. He is apprehending him on suspicion.

Subhạbadiñae. He suspected, or blamed me.

Subhạbte kombṛoko metaekana. They are calling him a thief on suspicion.

Monere subhạb hećañkana pase jahankoko jomkede. I have a suspicion that perhaps some creatures devoured him.

Subitạ. Well, excellent, opportune, convenient; satisfaction, opportunity.

Bes subitạñ ạikạueda. I feel excellently well.

Kạmi reaḱ subita bạnuḱtiñ. I have no satisfaction in my work.

Subod. Subud. Good tempered, gentle, upright, straightforward, docile.

Subud ḍahra. A good tempered bullock.

Subud hoṛ. An upright man.

Suboria. Suburia. Patient, long-suffering, able to control one's temper.

Subur subur. Too much liquid, too thin to be eaten comfortably with the fingers, and too thick to be taken up by a leaf used as a spoon.

Subur suburko daḱ mạṇḍiakaća. They have cooked the rice with too much liquid in it.

Suć. To pick off the stamens of the flower of the matkom (q. v.) tree previous to cooking.

Matkome sućeda. She is picking off the stamens from matkom (q. v.)

Matkom sujme. Prepare matkom for cooking by picking off the stamens.

Suć cẽṛẽ. The Purple Sun-bird, *Aruchnechthra asiatica.*

Suca̤. M. } **Suci. F.** } Good, faultless, true, truthful, faithful.

A̤ḍi sucae la̤ioḱkana. He is calling himself very good, he is making himself out to be very good.

Sud. } **Sod.** } Interest, usury.

Sud karateń oḍokakaťa. I have got it on interest.

Sude mule. Principal and interest.

Sude muleń emkeda. I repaid principal and interest.

Sud. } **Sudh.** } To pay off, to liquidate, as a debt. Cf. sod.

Sude mule. Principal and interest. Cf. sud.

Sudh. } **Sudho.** } Pure, unpolluted, accurate, correct, to purify, to cleanse.

Sudha̤. } **Sudha̤u.** } To pet or soothe by stroking or rubbing, as a cat, horse, bullock, &c. at which the animal is pleased.

Pusiń sudha̤kedea. I stroked the cat (at which it was pleased and purred.)

Sudha̤. The whole, along with, also.

Ato sudha̤koko jomakaťa. The people of the whole village have eaten.

Reheť sudha̤ toť giḍime. Pull it up by the root (root and all) and throw it away.

Am sudha̤ko seleťeťmea. They also include you.

Sudha̤r. To repair, to put to rights, to mend.

Sudha̤u. Cf. sudha̤.

Sudhe. Empty, only.

Sudhegeye rua̤ṛena. He returned empty.

Sudheť. } **Sudheť sudheť.** } To calm a restive cow by patting her and saying sudheť sudheť.

Sudheťedekanae. She is calming her by patting and saying sudheť sudheť.

Sudhra̤u. } **Sudra̤u.** } **Suḍra̤u.** } To repair, to mend, to put to rights, to make right, to correct faults or inaccuracies, to bring to a proper state of mind.

Dal sudhra̤ukedeae. He made him be right by beating him.

Kuṛhia ḍaṅrae sudhra̤ukedea. He made the lazy bullock right.

Nui ba̤hu ma a̤ḍiye da̤ṛkan tahẽkana, nitoḱ doe sudra̤uena. This bride was given to running away, but now she is all right (no longer runs away.)

Suḍra̤u. To flow freely, as blood; to spout, to leak, as a roof, &c.

Kha̤pra oṛaḱ suḍra̤uḱgea. Tiled houses leak.

Mayam suḍra̤uḱkana. Blood is flowing freely.

Sudri. To make manifest, to make public, to become known, to bring to light, to expose. Cf. sodor.

Sudrite idime. Take it away openly.

Sudrienae. He is exposed.

Sudro budro. Hairy, shaggy, rough. Cf. sodro bodro.

Suḍsuḍa̤u. } **Suḍusuḍu.** } Sound of water dripping, to drip.

Daḱ suḍsuḍa̤uḱkana. Water is dripping.

Daḱ suḍu suḍu joroḱkana. Water is falling drip, drip.

Suḍur. } **Suḍur suḍur.** } Too much liquid or moisture, thin owing to the presence of too much liquid.

Suḍur suḍurko daḱ ma̤nḍiakaťa. They have cooked the rice with too much water.

Suḍur suḍur. Noise of dripping or falling water, to lift boiling water out of a pot and pour it back again to prevent boiling over.

Suḍur suḍur joroḱkana. It is dripping.

Suḍusuḍu. Sound of water dripping, to drip. Cf. suḍsuḍa̤u.

Sug. To enquire, to enquire for some one lost or wanted.

Sug ńamkedeań. I enquired for him and found him.

Sug ba̤ṛaedae. He is making inquiry for some one lost (or wanted.)

Nui koṛa la̤giť ba̤hu suga̤ńme. Look out for a bride for me for this young man (son) of mine.

Ba̤huko sug ba̤ṛaeťkoa. They are enquiring for brides (marriagable girls.)

Suga̤m ba̤i. Coma.

Sug batra. News, intelligence.

**Ceťko sug batram a̤guakaťa.? ** What news have you brought?

Ape senaḱ sug batra la̤ime ceť lekana. Tell the news of your place what they are like.

Sughoṛ. Good, beautiful, excellent, grand, often used in fault-finding and sarcasm.

Bee sughoṛ ba̤hu kanae. She is a beautiful bride.

A̤ḍi sughoṛko isinakaťa, ba̤ń joma. They have cooked it excellently, I will not eat it.

A̤ḍi sughoṛiko ńamakadea. They have got a very excellent one (daughter-in-law.)

Sugi cẽṛẽ. A small bird so named from its call.

Sugubugu. To move or struggle, as shrimps out of water or as a swarm of ants, to be cowed and speechless.

Haraolenkhane oeṭ hõ sugubugu bạnuḱtaea. When he is defeated there is no movement in him.

Sugui sugui. Gently, as wind.

Sugum sugum. Stealthily, without making noise, noiselessly.

Sugum sugum ńindạe darankana. He is going about at night stealthily.

Suhi. To sign, pledge, agree, promise, attest, ratify, prove; testimony, signature.

Pańja suhi. To trace, to track.
Jahãe rengeye suhiḱ unigeye ńamea. Whoever it is proved to belong to he will get it.
Pańjaliń suhi ạguakaṭa. We have tracked the foot marks.
Ol suhikedae. He signed it, he receipted it.
Uniaḱ suhi do bań kana. It is not his signature.

Suhu. To boast, to praise.

Ińiń jutakaṭa, aće suhuḱkana. I put it to rights and he is taking the credit to himself.
Ohoń suhu ocolema, ṭhikgeń lạia. I will not allow you to boast, I will tell accurately (what took place.)
Suhuḱ lạgiṭe laha baṛaekana. He is acting officiously to make himself appear great.
Amte do ohom suhu daṛelena. You cannot praise yourself.

Sui. A needle, to spire, to sprout up pyramidically, to pout.

Sui bhugạḱ. The eye of a needle.
Sui ilakanako cẽṛẽ hoponko do. The feathers of the young birds have spired.
Jondra suiakana. The Indian corn has spired.
Sui suioḱkana. (The grain) is sprouting.
Caḱem sui suioḱkana? Why are you pouting?

Sui parjat. Not even a needle, nothing at all.

Sui parjat hõ bako bạgiada. They did not leave even a needle.

Sui topa. A children's game.

Sui gutu. A children's game so called.

Suiạ. Quarrelsome, ill-tempered.

Suikạr. To make private enquiry, to enquire privately.

Suikạr baṛaedae. He is privately seeking information.

Suikạriạ. One who makes private enquiry.

Suikạriạ kanae. He is one who is privately making enquiries.
Okoe kanae? Suikạriạ do. Who is he? He is a private enquirer.

Suilạ. M. } Long and sharp-pointed
Soela. M. } tall. Cf. soela.

Suili gại. A cow with long sharp pointed horns.

Suipạḱ. Quarrelsome, ill-tempered.

Suipạḱ mara gidrạ. An ill tempered rascal of a child.
Nui suipạḱ mara ạimại. A quarrelsome jade.

Suj. } Understanding, reasoning
Suj buj. } powers, sense, power of comprehension.

Nuiaḱ suj buj bạnuḱtaea. This (man) has no understanding, or has no power of reasoning.

Sujat. Docile, good tempered.

Sujhạu. To see, to see anything particularly.

Meṭ bań sujhạuḱkantama? Do your eyes not see?
Bań sujhạuḱkantaea. He does not see.

Sujoḱ. Cf. suć.

Suk. Ease, tranquility, content, happiness, easy circumstances.

Suktege menaḱkoa. They are living at ease.
Sukregeko tahenkana. They are living in ease.
Bae suk bhogleda. He did not enjoy it.
Bako suklena. They were not at ease, or they did not escape suffering or poverty.
Jom suk joṅkanako. They have a sufficiency of food.
Iń doko roṛ sukkedińa. They annoyed me by continual fault finding.
Iń doko ruheṭ sukkedińa. They annoyed me by continual scolding.
Iń doko ạou sukkedińa. They annoyed me by continually telling me to do something.

Sukạr. } The planet Venus as Evening
Sukor. } star.

Sukạr } Friday.
Sukạr hiloḱ }

Sukạu. } To dry up, to become em-
Sukhạu. } aciated.

Sukhi. Accustomed to ease, brought up in comfortable circumstances.

Nui do sukhi hoṛ kanae. This is a man accustomed to ease.
Ạdi din khone sukhiakana. He has lived in ease for a long time.

Sukhle. Empty-handed, dry, only.

Tehen dole sukhlegea, oeṭ hõ bạnuḱtalea. We are empty-handed to-day, we have nothing.
Sukhlegele ruạṛena. We returned empty-handed.
Sukhle bạdgetińa. I have only got third class rice lands.

Sukhwạr. } Accustomed to ease, sedent-
Sukwạr. } ary.

Sukhwạr hoṛ kanae. He is a man accustomed to ease.

Suki. A small silver coin, a four anna or two anna bit.

Sukri. A pig, a partridge, in hunting parlance.

Ato sukri. A domesticated pig.
Bir sukri. A wild pig.
Sukri hopon. A young pig.
Sukri kuḍu. A boar.
Sukri bạdhiạ. A castrated swine, a hog.
Sukri pạṭhi. A young sow before littering.
Sukri eṅga. A sow.
Datela sukri. A wild boar.
Sukri bãṛã. A pigsty, ringworm.
Sukri ḍakaḍak̆. A pig's trough.
Bata sukri. A bear in hunting parlance.
Sukri gạli tol. A method of tying used mainly when tying the feet of a pig to be carried swung on a pole.
Leg sohag bae em purạu ocolekokhanko sukri bãṛãea. Bạhu seṙenko sukri bãṛãwa. If he does not cause the whole of the customary presents to be given he is put in a pigsty. The bride's party do the pigstying.

Sukol.
Sukol hilok̆.
Sukolwar.
Sukolwar hilok̆. } Friday, the sixth day of the week.

Sukor.
Sukorwar.
Sukorwar hilok̆. } Friday, the sixth day of the week.

Sukraj. In comfort, at ease, ease loving.

Aṅge sukraje duṛuṭakana, ar ale doe kạmi ococtlea. He is sitting at his ease and making us work.
Marañ sukraje hoyok̆kana. He is becoming a great molly coddle.

Suktạu. To be pleased with.

Sukti. Strength, power. Cf. sạkti.

Sukur.
Sukurwar.
Sukạr hilok̆. } Friday, the sixth day of the week.

Sukurdum. Cf. sakardom.

Sukwạr. Accustomed to ease, sedentary.

Sul. Dysentery.

Pond sul.
Arak̆ sul. } Bloody dysentery.
Sule oḍokok̆kana. He is suffering from dysentery.
Sul ñamakadea. He has got an attack of dysentery.

Sulạk. A long thatching needle, a kind of hairpin.

Jhurjhuri sulạk. A kind of hair pin to which several little dangling chains are attached.

Sulạñ. To deport oneself properly, to enjoy oneself.

Sulañ joñ reak̆ katha malkar hoṛ reak̆.

Sulgạu. To kindle, to light, to cause to burn, to inflame, to be at its height, as harvest, or a fruit season. Cf. salgao.

Suli. A kind of raft generally made of sol (q. v.), used to cross rivers when in flood.

Suliteñ paromena. I crossed by a raft.

Suli. A measure of ten seers.

Mit̆ suli hoṛo. Ten seers of dhan.

Sulo. Sixteen.

Sulo ana. The whole, the full complement.
Ato ren sulo anale heċakana. The whole of the villagers have come.

Sụlo soñjok. Cf. solo soñjok.

Sulok. Cf. suluk.

Suloñ. Friendship.

Nukin do ạḍi sulontakin. These two have great friendship with each other.

Sultạ. To twist the edge of a cloth or a piece of rag into a sharp point, a piece of rag twisted to make a lamp wick.

Sultạwaeme. Twist the edge of a cloth into a sharp point and insert it into his ear to clean it.
Sultạ uskạuam. Raise up the lamp wick a little.

Sulući. Snot, mucus discharged from the nose.

Sulujok̆kanae. Mucus is discharging from his nose.

Sului lundui cẽṛẽ. The small Minivet, *Pericrocotus peregrinus.*

Suluk. Peace, harmony, to be at peace, to be in harmony.

Sulukte tahenpe. Live in harmony.
Supulukok̆pe. Live in harmony with each other.
Sulukok̆pe. Be harmonious.
Suluk okoci. A peacemaker.

Sum. Niggardly, parsimonious, miserly.

Sum.
Sumbh.
Sund.
Suñ. } A mine, a pit, the opening into a mine, the shaft of a mine.

Sum bhugạk̆. The entrance to a mine, pit's mouth.

Sumạn. To become quiet, to desist, to come out and leave as a spirit which had possessed one.

Sadom, catom, danapani komgea, beren baṭena, men ado akasok̆pe. Adoko sumạnenge.

Sumaṛ. To complete, to finish, to end, to do anything outright.
Jom sumaṛkedako. They ate up all.
Sumaṛkedale. We finished it.
Sumaṛkedeako. They killed him outright.

Sumbhrau. } To bear, to suffer, to experience, to go through.
Sumbrau. }
Ạḍi duke sumbhrạuakaṭa. He has gone through much affliction.
Oṛak duạrae, duk sumbhrạu hoṛ kanae. She will guide the house well, she is a person who has experienced suffering.
Sanamak̃e sumbhrạuakaṭa. She has gone through it all, she has experienced it all.

Sumdhi. } Used by the fathers of a married couple when addressing each other.
Sạmdhi. }

Sumjhạu. To entrust to, to deliver over, to make over to, to give in charge.
Bicạrreko sumjhạukedea. They delivered him to judgment.
Uni dole sumjhạuakadea. We have delivered her over (to her parents.)
Khajna ṭakañ sumjhạu oṭokəda. I made over the rent money and came away.
Noa kathae sumjhạuakawadiña. He has charged me with this matter.

Sumjhạuni. Delivery, a present given when anything is made over to the owner or the person for whom it was intended.
Ṭukuć sumjhạuni. A present given to the cooks when the cooking pots are delivered up.
Ado ṭukuć sumjhạuni bar khalak leṭoko ñama. Then on the delivery of the cooking pots they get two large leaf cups full of tripe. Cf. leṭo.

Sumtu bukuć. } A common fodder grass, *Eleusine œgyptiaca, Pers.*
Suntu bukuć. }

Sumuk. Cf. sonmuk.

Sumuṅ. Just as much as, fully.
Jom sumuṅ dakaepe. Cook just as much as will be eaten.
Inạk getaea jaega si sumuṅ. He has just as much land as he can plough.
Hạṛup sumuṅ dare kana. It is a tree which one can just encircle with his arms.
Ạyup sumuṅ. Fully evening.
Ạyup sumuṅle seṭerena. It was fully evening when we arrived.
Pereć sumuṅ. Just as much as it will hold.
Lekha sumuṅko duṛuplena daka jom. The full number counted, or just as many as were provided for sat down to food.
Ṭaka sumuṅe damlena. He was valued at a full rupee.
Unum sumuṅ dak. Just as much water as will cover the head of a person standing.
Noa ṭheṅga sumuṅ dak. There is just as much water as will cover this stick, the water is the depth of this stick.

Sumuṛguć. Huddled up, compactly.
Sumuṛguće gitićakana. He is lying huddled up.
Sumuṛgućko samṭaoakaṭa. They have gathered it together compactly.

Sun. Empty, to be empty.
Goṛa sunena. The cow shed is empty.
Lać oḍok sunenae.
Oḍok sunenteye gocena.

Sunạ. Empty, untenanted, desolate.
Sunạ oṛak. An untenanted house, a desolate house.

Sunạn. } To cause to hear, to tell, to inform, to hear, to listen to, to have effect, as medicine.
Sunạni. }
Sunạniadeale. We told him, we informed him.
Iń do bako sunạniadiña. They did not inform me.
Ran bań sunạnilentiña. My medicine had no effect.
Katha do bań sunạnlentiña. My story was not listened to.

Sunạt. Circumcision.

Sun bajik. To throw a somersault in the air.

Sunḍ. An elephant's trunk, the uvula of human beings.

Sund. A pit. Cf. sum.

Sunḍi. A semi-Hinduised aboriginal caste.
This caste are the distillers and liquor sellers.
Sunḍi gạḍi. A liquor shop.
Sunḍi gạḍitem senlena? Did you go to the liquor shop?

Sundaṛ. } Beautiful, pretty, good.
Sundor. }
Maha sundar ñelokkana. It looks very beautiful.

Sundor mukhi. Good looking, beautiful.

Sundor mukhi. A kind of rice.

Sunduć. To go or push oneself in head foremost, as an animal to hide among leaves, straw, grass, &c.
Sim okare coe sundućena. The fowl has hidden herself some where.
Hoṛ gadelreye sunduć boloena. He pushed his way into the crowd of people.

Sunduk. A box, a chest.
Ạn sunduk. The ark of the Covenant.

Suṅgạ. A sting, an awn, as of grain, grass, &c.
Suṅgạwanić kanae. It has a sting.
Suṅgạ hoṛo hõ menaka. There is also dhan that has awns.

Suṅkhạl. The Shell Ibis, *Anastomus oscitans.*

Suniạ. A present offered to a superior.

Sunsạn. } Untenanted, empty, desol-
Sunsun. } ate.

Sunsunge ṣikạuka. It feels desolate.

Sunsuni. } A large gorgeously colour-
Sunsunia. } ed beetle, *Sternocera chrysis, Fabricius*, belonging to the family *Bupristidæ*.

Sunsuni. } A common small flow-
Ṭạnḍi sunsuni. } ering plant, *Desmodium triflorum, D. C.*

Sunsuni. } A plant found in moist
Dak sunsuni. } places, *Marsilia quadrifolia, Linn.*

Suntu bukuć. A common fodder grass, *Eleusine ægyptiaca, Pers.* Cf. sumtu bukuć.

Santal tradition has it that the first man and woman lived on the grain of this grass.

Sunuḍur. A waterfall. Cf. sonoḍor.

Sunum. Oil.

Sunum len. To express oil.
Sunum lelen pạṭi. A native oil press.
Kuiḍi sunum. Oil yielded by the fruit of *Bassia latifolia*, Roxb.
Utiń sunum. }
Kẹrụẹ sunum. } Mustard oil.
Tuṛi sunum. }
Eraḍom sunum. Castor oil.
Surgujạ sunum. Niger seed oil, yielded by the seeds of *Guizotia abyssynica, Pers.*
Tilmiń sunum. Gingelly or sesame oil, yielded by the seeds of *Sesamum indicum, L.*
Kujri sunum. Oil yielded by the seeds of *Celastrus paniculata, Willd.*
Bando sunum. Oil yielded by the seeds of *Spatholobus Roxburghii, Benth.*
Boṅga sarjom sunum. Oil yielded by the seeds of *Ventilago calyculata, Tulasne.*
Nim sunum. Oil yielded by *Melia Azadirachta, Linn.*
Bherenḍa sunum. Oil yielded by the seeds of *Jatropha curcus, Linn.*
Bạru sunum. Oil yielded by the seeds of *Schleichera trijuga, Willd.*
Ṭisiạ sunum. }
Ṭhisiạ sunum. } Linseed oil.
Lopoṅ sunum. Oil yielded by the kernels of the fruit of *Terminalia belerica, Roxb.*
Kudrum sunum. Oil yielded by the seeds of *Hibiscus sabdariffa, Linn.*, and of *Hibiscus cannabinus, Linn.*
Tạrpin sunum. Turpentine.
Kuilạ sunum. Gas or coal tar.
Gotom sunum. }
So sunum. } Ghee, clarified butter.
Hasa sunum. Earth oil, kerosene.
Sunum piṭhạ. Cakes fried in oil.
Noatele sunuma. We will supply ourselves with oil from this.

Sunum pańja. } To divine by means
Sunum boṅga. } of oil and leaves.

Sunum pańja ạguańpe. Go and enquire for me if the sick one will recover.

Sunum muć. A species of black ant.

Sunum bið. A small burrowing snake of the species *Typhlops braminus, Cuv.*

Sunum joṛ. } A species of wild fig
Sunum joṛ dare. } tree, *Ficus cordifolia, Roxb.*

Supoṭ. Good, excellent.

Bes supoṭe benaoakaṭa. He has made it very good.

Supotia. } Gentle, quiet, peaceable,
Sapotia. } pacific.

Sạprud. } To entrust, to deliver over to,
Soprot. } to give or put in charge.

Noa doe suprudadińa. He gave this into my charge.

Supṭạu. To be good, as a crop; to grow or yield well, to cause to be excellent.

Cas bes supṭạuakana. The crops have grown well.
Noa jaega bese supṭạuakaṭa. He has caused this field to yield well.
Jonḍra bese supṭạuakaṭa. He has raised a good crop of Indian corn.
Nes bes supṭạulena cas. There was a good yield of the crops this year.
Ḍahrạ supṭạuenae. The bullock has become docile.

Supṭić. The instep, the dorsal surface of the foot as opposed to *talka* the planter surface or sole.

Supṭić. A small winnowing fan of the same shape as a haṭak (q. v.), mainly used by children when playing at doing household work.

Supud. Gentle, quiet, peaceable, pacific.

Bes supud bạhu kanae. She is a very gentle bride.

Supuluk. The reciprocal form of suluk (q. v.)

Supurd. Cf. suprud.

Sur. Excitation of feeling, intoxication, frenzy.

Sur deṅakawadea. He is excited.
Ńu surakanae. He is excited or frenzied with drink, he has drunk to excitation.
Bại reak sur bah cabaakantaea. The excitation of the fit has not yet passed away.
Edre sur deṅakawadea. He is excited with anger.

Sur marte. } With one rapid move-
Sur mente. } ment, with a rush or dart.

Sur marte calao goćenae. He went off with a rush.

Suṛą. A common Cyperus or sedge, *Cyperus tegetum*. *Roxb.*
Suṛą sagenem sagenoka. You will flourish like the sedges.
The culms of this plant are woven into mats At a cremation a piece of cotton yarn twisted round a culm of this plant is set fire to and applied to the mouth of the corpse to be cremated, after which the funeral pyre is lighted.

Suṛą nąngin boṅga. Name of a Santal godlet.

Suṛą maṭha.
Suṛą maṭha. } Cf. maṭha suṛą.
Maṭha suṛą.

Suṛąg. Search, enquiry, trace. track, clue, to search, to seek, to inquire for.
Suṛągiń lagaokatą. I am following up a clue.
Suṛąg baṛaedań. I am making enquiries.

Surąhi. A porous earthenware water bottle.

Suraj.
Suruj. } The sun.

Suraj mukhi.
Suruj mukhi. } The Sun flower, *Helianthus annuus, Linn.*

Suraj mukhi.
Suruj mukhi. } The Indian Scaly Ant-eater, *Manis pentadactyla. Cf. arba* and *harba.*

Surąs. To use up all moisture in food being cooked, to finish, dried up.
Jom surąskedako. They ate up all.
Jelko teke surąskedako. They cooked the meat and in doing so used up all the liquid (and left the meat dry.)

Sur bań. Anger.
Surbań caṭhakkantaea. He is angry.

Suṛe. To cook along with rice, cooked along with rice.
Jel suṛe. Flesh meat and rice cooked together.
Aṛak suṛe. Vegetables and rice cooked together.
Hako suṛe. Fish and rice cooked together.
Simko suṛe jomkoa. They cook fowls along with rice and eat them.

Suṛe Baske. A sub-sept of the Santal sept Baske (q. v.)

Surgi baha. A wild flowering plant, *Anisomeles ovata, R. Br.*

Surguja. A cultivated plant, which yields the Niger seed and oil of commerce, *Guizotia abyssynica, Cass.*

Surhi. Blotches on the skin supposed by Santals to be produced by a parasite.
Surhiko jomekana. The surhi is eating him, his skin is blotched.

Surhi. A kind of weevil which infests stored dhan.

Suriąu. Cf. sariąu.

Suṛiąu. Cf. sunduć.

Surik. Manner, mode, like, calculation.
Ona surikte emaeme. Give him according to that calculation.

Surjąhi boṅga. The Sun god.

Surką.
Surkąu. } To strip off, as the leaves off a switch, &c., by running through the hand.

Surką baber. A piece of rope used in setting a net for hares. The net slides down this rope when the top support falls.

Surkąu. To sniff, to suck up, to draw up as by a syringe or pump.
Surkąu aderme. Sniff it up (the nose.)
Sunumko surkąu aṭkara. They sniff oil to test it (whether good or bad.)

Surkąu. Cf. surką.

Surki.
Surti. } Bricks ground to powder which takes the place of sand in making mortar in Bengal.

Surma.
Surmąn. } To be excited, to be frenzied, to suffer from a paroxysm of anger, fury, desperation, impatience.
Surmąakan hoṛ cetem metaea? What can you say to an excited man?

Surmą surmi. Quickly, as one excited, or in a fury.
Surmą surmiye hećena are ruąṛ goćena. He came excited with anger and returned immediately.

Surpil. Hot tempered, applied to females.

Surpuṭ.
Surpuṭ surpuṭ. } Cf. soṛpoṭ.
Suṛpuṭ surpuṭ.

Surpuṭ marte.
Surpuṭ mente. } Cf. soṛpoṭ marte.

Suṛuć suṛuć. Imitative of the warble of the Finch lark.
Lipi cẽṛẽ ãṛgon jokheć suṛuć suṛućko raga.

Sursą. A disease affecting cattle, perforation of palate.

Sursą. } The sharp ends of a bow.
Ak sursą. }

Sursunduć. To cow, to daunt, to depress with fear or shame, to render speechless.
Ruhet sursunduc̓kedeako. They scolded and cowed him.
Sursunduće duṛuṗakana. He is sitting cowed.
Sursunduć thirenae. He is cowed and silent.

Sursur. } To move rapidly, to dart,
Sursurąu. } impetuously.
Hakoko sursur baṛaekana. The fish are darting about.
Sursurąu rakaṗgoćenae hako do. The fish darted to the surface.
Sursurąu calaoenae. He rushed away.

Suṛsuṛią. Narrow.
Suṛsuṛiako aṛeakata. They have made a narrow ridge.
Suṛsuṛią hor. A narrow path.
Suṛsuṛią bhugak. A narrow, strait or small hole or opening.

Suṛuć. Narrow.
Suṛuć hor. A narrow path, a foot path.

Suṛuć. To insert, to go into or among.
Doho suṛućkedae okare coṅ. He inserted it some where to keep it.
Suṛuć aćena okare coṅ. It is lost some where by gettng into some thing (among grass, &c.)
Ghāsre suṛujoka sar do. The arrow will get among the grass.
Sąuṛi cẽṛẽ ghāsre ạdiko suṛujoka. The sąuṛi bird is very much given to hiding in the grass i. e. to boring its way through the grass.

Suruć. } To sob, to snuffle.
Suruć suruć. }
Eken surućteṭge aṅjomokkana. Only the sob is heard.

Suruj bại. A kind of fit or convulsion, sunstroke.

Suruj mukhi baha. Cf. sụraj mukhi.

Suruj mukhi. The Indian Scaly Ant-eater. Cf. suraj mukhi.

Sũṛũkuć. A small bush, *Salix tetrasperma, Roxb.* Cf. gạda sigrik.

Suruṅ. To bore a hole in a rock for blasting, a hole bored in a rock for blasting.

Surusuć. To huddle up oneself, as from cold.
Dakte lohoć surusućenae. He is wet and huddled up owing to being cold.

Susạṅ. Dreary, desolate.

Susạr. To take care of, to nurse, to minister to, emergency.
Ajak hoṛmo hõ bae susạrettaea. He does not even take care of his own person.
Susạr calaokatiṅ me. Help me through this emergency.
Ạdiko susạr samarkedea, enhõ bae baṅcaolena. They nursed him very carefully, nevertheless he did not live.

Susạri. } The appellation of the priest
Susạrią. } who officiates at the Jatra (q. v.) festival.

Susạria. A nurse, a dresser in a hospital, one who ministers.

Susraṛ. Cf. sạsraṛ.

Susti. Slow, lazy, idle.
Ạdi sustigetaea nuiak kạmi. This (man's) work is very slow.
Sustige taṛamae. He walks slowly.

Susto. To improve or recover, as from an illness.
Susto ṅogokkanae netar do. He is improving a little now-a-days.

Susṭob. } Kindness, impartiality, ab-
Susṭop. } sence of anxiety.
Susṭobteko jomkeda. They ate without anxiety.

Susṭok. Good, well, absence of defect.
Susṭok kathae metadiṅa. He spoke to me affably.

Sũsũ. } To sniff, to snuff, to snort.
Susu. }
Sũsũ sahedokkanae. He is sniffing, or breathing strongly through the nose.
Sũsũkkanae rorok lạgit. He (bull) is snorting, he is about to charge.

Susuą. } To chitter and produce a
Suswąu. } hissing sound resembling
Susuąu. } susu susu, to shiver.
Enaṅrem susuąkkan tahẽkana. You were chittering awhile ago.
Enaṅrem susuąulena. You chittered awhile ago.

Susulṭak. In good condition physically, to be bright, as the countenance.
Sanam hoṛkoak metãhã raskạte susulṭagoka.

Susum. To heat, as water over a fire.
Dak susum ṅogme. Heat the water a little.
Dakko susumakata. They have heated the water.
Susum dak. Hot, warm, or tepid water.
Susum dake ṅuieda. He is drinking warm water.

Susurbaṅ. A wasp.
Khudią susurbaṅ. }
Sehgel susurbaṅ. } Different kinds of wasps.
Bana susurbaṅ. }
Careć susurbaṅ. }

Susurṭak̕. Robust, flourishing, as a healthy plant, in good condition physically, plump.
Susurṭak̕e moṭaakana. He is plumply fat.
N̕elkedean susurṭagok̕kanae. I saw him, he is becoming plump.

Susu susu. To chitter, the sound produced through the teeth when chittering or shivering.
Rabañte susu susuk̕kanae. He is chittering with cold.

Suc̕. To hollow out a cavity in sand and allow water to percolate into it.
Dak̕ko suda. They hollow out a cavity in the sand and allow water to percolate into it.
Suc̕ dak̕. Water that has percolated into a cavity hollowed out in the sand.

Suc̕. To dress or tie up the hair.
Rok̕ suc̕. / Roc̕ suc̕. } A method of tying up the hair by binding it with something or fixing it with hair pins, applied to women.
Tukạ suc̕. A method of fixing up the hair without tying or using hair pins. Women only use this method.
Peṭer suc̕. A method of fixing the hair by twisting it into a coil at the back of the head.
Tikia suc̕. The hair tied in a knot on the top of the head (by men.)
Laṛa suc̕. The hair tied in a bunch or knot on the side of the head (of males.)
Laṛi suc̕. The hair tied in a bunch or knot on the side of the head, (of females.)
Baha bõko sudok̕a. They also dress the hair with flowers.

Sũṭ. Dry ginger.

Suṭạm. Thread, yarn, any filmy substance produced by insects, such as spiders, silkworms, &c., &c.
Ponḍ suṭạm. White thread.
Arak̕ suṭạm. Red thead.
Lumạm suṭạm. Silk thread of the Tassar silk worm.
Guli suṭạm. A ball of thread, or a thread ball.
Ril suṭạm. A reel of thread, thread that is sold on reels.
Suṭạm or. To prepare the warp of a web of cloth. Cf. or.
Bindi suṭạm. Thread spun by a spider.
Toṛe suṭạm. Gossamer.
Nia kaskomle suṭạmạ. We will make this cotton into thread.

Suṭạm. / **Toṛe suṭạm.** } Gossamer.

Suṭạm orok̕. A children's game so called.

Suthar. Fine, grand, beautiful, used mainly in sarcasm.
Ạdi sutharem n̕elok̕kana. You appear very grand.
Ạdi sutharem oṛak̕akac̕a. You have built a grand house.

Suthni. A little, a pinch, a grain.
Mic̕ suthniye emadin̕a. He gave me a pinch.

Suthni. A plant, *Dioscorea fasciculata, Roxb.*, the root tubers of which are eaten.

Suthrại. Well, properly, nicely, grandly.
Suthrạiko pinḍạakac̕a. They have made a nice pinḍạ (q. v.)
Suthrạiye duṛupakana. He is sitting grandly (like a great man when others are working.)
Suthrạiye gitic̕ jok̕kana. He is sleeping quietly.

Suṭi. / **Munga suṭi.** } A long whip-like bean the fruit of the Horse Radish on Ben-nut tree, *Moringa pterygosperma, Gaertn.*

Suṭik. To enquire.
Kathae suṭik baṛaeda. He is making enquiries into the matter.
Suṭikpe okoe onare lek kanae. Enquire as to who in that (village) is worthy.

Sutrạu. To enquire, to enquire into, to investigate,.
Onko ṭhene sutrạuana. He enquired of them.

Sutri. A kind of cultivated pulse. *Phaseolus calcaratus, Roxb.*

Sutruc̕. Small, insignificant.
Sutruc̕ mara gidrạ. A little imp of a child.

Suṭuc̕. To search for by feeling with the fingers, or by lifting or removing small objects.
Cec̕em suṭuc̕ baṛaeda? What are you searching for?
Suṭuc̕ n̕amkedae. He felt for it and found it.
Dakatec̕ do bae jomeda, jelge suṭuc̕ baṛaedae. He is not eating the rice, he is fishing out the bits of meat.

Suṭuk̕. / **Suṭuk̕ suṭuk̕.** } Sound produced by water falling on the ground.
Suṭuk̕ suṭuk̕ mic̕ n̕indạe dak̕keda. It rained the whole night, drip drip.
Suṭuk̕ suṭuk̕ sadekana. It sounds drip drip.

Suṭuk̕ marte. / **Suṭuk̕ mente.** } With a drip, with a sound of water falling on the ground.
Suṭuk̕ marte sadeana.

Suṭur. / **Suṭur suṭur.** } Sound of nibbling or crunching, as by rats.
Suṭur suṭure jomeda. He is nibbling.
Suṭur maraokedae. He nibbled it up.
Ontereye suṭurkeda. He made a nibbling sound over there.

Sutur na gatar. The opposite of what is fit and proper.

Sutur na gatarem ńelońkana. You look untidy, or slovenly.
Sutur na gatarem roṛećkana. You are speaking improperly.
Sutur na gatarem kạmiakaťa. You have done the work badly.

Suyuṛ / **Suyuṛ suyuṛ.** To whistle through the teeth, as when whistling to a dog.

Suyuṛ maraokedae. He gave a whistle.
Suyuṛ suyuṛe goleda. He is whistling or hissing through his teeth.

Suyuṛ marte. / **Suyuṛ mente.** With a whistle, with a hiss through the teeth.
Suyuṛ marteye golkeda. He whistled with a hiss through the teeth.

Swabhab. / **Swabhao.** Nature, disposition.

Swadhin. Independent, one's own master.

T

Tab. Cf. tap̣.

Ṭabać ṭubuć. To splash in water, to cause a splashing sound.
Ṭabać ṭubućko paerańkana. They are swimming and splashing.
Ṭabać ṭubućko calańkana. They go making a splashing noise.

Ṭabak ṭabuk. / **Ṭabak ṭubuk.** To splash, to cause a sound of splashing.
Ṭabak ṭubukko don baṛaeda. They are jumping about and splashing (frogs.)

Ṭaba ṭubu. Imitative of the sound produced by striking the water with the feet when swimming.
Ṭaba ṭubuko paerańkana. They are swimming and making a sound resembling ṭaba ṭubu.

Ṭabuk marte. / **Ṭabuk mente.** With a splash.
Ṭabuk marte saḍeěna. It sounded splash.

Tabe. Dependent, subject.
Tabere. Under authority, subject to, dependent on.
Okoe tabere menaea? To whom is he subject, on whom is he dependent?
Tabeteć. Dependence, subjection.
Be-tabe. Independent, free.
Be-tabeteć. Independence, freedom.

Tabedar. A dependent, a follower, a subject.
Amren tabedar doń bań kana. I am not a dependent of yours.

Taben. A kind of parched rice, to make rice into *taben*.
Hoṛoko tabena. They make rice into *taben*.
Taben hoṛoko idiakaťa. They have taken away dhan to make into *taben*.

Taben il. Very young feathers on a young bird.
The name is given to feathers at the stage when they resemble the flat grains of *taben*.

Taben aṛak. A kind of wild plant used as a pot-herb.

Taben. Yours (dual.)
Okare taben oṛak? Where is your house?

Taber. Face downwards, upper side down.
Taberakanae. He is lying on his face, or stomach.
Taberteye gitiċakanae. He is lying on his face.
Taberteye gurena. He fell forward on his face.

Tạbij. An ornament worn on the upper arm.

Tabla. A kind of small drum beaten with the fingers, a small hatchet or axe.

Tabo. / **Tabon.** Ours, our, belonging to us. (inclusive of person addressed.)
Senakantabonae. He belonging to us has gone, our (brother, sister, &c.) has gone.

Tạbuć. Not thoroughly dry, moist, damp.
Alope bạndia tạbućgea. Do not put it up in *bandia* (q. v.) it is not thoroughly dry.

Ṭạbuk. / **Ṭạbuk ṭạbuk.** / **Ṭạbuk.** / **Ṭạbuk ṭạbuk.** Sound of water agitated in a hole, cavern or water pot.
Ṭạbuk ṭạbuk sadekana. It sounds ṭạbuk ṭạbuk.

Ṭạbuk marte. / **Ṭạbuk mente.** With a splash, as of water in a waterpot.

Ṭaḍ. An ornament worn on the upper arm by women.

Ṭaḍa. A pole carried on the shoulders of two or more men from which anything to be carried is slung, to carry slung on a pole.
Ṭaḍatekin gok ạgukeda. They brought it swung on a pole on their shoulders.

Tadarat. / **Tadarot.** / **Todarot.** To investigate, to enquire into.
Ona kathale tadarotkeda, bań sạbudlena. We enquired into that matter, it was not proved.

Tạdbir. } To deliberate, to take counsel,
Tạtbir. } opinion or advice.

Ṭaḍe. To lean upon a stick, crutch, &c., placed under the arm; to lean against, to cause to lean against.
Ṭheṅgare ṭaḍeakanae. He is leaning on a stick placed under the arm.
Silpiṅko ṭaḍeakaťa. They have leaned something against the door.

Ṭaeni ṭheṅga. Cf. ṭaini.

Taenom. Behind.
Taenom seć. Backwards.
Taenomre menaea. He is behind.

Tagada. To enquire into, to take to do with, to investigate.
Noa tagadae reaṅ oeť kantama? What right have you to enquire into this?

Tagaja. To insist upon a thing being done at once, to cause to do quickly, to be prompt.
Noa ṭaka ạḍi tagajakate uṭhạupe. Collect this money at once.

Tagaṛ. A trough.
Tagaṛre surti ar cunko sipia. They mix surti (q. v.) and lime in a trough.

Tagatusạ. } In disorder, disorderly, con-
Tạgutạsu. } fusion, to shake up, as straw for a bed, &c., littered.
Tạgutạsu noakoreko dohoakaťa. They have placed them about here in disorder.
Alope tạgutạsuia kicrić do. Do not disorder or disarrange the cloth.
Tạgutạsu ạrisge ńelokkana, oṛak sephaepe. It is littered and looks unseemly, clean the house.
Tạgutạsu busuṕ aṭećkateko gitićakana. They shook out the straw and are lying on it

Ṭaghen. } A prop, a catch, as anything
Ṭhagen. } put against a door to keep it open; to lean against.
Ṭaghenakaťaṅ. I have put something against it to keep it open.
Dhirite ṭaghenme. Put a stone to it to keep it open.
Ṭaghen sakom. A "guard" bracelet.
Onare ṭaghenoka. It will lean against that.

Tagoj. Strength.

Tagum. To eat in big mouthfuls.
Tạgum goťkadae. He devoured it.

Tạgidar. An overseer.

Tagoť aṛak. A wild plant used as a pot-herb. Cf. togoť aṛak.

Ṭagri hạnḍi. Pachwae, liquor made from rice, rice beer.

Tạgutạsu. Cf. tagatusạ.

Tãhã. That, that same.
Nasenak biswạs hõ tãhã bạnuktaea. Even a little faith that same he has not.

Tahã reseť. On the contrary. Cf. reseť.

Tãhã. There, in that place.
Jahã ạyuṕ tãhãm aṅgaena. Wherever night befel you there you stayed till morning.
Jahã mon tãhãṅ calakạ. Where my fancy leads me there I will go.

Tãhã. Certainly, without doubt.
Onḍege tãhãm aṅgaena adom meneda, ńindạregeṅ heťena. You were certainly there till dawn and you say I came (home) during the night.

Tãhã. } In some places.
Jãhã tãhã. }
Jãhã tãhã dakkedae, ar jãhã tãhã do bạṅ. It rained in some places and not in others.

Ṭahaka. } Distinctly, clearly, easily,
Ṭahãka. } without hindrance.
Khub ṭahakae roṛeda. He speaks very distinctly.
Ona ṭạnḍire do behaj ṭahakakin senokkan tahẽkana. On that plain they were walking with great freedom.

Ṭahalao. } To take or give an airing.
Ṭahlao. }
Ṭahalaok lạgiť band sećle senlena. We went towards the tank for an airing.
Sadomko ṭahlaoeťkoa. They are giving the horses an airing.

Taham tukuć. Stumbling.
Taham tukuć ńut. Pitch dark, in which one stumbles.
Taham tukuć baṛae kanae. He is going stumbling along.
Andheť dundheť taham tukuć okatepe calak kana? Where are you going to floundering and stumbling?

Tahao. } Feeling the way, groping
Tahaote. } as with a stick to try the depth of water, or in darkness.
Tahao ạṭkarkedae. He felt the depth (with a stick.)
Tahao tahaote calakme. Go feeling your way.
Tahao tahaote roṛme, ạuri sạuri alom roṛa. Speak carefully, do not speak at random.

Tahaṕ ṭaṭuṕ. } Stumbling, floundering,
Tạhuṕ ṭaṭuṕ. } as one walking in the dark; to go slap dash.
Tahaṕ ṭạṭuṕle heťena. We came floundering along.

Tahãṛ bihãṛ. All about, here and there, lying about, scattered here and there.
Tahãṛ bihãṛko gitića setoṅ dinre. In the hot weather they sleep here and there.
Tahãṛ bihãṛ mihũ merom menakkoa. The cattle are scattered here and there.
Tahãṛ bihãṛko bạgiakaťa. They have left (the things) lying about.

Ṭaharao. Cf. ṭarhao.

Tāhā reset. On the contrary.

Iñ doñ menkeda cele mundhạṭge ạtu hijuḱkana, ñelkede doñ tāhā reset mić goṭen hoṛe ạtu hijuḱkan. I said it must be a log that comes floating, I saw that on the contrary it was a man coming floating.

Tāhā reta. A preliminary to a song to get the time to which it should be sung as the lines of Santal songs sung to the same tune are not always of the same length.

Tāhā reta nana tarana tāhā reta nanare, Tāhā reta, nana tarana na nanare.

Tahạri. Ṭạhri. Ṭạhri ṭạhri. } Slowly, gently.

Ṭahạrite taṛamme. Walk slowly.
Ṭạhrite roṛme. Speak gently.
Ṭạhri alope sereña, cogoṛ baṛe serenpe. Do not sing slowly, sing quickly.

Tahāṛ tahāṛoḱ. To wander about.

Tahas. Tahas nahas. Tahās nahas. } To waste, squander.

Taha tạhi. Quickly, industriously, rapidly, at high pressure.

Taha tạhiko kạmikana. They are working at high pressure.
Oṛaḱre jomaḱ sanampe tahas nahasketṭạbona. You wasted all the food we had in the house.

Tạhbi. Quickly, without delay.

Tahē. Tahen. } To remain, to reside, to stay.

Birre tahenkanae, oṛaḱte do bae hijuḱa. He resides in the forest, he does not come home.
Uni do birreye tahēena, iñgeñ heċena. He remained in the forest, I have come.
Tahēteċge ohoko tahē ñawana. They will on no account be allowed to remain.

Tahē tuluċ. While, along with.
Tahē ñogoḱ. To stay for a little.
Tahē urić. To remain steadfast.
Tahē thir. To remain still.

Tahēkana. Was, were.

Tahēkanañ. I was.
Tahēkanale. We were.

Taher. A kind of cucumber, *Cucumis sativus, Linn.*

Tahka bahka. Hurriedly, quickly.

Tahka bahkañ oḍok goċena, hiṛiñ oṭoakadañ. I left hurriedly, and forgot it.
Tahka bahkaakanale. We are hurrying.

Tạhkiạt. To take care of, to take oversight of.

Saname tạhkiạteḱkana. He is taking the oversight of all.

Ṭahlao. To give or take an airing, to lead about, to cause to walk backwards and forwards, as a horse, &c.

Sadomko ṭahlaokoa. They give horses an airing.

Ṭahrao. To fix, settle, come to a decision or determination, to appoint, to establish, to stop, to stay, to remain, to be permanent, to make a fixture.

Noale ṭahraokeda. We came to this decision.
Aṛe ṭahraokedale. We made the dam a fixture, we caused it to be permanent.
Teheñ khonbo ṭahraokeda banar bela kạmi hoyoḱa. We decided that from to-day work would be carried on both forenoon and afternoon.
Gupiiċle ṭahraokedea teheñ khon. We appointed him cattle herd from to-day.
Aṛekedale, menkhan bañ ṭahraolena. We made the dam, but it did not stand.
Ḍahrañ saṗ ṭahraokedea. I caught and held the bullock.

Ṭạhri. Ṭạhri ṭạhri. } Slowly, gently.

Ṭạhri ṭạhri roṛme. Speak gently.
Ṭạhrigeye taṛamoda. He walks slowly.

Tạhsil. Tạsil. } To collect dues.

Tạḱsile heċakana. He has come to collect (rent, &c.)

Tạhsildar. Tạsildar. } A collector of rents, dues, &c.

Tahtahao. To be on the alert, to watch eagerly for, to stand in readiness to act on the instant, to be eager.

Tahtahao baṛaekanae. He is standing ready to act (as with arrow on string ready to shoot an animal as soon as it appears.)
Tahtahaoakanae kulại capade lạgić. He is ready to throw at the hare the instant it appears.
Ñeñel lạgićko tahtahao baṛaekana. They are eager to go to the fair.

Ṭạhuċ ṭạhuċ. Taking long steps, striding.

Ṭạhuċ ṭạhuċe taṛameda. He goes striding along.

Tạhuṗ tạhuṗ. Cf. tahaṗ ṭạtuṗ.

Tạhuṛ. To eat in large mouthfuls, to devour, to tear as a beast of prey a carcase.

Kule tạhuṛkedea. A tiger devoured him.
Tạhuṛ jomkedeae. He devoured him.
Tạhuṛ cooketkoae. He allowed them to be devoured (by a tiger.)

Tại tại. A call to pigeons.

Tại tại parwako hohoakoa. They call tại tại to pigeons.

Ṭaini.
Ṭaeni.
Ṭaini ṭheṅga. } A stick higher than a man with iron rings fixed loosely on the top which sound as the stick is struck on the ground.

The ṭaini ṭheṅga was till very recently employed to beat time when dancing.

Ṭaini.
Boṅga ṭaini. } A common jungle plant, *Tacca pinnatifida*, *Linn.*, the umbel of which on its stalk bears a resemblance to the ṭaini ṭheṅga (q. v.)

Taj.
Taja. } Fresh, fat, green, raw.

Tajaenae. He is fat.
Taja jel. Fresh meat, good flesh meat.

Taja. To recover from an illness.

Taji. Spirited, quick, energetic.

Nui ḍaṅra khube tạjia. This bullock is very spirited.

Tajia. The *tazia* of the Mohamedans. Cf. daha.

Tạjbij. To enquire into, to examine, to consider, to judge, to estimate.

Tak. Doubled once without cutting, as a thread, &c.

Bar tak. Doubled twice or quadrupled without cutting.
Pe tak. Thrice doubled without cutting.

Tak. Time, season, opportunity, proper time, nick of time, crisis.

Sanam senaƙ take dohoeda. He attends to every thing in its proper time.
Tak bae jogao daṛeada. He could not attend to it at the proper time.
Inạ takrege uniye heć goćena. He arrived at that particular time.
Jojom takregem hećena. You have come at meal-time.

Ṭak. Stock still.

Ṭak lekae teṅgoakana. He is standing stock still.
Teṅgo ṭakakanae. He is standing stock still.

Tak batar. Season, proper season, proper time, seasonably.

Tak batar ńelteko era. They watch for a favourable time to sow.
Tak batarre bae caslaƙa. He did not cultivate seasonably.

Tak rokom. Method, mode, ins and outs, habits and ways.

Tak rokom ạuriye saba kạmi reaƙ. He has not yet got into the ins and outs of the work.
Polis reaƙ takrokom ạuriye saba. He has not yet got into the habits and ways of the police.

Ṭaƙ. In composition one.

Okoe-ṭaƙ-em hataoea? Which one (animate) will you take?
Oka-ṭaƙ-em hataoa? Which one (inanimate) will you take?
Nui-ṭaƙ iń hataoea. I will take this one (animate.)
Noa-ṭaƙ iń hataoa. I will take this one (inanimate.)
Tala-ṭaƙạguime. Bring the middle one.

Ṭaka. Silver, a rupee, money.

Ṭaka reaƙ. Of silver, made of silver.
Ṭaka kạnḍi. Money.

Takao. To look at, to watch, to look intently.

Kule takaoedekan tahẽkana. The tiger was watching him.

Takap̣ takap̣.
Tokop̣ tokop̣. } To make a noise when eating.

Takap̣ takap̣e jomkeda. He gobbled up the food.

Takạr. Of that, of this.

Takar adhako ạgukina. They fine them the half of that.

Takia. A pillow.

Noań tạkiạia. I will make a pillow of this.

Tạkić. To come in contact with, to stumble, to meet with an obstacle, difficulty or hindrance; to strike the foot, head, &c. against an obstacle, to be offended, to be hindered.

Cạndire tạkićenae. His brow came in contact with (a branch.)
Santao hoelenkhanko tạkić godoƙa. When persecution arises they become offended.

Tạkin. Their, theirs, (dual.)

Oṛaƙ tạkin. Their house.

Tạkiť. Cf. tạkić.

Ṭaknaƙ. A small earthenware vessel.

Ṭaknaƙ ṭoknaƙreko dohoakaťa. They have put it in small earthenware vessels (of different kinds.)

Tako. Their, in comp.

Oṛaƙtako. Their house.

Takoe.. To spin on the *charkha* or spinning wheel.

Sutạmko takoekeda. They spun the thread.
Taƙkoeić. A spinner.
Taƙkoe kanae. She is spinning.

Takonia. Staring, starer.

Takonia hoṛ kanae. He is a staring man.
Takonia kanae. He is a starer.

Takraṛ. To dispute, to jangle, to argue, to wrangle, to quarrel.

Ona kathae takraṛeć kana. He has raised a dispute about that matter, he is disputing that matter.
Noa katha ạdim takraṛedińkana. You are hotly arguing this matter with me.
Jomaƙ reaƙ takraṛ kana. It is a dispute about food.
Uni takraṛe lagaoeda. He is raising a dispute.

Ṭakra ṭukra. } Pieces, fragments, broken
Ṭakra ṭukra. } pieces, to break into pieces or fragments.

Takta. A plank, a board.
Noale taktaea. We will make planks of this.

Ṭakṭak. Desolate.
Maraṅ ṭakṭak ṭanḍi. A wide desolate plain.

Ṭakṭak. } To click, as a watch or clock.
Ṭokṭok. }
Ghaṛi ṭakṭak saḍekana. The watch is sounding click click.

Ṭakṭaki. Stockstill, startled and deprived of power of motion.
Teṅgo ṭakṭakikanae. He is standing stockstill.

Ṭakṭaki. } To strike the end of a stick
Ṭhakṭhaki. } repeatedly on the ground.
Ṭakṭakiye calaokeda. He divined by means of striking a stick on the ground.
Santals have a superstition that if an enemy buries anything near a house the inhabitants will be injured. When there is a suspicion of something having been thus buried an *ojha* is brought who repeating an incantation strikes his stick all over the place. His hand is guided to the spot where the thing is buried. It is then dug up and thrown away and the spell removed. If a man's cows give a large quantity of milk, milk is buried under the impression that this will decrease the supply. If it is desired to injure a man's rice crops, rice is buried, and if his death is intended a bone is buried.

Ṭaku. The spinning axle of a spinning wheel, on which the thread is wound as it is spun.

Ṭaku. A blight which affects the rice plant in certain cases where there is too much water during an early stage of its growth.

Ṭal. Equal, without change, musical time or measure.
Mit ṭalgeakin nukin ḍaṅra do. These two bullocks are equal or alike.
Mit ṭalgekin calaka. They keep step.
Mit ṭale dakkeda. It rained without change.
Mit ṭalge ruạkkanae. His fever is continuous.
Ṭalge bae emetkana. He does not keep time.

Tal. } Subject. topic, theme,
Taṛ. }
Khub tale uthạuakaṭa maraṅ maraṅ katha reak. He is discoursing on an interesting and important subject.
Bes taṛe uthạuakaṭa. He is discoursing on an interesting topic.
Bes katha reak taṛe uthạuakaṭa. He is discoursing on an interesting theme.

Tala. Middle, centre.
Tala mala. The centre, the middle.
Tala malare. In the centre.
Talare. In the midst, in the middle, among, amongst.
Tala oṛakre duṛupakanae. He is sitting in the middle of the house.
Oṛak talareye duṛupakana. He is sitting in the middle of the houses.
Tala setoṅ. The direct rays of the sun.
Tala kạṭup. The middle finger.
Talaiċ. The middle one, the second in point of birth when there are three or more.
Tala koṛa. The second son when there are three or more, the stomach.
Tala kuṛi. The second daughter when there are three or more daughters.
Tala bạhu. The wife of the second son when there are three or more sons.
Tala jãwãe. Husband of the second daughter when there are three or more daughters,
Tala koraṅ bạhuaea. I will take food.
Peṛa talakedeako. They restored him to his caste privileges.

Tala. To help, to assist.

Tala. To put dhan the second time through the husking process.

Tala. The sole of a boot or shoe.
Tala ma besgea, cetan cadrateṭ baṛiċena. The soles are good, the uppers are bad.

Tala. } Half.
Tara. }
Mit din tala din. A day and a half.
Mit cando tala. A month and a half.
La tala po tala inạte hõle purungea.

Tala. A lock, a padlock.
Tala cạbhi. A padlock and key.
Silpiṅ tala oṭoa kaṭaṅ. I left the door locked, I locked the door before leaving.

Talaṅ. } A small piece or quanti-
Kaṭiċ talaṅ. } ty.
Kaṭiċ talaṅ emadiṅae. He gave me a little piece.

Talaṅ. In comp. ours (dual.)

Tala ṭanḍi. Friendless, without a guardian, alone, out on the plain.
Nitoke tala ṭanḍiena. Now he is friendless.

Ṭalao. To break, to transgress.
Hukum ṭalao. To break or transgress a command or order.

Ṭalao. To spend or pass, as time.
Jabãlekate dine ṭalaoeda. He spends or passes the time anyway.
Ajarete dine ṭalaoeda. She spends her time in gossipping, or visiting her neighbours.
Din ṭaklaoiċ kanae. He is an hireling, one whose aim is only to pass the day.

Talao. } Without intermission, con-
Mit talao. } tinually.
Mit talaoko roṛekana. They are continually finding fault with him.
Mit talaoge dakedae. It rains without intermission.

Talao. To warn.

Talbhaṅ. Respite, pause, interval, cessation.
Talbhaṅ bae emakokana. He gives them no respite.

Ṭalbi. To hurry, to cause to act without delay, promptly, quickly.
Adiye ṭalbieťlea. He is hurrying us much.
Adi ṭalbiko khojkana. They want it very promptly.

Tale. In comp. our.
Oṛak-tale. Our house.

Tale. } The Palmyra palm, *Borassus flabelliformis, Linn.*
Tale dare. }

Tale hako. A kind of fish.

Tale siń. The Palmyra palm. Cf. tale.
Rohoealah mairi ule siń tale siń,
Gujukre gurokre ńutum tahena. Doń sereń.

Talebor. Rich, great.
Khub talebor hoṛ kanae. He is a very rich man.

Taletal. Without intermission, continuously.
Taletal hoṛko hijuk̇kana. People are coming continuously.

Talgataṭuak̇. To crush, to bruize, to disintegrate, to break into pieces, as straw by being trampled on.
Hoṛeko dal talgataṭuak̇akaťa.
Sanamko jom talgataṭuak̇akaťa.

Ṭalha. A short stick, used to throw at small game, or to knock down fruit, &c.
Ṭalhate bele ulko capať ńura. They knock down ripe mangoes with the ṭalha.

Ṭali. } A branch on which tassar silk worms are transferred from one tree to another.
Lumam ṭali. }
Tassar silk worms having consumed all the leaves off a tree are collected on a small branch. This branch—ṭali—is fixed on to another tree and the caterpillars spread themselves over it.
The *ṭali* is never used as firewood as there is a superstition that if it is burned the silk worms will die from disease.

Ṭali. }
Toli. } Underneath, root, foundation.
Tuli. }
Ṭalire dak̇ menak̇a, arhõ la ńogme. There is water underneath, dig down a little more.

Ṭaliạu. } Belonging to an old well-to do family, wealthy, rich.
Tuliạu. }
Ṭaliạu hoṛ kanae. He belongs to an old well-to-do family.
Nek̇e tuliạuk̇kana. He is just now becoming rich.

Ṭali iṭạ. A broad flat tile.

Ṭalik. To take care of, to ward, to act as guardian or caretaker.
Hoṛe ṭalikeťkoa. He is looking after the people.

Ṭalikạ. } Inventory, a list of articles, number, to count, to number.
Ṭalkhạ. }
Hoṛko talkhạeťkoa. They are counting the people.
Mihũ merom reak̇ ṭalikạko hataoeda. They are taking the number of the cattle.

Ṭalim. To teach, to instruct, to impart knowledge, tuition, instruction.
Bese ṭalimakana. He is well instructed.
Nui gidrạ ṭalimkaetińme. Instruct this child of mine.

Ṭalin. In comp. our (dual.)
Oṛak̇-ṭaliń. Our house.

Talka. The palm of the hand, sole of the foot.
Jańga talka. Sole of foot.
Ti talka. Palm of hand.

Ṭalkha. Cf. ṭalikạ.

Ṭalmalao. Cf. ṭolṭol.

Ṭalmal. } To heave, shake, quiver, tremble.
Ṭalmalao. }

Talom. To overtop.
Pinḍhe talomkedae dak̇te. The water overtopped the embankment.
Hara talomkedeae. He grew and overtopped him, he outgrew him.

Talsa. Measles.
Talsa rakapakawadea. Measles have broken out on him.
Talsa ruạ ńamakadea. He has caught measles.

Talsa. Flour.
Talsa is prepared by first roasting the grain and grinding it. It is eaten without cooking, sometimes dry and sometimes mixed with water.

Talse. Cf. tarse.

Taltul. To begin, to take in hand, to get in readiness, to make preliminary preparations.
Dakae lạgiťko taltul baṛak̇kana. They are preparing to cook food.
Nit hõ bape taltulok̇kana, ar ṭak̇ngipe metańkana. You are not even now beginning to make preparations (for cooking) and you are telling me to wait.

Taltalao. To cause to haste, to hasten, to cause to hurry, to hurry, to dragoon, to constrain, to drive,
Taltalao oḍokkeťkoae. He hurried them out.
Khajna reak̇ko taltalaokeťlea. They are hurrying us to pay our rent.
Biṭhiko taltalaoakaťlea. They dragooned us into doing forced labour.
Kạmikoe taltalaoeťkoa. He is hurrying the work people.

Ṭaluk. A lease in perpetuity, a subdivision of a zila or county, the latter consisting of several ṭaluks.

Tạlukdar. A landlord, the holder or proprietor of a tạluk.

Tạlukdạri. The tenure, office, or estate of a tạlukdar.

Tạlukdariedae. He holds the tenure of a tạlukdar.

Tam. To seize with both arms and throw down.

Tapam. To wrestle. Reciprocal form of tam.
Tam gitićkedeae. He seized him in his arms and laid him down.
Tamkedeae. He threw him down.
Tam gur goťkedeae. He seized him in his arms and threw him down.

Tam. In comp. thine.

Ṭheṅga-tam halaṅme. Take up your stick.

Tamadi. Limitation as to time which bars a civil suit.

Katha do tamadientama. Your matter is out of date, cannot now be gone into as it has been brought up too late.

Tamae tomoe. To loaf about.

Tamae tomoe baṛaekanape, kami seć do bape calaǩkana. You are loafing about, you will not go to work.

Tạmại. Respect, reverence, deference.

Mạṅjhi reaǩ tạmại do bae dohoeda. He does not pay respect to the Mạṅjhi (q. v.)

Ṭamak. A kind of kettle drum.

Ṭamak khol. The iron portion of the ṭamak kettle drum when not covered with hide.
Ṭamak ru. To beat the ṭamạk or kettle-drum.

Ṭamak ṭumuk. } To convalesce, to re-
Ṭanak ṭunuk. } cover from illness.

Ruạ khone ṭamak ṭumukakana. He is recovering from an attack of fever.

Tamakhur. } Tobacco.
Thamakhur. }

Maraṅ tamakhur. Ganja.
Tin tamakhur. A mixture of ganja, chewing and smoking tobacco, which is smoked.

Taman. Exactly, precisely.

Taman uni lekageń ńelkedea. He appeared to me to be exactly like him.

Tamao. To be enraged, to be excited with anger.

Roṛ roṛte tamaoenae. He is angry with having had continually to find fault.
Tamaoakanae, alope bolaoea. He is enraged, do not disturb him.

Tamardaǩ. To weary out, to annoy, to worry, to trouble.

Tamardaǩkedińae. He wearied me out with work.
Tamardaǩkedińae nui gidrạ do. This child wearied me out.

Tamasa. An entertainment, a spectacle, a show.

Khubko tamasaeda. They are giving a grand show.
Ceť nondepe tamasaeda? What entertainment are you giving here? What are you doing?
Tamasa ńel lạgiťko senakana. They are gone to see the show.

Tamasuk. } A note of hand, bond, ob-
Tomosuk. } ligation.

Tamba. Copper.

Tamba reaṅ. } Made of copper.
Tamba reaǩ. }

Tambae tomboe. To loaf about.

Tambhao. } To stand still, to stop, to
Thambhao. } cease, to restrain, to support.

Miť ghuṛi hape tambhaoǩme. Remain silent a little time.
Nui ruạ dole tambhaokedea. We restrained this sick man, we kept him alive.
Dạṛkan taheǩanae, adole thambhaokedea. He was fleeing and we stopped him.
Baṅle tambhao dạṛeadea, goć ocokedeale. We were not able to restrain him, we allowed him to die.

Tamboṛ. } Uncomely, ugly.
Tamboṛae. }

Tạmbu. A tent.

Tạmbuko beretakaťa. They have pitched the tent.
Tạmbuko uthạukeda. They took down and removed the tent.
Tạmbuko rạpuťakaťtakoa. They have struck their tents.

Ṭạmbuć ṭambuć. Quickly, rapidly, applied to walking.

Ṭạmbuć ṭạmbuće calaǩkana. He is walking rapidly.

Ṭamḍa ṭạmḍi. To grope, or feel here and there.

Ṭamḍa ṭạmḍi baṛaekanae. He is groping here and there.

Ṭạmḍao. To grope, to feel with hands or feet, as in the dark or in water, to search or try to find in the dark or in water.

Daǩre hakoko ṭamḍao baṛaeťkoa. They are groping in the water for fish.
Ńutre ṭamḍao baṛaedae. He is groping (for something) in the dark.

Tạmil. To put in force, as a decree; to take possession of, to be in charge, to appoint.

Atoe tạmilakaťa. He has taken possession of the village.
Iń do miťṭać rajosṭiń tạmilapekana, ceť leka iń ạpuń ińe tạmilạdińa. I appoint unto you a kingdom as my father appointed unto me.

Ṭamka ṭakur. Numerous objects of different kinds hanging or clustering together, to hang in clusters, or bunches.

Ṭamka ṭakurko akakaeṭa. They have hung them up in bunches.

Ṭamka ṭakurko bharia idieda. They are carrying (the things) in *bhangies* and they are hanging over the sides in bunches.

Ṭamka ṭakur joakana. The fruit is in clusters, or it has fruited in clusters.

Kahu barduṛūć ṭamka ṭakurko akakoka. The Vampire bats hang in clusters.

Ṭamkia. An adept at beating the ṭamak drum.

Ṭamkur. To hang down loosely.

Latar seć ṭamkurakanan baber. The string is hanging down.

Ṭamna. Ṭamna kuḍi. Ṭamni. Ṭamni kuḍi. A kind of digging implement worked in the same way as a kudali or hoe.

Ṭampa ṭuṛa. Ṭampu ṭaṛuṅ. Long shanked, as a wading bird, long-legged, tall and lanky.

Ũṭko ṭampa ṭuṛageako. Camels have long legs.

Ṭampur. Long-legged.

Tamtamao. To rage, to be excited with anger.

Tamtamao baṛaekanae dadal lagić. He is raging about seeking an opportunity to assault (some one.)

Tamtamao heć goṭenae. He came raging.

Tamtase. Tamtaseć. To scatter, to disperse, scattered, dispersed.

Gai adipe tamtase ocoakaćkoa. You have allowed the cows to become very much scattered.

Alope tamtaseja. Do not scatter them (things.)

Ṭamuṭi. To reap grain in small quantity and thresh it without the aid of bullocks for immediate use.

Hoṛole ṭamuṭi baṛaeda. We are reaping small quantities of grain for immediate use.

Tan. The wild Dog of India, *Cuon rutilans.*

Ṭan. To be scarce, to be insufficient, to be badly off for, scarcity, dearth, want, need, lack.

Nes do dake ṭankeda. There was a lack of rain this year.

Kicriće adile ṭanakana. We are badly off for clothing.

Jomakte adile ṭangea. We have a scarcity of food.

Hoṛtele ṭangea. We have an insufficiency of labourers.

Kalom do ṭanok coṅ ceć coṅ. Who knows if there is likely to be a dearth next year.

Ṭan koṛra. A certain renal affection so called, diabetes, sensation of "burning" urine.

Tanabhana. To make preparations to begin a work.

Kedokko tanabhanaea. They begin to make preparations to cook the supper.

Tanak. Ṭanić. Or such like, or some one or something similar; perhaps, when used with a verb.

Kul tanak. Kul ṭanić. A tiger or some animal like it.

Tanak busak. Numerously, in large numbers.

Tanak busakko gujukkana. They are dying in large numbers.

Ṭanak ṭunuk. Convalescent.

Ṭanak ṭunuk nege phariaakanae ruakhon. He is convalescent, he has just got over his fever.

Ṭanao. To draw out, to stretch, to drag, pull, to be drawn, to be attracted, to be allured.

Harta ṭanaokateko rohoṛa. They stretch hides and dry them.

Kacahariteye ṭanaokediña. He dragged me to [the court.

Khad seć adi hoṛko ṭanaokkana. Many people are being attracted to the mines.

Ṭanaṭani. To be at loggerheads, to be at variance, to contend, to be at strife, to pull at each other.

Nukin do katha ṭanaṭanientakina. These two do not agree.

Mone ṭanaṭanikkantiña. I am undecided.

Ṭanaṭani. To be scarce, to be insufficient, to be badly off, scarcity, dearth, want, need, lack.

Jomakte ṭanaṭanikkana. We are badly off for food, we have an insufficiency of food.

Ṭanaṭani din. Time of scarcity.

Ṭana ṭukṛa. To cut or tear into pieces.

Kurta benao lagić kicrićko ṭana ṭukṛaia. To make a jacket they cut cloth into pieces.

Ṭanḍa. To straddle, to keep the legs far apart from each other.

Ṭanḍa paromkedeae. He stepped over him.

Ṭanḍakate teṅgoakanae. He is standing with his legs far apart.

Ṭanḍakateye duṛupakana. He is sitting with his legs far apart from each other.

Bhugake ṭanḍa eseṭakaṭa. He is standing in front of the hole with his legs far apart.

Ṭanḍao. To do sufficient to bar the claim of others without committing oneself.

Ṭandaoakadeako eṭak seć aloko jãwãeyea mente. They have done sufficient to prevent her being given in marriage to another.

Noa soḍok doe ṭanḍao eseṭakaṭa. He has done sufficient to this soḍok (q. v.) to prevent any other claiming it.

Ṭanḍha. } Cold, chill, mild, placid,
Ṭhanḍha. } gentle, comforted, assuaged, pacified.
Ṭanḍha mone hoṛ kanae. He is a man of mild disposition.

Ṭanḍi. A plain, to make plain, to clear, bare.
Birko mak ṭanḍiakaṭa. They have hewn and cleared the forest.
Ir ṭanḍiakaṭako. They have cleared (the ground) by reaping the crops.
Upko kapci ṭanḍikeṭtaea. They cut his hair bare.
Simko poṭor ṭanḍikoa. They scald fowls bare, they remove the feathers by scalding.
Dhiriko halaṅ ṭanḍikeda. They collected the stones and made (the ground) bare.
Aḍa ṭanḍi. The place where cattle are kept for a short time in the middle of the day when the herd is taking his food.
Goṭa ṭanḍi. } Every where.
Sanam ṭanḍi. }
Melan ṭanḍi. A wide plain.
Tala ṭanḍi. Cf. tala ṭanḍi.

Ṭanḍi bhiḍi janeṭeṭ. A wild plant, *Desmodium gangeticum, D. C.*

Ṭanḍi catom aṛak. A very common little annual plant, *Desmodium triflorum, D. C.*

Ṭanḍi jhapni. A small sensitive plant, *Zornia dyphylla, Pers.*
This plant like many others folds up its leaves at night, and on this account it is employed as a remedy in sleeplessness.

Ṭanḍi khode baha. Two small wild plants receive this name, one *Indigofera linifolia, Retz.*, and the other *Evolvulus alsinoides, Linn.*

Ṭanḍi meral. Two small wild plants, *Phyllanthus simplex, Linn.*, and *Phyllanthus urinaria, Linn.* receive this name.

Ṭanḍi sol. A small wild plant, *Ionidium suffruticosum, Ging.*

Ṭanḍi sunsuni. Cf. ṭanḍi catom aṛak.

Ṭanḍi suṛa. A common sedge *Cyperus rotundus, Linn.*

Ṭanḍi hoṛo. A species of tortoise.

Ṭanḍi seć. To go to stool.
Ṭanḍi seće senakana. He has gone to ease himself.

Ṭanḍi ṭikur. } Plain and rising ground.
Ṭanḍi ṭukur. }
Ṭanḍi ṭikur dak aṭukkana. The water is flowing over the face of the country.

Taṅ. To tilt up a vessel containing liquid so as to cause it to flow out into another vessel held in the hand.
Baṭire dak taṅme. Pour water into a cup.
Taṅ haṇḍi. The first brew of liquor which is run off the grain, for the second the grain is squeezed.

Ṭaṅ. Used with the numeral one (miṭ) to form the indefinite article a or an; a single animal or thing.
Miṭ ṭaṅ hakoe koelere baṅ do miṭ ṭaṅ biṅe calae? If he ask a fish will he give him a serpent?
Miṭ ṭaṅiń aguketa. I brought one.
Miṭ ṭaṅ dare ńuradea. A tree fell on him.

Ṭaṅga. A large axe.
Ṭeṅgoć. A small axe.

Ṭaṅgabeṭ. A kind of rice.

Ṭaṅgadar. The cut made with an axe.

Ṭaṅgao. To hang up, to suspend.
Ḍher lumame ṭaṅgaoakaṭkoa. He has hung up very many tassar silk cocoons.

Taṅgar maṭua. } Slightly intoxicated.
Talgal maṭua. }
Ńu taṅgar maṭualenkhan aḍiko roṛa. When they have drunk to slight intoxication, they speak much.

Taṅgaṭ. But just then, precisely.
Taṅgaṭ do unjokheege. Precisely at that time.

Taṅgi. To wait for, tarry for.
Taṅgikedeako. They waited for him.

Ṭaṅgi. } A dove-cot.
Parwa ṭaṅgi }

Ṭaṅgna. A peg, or anything on which anything is hung or placed.
Taṅgnare akaakaṭae. He has hung it on a peg.

Ṭankhi. To number, to see that all is right, to take care of, verification of accounts or number.
Hoṛe ṭankhieṭkoa. He is numbering the people.
Mihũ merom oṛakteko bolok jokbeċko ṭankhikoa, ńela mente sanamko menakkoa se baha. At the time the cattle enter the shed they count them to see if all are there or not.

Ṭanić. Or such like, or something similar.
Kul ṭaniće jomakadea. A tiger, or such like has devoured him.

Ṭankao. To be strengthened, to be refreshed, to be relieved.
Jom ṭankaoenae. He has eaten and is refreshed.
Jorok ṭankaoenae. He has warmed himself at the fire and is strengthened.
Netar doe ṭankao ńokena. Now he has gained a little strength.

Tankha Wages.

Tan kurte. In the meanwhile.

Tanman. Exactly, precisely with heart and soul, intently.
Tanman uni lekageye ńeloǩkana. He resembles him in every respect.
Tanmane ńeńelkana. He is looking intently.

Ṭan paṅgla. A disease which affects old people, senile decay.

Ṭanṭan. Tight, taut, tense.
Ṭanṭan tidakaćako, They have stretched it out (twine, rope, wire, &c.) tightly, they have pulled it taut.
Ṭanṭan hasoedińkana. I feel a pain as of tenseness.

Ṭanṭanao. To tighten by pulling or stretching, as a rope, &c., to stretch to stiffness.
Tol ṭanṭanaokadeako. They tied him tightly.

Ṭanuạ. }
Ṭanwạ. } Liable to dry up, as a rice field, innutritious, as food.
Gundli daka ṭạnuạgea. Boiled gundli (q. v.) is innutritious.

Tao. }
Taoao. } To heat, to be heated, to be excited, to heat to a white heat, as iron.
Em hoćaeme, taoaǩae nahaǩ. Give to him at once, he will get hot presently, get angry.
Edrete taoaoenae. He is heated, or excited, with anger.
Khubko tao ocoakaća. They have heated it very hot, to a white heat.

Taoa tạwi. }
Tawa tạwi. } To be heated, to be angry.
Taoa tạwi baṛaekanae. He is angry.
Taoa tạwi calaoenae. He went away in anger.

Taogar. Elastic.

Ṭãoge. }
Purwa ṭãoge. } A dove-cot.

Ṭãohẽ. }
Ṭhãohẽ. } Closely, close to each other, with little space or interval between. Cf. ṭạ̃uhẽ.

Tap. Time, juncture, a particular point of time rendered critical or important by a concurrence of circumstances.
Inạ taptegeye heć goćena. He arrived at that particular time.

Taþ. To pass through.
Saṛim bhugạǩgete ipilko ńel taboǩkana. The stars are seen through a hole in the roof.
Phạriạ daǩ hõ ńel taboǩa. Clear water can also be seen through.
Ńel taboǩaǩ. Anything transparent or that can be seen through.
La taþkedae. He dug through.
Gutu taþkedae. He pushed it through (a thread through a needle eye, a bead, &c.)

Ńel taþkeć lekam roṛkeda. You spoke as if you foresaw it, (as if you looked through into the future.)
Kạṭić hako jhạlikhonko taþena. The small fishes passed through from the net.
Dạṛ taþkedae. He fled right away.
Taboǩa. It will pass through.

Ṭap. Force, impulse, intensity.
Edre tapteye roṛkeda, sahaokam. He spoke through the impulse of anger, bear it.
Ạḍi tapte ruạ hećena. The fever came with great intensity.

Ṭapa. An open woven bamboo-basket like arrangement under which chickens, &c. are kept, a kind of hen-coop.

Tapaǩ. To jerk or throw anything into the mouth, to throw anything that will stick at or on.
Goṛa khunṭire holoń daǩko tapaǩaǩa. They sprinkle water in which flour has been mixed on the posts of the cow shed.
Tapaǩ ran. Medicine in the form of a powder.

Ṭapać ṭipić. }
Ṭipić ṭapaǩ. } Applied to rain when only a few large drops fall.
Ṭapać ṭipiće daǩkeda. A few large drops of rain fell.

Ṭapać ṭupuć. }
Ṭipoć ṭopoć. } To be enfeebled, feebly.
Ruạlente ṭapać ṭupućenae. He is enfeebled through having had fever.

Tapahen. Reciprocal form of tahen (q. v.)
Mićte baṛe tapahenben, aloben apan ạpinoǩa. Live together, do not separate.

Tapakić. Reciprocal form of ṭạkić (q. v.)

Tapam. To wrestle, the Reciprocal form of tam (q. v.)
Tapamkanakin. They are wrestling, or seizing and trying to throw each other down.

Tapandaǩ. A veiled name for rice beer.

Tapań. Reciprocal form of tań (q. v.)

Ṭapań. }
Ṭapań ṭapań. } Sound produced by metallic objects coming into contact with each other.
Ṭapań ṭapań saḍekana. There is a sound of clanging.

Ṭapań marte. }
Ṭapań mente. } With a clang.
Ṭapań marte saḍe goćena. It sounded with a clang.

Tapaṅgi. Reciprocal form of tạṅgi (q. v.)
Tapaṅgikanako. They are waiting for each other.

Tapar.
Ṭuạr ṭapar. } Orphans, orphaned.
Ṭuạr ṭapar kanako. They are orphans.

Taphim. To recognize, to know.
Taphimkedeań. I recognized him.
Bạń taphim daṛeadea. I could not recognize him.

Ṭapi. To deceive.
Aḍiye ṭạpikedińa. He greatly deceived me.

Tapiń. To knock the forehead against, to be knocked on the forehead, to mourn, to lament, to repercuss, to be reflected or reverberated, as sound; to strike against, as waves on a boat, &c.
Aḍi ṭhen tạpiń idiḱa. Will echo many times.
Silpińre tạpińenae. He hit his head against the door.
Ḍheoko do lạuka bhitrite tạpiń paromoḱkan tahẽkana. The waves were beating into the boat.

Tapis. Force, energy, violence, vehemence, impetuosity, rage, fury.
Aḍi tạpisteye roṛkeda. He spoke with great vehemence.
Aḍi tạpisteye dalkedea. He struck him with great force.
Tạpisteye tuńkedea. He shot him with great force.
Tạpiskateye calaoena. He left in a rage.
Noa aḱ reaḱ tạpis bạnuḱan. This bow has no spring.

Ṭapoḱ. A kind of bird trap.
A string is pulled and the trap falls on the bird.
Citriko ṭapoḱkoa. They trap partridges with the ṭapoḱ.
Ṭapoḱe oḍaoakaća. He has set the ṭapoḱ bird-trap.

Tapol. Lowlying, low, as a field, piece of ground, &c.
Onte ghuṭugea, note do tapolgea. Over there is rising ground, here it is low.
Tapol jaega. A low-lying place or field.

Tapos. To take care of, to nurse.
Taposkotińme. Take care of them for me.

Ṭapra ṭopra. Very small, as fields; plots. Cf. ṭopra ṭupri.
Ṭapra ṭopra khet kana. They are very small fields.

Tapra. Part uncooked.
Tapra ocokedam. You allowed part to be uncooked.
Tapraena. Part is uncooked.

Tapseć. To jerk the coarse material out of the hạtaḱ (q. v.) Cf. leceć.
Tapseć goćkam. Jerk it out.

Ṭaṗṭaṗ.
Ṭaptap. } Imitative of a sound of tapping, or short, quick, light taps.
Nui sadom ṭaṗṭaṗe taṛameda. This horse makes a sound resembling ṭaṗṭaṗ when walking.

Ṭapṭapa. Wide apart, wide spread, sprawling.
Ṭapṭapae dereńana. It has wide-spread horns.
Jańgae ṭapṭapaakaća. He is striding.
Ṭapṭapae gitićakana. He is lying with his legs and arms wide apart.

Tạpu. An island, to overflow or flood as water.
Daḱte saname ṭạpu idikeda. Water overflowed it and carried all away.

Tạpuḱ. To alight on the ground, applied to birds of short flight, such as partridges, wild jungle fowl, &c. &c., to settle, as dregs, &c.
Citri onḍegeye tạpuḱena. The partridge has alighted there.
Daḱ reaḱ mailạteć tạpuḱena. The dirt in the water has settled to the bottom.

Tạpuḱ. Applied to a thread which has not been raised when weaving.
Mić bar ṭhen sutạmpe tạpuḱ ocokeda teńoḱre. When weaving you failed to raise the threads in one or two places.

Tạpus. To enquire.
Adope khojkeć tạpuskećkhan buru leka jiwi haraena. You having made enquiry (regarding our welfare) our spirits have grown like a hill (we are greatly delighted.)

Tạr.
Tar. } Wire, the telegraph.
Tạr sutạm. Thin wire.
Tar reaḱ khaber taṛak mente ńam godoḱa. A telegraph message is received instantly.

Tar. Proper way or method, meaning, import.
Roṛ reaḱ tarteć iń ńamkeda. I understood the import of the speech.

Tara.
Tara tara. } A half, half.
Tara kecaḱ. A half, one half of anything broken in two, a widower, or widow.
Tara kecaḱ menaea. He is a widower, or she is a widow.
Tara tarako emkeda. They gave part, they did not give or pay in full.
Tara atrae kạmikeda. He did not do all the work.
Tara atrae daḱkeda. The rain was not general.
Tara din. Half a day.

Tara mara. Inefficiently, not fully.
Tara mara racae joḱkeda. She swept the court yard inefficiently.
Tara marae kạmikeda. He did the work inefficiently, he scamped the work.

Tara tapra. Part uncooked, or only half cooked, half and half, incomplete, partially.
Tara tapra isinena. It is not all thoroughly cooked.

Tara siń. Applied to the time of day when the sun is past the meridian, afternoon from noon to 3 p. m.
Marah tarasiń. About 2 p. m.
Hudiń tarasiń. 3 p. m.
Tarasińenae. He is past middle age.

Taṛa taṛi. To hurry, to do quickly.
Taṛa taṛiko calaoena. They went away in a hurry.
Taṛa taṛi kami hoyoktińa. I must work quickly.
Taṛa taṛile sapraokkana. We are hurrying on preparations.

Taṛa toṛo. In company.
Taṛa toṛoliń heóena. We came in company.

Tarae toroe. In succession, one after another.
Tarae toroeko odok hijukkana. They are emerging one after another.
Tarae toroeko odokokkana duarre mifte do bako sahoba. They are coming out one after the other, the door cannot contain all at once.

Taraj garaj. Loudly, to shout.
Taraj garaje hoho baṛaeda. He is shouting loudly.
Taraj garajokkanae. He is shouting.

Tăṛăk. To lie in wait, to lie in ambush, to watch for.
Kul do hoṛ jomko lagite tăṛăkakana. The tiger is lying in wait to eat people.
Hoṛ kul goje lagite tăṛăkakana. The man is lying in ambush to kill the tiger.
Kulko tăṛăkakoa. They lie in wait for tigers.

Taṛak marte. }
Taṛak mente. } Quickly, instantly, instantaneously, immediately, at once.
Taṛak mente nitge ruaṛ hodokme. Return instantly.
Tar reak khaber taṛak mente ńam godoka. A telegram is received instantaneously.

Tarak birak. Hither and thither, here and there, to disperse, to be scattered, to wander.
Tarak birakenako. They are scattered here and there.
Tarak birakko calaoena. They have dispersed, gone hither and thither.

Taral basal. Scattered, dispersed, here and there, sparse.
Taral basalpe dohoakata. You have put the things here and there, you have not put them all together.
Gaiko taral basalenako. The cows are scattered.

Taṛam. To step, a step.
Mit taṛam. One step.
Mit taṛam tayom seó paoenae. He receded one step.
Bar pe taṛame lahagotena. He advanced two or three steps.
Adi ăte taṛamkeda. He stepped very rapidly, he walked rapidly.
Taṛam piche doho idime. Place, or put down (one) after each step.

Taṛam gande. Solatium, usually two rupees, given to an elder sister on a younger being married before her.

Taṛań. }
Taṛań taṛań. } Sound as of the rolling of drums.
Tumdak sadekana taṛań taṛań. The kettle drums are rolling.

Taṛań marte. }
Taṛań mente. } With a roll, as of drums.
Taṛań marte sade gotena. It sounded with a roll.

Ṭaṛań. }
Ṭaṛań ṭaṛań. } Ringing sound (imitative.)
Ghanṭako ruieda, ṭaṛań ṭaṛań sadekana. They are ringing the bell, it sounds ṭaṛań ṭaṛań.

Ṭaṛań marte. }
Ṭaṛań mente, } With a ringing sound.

Taṛań tiṛiń. To speak angrily, to speak loudly as one angry.
Nui hoṛ do adi taṛań tiṛińe roṛa. This man speaks very angrily.
Edrete taṛań tiṛińokkanae. He is speaking loudly through anger.

Ṭaṛań ṭuṛuń. Tinkling sound, as that produced by a small bell.
Ghanṭi ṭaṛań ṭuṛuń sadekana. The small bell tinkles.

Tarantar. Half, a part, a portion.
Tarantar dakako emkeda. They did not give food to all.

Taṛao. To dig out, to averruncate, to tear up by the roots.
Hurut khunṭute taṛaoakata.
Noa khet benaore adi hurut khunṭute taṛaoakada.

Ṭaṛao. To deflect, to turn aside, to remove by pushing away or drawing towards.
Kudite hasako ṭaraokeda. They remove the soil by drawing it aside with a kudali.
Kathae ṭarao gidikettińa. He gave my subject another direction.
Ṭarao phăkkateye paromena. He pushed a way for himself and passed through.
Katwar ṭhengate ṭarao gotkam. Push aside the rubbish with a stick.
Dak ṭarao gidikate hakobon goókoa. We will lead the water away (by damming) and kill the fish.
Nahel iń ṭarao baṛaakata. I have roughly shaped the plough.
Dak ṭaraotabonme. Turn the rain away from us.
Sometimes when there is a likelihood of rain coming a person will stretch out the left arm and pointing with the little finger make a half circle in the air indicating the direction in which the rain cloud is desired to go.

Taraṛ. To tear, to rend, to crack, to split.
Kicrič taraṛena. The cloth is torn.
Kaḍae hoṭaǩ taraṛkedea. The buffaloe horned and tore him, the buffaloe tore his flesh with its horn.

Taras. To growl, to roar, as a wild beast, to boast.
Kulko tarasa. Tigers roar.
Ạdiye taraseť tahẽkana, adoe bhagaoena. He was boasting very much, and then he was conquered.

Taṛa tuṛa. To vituperate, to rate, to rail, to reproach.
Ạdiko taṛa tuṛạkeťlea. They rated us soundly.
Ạdiko taṛa tuṛạkediñ, bes okoṭe gạt ṭekaoko-pe. They rated me soundly, look well after the cows.

Taṛbaṛia. Energetic.

Tạrbhuj. }
Tạrbuj. } The Sweet melon, *Cucumis Melo, Linn.*
Tạrmuj. }

Tarcha. }
Tarchao. } Slanting, at an angle, obliquely, slope, curve, off the straight.
Tircha. }
Tirchau. }
Tarchaote gedme. Cut it slantingly.
Tarcha tarchateye calaoena. He went away holding to the side.

Taren. The shoulder of a human being, the neck of an animal on which the yoke rests.
Kaḍape taren oookedea. You allowed the neck of the buffaloe to be galled by the yoke.

Targal. }
Targalaǩ. } Confused, confusion, profusion.
Katha targalaǩpe bạgiada. You left the matter in confusion.
Targalaǩge tahẽena. It remains confused, or undecided.
Katwar targalaǩge menaǩa racare. There is much rubbish in the courtyard.
Matkom targalaǩ ňurakana. Much *matkom* (q. v.) has fallen.

Targhar. Method, proper time, proper way, customs, ins and outs, import.
Kạmi reaǩ targhar ạuriye ceda. He has not yet learned the ins and outs of the work.
Noa ato reaǩ targhar ạuriñ saba. I have not yet mastered the ins and outs of this village.
Noa disom reaǩ targhar bae bạdaea. He does not know the customs of this country.

Tạrgum. To scold, to rage, to speak harshly.

Ṭarhao. }
Ṭahrao. } To fix, to settle, to come to a decision or determination, to stop, to rest, to remain, to be determined, to be established.
Aṛe doe ṭarhaokeda. He made the dam stable.
Nui bohga dọ daǩ sunumreñ ṭarhaokedea I found this to be the bohga (q. v.) by divining with water and oil.
Luture ger ṭarhaokedea. He seized it by the ear with his teeth and held it fast.

Tạri. Liquor made from the juice of of the toddy palm, *Phœnix sylvestris, Roxb.*, also from that of the Palmyra palm, *Borassus flabelliformis, Linn.*, leaven, yeast.

Tạri. }
Tuṛi. } Below, down, underneath, under, to overtop.
Hara tạrikedeae. He grew and *belowed* him, he outgrew him.
Tạri oooenae. He is *undered*, he is overtopped.
Ceť lahakeťte onko pạhilkoe tạrikeťkoa.
Uni tạrire menaña. I am under him.

Tạri ghaṛi. }
Tuṛi ghuṛi. } To hurry, to do quickly.
Ạdiye tạri ghạṛikediña. He hurried me greatly.

Tạribos. Good, savoury, applied to food.
Bes tạribosko isinakaťa. They have cooked it very savoury.
Khubko tạribosakaťa. They have provided good food.

Tạrik. }
Tarikh. } Date, date of the month.
Aghãṛ reaǩ dosar tạrik. The 2nd of Aghãṛ.

Tạrjuạ. The Black Ibis, *Geronticus papillosus, Semm.*

Tarjuma. To translate, translation.
Hoṛ roṛte tạrjumaeme. Translate it into the Santal language.

Tarka irki. To be impatient, quickly, as one impatient.
Calaǩ lạgiť tarka irki baṛaokanae. He is impatient to go.
Tarka irki calaoenae. He left quickly, as one impatient.

Ṭarkao. To send away, to send away by the employment of artifice so as not to convey the idea that one is being got rid of.
Baretko peṛako lạgiť aboe ṭarkaoeťbona. She is sending us away so that she may entertain her brothers.

Tarkao. To relish, to enjoy, as food.
Jom tarkaoakadae. He has eaten and relished it.
Jom tarkaoakanae kul do, onte merom alope idikoa. The tiger has eaten and relished, do not take the goats over that way.

Taṛkha taṛkhi. To be seized with spasms, spasmodic twitching of the muscles.
Sạrdi ruạǩ jokhed oka doko taṛkha taṛkhi baṛaea. When fever is high they sometimes are seized with spasms.

Taṛkhạ. To threaten, to speak loudly and threateningly, violently, forcibly, vehemently.
Onko ḍaku sen tioẖkate taṛkhaikateko motadea, hapeya, teṅgolenme. Those robbers overtaking him said to him threateningly, Stop, stand.

Taṛkhao. To become rigid, as the body during a fit, to swoon.
Taṛkhaoẖako. They swoon.

Tarko. To be affected by vibration or motion, as a person riding in a railway carriage, &c., or as one holding anything when it is struck, to jolt, to shake.
Ạḍi tawaẖ tarkole paromena. We were tossed about in crossing.
Ạḍi tawaẖ tarkole hečena ạḍi ńut. We stumbled much in coming, it was very dark.
Ạḍi tawaẖ tarkoko raẖkeda. They wept much swaying their bodies.

Tãṛkuč. To tilt up, to bend down, as the branch of a tree.
Sin̈ saraẖ sič lagič ḍar tãṛkujme. Bend down the branch to pluck the sin̈ (q. v.) potherb.
Tãṛkučkateye ạbukena. He tilted up the waterpot and washed his hands.

Tarkur. The kernel of the fruit of the Palmyra palm.

Taṛmuj. Cf. taṛbhuj.

Tarop. } **Tarop dare.** } A small tree, *Buchanania latifolia, Roxb.*
Tarop. } Tarop jo. } The fruit of the tarop tree which is eaten.

Tarpin sunum. Turpentine.

Tarse. To be scattered by falling.
Haṭaẖre hoṛoe idieč tahẽkana, gurente sanam tarse gočena. He was carrying rice in a haṭaẖ (q. v.) by his falling it was all scattered.
Hoṛmo ṭakičentaete tarse hiričena. By his coming violently in contact (with something) it was scattered by falling.
Bae sambṛaolaẖa tarsekedae. He could not hold it, he allowed it to fall and be scattered.

Tarse koṭap. A small bush, *Grewia villosa, Willd.*

Tarse koṭap cẽṛẽ. A species of vulture.

Tartaṛiạ. Clear, clearly, distinctly, clean, fresh, without admixture, without defect.
Tartạriạ daẖ. Clear water.
Khub tartạriạ hoṛo kana. It is good clean rice (no admixture in it.)
Jel tartạriạgea. The meat is fresh.
Beṅgečedae, bes tartạriạge. He sees very clearly.

Taṛu. The hard palate.
Tạru lạndupentaea. The bridge of his nose has fallen in.

Taṛup. An animal of the tiger kind, a leopard.
Napṛaẖ tạrup. } Marań tạrup. } A tiger.[1]
Poṭea tạrup. A small species of leopard.
Sona citạ tạrup. A leopard.
Kurse baha tạrup. A panther.

Tarwạ. To pain, to become tender.
Din bhor dãṛã dãṛãte jaṅga tarwạena. The feet have become tender through travelling the whole day.

Tarwaṛe. A sword.
Tarwaṛe boč. To draw a sword.
Tarwaṛe ṭhema. To carry a sword under the arm.

Tas. } **Taspas.** } Playing cards.
Tas eneč. To play cards.

Ṭasak. } **Ṭhasak.** } To move, to shake, to cause to stir, to affect, to overcome.
Bạń ṭasak daṛeadea. I could not move him.
Nui do nunạẖ akalrebõ bańe ṭasaklena. This (person) even in so great a famine was not moved (was not affected.)

Tasaẖ. } **Dhubi tasaẖ.** } A larger or smaller quantity of Dhubi grass (*Cynodon Dactylon, Pers.*) when used in the ceremony of marriage or gai cumạuṛa (q. v.)

Tasań. } **Tumạl tasań.** } Poor, indigent.
Tumạl tasań hoṛ. A poor person.

Tase. To spread out to dry.
Hoṛo tasekam. Spread out the dhan to dry.
Lohoč kičrič tasekam. Lay out the wet cloth to dry.
Tase rohoṛkedale. We spread it out and dried it.

Tạsil. Strong, sharp, pungent, rich, as soil.
Tạsil hạnḍi. Strong rice beer.
Tuṛi sunum ạḍi tạsila. Mustard oil is very pungent.
Nui ren gunḍri ạdiye tạsila. This person's quail is very sharp (it at once obeys the signs given to it.)

Ṭaskao. } **Ṭhaskao.** } To move, to cause to stir, to shake.
Bań ṭaskaoẖkana. It is not being moved, it is not moving.

Tasla. A brass vessel used to cook in.

Tasṛao. } **Thasṛao.** } To throw on the ground, to throw down.
Tasṛao gočkadae. He threw it on the ground.
Gidrạ usạčente tasṛao gočenae. The child being sulky threw itself on the ground.

Tasra tasri. } To throw down repeat-
Thasra thasri. } edly, or many things; disorderly, scattered about.
  Tasra tasri baraekanae. He is throwing himself on the ground.
  Thasra thasriko dohoakata. They have put the things down in disorder.

Tasu. A finger's breadth.
  Pon tasu. Four fingers' breadth.

Tăt. Catgut, strong fibre found over the cervicle vertebræ of animals twisted, and used as strings for musical instruments and many other purposes.

Ṭaṭ. Sackcloth, gunny cloth.

Tata. Grandfather.
  Tataṅ. My grandfather.
  Tatam. Thy grandfather.
  Tatatteṭ. His grandfather, the grandfather.

Tataea. The relationship between grandfather and grandchild.
  Tataea kanakin. They are grandfather and grandson.

Ṭaṭak. Suddenly.
  Ṭaṭakgeye goćena. He died suddenly.

Ṭaṭak. A juggler, a conjurer.

Ṭaṭao. To be numb, to be seized with cramp, to be stiff, to be crisp, to be over dry.
  Ti jaṅga ṭaṭaoentaea. His hands and feet are numb.
  Horope rohor ṭaṭao ocoakata. You have dried the dhan until it has become crisp.
  Reṅgeć ṭaṭao ocoketkoae perako. He allowed his visitors to be numb with hunger.
  Sir ṭaṭao. To sympathise with, compassionate.

Tatao. To warm, to heat, to stir up, to energise.
  Reṅgećteko tataoena. They are heated with hunger (fever of starvation.)
  Dak tataoena. The water is heated.
  Nui hor tataoge bae tataoka. This man will not be energised.

Ṭaṭarbaṅ. Lanky, tall and slim.

Tataya. Cf. tataea.

Tatbir. } To take care of, to look after.
Totbir. }
  Sanamak bes okoćtem tatbira. You will carefully look after all things.

Ṭaṭhe. To strike or beat with a stick, to strike with a stick at random.

Tathić. An intensive particle.
  Aćge tathiće kombrokeda ar iñe badaṅkana. He stole it himself, and he blames me.

Ṭaṭhra. A coarse bamboo mat.

Taṭiaha. Lean, slim, lanky.

Tăti. }
Tanti. } A Hindu caste of weavers.
Tănti. }
  Tăti kicrić. Cloth woven by a tăti.

Ṭaṭi. A screen, a shutter or door of matting, branches, &c.

Ṭaṭiol bhit. A kind of wattle and daub wall.

Ṭaṭka. New, fresh, recent.

Ṭaṭka. To be numbed, as with fear.
  Botorte ṭaṭka goćenae. He at once became numb with fear.

Ṭaṭka birki. To fear, to be alarmed.
  Ṭaṭka birki baraikanale. We are in fear.

Ṭaṭka mar. Suddenly, quickly, immediately, without delay, at once.
  Ṭaṭka mar gele rohoekeda. We hurriedly planted (our dhan.)
  Ṭaṭka margeye heć goćena. He suddenly arrived.
  Ṭaṭka mare goćena. He died suddenly.

Tatla. Half.
  Tatla paikate emakom. Give each a half pai (q. v.), give half a pai to each.

Tatle. Often, continually in quick succession.
  Tatlegeko hijukkana. They are continually coming.
  Tatle geye dakeda. It rains continually.
  Tatlege perako hijukkana. Visitors are continually coming.

Tatle mar. Often, repeatedly, in quick succession.
  Tatle mare uyukadea. He struck him repeatedly.
  Tatle margeye jomkeda. He ate very often.

Ṭaṭok. } A conjurer.
Ṭaṭokdar. }

Ṭaṭuk. Cf. tawak ṭaṭuk.

Ṭăuhĕ. } Closely, close to each other,
Ṭhăuhĕ. } with little space or interval between.
  Ṭăuhĕko tolakata. They have put the lashings close to each other.
  Ṭăuhĕko dohoakata. They have put them close to each other.

Tawa. A kind of flat earthenware vessel.

Tawak. To dash down, to throw down.
  Tawak posakkedae. He dashed it down and broke it.

Tawak ṭaṭuk. Stumblingly, flounderingly.
  Tawak ṭaṭukle hećena. We came stumblingly.

Tawar tawar. To shake, to move to, dangle, to hang and swing, to vibrate. Cf. lawar lawar.

Tawar tawar gidr̤e heo bar̤akedea. She carried the child with its legs dangling.

Ṭawić. To boast, to challenge, to snort and paw the ground as a bull, &c. challenging another.

Ạdim tawićetkan tahẽkana, okorem dar̤elena? You were boasting greatly, where did you conquer?

Ṭayal ṭuyul. To rise or protrude so as to be seen.

Pukhrire puṭhi hako ṭayal ṭuyulko don bar̤aekana.

Erleć hor̤o bhage do bań menakŕa, ṭayal ṭuyul.

Gundli do nekŕege jahã kahã ṭayal ṭuyul gelekŕkana.

Tayan. An crocodile.

Tayar baha. A wild plant, *Justicia Belonica, Linn.*

Tayo tayo. A children's game.

Tayo. } To clap the hands.
Thayo. }

Ti tayokateye boloena. He clapped his hands and entered, i. e. he brought nothing in his hands, was unsuccessful.

Ṭayokŕ. } Cf. asokŕ ṭayokŕ.
Asokŕ ṭayokŕ. }

Tayom. To be behind, to fall behind, to be after or in the rear, after, behind.

Tayomre. Behind, after, in the rear.
Tayomte. Behind, after, afterwards.
Otoh tayom. Following, in single file.
Thor̤ageko tayom mar̤aṅa, bańkhan mić tegeko heoena. They were a little before and after each other, otherwise they came together.
Alope tayom mar̤aṅokŕa, mićtege calakŕpe. Do not fall behind or go before, go all together.
Tayomte arhõń emama. I will give you more afterwards.
Tayom daram. The future.
Tayomenae. He is behind.
Tayomkedeae. He put him behind.
Tayomokŕam. You will be behind, or late.
Tayomr̤eye tahẽena. He stayed behind.

Tayo sar̤ap. To clap the hands.

Te. Into, in, by, with, because, as; used also to form adverbs.

Theṅgateye dalkedea. He struck him with a stick.
Cećteye dalkedea? With what did he hit him?
Hor̤o setoṅte goćena. The dhan died by the heat of the sun.
Ińtege. By myself.
Dal ocoenteye rakŕeda. He is crying because he was struck.
Aćṭiteye goćena. He died by his own hand.

Te. To winnow.

Hor̤oko tetekana. They are winnowing dhan.
Hor̤o tekateko bạndia. After winnowing dhan they put it up in bạndis (q. v.)

Te. To apply sindur to the forehead, used of forcibly marking an unmarried woman.

Sindur dại nae teadiń. Oh! sister, he put sindur on my forehead.

Teag. To leave, to abandon, to desert, to forsake, to quit, to abdicate, to give up.

Jiwiye teagkeda. He gave up the ghost.
Or̤akŕ duạre teagkeda. He abandoned his family.

Tear. To prepare, to get ready; ready, prepared, fat, wealthy, finished, complete.

Dakako tearkeda. They prepared the food.
Sapr̤ao tearenako. They have completed preparations.
Bapla reakŕko tear sạtkeda. They completed all matters connected with the marriage.
Sen tearakanae. He has gone and is in readiness.
Nui ḍahra khube tearena. This ox is very fat.
Nui hor̤ do bese tearena. This man is very wealthy.
Tearakŕ ạguime. Bring a finished one.

Tebakŕ. To forestall, to anticipate, to overtake, to see in the act.

Dakako jom tebakŕkeda. They had eaten the food before I arrived.
Kombr̤okoń tebakŕkeṭkoa. I saw the thieves in the act of stealing.
Iń hõ bań tebakŕledea. I also did not overtake or see him (as he had left before I arrived.)
Amem heć tebakŕena, bańkhanem ńamkea. You have come late, otherwise you would have got.
Bae tebakŕakan khan. If he were not seen in the act.
Parom tebakŕentem bańcaoena. Having crossed before (the engine came) you are saved.

Ṭebeć ṭebeć. Quickly, with short quick steps, said of small males.

Ṭebeć ṭebeće calakŕkana. He trips along.

Ṭebe ṭebe. To be overweighted, to be cumbered.

Bạń dar̤ dar̤eakŕkana ṭebe ṭebeẽnań. I cannot run I am overweighted (having eaten too much.)
Hamalte ṭebeṭebeẽnae. He is overweighted with the heavy weight.
Gidr̤ạ ṭebeṭebeye dạr̤eda. The child runs heavily, (having eaten too much.)

Tebor̤. } Thrice, three times.
Tebr̤a. }

Ona reakŕ tebor̤iń hataoa. I will take three times that.
Tebr̤age emokŕ hoyokŕtama. You will have to give three times that.

Ṭebra. M. } Small, short of stature with
Ṭibri. F. } large stomach.

Ṭebra mara gidrą. A little imp of a child.

Tebṛa. Thrice, three times. Cf. teboṛ.

Ṭebṭebe. To be satiated and stomach distended.

Jom ṭebṭebeakanae. He has eaten to satiety and his stomach is distended.

Ṭeć. Used with the numeral one (miť) to form the indefinite article a or an; a single animal or thing.

Miť ṭeć piṭhąe koelere baṅ do miť ṭeć dhiriye calae? If he ask a loaf will he give him a stone?

Miť ṭeć ąguime. Bring one.

Ṭeć ṭeć. } To produce a knocking or
Ṭheć ṭheć. } tapping sound, (imitative.)

Dhiriko koṭeja ṭheć ṭheć. They break stones and make a sound resembling ṭheć ṭheć.

Ṭeć ṭeć saḍekana. It sounds ṭeć ṭeć, or tap tap.

Tegar. To mar in trying to improve.

Egarkatem tegarkada. You tried to improve it and you marred it.

Tegeć masak. Much, of all kinds, of many kinds.

Tegeć masaḱe roṛeda. He says all kinds of things.

Tegeć masaḱe egereda. She gives all kinds of abuse.

Tegeć masaḱe arjaoakaťa, bae rehgejoḱa. He has raised good crops of all kinds, he will not suffer hunger.

Tegeć tągum. Voraciously, unseemly, unbefitting, objectionable.

Tegeć tągume jomkeda. He ate voraciously.

Siṅ sąṭup tegeć tągume roṛeda. He is always saying objectionable things.

Tegeń. } To quarrel, to dispute,
Regeń tegeń. } to altercate, to squabble, to wrangle, to bicker.

Regeń tegeńoḱkanako. They are wrangling.

Regeńre tegeńre. In quarrels and squabbles.

Tege neṛe. To pull, to tug, to tear, to pull against each other, pulling, tugging, wrenching.

Tege neṛeko jojomkana. They are tearing the (flesh meat) when eating, not biting off.

Nui do bae dhejana tege neṛe gegeťkanae. This (person) cannot cut (flesh meat), he is tearing it apart.

Tege neṛe gidi kuṛiťko jomkeda. The vultures and kites tore (the flesh) and ate it.

Tege neṛeko or oḍokkedea. They pulled him out.

Tege tege. } To pull, to pull at, to pull
Tegtege. } out, as a piece of elastic, to stretch.

Or tegtegekedeakin. They pulled at him.

Mocae tegtegekeťtaea. He stretched, or widened his mouth.

Ṭeghan. } A prop, anything placed so
Theghan. } as to keep an object from
Ṭeghen. } falling or changing its position, as a catch or check to keep a door open, &c.

Ṭeghen daramakaťako. They have put a prop under it to keep it from falling, or (if a door) to keep it open or prevent it closing.

Tegtege. Cf. tege tege.

Ṭehaḍ. } To be supported by leaning
Ṭhehaḍ. } or resting on something, to lean on, to be propped up, to be dependent on, to be under the shield of, to be under patronage, to entrust to for nourishing and cherishing, to give in marriage.

Ṭeḱbaḍak. A prop.

Ṭehaḍak. That which is propped up.

Ṭehaḍkedeako. They gave her in marriage, put her in a position to look to another for protection.

Ąuriye ṭehaḍoḱa. She is not yet married.

Tehaṛa. } A pillar or mark placed at the
Tehṛa. } junction of three boundaries.

Ṭehẽ. } To cry as an infant (imita-
Ṭehẽṭehẽ. } tive.)

Ṭehẽ ṭehẽye raḱeda. It is crying ṭehẽ ṭehẽ.

Ṭehẽ ṭehẽedae. It is crying.

Tehe tehe. Very, extremely, applied to whiteness.

Tehe tehe pondge ńeloḱkana. It appears very white.

Tehe mẽhẽ. To linger, to put off time, to dawdle.

Tehe mẽhẽ bako oḍok hodoḱkana. They are dawdling and not coming out quickly.

Tehe mẽhẽye bilomeť tahẽkana. He was lingering without reason.

Teheń. } To-day.
Teheńoḱ. }

Teheń gapa. Now-a-days.

Teheńaḱ kuṛąi baṛe emańme. Please give me to-day's wages.

Teheńoḱe hijuḱa. He will come to-day and presently.

Ṭehõ. } To cry as an infant (imita-
Ṭehõ ṭehõ. } tive.)

Ṭehõ ṭịhĩ. To cry together as infants.

Tej. Sharp, pungent, spirited, strong.

Noa churi do ąḍi teja. This knife is very sharp.

Bilạti thamakhur do ąḍi teja. English tobacco is very pungent or strong.

Nui do ąḍi tej ḍaṅra kanae. This is a very spirited bullock.

Tejo. A maggot, a creeping insect, a caterpillar, applied to the larvæ of all kinds of insects.

Tejokedeako. Maggots bred in him.
Tejoskaťako. Insects have eaten it, or caterpillars have infested it.
Kuĩṇḍi tejo. A caterpillar-like insect found in the kuĩṇḍi (q. v.) fruit.
Baṛe tejo. An insect found in the ripe fruit of the Banyan tree.
Lowa tejo. An insect found in a certain kind of ripe fig.

Tejo aṛak̕. Pot-herbs eaten by caterpillars, worm-eaten.

Tejo aṛak̕ hõ aloe ńamma. May he not even get worm-eaten pot herbs.

Tejo mala. A common wayside climbing plant, *Cissampelos Pareira, Linn.*

Tejpat. The leaf of *Laurus cassia*, used as a spice.

Ṭek. To live, survive, be living, stop, stay, to hinder, to obstruct.

Hoṛote khuble ṭekkeda. We lived a long time on the rice.
Nit hạli ṭekakanae ruạk̕ić do. The sick one is alive at present.
Ceť coṅko ṭeken nit hõ bako hijuk̕kana. What can have hindered them, they are not even coming now.

Ṭek. About one.

Mạhnạ ṭek hoyok̕kana. It is about one month.

Ṭekao. To bar, to obstruct, to prevent; to obstruct, prevent or hinder by interposing an obstacle.

Ṭekao ruạṛkedeako. They turned him back, they barred his way and turned him back.
Gai ṭekaoe senakana. He has gone to prevent the cows (from straying.)
Dak̕ dokin ṭekaokeda. They barred the way of the water, dammed it.

Teke. To boil, to cook by boiling.

Aṛak̕ko tekea. They cook pot-herbs.
Kicrićko tekea. They boil clothes (before washing.)
Teke matkom. Cooked matkom.
Abobo siťle baṅko tekeabona. We must first gather (the pot-herbs) then they will cook them for us.
Aṛak̕ tek̕keić. A wife.

Ṭeke ṭeke. To sound as a wooden bell on a cow's neck, or as food being stirred in a small pot.

Ṭeke ṭeke sạḍekana ṭoṭko do. The bell on the cow's neck sounds ṭeke ṭeke.
Male ṭeke ṭeke goťama nahak̕. We will presently make the sound of ṭeke ṭeke for you (we will presently cook you some food and in stirring it will make the sound of ṭeke ṭeke.)

Tekeć. / **Tekeć tekeć.** To jingle.

Tekeć tekeć sạḍekana sakom do. The wristlets are jingling.

Tekeć marte. / **Tekeć mente.** With a jingle.

Tekeć mente sạḍẹńa. It sounded jingle.

Tekek̕. / **Tekek̕ tekek̕.** To jingle. Cf. tekeć.

Tekek̕ marte. / **Tekek̕ mente.** With a jingle. Cf. tekeć marte.

Ṭeker ṭeker. The sound produced by a bell made of the wood of the Palmyra palm.

Tale ṭoṭko ṭeker ṭeker sạḍea. The cow's bell made of the wood of the Palmyra palm sounds ṭeker ṭeker.

Tekhar. Times.

Bar pe tekhar iń ńelkedea. I saw him two or three times.

Tekhrao. To repeat a question, to question or interrogate repeatedly.

Ạḍiko tekhraokedea, enhõ bae lạilak̕a. They interrogated him repeatedly, still he would not tell.
Arhõe tekhraokedea. He again repeated the question, he again re-examined him.

Tekhraṛ. To dispute, to altercate.

Tekhraṛe lagaokaťa. He is disputing.

Tekhra tikhri. To squabble, to dispute.

Ạḍikin tekhra tikhriena. They wrangled fiercely.

Teko. In comp., the person or persons in company with.

Mańjhitekoko bicạrkeda. The Mańjhi (q. v.) and those in company with him judged it.

Ṭekos. / **Ṭekos ṭekos.** Imitative of the sound produced by the *charkha* or spinning wheel, to whir.

Ṭekos ṭekos sạḍekana carkha do. The spinning wheel sounds whir whir.

Ṭekos marte. / **Ṭekos mente.** With a whir. Cf. ṭekos.

Ṭekos marte sạḍe goťenạ. It gave a whir, it sounded whir.

Ṭekoskoť. / **Ṭekoskoť ṭekoskoť.** Imitative of the whirring sound produced when the spinning wheel is reversed to wind the spun thread on to the spindle.

Tekra tikri. To squabble, to dispute. Cf. tekhra tikhri.

Tel. Oil.

Tel nahan. A ceremony observed five days after a death.

Tel khaṛ. }
Tel khaṛi } A ceremony observed three days after a death.
Gapale tel khaṛoka. To-morrow we will observe the *telkhar* ceremony.

Tela. To procure for another, to go surety for another, to take, to receive, to give.
Paurąe telaadea. He procured liquor for him.
Niąge kusite kusąlte ataṅke telakeam. Accept this with pleasure.

Ṭela. Able to run, applied mainly to leverets.
Ṭela kuląi iṅ goćkedea. I killed a leveret.

Tele. Young lice of the species *Pediculus capitis.*

Tele. To gather with the hand and put back into the mortar the rice or other grain which has escaped when being husked, cleaned or pounded.
Teleaḱkanae caole. She is putting the rice which has escaped back into the mortar.

Telgar. Fat, in good condition, rich, well-to-do.
Bese telgarakana nui khąsi do. This wether is fine and fat (will yield much suet.)

Telhan. A cess paid in oil.
Lagaoalekana telhan. We have to pay the cess in oil.

Telheć. }
Telheć dare. } A large forest tree, *Sterculia urens, Roxb.*

Teli. }
Tili. } A caste of Hindus who make and sell oil, an oilman.

Telṅjo. To stretch out, as the legs.
Telṅjokateye gitićakana. He is lying with his legs stretched out.
Jaṅga telṅjoetam. Stretch out your legs.

Telpeṅ. Shallow.
Noa gaḍa do telpeṅgea. This river is shallow.
Telpeṅ thąriye kiriṅakaća. He has bought a shallow brass plate.

Telsãoar. Fairish, in complexion.
Telsãoar koṛa. A fairish youth.
Telsãoar kuṛi. A fairish girl.

Ṭembe ṭuṛa. M. }
Ṭembe ṭuri. F. } Small, applied to children.

Ṭembeć ṭuruć. Small.
Ṭembeć ṭuruć gidrą menaḱkotaea. He has a lot of small children.

Ṭembros. The Guava.

Ṭembroṫ. Small, little.

Ṭemeć. Shallow.
Onkage khąndri ar ṭemeć daḱem ṅama. Thus you will find deep and shallow water.
Aṛe aṛete ṭemećgea. It is shallow at the edges.

Ṭemel. }
Ṭemel ṭemel. } Little, dwarfish, trippingly.
Ṭemel ṭemele dąṛã baṛaekana. He is small, tripping about.
Ṭemel mara gidrą. A little rascally child.

Ṭemna. }
Ṭimni. } Cf. ṭamna ṭamni.

Ṭemreṫ. }
Ṭemreṫ ṭemreṫ. } Small, little.
Tinmarahae? ṭemreṫ ṭemreṫgeae. How big is she? she is very small.

Ṭemso. }
Ṭemsoḱ. } Short in stature.
Ṭemsoḱgeae bąhu do. The bride is short of stature.

Ṭemṭeṛem. Quite, applied to fullness of water. Cf. cemceṛem.
Khetre daḱ ṭemṭeṛem peṛećakana. The fields are quite filled with water.
Band ṭemṭeṛem peṛećakana. The tank is quite full.

Ten. To be pressed down by something lying on the top, to cause to be pressed down by putting something on the top.
Kaṭṭeye tenena. He is pressed under a log, a log is lying on the top of him.
Tiye tenkedea. He pressed his hand (under something.)
Mone tentam. Control your grief, control your spirit.

Ten. In comp. added to nouns to form adjectives
Sadom tenko hoṛ. The mounted men.
Hortenrenko hoṛ. Those people on the road, or travelling people.
Birtenko hoṛ. Those people in the forest.
Hortenić. The traveller, the one on the road.
Pąhiltenko. Those first.

Teṅ. To weave.
Kicrićko teṅa. They weave cloth.
Teteṅić. The person weaving, a weaver.

Ṭen. }
Ṭaṅ. } Used with the numeral one (miṫ) to form the indefinite article a or an; also a single animal or thing.
Miṫ ṭen. One individual.
Miṫ ṭen hoṛe calaḱkana. A man is going.

Ṭena. A stand on which a tame parrokeet is kept chained.
Ṭena miru apeaḱ ṭena khon aleaḱ ṭenarele ucąṛakadea. We have removed your tame parrokeet from its stand to our stand, i. e. we have taken one of your daughters to our house as a bride.

Ṭena ḍaṅ. A lever by means of which water is raised from a well.

Teńa. The relationship between the husband of an elder sister and her brothers and sisters.

Teńań. My elder sister's husband.
Teńat. His elder sister's husband.

Teńaea. } Brothers-in-law, the relation
Teńaya. } ship between a brother and his elder sister's husband, and vice versa.

Teńaeaḱakin. They are brothers-in-law.
Teńaeakin calaoena. The brothers-in-law went away.

Teńa era. Brothers-in-law, the relationship between a brother and his elder sister's husband.

Teńaera kanakin. } They are brothers-in-law.
Teńaeraḱakin. }
Teńaera sangaikantakoa. Their assumed relationship is that of brothers-in-law.

Tenae gandke. } A scoundrel, scoun-
Tenae garke. } drelly, used only by women.

Teńat. His elder sister's husband.

Teńaya. Cf. teńaca.

Ṭenḍa bayar. } A young buffaloe with
Cenḍa bayar. } six teeth.

Ṭenḍar. To lean against or on.

Ṭenḍar maci. A chair or stool with a back.
Ṭenḍar aḱ sar. A name given to a present made by the bridegroom's father to the bride's brothers.
Caini bhitreko ṭenḍarakaťa. They have leaned the ladder against the wall.

Ṭenḍos. Defiant, contentious, stubborn.

Ṭenḍoseť kanae. He is opposing.

Ṭenḍosia. A defiant, contentious or stubborn person.

Tenḍosia kanae. He is a contentious person.

Teṅgen. To kill for sacrifice by cutting off the head with a knife.

Mase sim sanḍi boṅgaem.
Mase juri parwa teṅgenem.
Come, sacrifice a cock,
Come, offer one of a pair of pigeons.
Doṅ sereń.

Teṅgo. } To stand, to stand still, to
Teṅgon. } assume an upright or per-
Tiṅgu. } pendicular position, to raise to an upright position, to appoint, to assume responsibility.

Teṅgo daram. To stand in front of, to oppose, to withstand.
Samahre kaḱthaió hõ banugiétińa,
Dea seére teṅgonió hõ banugiétińa.
I have no one to speak for me in front,
I have no one to stand at my back.
Teṅgo daḱ. Rain without wind when the drops fall perpendicularly.
Teṅgo ruą. The standing fever, hunger, starvation.
Ale seď teṅgo ruą do ḍhergea. There is much hunger over our way.

Ṭeṅgoć. A small axe.

Ṭaṅga. A large axe.
Tala ṭaṅga. A middle-sized axe.
Potam cupi ṭeṅgoć. A small sized axe of a peculiar shape.

Teṅgon. Cf. teṅgo.

Ṭeṅgra hako. A species of river fish.

Teńjao. } To exercise the body, to keep
Tińjau. } in training, to inure, to accustom to, to harden the body.

Kami teńjaoakanae. He is accustomed to work.
Ruąḱiće dąrã teńjaoakana. The sick one is now used to walking.
Sadom teńjaoko lagiť bahreteko idikoa. They take out horses to keep them in training.

Teńjlo. To stretch out, as the legs. Cf. telńjo.

Teńoḱ barã. The price paid for weaving; this is calculated at so much per cubit.

Ṭenṭa. A fish spear.

Ṭenṭha. } Worn small, small, mischiev-
Thenṭha. } ous.

Ṭenṭha sagar. A wheel worn small.
Ṭenṭha nahel. A plough worn small by use.
Ṭenṭha mara gidrą. A little rascal of a child.

Ṭeń teń. To become taut, tight or rigid, to contract and become tight, to be tightly strung.

Baberko ṭanao ṭeńṭeńakaťa. They have pulled the string tight.
Lohoťlenkhan aćtege ṭeńṭeńoḱa baber do. When it gets wet twine tightens of itself.

Ṭẽo ṭẽo. To jabber, to talk much.

Nui hoṛ do ądi ṭẽo ṭẽoḱkanae. This man is jabbering much.
Oṛaḱ na siraḱem ṭẽo ṭẽoḱkana. You are jabbering nonsense.

Ṭep. Corner of a piece of cloth, state, position, gist.

Noa katha reaḱ ṭep bań ńamakaťa. I have not caught the gist of this matter.
Kiorié reaḱ ṭepregeń lo ocoakaťa. I have burnt the corner of the cloth.
Ṭeprege jahãnaḱko ghẽṭa. They tie things in the corner of a cloth.

Ṭepa ṭepe. Small, little.

Ṭepeń. } Narrow in width and
Ṭepeń ṭepeń. } short when worn round the waist.

Noa kiorié do ṭepeńgea. This cloth is short.
Ṭepeń ṭepeńe bandeakaťa. She is wearing her garment very short.

Tepen. The reciprocal form of ten (q. v.), to rest on each other, to be superimposed.

Parkom baber alope tepen ocoea, bańkhan ạdi kukmuǩa. Do not allow the twine with which the bed is woven to overlap, or else it will cause much dreaming.

Alope tepen ocoea. Do not superimpose them.

Tepeť. To block up, to close up, to stop up.

Nunạǩe arjaoakaťa nes oṛaǩe ader tepeťakaťa. He has gathered such a good crop this year that in storing it he has blocked up the house.

Bhugaǩ tepeťkaǩme rabań boloǩkana. Stop up the hole cold is coming in.

Ṭepoǩ. A kind of bird trap. Cf. ṭapoǩ.

Ṭep̣ṭep̣. } Hard, as the stomach when
Ḍep̣ ḍep̣. } full.

Ṭep̣ṭep̣geye jom biakana. He has eaten his belly full.

Ṭepṭepe. Hard, stiff, to die.

Jom ṭepṭepeakanae. He has eaten till his stomach is hard.

Ota ṭepṭepekedeae. He held him firmly down.

Goć ṭepṭepeěnae. He is dead and stiff.

Ṭera. } Squinting, oblique-eyed.
Ṭeraṭera. }

Ṭerageye beńgeťeda. He squints.

Ṭeraṭerae beńgeťadińa. He looked at me squintingly.

Ṭera M. } Squinting, oblique-eyed, cock-
Ṭiri F. } eyed.

Nui do ṭerageae. This (person) squints.

Nui do ṭirigeae. This (female) squints.

Terań. To shoot an arrow so as to allow for trajection, a bow shot.

Tinạǩ sạngińa? Miť terań hoyoǩa. How far is it? A bow shot.

Terań tioǩkedeae. He shot an arrow to where he was.

Terdeć. To shine, as the moon, moonshine, moonlight.

Terdećakaťae. The moon is shining.

Terdeć ńindae calaoena. He left after the moon had risen, he left by moonlight.

Terdeć marsal netar do. There is moonlight at present.

Ḍigḍige terdećakaťa. There is bright moonlight.

Nahaǩe terdejoǩa. The moon will rise presently, there will be moonlight presently.

Tere. A ceremony observed at a marriage, to anoint with oil and turmeric.

Bạhu jãwãeko terekina. They anoint a bride and bridegroom with oil and turmeric.

Tetre kuṛi. The girls who anoint the bride and bridegroom at a marriage

Ṭereć. } The call of the parrokeet
Ṭereć ṭereć. } when sitting, (imitative.

Ṭereć maraokedae. (The parrokeet) called out once.

Ṭereć ṭereće raǩkeda. (The parrokeet) is calling ṭereć ṭereć.

Ṭẽṛẽć ṭẽṛẽć. Shrilly, in a high key.

Miru ṭẽṛẽć ṭẽṛẽće roṛeda. The parrot speaks in a high key.

Tẽṛẽjhaǩ. Big, huge, applied to huge objects lying on the ground.

Gitićakan tẽṛẽjhaǩe ńamkeda. He found him lying with his huge bulk on the ground.

Dare tẽṛẽjhaǩ gurakana. The tree has fallen with its huge length on the ground.

Terel. } The Indian Ebony tree,
Terel dare. } *Diospyros tomentosa, Roxb.*

Terel mańj. Ebony.

Ṭeremere. Under the influence of liquor or a narcotic, to be intoxicated.

Ṭeremereěnako. They are intoxicated.

Pạurạ ńukate ṭeremereěnae. He is intoxicated with drinking liquor.

Ṭeṛem ṭeṛem. Quite, applied to fullness. Cf. ceṛem ceṛem.

Band ṭeṛem ṭeṛem perećakana. The tank is quite full.

Teṛeń goṛeń. Anywhere, anyway, all ways, every where.

Teṛeń goṛeńko gitićakana. They are lying every where.

Dare khub teṛeń goṛeńko gurakaťa. They have felled the trees every where.

Teṛeť boṛeť. Repeatedly, time after time, over and over again.

Teṛeť boṛeťe kulikedińa. He questioned me again and again.

Teṛeť boṛeť ghạri ghạri inạgeye roṛeda. He keeps continually saying the same thing.

Ṭereṭere. Applied to the croaking of small frogs and to the thin or weak voice of a small person, to vaunt or boast, applied to insignificant persons.

Ṭereṭereye roṛeda. He is speaking in a thin or feeble voice.

Ạdim ṭereṭereǩkana. You are jabbering a great deal, in a thin voice.

Teretese. Abundantly, in large quantity, applied mainly to matkom (q. v.) fallen from the tree.

Matkom ńurakana teretese. Matkom has fallen in large quantity.

Teretese taseakať leka ńurakana. It (matkom) has fallen in large quantity, as if it had been spread out.

Tŏṛga. Not parallel, perverse, twisted, warped.

Sarjom takta bar pe boobor dobolekhan tĕṛgaǩa. If a *sal* board be kept for two or three years it will warp.

Bicạr bae jomeda, tĕṛgaǩkanae. He does not accept the decision, he is perverse.

Tergeń. / Tergeń tergeń. To nag, to find fault, to chide angrily, to upbraid, to vituperate, to objurgate.

Tergeń tergeńe roṛeda. She is nagging.

Tergeń tergeńoǩkanae. She is nagging.

Tergeń marte. / Tergeń mente. With a snap. Cf. tergeń.

Tergeń marteye roṛkediña. He snapped at me.

Terges. To nag, to find fault with angrily. Cf. tergeń.

Ṭeṛha. Crooked, slanting, oblique.

Terheć. A large forest tree, *Sterculia urens, Roxb.* Cf. telheć.

Ṭermerao. To be under the influence of an intoxicant or a narcotic, to be intoxicated.

Gańjateko ṭermeraoakana. They are under the influence of ganja (q. v.)

Ṭeroǩ. / Ṭeroǩ ṭeroǩ. To hop, to walk or trip like a dwarf or a little child.

Ṭeroǩ ṭeroǩe calaǩkana. He goes hopping along.

Ṭeroǩ ṭeroǩe don idieda. He goes hopping along.

Ṭeroǩ Phạgu. Little Phagu.

Terom. A kind of wild honey bee.

Terom rasa. The honey of the *terom* bee.

Teroń. Because, on account of.

Ona terońem dal ocolena. Because of that you were beaten.

Onkam roṛkeć terońko edreaćmea. They were angry with you because you spoke thus.

Ṭes. / Ṭes ṭes. Imitative of the noise produced by anything brittle snapping or clicking. Cf. thes.

Ṭes ṭes sadekana. It sounds ṭesṭes, it is snapping.

Ṭesa. To shore, to prop, to support by a post or buttress. Cf. ṭhesa.

Ṭesao. / Ṭhesao. To put close to, to cause to reach or be close to. Cf. ṭhesao.

Tesar. / Tesra. Third.

Tesar din. The third day.

Tesra din. The third day.

Tesar dhao. The third time.

Tesar serma. The third year.

Tesarić. The third one (animate.)

Tesaraǩ. The third one (inanimate.)

Ṭesaṭes. Close together, touching each other. Cf. ṭhesaṭhes.

Tese. Through, on account of, by reason of, owing to.

Onatese bań senlena. On that account I did not go.

Tesnek. As it was, in its first state, without change or detriment, equal.

Pạhil rin do tesnekge tahĕena. The former debt remained as it was.

Tesneke ńam ruaṛkedea. He received him back without having received any detriment.

Tesra. Third. Cf. tesar.

Ṭesra. M. / Ṭisri. F. One-eyed, blind of one eye, one eye imperfect, having imperfect vision.

Ṭesrageae. He is one-eyed.

Ṭisrigeae. She is one-eyed.

Ṭesṭa. To seek for, to endeavour, to apply one's mind to, to exert oneself.

Khoroc ṭesṭaabonme cabaǩkana. Exert yourself to provide food for us, (our supply) is coming to an end. [to anything.

Ceć hŏ bae ṭesṭaea. He does not apply his mind

Teć. A particle affixed to nouns adds emphasis or definiteness, also employed to form abstract nouns.

Hendeteć. The blackness.

Marańteć. The greatness.

Gećteć. The cut.

Hoponteć. The son.

Kakatteć. The uncle.

Aćteć. Himself.

Ạditeće ruaǩkana. He is seriously ill.

Ḍherteć cabaena. The greater part is finished.

Tetań. Thirst, to thirst, to be thirsty.

Daǩ tetańedekana. He is thirsty.

Daǩ tetạńe maraokećtaea. He quenched his thirst.

Daǩ tetań bań maraoakantaea. His thirst is not being quenched.

Tetańediǹkana. I am thirsty.

Ạdi tetańkedea. He was very thirsty.

Reńgeć tetańe kạmikana. He is labouring in hunger and thirst.

Reńgeć tetań bam kạmilekhan ceć hoyoǩa? If you do not labour in hunger and thirst what will you get?

Ṭĕṭĕ. Applied to the crying of an infant. (imitative.)

Cedaǩ ṭĕṭĕpe raǩ ocoedekana? Why are you making the infant cry?

Ṭĕṭĕ. Applied to the call of the Kerkeṭa (q. v.) or Shrike.

Kerkeṭako raga ṭĕṭĕ. The Kerkeṭa calls ṭĕṭĕ.

Ṭeṭeć. Imitative of the cry of certain birds. Cf. ṭeć.

Cĕṛĕ hŏko ṭeṭeća. Birds also chirp.

Ṭeṭeṭeṅgoć ćeṛe. This name is given to two species of Lapwing. *Sarcicophorus bilobus*, and *Lobivanellus goensis*.

Tetha. Cf. thetha.

Ṭeṭoas. To be thirsty.
Ạḍi ṭeṭoasoḱkanae. He is very thirsty.

Tethoṛ. Obstinate, heady, rude. Cf. thethoṛ.

Tetre. } Tekre. } Anointers, those who at a marriage anoint the bride and bridegroom with oil and turmeric. Cf. ṭere.
Tetreko kanako. They are anointers.
Tetreić. An anointer.

Ṭeć ṭeć. Ticking sound (imitative.)
Ghạṛi ṭeć ṭeć saḍekana. The watch sounds tick tick.

Ṭewan. To search for, to find.
Bạhuko ṭewanakadea. They have found a bride.
Ṭewan baṛaedae. He is searching.
Onaḱ reaḱ tewange bah ńamoḱkana.

Tewelgać. Weak, feeble, poor, faint, unconscious.
Aṭha saṭha bạnuḱtaea, tewelgaćenae. He has no strength, he has become feeble.

Teweń. To hold and carry suspended in the hand.
Laltene teweńakaća. He carries the lantern suspended from his hand.

Teweń jiweć. To hang on to life, to keep alive.
Niạ matkomtele teweń jiwećena. Owing to this *matkom* (q. v.) we are hanging on to life.

Ṭeweć. To silence, to confute, with negative to obey, to move.
Katha bae ṭewećada. He did not obey the order.
Lutur hõ bae ṭewećlaḱa. He did not even move his ears, he did not obey.
Mić kathategeye ṭewećkećkoa. He silenced them with one word.
Ona ńelte ḍạn ar onko ren herelko ṭewećena. Seeing that the witches and their husbands were silenced.

Ṭhaba ṭhobo. In a cluster, applied to fruit.

Ṭhaba ṭhube. In clusters, in a cluster.
Ḍạhu ṭhaba ṭhube joakana. The dạhu (q. v.) has fruited in clusters.

Ṭhạbu. } Ṭhạbu ṭhạbu. } Large, big, very large, very big.
Ṭhạbu ṭhạbu joạkana. Its fruit is very large.
Ṭhạbu ṭhạbuko kuṭiakaća. They have cut the meat into very big pieces.

Ṭhae. } Thae ṭhae. } Imitative of the ringing sound produced when anything hard is struck.
Thae ṭhae saḍea. It rings, it emits a ringing sound.
Ṭhae ṭhae keṭeća. It is so hard as to ring.

Ṭhae marte. } Ṭhae mente. } With a ring.

Ṭhae. } Ṭhae ṭhae. } Absolutely, actually, positively, used only in connection with fasting or starvation.
Thae ṭhae reṅgećtege menaḱlea. We are positively starving.
Ṭhae upạstege din bhor menaḱlea. I have absolutely fasted the whole day.
Ṭhae upas menaḱlea. We are absolutely fasting.

Ṭhaekoḱ. } Ṭhaekoć. } Old, past child bearing.

Ṭhae ṭhui. Imitative of ringing or clanging sounds of different tones, as for instance when iron is struck alternately by a heavy and light hammer.
Ṭhae ṭhuiko koṭećeda. They are hammering and producing a sound resembling ṭhae ṭhui, ṭhae ṭhui.

Thag. To deceive, to oppose, to swindle

Thagal. } Thaglao. } Thagal thagal. } To bite as a snake by darting.
Biṅe thaglao goćkedea. The snake made a dart and bit him.

Thagla thagli. To bite at each other as snakes. Cf. thagal.

Thah. Bottom, to fathom.
Oka thahge bah ńamoḱkana. No bottom can be found.
Niạ daḱ reaḱ thah bạnuḱanah. This water has no bottom, this water is bottomless.
Thah baṛakedań bạhu reań, okare hõ thah bań ńamlaḱa.

Ṭhạhri. } Ṭhạhri ṭhạhri. } Slowly, gently, disjointedly.
Ṭhạhri ṭhạhriye roṛa. He speaks disjointedly.
Ạḍi ṭhạhriko sereńa. They sing gently.

Ṭhạị. } Ṭhão. } A place, to place, to give in marriage.
Ṭhạị ṭhạire. In divers places.
Ṭhạị bạnuḱanah duṛup ḷạgić. There is no place to sit.
Aurile ṭhạoea. We have not yet given her in marriage.

Ṭhạị ṭhạị. Close together, near to each other.

Ṭhạị ṭhạị. } Ṭhãe ṭhãe. } Dry, as a cough.
Ṭhạị ṭhạiye khoḱeda. He has a dry cough.

Thaiạ. A game so called.

Ṭhaicạ. A quarrel, a wrangle, a dispute.
Nuige ṭhaicạe ňambaṛakana. This (person) is seeking a quarrel.
Ṭhạicạgeye ehoba. He will begin a quarrel.

Ṭhaikạ. Cf. ṭhaicạ.

Thạili. } A bag.
Thạilạk'. }

Thạiyạ. To kick with the sole of the foot, to stamp on with the foot.
Thạiyạkediňa. He kicked me.
Losoṭe thạiyạkeda. He kicked off the mud (adhering to his feet.)
Thạiya thokae heċena. He came with his feet covered with mud.

Thạiyo hạrup. A game so called.

Thak. } A division, a pile, a company, a band, a lot.
Thok. }
Thak thakko dohoakaṭa. They have placed it in divisions or in lots.
Palṭonko thak thakko hijuk'kana. The soldiers are coming in companies, or regiments.

Ṭhak'. } Imitative of a clicking sound.
Ṭhak' ṭhak'. }
Ṭhak' ṭhak'e sạḍe ocoeda. He is making a clicking sound.

Ṭhak'. Near.

Ṭhak. }
Ṭhakna. } To deceive, to cheat.
Ṭhakua. }
Ṭhakkediňae. He cheated me.

Ṭhak. To astonish, to amaze, to cause to wonder.
Joto gadel hoṛko ṭhakena. All the multitude wondered.
Ṭhakkediňae. He astonished me.

Thakaman. Well-to-do, rich.
Thakaman hoṛ kanae. He is a well-to-do man.

Thakao. To be tired, to be exhausted through illness.
Thakao heċenae. He came tired.
Alom calak'a thakaok'am. Do not go, you will tire.
Ruạ thakaoakanae. } He is very ill and exhausted.
Thakaoakanae. }

Thakar bakar. } Greasy, dirty owing to moist stuff, as clay, grease, &c., &c., adhering to the person.
Thokor bokor. }
Thakar bakare lohoṭ heċakana. He has come covered with mud.
Thokor bokor losoṭ laṭkaoakawadea. He is dirty with mud sticking to him.

Thakar bakar. Tired, wearied.

Thaka thạki. Tired, wearied.
Thaka thạkienale kạmi kạmite. We are tired with continued working.

Thakdama. } To disappoint.
Thakdoma. }
Thakdamakediňte eskarge calak' hoeėntiňa. Through his disappointing me I had to go alone.

Ṭhaket'. } To come into contact with and be brought to a stop.
Ṭheket'. }
Ṭhaket' dohokediňae. He detained me.
Ṭhaket' tahẽenae. He was detained.
Gạḍi darere ṭhaket'ena. The cart came in contact with the tree.
Sojhete lagaeme, jahã darere alom ṭhaket' ocoea. Drive straight, do not cause it to come in contact with any tree.

Ṭhaket' ṭhaket'. } With many interruptions, repeatedly coming into contact with obstacles.
Ṭheket' ṭheket'. }
Ṭhaket' ṭhaket'teye metadiňa. He said to me in broken words.
Ṭhaket' ṭhaket'tele heċena. We were stopped, or detained, many times on our way.

Thake thak. In heaps, in bands. Cf. thak.

Ṭhakna. M. } A deceiver, a cheat, deceiving, cheating.
Ṭhạkni. F. }

Ṭhakna. To deceive, to cheat.

Ṭhakrao. } To upbraid, to twit, to threaten, bring up an old matter.
Ṭhokrao. }
Baň em daṛeaekanteye ṭhakraoediňkana. Because I cannot pay him he is upbraiding me.

Ṭhakṛok'. } Applied to the sound produced by driving the thread home when weaving.
Ṭhakṛok' ṭhakṛok'. }
Mạku sohor piche ṭhakṛok'. Every time the shuttle is thrown there is the sound ṭhakṛok', the sound produced by driving home the thread.

Ṭhak ṭhak. } To be ready, eager, prepared.
Ṭhak ṭhakao. }
Laṛhạị lagiṭ ṭhakṭhakao baṛaekanae. He is eager for a fight.
Laṛhạikin ṭhakṭhakaoena. They are prepared to fight.

Thak ṭhak. } Shivering, to shiver.
Thak ṭhakao. }
Ṭhak ṭhak rabaň. It is shivering cold.
Ṭhakṭhakaok'kanae. He is shivering.

Thakthakao. To hinder, to impede.
Nui hoṛe thakthakaoket'bona. This man hindered us.

Thak thạki. Cf. ṭakṭaki.

Ṭhakṭhok. Imitative of the sound of hammering, mainly applied to hammering or striking wood.
Ṭhak ṭhokko ehopakaṭa kaṭ mistri do. The carpenters have begun to hammer.

Ṭhaḱ ṭhoḱ. To rap, as on the ground with the end of a stick; fearlessly, plainly, without reserve.
Ṭhaḱ ṭhoḱateye boloena. He went in rapping on the ground with his stick (to announce his coming.)
Katha alom okoea, ṭhaḱ ṭhoḱ baṛe lạime. Do not hide the matter, rap it out, tell it without reserve.

Ṭhaḱ ṭhuḱ. Imitative of the sound produced by hammering, or one object coming into contact violently with another.
Mẽṛhet kanḍa reaḱ ṭhaḱ ṭhuḱ baṅ aṅjomlena. No sound of hammering with an iron instrument was heard.
Ṭhaḱ ṭhuḱkin dapalena. They hammered each other.

Ṭhạkuạ. To deceive, to cheat. Cf. ṭhaḱ.

Ṭhạkumṭhaḱ. In clusters, as the fruit of the Papita, Palmyra palm, &c.
Marań utạre ghẽṭakaṭ ṭhạkumṭhaḱ.
Ṭhạkumṭhaḱ joakana. It has fruited in clusters.

Ṭhạkur.
Ṭhạkurjiu. } The supreme being.

Ṭhạkur. A title inferior to raja, a title given to Brahmins, a deity.

Ṭhạkur.
Murmu ṭhạkur. } The name of one of the Santal septs.

Thalbalao. To be near parturition.

Thalbạli. To be near to parturition, of animals.
Thalbạliakanae gại do. The cow is near parturition.

Thalaḱ thuluḱ.
Thalak thuluk. } Unsteady, as a child beginning to walk.
Thalaḱ thuluḱe cacoḱkana.

Thale.
Jale thale. } Cf. jale thale.

Thalhalao. To be ravaged by, to be reduced to the last extremity, to be in evil plight, to be stricken.
Lạ̃ basoteko thalhalaoena. They are cholera stricken.
Reṅgeṭteko thalhalaoena. They are reduced to the last extremity through hunger, they are famine stricken.

Thạli. To sink, as in a bog, quicksand, mud, &c.
Losoṭre thạlienae. He has sunk in the mud.
Gitilre thạli ṭhekomenae. He has sunk and stuck in a quicksand.

Thalpe. Slow, sluggish, inactive, applied to females.
Thalpegeae nui ạimại do. This woman is slow.
Nui gại do thalpegeae. This cow is sluggish.

Thal thal. Shaking, quivering, as a bog or semi-liquid mud.
Losoṭena thal thal. The mud is soft to quivering.
Thal thalko losoṭakaṭa. They have mixed up the mud and water till it quivers.

Ṭhal ṭhal.
Thal thal. } To roll about in globules, as quicksilver &c., having the property of always resolving itself into globules.
Poraeni sakamre daḱ ṭhalṭhalao baṛaea, baṅ lạṭkaoḱa. Water rolls about on the leaf of the poraeni (q. v.), it does not stick.
Ṭhal ṭhal baṛaekana daḱ. The water rolls about in drops.

Thạluḱ thạluḱ. Shaking or quivering as the adipose tissue of a fat person when walking, to waddle, as a fat tired person.
Thạluḱ thạluḱe taṛameda. He is waddling.

Thạluḱ thạpuḱ.
Thạluk thạpuk. } Tottering, shaking, feebly, as an old or feeble person.
Thạluk thạpuke calaḱkana. He walks totteringly.

Tham. A prop, a pier, as of a bridge.
Pul reaḱ tinạḱ tham menaḱa? How many piers has the bridge?
Thamakaṭako. They have applied a prop or props.

Tham. To stop, cease.

Tham khunṭi.
Kham khunṭi. } A king post.

Ṭhamae ṭhukại. Impedimenta, to be impeded, to have more articles than can be conveniently carried.
Ṭhamae ṭhukại ạḍi utạr mənaḱtińa. I have more things than I can conveniently carry.
Iḱdiye ṭhamae ṭhukạioḱkana. He cannot conveniently take all with him.

Thamakhur. Tobacco.
Jom thamakhur. Chewing tobacco.
Ńui thamakhur. Smoking tobacco.
Bilạti thamakhur. Tobacco prepared in the European method.
Surti thamakhur.
Moera thamakhur. } Uncured tobacco.
Kạcri thamakhur. Locally produced tobacco.

Thamar. Tobacco.
Hukạ thamar tanaḱ alope jom ńuitaea. Do not chew or smoke with him.

Thambhao. To settle, to remain, to be firm, to be permanent.
Unạḱe arjaoeṭrehõ oṛaḱre bam thambhaoḱkantaea, ublạ ḍublạedae. Although he raises such good crops it does not remain in his house, he squanders it.
Jiwi do thambhaoentaea. His life remains to him.

Tham gaḍi. To settle, to take up one's residence; dwelling, residence.
Danderkore thamgaḍi tahẽkantaea. His dwelling was in the caves.
Nagraharaye thamgaḍiona. He settled in the city.

Ṭhamkao. To cease flowing, to be stanched, applied mainly to blood.
Mayam ṭhamkaoena. The blood has ceased to flow.

Than. A piece or web of cloth.
Kiorić than. } A web of cloth, a piece of cloth.
Than kiorić. }

Than. Place, the place where a deity is supposed to reside.
Mạńjhi than. The rude temple-like erection in every Santal village where the manes of the deceased Mańjhi or village head man is worshipped.
Boṅga than. The place where a deity is supposed to reside.
Jaher than. The sacred grove in which the village deities are supposed to reside.

Than baisạu. To set up an idol or fetich.

Than oraḱ. An idol house, a temple.

Thana. A police station.

Thanadar. The person in charge of a police station.

Ṭhanao. To determine, to resolve, to settle.
Monereye ṭhanaokeda. He determined in his mind.

Ṭhanḍga. } Hair cropped very short,
Ṭhunḍga. } hairless, bare, as a tree of branches.

Ṭhanḍgać. } Having hair cropped very
Ṭhunḍguć. } short or shaved, bare.

Ṭhanḍgać thunḍguć. Having hair cut very short, having the head cropped bare or shaved.
Ṭhanḍgać ṭhunḍgućko hecakana. The people with cropped heads have come, or the people with shaved heads have come.

Ṭhanḍa. } Cold, to make cool, to com-
Ṭhanḍha. } fort, to assuage, to refresh.
Jom ṭhanḍaenako. They have eaten and are refreshed.
Jiwi ṭhanḍaentaea. His spirit is comforted, or his sorrow is assuaged.

Thanel. The female breasts, the udder of an animal.

Ṭhaṅ. } Imitative of a clanging
Ṭhaṅ ṭhaṅ. } sound, to clang.
Ṭhaṅ ṭhaṅ sadekana. It is sounding clang, clang, it is clanging.
Ghanṭako ruia ṭhaṅ ṭhaṅ. They ring the bell clang, clang.

Ṭhaṅ marte. } With a clang.
Ṭhaṅ mente. }
Ṭhaṅ marte sade goćena. It sounded with a clang, it sounded clang.

Ṭhaṅgal thuṅgul. } Dizzy, head swim-
Thuṅgul muṅgul. } ming.
Ṭhaṅgal thuṅguliń ṭikaueda. I feel dizzy.

Ṭhaṅgar ṭhuṅgur. Big and little.

Ṭhaṇi. Place.
Aliṅaḱ jonom ṭhạni khonliń hijuḱkana. We are coming from our native country or birth place.

Ṭhaṅka ṭhoraṅ. Loud rapping sound, without reserve, fearlessly, openly.
Mać ṭheṅgateko koṭaḱlekhan ṭhaṅka ṭhoraṅ sadea. If one raps with a bamboo stick a loud rapping sound resembling ṭhaṅka ṭhoraṅ will be produced.
Jegeye ńellaḱa monere bae doholaḱa, ṭhaṅka ṭhoraṅe roṛkeda. What he saw, he did not keep to himself, but spoke it out fearlessly.

Ṭhaṅ ṭhuṅ. Imitative of the sound produced when iron is struck by iron.
Mẽṛhećko dala ṭhaṅ ṭhuṅ. They hammer iron and produce a sound resembling ṭhaṅ ṭhuṅ.

Ṭhaṇit. Residence, place, camping ground.
Ińaḱ jonom ṭhạnit. My birth place.

Ṭhankao. To do enthusiastically, with heart and soul, to warm up.
Ṭhankaome se mandạria,
Lolo setoṅ alom bataoa.
Warm to your work drummer,
Heed not the fierce rays of the sun.

Ṭhankao. To cease, to become less, to decrease.
Ruạ ṭhankao ńoḱentaea. His fever has decreased a little.

Ṭhanka ṭhạnki. To scold, to give abuse.
Ṭhanka ṭhạnki baṛaekanae. He is going about scolding.

Ṭhanṭạratiń. } Here and there, from
Ṭhonṭạratiń. } place to place.
Ṭhanṭạratińe ńam baṛaeda. He is searching for it here and there.

Ṭhanṭhanao. To be intent on, to be eager, to be in readiness.
Kạmi do baṅataea, jom lạgiće ṭhanṭhanao baṛaekana. He has no mind to work, he is intent on eating.
Dadal lạgiće ṭhanṭhanao baṛaekana. He is intent on striking (some one.)

Ṭhanṭhania. Dry, very dry.
Ot do ṭhanṭhaniagea. The soil is very dry.

Ṭhāo. A place, to place, to give in marriage.
Duṛuṕ ṭhāo aṛaǩaepe. Make room for him to sit.
Gitić ṭhāo nonḍe menaǩa, se baṅ? Is there a place to sleep here or not?
Ṭhāo bạnuǩan. There is no room.
Mạipe ṭhāokadea se baṅ? Have you given the girl in marriage or not?
Ṭhāoakadeale. We have given her in marriage.
Ṭhāṭhāokanae. He is making room, or clearing a place.

Ṭhāo ku ṭhāo. In some places and not in others.
Ṭhāo ku ṭhāoreye daǩkeda. It rained in some places and not in others.

Ṭhāo ghurghur. } Turn where you are,
Ṭhāo gurgur. } said to bullocks
Ṭhāoe gurgur. } when turning them in little space.

Ṭhāoe ṭhāo. Cf. ṭhāohe ṭhāohe.

Ṭhāohe. } Near to each other,
Ṭhāohe ṭhāo. } close together.
Ṭhāohe ṭhāohe. }
Ṭhāohe ṭhāoheko oṛaǩakaṭa. They have built their houses close together.

Ṭhap. A kind of performing doll which the performer causes to clap its hands producing a sound resembling ṭhap, ṭhap.

Thap. Respect, honour, trustworthiness.
Iñaǩ thapko uṭhạukeda. They have ceased to respect me.
Uniaǩ thap cabaentaea. He is no longer [respected.

Ṭhaṕ. } To produce a loud clapp-
Ṭhaṕ ṭhaṕ. } ing or tapping sound, (imitative.)
Sim sạnḍi ṭhaṕ ṭhaṕleeneće raga. The cock first claps its wings then it crows.
Ṭhaṕ ṭhaboǩkanako. They are clapping (wings.)

Ṭhaṕ marte. } With a clap or loud
Ṭhaṕ mente. } tapping sound.
Ṭhap marte saḍe goṭena. It sounded clap.

Thapa. To slap, to hit, to beat lightly, to come slightly into contact with.
Thapameaṅ. I shall slap you.
Hoe jokheć ḍạr ḍạr thapaǩa. When it blows the branches come into contact with each other.
Kaḍae thapakedea. The buffaloe hit him lightly with his horn.

Ṭhapa ṭhapa. Slight tapping or rustling sound, as that produced by leaves, &c., striking against each other.
Ṭhapa ṭhapa saḍekana. There is a sound of light tapping.

Ṭhapa ṭhopo. To slap each other, to pat.
Ṭhapa ṭhopoenakin. They slapped each other.

Ṭhapa ṭhuǩ. To come in contact with, to strike against, to bump against.
Kanḍa alom ṭhapa ṭhuǩ oćoea. Do not allow the waterpots to bump against each other.
Balaea do taren tarenko ṭhapa ṭhugoǩa. Balaeas (q. v.) bump shoulders.

Ṭhapar. } Applied to the sound
Ṭhapar ṭhapar. } produced by light objects coming into contact with each other, a light tapping or rustling sound.
Ṭhapar ṭhapar sakam saḍekana. The leaves are rustling.
Ṭhapar ṭhapar miṭ ñindạko enećkana. They have danced and tapped (the drums) all night.

Ṭhapar marte. } With a tap or rustle.
Ṭhapar mente. }
Ṭhapar marte saḍeena. It sounded with rustle.

Thapna. } To erect, to set up, as an
Thapni. } idol; to introduce a spirit by incantations, &c. into a place or house.
Ḍạnge boṅgako thapnakoa jahāe oṛaǩre. Witches by incantations introduce spirits into any one's house.
Thapna boṅga dole oćoǩkedea. We removed, or exorcised, the spirit that had been introduced by incantations.

Thapna thạpni. To introduce spirits by incantations.
Jaherre boṅgako thapna thạpnikeṭkoa. They introduced boṅgas (q. v.) into the sacred grove.

Thapo thapo. To pat.
Ma uni gidrạ thapo thapokaeme raǩedae. Pat that child, he is crying.

Thapo thapo. A children's game so called.

Thapṛe. To pat, to come slightly in contact with.

Thapṛoǩ. Short of destination or proper place.
Atraregoye thapṛoǩkada. He placed it short of its proper place, he threw it down half-way.
Laṅgaenae, ontegeye thapṛoǩ tahēena. He is tired, he stayed behind there.

Thap thop. To put at rest for the present, to pacify for a time.
Noa kathale thap thopakaṭa. We have put this matter at rest for the present.
Mahajon nesiṅ thap thopakaṭkoa. I have pacified the moneylenders for this year.

Thar. } A line, a row, in lines, in
Thar thar. } rows.

Mit́ tharko teṅgoakana. They are standing in line.

Thar tharko duṛupakana. They are sitting in rows.

Thar ke thar. In lines, in rows.

Tharke tharko duṛupakana. They are sitting in rows.

Ṭhar. To deceive, to dupe, to play one false.

Nui kathategeye ṭhar baṛaediṅkana. This (person) is deceiving me with words.

Ṭhạr. } There, on the spot.
Ṭhor. }

Ṭhạrregeṅ gurkedea. I knocked him over on the spot.

Ṭhorregeṅ dohokedea. I kept him on the spot.

Thara. } A brass plate used to eat
Thạri. } from.

Ṭhaṛaḱ ṭhuṛuk. Imitative of the sound produced by two persons pounding in the same ukhuṛ (q. v.)

Ṭhaṛak ṭhuṛukkin huṛuṅeda.

Tharam thurum. To totter, to walk unsteadily as an old person or one walking on a rough road in the dark.

Tharam thurume calakkana He walks unsteadily.

Tharam thurumenae. He is tottering.

Tharam thurumle heċena. We came stumbling (in the dark.)

Ṭhaṛaṅ ṭhuṛuṅ. To sound in succession as two bells of different tones (imitative.)

Hạthi ghạnṭi ṭhaṛaṅ ṭhuṛuṅ saḍekana. The elephant's bells sound ṭhaṛaṅ ṭhuṛuṅ.

Thara thạr. In rows, in lines.

Thara thạrko calakkana. They are walking in line.

Tharat́ thorot́. Limping, hobbling through fatigue or sore feet.

Laṅgaenako tharat́ thorot́. They are tired and limping.

Unkin tayom tharat́ thorot́e sen idiena. He hobbled after them.

Tharbasao. } To wonder, to be as-
Tharbhasao. } tonished, to be amazed, to be terror struck.

Kul ńelte tharbasao got́enae. He was terror struck through seeing the tiger.

Thare mare. To push to the front, without orders.

Thare mare jojom lạgidokkanae. He is beginning to eat before he is fully served.

Hoṛo irok bam ạculedea, actege thare mare irokkanae. You did not hire him to reap dhan, he is reaping without orders.

Ṭhare ṭhore. Ambiguously, equivocally, hintingly.

Ṭhare ṭhorekin lạpạiena. They conversed together hintingly.

Thare thar. In lines, in rows.

Thare tharko teṅgoakana. They are standing in rows.

Thari. A brass plate. Cf. thara.

Tharṛao. To be tired, to be fatigued. Cf. thorṛao.

Tharsat́ thorsot́. Slowly, slowly and feeling the way with the feet as one walking in the dark.

Tharsat́ thorsot́ [illegible] kanae. He is shuffling and feeling the way with his feet.

Thar thar. To shake, to tremble, to start.

Thartbargeṅ ṣikṣueda. I feel myself trembling.

Reṅgeċte thartharo aṭkareda. He feels a trembling through hunger.

Thartharao. To shake, to tremble, to start.

Botorte thartharaokkanae. He is trembling through fear.

Thartharao. To be eager, to be intent on, to be desirous, to have a longing for, to be very anxious about. Cf. thurthuṛau.

Ṭhas. } Applied to the sound
Ṭhas ṭhas. } produced by anything brittle, as glass, &c, breaking, to snap or crack as anything brittle.

Ṭhas ṭhas rapudokkana. It is breaking with a series of snaps.

Ṭhas marte. } With a snap or crack,
Ṭhas mente. } with ease, easily.

Ṭhas marte rạput́ got́ena. It broke with a snap.

Ṭhasaha. Brittle, easily broken.

Kão ṭhasahagea. Glass is brittle.

Ṭhasak. } To move, to cause to stir, to
Ṭasak. } affect, to overcome.

Baṅ ṭhasak daṛeaka. I cannot move it.

Noa daka ohoṅ ṭhasak daṛelea. I cannot overcome all this boiled rice, I cannot consume all this boiled rice.

Ṭhasao. To do for, used in threats.

Kacahạrire idikatele ṭhasaomea. We will take you to the court and do for you.

Thasao. To mix by kneading, to press clay into a crack of a wall, floor, &c.

Khapra hasako thasaoeda. They are mixing by kneading (by hands or feet) clay to make tiles with.

Ṭhasiạu. To overcome, to conquer, to defeat, to vanquish, to over match, to over power, to rout, to master.

Nui hoṛiń ṭhạsiạuakadea. I have defeated this man.

Kạmiteń ṭhạsiạuakadea. I have defeated him in working.

Jom ṭhạsiạu ocokedeań. I gave him so much that he could not eat it all.

Ṭhaskao. To move, to cause to stir, to shake.

Bań ṭhaskaoḱkana. It is not stirring.

Thasṛao. To fall down, to throw down, to throw oneself down.

Dakae thasṛaokeda. He threw down the cooked rice.

Gidrạe thasṛaokedea. She threw the child down (when she herself slipped.)

Ṭhaṭarbaj.
Ṭhaṭharbaj. } Boastful.

Ṭhaṭarbaj hoṛ kanae. He is a boastful fellow.

Ṭhāṭ. Barren, childless.

Ṭhaṭgeae. She is barren, or children all dead.

Ṭhạṭbond. To adorn, to beautify, grand.

Khubko ṭhaṭbondakaṭa. They have made it very grand.

Bes ṭhạṭbond horoḱkateye heǹakana. He has come grandly clothed.

Ṭhaṭe.
Ṭhaṭhe. } To hit, to strike.

Ṭhaṭekedeako. They hit him.

Ạdiye mocaana, ma ṭhaṭheẽpe. He is too glib, hit him.

Ṭhaṭera. A brazier, a caste who manufacture and sell brass ware.

Ṭhaṭha. To make fun, to make sport, to joke, to jest.

Ṭhaṭhaedińkanae. He is making fun of me.

Noa do ṭhaṭha katha do bań kana. This is not a matter of jest, this matter is not a jest.

Ṭhaṭhao. To spend time, to remain, to live.

Noa atore besko ṭhaṭhaoakaṭa. They have enjoyed good health in this village.

Ḍher bochore ṭhaṭhaoakaṭa. He has lived many years.

Noa atore bako ṭhaṭhao daṛeada. They could not remain in this village, (not having good health.)

Okoeko tahena, onkoko ṭhaṭhaoa, ar okoe bako tahen daṛeaḱa, onko bako ṭhaṭhao daṛeaḱa.

Ṭhāṭhāo. Cf. ṭhāo.

Ṭhāṭhāokanae. He is making room, he is making or clearing a place.

Ṭhaṭhar. Cf. ṭhar.

Ṭhaṭori. A worker in brass, a goldsmith.

Ṭhaṭra. A kind of bamboo mat.

Ṭhaṭra. M.
Ṭhaṭri. F. } Emaciated.

Ṭhaṭragea ḍaṅra do. The bullock is emaciated.

Ṭhaṭra ṭhaṭri. Emaciated.

Ṭhaṭra ṭhaṭri cabaenako merom do. The goats are completely emaciated, or the goats are all emaciated.

Thaṭ thoṭ. Stammeringly, indistinctly.

Thaṭ thoṭe roṛeda. He speaks stammeringly.

That thot. Stammeringly, falteringly, to stammer, to falter in speech, to mumble.

That thote roṛeda. He speaks falteringly.

That thotenae. He is stammering.

Ṭhạukạ. The whole piece, as opposed to a part, total, a large quantity.

Ṭhạukạkaṭale. We have totalled it.

Ṭhạukạ hataokhan ńel ńamoḱa. If a whole piece, or a large quantity, is taken it can be seen.

Ṭhạurạ. To assemble, to gather together, to crowd together.

Boloḱa mente duạr ṭhenko ṭhạurạakana. They are assembled at the door for the purpose of entering.

Thạwi. To reside, to lodge, to be in residence, to abide.

Nonḍele thạwiakana. We are residing here.

Ṭheć. Place, the sign of the Dative case.

Iń ṭheć menaḱa. It is with me, I have it.

Uni ṭheć khon hataome. Take it from him.

Pe ṭheć tolpe. Tie it in three places.

Miṭ ṭhećko jaoraakana. They are assembled in one place, they are assembled together.

Barpe ṭhećiń ńeleḱkoa. I saw them in two or three places.

Ṭheć ṭheć. Imitative of the sound produced by breaking stones with a hammer.

Ṭheć ṭheće koṭećḱkana. He is breaking stones and producing a sound resembling ṭheć ṭheć.

Ṭhegan.
Ṭeghan. } A prop, a catch, something put against another to keep it in place, or open, as a door. Cf ṭaghen.

Thegṛao. To strike with the heel of the fist, a wristlet, &c., to strike with a stick.

Thegṛaokedeae. He hit him with the heel of his fist.

Ṭhek. Hindrance, obstacle, impediment.
Cet ooh ṭhek lagaoena, onate bae hedlena. Some hindrance has occurred, for that reason he has not come.
Dhirire ṭhek lagaoena gaḍi do. The cart has met with an obstacle in the stone, the cart is impeded by having come into contact with a stone.

Ṭhek. A prop, to prop, to shore.
Ṭhekko lagaoakaṭa. They have put in a prop.

Ṭhek. A storehouse for grain.

Ṭheka. A large bamboo basket.

Ṭhekan. } To find out, to trace, to detect,
Ṭhikaṇ. } to place, to fix, to settle, to ascertain.
Aurile ṭhekana. We have not yet fixed (the date, place, &c.)
Ṭhekanadińae phalna din hijuk̔me. He fixed a date for me to come.
Tehen̔ do ṭhekan din kana. To-day is the day fixed.
Be-ṭhekan. At random, without previous arrangement.

Ṭhekao. To push into a fire, as firewood.
Sahan ṭhekaoak̔me. Push firewood into the fire.
Sahane ṭhekaokeda. He pushed firewood into the fire.

Ṭhekao. To begin, to engage in.
Sek̔reńe ṭhekaoena. He began to sing.
Sek̔reń iń ṭhekaokedea. I made him begin to sing.

Ṭheke ṭheke. Close to each other.
Ṭheke ṭhekeko oṛak̔kaṭa. They have built their houses close to each other.

Ṭhekom. To stick, to adhere, united, close or crowded together.
Ṭhekom ṭhekom joakana. It is covered with fruit.
Ṭhali ṭhekomenae. He sank and stuck (in the quicksand.)
Dal ṭhekomkedeae. He struck him and fixed him to the place, made him unable to leave the place, disabled him.

Ṭhekra. A wooden bell tied to the neck of a cow or bullock. Cf. ṭoṭko.

Ṭhekro potam. } The little Brown Dove
Ṭhikri potam. } *Turtur Cambayensis*. Cf. potam.

Ṭhel. A silver ornament worn on the wrist, or upper arm.
Horogińpe baba sopore rupa ṭhel do.

Ṭhela. To push, to shove.
Eṭak̔ hoṛko dań ṭhelaakoa. They throw suspicion, or blame, on other people.

Ṭhela. To become callous or hardened.
Gok̔ gok̔te taren ṭhelaakantaea. His shoulder has become callous by continually carrying on it.

Ṭhela gaḍi. A carriage pushed by men, a perambulator.

Ṭhela jal. A fish net fixed on a handle and worked by being pushed through the water.

Ṭhela ṭhili. To push or shove, as in a crowd, crowded.
Ṭhela ṭhilikateń boloena. I pushed this one and that one and entered (into the crowd.)

Ṭhelao. To push, to shove, to put back, as a date.
Ṭhelao gurkedeae. He pushed him and made him fall, he pushed him down.
Ṭheńgateye ṭhelao ńurkeda. He pushed it down with a stick.
Baplako ṭhelao ńok̔keda. They put back the marriage a few days.
Baplako ṭhelao lahakeda. They put back the date of the marriage.

Ṭhelepaese. To push, to shove, to elbow, as one's way in a crowd.
Ṭhelepaeseye boloena. He elbowed his way in (to the crowd.)
Uni joṭede lagiṭko ṭhelepaesek̔kan tahẽkana. They were pushing their way into the crowd to touch him.

Ṭhele ṭhele. Ample, more than sufficient, as food.

Ṭhema. To stick in, as a knife, &c. in the belt.
Churiye ṭhemakeda. He stuck a knife in his belt.
Cun thamakhure emadea, ona doe ṭhemakeṭa. He gave him lime and tobacco, he stuck it in (his waist cloth.)

Ṭhemka. M. } Small, short in stature.
Ṭhimki. F. }
Ṭhemka hoṛ. A short man.
Ṭhimki ạimạị. A short woman.

Ṭhemsok̔. Short in stature, applied to females.
Ṭhemsok̔geae. She is short in stature.

Ṭhen. Place, sign of the Dative case.
Iń ṭhen menak̔a. It is with me, I have it.
Mit̔ ṭhenren hoṛko. People of the same place.
Amṭhen khonią́ hataoa. I will take it from you.
Ac̔ ṭhen menak̔. He has it himself.
Ac̔ ṭhene dohokeda. He kept it.
Phalna ṭhen menak̔a. A certain person has it.
Uniak̔ oṛak̔ ṭhen menak̔a. It is near his house.

Ṭheń. } Imitative of a sound of
Ṭheń ṭheń. } clanging or clinking.
Ṭheń ṭheń sadekana. It is clinking.

Ṭheń marte. } With a clang or clink.
Ṭheń mente. }
Ṭheń mente sade goṭena. It sounded with a clink.

Ţheṅga. A staff, a club, a cudgel, a blow with a staff or cudgel.
Mutạk ţheṅga. A club, a bludgeon.
Ţheṅga bạnduk. A combined staff and gun.
Bar pe ţheṅgae dalkedea. He struck him two or three blows with a staff.

Ţhenţa. / **Ţhenţha.** / **Ţenţha.** Worn small as an implement with use, mischievous, disrespectful, as a child to a grown up person. Cf. ţenţha.
Ţhenţa nahel. A plough worn small.
Ţhenţha kuḍi. A kudali worn small.

Ţhep. To put the thumb under anything and send it off with force, as when playing at marbles, to knuckle, as when playing at marbles.
Ţakako ţhep aţkara. They put a rupee on the thumb and send it off with force to test it by causing it to ring.

Ţhepca. M. / **Ţhipci. F.** Small, short of stature.

Ţhepe. / **Ţhepe ţhepe.** To shake the ears or head, to wag the tail.
Luturko ţhepea. They shake the ears.
Canḍbolko ţhepe ţhepea. They wag their tails.

Ţhepelao. The reciprocal form of ţhelao (q. v.)

Ţhepo. To defy, to shew the thumb as a sign of defiance.
Ţhepo udukadiṅae. He shewed me his thumb, he defied me.
Ţhepokedam. You defied, you shewed your thumb.

Ţhepo. Short, as a measure.
Ţhepo pailạteye emadiṅa. He measured it to me in a short measure.

Ţher. To brag, to bluster, to talk big, to contradict, to be antagonistic, to be recalcitrant.
Ạḍim ţherkana pạhil dhaoem jitạuente. You are bragging greatly because you won the first time.
Ţher do oeć hõ bae ţher baṛaleda, hapeṛeye tahẽena. He was not in the least recalcitrant, he remained mute.

Ţher. / **Ţherţher.** / **Ţherţherao.** To peal, as thunder, to boom.
Bijli do ţherţher saḍeḱkane aṅjomkeda. He heard the lightning (thunder) pealing.
Ceţer ṅurena ţherţher. The thunder bolt fell pealing.
Ceţer ţherţherao ṅurena. The thunder bolt fell, peal on peal.
Rimil do ţherţher saḍeena. The thunder pealed.

Ţher marte. / **Ţher mente.** With a peal.

Ţhĕṛboḱ. / **Ţhŏṛboḱ.** Stunted, dwarfish, little.

Therethepe. Thicker or closer than usual.
Therethepe hoṛoko rohoeakaťa. They have planted the dhan closer than is usual.
Hoṛeĉko'era therethepe. They sow hoṛeć (q. v.) very thickly.

Ţheṛeţhepe. To shake, as the ears; to wag, as the tail.
Canḍbole ţheṛeţhepeeť tahẽkana. He was wagging his tail.

Ţhes. / **Ţhes ţhes.** Applied to a sound of snapping or clicking.
Ţhes ţhes saḍekana. It is clicking.

Ţhes marte. / **Ţhes mente.** With a snap, with a click.
Ţhes marte saḍe goťena. It sounded click.

Ţhẽs. / **Ţhẽs ţhẽs.** Imitative of the sound produced when breathing is effected with difficulty, to wheeze.
Ţhẽs ţhẽse sahećeda. When breathing he produces a sound resembling ţhẽs ţhẽs.

Ţhẽs marte. / **Ţhẽs mente.** With a wheeze.
Ţhẽs marteye saheťkeda. He breathed with a wheeze.

Ţhesa. A guard to prevent a ring or other ornament coming off.

Ţhesa. To shore, to prop, to support by a post or buttress.
Ţhesa daramakaťako. They have propped it up.
Rapudoḱkante ţhesakedako. They propped it because it is breaking.
Bạnduk ţhesa. A prop for a long gun.

Ţhesa ţhes. Close together, touching each other.
Duṛuṗakanako ţhesa ţhes. They are sitting close together.
Ţhesa ţhes oṛaḱko benaoakaťa. They have built the houses touching each other.

Ţhesao. To put close, to cause to reach or be close to.
Bhitre ţhesaokam. Put it against the wall.
Baṛakar hạbiĉko dal ţhesaokeťkoa. They beat them and drove them up to the Barakar (river.)

Ţhesra. M. / **Ţhisri. F.** One-eyed, blind of one eye, one eye imperfect, having imperfect vision, squint-eyed.

Ţheţha. Worn small by use.

Thetha. } To ask a question a second
Tetha. } time or repeatedly, perverse, cross.

Ma thethaem. Question him again.
Kuli thethaem. Question him over again.

Ṭheṭham. Obstinate, heady, cantankerous.

Thethmet. } Again and again.
Uṭi uṭi. }

Thethmete kulieťkos. He is questioning them again and again.

Thethoṛ. } Obstinate, heady, rude.
Tethoṛ. }

Thethoṛ hoṛ kanae. He is an obstinate man.

Thethṛamu. } Obstinate, cantankerous,
Thethramu. } pig-headed.

Thethramu hoṛ kanae. He is a cantankerous fellow.

Ṭhik. Exact, right, correct, accurate.

Bes ṭhik. Exactly right.
Ṭhikgem roṛkeda. You spoke correctly.
Ṭhik goťkam. Put it right.
Bań ṭhika. It is not correct.
Ṭhikte baṛe roṛme. Speak correctly, speak accurately.

Ṭhikạ. Lease, contract.

Ṭhikạteń hataoakaťa. I have taken it on contract.
Ṭhikạtele kạmikana. We are working by contract, or by piece work.
Noa atoń ṭhikạakaťa. I have taken a lease of this village.
Ṭhikạteń emaťkoa. I gave it to them on contract, or on lease.

Ṭhikạdar. A contractor, a lessee.

Ṭhikạn. To find out, to trace, to detect, to place, to fix, to settle, to ascertain. Cf. ṭhekan.

Ṭhikạri. Sunshine.

Ṭhikạrireye duṛuṗakana. He is sitting in the sunshine.

Ṭhikạri. A ring worn on the fingers or toes.

Ṭhikedar. A contractor, a lessee.

Ṭhikrạ ṭhikri. Resilient, rebounding.

Jom ṭhikrạ ṭhikrienako. They have eaten to satiety.

Ṭhikrạu. To fly back by force of impact, to rebound.

Jom ṭhikrạuenako. They have eaten to satiety.

Ṭhikri. Small, a short woman, a female dwarf.

Ṭhikri potam. The little brown dove, *Turtur Cambayensis.*

Ṭhik ṭhak. Right, correct, exact, accurate, to make right, correct, exact, accurate.

Jotoaǩe ṭhikṭhakkeda. He made all things right.

Ṭhili. A small earthenware water pot.

Ṭhili daǩ. A girl about 7 or 8 years of age who can carry a ṭhili of water on her head.

Ṭhili. } A small earthenware
Kărwas ṭhili. } vessel in which a little dhan is placed and sent with a bride to her new home. The pot is ornamented with figures drawn in white.

Ṭhimki. F. } Small, short in stature,
Ṭhemka. M. } applied to females. Cf. ṭhemka.

Ṭhimki ṭimạṭi. A small woman.

Ṭhiń. } Imitative of the sound of
Ṭhiń ṭhiń. } ringing as when an anvil or iron is struck with a hammer.

Ṭhiń marte. } With a ring, or ringing
Ṭhiń mente. } sound. Cf. ṭhiń.

Ṭhiń marte saḍeǒna. It sounded with a ring.

Ṭhiń ṭhoṗ. Imitative of the sound produced when iron, &c., is being struck alternately by a light and heavy hammer.

Ṭhiń ṭhoṗ, ṭhiń ṭhoṗko piṭạueda. They are hammering and producing a sound resembling ṭhiń ṭhoṗ, ṭhiń ṭhoṗ.

Ṭhińgi mať. A species of solid bamboo with very short spaces between the nodes.

Ṭhipci. F. } Small, short of stature.
Ṭhepca. M. }

Ṭhipi. A cork, a stopper, anything used to stop a bottle, &c.

Ṭhipiteť lagaoaǩme. Put in the stopper.

Ṭhir. To cease, to stop, to become quiet or still.

Ṭhir hataṛ. To cease for the present, to cease in the meantime.
Ṭhiroǩme. Cease, be quiet.
Teńgo ṭhirenae. He stood still.
Ṭhir hapeǒnae. He became quiet, ceased speaking.

Ṭhiṛiń. } Imitative of the sound
Ṭhiṛiń ṭhiṛiń. } produced by light
Ṭiṛiń. } cymbals, or the tinkl-
Ṭiṛiń ṭiṛiń. } ing of a small bell.

Ghạnṭi ṭhiṛiń ṭhiṛiń saḍekana. The bell tinkles.

Ṭhiṛiń marte. } With a tinkle.
Ṭhiṛiń mente. }

Thirsoť thorsoť. } Slowly, feeling with
Tirsoť torsoť. } the feet, as when walking in the dark, shuffling.
Thirsoť thorsoťe taṛameda. He walks shufflingly.

Ṭhirṭhiṛau. } To shake, to tremble.
Ṭhurṭhuṛau. }
Rebańte ṭhirṭhiṛauǩkanae. He is shaking or shivering with cold.

Ṭhisi. } The Linseed plant, *Linum*
Ṭhisiạ. } *usitatissima*, *Linn.*, and its products.
Ṭhisiạ holoń. Linseed meal.
Ṭhisiạ sunum. Linseed oil.
Ṭhisiạ kaṛe. Linseed oil cake.

Ṭhisi. A guard to prevent a ring or other ornament coming off.

Ṭhisri. F. } One-eyed, blind of one eye,
Ṭhesri F. } having defective vision, squint-eyed. Cf. ṭisri.

Thit. Security for a loan.
Disomko thitaťkoa. They gave the country to them as security for a loan.
Thit mal. Domestic animals given as security for a loan.
Thitko udukaťkoa. They shewed them the security for the loan.

Ṭhiṭṛãǩ. The calf of the leg, the leg between the calf and the heel, the shin.

Tho. To spit, to expectorate, spittle.
Thoadeae. He spat on him.

Tho. An emphatic particle.
Hẽ tho. Yes certainly, just so.
Khange tho. Just then, at that precise time.
Onatege tho. Just on that account.
Calaǩme tho raj ṭheć. Go then to the king.
Amge thom baṛiclaǩa. It was yourself who did the injury.

Thobla. } A cluster, in clusters.
Thobla thobla. }
Thobla thobla joakana. It has fruited in clusters.
Miť thobla. One cluster.

Ṭhoć. To cause the joints to crack, mainly the finger joints, to crack between the thumb nails.
Kaṭupko ṭhoja. They crack the finger joints.
Ṭhoć cabakedale. We have cracked all, i. e. we have eaten up all.

Ṭhoć. A common plant, *Physalis minima. L.*

Ṭhoć. A children's game.

Ṭhoe. } Ringing sound produced
Ṭhoe ṭhoe. } by striking a hollow object.
Ṭhoe ṭhoe saḍekana. It rings.

Ṭhoe marte. } With a ring.
Ṭhoe mente. }
Ṭhoe marte saḍeċna. It sounded with a ring.

Ṭhoekoǩ. } Lean, emaciated, past child
Ṭhoekoť. } bearing.
Nui ṭhoekoť mara ṣimạı. This lean harridan.

Ṭhoeraǩ. Hollow-eyed.
Nui 'ṭhoeraǩ mara buḍhi. This hollow-eyed old scrub.

Ṭhoeraǩ. } A hollow, a hole
Ṭhoeraǩ ṭhoeraǩ. } or small cave.
Ṭhoeraǩ ṭhoeraǩ oyońpe. Look into every hollow or hole.

Ṭhohor. To recognize, to know, to take note of, to consider. Cf. ṭohor.

Ṭhok. } To deceive, to swindle, to opp-
Ṭhag. } ose. to strive with.
Aḍi ṭhok hoṛ kanae. He is a great swindler.

Thok. } Community, sect, band, comp-
Thuk. } any, heap, file, division, party.
Thok thokko dohoakaťa. They have placed it in heaps.
Nagraha renko doko bar thokena. The people of the city became two parties, espoused two different sides.

Ṭhoǩ. } Imitative of the sound
Ṭhoǩ ṭhoǩ. } produced when anything hard is struck, to ring.
Ṭhoǩ ṭhoǩjańreye dalkedea. He struck him on the bones and produced a sound resembling ṭhoǩ ṭhoǩ.
Ṭhoǩ ṭhoǩ saḍekana. It sounds ṭhoǩ ṭhoǩ.

Ṭhoǩ marte. } With a thud, or knock-
Ṭhoǩ mente. } ing or hammerimg sound.
Ṭhoǩ marte saḍe goťena. It sounded ṭhoǩ.

Ṭhokao. To hammer, to hammer in, as a nail.
Tạmbu khunṭi ṭhokaope. Hammer, or drive, in the tent pegs.

Thoke thok. In heaps, in bands, &c. Cf. thok.
Thoke thokko dohoakaťa. They have placed it in heaps.

Ṭhokiã bajiã. To tap and cause to sound,
Ṭhokiã bajiãkate bhajana bachao oḍokkeda. Having tapped and caused the earthen pots to sound he chose out (a sound one.)

Thokoboko. } Dirty, as with mud,
Thoroboko. } blood, &c., &c., adhering to the person. Scottice, *slaistered.*

Thokoboko losoť laṭkaoakawadea.

Thokor bokor. Dirty, as with soft clay, mud, blood, &c., adhering to the person.

Ṭhokrao. To upbraid, to twit, to threaten, to bring up an old matter.

Baṅ em daṛeaekanteye ṭhokraoediṅkana. Owing to my not being able to pay him he is upbraiding me.

Thokṛe. } To adhere to, to stick to, as
Tokṛe. } clay to the feet.

Jaṅgare losoť thokṛeakana. Mud is sticking to his feet.

Thok thak. In heaps, in bands. Cf. thok.

Thol. Place, abode, to abide, to repose.

Aboǩ reaǩ thol bae ṅamleťte Nuh ṭhene ruaṛ heďena. As it did not find a place on which to alight it came back to Noah.

Tahen reaǩ thol bạnuǩtaea. He has no place to stay in.

Unạǩe arjaoeťrebõ tholge bạnuǩtaea Although he reaps such good crops he is never at rest, or is always in search of some thing which he needs.

Unirege tholoǩa. It will remain or abide on him.

Ṭhol ṭhol. } To roll about in globules
Ṭhol ṭholao. } as mercury or quicksilver; having the property of always resolving itself into globules as quicksilver. Cf. ṭhal ṭhal.

Ṭhomsoǩ. } Short in stature, squat,
Ṭhemsoǩ. } applied to females

Thom thoroǩ. Bull-necked, corpulent.

Ṭhona ṭhuni. To dispute, to be at variance, to be at loggerheads.

Ṭhona ṭhunienaliṅ uniteliṅ. He and I are at variance.

Jomi bisoero ṭhona ṭhuniakanakin. They are at variance with each other about land.

Ṭhoṅga. A piece of hollow bamboo put to various uses.

Laṭha ṭhoṅga. A piece of hollow bamboo in which birdlime is kept.

Sunum ṭhoṅga. A piece of hollow bamboo in which oil is kept.

Ṭhonk. } Solicitude, yearnig, longing,
Ṭok. } force of habit, or affection.

Hopon maya nun maraṅ ṭhonkteť.

Ṭhonkao. } To do enthusiastically, with
Ṭhankao. } heart and soul, to warm up. Cf. ṭhankao.

Ṭhonko. Dry.

Bes ṭhonko jaegarebon duṛupa. We will sit on a good dry place.

Onte do odagea, nonḍe bes ṭhonkogea. It is damp over there, here it is nice and dry.

Ṭhonok. Ornate, elegant, gorgeous, splendid, resplendent, beautiful, magnificent, glorious, glory, splendour, magnificence.

Bes ṭhonokko banaoakaťa. They have made it very beautiful.

Ṭhonṭa. } The bill or beak of a bird.
Ṭhonṭha. }

Datrom ṭhonṭa. The sharp point of a sickle.

Kuṭis ṭhonṭha lekan katha menaǩtiṅa. I have a statement like the beak of the Kuṭis bird, i. e. very short.

Ṭhonṭaṛatiṅ. Here and there. Cf. ṭhanṭaṛatiṅ.

Ṭhonṭha. Cf. ṭhonṭa.

Ṭhoṗ. A drop.

Miť ṭhoṗ daǩ. One drop of water.

Ṭhoṗ ṭhoṗ joroǩkana. It is dripping.

Ṭhoṗ ṭhoṗ. Sound of rapping or tapping, to rap, to tap. Cf. ḍhoṗ ḍhoṗ.

Ṭhoṗ ṭheṗpe ado jhiďapea. Tap and it shall be opened unto you.

Thopa. } A cluster, bunch, in
Thopa thopa. } clusters, in bunches.

Ti thopa. The hand and fingers.

Jaṅga thopa. The foot with the toes.

Kul thopa. The foot and toes of a tiger.

Thopnaǩ. The hand from the wrist, branched, as a tree.

Thopnaǩreye dalkedea. He hit him on the hand.

Ṭhopoṅ. } Exhausted through
Ṭhopoṅ ṭhopoṅ. } fatigue, hunger and thirst.

Ṭhopoṅ ṭhopoṅe heďena. He arrived exhausted.

Ayur ṭhopoṅedekana. He is tiring him by leading him on.

Ṭhopoṅ ṭhopoṅtege menaea. He is exhausted.

Ṭhopor. } Applied to the sound
Ṭhopor ṭhopoṙ. } produced by light objects coming into contact with each other, a light tapping or rustling sound. Cf. ṭhapar.

Ṭhopor marte. } With a tap or rustle.
Ṭhopor mente. }

Thopram. To plaister, to smear.

Hasako thopramakawada. They have plaistered it with mud.

Ranko thopramakoa. They plaister medicine on them.

Thopro. To assemble, to collect together.
Mit ṭhečko thoproakana. They are assembled together.
Ghaore roko thoproka. Flies collect on a wound.
Disom hoṛe thopro ocoketkoa. He assembled the country people together.
Jāhārege māṛi tāhena, ondege gidi hōko thoproka. Where the carcase is there will the eagles be gathered together.

Thopro bir. A scrub jungle, a jungle in which there are no large trees.

Thor. An emphatic particle.
Ape hō onka jompe thor iń lekape moṭaka. You also eat thus and you will become fat like me.
Iń hō thor amren hopon. I also am your son.

Ṭhor. }
Ṭhaṛ. } There, on the spot. Cf. ṭhaṛ.
Ṭhaṛregeń gurkedea. I knocked him over on the spot.

Thoṛa. }
Thoṛa thoṛa. } A little.
Thoṛa thoṛate jompe. Eat a little at a time.
Alom thoṛaea. Do not scrimp him.

Thoṛa thuṛi. A little.
Thoṛa thuṛile emama. We will give you a little.

Thoṛa bahut. }
Thoṛa bohut. } A little.
Thoṛa bohutko emadińa. They gave me a little.

Ṭhōṛbok. M. }
Ṭhēṛbok. F. } Stunted, dwarfish, little.

Ṭhōṛē. }
Ṭhōṛē jań. } The ankle bone, shinbone, elbow bone.
Moka ṭhōṛē. The elbow bone or joint, the cubit bone.

Thorio. Feeble.
Haṛam thorioenae. He is old and feeble.

Thoroboko. Dirty, as with soft clay mud, blood, &c., adhering to the person.
Thoroboko losot laṭkaoakawadea.

Thoroń thopoń. Dirty, as hands and face with eating.
Nui gidrạ do thoroń thopońgese ạbukkaeme. This child's hands and face are dirty with eating, wash him.
Thoroń thopońakanae, ạbukkaeme. His hands and face are dirty with eating, wash him.

Thoro thopo. Stunted, as trees and field crops.
Thorothopoge darelena, dak bah ńamlette. Not getting sufficient water it grew stunted.

Thorothopo. Roughly, as plaster; to plaster with mud or clay the first time which is done roughly, to plaister.
Pạhil dole thorothopokakkana. We are giving it the first rough coat of plaster.
Jāhālekako thorothopoakata. They have put on the first coat of plaster anyway.
Losotteye thorothopoakana. He is plaistered with mud.
Mayamte thorothopoakanae. He is plaistered with blood.

Thoro thoto. Imitative of a tooting sound.
Thoro thotoko oroheda. They are tooting (on a horn.)

Thorot thorot. To limp, to walk feebly, as from fatigue or age; noise produced by old and battered shoes.
Dāṛā dāṛāte thorot thorotenae. He is limping with much travelling.

Thorṛao. }
Tharṛao. } To be tired, to be fatigued.
Roṛ roṛteń thorṛaoena, bae añjoma, cekaeań? I am tired speaking to him, he will not obey, what can I do to him?

Ṭhos. Cheap.
Netar matkom do ṭhosgea. Just now the matkom (q. v.) is cheap.
Hoṛoko enlekhan caole ṭhosoka. When they thresh the dhan rice will be cheap.
Unre caole khub ṭhosge tahēkana. At that time rice was very cheap.

Ṭhosgar. }
Ṭhoskor. } Cf. ṭhosok.

Ṭhosok. Splendour, grandeur, glory. Cf. ṭhonok.
Ṭhosok kiṛiċan te. Gorgeously apparelled.
Bes ṭhosok oṛak benaoakata. He has built a very grand house.
Ṭhosok ṭhosok ńelok kana. It looks very grand.

Thosot morgot. Fusionless and slovenly, deficient in stamina and slovenly, pithless and slovenly.
Thosot morgotgeae. He is pithless and slovenly

Thotha. }
Totha. } An arrow without a point.

Thotha. }
Totha. }
Thothea. } Having a defect in speech, slow of speech.

Ṭhoṭheo. Hollowed out to a shell, only the shell remaining.
Cele coń terelko jom ṭhoṭheoakat. Something has eaten and hollowed out the terel (q. v.) fruit to a shell.

Thothiạ. Having a defect in speech, slow and halting in speech.

Ṭhoṭhkao. To peck, as a bird.

Thothma. }
Thuthmạ. } M. }
Thuthmi. F. } Very fat and dumpy.

Thotho. Very, applied to obesity; unintelligent, witless, dull-witted.
Thothoe moṭaakana. He is very fat.

Ṭhoṭho. To plough.
Okoe nonḍeko ṭhoṭhokeda? Who ploughed here?

Ṭhõṭhõ. } Said to bullocks when they
Ṭhõgur. } are required to turn where they stand.

Thotho motho. To hurry, to rush through, as work.
Iñ do thotho motho goẽenañ. I hurried.

Thothomthorok̕. Very, extremely, applied to obesity.

Thothot̕. } Applied to urinous smells
Tothot̕. } generally.
Thothot̕ge sokana.

Thothot̕. Speechless, without anything to say as one convicted.
Thethot̕enae. He is speechless.

Thothṛa. M. } Having a defect in
Thuthṛi. F. } speech, slow of speech.
Thothṛageae ṛui hoṛ do. This man has a defect in his speech.

Ṭhoṭkao. } To touch with the point of
Ṭhoṭrao. } anything, to employ the point of anything to remove, extract, &c.
Kaṭupteye ṭhoṭkaokediña. He tapped or touched me with the point of his finger.
Ere cẽrẽ darereko ṭhoṭkaoa. Woodpeckers tap on the trees (with their beaks.)
Sim bhukuko ṭhoṭkao jomkoa. Fowls remove the earth from above the white ants with their bills and eat them.

Thotna. Snout, mouth.
Thotnare thapayem aḍiye roṛa. Slap him on the snout, he speaks a great deal.

Thoto thoro. Imitative of a tooting sound. Cf. thoro thoto.

Thotṛa. M. } Having a defect in speech,
Thutṛi. F. } slow of speech.
Ṭhoṭrao. Cf. ṭhoṭkao.

Thoya. An emphatic particle. Cf. tho.
Do thoya pharakte idikate ñapamkinpe. Take them to a distance and confront them with each other.

Ṭhoyo. Hollowed out to a shell.
Jom ṭhoyoakat̕ako. They have eaten it into a shell, have eaten all the inside of the fruit and left only a shell.
Ṭhoyo mara buḍhi. A hollow hag.

Ṭhoyot̕ ṭhoyot̕. Imitative of the sound produced by an old or tired person shuffling along.
Ṭhoyot̕ ṭhoyot̕ko calak̕kana. They go shuffling along.

Ṭhu. To shoot with a gun, to cause a cracking sound, to cause a report, sound produced by anything bursting or exploding, used also by women when scolding.
Ṭhu goć kedeañ. I shot him (and) killed him, I shot him dead.
Meṭ ṭhuk̕tama, Your eye will burst (and produce a sound when doing so.)

Ṭhube. } In a cluster, in clusters,
Ṭhube ṭhube. } close or crowded together.
Jo ṭhubeakana. It has fruited in clusters.
Ṭhube ṭhube joakana. The fruit is in clusters or crowded together.
Tol ṭhubeakat̕ako bah raṛa godok̕a. They have knotted it many times, (made a cluster of knots) it will not easily untie.

Thubṛe. To adhere or stick to, as clay to boots, or grass, weeds, &c. to plough.
Nahelre thubṛeõntama, ocok̕kam. Your plough is clogged, remove it.

Thugul. } Applied to chopping
Thugul thugul. } with a blunt instrument, a dull thudding sound.
Jañ thugul thugule samak̕eda.

Thugul marte. } With a dull thud.
Thugul mente. }
Thugul marteye uyuk̕keda. He hit one blow with a blunt chopping instrument, but did not cut through.
Thugul marteye samak̕keda. He hit it with a dull thud.

Ṭhuiak̕. A cocoon of the Tassar silk worm with one end cut off.

Ṭhuiak̕ arak̕. A wild plant used as a pot-herb, *Melochia corchorifolia, Linn.*

Ṭhuk̕. To knock against, applied mainly to the head.
Ṭhuk̕enañ. I have bumped my head (door being too low.)
Ṭhapa ṭhuk̕. To strike or bump against each other.

Thukau. } To be resolute, to be
Dil ṭhukau. } determined, to brace up the spirits, brace up one's loins, to nerve oneself.
Dil ṭhukaukateye calaoena. He braced up his spirits and went.

Thukiã bajiã. Cf. ṭhokea bajiã.

Thukit. To be tired, to be weary, to be perplexed.

Thukṛa thukṛi. Imitative of the sound produced by knocking against several objects in succession.
Thukṛa thukṛi ńam baṛaeťkanae. He is searching for it and knocking against things.

Thukṛau. To knock against, to come in contact with, to push with the head, foot, &c., to grope with the feet in the dark.
Cele coe thukṛaukediña. Some living thing or other knocked against me.

Ṭhukṛau. } Ṭhokrao. } To upbraid, to twit, to threaten, to bring up an old matter. Cf. ṭhokrao.

Thukṛi. To touch, to nudge, to slightly touch one as a hint.
Thukṛikediñae. He touched me, or nudged me.

Ṭhuk ṭhuk. } Ṭuk ṭuk. } Shivering, to shiver. Cf. ṭhak ṭhak.
Ṭhuk ṭhuk rabañedińkana. I am shivering with cold.

Ṭhuk ṭhukạu. To shiver.
Rabañteye ṭhuk ṭhukạuǩkana. He is shivering with cold.

Thukum. Stop, out, used in certain games when a player is caught or put out of the game.

Thul. } Thur. } To get ready, to complete, entire, complete, undiminished.
Ninạǩ ṭakań thulakaťa. I have got ready so much money.
Lekha thulkeťkoań. I totalled them up.

Thuluǩ. } Thuluǩ thuluǩ. } Imitative of a dull sound produced by a blow or blows.

Thuluǩ marte. } Thuluǩ mente. } With a dull sound as of a blow.

Thum. A kind of game.

Thum. A boundary mark, post, pillar, &c.
Beṛhaete thumko biť ạcura. They fix boundary pillars all round.

Ṭhundga. Bare, as a tree of branches, or a head of hair.
Ṭhundgạ dare. A branchless tree.
Ṭhundgạ bohoǩ. A hairless head.

Ṭhundga. M. } Ṭhundgi. F. } Hairless, cropped bare, as the head.

Ṭhundguť. Bare, branchless, hairless.

Ṭhuṅ marte. } Ṭhuṅ mente. } With a crack, with a ring, with a snap. (imitative.)
Ṭhuṅ marte rạpuťena. It broke with a crack.

Thuṅgla. M. } Thuṅgli. F. } Simple, a simpleton, a simple Simon.
Thuṅgli geae. She is simple.

Thuṅgul muṅgul. Dull feeling in head, dizzy.
Bohoǩ hasote thuṅgul muṅgul iǩ ạikạueda. Owing to a head ache I have a dull feeling in the head.

Ṭhuni. A projecting pin to prevent anything slipping or coming off.

Thuni. To cut into short lengths, a cutting.
Leṅoǩ lạgiť ạkko ṭhunia. They cut sugar cane into short lengths for the purpose of pressing the juice from it.

Ṭhunṭa. M. } Ṭhunṭi. F. } Maimed in a limb or limbs. Cf. ṭhunṭha.
Ti ṭhunṭạgetaea. His hand is maimed.

Ṭhunṭha. M. } Ṭhunṭhi. F. } Maimed in a limb or limbs.
Ṭhunṭhạgeae. He is maimed.
Ṭhunṭhigeae. She is maimed.
Ti ṭhunṭhigetaea. Her hand is maimed.
Ṭhuṭhạ dare. A maimed or pollarded tree.

Ṭhunṭi. Maimed in a limb or limbs, applied to females.

Thupi. A small wooden mallet used mainly to beat plaster. Cf. thapi.

Ṭhupuṭhuǩ. Reciprocal from of ṭhuǩ. (q. v.)

Thur. To get ready, to complete, to total.
Pạhil sanam thurlem. Collect all first.
Heč thurenako. They have all come.
Jom thurenale. We have eaten and rested.
Isin thurakaťale. We have completed cooking.
Jaora thuroǩpe. Assemble all together.

Thuriạ ukhuṛ. A veiled name for daughters.

Ṭhurṭhurạu. To shake, to tremble.
Rabañte ṭhurṭhurạuǩkanae. He is shivering with cold.

Ṭhurkạ. } Ṭhurki. } Short in stature, a little man, a little woman. a dwarf.

Thurthurạu. To be eager, to be desirous, to have a longing for, to be very anxious about, to be solicitous.
Ạuri khonge jom lạgiť thurthurạuǩkanae.
Aćtege kạmi lạgiťe thurthurạu baṛaekanae.

Ṭhus. } Ṭhus ṭhus. } Imitative of the sound produced by any brittle object cracking or snapping.
Ṭhus ṭhus rạpudoǩkana. It is breaking with a series of snaps or cracks.

Ṭhus marte. } With a snap or crack.
Ṭhus mente. }

Ṭhus marte rạpudok̀a. It will break with a snap.

Rạpudok̀ jokheć ṭhus marte saḍea. When it breaks it will sound crack.

Thutba. } Thick.
Thutma. }

Thutma ṭhenga. A thick staff.

Thutba thotna. Short, thick snout.

Ṭhuṭhạ. M. } Maimed, short.
Ṭhuṭhi. F. }

Ṭhuṭhạgeae. He is maimed.

Ṭhuṭhigeae. She is maimed.

Ṭhuṭhạ ṭhenga. A short baton-like stick.

Ṭhuṭhạ. Shorter than the proper length.

Tengoć reak̀ ḍanḍom ṭhuṭhạgea. The handle of the axe is shorter than the proper length.

Thuthi. Memory.

Am do olkatem joṛaoa, iń do thuthiregeń joṛaoa. You write it down and add it up, I add it up in my memory.

Puthi reak̀ khon thuthi reak̀ serosa. The memory is superior to a book. (This shews the estimate in which oral tradition is held by the Santals.)

Thuthi kuṭạ. Loquacious, prating, glib.

Ṭhuṭhukur. A turkey cock.

Ṭhuṭhukur. A children's game.

Ṭhuṭkạ. M. } Short in stature.
Ṭhuṭki. F. }

Ṭhuṭki. To be worn small through use, to become small as anything through use.

Ṭhuṭki jonok̀. A worn broom.

Jonok̀ heṛ ṭhuṭkiena. The broom is worn small.

Ṭhuṭkuć. Short, small, as a piece of wood.

Lo ṭhuṭkućena. It is burnt short or small.

Giri ṭhuṭkućakaćako. They have cut it short.

Mić ṭhuṭkuć sahan. A small piece of fire wood burnt short.

Ṭhuṭ langaṭ.* Poor people. Cf. ṭuṭ langaṭ.

Thutmạ. M. } Stout.
Thutmi. F. }

Thutmạ. Cf. thutbạ.

Thutṛi. F. } Having a defect in speech.
Thotṛa M. }

Thutṛi biń. } A species of snake.
Thutri biń. }

Thutwa. Stout, thick, a small bạndi (q. v.)

Thutwae moṭaakana. He is dumpy.

Thutwae ńelok̀kana. He looks dumpy, or stout.

Matkom thutwa latarre menak̀a. It is under the parcel of matkom (q. v.)

Pe pon muṛi bạndikate thutwako metak̀a. They call a bạndi of 3 or 4 maunds a thutwa.

Ti. The hand.

Ti calao. To lay hands on, to strike.

Ti alom calaoa. Do not strike.

Ti jaṅga. Hands and feet, limbs.

Ti bạisạu. To become expert, to be accomplished.

Ti ṣuri bạisạuk̀taea. He has not yet become expert.

Ti ol. Lines on the palms of the hand.

Ti thopa. The hand with fingers.

Ti jaṅgare giḍi. To throw oneself at another's feet, to implore.

Tiạg. } To give up, forsake.
Teag. }

Jiwiye tiạgkeṭaea. He gave up the ghost.

Jomak̀e tiạgakaṭa. He has given up partaking of food.

Tiạk̀. To lead by the hand, or stick, rope, chain, &c.

Merome tiạk̀ idiedekana. He is leading away the goat.

Tiạk̀. To bend, as a bow.

Ak̀ sare sạpkeda, metadeae tiạgme, khane tiạk̀keda. He seized the bow and arrow, he said to him bend it, then he bent it.

Tiạk̀. } A sacrificial fowl, used in connection with sacrifice.
Sim tiạk̀. }

Sim tiạk̀bo boṅgakoa. We sacrifice devoted fowls.

Tiạr. To stretch.

Ti tiạr. To stretch out the hand.

Baber tiạrme. Stretch the twine.

Ṭibhi. } To prop by means of a post with a V shaped head, a prop with a V shaped head.
Ṭighi. }

Ṭibhi lagaoak̀pe. Put in a prop.

Ṭibhi daramakaṭako. They have propped it up.

Ṭibić ṭibić. } Quickly, trippingly, said of small females.
Ṭibik̀ ṭibik̀. }

Ṭibić ṭibiće calak̀kana. She goes trippingly.

Tić. To stretch, to elongate.

Bińe tićakana horrege. The snake is stretched out on the road.

Baber tijme. Stretch the twine.

Tić. To be equal to, to resemble, to be similar, to be like.

Ona do noa tuluć bań tićlena. That does not resemble this.

Ṭićṭorok̀. } The Indian Bulbul, *Pycnonotus pygæus.*
Ṭićṭorok̀ ceṛẽ. }

Ṭiḍwi. } Obstinate, headstrong, stubborn, obdurate, opinionative.
Ṭiṛwi. }

Nui hoṛ do ạḍi ṭiḍwi kanae. This man is very obstinate.

Ṭigaṭage. To walk heavily, to bring the feet round with a sweep when walking.

Ṭighi. Cf. ṭibhi.

Ṭihạ ṭahe. Rolling, walking heavily.
Ṭihạ ṭahe taṛamedae, nui gạiye sorakana. She is rolling, this cow's time to calve is near.

Ṭihkạ ṭihki. Painful, as a boil, hot and painful.
Ṭihkạ ṭihki hasoediñkana. I feel it hot and painful.

Ṭihkạu. To be hot and painful, throbbing, applied to the sensation which accompanies inflammation.
Ojo tihkạuḱkantaea. His boil is hot and painful.

Ṭihon. A kind of climbing plant, *Canavalia ensiformis, D. C.*

Tij. } A thing, an article, property,
Cij. } goods.
Tij durib. } Goods and chattels.
Tij bạsut. }
Khube tijakaṭa. He has much moveable property.

Ṭik. A tick.

Ṭikạ. To vaccinate, vaccination scar.
Ṭikạkedeae. He vaccinated him.
Bae ṭikạlena. He is not vaccinated.
Ṭikạ babṛẽ. A Brahmin vaccinator.

Ṭikạ. To put a mark on the forehead.
It is customary when certain rajas succeed to their estates for the neighbouring rajas to meet together and mark the forehead with redlead as a sign that he has succeeded to the throne. This is equivalent to coronation.
Tikạdar raj. A king who has received the ṭikạ, a crowned king.
Bin ṭikạ raj. An uncrowned king, Santal chief or pargana (q. v.) who although uncrowned is like a king among his people.

Ṭikạ Murmu. A sub-sept of the Santal sept Murmu.

Ṭikạḱ. To mark with the tip of the finger previously dipped in some colouring matter.
Mõṛẽ ṭikạḱ sindurteko bundikedea. They marked her five times on the forehead with red lead.
Ona beṛhaete pe ṭhen sindure ṭikạga. He makes five marks round it with red lead.

Ṭikạs. } A ticket, stamp, an adhesive
Ṭikạṭ. } stamp.
Ṭikạsle kaṭaoakaṭa. We have purchased tickets.
Ṭikase lagaoakaṭa. He has affixed a stamp.

Ṭikeṭ. The title borne by the eldest son of a Bhuiya raja.

Ṭikạu. To remain, to last, to be stable, to live, survive, be living.
Baṅ ṭikạuḱa. It will not remain.
Aṛe ṭikạukedale. We put up a stable dam, or embankment.
Ohoe ṭikạulena, laṅga cabaenae. He will not live, he is completely exhausted.

Ṭikiạ. A small cake of prepared charcoal for smoking tobacco in the chilum (q. v.)

Tikin. The meridian, mid-day, noon.
Candoe tikinena. The sun is on the meridian, it is mid-day.
Ạuri tikinoḱre. Before the sun reaches the meridian.
Tikin eṛaḱ. A little past the meridian, about 1 p. m.
Tikin hor. A journey that can be accomplished by mid-day.
Tikin loṛaḱ. A little past the meridian, a little after mid-day.

Ṭikis. } A ticket, an adhesive stamp.
Ṭikiṭ. }

Ṭiklạ. M. } Having a white blaze on
Ṭikli. F. } the forehead.
Ṭiklạ daṅra. A bullock with a white blaze on the forehead.
Ṭikli gại. A cow with a white blaze on the [forehead.

Ṭiklạ ṭikli. Each having a white blaze on the forehead.
Ṭiklạ ṭikli geako. They have each a white blaze on the forehead.

Ṭikli. A wafer ornament worn on the forehead by Hindu women, a spangle.

Ṭikmiń cẽṛẽ. A species of kestrel.

Ṭikor ṭokor. Imitative of the sound of an alternately high and low note or tone.
Ṭikor ṭokor saḍekana ṭoṭko do. The ṭoṭkoe (q. v.) sound alternately a high and low note.

Ṭikor ṭokor. Carrying dangling, driving, &c., as one a large number of small children.
Saname idikeṭkoa, ṭikor ṭokor. She took them all away, carrying, leading and driving.

Tikor tokor. Hanging down, as mucus from the nose or viscid saliva from the mouth.
Tikor tokor ulidaḱe aṛaḱ gidikeda.
Tikor tokor suluć joroḱkantaea.

Ṭikur. A small plot of land surrounded by water, a piece of highland surrounded by fields that are submerged during the rains.
Gobindpur band talare ṭikur menaḱa. There is a small island in the middle of the Gobindpur tank.

Ṭandi ṭikur. Plain and island, all varieties of land.

Ṭandi ṭikur casko lagaoakaṭa. They have cultivated all kinds of land.

Ṭilha ṭikurko oṛakakaṭa. They have built houses on the rising grounds.

Ṭikuria. Of or belonging to an island, rising ground of small area. Cf. ṭikur.

Til. } The plant which yields the
Tilmiń. } Gingelly or Sesame oil, *Sesamum indicum, Linn.*

Tilai dare. A small bush, *Wendlandia tinctoria, D. C.*

Tilai potam. The Ring dove.

Tilak. } A mark which Hindus make
Tilok. } on their foreheads with coloured earths or unguents, to mark the forehead.

Tila sar. A kind of rice.

Ṭilha. A small rising ground, a mound.

Ṭilha ṭikurko oṛakakawana. They have built their houses on mounds.

Tili. A Hindu caste of oilmen.

Tili ṭopar. The leather arrangement by means of which an oil man blindfolds his bullock when turning the oil press, blinders.

Tili ṭopare lagaoakawadea. He has blindfolded him (a bullock.)

Til kancan. A kind of rice.

Tilki bilki. To be elated, to be jubilant.

Calak lagiṭ tilki bilki baṛaekanako. They are elated at the prospect of going.

Tilki bilkikkanako. They are jubilant.

Tilmaṅ talmaṅ. Applied to the flapping of long garments.

Tilmaṅ talmaṅe taṛameda. She walks flappingly, as she walks her garments flap.

Tilmaṅ talmaṅ aṅgrope horokakaṭa. He has on a long coat which flaps.

Tilmiń. The plant which yields the Gingelly or Sesame oil, *Sesamum idicum, D. C.*

Pond tilmiń. The White variety.

Hende tilmiń. The Black variety.

Tilok. Cf. tilak.

Tilpaṅ talpaṅ. Applied to the movements of a long robe when the wearer walks; long, as a choga or robe.

Tilpaṅ talpaṅake horokakaṭa. He is wearing a long robe.

Ṭilṭilau. To be superabundant, to be congested, to be more than enough, to be distended by some internal agent or expansive force, to be tense.

Bele ṭilṭilauena. The gathering is tense (being distended with pus.)

Pereć ṭilṭilauena band do. The tank is full super-abundantly.

Toa seteń ṭilṭilauentaea.gai do. The cow's udder is congested with milk.

Ṭimba ṭambe. Heavily, as one moving under a heavy burden or fatigued, to be fatigued or burdened and shew it in the movements.

Hamalte ṭimba ṭambeye calakkana. He moves heavily owing to the burden.

Ṭimba ṭambeenae. He is burdened and moves heavily.

Ṭimbok ṭombok. } At a fair pace.
Ṭambuk ṭombok. }

Ṭambak ṭomboke calakkana. He is going at a fair pace.

Timin. How.

Timin marań menaea? How big is he?

Timin sangiń? How far?

Timin sangińre dada Gua nai? Yohaere, timinak coń dak doe jaṛi. How far away is the Gua river, brother? Yohaere, Who can tell how much it it may rain.

Bahutale timin marań? How big is our bride?

Timinak. } When, how much.
Timinań. }

Timinańre coe tiog. When may he arrive.

Timinańeneć coe tiog. When may he arrive.

Ṭimpa ṭaṛe. Applied to the walking of a feeble, burdened or tired person who does not step out but straddles.

Ṭimpa ṭaṛeye taṛamećkana. He straddles when walking.

Ṭimpi ṭiriń. Imitative of the ringing of a small bell, to tinkle as a small bell.

Ṭimpi ṭiriń sadekana ghanṭi do. The small bell is tinkling.

Tin. Three.

Ṭin. Tin, a canister or tin of any kind.

Tin. How many, how much, how.

Tin din hoeena? How many days have passed?

Tin habić. } How long, till when (to-day.)
Tin dhabić. }

Tin jokheć. At what time, when (to-day.)

Tinre. When, at what time (to-day.)

Tin ghaṛi? How long?

Tin tiriṭ? How much?

Tin marań? How big?

Tin sangińa? How far is it?

Tin uḍi. } How much, applied to small quanti-
Tin uḍli. } ties.
Tin hạbiċem tahena? Till when will you stay? how long will you stay?
Tin jokhedem calaka? When will you go? at what time will you go?
Tin ghạṛi nonḍem tahena? Bar ghanṭa gan. How long will you stay here? About two hours.
Tin uḍim jomkeda. You ate very little.
Tin uḍim emadińa. What a little you gave me.
Tin tiriċe emaćpea? How much did he give you?

Tiń. Mine, of me, used in comp.
Oṛak tiń. My house.
Merome goćkede tińa. He killed my goat.

Tiń. To stone, to throw a heavy stone on.
Tiń goćkedeae. He threw a heavy stone on it and killed it.

Ṭiṅgi. } To be elated, to be jubil-
Riṅgi ṭiṅgi. } ant.

Tiṅgi. To put fuel on a fire, to light a fire.
Tiṅgi cabakedako sahan do. They used up all the firewood, burnt it all.

Tiṅgiċ. To tingle, as the ears; to lose for a time the sense of hearing owing to a loud sound, ear-piercing, ear-splitting, deafening.
Roṛ tiṅgiċkedeako. They spoke him deaf.
Raheċ tiṅgiċkedeako. They deafened him with scolding.
Lutur tiṅgidok lekako bohoeċkana. They are shouting fit to split the ears.
Oka do bạnduk sạḍete lutur tiṅgidoka. At times through the report of a gun the ears are deafened.
Ruạ tiṅgiċena. He is dull of hearing owing to fever.

Tiṅgu. } Cf. teṅgo.
Tiṅgun. }

Tinik likiṛ. Applied to certain pieces of a carcase which only elderly people, as a rule, will eat, as brains, tongue and womb.

Tińjạu. To accustom, to train, to season, to habituate, to revive, to reinvigorate, to refresh.
Dāṛā tińjạuenae. He has refreshed himself by walking.
Kạmi tińjạu hoṛ kanae. He is a man inured to labour.

Tinrenań. At what time, when, (to-day.)

Ṭiń ṭiń. Thin, as liquid; clear, transparent, as water.
Dak leka ṭiń ṭiń dak mẹnḍi. Thin rice water, like water.
Dak hõ ṭińṭiń phạriạka. The water is also clear to transparency.

Tin topor khana. To injure, to cause injury, trouble, or suffering.
Tin topor khanakedińae. He caused me much trouble.
Tin topor khanakeċtińa. They caused me much damage.

Tińyạń. My brother-in-law.

Tiok. To reach, to arrive, to overtake, to reach up and pull down or off.
Tiokańme. Get it down for me.
Okatepe calakkana? Sarjom tiokle calakkana. Where are you going? We are going to knock down and gather sarjom (q. v.) fruit.
Bań sen tiokledea, sen tebakenae. I did not find him, he had left before my arrival.
Iń do bạń ańjom tioklaka. I did not hear, it did not reach my ears.
Bań tiok ocoleċkoa. I did not reach all, I had not sufficient to give to all.
Bạń tiokena. I was not reached, I got nothing.
Hinạ boṭkoe ṭheniń sen tiokkedea. I overtook him at that hill.
Tiogea menteń senlena, bạń tiok dạṛeadea. I went to overtake him, I could not overtake him.

Ṭipạk. A drop, to drop as rain.
Dake ṭipạkeda. Rain is dropping, a few drops of rain are falling.

Ṭipạn. To fasten the small leaf bag in which are the eggs of the Tassar (q. v.) silk moth on to the tree on which the caterpillars when hatched are to feed.
Lumạmko ṭipạnkoa.

Tipiạk. The reciprocal form of tiạk (q. v.)

Ṭipiń ṭipiń. } Short, as a garment worn
Ṭepeń ṭepeń. } round the waist.
Ṭipiń ṭipińe bandeakaċa. She is wearing her garment short.

Ṭipiń ṭipiń. Imitative of the sound produced by a small bell, to tinkle.
Ṭipiń ṭipiń sạḍekana ghạnṭi do. The bell tinkles.

Tipiok. The reciprocal form of tiok (q. v.)
Tipiokkanakin. The are overtaking each other.
Tipiokako nahak. They will overtake each other presently.

Ṭipi ṭipi. To tinkle, a tinkling sound.
Ṭipi ṭipi sạḍekana. It sounds tinkle, tinkle.

Ṭipi ṭipi. Applied to the call of the *ghardidi* (q. v.) or small Tailor bird.

Ṭipkạ. Float of a fishing line.

Ṭipkạ. A method of catching a certain kind of small fish (coḍgoć hako) without a hook.

A number of worms are threaded on a thin line and put into the water. The fish not being able to swallow the worm, owing to the thread in the inside, chew it and hold on so tightly that they allow themselves to be pulled gently out of the water.

Ṭipoć.
Ot ṭipoć. } A kind of plant.

Ṭipoć dak̃te aḍ baṛakeḍiñae. He washed my face with ṭipoć water, i, e, he cheated me.

Ṭipok̃ ṭopok̃.
Ṭipok̃ ṭoṛok̃. } In drops, drippingly.

Ṭipok̃ ṭopok̃ jorok̃kana. It is leaking in drops, or is dripping.
Mayam ṭipok̃ ṭopok̃ jorok̃kana. The blood is dripping.

Ṭipṭap. Imitative of the sound produced by light objects falling on the ground, pitapat.

Ṭipṭap matkom (q. v.) ñurok̃kana. The matkom is falling pit a pat.

Ṭir. A handle, a plough handle.

Ṭir eneć. A children's game.

Ṭirạ. The male moth of the various species of silk producers, the male quail; small, applied as a depreciatory term to small men.

Lumạm ṭira. The male of *Antheræa mylitta*, the Tassar Silk moth.
Bhạruạ ṭira. The male of *Attacus Atlas* and *Actias selene*.
Gunḍri ṭirạ. The male Quail.
Ṭirạ Phagu. The little (man) Phagu.

Ṭirań. Not to have sufficient means of subsistence, to be very poor, to be hard up.

Aḍiko tirańakana. They are very hard up.
Jom ñui reak̃ tirańko tahẽkana. They were badly off for food.

Ṭiṛanicạ. To be hard pressed, to be short handed, to be pressed for labourers.

Netar dole tiṛa nicạakana, ohole ganlena. We are hard pressed at present for persons to do our work, it is out of our power.
Kạmi iạte hoṛkole tiṛạ nicạakana. On account of the work we are hard pressed for labourers.

Ṭiṛạs.
Ṭiṛạsa. } Thirst.

Upạsa tirạsale kạmiakat́a. We have worked in hunger and thirst.

Tirchạ.
Tirchạu. } At an angle, slantingly.

Tirchạgem mak̃keda. You cut it slantingly.

Tirchạ tirchi. Off the straight, slanting, crooked.

Tirchạ tirchipe banaoakat́a. You have made it crooked.
Tirchạ tirchiko rakaḅakat́a bhit do. They have built up the wall off the straight.

Tire juge. All one's life, life long, always.

Tire juge apạsulkin menakawana. They agreed to cherish each other all their days.
Tire juge lạgit́. For ever, always.

Tirhol. To rub in the hands, to rub the eyes, to twist by rubbing in the palms of the hands.

Met́ tirhol tirholteń kạmiakat́a. I have worked continually rubbing my eyes, (I have laboured so hard that sweat continually blinded my eyes and I had to rub them to be able to see.)
Ṭhik do bako tirholakat́a, bhạruṛ bhạruṛ ge ñelok̃kana. They have not twisted it properly, it looks rough (twine.)
Kombṛoko hoṛo geleko tirhola. Thieves rub the ears of dhan in their hands.

Tiri. Used by husband and wife when addressing each other in private.

Tiri purus. Husband and wife.

Tiriạu.
Tiriyạu. } To extend, to extend in line, to stretch out.

Sendra hoṛko tiriạuakana. The hunters are extended in line.

Ṭiṛiń. To fly into a rage, to get into a passion, to flare up.

Aḍi tiṛiń goćenae. He flew into a great rage.

Ṭiṛiń taṛań.
Taṛań tiṛiń. } To speak angrily, to speak loudly as one angry, to get angry.

Tiṛiń taṛań godok̃ae. He flares up at once.

Ṭiṛiń.
Ṭiṛiń ṭiṛiń. } Imitative of the tinkle of a bell, to tinkle.

Ghạnṭi ṭiṛiń ṭiṛiń saḍekana. The bell sounds tinkle, tinkle.

Ṭiṛiń marte.
Ṭiṛiń mente. } With a tinkle.

Ṭiṛiń marte saḍegoćena. It sounded tinkle.

Ṭiṛiń goṛiń. To cry or speak like a petulant or cantankerous child, whiningly, pulingly.

Jomak̃ lạgit́ tiṛiń goṛiń baṛae kanae. He is whining for food.

Ṭiṛiń ṭipiń. Tinklingly.

Ṭiṛiń ṭipiń saḍekana. It sounds tinklingly.

Tirio. A flute.

Tirio orań. To play the flute.

Ṭiriot́ ṭoriot́. Cry of small parrot.

Miru ṭiriot́ ṭoriot́ko raga. Parrots call out ṭiriot́ ṭoriot́.

Tiris jug.
Tiris kal. } Always, for ever.
Tiriskal onko then toa hoyokkana. They have always milk.

Tiris baris. Always, all the year, annually.

Tirić.
Tin tirić. } How much, how many.
Tin tiriće ematpea? How much did he give you?
Tin tirić poesae ematpea? How many pice did he give you?
Tin tirićko haraakana? How much, or how big, have they grown?

Tirić.
Un tirić. } So much as that, so many as that.
Un tiriće ematpe rehõ bape kusilena. Although he gave you so much as that you were not satisfied.

Tirić.
In tirić. } As much as this.
In tirićko haraakana. They have grown as much as this.

Tirić.
Nin tirić. } As much as this.
Nin tirićko haraakana. They have grown as much as this.

Tirić.
Nun tirić. } As much as this.
Nuntirić takako agukeclea. They charged us as much money as this.

Tirić.
Khub tirić. } A large quantity.
Khub tirić tohobme. Seize a large quantity.

Tirić.
Ạdi tirić. } Very much, very many.
Ạdi tirić alom emakoa. Do not give them very much, a very large quantity.

Tirić leka. Exceedingly, vehemently.
Nonka hohoate tirić leka dạṛ idikedae. Calling out thus he fled.

Tiriyạu. Cf. tiriạu.

Tirkõṭ.
Tirkoṭ.
Tirkũṭ.
Tirkuṭ. } Very many, on all sides.
Tirkõṭ hoṛko jarwalena. Very many people were assembled.

Tirlik.
Ṭunṭi. } To spurt out, as blood from an artery, &c.
Mayam tirlik oḍokena. The blood spurted out.

Tirmirạu. To be enfeebled, to lose strength or vitality, to be dizzy, to tremble, to flutter.
Rehgeõte tirmirạuenae. He is enfeebled through starvation.
Dak tetahte tirmirạuenae. He is enfeebled through thirst.
Hoṛo aphor setohte tirmirạuena. The dhan seedlings are losing their vitality through the heat of the sun.
Gujuk leka tirmirạuenae. He is so feeble that he is like dying.

Tirmić. To twist, squeeze or rub between a finger and the thumb.
Tirmić gočkedeañ. I squeezed it between my finger and thumb and killed it.

Tirmuti cẽṛẽ. A species of kestrel, *Tinnunculus alandarius.*

Tiṛoć toṛoć.
Liṛoć toṛoć. } Slimy, ropy, mucilaginous.

Ṭirom hako. A species of fish.

Ṭirom cẽṛẽ. The Indian Bee-eater, *Merops viridis.*

Ṭirom hasa. A kind of friable earth.

Ṭiroṅ. The Sun-bird.

Tiṛotoṛo. Hanging like a string of some tenacious, viscous, ropy or glutinous substance, aptness to draw out into a string as of glutinous substances.
Tiṛo toṛo uli dak jorokkantaea. Saliva is hanging like a string from his mouth.
Ạdi jut tiṛo toṛo ologoka. It is beautifully stringy and marks nicely.

Tirpit. To satisfy.
Dakte baṅ tirpitlena. I was not satisfied with water.
Tirpitok leka bae emadiña. He did not give so as to satisfy me.

Tirṛạ. A gigantic climbing plant, *Pueraria tuberosa, D. C.*
Tirṛạ da. The edible tuber of tirṛạ.

Tirsul.
Tirsuṛ. } A form of inflammation of the eye.
Tirsulakanae. He is suffering from inflammation of the eyes.

Tirsul. A trident, or three pronged lance.

Tirsuṛ. Cf. tirsul.

Tirtirạu. Cf. tirmirạu.

Tiruṅ miruṅ. Whiningly, petulantly, importunately.
Tiruṅ miruṅe kokoekana. He is begging whiningly.
Tiruṅ miruṅokkanae. He is whining.

Tirup̣. To lean forward, to lean against each other, to hang the head, to bow the head.
Ṭheṅgateye tirup̣akana. He is leaning on a staff.
Raj noa ñelkateye tirup̣ goćena. The king saw this and bowed his head.
Mić goṭeć kumbạ uni mukhia hoṛ lạgićko tirup̣a. They make a shelter of sticks leaning against each other for that chief.

Tis. When (not to day.)
Tisem calak̇a? Meañ iñ calak̇a. When will you go? I will go the day after to-morrow.
Tis hõ bañ. Never.
Tisre hõ bañ. At no time, never.

Tis hõ. Ever, at any time.
Tis hõ bañ. At no time, never.
Tis hõ alo. At no time, never, (prohibitive.)
Tis hõ oho. At no time, never, (assuring.)
Onka do tis hõ bañ hoyok̇a. It will never be thus.
Onḍe do tis hõ alom calak̇a. Do not at any time go there, never go there.
Alom botorok̇a, tis hõ ohoko dallema. Do not fear, they will at no time beat you, they will never beat you.

Ṭisi. Ṭhisi. Ṭisiạ. Ṭhisiạ. The Linseed plant, *Linum usitatissima, Linn.*, and its products.
Ṭisiạ holoñ. Linseed meal.
Ṭisiạ sunum. Linseed oil.
Ṭisiạ kaṛe. Linseed oil cake.

Tisok̇. Tisoñ. When (not to-day.
Tisoñ coñ ohoñ men daṛeleа. I am unable to say when.
Tisok̇ coñ, bañ baḍaea. I do not know when.

Ṭisri. F. Ṭesra. M. Ṭhisri. F. Ṭhesra. M. One-eyed, blind of an eye, one eye imperfect, having imperfect vision.
Ṭisri geae. She is one-eyed.

Tit. Utit. An ascetic, to become an a scetic.
Onkoko titakat̕a. They have become ascetics.

Tit mantar. An incantation.

Tiṭạ titi. To weary, to worry, to annoy.
Tiṭạ titikediñako, cet̕ hõ bako k̇ami ocoañ. They annoyed me, they allowed me to do no work.

Tiṭạu. To be wearied, to be worried, to be annoyed.
Nokoko tiṭạukediña. These people annoyed me.
Gitic̕ gitic̕teñ tiṭạuena. I am worried with continued lying, (as a sick person.)

Titi. Bitter, pungent, acrid, sour. Cf. tito.

Titikhạk̇. To be troubled, to be perplexed, to be anxious.

Ṭiṭiṛhic̕ cẽṛẽ. This name is given to two species of Lapwing, *Sarcicophorus bilobus*, and *Lobivanellus goensis*. Cf. ṭeṭe ṭeṅgoc̕ cẽṛẽ.

Titic̕. Aḍi titic̕. Very much, a large quatity.
Aḍi titic̕ko emat̕koa. They gave them a large quantity.

Titic̕. Untitic̕. So much, as much as that.
Un titic̕ko emat̕koa. They gave them so much.

Titic̕. Nin titic̕. So much, so much as this.
Nin titic̕ko emadiña. They gave me so much.

Titic̕. Nun titic̕. So much, this much.
Nun titic̕le emat̕koa. We gave them this much.

Tito. Bitter, pungent, acrid.
Jiwi titoentiña. My spirit is embittered.
Bugite rinakat̕ae, titoenae. He has incurred much debt, he is embittered.

Tito miṭho. Bitter and sweet.
Nui doe tito coe miṭho coe iñ do bañ baḍaea. Whether this man is untrustworthy or trustworthy I do not know.

Tiwạr tawar. Tawar tawar. Dangling.
Tiwạr tawar gidrạe hecakadea. She is carrying the child with its legs dangling.

Ṭiwic̕. Ṭiwic̕ ṭiwic̕. To shake, to wag.
Gaḍa cạñcir cẽṛẽ cupiko ṭiwic̕ ṭiwija. The Water-wag-tail birds wag their tails.

Ṭiyạl ṭapal. Flapping, as strips.
Kicric̕ oṛec̕entaea, ṭiyạl ṭapal. His cloth is torn and flaps.

Ṭiyạl ṭiyạl. Shaking, as the tail of a dog, far, as far as the eye can reach.
Ṭiyạl ṭiyạle lagaedek̇ana. He is chasing him with his tail shaking.
Ṭiyạl ṭiyale laga idikedea. He pursued him as far as the eye could reach.

To. An emphatic particle.
Ạkhir toñ gujuk̇gea. At the end I shall die.
Jawabañgea tom, ar cetem cekaea? Dismiss me you will, what more will you do?
Iñ ṭhenem hataogea to ṭaka. From me you will take the money.

Toa. Milk, the female breast.
Gại toa. Cow's milk.
Merom toa. Goat's milk.
Toa daka. Rice cooked in milk.
Hoṛo ạuri belek̇a, toa peredakana. The rice is not yet ripe, it is filled with milk.
Toa ḍaṭa. The first teeth.
Nui gạy khube toaea. This cow gives much milk.
Toa beleakantaea. Her breast is suppurating, (milk abscess.)
Toa dare. The milk tree, i. e. mother.
Haere, toa dare bạgiadiñae. Alas, my mother has forsaken me (died.)

Toa kaṭkom. A species of crab. Cf. kaṭkom.

Toa aṛak̇. A wild plant used as a pot-herb.

Toa baha. The milk flower, a small garden shrub with a pure white flower.

Tobaǩ. To brand with a hot iron, to cauterize, to peck.
Datrom dhipạukateye tobaǩkedea. He branded him with a red hot sickle.
Kạhu ṭhen alope tobaǩ ocokoa. Do not allow the crows to peck at them (cattle with sores.)

Tobe. Then.
Tobe, okatem heđakana? Then, where have you come to?
Johar, tobe emam calamkanale. Johar (q. v.) then we are presenting to you.

Tobe nạhī. Then only.
Kạmime tobe nạhīm joma.

Tobe khać. } Then.
Tobe khan.
Tobekhan ma niạge jomme. Then, come eat this.

Tobe eṛoń. } Therefore, for that reason, on that account.
Tube teṛoń.
Tobe teṛoń ape do bape arjaoa. For that reason you do not raise good crops.

Tobo. } To be cloyed, to be surfeited, to be filled to satiety and loathing, to glut, to be exhausted.
Tobo tobo.
Jom jomte tobo toboenae. He has eaten till he is cloyed.
Daǩ daǩte tobo tobokeďlea. We have had a surfeit of rain.
Jom toboenae. He has eaten till he is cloyed.

Tobṛe. To gather together, to assemble. Cf. tombṛe.

Toć toć. Stretched out.
Toćtoće gitićakana. He is lying stretched out.

Ṭoḍa. The sharp point of a wooden plough in which the share is fixed.

Todarot. } To investigate, to enquire into.
Tadarat.
Todonto.
Ona kathale todarotkeda, bań sạbudlena. We enquired into that matter, it was not proved.

Ṭoḍor. A wristlet, worn by males.
Pitạr ṭoḍor. A brass wristlet.
Rań ṭoḍor. A pewter wristlet.
Rupạ ṭoḍor. A silver wristlet.

Toe. Off the square, not at a right angle, slanting.
Cạukaṭha do toyena. The door frame is not perpendicular.

Toe. A part of the female organ.

Toenat. To prepare, to make ready.
Isin toenatkedale. We cooked and made ready.
Senoǩ lạgiťko toenatakana. They are ready to start.
Ape lạgiť jaega toenatiń calaǩkana. I go to prepare a place for you.

Togoć. To break into small pieces with the teeth and prepare for swallowing, to masticate, to chew, to gnaw, to crunch, to nibble, to grind the teeth.
Togoć ḍaṭa. To fix the teeth firmly together, to suffer from tetanus or lock jaw, to gnash the teeth.
Ran ańuae botorte togoć ḍaṭakedae. Through fear of being given medicine to take he fixed his teeth firmly together.
Bạilenre hõko togoć ḍaṭaea. During convulsions they also grind the teeth.
Togoć lạhuťkateye uťkeda. He masticated it well and swallowed it.
Togoć rạṭuǩkedae. He crunched it in his teeth (as a dog a bone.)
Togoć gejerkedae. He broke it into small pieces with his teeth.
Okate coń togoćkedetalea. Ours (husband, son, &c.) has gone somewhere.

Togoť. A kind of wild cat.

Togoť. } Soft, very soft.
Togoť togoť.
Togoť togoť aṭkaroǩkana. It feels very soft.
Noa kaṭ do togoťgea. This log is soft.

Togoť araǩ. } A wild plant used as a pot herb, *Gnaphalium indicum, Linn.*
Tagoť araǩ.

Toho. Cf. oho.
Tohoń senlena. I cannot go.

Tohoć tohoć. Long, rank.
Tohoć tohoć gelećna. The ears of grain are long.

Ṭohok. } Distinctly.
Ṭohoka.
Ṭohokań ńelkedea. I saw him distinctly.
Ṭohokań ańjomkeda. I heard distinctly.
Ṭohokań ńelkedea kul do. I saw the tiger distinctly.

Tohoṗ. To grasp, a handful, as much as one can grasp.
Tohoṗ sumuńe irkeda. He reaped as much as he could grasp, a handful.
Barpe tohoṗko binḍạkaťa. They have made a sheaf of two or three handfuls, they have made sheaves of two or three handfuls each.
Miť tohoṗ hoṛoko emadińa. They gave me a handful of dhan (in the straw.)
Miť tohoṗ bahae siť ạgukeda. He plucked and brought a handful of flowers.
Khub tiriť tohobme. Take a good big handful.

Ṭohor. }
Ṭhohor. } To recognise, to know, to take note of, to consider.

Onde amren gạiń ṭohorkedea. I recognized your cow there.

Ḍher sạṅgiń bań ṭohor daṛeakoa. I cannot recognize them (men, cows, &c.) at a great distance.

Bae ṭohorleťte onareye khańjoena. Through not having taken note of it he fell into it.

Ṭohor ṭohor baṛe lạiańme. Tell me carefully.

Amaḱ meťre menaḱ kowale bam ṭohoreda. Thou dost not take note of the beam in thine own eye.

Tohoť. To strike the foot against anything lying on or fixed in the ground, to stumble.

Dhirire tohoťenań. I struck my foot against a stone.

Tohoť gurenae. He struck his foot against (something) and fell.

Tohoť ṭạṭuṗe calaoena. He went away stumbling.

Tohoť ṭạkiće calaoena. He went away stumbling and striking himself against obstacles.

Tojahi. Stingy, niggardly, lazy.

Tojahigeae, bae emoḱa. He is stingy, he will not give.

Tojbij. To enquire into, to examine, to consider, to estimate.

Beske tojbijakaťa. They have enquired into it carefully.

Tok. A large pestle, used to husk and clean grain. Cf. ukhuṛ.

Ṭok. Desire.

Jom reaḱ ṭok hedadińa. I have a desire to eat.

Ṭok leka thoṛage ńuime. Drink only a little.

Ṭok leka baṛe jomme. Eat only a little.

Toka. Where.

Tokare menaea? Where is he?

Ṭokaḱ. A small earthenware vessel.

Ṭokao. To interrogate, to challenge, to accost, to prevent.

Iḱdi jokhećko ṭokaokedea. They challenged him when he was taking it away.

Ṭoke. A sty or inflamed tumour on the edge of the eyelid.

Ṭokeakanae. }
Ṭoke janamakawadea. } He is suffering from a sty.

Ạḍim eḱṛea onatem ṭokeakana. You are given to deceit, therefore you have got a sty on the eyelid.

Toke. To tie the hair up in a certain way.

Tokeakaťae uṗ do.

Ṭoklaḱ. }
Ṭoknaḱ. } A small earthenware vessel.

Ṭoklaḱ hoṛo. A species of crab.

Tokoṗ. }
Tokoṗ tokoṗ. } With gusto, to eat with gusto.

Tokoṗ maraokedae. He ate it up with gusto.

Tokoṗ tokoṗe jomeda. He is eating with gusto.

Ṭokor. }
Ṭokor ṭokor. } Jinglingly, to jingle.

Ṭokor ṭokor sadekana. It sounds jinglingly, it jingles.

Ṭokor marte. }
Ṭokor mente. } With a jingle.

Tokor tokor. Glutinous, tenacious, stringy, viscid, the property possessed by a semi-liquid which admits of its being drawn out without breaking.

Tokor tokor sulué ḍoroḱkantaea.

Tokor tokor kharaḱ oḍokoḱkantaea.

Ṭokrao. To upbraid, to twit, to threaten, to bring up an old matter. Cf. ṭhokrao.

Tokraṛ. To re-iterate, to repeat, to persevere, to dispute, to altercate.

Ạḍiye tokraṛediṅkana. He is asking me repeatedly.

Tokṛe. }
Thokṛe. } To adhere, to stick to, as clay to the feet.

Losoť tokṛeĕna jańgare. Mud is sticking to the feet.

Ṭokṭoko. To hinder, to block, to stick up or out, to hinder, block or incommode by projecting or causing to project.

Ṭokṭokoe teṅgoakana. He is standing straight up.

Ṭokṭokoko biťakaťa. They have fixed it so that it sticks up.

Horre ṭokṭokoko dohoakaťa. They have placed it projecting on to the road.

Jańgae ṭokṭokoakaťa. He has stretched his legs and is in the way.

Hoṛko talare bạnduk ṭokṭokoe goḱ baṛaeda. He is carrying his gun among the people projecting over his shoulder.

Toḱ. To tie, to bind, to fasten, to build with bricks or stones.

Ti jańgako toḱkeťtaea. They bound him hand and foot.

Toḱ samṭao. To tie up together, tie into a bunch or bundle.

Toḱ urić. To tie or bind tightly.

Iṭạte toḱ. To build with bricks.

Dhirite toḱ. To build with stones.

Kūi iṭạteko toḱakaťa. They have built the well with bricks.

Hoṛmo toloḱ. Person to become mature.

Hoṛmo bań toḱakantaea. His person is immature.

Ạuri hoṛmo toloḱtaea. His person is not yet mature.

Hoṛmo do toḱentaea. His person is mature.

Tola. A weight almost equal to half an ounce.

Ṭola. An out-lying hamlet or part of a village.
Muci ṭola. The part of a village inhabited by the mochi or shoemaker caste.
Hoṛ ṭola. The part of a village inhabited by Santals.
Deko ṭola. The part of a village inhabited by Hindus.

Tolao. To assess, to tax, to exact, to collect.
Oṛak̕ oṛak̕ mimiť cukạk̕kateko tolaoa. They assess each house at one cukạk̕ (q. v.) of oil.)

Tolgoyam. Fine, soft.
Tolgoyam ghās. Soft grass.
Tolgoyam uṗ. Down, soft hair on body at birth.
Tolgoyam il. Down, soft hair on body of feathered creatures when hatched.

Tolhāṭ. Neighbourhood, vicinity.
Inạ tolhāṭ ren sanamko baḍaea. All of that neighbourhood know.

Tolmoć. To begin to wither, to wilt.
Setoṅte sakam tolmojok̕kana. The leaves are wilting owing to heat of the sun.

Ṭolmol. } **Ṭolmolao.** } To heave, to shake, to quiver, to tremble.
Rengećteko ṭolmolaoena. They are trembling owing to starvation.
Ḍheote lạukạ ṭolmolaok̕kana. The boat is heaving owing to the waves.

Tolob. } **Tolop.** } Pay, wages.

Tolob. } **Tolop.** } To feel a call of nature, to call, to summon.
Dak̕ seć tolobkedea. He felt a call to go to stool.
Raca sen tolobkedea. He felt a call to urinate.
Ona nakhạren hoṛkoe tolopkoa. He summons the people of that neighbourhood.

Toloć. To squeeze out, as the stone of a ripe fruit.
Kuinḍi ma tolojme. Squeeze out the stone of the Kuinḍi (q. v.)

Toloke. Proud flesh, large granulations.
Toloke haraakana. Proud flesh has grown.

Toloṅ. Part of bhạgwạ (q. v.) hanging down in front.
Toloṅe aṛak̕akaťa. He has caused a part of his bhạgwạ (q. v.) to hang down in front.

Tolop. Pay, wages.

Tolop. Cf. tolob.

Tolsaṅ. To lie on the ground.
Ńu bulenteko tolsaṅena. They are drunk and lying on the ground.

Toltolao. To cause to haste, to hasten, to cause to hurry, to dragoon, to constrain, to drive. Cf. taltalao.
Toltolao oḍokkeťkoae. He hurried them out.
Toltolaoede kanako kạmi lạgiť. They are driving him to work.

Ṭolṭolao. Cf. ṭilṭilạu.

Ṭomba. } **Ṭombao.** } To accumulate, as water in a hollow, &c., full.
Dak̕ ṭombaakana. Water has accumulated.

Tomboṅ. To put close to, to put so close as to touch.
Sengel tahen lagiť munḍhạť tomboṅkak̕pe. Place the log touching the fire so that it may retain the fire.

Tombṛe. } **Tobṛe.** } To gather together, to assemble, to huddle.
Miť ṭhenko tombṛeakana. They are assembled in one place.
Hạṛuṗ tombṛeakanako. They are huddled up with the arms across the chest (owing to the cold.)

Tombṛe. } **Liṭa tombṛe.** } A species of wasp.

Tombroť. Short-necked, bull-necked.
Tombroťe moṭaakana. He is so fat as to be short-necked.
Tombroťge ńelok̕kanae. He appears to be bull-necked, or, he is bull-necked.

Tomol dak̕. To be wearied, worried, bothered, annoyed.
Hijuk̕ senok̕te tomol dagok̕kanae. He is becoming wearied by coming and going.
Nui gidrạ tomol dak̕kediṅae. This child worried me, this child bothered me.

Tomosuk. A note of hand, bond, obligation.

Tomtom. Silent, silent through being [sulky.
Tomtomakanae. He is silent.
Tomtome thirakanae. He has become silent.

Ṭomṭombao. To the brim, full to the brim.
Band pereć ṭomṭombaoena. The tank is full to the brim.
Dul ṭomṭombaoakaťako. They have poured in till it is full to the brim.

Ṭona. To cut into lengths.

Ṭona ṭuni. To cut into lengths or pieces.

Tońcok. A fault, a defect, doubt, [suspicion.
Uni hoṛak̕ kathare tońcok menak̕a. There is dubiety about that man's statement.
Amak̕ tońcok bako ńamlekhan ohoko ruhet̕lema. If they had not found a fault in you they would not have scolded you.
Ạḍi tońcokgea noa katha. This story is very suspicious.
Kạṭić talaṅ lạgiće tońcokkeda. On account of a very little he refused assent.

Ṭonḍaṅ. Rising ground, dry land, dry ridge.
Ṭonḍaṅ ṭonḍaṅte calaḱme. Go along the dry land.

Tondehi. } **Tondohi.** } To investigate, to enquire into.
Khube tondohiakaťa. He has investigated it carefully.

Tondori. To investigate, to enquire into.

Toṅge. To join, to unite, to join end to end, to tie two ends together.
Baberko toṅgeakaťa. They have tied the ends of the strings together.
Laċ topaḱakantalea, ladle toṅgea. Our bellies have snapped in two, we will piece our stomachs together, i. e. we are hungry, we will take food.

Ṭoṅkor. To hang down, to hang down loosely.
Baber ṭoṅkorakana. The string is hanging down loosely.

Ṭoṅ ṭoṅ. Very high, very lofty.
Ṭoṅṭoṅ oṛaḱko bereťakaťa. They have made the house very high.
Chata ṭoṅ ṭoṅko bereda porobre. At the festival they raise the umbrella very high.

Tonkha. Wages, salary.

Ṭonko. To be refreshed, to recover, to recruit, to be re-invigorated.
Jom ńu ṭonkoenae. He ate and drank and was refreshed.
Joroḱ ṭonkoenae. He warmed himself at the fire and is re-invigorated.
Ruạ khon ṭonko ńoḱenae. He has recovered a little from his fever.

Tonol. A fastening, what is used to tie or fasten with. Cf. tol.

Tonoṛ. An addition to the length of a house on a gable end.

Ṭonṭa. To lack, to be in need of, to have an insufficient supply of, to be scarce.
Daḱ reaḥ ạdi ṭonṭa. Water is very scarce.
Ṭanre do ṭonṭare do sãwãealeme. In dearth and scarcity give us a full supply of water.

Ṭonṭoṛoċ. A spout, a faucet.

Ṭop. A drop, to drop. Cf. ṭopoḱ.

Top. A cannon.
Top aṛaḱ. } Top jereť. } To fire a cannon.

Topa. To bury, to cover over.
Ṭakako topa mareakaťa. They have buried money for a long time.
Ṭakate topaakanae. He is buried in wealth.
Kicriċteye topaạkana. He is buried under cloth, he has a great deal of clothing above him (as when in bed.)
Topakadeako. They buried him.

Topaḱ. To break, to snap.
Topaḱ ńurbaena. It snapped and fell.
Riniń topaḱkeda. I paid off my debt.
Kathako topaḱkeda. They broke the agreement, put an end to the agreement.
Maḱ topaḱ. To cut through, as with an axe, sword, &c.
Dare maḱ topaḱkedae. He hewed through the tree.
Topaḱ topaḱe roṛeťkana. He is speaking hesitatingly.
Topaḱ topaḱ ạtuḱkana. It is flowing in driblets.

Ṭopar. To cover, to blindfold.
Hoṛmo hartate ṭoparakana. The body is covered with skin.
Tili do ghạni ḍaṅrako ṭoparkoa. Oil men blindfold the bullocks that turn the oil presses.
Bạgi sadomko ṭoparkoa. They put blinkers on carriage horses.

Tope. To cut, to clip, to cut the hair short so that it reach only to the beginning of the neck, to dock a horse, to cut the tail of a fowl.
Tope uḅ. Hair cut so as to reach down to the neck.

Tope sarjom. A kind of tree mentioned in Santal traditions.

Tope tope. Short, as hair.
Tope tope uḅtae. His hair is short.

Tophad. } **Tophat.** } **Taphat.** } Distance, difference, distinction, disparity, distant, separate, far away, remote.
Ạdi tophat khonińi jereťledea. I shot him from a great distance.
Ạdi tophatgea. It is very distant.
Unkinaḱ katha tophatgetakina. There is a disparity in their statements.
Tophat tophatreko oṛaḱakaťa. They have built their houses at a distance from each other.
Taphat ńoḱre tahenme. Remain at a little distance.

Topo. To immerse.
Daḱreye topo goċena. He was drowned.
Topo dakako joma setoṅ dinre. In the hot weather they eat rice that has been immersed in water.
Topo jojoakaťako. They have kept it immersed in water until it has become sour.

Ṭopoḱ. } **Ṭhopoḱ.** } To drop, to drip.
Daḱ ṭopogoḱkana sate khon. Water is dripping from the eaves.
Ṭopoḱ ṭopoḱ joroḱkana. It is falling in drops.
Daḱ ṭopoḱena. Water has dropped.

Topol. Reciprocal form of tol. (q. v.)
Topol sạgạị. Relation by marriage.

Topolas. Reciprocal form of tolas (q. v.)

Topond. The mark made by the goad, especially on buffaloes.

Topond thene ghaoakana. He has a sore at the goad mark.

Ṭopor. } Rattling sound as that
Ṭopor topor. } produced by the tongue of a wooden bell.

Ṭopor ṭopor ṭoṭko sadea. The wooden bell sounds ṭopor ṭopor.

Ṭopor marte. } With a rattle.
Ṭopor mente. }

Ṭopor marte sadeana. It sounded with a rattle.

Topoć. A kind of small bug, which lives in the ground and whose bite is very painful.

Topoć. A kind of pimple which sometimes appears on the faces of persons attaining adolescence, acne.

Topoć. The opening by which rats go in and out of their underground residence.

Topoć. Reciprocal form of toć (q. v.), to peck at each, as fowls, to pull each other's hair when quarrelling.

Simko topoća. Fowls peck at each other.

Ṭopra. A small plot of rice land.

Toṛ. Force, velocity, as of a current or bullet, energetically.

Alope ãṛgona daḱ reaḱ ạdi toṛ. Do not go in the current is very strong.

Nạliteć khaṭo banduk ạdi do bae toṛa, jeleń nạli khube toṛa. Short barrelled guns have not much force, long barrels have great force.

Khube toṛkeda. He was very energetic, or he infused energy (into all.)

Toṛ. To sting.

Kidiń kaṭkome toṛkedea. A scorpion stung him.

Susurbańko totoṛa. Wasps sting.

Toṛ. The common striped squirrel, *Sciurus palmarum.*

Tor. } Applied to the croaking of
Ṭorṭor. } frogs, to croak, to croak
Ṭorṭorao. } incessantly, to give no peace, to keep at it.

Ṭorṭore raḱeda. He is croaking.

Roṭe ṭorṭoraoḱkanae. The frog is croaking.

Ṭor maraokedae. He gave a croak.

Ṭorṭorao idiećkoae kuliko. He gave the coolies no peace till they went with him.

Toṛ candbol. A common grass, *Eragrostis ciliaris, Linn.*

Toṛa. A bag for holding money carried bound round the waist underneath the clothing, a long narrow purse.

Tora. Immediataly after.

Boṛ torage omon goćena. He spoke and it sprang up. [after being beaten.

Dal torageye goć goćena. He died immediately

Heć torage jojome duṛupena. Immediately after he came he sat down to his food.

Ńu torageye goć goćena. He drank it and immediately died.

Tora. In comp, means that something occurs immediately preceding the leaving of a certain place.

Idi toraeme. Take it with you.

Ańjom toraeme. Hear and go away.

Jom toraeme. Eat and go.

Ńel toraeme. See and go. [away.

Daltorakadeako. They struck him in going

Tora. In composition gives the idea of going away from the speaker.

Hạni torae calaḱkan. There he is going away.

Hanko torako calaḱkan. There they are going away.

Tora. } Gives the idea of going at
Okoe tora. } once or without delay.

Menwanae, okoe tora noa buṛhtegeń koe baṛa joha. He said I will beg by means of this buṛh. (q. v.)

Okoe tora calaḱṇń nitoḱ. I will go at once.

Tora. A particle having a plural signification.

Ale tora lekangeae, ạdi kisạṛ doe bah kana. He is like us, he is not very rich.

Ape tora dohaete bugi baṛageale.

Toṛahêć. Embellishment, to embellish, expand or exaggerate a statement or narrative.

Katha reaḱ toṛahêćteć. The embellishment of the narration.

Toraju. Scales. [choose.

Torajut. To prepare, to repair, to

Toṛao. To repay, as a debt, to clear away by breaking.

Mahajon iń toṛaoakadea. I have cleared my debt to the money lender.

Noa birre ạdi huraćko toṛaoakaća. They have cleared out many tree stumps from this jungle.

Torao. To surmount a difficulty, to overcome a difficulty, to get over a difficulty, to aid, help, assist, profit.

Ona gạr khonih toraoena. I have surmounted that difficulty.

Ona gạr khonih torao kedea. I got him over that difficulty.

Okaṭaḱ hotetem toraokoḱa ona do samahoḱaḱ. By whatsoever thou may'st be profited that is an offering.

Toṛao. To pause, as between the ending of one song and the beginning of another, to pause in the execution of a dance preparatory to a reverse movement.
Eneċko toṛawa. They pause in dancing.
Sereñko toṛawa. They pause in singing.

Toṛaoni. Gonoṅ toṛaoni. } Food and liquor given to the bridegroom's party on the payment in full to the bride's father of the amount of gonoṅ pon (q. v.) or price of the bride agreed on between the parties.

Ṭoras. To be troubled, to be frightened.
Ona añjomkateye torasena. Having heard that he was troubled.

Toṛe sutạm. Gossamer.

Toṛe pokhori. Tuṛi pukhuri. } The name of a tank mentioned in Santal traditions.

Toreć. To be satiated.
Jom toreċenae. He has eaten to satiety.
Ñu toreċenae, dạṛkedae. He drank to satiety and went away.

Torhoć. A species of large lizard.

Torkal. Light-sleeping, easily wakened.
Khub torkal hoṛ kanae. He is a very light sleeper.

Torko morko. Quickly, without delay.
Torko morkoe heċ goċena. He came quickly.

Torlad. Torlać. } To cause trouble, annoyance or distress, to become tired, or wearied.
Torlaċkediñae. He caused me trouble.
Roṛ roṛteñ torlaċena. I am wearied with speaking.

Torlad. Tin torlad. Torlat. Tin torlat. } To cause various kinds of trouble, annoyance or distress.
Tin torlatkeċkoae. He caused them much trouble.

Torlao. To melt, to fuse.

Torlo morlo. To bear a distressed look, to look haggard or squalid, to appear like one not thoroughly awake, dull, distressed.
Reṅgeċteko torlomorloena. They are distressed looking through starvation.
Dal torlomorlokedeae. He beat him and caused him to look haggard.
Bul torlo morloenae. He is drunk and squalid.

Tormak̕. Jarmak̕ tormak̕. Tormać. Jarmać tormać. } Forlorn, like a vagabond, aimlessly.

Tormaṛ oć. A form of edible mushroom.

Tormuj. Cf. tạrbuj.

Toroć. Ashes, to reduce to ashes.
Lo toroċena. It is burnt to ashes.
Lo torojok̕a. It will burn to ashes.

Ṭoroḍaṅ. A kind of fish trap.
Tale ṭoroḍaṅ. The ṭoroḍaṅ made out of strips of the Palmyra palm leaf.
Kạsi ṭoroḍaṅ. The ṭoroḍaṅ made out of Kạsi (q. v.) grass.
Mać ṭoroḍaṅ. The ṭoroḍaṅ made out of strips of bamboo.
Meral ṭoroḍaṅ. The ṭoroḍaṅ made out of thin twigs of the Meral (q. v.) tree.

Ṭorok̕ ṭorok̕. Sound of water dropping.

Torop. Toroph. } Direction, side, towards.
Uni torophakanae. He is on his side.
Uni torop baṛe roṛme. Speak in defence of him.
Toropte. Through, by means of, by.
Mạñjhi toropte hoeakana. It was brought about by the Mạñjhi (q. v.)

Torop. To be tasty, good, delicious.
Noa utu do ạdi toropakana. This relish is very tasty.

Toropdar. Torophdar. } Partisan.
Uni ren toropdar kanae. He is a partisan of his.

Toroć. To knock the foot against an obstacle, to stumble.
Tohoć toroċiñ heċena. I came stumbling along.
Somboć toroċliṅ heċena. We came floundering along.

Ṭoroć. Ṭoroć toroć. } Imitative of the croak of the tree frog. Cf. ceṭer roṭe.

Toropdạri. Torophdạri. } Partial, prejudiced.
Toropdạrieć kanae. He is acting partially.

Torphan. Company, side, heap, pile, division.
Torphan torphanko dohoakaċa. They have placed it in separate piles or divisions.

Toṛphaṛ. Unreservedly, keeping nothing back.
Toṛphaṛe roṛkeda. He spoke unreservedly, he made a clean breast of it.

Toṛṛe. A trumpet.
Toṛṛeko oroṅeda. They are blowing trumpets.

Toṛṛe khunṭi. A post fixed at each of the four corners of a funeral pyre to retain the fuel in place.

Toṛtoṛ. Viscous, tenacious glutinous.
Atnaƙ sakam reaƙ daƙ toṛtoṛa. The water in which the leaves of the Atnaƙ (q. v.) tree have been mixed is glutinous.

Ṭoṛṭor. Ṭoṛṭorao. } Cf. ṭor.

Ṭoseạ. Ṭhoseạ. } To circumcise, useless.

Ṭosgor. Ṭhosgor. Ṭoskor. } Good, well, beautiful.
Ạdi ṭoskore taṛam idieda. He walks very well.
Ạdi ṭoskorko benaoakaƫa. They have made it very well.

Ṭosok. Cf. ṭhosok.

Tosot morgot. Thosot morgot. } Fusionless and slovenly, deficient in stamina and slovenly, pithless and slovenly.

Toƫ. To peck.
Sim enga gidrạe todekana. The hen is pecking the child.

Toƫ. To pull out, to extract, to come out, to bring or put out, to pluck, to pick.
Kaskome toƫeƫkana. 'She is picking cotton (from the bush.)
Daṭae toƫkeƫtaea. He pulled out his tooth.
Laga toƫkedeae. He drove him out.
Ńir toƫenae. He came out running.
Kul do ṭạṇḍite ńir toƫenae. The tiger ran out into the open.
Boṛ bań todoƙkantaea. He is unable to speak, he is speechless.

Ṭota. A cartridge.
Ṭota bạnduk. A breech-loading gun.

Ṭota. To shoot a second time when the game has not been brought down by the first arrow.
Ṭota phạṛi. The half of a shoulder of venison which falls to the share of him who has shot a deer a second time when the first arrow did not kill or disable it.
Uni ṭoṭakedeić ṭota phạṛiye ńama. The man who shot it the second time gets half of the shoulder.

Ṭoṭe. To carry a child astride on the hip. Cf. heo.
Gidrạ geye ṭoṭekae siń sạṭup. She carries the child all day.
Gidrạe ṭoṭeakadea. He has taken up the child astride on his hip.

Ṭoṭe. A small gourd hollowed out and used as a drinking vessel, or to keep anything in.

Ṭoṭha. Neighbourhood, vicinity.
Noa ṭoṭhare do bạnuƙanah. There is none in this neighbourhood.

Totha. Totheya. } Having a defect in speech.

Ṭoṭhkao. Ṭoṭkhao. } To peck, as a bird. Cf. ṭhoṭkao.
Ṭoṭhkao jomkedae. He pecked it and ate it.

Tothna. Snout.

Tothoƫ. Smell of stale urine.

Totka. Nape of the neck.

Totka gaḍa. The hollow below the occipital protuberance.

Ṭoṭkhao. Cf. ṭoṭhkao.

Ṭoṭko. A wooden bell hung round a cow or bullock's neck, a veiled name for a wife.
Ṭoṭkoanae se bań? Is he married or not? has he a wife or not?
Ṭoṭkole akawaƫmea. We have given you a wife, we have hung a wooden bell on your neck.

Ṭoṭoƙ. A kind of wild cat.

Ṭoṭok. Ṭaṭok. } A sorceter.

Totonopaƙ. Totonapaƙ dare. } A wild fruit tree, *Eugenia operculata, Roxb.*

Ṭoṭŏṛbaƙ. A small receptacle made by twisting a leaf, &c. into a spiral at one end, like a grocer's bag.

Totṛa. Thotṛa } Having a defect in speech.
Uni doe totṛagea. He has a defect in his speech.

Totro. To roll up as a scroll, anything rolled up as a scroll.
Sakam totroakana. The leaf is rolled up.
Sakam totroakaƫae. He has rolled up the leaf.
Totroko oroha. They play on a rolled up leaf. A part of the leaf of the Palmyra palm is rolled up like a scroll and when blown into emits a sound.

Ṭoya. Ṭoya cĕṛĕ. } The Blue-Jay.

Ṭoya dhaca. An ornament made of the feathers of the Blue Jay worn fixed to the knot of hair on the back of the head.

Toyo. The Jackal, *Canis aureus.*

Toyo hoḍgor potam. A species of wild pigeon so called from its note.

Tṛaṅ tṛaṅ. } Loud and distinct, clang-
Ṭaṛaṅ ṭaṛaṅ. } ing, applied to sounds such as that of a gong, kettle drum, &c.

Tṛaṅ tṛaṅ tumdaḱ saḍekana. The kettle drum sounds tṛaṅ tṛaṅ. [tinctly.
Tṛaṅ tṛahe roṛeda. He speaks loudly and dis-

Tuạṅ. To bruise, to contuse.

Dal tuạṅkedeako. They struck and made contused wounds.
Ememteṅ tuạṅena. I am bruised, reduced to poverty, by continual giving.

Ṭuạr. An orphan, to become an orphan.

Apat ṭuạr. Fatherless.
Engat ṭuạr. Motherless. [orphan children.
Pea gidrạ ṭuạr oṭokaćkoae. She left three

Ṭuạr ṭapar. } Orphans.
Ṭuạr amar. }

Gupi lạgiťiṅ ṅamkana ṭuạr amar menaḱkokhan. If there are orphans I am seeking (some one) to herd cattle.

Tubeć. To stuff, to plug, to cram in.

Oka do lutur tulạmteko tubeda. Sometimes they plug the ears with cotton wool.
Nunạḱe arjaoakaťa, tubeć rebeć oṛaḱreye ader peređakaťa, enrehõ niniạḱkanae. He has reaped such good crops, crammed his house full, nevertheless he calls out poverty.

Ṭũć. To pull out the ear of a straw or grass, to pull out the upper part of a grass.

Hoṛoko ṭũja. They pull out the ears of dhan from the straw.

Ṭũḍạ. } To touch lightly with the point
Ṭunḍạ. } of anything, a stick, the finger, &c.

Kaḍa ḍaṅra sioḱ jokheđko ṭũḍạkoa. When ploughing they poke the buffaloes and bullocks (with a stick.)

Ṭuḍạḱ. To dip into, as a pen into ink; to put the tip of the finger into anything that will adhere to it.

Buluhe ṭuḍạḱ jomeda. He is putting his finger into salt and eating what adheres to it.
Mić ṭuḍạḱte bar pe katha ologoḱa. With one dip two or three words are written.
Mić ṭuḍạḱ guṛ hõ bae emadiṅa. He did not even give me as much guṛ as would adhere to the finger (if dipped in it.)

Tude. A poetical name for the Tuť bird (q. v.)

Tudrạ. To assemble together, to crowd together, to cluster.

Mić ṭhenpe tudrạakana. You are assembled in one place.
Tudrạko do alom otoṅkoa bạrić lạgiťko. Follow not the multitude to do evil.

Tugum tugum. Throbbing, as pain in the ear.

Lutur tugum tugum hasoediṅkana. I feel a throbbing pain in my ear.

Tuhel. To be full.

Jom tuhelakanae. He ate and is full.
Gaḍa peređ tuhelakana. The river is filled full.
Bul tuhelenae. He is dead drunk.

Tuheť. To fill full, to cram full, as a store, &c.

Noa oṛaḱ oas reaḱ arjaoaḱte tuheťakaťako. They have filled this house full with agricultural produce.

Tuhkiť. To recognize, to know for a fact, to know for certain, to search out.

Uni ḍaṅraṅ tuhkiť oṭoakadea. I recognised the bullock and came away.
Khubem tuhkiťakadea? Hẽ, tuhkiťakadeaṅ. Did you clearly recognise him? yes I recognised him.
Noa katha tuhkitem baḍaea? Do you know this matter for a certainty?

Ṭuilạ. M. } A lock of hair left on the
Ṭuili. F. } crown, having a lock of hair on the crown, slim, lanky.

Ṭuilạ. To make water, of children.

Ṭui ṭui. Very high, lofty, tall, satiated.

Jom ṭui ṭuienae. He has eaten to satiety, i. e. till it appears on his stomach.
Ṭui ṭui usulae. He is very high.

Tukạ. A nest, to make or build a nest.

Netar ćẽṛẽko tukạeda. Just now birds are building their nests.

Tukạ suť. A method of tying up the back hair.

Tukạ. The hard core of a boil or gathering.

Ṭukin. Only, nothing more than.

Jiwi ṭukin menaḱtiṅa. I have only my life.

Ṭukin. } How much.
Tin ṭukin. }

Tin ṭukine emaťmea? How much did he give you?

Ṭukin. } This much.
Nin ṭukin. }

Nin ṭukine emadiṅa. This much he gave me.

Ṭukṛạ. } A piece, a fraction, to make
Ṭukrạ. } into pieces.

Mić ṭukṛạko emadiṅa. They gave me one piece.
Dal ṭukṛạkedae. He hit it and broke it into pieces.

Ṭukṛạ ṭukṛi. } Pieces, bits, broken
Ṭukṛạ ṭukṛi. } pieces, to make into pieces.

Ṭukṛạ ṭukṛiṅ ạgukeda. I brought broken pieces, or pieces.

Ṭukri. A kind of bamboo basket.

Ṭukuć. A small earthen pot.
Ṭukuć ṭukuće dakaakaća. She has cooked several pots of rice.

Tukuć. To nudge, to touch lightly.
Tukuć ganeme. Nudge him again.
Tukujem. Nudge him.
Hijuk̕ hijuk̕teye tukuć ganiń. Lest by her continued coming she weary me.

Ṭukuć.
Kuṛi ṭukuć cẽṛẽ. } A species of Lapwing.

Tukuć.
Taham tukuć. } Stumbling.

Ṭukuć hoṛo. A species of tortoise.

Tukun. To become numb, numb.
Rabańte tukunenae. He is numb with cold.

Tukuṗ tukuṗ. Old and feeble.
Tukuṗ tukuṗe haṛamena. He is old to feebleness.

Ṭuku ṭuku. Hastily and a small quantity in a small pot.
Ṭuku ṭuku isin goćkadae. She hastily cooked a small quantity.

Tul. To lift, to raise, used as to go when scolding.
Tul rakaṗkedeae. He raised it up.
Tiye tulkeda. He raised his hand.
Okatem tullena? Where did you go?
Bale tul daṛeak̕kana. We cannot lift it.
Tutulko. Lifters, bearers.

Tulạ. Scales, a balance, to weigh.
Tulạedako. They are weighing.
Tuk̕lạić. A weigher.
Tulạ ḍạṇḍić. Beam of scales.
Kạsi tulạ. A lever balance.
Taraju tulạ. A common balance in which scales and weights are used.
Nikti tulạ. Small scales in which valuable articles are weighed.

Tulạm. Ginned cotton.
Piteć tulạm. Carded cotton.
Rić tulạm. Ginned cotton.

Tulạni. Market dues, claimed by the official who measures and weighs.
Tulạniko uṭhạua. They collect market dues.

Tulạu. To compare, to copy, to raise an old embankment, to collect, to weigh.
Katha tulạupe. Compare the statements, or weigh the matter.
Eṭagak̕ kagojre tulạukatińme. Copy it for me on to another piece of paper.
Pinḍhe kạṭićgea, tulạupe, khan dak̕ teńgona. The embankment is low, raise it, then it will hold water.
Oṛak̕ oṛak̕ tulạu baṛakateń emaćkoa? I collected from each house and gave to them.
Mokordoma tulạu. To withdraw a complaint.
Mokordomale tulạukeda. We withdrew our complaint.
Tulạu phen katha. A pun, a comparison.

Tuli.
Tuliạu. } Rich, well-to-do, to rise in social position.
Jom tuliạu akanae. He has eaten his fill.
Tuliạu hoṛ kanae. He is a rich man.
Nui do sor din khone tuliạuakana. This (person) has only recently become well-to-do.

Tuli. Foundation, as of a wall.
Kạt reak̕ tuli. The foundation of a mud wall.

Tulkuṗ. Short and branchy, as a tree, to bend as ears of grain when ripe, short, as hair.
Gele tulkuṗena. The ears of grain are bent.
Hoṛo bele tulkuṗena. The dhan is ripe and the ears are hanging down.
Tulkuṗ uṗ kantaea. His hair is short.

Tulni. Equal to, like, similar, a partisan.
Goć tulni. Like dead.
Iń do uni sohgepe tulniedińkana. You are making me a partisan of his.
Noko do Saheb tulni hoṛ kanako. These are partisans of the English.

Tulpạ. M.
Tulpi. F. } Having short hair.

Tulpạ. Low and short branched, as a tree.
Ona Baṛe tulpạbo beć ńamkeda, nitok̕ do khub ḍaṛana. That Banyan tree when we came was low and short branched, now it is well branched.

Tulpi. Cf. tulpạ.

Tulsi dare.
Ṭursi dare. } Holy Basil, *Ocymum sanctum, Willd.*, a plant carefully tended and worshipped by Hindu women.
Tulsi sakam. The leaf of Holy Basil.

Ṭulṭulạu. To the brim, full to the brim.
Band pereć ṭulṭulạuena. The tank is full to the brim.
Kanḍako lo pereć ṭalṭulauakaća. They have dipped the water pots in the water and filled them to the brim.

Tultulạu. To cause to haste, to hasten, to cause to hurry, to hurry, to dragoon, to constrain, to drive. Cf. taltalao.

Tuluć. With, along with, in company [with.
Uni tuluće calaoena. He went with him.
Calak̕ tuluće jạpićidieda. He sleeps as he walks. [with them.
Alom onko tulujok̕a. Do not be one of them, do not unite with them, do not company
Iń tuluć alom ropoṛa. Do not dispute with me.

Tuluć tupuć.
Dhuluć dhupuć. } Unevenly, big and little, long and short.
Tuluć tupuć geleakana. The grain has eared unevenly.

Ṭum. Small, insignificant, frivolous.
Ṭum katha. A frivolous matter.
Mit ṭum heć ńogokme. Come near for a little.

Tumạl. To glean.
Tumạl baṛaedako. They are gleaning.

Tumạl tasaṅ. } Gleaning.
Tumạl tosoṅ. }
Tumạl tasaṅteko ạsulokkana. They live by gleaning.
Tumạl tasaṅ hoṛ kanae. He is a gleaning man, i. e. poor.

Ṭumạṅ. } An earthen pot larger than
Ṭumnạṅ. } a celaṅ (q. v.) and smaller than a ṭukuć.

Tumbạ. } A water bottle made out of
Tumbṛi. } a hollowed gourd.
A tumbạ is said to have the property of keeping water cool in the hottest weather.
Tumbạ dak. A tumbạ bottle of water.

Tumbạ oṭ. An edible form of puff ball.

Tumbṛi. Cf. tumbạ.

Tumbri. A small drum used by snake charmers and made out of a hollow gourd.

Tumbuṭ. To bow the head, to hang the head, to put close to.
Boṛ tumbuṭkedeako. They spoke to him and made him hang his head.
Lajaote mit tumbuṭgeye tahẽena. He never lifted his head through shame, he kept his head down all the time through shame.
Seṅgelre mundhạṭ tumbuṭkam. Push the log close to the fire.
Sahan tumbuṭakme. Put the firewood touching the fire.

Tumdak. A kind of drum.
The body of the drum is of burnt clay, the end beaten by the left hand is of bullock's hide, and that beaten by the right hand is of goat's skin, the whole is laced with strips of bullock's hide.

Ṭumnạ. A kind of earthenware vessel.

Tumsaṅ. Very corpulent, very fat.
Tumsaṅe moṭaakana. He is very fat.
Tumsaṅe ńelokkana. He looks very fat.

Tumul. Marrow.
Tumul dakentaea. His marrow has become water, he has become feeble.

Tuń. To shoot with bow and arrow.
Tuń ńamkedeań. I shot and hit him.
Khub tutuń hoṛ kanae. He is a good shooter with the bow.

Ṭuṅ. A little.
Ṭuṅtegeye haraoena. He was beaten by a very little.
Ṭuṅ katha. A trifling or frivolous matter.
Mitṭuṅ hõ bae botorlena. He was not in the least afraid.
Mit ṭuṅ hõ bae monduklena. He was not in the least sorrowful.
Ṭuṅtegeye goćena. He died suddenly.

Ṭuṅ ghuṛi. A little time.
Ṭuṅ ghuṛitege heć ruạṛenae. He returned in a little time.

Ṭuṅ marte. } With a ring, with a snap,
Ṭun marte. } crack, (imitative.)
Ṭhun marte. }
Ṭhuṅ marte. }
Ṭuṅ marteko dalkeda. They struck it once and caused it to ring.
Ṭuṅ marte sade goćena. It sounded with a ring.

Ṭuṅ mente. } Cf. ṭuṅ marte.
Ṭun mente. }
Ṭhun mente. }
Ṭhuṅ mente. }
Ṭuṅ mente rạpućena. It broke at once with a crack.

Ṭunạ. M. } Small, very little.
Ṭuni. F. }

Ṭunḍạ. } To prod, to poke at as with a
Ṭunḍu. } stick.
Ḍaṅrako ṭunḍạkoa. They poke at bullocks with a stick (when driving them.)

Ṭunḍạṅ. To move along anything narrow and raised above the ground.
Hiṅạ ḍạr niạ ḍạre ṭunḍạṅ ạcurokkana. He is going round from this branch to that.

Ṭunḍạṅ bhor. As long as life, the whole of one's life.
Ṭunḍạṅ bhoriń joma. I will enjoy it the whole of my life.

Ṭunḍi. The point where the shafts of a bullock cart unite, and where the yoke is attached.

Ṭunḍu. To prod, to poke at with a stick. Cf. ṭunḍạ.

Ṭuṅgạu. To snip off with the fingers, to break off.
Okoe koṛa coṅ go ḍoge ṭuṅgạukeṭ. Some young man or other, mother, has snipped off the sprout.

Ṭuṅgạu. To reach unto, to extend to, to fill or be full to full extent or capacity.
Dhuạ̃ serma ṭuṅgạu hạbić rakapạkana. The smoke has risen up to the skies, or has filled all the space up to the sky.
Dakko dul ṭuṅgaukeda. They poured water into the water pots filling all the space, they filled the waterpots to the brim.

Ṭuṅki. A small bamboo basket with a contracted opening.

Ṭuṅki dipil bapla. A form of marriage suited to poor people.
In this form of marriage the bride goes to the bridegroom's house and the marriage ceremony is performed there.

Ṭuṅ ṭuṅ. Tight, tense.
Ṭuṅ ṭuṅ moakana. It is swollen and tense.
Ṭamak ṭuṅ ṭuṅ saḍekana. The kettle drum sounds tense, i. e. the sound produced when tightly braced.

Ṭuni. } Small, very small.
Ṭuni ṭuni. }
Ṭuni ṭuniṅ aguakaṭa. I have brought a very small one.
Nin marań ṭuni gidrạ. A small child of this size.

Ṭuni. F. } Small, very small.
Ṭunạ M. }
Kạṭićgiako ṭuni ṭuni. They are little things.
Ṭunạgeae. He is small or little.

Ṭuniạu. To fit arrow on bow string ready to shoot.
Sare ṭuniạuakaṭa. He has fixed the arrow on the bow string ready to shoot.

Ṭunkạu. } To huddle up.
Ṭunkuć. }
Rabańte ṭunkạuenae. He is huddled up owing to the cold.
Rabańte ṭunkućenae. He is huddled up owing to the cold.

Tunkhi. Cf. ṭankhi.
Ṭunkuć. Cf. ṭunkạu.

Ṭunṭhạ. M. } Maimed.
Ṭunṭhi. F. }
Ṭunṭhạgeae. He is maimed.
Ti ṭunṭhigeae. She is maimed in the hand.

Ṭunṭi. To spurt, to issue with force through a small opening.
Meyam ṭunṭi oḍokoḱkana. Blood is spurting out.
Kanḍa bhugạḱena, dak ṭunṭi oḍokoḱkana. The waterpot is holed, the water is spurting out.
Ṭunṭiḱa. It will spurt out.

Ṭunṭi loṭa. A loṭa (q. v.) with a spout.

Ṭuuṭunạu. To huddle up oneself and shake or shiver.
Rabańte ṭunṭunạuenae. He is huddled up and shaking owing to the cold.

Tunum. To feel with the hand.
Ti tunum. To feel the pulse.
Ti tunumem baḍaea? Do you know how to feel the pulse?
Tunum ńamkedae. He felt for and found it.

Tunuń. A kind of rat trap in which a small bow and arrow are fixed the arrow of which when released transfixes the rat through the head.

Tuphim. } To know, to recognise, to take
Tuphin. } particular notice of, to mark.
Laha ṭhạikoko bachao johkan tabọ̃kan tuphinkeṭte. When he marked how they were choosing the front places.

Ṭupi. A percussion cap.
Ṭuplạḱ. A small bamboo basket.
Ṭupliḱ. A bamboo basket smaller than a ṭuplạḱ (q. v.)

Ṭupri. A hat, a cap, head gear, to put on a hat or cap.
Jolha ṭupri. A cap of the shape worn by Musalmans.
Raj ṭupri. A gold laced cap worn by rich men, a king's crown.
Saheb ṭupri. English hats, hats or bonnets of the kinds worn by Europeans.
Ṭuprikedeako. They hatted him, they put on him a hat.
Ṭupriko horoḱadea. They put on him a hat.
Ṭupriḱae. He will wear a hat, he will have on a hat.

Tupuć. To fall head foremost, to fall headlong, headforemost, headlong.
Tupuć goćenae. He fell headforemost and died.
Buru kańkha hạbićko idikedea tupuć ńurhạea mente. They took him to the brow of the hill for the purpose of casting him down headlong.

Tupuń. The Reciprocal form of tuń (q. v.); to shoot at each with bows and arrows.
Hulreko tupuńena. In the rebellion they shot at each other with bows and arrows.

Tur. The roller on which the cloth is rolled by the weaver as he weaves

Tur. Age.
Mit tur kangeako. They are of an age.

Tur. Species, breed.
Onkoaḱ tur calaḱa mente. So that their species might continue.
Nãwã turiń rakapkeda. I obtained a new species or breed.

Ṭurạ. M. } Small, little.
Ṭuri. F. }

Turãt. Immediately, instantly, on the instant, at once, without delay.
Turãt geye ruạṛ goćena. He returned immediately.

Ṭurạ ṭuri. Big and little, small and smaller.
Ṭurạ ṭuriye busạḱakaṭkoa. There are big and little in her litter.
Kạṭić geako ṭurạ ṭuri. They are small, small and smaller.

Tuṛbuṛạu. } To cause to hurry, to hasten, to drive, to whip up.
Taṛbaṛao. }
Aḍiye tuṛbuṛạueṭkoa. He is hurrying them greatly.

Tarbariạ. } Energetic,

Ạdi turburiạ hoṛ kanae. He is a very energetic man.
Turburiạ geạe. He is energetic.

Tuṛi. The plant which yields the Mustard or Colza oil, *Brassica campestris, Linn.*

Thọdiạ tuṛi. }
Luṭni tuṛi. } Varieties of *Brassica campestris,*
Man tuṛi. } *Linn.*
Rại tuṛi. }

Tuṛi parhao. To recite an incantation over mustard seed. Cf. tuṛi.

An incantation is recited over some mustard seed, after which a few seeds wrapped in a piece of cloth are attached to a string round the neck or loins and worn as a charm against witchcraft, the evil eye, &c.

Tuṛi. A semi-Hinduized caste of aborigines, by profession drummers.

Tuṛi cẽṛẽ. A small bird which frequents the fields in which mustard is grown.

Tuṛi sim. A plant, *Orobanche indica, Ham.,* the roots of which adhere to those of other plants. In the Santal country it is found mainly on the tuṛi or mustard plant, hence the name.

Turiạ. Age.
Miṭ turiạ kanako. They are of an age.

Tursi phul. A kind of rice.

Tursi dare. Cf. tulsi dare.

Turtạ. To invent, to fabricate, to concoct, to trump up.
Turtạkateye lạikeda. He concocted and told, he concocted what he said.
Turtạ katha kana. It is a fabricated statement.

Turte. Immediately, instantly, on the instant, at once, without delay.
Turtegeye em goṭena. He gave at once.
Turte turte epemge besa. To give without delay is best.

Turui. Six.
Turui ṭaka. Six rupees.

Turu dhum. Unseemly, unsightly, applied to rubbish, &c. lying about.
Turu dhum katwarakana. It is unsightly with rubbish.
Turu dhum ñeloḳkana, niạ hõ bape saphaeda. It looks unsightly, even this you do not clean.

Turuk. Musalman cavalry.

Turuk turuk. } Trippingly, with short
Ṭarak turuk. } and quick steps.
Geḍra hoṛ ṭuruk ṭuruke calaḳkana. The little man goes tripping.
Ṭuruk ṭuruk baṛaekanae. He goes tripping about.

Turuñ. A heavy piece of wood with a hole through it into which the foot of a criminal is placed and then wedged tightly.
Turuñko horoḳadea. They put a turuñ on him.
Turuñadeako. They fixed his foot in a turuñ.

Turuñ. To fill.
Jom turuñense. He has eaten and is full.
Bạndiye ader turuñkeda. He brought in bạndis (q. v.) and filled it (storehouse.)

Turutukạ. Litter, rubbish, unsightly or unseemly owing to the presence of litter or rubbish.
Oṛaḳ turutukạakana. The house is littered.
Turutukạ ñeloḳkana, joḳ giḍikaḳpe. It is unsightly owing to the presence of litter, sweep it up and throw it away.

Turyuṭ turyuṭ. To croak, as a young frog.
Turyuṭ ṭuryuṭ roṭeye raḳeda. The frog is croaking.
Turyuṭ ṭuryudoḳ kanae roṭe do. The frog is croaking.

Ṭusạ. A bud, a leaf bud, a shoot, the tip.
Sarjom ṭusạ. A bud of the sarjom (q. v.) tree.
Maṭkom ṭusạ. A bud of the maṭkom (q. v.) tree.
Pe ṭusạ dhubi ghãs. Three tips of dhubi (q. v.) grass.

Tuskạ. } A certain one, so and
Phạlna tuskạ. } so.
Phạlna tuskạ nite lạieṭkoa. She is now saying it is so and so.

Tuskil. Fault, offence, delinquency, misconduct.
Ceṭe tuskilkeṭtama? What offence is he guilty of against you?
Ceṭ tuskil unirepe ñamkeda, onatepe ḍandomkedea? What fault did you find in him, for which you fined him?
Amaḳ tuskil kana, onateko sạjạikeṭmea. It is your fault, therefore they punished you.

Ṭuṭ. }
Ṭuṭi. } Loss, to suffer loss or damage.
Ạdi ṭuṭ paṛaoentiña. I suffered much loss.
Mon ṭuṭ. To be very sorrowful.

Ṭuṭ dare. The Mulberry tree.

Ṭuṭ cẽṛẽ. A small bird, *Xantholœma haematocephala.*

Ṭuṭ kuriạ. A very small hut.

Ṭuṭ laṅgaṭ. } Poor people.
Ṭhuṭ laṅgaṭ. }

Ṭuṭạ bhaṅga. Fragments, pieces, broken, cracked, damaged.
Ṭuṭạ bhaṅga tahẽkantiṅa, bodolkedaṅ. I had damaged ones, I exchanged them.

Ṭuṭạu. To be broken, to be fractured, to be broken up, to be reduced to poverty, to be ruined.
Mon ṭuṭạu. To be broken in spirit, to be very sorrowful.
Iskul do ṭuṭạuena. The school is broken up.

Ṭuṭhạ. } **Ṭuṭhạ ṭuṭhạ.** } Shorter than the proper length.
Candbol ṭuṭhạgetaea. His tail is short.

Ṭuṭi. A blunt arrow, to shoot a blunt arrow, to hit, as hail.
Mać ṭuṭi. The blunt point of bamboo on an arrow.
Dereṅ ṭuṭi. The blunt point of horn.
Lopoṅ ṭuṭi. The blunt point of the lopoṅ (q. v.) fruit.
Soso ṭuṭi. The blunt point of the stone of the soso (q. v.) fruit.
Cẽṛẽko arelte ṭuṭi goćketkoae. Birds were killed by hail stones hitting them.

Ṭuṭi. To suffer loss, to sustain damage, loss, damage. Cf. ṭuṭ.

Tutiyạ. Sulphate of copper, blue stone.

Ṭuṭki } **Ṭhuṭhki.** } Worn small with use.
Ṭuṭki jonok. A worn broom.

Tutri biṅ. A species of snake.

Tuć tuć. In large volume, applied to smoke.
Tućtuć dhũakkana. There is a large volume of smoke.
Tućtuć dhũa rakaṭkana. Smoke is rising in large volumes.

Tutur. In sixes.
Tutur goṭećkate emakom. Give each six.

Ṭuṭuri. To cover the head, as with cloth; to veil the face by pulling the garment over it, as is the custom with native females.
Setoṅ jokhećko ṭuṭurika. They cover the head when the sun is hot.

Ṭuṭuri. } **Bahu ṭuṭuri.** } A small plant, *Vernonia cinerea, Less.*

Ṭuṭuri baṭuri. To cover the head, of females.
Ṭuṭuri baṭuriko heđena. They came with their heads covered.
Ṭuṭuri baṭuri kateko heđakana. They are come with their cloth over their heads.

Tutu tutu. To toot, as on a horn; to blow a blast on the horn; imitative of the sound produced by blowing on a horn.
Sakwako oroha tutu tutu. They are tooting the horn tutu tutu.
Tutu tutuiedako. They are tooting (on horns.)

Tuwạṅ. Cf. tuạṅ.

Tuwel. } **Tuhel.** } Unconscious, as one intoxicated.
Bul tuwelenae. He is dead drunk.

Tuweć. } **Tubeć.** } To stuff, to plug, to cram in.
Tuwećanme. Partake of food.
Ma tuweć johme, iṅ do baṅ tahena. Eat, I will not stay.

Ṭuyul ṭuyul. Bobbing up and down, in spurts.
Ńirak jokheć ṭuilạ ṭuyul ṭuyul hilạuka. When running the lock of hair on the crown bobs up and down.

U

Uạị. Another, a stranger, another's, a stranger's.
Uạị sate uạị kuḍạm aloben dohoea. Do not put him under the eaves or at the back of another's house. (A prayer offered for a dead person.)

Uạkep. } **Uạkhep.** } Experienced, intelligent, knowing, sensible, to be on the alert, to be cautious, to consider, to ponder.
Uạkep tabonpe. Be on the alert, be careful.

Ubạṛ khabaṛ. Rough, bad, full of holes as a road.
Onḍe do ḍahar ubạṛ khabạṛ iạteko bagiada. On account of the road being bad there they left it.
Ubạṛ khabạṛ hor do baṅ juta. The road is not good, it is full of holes.

Uber. } **Ubeṛ.** } To clear up after rain.
Nitok do uberakaćae. Now it has cleared up.

Ublạ ḍublạ. To squander, to waste, to fritter away.
Sanam dhonko ublạ ḍublạkećtakoa. They squandered all their substance.

Uboṛ suboṛ. To leave over from a meal.
Uboṛ suboṛak ńelpe, menakkhan emaepe. See if there is anything left over, if there is give it to him.
Uboṛ suboṛ ocoakaćako. They have left some, have not eaten all.

Ubri. F. } **Obra. M.** } Big-bellied.

Uć. To jump about, to skip, to talk big, to vaunt, to boast.
Damkom ḍahra etoko jokhećko uć baṛaea. When young bullocks are being broken in they jump about.
Aḍiye uć baṛaekan tahẽkana, men do bae daṛelena. He was talking very big, but he did not win.
Raskạteko uć baṛaekana. They are dancing with joy.

Ucạṛ. To transfer, to remove from one place to another, to displace, to shift, to be contagious or infectious.

Ol ucạṛ. To copy as a writing or drawing.
Niạ ol ucạṛkạtiñme. Copy this for me.
Guṭi do ucạṛok duk kana. Smallpox is an infectious disease.
Rohoe ucạṛ. To transplant.
Oṛakko ucạṛkeṭtakoa. They have removed their house.
Onḍe khonko ucạṛena. They have flitted from there.

Ucạṛ nacaṛ. To change place of residence often, to shift from place to place.

Ucạṛ nacaṛ baṛaekanae. He keeps changing his place of residence.
Ucạṛ nacaṛ ocoediñkanae. He causes me often to change my residence
Hanḍe nanḍe ucạṛ nacaṛ baṛaedae. He keeps shifting it from place to place.

Ucạran. To pronounce.

Ṭhik do bae ucạran daṛeakkana. He cannot pronounce well, or correctly.
Ucạran do bañ ṭhiktaea. His pronunciation is not correct.

Ucạṭ. To bring pressure to bear on one, to make uncomfortable.

Ạuri ḍanḍe emok hạbiẹko ucạṭakadea. They have brought pressure to bear on him until he pays the fine.

Uchạd. To annihilate, to destroy, to ruin, to devastate.

Ḍañrako jom uchạdakaṭa. The bullocks have grazed it and destroyed it.
Uchạdena hoṛo do. The dhan is ruined.
Uchạdenako, sanamko goć cabaenako. They are annihilated, they have all died out.

Uchạn. Without peace or joy, unhappy.

Uchlạu. To vomit, to spue, to retch, to throw up.

Rane uchlạu giḍikada. He threw up the medicine.

Ucit. To be intelligent, to be attentive, mindful, observant, regardful, wise.

Nit hõ bam ucitokkana. You are not even yet observant.

Ucrạn. Pronunciation, to pronounce. Cf. ucạran.

Ucrạnrem sabokа. You will be known by your pronunciation.

Ucrạu. To be seized, as by a fit or convulsions, or a fit of insanity.

Mirgi arhõ ucrạu ruạṛkedea. He has again been seized by an epileptic fit.
Kohkak nit ucrạu ruạṛkedea. He has now been seized by another fit of insanity.

Ucuñ. To nudge with the elbow, to hit with or dig the elbow into one.

Ucuñkediñae. He dug his elbow into me, or he nudged me with his elbow.

Udạcal. A rumour, a fiction, groundless, a fugitive.

Udạcal katha kana. It is a rumoured matter.
Am do dhạrtire udạcal ar ñir baṛaeićem hoẽna.
Udạcal kana noa do. This is a traveller's tale.

Udại paḍae. } **Udại puḍại.** } To waste, to squander, to misuse, to fritter away, wastefully.

Udại paḍae giḍiedape. You are throwing it away uselessly.
Ạuriak udại paḍaepe khoroceda. You are spending it wastefully.

Udạl. A large forest tree, *Sterculia colorata, Roxb.*

Udạm. Work, trade, profession.

Kam udạm din. The time when there is work to do from an agriculturist's point of view.

Udạm. Lying about, out of place, not cleared away after use, littered, applied to things left lying about a house.

Udạmko bạgi giḍiakawada. They have left them lying about.
Udạmge tahẽena. They remained lying about.
Udạm geñ heć ñamkeda, hoṛ bạnukkoa. I found the things lying about when I came, there was no person there.

Uḍar. To disperse, to let out cattle after the mid-day rest.

Sanam hoṛko uḍarena. All the people are dispersed.
Gạiko uḍarena goṭa ṭanḍire. The cows are dispersed all over the place. [cattle.
Gại uḍar ber hoẽna. It is time to let out the
Tinrem oḍokena oṛakkhon? gại uḍarko jokheć. When did you leave home? at the time of letting out the cattle, i. e. about 2 p. m.

Udạs. To look distressed, to look out of sorts, to be distressed or sorrowful, desolate.

Mone udạsentaea. His spirit is sorrowful.
Duken iạte netar do udạse ñelokkana. He looks distressed through being in affliction.
Cas samṭaoenkhan netar do udạsge aṭkarokkana. Now that the crops have been gathered in it feels desolate.

Udạu. To fly, to squander, to waste, to dissipate.

Iñak kathako udạukeṭtiña. They passed my matter over. [their wealth.
Dhon doko udạukeṭtakoa. They squandered
Cẽṛẽ udạukae nahak. The bird will fly away presently.
Coṭte udạuktenko. Birds, fowls of the air.

Udạu. } **Udạ̃u.** } A rumour, a current story passing from one person to another without any known authority for the truth of it.

Mit goṭeć udạ̃u añjomkate aćak disomteye ruạṛ calaoena. Having heard a rumour he returned to his own country.

Goṭa disomre udgąuena. It is rumoured all over the country, the rumour has spread all over the country.

Udgar. Heat, hot, to become hot.
Udgąr din kana netar do. At present it is the hot weather.
Setoñ dinre udgąr ięte bahrereko gitića. In the hot weather on account of the heat they sleep in the open, or in the open air.

Udgąu. To urge, to exhort, to egg on, to stir up, to incite.
Kąmire udgąuećkoae. He is inciting them to work, or he is urging them on to work.
Uni piṭiakan biñ alom udgąuea. Do not stir up that coiled up snake.

Udguć. } Udgup. } Fairly, moderately, applied to fatness.
Udgupe moṭaakana netar do. Just now he is moderately fat.

Udhąr. On credit, not paying ready money.
Udhąrteñ ągukeda. I bought in on credit.

Uḍhąu To hold a house warming, to take possession of a new house, to use a new article for the first time.
Oṛaǩ uḍhąu lągićko jarwalena. They were assembled to hold a house warming.
Noa tukuć ąurile uḍhąua. We have not yet used this pot.

Udhiąu. To boil over.
Toa do udhiąuǩa, ḍher alope tihgiaǩa. The milk will boil over, do not put on too much firewood.

Udhin. Submission, subjection, dependence.
Uni udhinre menaña. I am subject to him.

Udhmą. } Udmą. } Free, unrestricted, without surveillance, unemployed.
Ḍąńri udhmąko aṛaǩakaćkoa. They have allowed the cattle to go at large. no one in charge of them.
Udhmą din. The hot weather when from an Indian agriculturist's point of view there is little work to be done.
Udhmą netarge menaea, kąmi bąnuǩtaea. At present he is unemployed, he has no work.

Udhuć udhuć. Applied to the walking of a very fat person, to waddle.
Udhuć udhuće calaǩkana, moṭa ięte. He is waddling through fatness.

Uḍi. Cf. ąḍi.
Uḍi utąrpe emadea. You gave him a great deal.
Tin uḍi emaćmeae? Nin uḍi. How much did he give you? As much as this.

Uḍi. } Uṛi. } Petulant, sulky.
Ąḍi uṛi kanae. He is very sulky.

Uḍią. } Uṛią. } The people of Orissa, the Uriyas.

Uḍią. A kind of bamboo basket.

Uḍią uḍii, } Uḍiyą uḍiyi. } Flying away, carried away by the wind, as the thatch on a roof, &c.
Oṛaǩ renko sanam uḍią uḍiiko oḍok calaoena. The whole household went flying away one after the other.
Sanam ąuṛiye uḍią uḍiikeda. He (the wind) carried away all the thatch.

Uḍiąu. To raise, as dust, to be carried by the wind.
Dhuṛiko uḍiąueda. They are raising the dust.
Alope onkaea, dhuṛi uḍiąuǩa. Do not do that, dust will be raised.

Udkhud. Food, means of subsistence.
Udkhud cetat hõ bąnuǩtaea are bakhaećkana. He has got no means of subsistence and he is talking much.
Udkhud oeć hõ bąnuǩtaea, eken bhakage ḍhertaea. He has nothing to eat, he has only a glib tongue.

Uḍhi A small bamboo basket.

Udmą din. Cf. udhmą.

Uḍmalao. To dance and wheel round armed with club, spear, &c.
Ado daram daǩ lągić bąriątko ṭhen uḍmalaoateko calaǩa. At the ceremony of taking water to the bridegroom's party, they go dancing and wheeling armed with clubs, &c.
Uḍmalao bąṛaekanae. He is dancing about, (as if challenging some one.)

Uḍrą uḍri. To go off in companies on the impulse of the moment on seeing, or hearing of, others going.
Uḍrą uḍriko calaoena aṛaǩ sić. They have gone off one after the other to gather pot-herbs.
Ńeńel uḍrą uḍriko calaoena. They have gone off in companies to see the fair.
Mić serma do hoṛ uḍrą uḍriko dąṛeć tahẽkana bototre. One year the people through fear were fleeing.
Huhul hoṛ do Bir disom khon uḍrą uḍri noa disomteko ńir heelena. Rebels from the Santal Pargannas fled in companies to this (part of the) country.

Uḍrąu. To go off on the impulse of the moment on seeing, or hearing of, others going.
Uḍrąu calaoenako ńeńel lągić. They have gone off to the fair.
Cele coe bhiṛkąukećkoa uḍrąuenako gąi do. Something frightened the cows, they have run off.

Udri. } Udri rog. } Dropsy.
Udriakanae. He has dropsy.

Uḍuć ḍubuć. Sinking below and then rising above, as in water.
Uḍuć ḍubućle paromena. We crossed (the river) at times under and at times above the water.
Uḍuć ḍubućko paeraǩkana. They are swimming sinking in and rising above the water.

Uḍu ḍubu To be immersed, to be overwhelmed.

Uḍuḍubuakanale kạmite. We are immersed in work, overwhelmed with work.

Uduk̕. To shew, to point out.

Uduk̕ kạṭup. } The index-finger, the fore-
Uk̕duk̕ kạṭup. } finger.

Ote uduk̕adiña. He pointed out the land to me.

Kewateye uduk̕adiña. He pointed it out to me with his chin.

Hor khone uduk̕aćkoa. He pointed it out to them from the road.

Ṭhuṭhuye uduk̕adiña. He shewed me his thumb, he defied me.

Uk̕duk̕ak̕. A pointer.

Uḍuṅ. Cf. oḍoṅ.

Udur. To snore.

Uduréḱanae. He is snoring.

Uduṛ dhumạ. Very, applied to stoutness, very stout, corpulent.

Uduṛ dhumạe moṭaakana. He is very stout.

Uduṛ dhumạe ńelok̕kana. He appears to be very corpulent.

Uduṛ dhupuṛ. With might and main, hastily, hurrying on, with least possible loss of time, distracted, perplexed.

Uduṛ dhupuṛko chuṭạuakana. They are at it full tilt.

Ạdi uduṛ dhupuṛko lagaoakana oṛak̕ bek̕nao. They are hurrying on the building of the house.

Ughạr samhar. To nurse, as a sick person.

Ạdile ughạr samharledea, enhõ bae bańcaolena. We nursed him assiduously, nevertheless he was not saved, did not survive.

Ughạṛ. Uncovered, exposed.

Ughạṛkediñae. He exposed me, told about me.

Ughạṛgeye gitićakana. He is lying without a covering.

Dakakate ughạṛgeko dohoakaṭa. Having cooked the rice they have left it uncovered.

Kicrićko ughạṛkedea. They stripped off his clothes.

Ughṛạu. To uncover, to expose.

Bhorom ughṛạukeććińae. He made me ashamed, he disgraced me.

Ugni monda. To become deranged, as the stomach.

Ugni mondaakantaea. His stomach is deranged.

Ugur. To esteem, to hold in esteem.

Kạmire khube ugurakana. He is greatly esteemed for his work.

Ti uguruk̕kantaea. He is liberal, or he is generous.

Ugur sundué. Industriously, harmless, quietly.

Ugur sunduće kạmi joña. He works industriously.

Jakob do ugur sundué tạmbukoreye tahena. Jacob dwelt quietly in tents.

Uh. Cry of pain, or sorrow, alas.

Uh! goćentińae hoponiń do. Alas! my son is dead.

Uh! nonḍe hasokediña. Oh! it pained me here.

Uhui uhui. Throbbing.

Uhui uhui hasoediñkana lutur do. There is a throbbing pain in my ear.

Ũhũk̕. Interjection of annoyance or regret.

Ũhũk̕! hiṛińkedań. Oh dear! I forgot it.

Ũhũk̕! bạń disạećkana. Oh dear! I do not remember.

Uhu uhu. An interjection of annoyance or regret.

Uhu uhu! thoṛań bańcaokedea. Dear me! I missed it by ever so little.

Uihạr. To think affectionately of, to yearn for, to long for, to remember with affection.

Ạdiń uihạrećmea. I am thinking of you with affection.

Janam disomiń uihạreda. I remember my native country with affection, or I am longing for my native country.

Uihạr uihạrteń ńuieda pạurạ. I am drinking liquor and thinking of the time when I may not be able to get it.

Uihạr uihạrteye rak̕ećkana. She is weeping owing to continued affectionate remembrance.

Ujạṛ. To lay waste, to desolate, to ruin, to devastate, deserted, desolate.

Ujạṛ ato. A deserted village.

Kaskomko ujạṛkeda. They ruined the (field of) cotton.

Peṛako jom ujạṛkeślea. Visitors ate us bare.

Casko jom ujạṛkeśtalea. They ate and devastated our crops.

Ujạṛ din kana netar do. This is the time when the fields are bare.

Ujạṛ kanṭa. A common prickly weed of cultivation, *Argemone mexicana, Linn.*

Ujhlạu. To pour out.

Kanḍate ujhlạuaeme. Pour it on him from a waterpot.

Dul ujhlạukedako dak̕. They poured out all the water.

Noa bahako dul ujhlạuak̕kana. They are pouring water on this flower.

Ujhlạu caba goćkam. Pour it all out.

Khaclạk̕ reak̕ hoṛo ujhlạu goćkam. Pour out the rice that is in the basket.

Hoṛoko ujhlạu giḍi baṛaakaṭa. They have spilled rice here and there.

Uji. A substitute.

Ujiń doho oṭoakadea. I have left a substitute.

Uni ujireń kạmikana. I am working as his substitute.

Ujil jhạmbil. } To keep moving articles from one place to
Ujil jhumbil. } another, to keep moving from one place to another, two days or so here and two days or so there.

Ujil jhạmbil bạṛaedae. He keeps moving (the articles) from one place to another.

Ujoḱ. Cf. uć.

Ujrạ. Cf. ujạṛ.

Uju. } True, accurate, honest,
Uju uju. } upright, straight forward.

Uju uju roṛpe. Speak truthfully.
Uju katha roṛme. Tell a true story.
Uju hoṛ kanae. He is an honest man, he is a straight forward man.

Ujuḱ. To fall from a standing position.

Ujuḱenae. He has fallen.
Ujuḱadea. It fell on him.

Ujur. To petition, to make application, to make an excuse; petition, representation, excuse.

Ujur do bań añjomoḱtama. Your excuse will not be listened to.
Iñaḱ ujur bań añjomlentiña. My petition was not heard, or was not granted.
Kaṭ lạgić iń ujurakaṭa. I have petitioned for timber.

Ujur mujur. To petition, to make application, to entreat, to beg, petition, excuse.

Ạdiye ujur mujurlaḱa. He earnestly entreated.
Ujur mujurkedae. bań añjomlentaea. He petitioned earnestly, his petition was not granted.

Ukạṭ pakaṭ. To disorder, to put into confusion, disorderly, disarranged, higgledy piggledy.

Sanam kagoje ukạṭ pakaṭkeda. He disarranged all the papers.
Busup̣ sanamko ukạṭ pakaṭkeda. They disordered all the straw.

Ukbuk. } Suffocating, to suffocate, to
Ukbukạu. } stifle, to gasp for want of breath.

Hoe bae hoeĕda, ukbukge aṭkaroḱkana. There is no breeze, it feels stifling.
Ukbukạu goćenae. He was suffocated to death.
Unumlenkhane ukbukạuḱa. If one goes under the water he is suffocated.

Ukhrạu. To pluck up, to eradicate, to be rooted up, to raise up, to stamp, to be imprinted.

Reheć sudhạko ukhrạukeda. They plucked it up root and all.
Oda otre pañja ukhrạuakana. The feet marks are imprinted on the damp soil.
Deare parkom reaḱ cinhạ ukhrạuakana. The marks of the bed are imprinted on his back.

Ukhṛi. Cf. ukhuṛ.

Ukhu pukhu. Stifling, stuffy.

Ukhu pukhu ạikạuḱkana, udgạrte. It feels stifling owing to the heat.

Ukhuṛ. A large wooden mortar in which rice and other grains are husked, cleaned or made into flour.

Ukhuṛ ḍạḍi. A spring of water in which a hollow log has been placed to prevent the sides falling in.

Ukil. A pleader, an advocate.

Ukilạtnama. Power of attorney.

Uktạu. Cf. ạktau.

Jom lạgiće uktạuḱkana. He is impatient to eat.

Duṛup̣ duṛup̣te uktạuenae. He is wearied with continued sitting.

Ukta ukti. To be impatient.

Uktạ ukti baṛae kanae calaḱ lạgić. He is shewing his impatience to go.

Ukti. Ability, means.

Ukti bạnuḱtiña. I have not got the means, I cannot afford.
Nạlis reaḱ ukti bạnuḱtiña. I have not got the where withal to sue in court.

Ukti. To raise, to bring forward, to bring to notice. Cf. upusti.

Noa kathako uktiećkana. They are bringing forward this matter.

Uku. Cf. oko.

Ukurić. Where, applied to animates.

Ukurić okare menaetapea baba do? Where is your father?
Okurićtako Isor do? Where is their God?

Ukurić. A small wild bulbous plant.

Ukuṛ sukuṛ. To be restless, unable to remain still, applied mainly to restlessness induced by cold.

Rabahte ukuṛ sukuṛoḱgeako. They become restless owing to cold.

Ukus pukus. To breathe and give signs of life by moving.

Ukus pukusoḱkanae. He is breathing and moving.

Ukuć bukuć. } Burning to tell, to know,
Ukuć buyuć. } to see, &c., unable to keep a secret.

Ukuć bukuć bae jiwi daṛeada, lại goćkedae. He could not keep it secret, he blabbed it out.

Ul. } The Mango tree, *Mangi-*
Ul dare. } *fera indica.*

Ul bele. A ripe mango fruit, unripe mangoes when boiled.
Ul jań. The stone of a mango.
Ul ạmsi. Unripe mangoes cut into pieces and dried in the sun. Cf. ạmsi.
Ul koyo. The kernel of a mango stone.
Ul kạñji. A drink made from unripe mangoes.
Ul rase. A relish made from unripe mangoes.

Ụl banda. The name given to several kinds of parasitic plants found on mango trees.

Ulạ. To eject from the mouth, to spit out, to vomit.

Baṅ sebelkedete ulạ giḍikedae. He spat it out as the taste was not good.

Ulạ. Metal bush fixed into the nave of a wheel on which the axle rests.

Ulạg. Lonely, deserted, desolate, deteriorated.

Ulạgge bujhạuk̕kana, cele hoṛ hõ baṅ. It feels desolate, there is no person about.

Algate tabẽnte ran do ulạgena. Through being exposed the medicine has become deteriorated, or lost its peculiar property.

Ulạr. To persuade, to induce, to incite, to instigate, to allure.

Okoe coṅko ulạr idiakadea. Some one has allured him away.

Ulạr. To tilt up as a cart loaded too heavily behind.

Gạḍi ulạrena. The cart has tilted up.

Ulạṭ palaṭ. } Upside down, topsy turvy,
Ulạṭ pulaṭ. } to disorder, to turn upside down, to confuse.

Sanam kathako ulạṭ palaṭkedako. They turned the matter inside out, examined it in all its bearings.

Ulbul. } Deceit, misrepresentation,
Ulbuliạ. } guile, imposition, wile, disorderly, wayward.

Okoeak̕ ulbuliạteye cạlaoena? Through whose imposition has he gone?

Onko sãote ulbuliạe calaoena. He has been inveigled into going with them.

Ulḍha. A plant which grows in tanks the root of which is eaten.

Ule sarjom. The name of a tree mentioned in Santal traditions.

Ule siṅ. A poetical name for the Mango tree.

Ule siṅ, tale siṅ rohoe alaṅ mạiri,
Gujuk̕re, gurok̕re ṅutum tahena.
My dear, we will plant the Mango and Palmyra palm,
When we are dead and gone our name will remain.

Uli dak̕. Saliva.

Uli dak̕ sarsao godok̕a. Saliva flows.

Uli dak̕ jorok̕kantaea. Saliva is dropping (from his mouth.)

Uli dak̕ baṅ todok̕kantaea. He has no flow of saliva.

Ulkhạnia. } Short-tempered, wanting
Alkhạnia. } in perseverance, wanting in self-control, impatient.

Ulkhạniạ hoṛ kanae. He is a short tempered man.

Ulkhu pulkhu. Stifling, stuffy, oppressive, suffocating.

Ulkhu pulkhu aṭkarok̕kana hoe baṅ bolok̕kante. It feels stuffy owing to the air not entering.

Ulmạl. From all directions, to be perplexed, to be troubled, to be distracted.

Hulre hoṛko ulmạlena. At the rebellion the people were in a state of confusion.

Ulmạle hoeĕda. It is blowing from all directions.

Ulphạ. Unemployed, rent free, unencumbered.

Ulphạ geye jojom kana. He enjoys it rent free.

Ulphạ din. Time when there is no work to be done.

Ulphạe dãṛã baṛaek̕ana, kạmi bạnuk̕taea. He is going about unemployed, he has no work.

Mạn do ulphạgea. Mạn (q. v.) land is rent free.

Ulṭạ. Reverse, opposite, the opposite of what is right and proper, contrary.

Ulṭạteye aṭeṫek̕ana. He is spreading the bed clothes the wrong way.

Ulṭạteye gitiċakana. He is lying contrary, his head where his feet should be.

Ulṭạgeye roṛeda. He is speaking contrarily.

Ulṭạ seċe gitiċakana. He is lying the reverse way.

Ulṭạ ulṭi. To turn from side to side, to roll over on one side and then on to the other.

Laċ hasoedekante ulṭạ ulṭi baṛaek̕anae. He is rolling from one side to the other owing to a pain in the stomach.

Ulṭạ palṭạ. } In disorder, in confusion,
Ulṭạ pulṭạ. } topsy turvy, upside down, disorderly, confusedly.

Ulṭạ pulṭạko dohoakaṫa. They have put the things down in disorder.

Ulṭạu. To reverse, to turn upside down, the opposite of what is right and proper, reversed, upside down, contrary, different.

Ulṭạute. Upside down.

Ulṭạuteko dohoakaṫa. They have placed them upside down.

Kaṇḍae ulṭạukeda. He overturned or upset the water pot.

Alaṅge baṅ ulṭạuk̕taea. He cannot speak, he is dumb.

Ulṭạu palṭao. To turn upside down, topsy turvy.

Sanamko ulṭạu palṭaokeda. They topsy turvied everything.

Ulṭi. } Inaccurately, the reverse
Ulṭi ulṭi. } of what is known to be right and proper.

Ulṭi ulṭigeye roṛek̕kana. He is speaking inaccurately.

Ulṭi pulṭi. In disorder, in confusion, topsy turvy, upside down, disorderly, confusedly, backwards and forwards, first one way and then another.
Ulṭi pulṭiye hoeṅda,, onte note khon. The wind blows shiftingly, from this side and that.

Ulṭi ghanṭa. The afternoon.

Ulṭu pulṭu. Cf. ulṭa palṭa.
Ulṭu pulṭukedako. They confused it.

Uluṅ. Naked.

Um. To immerse, to bathe, baptize.
Um hoṛ. A baptized person, a Christian.
Umoḱe senakana. He has gone to bathe.
Holako umkedea. The bathed him yesterday.

Umadha. / Umadha jote. } The thong which binds the yoke to the plough beam.
Umadhae lagaokeda. He contradicted him.

Um ạmiṅ. Ceremonial washing or cleansing, ceremonial purification.
Um ạmiṅenae se baṅ? Hẽ, um ạmiṅenae. Has she been purified or not? Yes, she has been purified. (A polite way of asking if a woman has been confined.)

Um ạndha. Cf. umadha.

Umạr. / Umer. / Umor. } Age.
Niạ umạr kanae. He is of this age.
Uniaḱ umạr tinạḱ hoeṅna? What is his age? how many years old is he?

Umạ̃r. To fill as full as it will hold, as a measure heaped full of grain, to give liberally.
Mae phạriạḱma, phạriạlenkhaniṅ pereṅme umạ̃rmeaṅ. May he recover, if he recovers I will give you as much as you can take. (a prayer for a sick person.)

Umạ̃r khạclạḱ. A basket used as a grain measure being as much as it will hold filled up.

Umạr samar. / Umạr sumạr. / Umạr tamar. } With might and main, determinedly.
Noko do umạr sumạrko kạmikana. These are working with might and main.

Um areć. Pouring, as if one were pouring water on himself for a bath.
Um areće daḱeda. It poured a deluge.
Um areć balbal daḱ joroḱkantaea. He is bathed in perspiration.
Um areć balbal daḱte lohoćenae. It is wet with pouring perspiration.

Umariạ. Age, aged.
Mit́ umariạ kanakin. They are aged alike, they are of the same age.

Umạa. Inabstinent, libidinous, incontinent, lustful, under the sway of the animal appetite.
Jom umạsenae. He has been well fed and has become libidinous.

Umbrạu. To become rich, to become fat or sleek, to be, under the sway of the animal appetite.
Jom umbrạu. To be well fed and sensual, or dissipated or libidinous.
Jom umbrạuakanae. He is well fed and has become sensual.
Khub umbrạu hoṛ kanae. He is a very rich man.
Netare umbrạuakana. Now he is fat, or in good condition physically.

Umrạ M. / Umri F. } Dissolute, inabstinent, libidinous, sensual, incontinent, unable to control the animal passions.
Umrạ umriko calaoena. The libidinous men and women have gone.

Umdhi. To be drowsy, to be very sleepy,
Ạḍi umdhiakanae. He is very drowsy.
Pe mạ̃hãe beṅgeṫkeda, ona umdhite losoṫ lekae jạpiṫkeda. He was awake three nights, owing to that drowsiness he slept like a log.

Umdhum. With all haste, full drive, full tilt, hurry scurry, full swing.
Umdhumko kạmikana. They are working with all haste.
Ạḍi umdhumko enećkana. They are dancing full swing.

Umer. Age. Cf. umạr.
Gidrạ umerre. In childhood.
Niạ umerrege ḍher iṅ ṅelakaṫa. I have seen much in this my day.
Koṛa umere ṅeloḱkana. He appears to be a youth.

Umjhạu. To drive or chase fish about in a pool to tire them so that they may the more easily be caught.
Hakoko umjhạuakaṫkoa. They have chased fish and caught them.
Hoṛko umjhạuḱa Sohrae Sakrat jokheć. At the time of the Sohrae (q. v.) and Sakrat (q. v.) festivals people get no rest (going from one village to another in the hope of getting liquor.)

Umjha umjhi. With rejoicing, in high spirits, jubilant.

Umkạu. To be actuated by animal appetites, to become voluptuous. Cf. umuk.

Umtạ M. } Actuated by animal ap-
Umti F. } petites, voluptuous, lascivious, dissipated.

Umtạ umtiko calaḱkana ńeńel lạgić. The men and women actuated by sensual appetites are going to the fair.

Umtạu. To be excited, to be intoxicated, to give rein to the animal appetites, to become voluptuous.

Jom umtạuenae. He is well fed and has become carnal.

Hạṇḍi paurạ ńuite hoṛko umtạuḱa. By drinking beer and spirits men become sensual.

Sohraereko ńu umtạuḱa hạṇḍite. At the Sohrae (q. v.) men drink and succumb to their animal appetites.

Umuk. To be actuated by the animal appetites, to become voluptuous.

Jom umukenae. He has become dissipated, or voluptuous, through being well fed.

Jom umuk iṭte nonkaenae. He has become like this owing to his being well fed and having become animalish.

Umuk. Authority, delegated authority.

Gati do kisạṛ reaḱ umukteye kạmikana. The servant is acting under the authority of the master.

Umuk. A certain (person.)

Umuk hoṛe lạiadińa. He told me of a certain man.

Umuk umuk ạdi utạre lạiketkoa. He blamed many, this one and that one and the other.

Umul. Shade, shadow, shelter, reflection.

Dare umulre. Under, or in the shade of the tree.

Ạrsire umultet ńeloḱa. The reflection, or image appears in the mirror.

Am umulre menańa. I am in your shadow, I am dependent on you, I trust in you.

Umulanpe, manewa, umulanpe. Take shelter, men, take shelter.

Umur. Age. Cf. umạr.

Umur tumạr. Cf. umạr tamar.

Uń. To twist, as strands into a thread, rope, &c, to curl up or contract, as a leaf in drought.

Baberko uńa. They twist twine.

Hoṛo setońte uńena. The leaves of the dhan have curled with the heat.

Un. } Then, at that time.
Unre. }

Unre bạń tahẽkana onḍe do. I was not there then.

Un jokha. } That time, then.
Un jokheć. }

Un jokhae daḱeć tahẽkana. It was raining at that time.

Un utạr. Then only, not till then.

Un utạr iń bạdaekeda. Not till then did I know.

Un dhạbić. } Up till then, up till that,
Un dharić. } up till there.
Un hạbić. }

Un tirit. } As much as that, so much.
Un titit. }

Un titrite emaḱlea. He gave us as much as that.

Un marań. As big as that, so big.

Kul un marańe tahẽkana. The tiger was as big as that.

Un aneć. Not till then, only then.

Un anećko lạiadińa. Only then did they inform me.

Un khon. Since then.

Un khon nonḍe menańa. I am here since then.

Unạḱ. as much as that, so much.

Unạḱ marahae. He is as big as that, or he is so big.

Unạḱ hõ bae emaḱlea. He did not even give us so much as that.

Unạḱ usulgea. It is as high as that.

Unạḱena. It is as much as that.

Cekate unạḱena nitoḱ do? How is it as much as that now?

Unạn. } To spread as a report, rumour,
Unạni. } &c. to become known, to become public.

Katha do unạniena. The matter has become widely known.

Unạniakana ona katha. That matter has become public.

Sańkha rạpud reaḱ unạniena. The report of the breaking of the *sańkhas* has spread.

Unạu. To over cloud, to be black and threatening as the sky with clouds.

Daḱe unạuakaḱa. The sky is black and threatening rain.

Undkup. } To infer, to judge, to ween.
Unkup. }

Onḍe dhorage jel menaea mente unkupkate sarko ạṛaḱkeda. Inferring that the deer was certainly there they let fly their arrows.

Uni. He, she, that.

Uni hoṛ doe hatạokeda. That man took it.

Unis. Nineteen.

Unis bisgeakin. They are nineteen and twenty, not far apart, much the same, differing little, nothing to pick and choose from.

Uńjhạ uńjhi. With rejoicing, in high spirits. Cf. umjha umjhi.

Uńjhạ uńjhiko calaḱkana ńeńel. They are going in high spirits to see (the fair.)

Unkạ. A little over and above the exact weight, given to the purchaser; into the bargain, extra, applied also to a younger sister's becoming co-wife to an elder one.

Unkạko emadea. They gave her to him over and above what he paid for, she was thrown into the bargain.

Unkup. To infer, to judge, to ween. Cf, undkup̣.

Unṭ. A camel.

Unu unu. } Of many kinds, various, of
Unu aṇu. } different degrees.

Unu unu hoṛ menaḱkoa. There are many kinds of men.
Unu unu katha añjomoḱkana disomre. Many kinds of stories are being heard in the country.

Unum. To submerge, to go under, to sink in water, a man's height from the feet to the crown of the head.

Unum sumuṅko laakaṭa. They have dug the full depth, or height of a man i. e. standing in the pit his head would not appear above the ground.
Unum goćenae. He was submerged and died, he was drowned.
Unum eneckanako. They are diving in playing in the water.
Rinte unumakanae. He is drowned in debt.
Jom unum. To receive and give nothing in return.
Eyae ṭakako jom unuma. They receive seven rupees and make no return presents.
Ṭaka doe jom unumkeḱtińa. He did not repay me any of the money.

Unum sumuṅ. The full height of a man, as deep as the height of a man.

Unum sumuṅ daḱ menaḱa. There is water to the depth of the height of a man.

Unum sunum. Cf. unum sumuṅ.

Up̣. Hair.

Bhiḍi up̣. Wool.
Bhiḍi up̣ reaḱ. Woollen, made of wool.
Piṭi up̣. Curly hair.
Up̣e aṛaḱakaṭa. She has let down her hair.
Tope up̣. Short hair, hair cut short.

Up̣. To pour out or forcibly eject from a basket, &c., &c., to tip out.

Ḍopka khon daḱko up̣ goćkaḱkana. They are pouring out the water from the ḍopka (q. v.)
Khaciaḱ khon hasako up̣ giḍieckana. They are throwing down earth from baskets.

Up̣ muć. A black ant which exudes a hair-like thread from the anus, hence the name.

Upạị. To make effort, to endeavour, to bestir oneself, to essay, to strive.

Upạị do bạnuḱtińa. I have no resource.
Nes do bạṅ ae upạilaḱa. I did not raise good crops this year.
De upạialeme. Do something for us.
Paesa reaḱ upạiń lagaoakaṭa. I am endeavouring to raise money.

Upạl baha. The Lotus, *Nymphaea Lotus, Willd.*

Pond upạl baha. The white Lotus.
Araḱ upal baha. The pink Lotus.

Upạn jhapan. To change from place to place, vicissitude, hardship, ups and downs, annoyance.

Upạn jhapankedińako. They annoyed me.

Upạr. To save from the necessity of borrowing ready cash.

Ṭaka bạṅ tahẽkantińte nuigeye upạrkedińa. As I had no money this (man) saved me from the necessity of borrowing money.
Tuṛi hoyoḱkanteń upạr idiḱkana. As I got crops of mustard seed I am saved from the necessity of borrowing money, I am getting rich.
Nes upạroḱa. There will be a full return this year, and no necessity to borrow.

Upạr. On, above, upon.

Nui do rin upạr rin henaḱtaea, enhõe ririnkana. This (man) has debt on debt, still he contracts more.
Sud upạr sude hisạbadińa. When he made up my account he charged me interest on interest

Upạrre. } Against, with.
Upạrte. }

Iń upạrreye lạlisakaṭa. He has laid a complaint against me.
Iń upạrreye edreãna. He is angry with me.

Upạrdom. Long heavy breathing, to pant, short of breath.

Upạrdom geye sahećeda. He is panting.
Dal dalteko upạrdomkedeạ. They beat him till he was short of breath.

Upạr khapar. To destroy, to pull down, to ruin, to dilapidate, to dismantle.

Oṛaḱko upạr khaparakaṭako. They have dismantled the house.

Upạs. To fast.

Teheń doe upạsakaṭa. He is fasting to-day.
Pe mãhã khonle upạsakaṭa. We have fasted, have been without food, for three days.

Upạsa tirạsa. Hunger and thirst, hungry and thirsty.

Upạsa tirasako kạmikana. They are working in hunger and thirst.

Upcạu. Cf. upjạu.

Upel. To arise, to come into existence, to appear, as an apparition or a ghostly visitant.

Mić goćeć upelića ńelakadea. He has seen an apparition.
Nonde boṅgae upelakana. A boṅga (q. v.) has arisen here.
Onde gosãeye upelakana. A gosãe has arisen there.

Upel baha. } The Lotus, *Nymphaea*
Upal baha. } *Lotus, Willd.*

Pond upel baha. The white Lotus.
Araḱ upel baha. The pink Lotus.

Uper khaper. To squander, to waste, to misuse, to carry away, as by wind; to damage, to injure.

Hạndi ńuite jotoko uper khapera. They squander all in drink.

Upgạr. To help, to assist, help, assistance.

Nuige upgạrkedińae. This (person) helped me.

Uphạd. Disaster, distress, calamity, judgment.

Uḍi uphạd calaḱkana, hoṛko gujuḱkana. There is a great calamity in progress, the people are dying.

Eli ar uni oṛakren cetanre uphạdiń kola. I will send a calamity upon Eli and his house.

Uphạdko janamkeda. They created a disturbance.

Ale ṭhen ạḍi uphạd calaḱkana, iń do ohoń ganlena. We are involved in great distress, it will not be convenient for me (to go.)

Uphạdiạ. Traitorous, disturbing the peace.

Uphạn. To shine, as the sun after dispersion of clouds.

Nitoḱ do uphạn ńoḱakana. Now there is a little sun shine.

Uphań. Opportunity, respite.

Nahaḱ do ạḍi hoṛ oka hiloḱ kạṭic talań uphańko ńamlere enhiloḱge ona jokhećko umoḱa. In the present day many people when they get a little respite on that day and at that time they bathe.

Uphãṇḍ. } The arrangement of twine
Uphạṛ. } at the foot of a bed by means of which the netting is tightened.

Uphãṇḍ topaḱ ṭaka. A rupee which the headman of a Santal village receives on a marriage taking place in his village.

Uphạr. Disaster, calamity, rumour.

Disom khon uphạr hećleare, bahma, mõṛẽko Turuiko usạćakana, unrehõko maḱ mõṛẽḱa.

Uphlạu. To rise to the surface and float.

Uphlạ uphli. To rise to the surface and float.

Daḱ saname uphlạ uphlikeda. The water raised it all to the surface and carried it away.

Uphrạ uphri. } Struggling, striving, one
Upra upri. } above an other, one close on the heels of another.

Uphrạ uphriko boloḱkana. They are struggling to get in.

Uphrạ uphriko goćena. They died one after the other, in close succession.

Uphrạ uphriko jom lagidoḱkana. They are striving as to who will eat first.

Rel gạḍire uphrạ uphriko dejoḱa. They struggle to get into the railway carriages.

Upi. } Applied to ants which at
Upi kalgat. } a certain stage of their existence assume wings.

Upi kalgat lekae oḍokena. He has gone never to return, like the winged white ants who when they leave their holes never return.

Upi leka hoṛko jarwaakana. The people are assembled like winged ants, i. e. in large numbers.

Upiạ̃s. Dandruff, scurf which forms on the head and comes off in small flakes.

Upjạ. } Crops, produce of the soil.
Upjạu. }

Upjạ bań hoelena nes. This year the crops were not good.

Bale upjạu ocolaḱa nes do. This year we did not raise good crops.

Upjạn. } Crops, produce of the soil.
Upjon. }

Upkar. To help, to assist, assistance, help.

Uniye upkạrkedińa. He assisted me, helped me in my difficulty.

Uplạu. To rise to the surface of water.

Rohoe hoṛo uplạukedae daḱte. The dhan which was planted was raised to the surface by water.

Unum goć hoṛe uplạuena. The person who was drowned has risen to the surface, the body of the man who was drowned has floated.

Upor. Above, superior.

Cela do guru upor doe bań kana. The disciple is not greater than his teacher.

Uporre. At that juncture, at that particular time.

Ona uporre iṅgeń senena. I went just at that time.

Uposti. Cf. upusti.

Uprạḱ. } To be offended, to be
Rag uprạḱ. } angry.

Alom rag upragoḱa, ale gele bạṛićkeda. Do not be offended, we made the mistake.

Uprạnd. Over and above, besides that, in addition to that, at that juncture, just then.

Onae hataokeḱtińa, ar ona uprạndre dal hõe dalkedińa. He took that from me, and in addition to that he beat me.

Ona uprạndre unigeye hećena. Just at that time he came.

Uprạ pạṛi. One above another, struggling, striving.

Uprạ pạṛiko boloḱkana. They are struggling to enter, they have to struggle to get in.

Uprạ pạṛi rel gạḍireko dejoḱkana. They are struggling to get into the railway carriage.

Uprạ upri. Struggling.

Upriạ. Strange, unknown, recent.
Upriạ hoṛ. A stranger.
Ale upriạ hoṛ cećle roṛa? am mare hoṛ roṛme. What can we recent comers say? you are an old resident, you speak.

Uptạn. To spring up, to take place, to come into being.
Botor ar as hõ banarge uptạnoḱkana. Fear and hope these both are springing up.

Upusạṭ. Reciprocal form of usạṭ (q. v.)

Upusti. To bring forward, to raise, to start.
Okoe noa kathae upustiḱeda? Who raised this matter?

Upuṭ. To have patience, to forbear, to tolerate, to bear, to be satisfied, make impression
Uni do bae upuṭlena. He could not have patience.
Uni do onate bae upuṭlente din hiloḱ ge ondeye ạcur baṛaea. Being dissatisfied with that she every day walked about there.
Miṭ ghạṛi hõ bae upuṭ daṛeada. He could not tolerate for even a little while.
Nui gidrạ miṭ ghạṛi hõ bae upuṭa. This child does not exercise patience for a little.

Uputhạu. Reciprocal form of uṭhạu (q. v.)

Uputkạu. Reciprocal form of uṭkạu (q. v.)

Ur. To cast the skin, to slough, to remove the skin or outer covering, to pick the grains of Indian corn from the cob.
Biṅko uroḱa. Snakes cast their skin.
Jondra urme. Separate the grains of Indian corn from the cob.

Urạl. To persuade, to induce, to incite, to instigate, allure.
Uni doko urạlkedea. They allured him away.

Urạle patale. } Attracted by the sight
Urạl patal. } of others, caught the infection.
Hako goć urạle pataleko calaoena. They went to catch fish being attracted by seeing others going.
Urạle patalele hedena, noḱõe bale ṅamleṭkoa. We followed them and see we did not find them.

Urạliạ. One who incites, induces, allures. Cf. urạl.
Urạliạ kanae. He is one who allures others.

Urạn. To destroy, to lay waste, to desolate, to devastate, to ruin.
Pohoko jom urạnkedako. The locusts devastated it.

Urão. The Oraons, an aboriginal tribe of Chutia Nagpur.

Urbhuṅ. } Stupid, foolish, ignorant,
Urbhuṅga. } brainless, beef-witted,
Urbhuṅgaha. } incapable, imbecile.
Uni raj do urbhuṅgageye tahẽkana. That king was foolish.

Urbudaha. Senseless, puerile, simple, ignorant.

Urgạn. Likeness, resemblance, image.
Apat urgạne ạguakaṭa. He has reproduced his father. he is a reproduction, of his father,
Isor do aćaḱ urgạnan do manwae sirjạukedea. God created man bearing his own likeness.

Urgum. Warm.
Urgum oṛaḱ kana. It is a warm house.
Bae goćakana, urgumgeae. He is not dead, he is warm.

Uṛhu buṛhu. Over head and ears, many times round.
Rabaṅ dinre uṛhu buṛhuko oyo poṭomoḱa. In the cold weather they wrap themselves up over head and ears.
Uṛhu buṛhue bedhaoakaṭa. He has wrapped it many times round.

Uṛiạ. }
Uḍiạ. } The people of Orissa, Uriyas.

Uriạu. To clean out and whitewash a house, to lay thatch on without tying it down, to chastise.
Oṛaḱ goé gurićkateko uriạu oḍoka. They plaister a house with cowdung and clean it out.
Uriạumeaḱo nahaḱ. They will chastise you presently.

Uriạu. To have presence of mind, to occur to one on the spur of the moment, to feel an impulse to, to suggest itself to.
Ceṭ hõ baṅ uriạulentiṅa. I lost all presence of mind, nothing suggested itself to me.

Urić. Tight, firm, steadfast.
Tolurićakaṭae. He has tied it tightly.
Beṅgeṭ urićakaṭ tahẽkanae. He was gazing steadfastly.
Mone urićkedae. He determined, he made up his mind.
Saḅ urijoḱme. Hold tightly, hold fast.
Urić utạrkedako. They proved it to the hilt.
Urićena. It is tight.
Baṅ urijoḱkana. It is not tightening.

Urić. A bullock.
Urić arạṛ. Plough cattle.
Adar urić. A bull kept for breeding purposes.
Damkom urić. A young bullock which has not got its full complement of teeth.

Uṛić. } A small bird, studied much
Uṛić cẽṛẽ. } as an omen.
Etom uṛić, koṅe ere, sarkeṭ sạgunaṭte, sikriạḱ mạkṛiạḱbo joṛaokeṭa. Having taken an omen from the Uṛić bird on the right and the Ere (q. v.) bird on the left we contracted marriages.

Urić hon. A species of large rat.

Urić alaṅ. } A small plant used
Urić alaṅ arak. } as a pot-herb, *Portulacca oleracia, Linn.*

Urić alaṅ. } A small wild plant,
Nanha urić alaṅ. } *Portulacca quadri folia, Linn.*

Urić utiń. A method of hiring bullocks for cultivation.

One member of a family gives his services in exchange for the loan of a pair of bullocks to do the cultivation of the family.

Uri horo. Wild rice, *Oryza sativa Linn*.

Urit. Cf. arit.

Urlau. To separate by brushing with the hand as straw, &c mixed with dhan, &c.

Busuṗko urlau gidia. They separate and throw aside the straw.

Urla urli. Brushing or separating with the hand. Cf. urlau.

Urla urlikate capat gidi gotkedae.

Urmal. Small hollow spheres of bell metal having little iron pellets inside, worn attached to a leather belt round the loins, and producing a tinkling sound when the wearer moves. They are worn when dancing.

Urni bir. Primeval forest, a large thick jungle.

Ursiń barsiń. A day or two, a short period, a few days.

Ursiń barsiń do tahẽ hatar oooae. Let it remain for a few days.

Uru. A beetle.

Kat uru. Beetles bred in timber.
Gurić uru. Beetles bred in dung.

Uru ghao. Scaldhead, eczema.

Uru eṅga. A kind of abscess of the scalp.

Uruć putuć. Fierce, scorching, applied to the heat of the sun.

Uruć putuć setońkana. It is scorchingly hot.

Uruć supuć. Greedily, applied to eating or drinking after one has been satisfied.

Uruć supuće ńuieda. He is drinking although he has had enough.

Uru kundel. To tumble or roll about on the ground like a beetle's dungball.

Uru kundele rakkeda. He is rolling on the ground and crying.

Urum surum. With a will, energetically, at high pressure, hard.

Urum surumko kamikana. They are working at high pressure.

Urum bhusum. } Dusty, dirty.
Uruṅ bhusuṅ. }

Katić gidra uruṅ bhusuṅ dhuṛireko enećа. Little children dirty themselves playing in the dust.

Uruṅ bhusuṅakanań, bań umlenkhan thik bań sikauka. I am dusty, if I do not bathe I shall not feel comfortable.

Uruń uruń. } To be displeased, to be
Uruń paruń. } dissatisfied, to look
Uruń puruń. } vexed, to sulk, to be in the dumps, to murmur.

Ńutren hoṛak raska ńelte alom uruń uruńoka. Do not murmur at seeing the pleasure of the people of darkness.

Uruń puruń baṛaekanae. She is going about sulking.

Uruṅ bhusuṅ. Cf. urum bhusum.

Uru suru. Out of sorts, indisposed owing to a catarrh.

Uru surue mandakkana. He is out of sorts owing to a cold.

Urut. To cause to spin round by pulling a string first one end and then the other, to rub on a stone, as when sharpening a knife, axe, &c. &c.

Apariye urut ooeloakata. He has ground the arrow to a sharp point.

Kuindi hoyoe lagit jhinuke urut bhugalakata. He has ground a hole in the shell with which to pare the skin off the kuindi (q. v.) fruit.

Kapiń urut laserakata. I have ground the battle axe sharp, I have sharpened the battle axe by grinding.

Urut dhiri. A stone on which implements are sharpened by rubbing.

Urut urut. To be impatient, to long for, to crave for.

Jom lagit urut urutokkanae. He is impatient to get food.

Usara. Quickly, without delay, expeditiously, to hasten, to make haste, to expedite.

Bań usarakkana kami do. The work is not proceeding expeditiously.

Usarate daka hodme. Make haste in cooking the rice.

Usarau. Cf. usrau.

Usas. To help, to assist, to minister, to give or get respite or relief.

Nui hoṛ adi usasa kawadińae. This man has greatly helped me.

Usasiń ńamkeda. I got respite, or relief.

Usaṭ. To sulk, to be in the dumps or doldrums.
Bạhui usạṭentalea. Our bride is in the dumps.

Usạṭ. To be exhausted, as soil; insipid, as food; faded, as a flower, to lose strength.
Barge usạṭentiña. The soil of my garden is exhausted.
Goć hoṛo reak̔ daka usạṭgea. Rice which has died before ripening when cooked is insipid.
Usạṭena noa ul dare do. This mango tree is past bearing fruit.
Roṅ usạṭena. The colour has faded.

Usić. To vaunt, to boast, to talk big.
Usić baṛaedae. He is vaunting

Usić. To puff or hiss, as a snake when angry, refers mainly to the cobra.
Biṅe usićadea. The snake puffed on him.
Santals believe that if a snake puffs its breath on a person it communicates its poison to him, and death is almost as certain as if it had bitten him.

Uskạu. To raise up, to move, to rise.
Ạdi hamala noa kaṭ do, bạṅ uskạu daṛeak̔kana This log is very heavy I cannot raise it.
Duṛup̔ khon bae uskạuk̔kana. He is not rising from his seat.
Caba kathako uskạukeda. They raised again a settled matter.

Usku pusku. To move about, to make a movement towards getting up from a sitting position.
Bereć lạgić usku puskuk̔ kanae, bae bereć daṛeak̔ kana. He is making a movement to get up, he cannot stand up.
Gitić khone usku puskuena. He awoke and made as if to get up.

Uskur. To rouse, incite, excite, stir up, to energise, to stimulate.
Seṅgel uskurak̔me. Stir up the fire.
Okoe coko uskur boloak̔kana. Some one is supplying the stimulus to this.

Uslạt. } **Uslạti.** } Acknowledgment of payment, to give credit to in an account, a receipt, from *usul* to repay.
Bin reak̔ uslạti bae emadiña. He did not give me an acknowledgment of payment of my debt.

Usnạ. Rice which has been boiled before being husked, having innoculation or vaccination marks on the person.
Usnạ caole. Rice which has been boiled preparatory to husking.
Nui hoṛ do usnạgeae. This man has vaccination marks.

Usrạu. To hasten, to succeed, successful, effective, ready, active. Cf. usarạ.
Jahã tinạk̔gem usrạu daṛeak̔a, unạk̔ hakopakoetalaṅme. Make all the haste you can.
Dadal bạṅ usrạulak̔a. I was not ready to strike, it did not occur to me to strike.
Boroṛ bạṅ usrạulak̔a. I was not ready to speak, it did not occur to me to speak.

Usṭạha. Exhausted, insipid, faded. Cf. usạṭ.

Usti. A piece or pieces of bone of a cremated corpse rescued from the ashes of the funeral pyre. Cf. jaṅ baha.

Usti pusti. } **Usṭi pusṭi.** } Many generations, generation after generation.
Usti pusti reak̔ kantalea. It has been ours for many generations.

Usuk̔ pusuk̔. Cf. uskupusku.

Usul. High, lofty, tall.
Ạdi usul dareakana. It has grown very high.
Unạk̔ do alom usula. Do not raise it so much, do not make it so high.
Usul hoṛ. A tall man.
Usulena. It is too high.

Usul. To pay up, to repay, to give credit in an account for money paid.
Ṭaka usulaṅme. Credit the money to me.
Ṭaka ṣuri usulok̔ hạbić kạmime. Work till the money is paid up.
Tamasuk reak̔ deare usul ṭakako oladea. They entered the money he paid on the back of the document.

Uswạu. To suffer a relapse, to reappear, as a disease, to return, as an illness; be retarded as recovery from an illness.
Ceć bataṛak̔coe jomkeda, onate uswạuena karon do. He ate something which did not agree with him, therefore the disease has reappeared.

Uć. To swallow.
Biṅe ućkedea. The snake swallowed it (frog.)
Uć cabakedae. He swallowed it all.
Uć bienae, ar nitok̔ doe roroṛkana. He has swallowed his fill, and now he is finding fault (used in scolding.)

Ūṭ. } **Ūṭh.** } A camel, a dromedary.

Uṭạ. To root, as swine; to turn up or lift up with the snout or head.
Celem hataoea, sakam oк̔ṛećić se ot uk̔ṭạić? Which will you take, a tearer of leaves (a goat) or a rooter of the earth (a pig)? (asked of a spirit to find out what sacrifice will be acceptable.)
Ḍahra bhite uṭạkeda The bullock raised up the wall with his head.
Ḍahra uṭạkediñae. The bullock hit me with his head (in raising it up.)

Utạhuli. With an interval of a day or two, one after another, before and after. Cf. otạ hole.

Utạr.
Uttạr. } The north.

Utạr nakha. The north.
Utạr mohnḍa. The north, northward.
Utạr sen.
Utạr seć. } The north, northwards.
Utạr sene mohnḍaakana. He is going towards the north, or he is facing the north.

Utạr. Answer, reply.

Utạr emoǩ. To give an answer, to reply.
Noa katha reaǩ utạr emoǩme. Give a reply to this matter.

Utạr. Added to other words is intensive implying highest in degree, perfection, completion, or absoluteness; very.

Sạri utạrge. It is perfectly true.
Sen utạrenae. He has left for good.
Heć utạrenako. They have come to stay.
Ạḍi utạr. Very many.
Tehen̕ utạrin̕ baḍaekeda. Only to-day did I know, not b fore to-day did I know.
Un utạrin̕ baḍaekeda. Then only did I know.
Maran̕ utạrgeae. He is very big.
Maran̕ utạraǩ. A very big one, or the biggest one.
Maran̕ utạrić. A very big one, or the biggest one (animate.)
Bạnuǩ utạrena. There is absolutely none.
Caba utạrentin̕a ṭaka do. My money is completely exhausted.
Tayom utạrre uni menaea. He is at the very end (of a line,) he is the very last.
Pea utạrako. They are full three, there are full three of them.
Aema utạr. An exceedingly large number.
Aema utạr hoṛko goć ocoena. An exceedingly large number of people were killed.
Sojhe utạrgea. It is perfectly straight.
Goć utạrenae. He is dead out right.
Kāṛā utạrenae. He is stone blind, he is perfectly blind.
Tayom utạrre uni hõe goćena. He died last of all, at last he also died.
Tayom utạrteye lạiadin̕a. At the very last he informed me.

Uṭeǩ. To obtain a living.

Phalna mạn̕jhi jahga latarre ạsuloǩ uṭedoǩa mente. To obtain a living under the wing of a certain Mạn̕jhi. (q. v.)

Uthạhuli. Cf. utạhuli.

Uṭhại paṭhae. With all one's possessions, for good.

Uṭhại paṭhaeko calaoena. They have left for good
Uṭhại paṭhaeko hećena. They have come bringing all they possessed with them, they have come to stay.

Uṭhạu. To raise, to abolish, to collect, as money; to break up camp, to leave a place where one has been resting or staying temporarily.

Onḍe khonko uṭhạuena. They have left that place (where they had been camping or resting.)
Ona dạstur do uṭhạuenạ. That custom has been abolished.
Ạḍi ṭakako uṭhạukeda. They raised or collected much money.
Ṭaka uǩṭhạu tege menaǩkoa. They are engaged in collecting money, they are still collecting money.

Uṭhạu. The third ploughing given to a field.

Uṭhi bạisi. To break up, as a panchayat.

Uṭhi bạisienale. We have risen from the panchayat, we have broken up the panchayat.

Uṭhulạǩ. A temporary fireplace made of three stones or clods of earth, &c.

Uṭhul uṭhul. Throbbing in the head when in pain.

Uthum.
Uthumte. } Owing to, in consequence of.

Ghao uthumte ruạǩkanae. In consequence of the wound he has fever.
Khoǩ manda uthumte bohoǩ hasoedekana. He has headache owing to a cold.

Uṭhuṭhu. Cf. uṭuṭu.

Uṭi. Joint, node, knot in timber.

Maǩ uṭi. The node of a bamboo.
Kạṭuḅ uṭi. A finger joint.
Uṭi uṭi hasoedin̕kana. My joints are paining me.

Uṭić. To horn, to hit with the horns by lifting up the head, to toss, as a bull with its horns.

Ḍan̕rae uṭićmea. The bullock will hit you with its horns (if it raises its head.)

Utin̕. To barter, to give in exchange.

Ḍan̕ran̕ utin̕kedea. I exchanged the bullock.
Barea ḍan̕ra kaḍaten̕ utin̕keṭkina. I gave two bullocks in exchange for a buffaloe.
Lạhite buluhin̕ utin̕ ạgukeda. I bartered lac for salt.

Utin̕ sunum. Mustard oil.

Utiǩ. An ascetic, a jogi gosãe (q. v.)

Utiǩ lekae oḍok calaoena. He forsook all and went away like an ascetic.

Utjog. To take in hand, get together what is needed, to set one's mind to, to seek, to endeavour.

Dakae lạgiǩ utjog lagaome. Take in hand the cooking of the food.
Goćkin lạgiǩko utjoga. They seek to kill them.

Uṭkạ paṭka. To turn up, to topsy turvy, to rake up old matters.

Uṭkạ paṭkae ruheǩkedin̕a. He scolded me raking up old matters.
Hasa uṭkạ paṭkae poeda. He is hoeing an turning over the soil.

Uṭkạu. To prize, to raise or force with a lever.
Mare mareak̓e uṭkạukedińa. He brought up very old matters against me.
Jonḍra doko si uṭkạukeda. They ploughed up the Indian corn.
Rehetko la uṭkạuakat̓a. They have dug up the root, or they have dug it up by the root.

Uṭkạu paṭkạu. } **Uṭkau paṭkao.** } To turn over, as soil; to rake up old matters.
Uṭkạu paṭkạukedińae. He raked up old matters against me.

Utkuć. To nudge, to draw attention.
Utkuć ńok̓kedeae. He nudged him slightly.

Utlạu. To raise anew, to rise to the surface, to become known, to make known, to boil up or over.
Noạ katha utlạuena. This matter has come to the surface, has become known.

Utpat. } **Utpatao.** } Restless, mischievous.
Nui gidrạ utpatao baṛaekanae. This child is continually getting into mischief.

Utpạtiạ. Restless and mischievous.
Ạḍi utpạtiạ gidrạ kanae. He is a very restless and mischievous child.

Utrạha. } **Utrạhi.** } Belonging to the north.
Utrạha hoṛ kanako. They are north country-men.

Utrạu. To copy, to translate, to turn out, to become, to develop.
Nui ḍaṅra bese utrạuakana. This bullock has turned out well, has developed into a good bullock.
Khub koṛae utrạuakana. He has developed into an excellent young man.
Hindi khon Santaliteko utrạuakat̓a. They have translated it from Hindi into Santali.

Utri dudhi. A species of climbing plant, *Cryptolepis Buchanani, R. & S.*

Utu. Relish, taken along with cooked rice, *Scottice*, kitchen.
Dạl utu. A relish made from different kinds of leguminous fruits.
Jel utu. Flesh meat.
Aṛak̓ utu. A vegetable relish.
Hako utu. A fish relish.

Utu dhutu. To hurry, to do with might and main.
Dak̓ lekhan jonḍra erok̓ lạgić ạḍiko utu dhutu baṛạea. If it rains they hurry on the sowing of the Indian corn.
Noko do jom reak̓ko utu dhutu baṛaeda. These (people) are hurrying on the cooking of the food.

Uṭu puṭu. To be impatient, to be anxious, to fret.
Ạḍiye uṭu puṭu baṛaekana. He is very impatient.
Kạmi lạgiće uṭu puṭu baṛaeda. He is anxious to get to work.

Uṭup̓ uṭup̓. } **Aṭap̓ uṭup̓.** } To move.
Lać uṭup̓ uṭubok̓kana. There is agitation in the stomach.
Cele coń uṭup̓ uṭup̓e laṛaok̓kana. Some creature is moving up and down.

Utuć tumbuć. } **Utuć tuṅguć.** } To be in dotage, to be feeble of understanding or mind, as old people.
Buḍhiente utuć tumbućenae. Through being old she is in her dotage.

Uṭ uṭu. Prominent, rising above the surrounding surface, bossed, hummocky, protuberant, bumpy.
Uṭ uṭu ńelok̓kana. It appears to be prominent.

Uu. The call of a species of quail.

Uyuk̓. To be born, to be given birth to.
Gidrạe uyuk̓ena. The child is born.

Uyuk̓. To bring down the hand, or the hand grasping anything, as if striking, to strike.
Mić dhao uyuk̓aeme. Bring the stick down on him once.

Uyuṅ. Cf. oyoṅ.

W

Wạkil. A pleader, an advocate.

Wakhep. Experienced, intelligent, knowing, sensible, to be on the alert, to be cautious, to consider, to ponder. Cf. uakep.

Waront. Cor. of the English word warrant of arrest.

Y

Ya. Used in addressing persons younger than the speaker, applied to males.
Celeya okatem heoena. Ho boy, where have you come to?

Yad. To commit to memory. Cf. ead.

Ye. Said when mocking or imitating a child.
Yeyeyeak̓kanae. He is yeyeing.

Yi. Used when mocking, or imitating.
Yiyiyiek̓kanae. He is mocking, saying yi yi yi.

Yohae. Cf. ohae.

Yoi. Exlamation of warning.
Men, yoi, kul daraekana. Look out, the tiger is coming.

Yore. Sometimes used as the preliminary to a song. Cf. tãhãreta.

SUPPLEMENT.

Abaṛ. To cry, to be peevish.
Gidrạ ạḍi ãṭe abaṛeťkana. The child is crying very much, or loudly.

Ạbir. A red powder used by Hindus at the *holi.*

Abjoṛ. To be littered, to be encumbered, to be hindered or impeded; litter or rubbish lying about.
Racare ạḍi abjoṛ menaťa There is much litter or rubbish in the courtyard.
Miťṭeć abjoṛko doho oṭoadiña. They left an encumbrance with me, something to encumber me.

Acaǩ. To rinse out the mouth and rub the face with the wet hand, used mainly of those possessed by a spirit at certain ceremonies for the dead.
Daǩle emamkana, acaǩme. We are giving you water, rinse out your mouth.
Ạuriye acagoǩre daǩ bae ńuia. He will not drink water until he has rinsed his mouth.

Acur soṛta. To recur, to break out again, as an epidemic, &c., recrudescence.
Ạcur soṛtaena. It has broken out again, there is a recrudescence.

Ạda umạr. Very many, numerous.
Ạda umạrko hećakana. Very many have come

Aḍe. } Aḍe aḍe. } Secretly, privately, keeping out of sight.
Aḍe aḍeteye calaoena. He passed keeping out of sight
Aḍe aḍeteye roṛeda. He is speaking privately.

Adhać udhuć. Unweildy through corpulence.
Adhać udhuće moṭaakana. He is fat to unweildiness.
Adhać udhuće calaǩkana. He is waddling (owing to corpulence.)

Adhan. Some, some...others.
Adhanko goćena, adhanko menaǩkoa. Some have died and others still exist.
Adhanko calaoena. Some have gone.

Aḍharo buḍharo. Old, aged, very old.
Aḍharo buḍharokateye goćena. He lived to be very old and died, he died at a great age.
Aḍharo buḍharokatekin goćena. The couple lived to a great age and died.

Adol. Authority, right, jurisdiction control, possession.
Niạ goṭa atore adoliń phirạueda. I exercise authority over the whole of this village.
Nuige adolkedae baṛge do. This person took possession of the baṛge (q. v.)

Aḍon. To shelter, to hide, to screen to cover, to fence.
Bale ńamledea, aḍonkedeako. We did not find him, they hid him.
Aḍon ńoǩkaǩpe, baṅkhan mihũ meromko bo loǩa. Fence it, or screen it a little, or else the cattle will come in

Adra. } Adra jạpuť. } The beginning of the rainy season, name of the sixth lunar mansion of Hindu astronomers.
Adra boloakana, alope dalkoa, ḍahra, poṭagoǩako. It is now the beginning of the rains, do not beat the bullocks, their skin will come off.

Adra. To sulk, to shew temper, to be ill humoured, to be petulant.

Adra ạdri. Cf. adra.
Bako kusiǩa, adra ạdriǩako. They will not be pleased, they will shew temper.

Aḍra ạdri. To bellow, used only in the plural. Cf. aḍrao.
Aḍra ạdriko calaoena. (The cattle) went away bellowing.

Aere. } Aere aere. } To deviate, to swerve, to diverge out of direct course, not to go or be carried directly to a given point.
Ti aereǩtaea. His hand will deviate.
Aere aereko calaǩkana. They are not going straight.

Aesun. To be necessitous, to be straitened in means, to be in embarrassed circumstances.
Nui hoṛ doe aesungea. This man is in straitened circumstances.

Ạgaṛ. Heavy in front as a loaded cart.

Agra ạgri. To shew temper, as a child.
Agra ạgri baṛaekanae. He is shewing temper.

Agra. } To refuse anything offered, to
Agrao. } refuse with disdain, or through ill temper.

Ahal ahal. } Distressed, as through
Ahal kahal. } hunger, thirst, toil,
Ahle kahle. } &c.

Rehgeốte ahal kahal aṭkaroḱkana. Distress is felt owing to hunger.

Tetañte ahal ahaliñ hedena. I came distressed with thirst.

Ahal ehel. Fat, corpulent, extremely, applied to corpulence.

Ahal ehele moṭaakana. He is extremely fat.

Ahal ehele ñeloḱkana. He appears to be very corpulent.

Ahạri. The person who offers sacrifices during the rearing of the Tassar silk worms.

Ahka ạhki. Panting, suffering from thirst.

Ahka ạhkiye hedena. He came distressed with thirst.

Ahle kahle. Cf. ahal ahal.

Ạiạ. Mother, used by little children.

Ãiṭhạ jũiṭhạ. Leavings of food, defiled as leavings of food, or as a plate from which food has been eaten.

Ãiṭhạ jũiṭhạko emadiña. They gave me food that had been left over.

Ạiyo. } An exclamation of annoy-
Ạiyo ge. } ance.

Ạiyo, nui ḍahra bae añjoma. Hang it! this bullock will not obey.

Akha makha. Without reason, causelessly.

Akhaṛ. One of a course, a stanza, a short song. Cf. akhṛa.

Akhṛa ạkhṛi. At variance, inharmoniously, given to quarrelling.

Ạki lañka. } Very far, distant, a long way
Ạki loñka. } off, a great distance.

Ạki loñkatem senlena. You went to a great distance.

Ạki loñkae calaoena. He went very far.

Akoṛ. Difficult, as a road.

Hạti bañkhan akoṛ horre calaḱ do ạdi harkheta. To go a difficult road without an elephant is very trying.

Akra. Dear, high priced.

Jom jinis ạdi akraena. Food stuffs are very dear.

Alabạsuạ. Cf. albạsuạ.

Alaklạnḍi. Vainly, purposelessly, aimlessly, pithlessly.

Metaekanañ, bes okoốte dipilañme, alaklạnḍiye tuleda. I say to her, lift it properly on to my head, and she lifts it pithlessly.

Alaklạnḍipe dãṛã baṛaekana, bape kạmikana. You are wandering about aimlessly, you are not working.

Ala mara. To be reduced to the last extremity.

Uni hoṛ do ala maraenteye duṛuṕakan tahẽkana. That person being reduced to the last extremity was sitting.

Alapala. } To be wearied, to be tired,
Alapalao. } to be worn out, as with illness, work, &c.

Alapalae ruạḱkana. He is worn out with fever.

Jom jomtele alapalaena. We are wearied with eating, we have eaten till we can eat no more.

Kạmi kạmitele alapalaena. We are worn out with continued working.

Alạriạ. To wish to be fondled or taken up in the arms, as a child.

Alạriạḱkanae. He wishes to be taken up in the arms.

Albạsuạ. } Deficient in intellect, dull-
Alabạsuạ. } witted.

Alabạsuạgeae uni koṛa do. That boy is dull-witted.

Ale. To be satisfied, to have enough.

Jom aleẽnae. He has eaten enough.

Aleẽnañ nitoḱ do. I have had sufficient now.

Ale jañje. To lounge or hang about in hope of getting something.

Rehgeốte ale jañje baṛaekanae. Being hungry he is hanging about hoping to get something.

Aleć. To ask for, to beg, to be in need.

Ḍahra lạgić iñ alećoḱkana. I am asking for a bullock, I am in need of a bullock.

Ạlkhaniạ. Short-tempered, wanting in patience and perseverance and greedy.

Ạlmạlao. To be confused, to be perplexed, to disorder; confused, orderless, from all directions. Cf. ạlmạl.

Aloṕ. } A little, a very little.
Aloṕ aloṕ. }

Aloṕ alope locakeda. He took very little.

Alta. A red pigment applied to the feet by women at a marriage, to apply *alta* to the feet.

Amal gañjal. } Applied to the *pata*
Ambal gañjal. } (q. v.) festivals observed after the 1st Baisakh (q. v.)

Amba gaura. A bunch of red cotton fixed on the back hair by women.

Amba phara. To separate, to split.
Ma nukinbo amba pharakakina. Come, we will separate these two (husband and wife.)

Amchola.} Thin, as the skin pared off a
Amcola. } mango.
Amcolagea. It is thin.

Amcola sakom. A variety of sakom (q. v.) or wristlet.

Amdạni. The season in which any merchandise generally comes into the market, anything gained over and above, ways and means, income.
Amdạni phirạu. To exercise authority.
Khub amdạni hoeakantaea. He has had good profit.
Aćaḱ amdạniye phirạukeda. He exercised his authority.

Ạmila. Abundant, unlimited, great in quantity or number. Cf. amela.

Ạmiń. To purify ceremonially. Cf. um ạmiń.

Anatań. The vessel into which anything is received.
Tuplạḱ do kokoeko reaḱ anatań kana. A small basket is the thing into which beggars receive (alms.)
Sate daḱre anatańko lagaoakata. They have placed a vessel to catch the water falling from the eaves.

Ancal. Neighbourhood, vicinity. Cf. oncol.
Niạ ancal ren horko jarwalena. The people of this neighbourhood were assembled.

Andha ondho. Blinking, the feeling of one who has just awaked from sleep.
Gitić bereć tora andha ondho aṭkaroḱa.

Andga. Testicle.

Anḍhoń. Cheap, low priced, from a seller's point of view; dear, high priced, from a buyer's point of view.
Bhao hõ anḍhońgea. The rate is also low, or high.
Ạḍi anḍhońgeń ạkriń keda. I sold it very cheap.

Anḍhoń manḍhoń. To sell at under value.
Anḍhoń manḍhoṅić ạkriń giḍikeda. I disposed of it for less than its value.

Andkao. To make a noise or din.
Andkaoedape. You are making a din.

Aṅgachao. To confess, to acknowledge.

Aṅge aṅge. Each, each one,
Aṅge aṅgere poesa do henaḱa, ạuriń uṭhạu jarwaea. The money is with each one, I have not yet collected it.
Aṅge aṅge thạri henaḱtalea, patra phuruḱ bań jạrurạlea. We each have a brass plate, we have no need for leaf plates or cups.
Aṅge aṅge catomiń kiriṅapea, alope repeda. I will buy each of you an umbrella, do not quarrel, or do not take one from the other.

Ạṅgrạu. To undertake, to accept, to agree to, to profess. Cf. aṅrạu.

Aogar. To sink or cut in deep.
Nahel aogarme. Cause the plough to go deep.

Apjos. Infamy, disgrace, misfortune.
Apjosiń hạrkeda. I have become disgraced.

Aptar. To be untidy, to be littered, to be dirty, litter, leaves, &c. lying about.
Ạḍi aptar menaḱa. There is much litter lying about.
Onḍe alom duṛuṕa, aptar menaḱa, pase jahãnko ko tahen. Do not sit there, there is litter, perhaps some creature (snake, &c.) may be there.

Ạpuc. Slighted, scorned, neglected, dis-esteemed.

Arạmin. Others, outsiders, non-relatives, the public.
Arạmin menaḱkoa. There are others also.
Peṛa doe bań kana, arạmin kanae. He is not a relative, he is an outsider.
Arạmin kạd oṛaḱreko bhoraoketkoa. They put them in the public prison.

Aṛe pase. Neighbourhood, vicinity, near. Cf. aḍe pase.

Aṛgoṅgaṛ. To confuse, to disorder, to misunderstand.
Bicạrpe aṛgoṅgaṛkeda. You have confused the decision.

Ạriyạn. } A dish prepared with meat
Ạryạn. } and flour resembling a very
Ạryhạn. } thick soup.

Aṛoń. Very much, very many.
Aṛoń sahańko ạguakata. They have brought very much firewood.
Aṛoń daḱ menaḱa. There is very much water.

Ạṛthi paṛthi. Uncultivated, fallow, odd corners that are not cultivated every year for want of water.
Sanamle rohoeakata ạṛthi paṛthi. We have planted all, even the parts that are not cultivated every year.

Aṛuć paṭuć. } To go smash at a thing,
Aṭuć paṭuć. } quickly, impetuously, headlong.
Aṛuć paṭućko kạmikana. They are going slap dash at the work.
Aṛuć paṭuće calaḱkana. He is going quickly.

Asạrthi. False, untrue.
Asạrthi gohae gujrạukeda. He gave false evidence.

Asbas. Tired, confused, perplexed. Cf. asbasao.

Aser. A jungle climbing plant the root of which is eaten.

Ạsin dạrin. Big, large, huge.

Ạsusạr. } **Osusạr.** } To be in a difficulty or strait, to be without resource.
Ạsusạrgeañ iñ do. I am in a difficulty.
Ạsusạrakanae. He is straitened, he is in a strait.

Atañ pinḍạ. A verandah joined on to another roof at a lower level.

Ate. Listen, hear, hark. Cf. ote.
Ate, cet sạdekạna? Hear, what is making a noise?

Aṭhaona paṭhaona. } **Aṭhạunạ paṭhạunạ.** } To go messages.
Aṭhaona paṭhaona lạgit́ mit́ hoṛle dohoakadea. We have engaged a man to go messages.

Ạṭuć pạṭuć. Cf. ạruć pạṭuć.

Ā̃unṭhi pā̃unṭhi. Odd corners and edges which are not cultivated every year for want of water.
Ā̃unṭhi pā̃unṭhi sanam nes rohoeok̀a. All odd corners and edges will be planted this year.

Ạurạha. Unbroken, untrained, uncultured, untutored, undrilled
Ạurạha ḍaṅra. An untrained bullock.

Awala. Conditioned.
Culti awala hoṛ kanae. He is a rich man.

Awañ ewer. To be utterly destitute, to be starving for want of food.
Reṅgeċte awañ ewerenale, aṛak̀ sakam hõ bañ ńamok̀kana, ar nalha hõ bañ.

Āyā. True, of a truth, really, just.
Āyāwak̀ baṛe emakope. Give them what is just.
Āyā katha baṛe galmaraome. Tell a true story.

Ayak̀. } **Sen ayak̀.** } To go out of sight, to go out of the way.
Sen ayak̀enae. He has gone out of the way.
Ayak̀akanae. He is keeping out of sight.
Noabon kạmia, alom ayagok̀a. We will do this work, do not go out of the way (so as to shirk it.)

Ayar. } **Ayar ayar.** } Straight, applied mainly to implements which should be more or less curved.
Ayar ayargepe benaoakat́a, bape liwet́akat́a. You have made it straight, you have not given it a curve.

Ayar. } **Ayar ayar.** } Oblique, obliquely, not at a right angle.
Ḍaṅra do ayar ayare calak̀kana. The bullock is going obliquely.
Noa ā̃rgom ayargepe benaoakat́a. You have made this harrow oblique, (the pole not at a right angle to the harrow.)

Ạyup lumbak̀. } **Ạyup lupạk̀.** } **Ạyup jopok̀.** } **Ạyup ńumbak̀.** } **Ạyup ńupạk̀.** } A little after nightfall.
Ạyup lumbạk̀le seṭerena. We arrived a little after nightfall.

B

Ba. Or, either.
Mit́ leka ba mit́ leka oṛak̀ benaokate onareko tahena. They make houses of one kind or another and live in them.
Jahā̃ṭak̀ ba jahā̃ṭak̀ rog janamea. He will be seized by one or other kind of disease.

Bacol. To spare, overlook.

Bacṛa. Immature, young.
Nui ḍaṅra alom etoea, bacṛageae. Do no break this bullock into the yoke, it is immature.

Bad. } **Badre.** } After, afterwards.
Pe ghanṭa badre. After three hours.

Bạḍ birit. Increase. Cf. bạḍ.
Khubko bạḍ biritakantaea. His (cattle) have increased well.

Baḍhaona. Increase.

Bạḍi. A flood.
Bạḍi ā̃rgona alope bolok̀a. The river is rising do not enter it.

Badla bạdli. To exchange, to requite, to take revenge.
Badla bạdlikedakin. They exchanged.

Badnam. } **Bodnam.** } To disgrace, to give a bad name to.
Badnam ocokediñae. He caused me to get a bad name.

Badoli. Born or married when it is raining, or cloudy.
Dak̀ dak̀tegeye janamena menkhan uni doko metaea badoli. If it is raining when he is born he (or she) is termed *badoli*.
Baplak̀ jokheće dak̀lekhan bana hoṛ unkin dokin badoli. If it rains when they are being married both are termed *badoli*.

Badom. A sail.

Bạghut boṅga. One of the lesser deities of the Santal pantheon.
Bạghut boṅga is the tiger deity and is propitiated every year at the Dasãe (q. v.) festival. The person who is supposed to be possessed for the time being by Baghut boṅga pounces upon the sacrificial fowl, as a tiger does his prey, and he does not cut off its head with a knife, as is the usual custom, but bites it off with his teeth.

Bagrạsiạu. Fearless, brave, courageous, as a tiger.

Nui hoṛ do ạdi bagrạsiạṅgeae, bae botoroḱa. This man is very courageous, he does not get alarmed.

Baha eneć. A dance so called.

Baha sereṅ. Songs sung during the dancing of the *Baha* dance.

Baha ru. Time beaten on the drums, to which the *Baha* dance is danced.

Baha raṛ. The tune or air to which the *Baha* songs are sung.

Baha careć. A long piu which fixed in a rafter forms a kind of hook, by means of which the rafter is hooked on to the ridge pole of the roof.

Baha bas. At the conclusion of a dance one or more of the musicians passes each a flower along the line of girl dancers. This is called *Baha bas.*

Eneć mokoṅlenkhanko baha basa. When they conclude a dance a flower is passed along the line of dancers.

Baha daḱ. At the Baha festival (q. v.) water is thrown by certain persons on others. This is known as *Baha daḱ* or Flower water.

To have water thus thrown on one is considered very lucky.

Hiliṅ daḱe arećadiṅa, ạdiye sawặeadiṅa. My sister-in-law threw water on me, she made me very lucky.

Bahka bạhki. To stray, to wander away, to deceive, to allure, to delude. Cf. bahkao.

Ḍher sạhgiṅe bahka bạhkiena, ohom tioḱlea. He has by this time wandered very far, you will not overtake him.

Bahka bạhki ocokećkoam. You allowed them to stray, or scatter (cattle.)

Bakaṭ bokoṭ. To chatter, to jabber, to scold.

Bakaṭ bokodoḱtege menaea. He is continually chattering.

Bakhradạri. Sharing in, participating in.

Bala saka. All who participate in the bala (q. v.) relationship, fathers, mothers, uncles, aunts, &c. of a married couple.

Bạl gada. Sand washed on to a field by a flow of water.

Saname bạlgadakeḟtalea. All our fields are full of sand brought down by a flow of water.

Bamka bạmki. To be at its height, to increase in intensity, to flare up, to rage, as fire.

Noa sengel do bamka bạmkiena, ohobo daṛelena. This fire has increased in intensity, we will not be able to master it.

Bạn. } Hire, wages.
Bạni. }

Bạn baṛa joṅkanae. He is working for wages, or he is earning wages.

Bandha. M. } Foolish, dull-witted, lum-
Bandhi. F. } pish.

Bandhe. To pledge, to pawn, to mortgage, security, pledge.

Bandheaḱaṭaṅ loṭa thạri. I have pledged my brass cups and plates.

Baṅgaṭ. } Libidinous, and keeping to
Baṅgoṭ. } no settled work.

Bạṅki. Poles fastened to a cart to increase its carrying capacity.

Bạni. Cf. bạn.

Baṅkạr. A hired worker.

Bapa purkhạ. Ancestors.

Bapa purkhạ khon hećakantalea. It has come to us from our ancestors.

Barat boroṭ. White, clean, tidy, shining.

Barak. Like, resembling. Cf. barag.

Barbar. } To germinate as grain
Barbarao. } steeped in water before being sown.

Hoṛo barbaraoakana. The dhan has germinated.

Baṛhantar. } Well-grown, big, healthy.
Baṛhansạr. }

Baṛhantargeako noko jaro do. Those of this stock are big.

Bạriạr. A common wild plant, *Sida humilis*, var, *morifolia, Willd.*

Baropheṭ. An indefinite number of.

Baromaeia ćṛe baropheṭe raga. The Baromaeia (q. v.) bird has twelve different calls. (an indefinite number.)

Barsa. } Hope, dependence, expecta-
Bharsa. } tion, confidence, trust, faith.

Barwari. A Hindu festival so named.

Bạsi mara. To allow a corpse to remain overnight in the house when it might have been disposed of before sunset.

Bat baḍohi. Lying to save trouble, to avoid having to do a thing, or to gain an end, talkative.

Baṭiau. To keep to oneself and defraud others.
Saname baṭiau idikeda. He kept it all to himself, he went away taking all with him.

Bat kaṭi. Stubborn, disobedient, talkative.

Baṭ paṛa. A highwayman, a spy.

Baṭul. To slight, to aggrieve, to dismiss.
Kami khonko baṭulkedea. They dismissed him from his work, or removed him from his employment.

Baul. M. } **Bawil** F. } Mad, insane, crazy.

Bauṛan. Insane, mad, crazy.

Bawil. F. } **Baul.** M. } Mad, insane, crazy.

Bebilonḍ. To be lost sight of, to be scattered to the wind, to be ruined or destroyed. C. babilonḍ.

Bebohar. Usage, practice, custom, conduct, behaviour, to comport oneself, to behave, to conduct oneself, to use. Cf. beohar.

Becol. Of bad behaviour, of bad character, unreasonable.
Becol ar baṛić hoṛko khonle dogokma. May we be preserved from unreasonable and wicked men.

Bede bede. Broad-faced. Cf. bed bede.

Bedha bidhi. Cross grained.

Beḍo beḍo. A rat tat beaten on the drum.
It is beaten when the duṅgeṛ (q. v.) dance is danced in the place where the hunters pass the night.

Beḍot rasa. Used in scolding and threatening.
As the expression is somewhat objectionable it is used by men to men and women to women.
Beḍot rasale ńurtama.

Behoea. Shameless, impertinent.

Bekup. Stupid, foolish.

Bele har. To be fully ripe, to be over ripe.
Bele harena jo do. The fruit is fully ripe.

Belok. Separate.

Belwaṛi malla. A necklace of beads, or beads, made from the hard rind of the fruit of the Bael tree, *Ægle Marmelos, Correa.*

Beńcok. To sulk.

Beńja bińji. Cf. bińja bińji.

Bephokoṭ. Without reason, unreasonably.
Bephokoṭ ṭaka lagaoadińa. I was charged without reason.

Bẽṛẽ bẽṛẽ. Heaped up, as much as it will hold.
Bẽṛẽ bẽṛẽko perećakaća. They have filled and heaped it up.
Jom bẽṛẽ bẽṛẽenae. He has eaten his fill.

Beṛńcok. To sulk.

Berosta. } **Birokto.** } To be annoyed, bothered, irritated, galled, provoked.
Noa iṣte onko do berostakte ḍher dhao cakri bagikateko calaka. Owing to this they through being irritated often leave their service and go away.

Beṭeń beṭeń. To snap at, to reply testily, talkative.

Bhac marte. } **Bhac mente.** } Quickly, rapidly, in a trice.
Bhac martebon areja. We will bale out the water quickly.

Bhadbhadao. To make a pattering noise, as a shower of fruit from a tree, to patter.
Kuinḍi bele bhadbhadao ńurena. The ripe kuinḍi fruit fell pattering.

Bhãe. } **Bhãe bhãe.** } Superstitious fear, alarm.
Goć oṛakre bhãe bhãe aṭkaroka. Fear is felt in a house in which there is a corpse.

Bhag bãṭ. } **Bhag bãṭa.** } Share, portion.
Bhag bãṭa bako emańkana. They are not giving me a share.

Bhaluk luka. A children's game.

Bhan. } **Bhanbhan.** } **Bhanbhanao.** } To hum, to buzz, as flies, &c, to drone, as beetles, &c.
Bhanbhanko saḍe ocoeda. They are causing a buzzing sound.
Bhan bhanaoko boloena bhugakte. They entered the hole buzzing.

Bhan marte. } **Bhan mente.** } With a buzz, with a drone.
Bhan marte oḍokenae uru do. The beetle flew out with a drone.

Bhanḍal bhunḍul. Naked, nude.
Gidrako bhanḍal bhunḍul dakreko enećkana. The children are playing in the water in a state of nudity.

Bhandal bhundul. Applied to the running of fat animals, as hares, jackals, &c. The plural of bhundul bhundul. (q. v.)

Bhandul } Applied to the runn-
Bhandul bhandul. } ing of a fat animal, as a hare, jackal, &c, bobbing, waddling.
Bhandul bhandule dạrkeda.

Bhandul marte. } With a bob.
Bhandul mente. }
Kulại bhandul marteye dạrkeda. The hare fled with a bob.

Bhạṅgrạ. Lazy, slothful.

Bhańj. A method of cultivation where two men have each one bullock each ploughing with the pair on alternate days.

Bhao baṭa. Rate, price.

Bhara. To swell, to puff out, to become distended, to fill up or out.
Hoṛmo bharak̕kantaea. His body is swelling. (as in dropsy.)
Hoṛmo ạuri bharak̕taea. His body is not yet filled out (said of a youth who has grown tall and is still lank.)

Bhasań bhusuń. One after the other.
Bhasań bhusuńko oḍokena bhugạk̕ khon. They came out of the hole one after the other.

Bhaskar. } Ugly, unshapely, inelegant,
Bhaskaria. } uncomely.
Ạdi bhaskạriạe ńelok̕kana. He looks very ugly.
Ạdi bhaskarko benaokeda. They made it very ugly.

Bhạsuḍań. } Dirty, slovenly.
Bhạsuḍań bhạsuḍań. }

Bhãt. Kinds, manner, way.
Ạdi bhãt hoṛ menak̕koa. There are many kinds of people.

Bhataha. Deceiver, deluder.
Nui bhatahage hoṛe bulạuakat̕koa. This deceiver has led the people astray.

Bhat dhuna. } Lazy, idle fellow.
Bhat dhunaha. }
Ceṫ hõ bae kạmia nui bhat dhunạ do. This lazy fellow will do no work.

Bhat mara. Lazy, idle.

Bhaṭ bhuṭ. To rumble, as the stomach.
Laċ bhaṭ bhuṭ sadekantaea. His stomach is rumbling.

Bhạunṭiạ jel. A species of deer.

Bhãwãr. To exercise as an athlete, to train, to break in, to accustom, to inure; expert, skilled, smart. Cf. bhãoar.

Bhạya. Brother.
Bhạyạ bhạyạkin lạṛhạikana. Brother is fighting with brother.

Bheao. To recognize, to know.
Nonkateye calak̕kan tahẽkana, bheaokedeań. He was going this way and I recognized him.

Bhede bhede. To chatter, to jabber continually.
Bhede bhedek̕kanae. She is chattering.

Bheńcok̕. To sulk and look away, to give way, move aside.

Bheṭra M. } Small, little.
Bhiṭri F. }

Bthetra bhiṭri. High rice lands, which do not produce good crops owing to want of moisture.

Bhinsạr eneċ. A dance so called.

Bhinsạr sereń. Songs sung during the dancing of the *Bhinsạr* dance.

Bhinsạr rạṛ. The time or air to which the *Bhinsạr* songs are sung.

Bhinsạr ru. The time beaten on the drums to which the *Bhinsạr* is danced.

Bhoc marte. } Quickly, rapidly, in a
Bhoc mente. } trice. Cf. bhac marte.

Bhogdar. One who enjoys the fruits, revenues, &c., of anything.

Bhojgoċ. } Loosely, insecurely, easily
Bojgoċ } loosened, as a knot.
Bhojgoċko bindạakaṫa hoṛo do. They have bound the dhan sheaves loosely.
Bhojgoċko tolakaṫa. They have tied it insecurely.

Bhokar. } To raise a dam, embankment,
Bokhar. } ridge, &c. by putting fresh earth on it.
Pinḍheko bhokarakaṫa. They have raised the embankment (of the dam.)

Bhokoṛ. } Bubbling up as water
Bhokoṛ bhokoṛ. } in a spring. Cf. bhukur.
Bhokoṛ bhokoṛ dak̕ seteńok̕kana. Water is coming bubbling up.

Bhokoṛ marte. } With a bubble, with
Bhokoṛ mente. } a spurt, as water from a hose.

Bhonḍa. Fat, corpulent, unweildy, large, thick-headed, dull-witted. Cf. bhõnḍa.

Bhonḍa kạhu. The Bow Billed Corby, *Corvus Levaillantii, Less.*

Bhonḍa miru. A species of large paroquet.

Bhonḍa kisni. The large Starling, *Gracula religiosa.*

Bhonḍ bogla. }
Bhonḍ boglaha. } Ill-shaped, ugly.

Bhondlo. }
Bhondlo bhondlo. } Loosely.

Bhondlo bhondlo baberko uńakaća. They have twisted the string loosely.
Bhondlogea. It is loose.

Bhonḍo. Blunt.

Bhondṛo. }
Bhondṛo bhondṛo. } Cf. bhondlo.

Bhosḍoṅ. }
Bhosnḍoṅ. } Dirty, untidy, slovenly.

Bhosoṅga. M. } Fat, stout, used mainly
Bhosoṅgi. F. } when scolding or finding fault.

Bhuḍ. } Imitative of the sound
Bhuḍ bhuḍ. } of a thud or thump.

Bhuḍ marte. }
Bhuḍ mente. } With a thud.

Bhuḍ marte ńurena. It fell with a thud.

Bhud bhudia̤. Soft, friable.

Bhuktạn. To pay in full.

Ḳhajna seó bhuktạn hoeẽna, ińpe emańa. I have settled up the rent, you will repay me.

Bhuktạu. To pay in full.

Ṭakań bhuktạukeda. I paid the money in full.
Jahã lekate khajnale bhuktạukeda. We paid our rent one way or another.

Bhula̤ bhạtua̤. Wandering, wandering about as a half-witted person, thoughtless, negligent, heedless.

Bhula̤ bhạtua̤e dãṛã baṛaekana. He is going wandering about.

Bhumkạu. To spring, as water, to well up.

Dak bhumkạkkana. Water is welling up.

Bhunḍi. F. }
Bhunḍa̤. M. } Fat, huge, corpulent.

Bhunḍla̤. M. } Naked, nude, and plump,
Bhunḍli F. } used of children.

Bhunḍli kateye umoḱkana. She is bathing in a nude state.

Bhusur bhusur. Soft.

Buṭko ataakaća bhusur bhusur. They have roasted the gram very soft.

Bhuṭạu. To be seized with a passion to take life, applied mainly to malevolent spirits.

Bhuṭ bhuṭia̤. Big-bellied.

Jom bhuṭ bhuṭia̤enae. He has eaten till he is big-bellied.

Bhut kilạu. To give up a good place or work without reason,

Bhut kilạukedea, oḍokena. He gave up a good position and left.

Bic mara. } Not to give even a return
Ita̤ mara. } of the seed sown.

Akal sermare bic maraena. In the famine year there was not even a return of the seed sown.

Biḍbiḍi. Stock still.

Biḍbiḍiko teṅgo baṛaekana. They are standing stock still.

Biddạn. Learned.

Bidhạn. Rites, as those observed at death, naming of a child, purification of a mother, &c.

Bidhạnko cabakeda. They have performed all the rites.

Bigria̤. Forced, as labour.

Bihạl era. A married wife.

Bijgoć bojgoć. Loosely, insecurely.

Bijgoć bojgoćko tolakaća hoṛo binḍa̤. They have bound the sheaves of dhan loosely.
Bijgoć bojgoće bandeakaća.

Bilis bilis. Flashing, flaring.

Bilo. To distribute, to serve out.

Marjatiaḱkoko biloeko bahalkećkoa. They appointed them to serve out food.

Bima̤s. To distribute, to share, to serve out, mainly cooked food.

Bisma̤skedako. They distributed it.

Biń oć. A poisonous kind of mushroom.

Bińja̤ bińji. } When hunting partridges
Beńja bińji. } having located one they go round and round it saying bińja̤ bińji, bińja̤ bińji.

Birbithan. } To scatter, to scatter and
Biri bithạn. } destroy.

Kul do pal ren ga̤i biri bithạnkećkoteye oalaoena. The tiger having scattered the cows of the herd went away.

Birgha̤. } To be ill-tempered, irritable,
Birgho. } angry.

Bić bidya̤. Staggering, going from side to side as one intoxicated.

Bitti. Trade, profession, work.

Hoṛ reaḱ bitti se ka̤mi. A man's trade or work.

Bituć. The posteriors.

Bitućạdińae. He showed me his posteriors.

Bo. To give any of the different kinds of *daka* (q. v.) out of the pot while still on the fire.
Culhạ cetan khon boadińae daka do. She gave me boiled rice out of the pot on the fire.

Boaǩ moca. Big or wide mouthed.

Bod. To soothe, to pacify, to wheedle. Cf. bodhao.
Solo sońjok dobo jumạulege atmabon boda. When we have gotten all the materials together then we may soothe our spirit.

Boḍboḍo. Lazy, idle, applied to females.

Bodgaǩ bidgạǩ. Deep, as a blow with a hoe in the soil, or an axe in wood. Cf. bodgaǩ bodgaǩ.

Bodnam. Cf. badnam.

Boeboe. Tall.
Boeboe haraakanae. He has grown tall.

Boesar. Part of a loom.

Bokcao. To take a handful out of a quantity, to hide in the armpit, to hide anything.
Tabene bokcaoana. He has taken a handful of parched rice.

Bokor bokor. Unwinding, running out, as a coil of rope, &c.

Boksi. F. } A witch, a warlock.
Boksa. M. }
Uni boksi ạimạiye ńel goćkaćlete cele hõ bale goćlećkoa. Owing to that witch woman having seen us we have killed nothing (no game.)

Bomborkeć. } Very fat and short-necked,
Bomborkoć. } having ruffled feathers like an angry sitting hen.
Bomborkoće duṛupạkana. He is sitting there fat and short-necked.

Bondis. Cf. bundis.

Bonḍo. } Blunt.
Bhonḍo. }

Bonto boyol. In a line or strip, extending in one direction.
Bonto boyolko oḍokena. They came out in a continuous stream (bees from hive.)

Borborao. To become soft, to be injured or destroyed.
Lohoć borboraoena hasa do. The clay has become wet and soft.

Bota. A part of the *huka,* or hubble bubble.

Botboto. Long.

Botolo. The entrance.
Botoloteć mićṭeć marah dhiritekin sińkaća. They closed the entrance with a large stone.

Buceṛ. To excess, over much. Cf. bhuceṛ.
Ńu buceṛenae. He has drunk to excess, he is drunk.

Buḍhạ kohna. Old men acquainted with the Santal traditions and customs.

Bud hara. To be at one's wit's end, to be non-plussed.
Ceć ran hõ bań disạ daṛeaǩa, bud haraenań. I cannot think of a medicine, I am nonplussed.

Bukạ lolo. To partake of food, or warm rice water.

Bulkạu. To steep Indian corn, gram, &c. in hot water previous to roasting. Cf. ata.

Buṛi. A small ball, a pill.

Bursạ pạí. A measure larger than the standard. Cf. pursạ pạí.

C

Cabcab. }
Cabhcabh. } Slushy, moist.
Cobcob. }
Ot cabcab lohoćena. The soil is wet to slushiness.

Cabhao. To swallow, to devour, to overspread, to increase.
Cando cabhaokedeae gahnaǩre. In the eclipse he swallowed the moon.
Kule cabhaokedea. The tiger devoured him.
Nitoǩe cabhaokedea. Now he has devoured him.
Dhạrtire do kạí cabhaoena. Sin overspread the world.

Cạbuk. A horse whip, a driving whip.

Cạbur. }
Cạbur cạbur. } Splashing.
Chạbur. }
Chạbur chạbur. }
Cạbur cạbure don idiǩeda. He went jumping away splashing.

Cạbur marte. } With a splash.
Cạbur mente. }
Cạbur menteye donkeda. He jumped with a splash.

Cacalkaṫ. To contract, to shrivel, to curl up.
Bohoṛ cacalkaćena. It has dried and contracted.

Căćcŭć. Imitative of the chirp of chickens, squeal of young rats or mice.

Sim hopon căć cŭćko raga. Chickens call chaé chué, or chickens chirp.

Caçhi. } **Chaçhi.** } To boil down, to evaporate by boiling, to cause a fluid substance to become thicker by evaporation.

Toa caçhikedae. He boiled down the milk,

Caego. Talkative, loquacious, clapper tongued, applied to females.

Caehar. Wide, as the mouth, opening of vessel, &c.

Ţukuć mocateć caeharges. The mouth of the ţukuć (q. v.) is wide.

Cahak mahak. To be forward, eager, alert, assiduous, intent; to swagger, to shew off.

Ńeńel calak lagić do adim cahak mahak baṛaekana. You are shewing great eagerness to go to the fair,

Kami sen onka ma bam cahak mahak baṛaea. You are not equally eager for work.

Cahăţ. Pressing, urgent. Cf. cohŏţ.

Cahla. To be slushy, slushy.

Hor adi cahlagea. The road is very slushy.

Cakendak. Very fat, big and fat.

Cakendake ńelokkana. He looks very fat.

Cakṛa cokṛo. Creased, crumpled, crushed out of shape.

Sanam kagoj cakṛa cokṛokedae. He creased all the paper.

Calcalua. Hurriedly, hastily, to be in a hurry, to be in haste.

Calcalua iń calak lagić. I am hurrying to go.
Calcaluae hećena. He came hurriedly.

Calcul. To begin to move, to make a movement, to make a start.

Dakae lagićko calculokkana. They are making a start to cook the food.

Nitok doko calcul baṛakkana. Now they are beginning to move.

Calak lagićko calculokkana. They are preparing to start.

Calha. } **Calha hako.** } A species of river fish.

Calti. } **Culti.** } Well-to-do, in easy circumstances.

Bes calti awala hoṛ kanae. He is a man in easy circumstances.

Camaeṭa. To sow seed after having ploughed the soil only once.

Muńiń camaeṭakeda. I sowed muń (q. v.) after only one ploughing.

Camal comol. To walk on tip toe through fear of making a noise, to be in terror, fearsome.

Camal comol atkarokа. It is fearsome.
Botorte camal comolenae. He is moving on tiptoe through fear.
Noa bir camal comoliń paromena. I passed through this jungle in terror.

Camdaṛak. Still, stockstill.

Camdaṛake teńgoakana kami bagikate. He has left his work and is standing still.

Camkau. To scourge, to beat with a wand or thin cane.

Camkau poṭak ar sasetenteko goćena. They through scourging and distress died.

Campur. Jesting, cozening.

Campurte. In jest, jestingly.
Adi campur hoṛ kanae nui do. He is a great cozening man this.

Camraṅga. The body, outwardly beautiful.

Cancan. } **Cancanao.** } To speak or cry out loudly.

Cancan baṛaekanae. He is bawling out, or speaking at the top of his voice.
Cancanaokkanae. He is speaking loudly.

Candak condok. To walk on the ball of the foot or on the toes.

Candak condoke calakkana. He is walking on the ball of the foot.

Candheṛ. To become a clump, a number of stalks to spring from one and become a bunch.

Hoṛo bes candheṛakana. The dhan has grown well into clumps.

Candoṭa. } **Candoṭare.** } Monthly, in the month.

Candoṭare pe dhao, Three times monthly, three times in a month.

Căo. } **Căocăo.** } Squealing, as a wooden axle without oil, to dingle in the ears, to tingle, as the ears.

Gaḍi niṅgha căocăo saḍekana. The cart axle is squealing.

Căo marao. To overspread, to tingle, as the ears.

Onde khon do goṭa disom căo marao goćena. From there it overspread the whole country.

Căora. M. } **Căuri.** F. } Having the long hairs in the tail more or less white.

Căorao. To turn round without moving from the spot.

Bandiko căorao acurkeda. They turned the bandi (q. v.) round where it stood.
Ḍaṅrako căoraokećkina. They turned the bullocks round without their moving from the spot.

Capan. } To remove tassar silk worms
Capon. } from one tree to another.
Mõṛẽ dareren capankeťkoa. I have removed the silk worms to five trees.

Cạpur cạpur. } Splashing, sound of
Chạpur chạpur. } splashing in water.
Cạpur cạpure laga paromkeťkoa. He drove them across splashing.

Carapiạ. } Live stock, an animal
Carapiạ dhon. } that grazes.
Carapiạ dhone jomkeda. The cattle ate it.
Carapiạ dhon ḍherge menaǩkotaea. He has much live stock.

Cạrit. To be on the look out for, to mark down, to watch, to take cognizance of, to note.
Merome cạriteťkoa kombṛo do. The thief is watching the goats.

Carmanḍo. To half thresh, as grain.
En carmanḍoakaťań. I have half threshed it.

Cạrpạṭ. To finish, to eat or graze up all.
Jom cạrpạṭkedako ucạṛkom. They have eaten up all, remove them (silk worms to another tree.)
Cạrpạṭkedae. It grazed it all.
Cạrpạṭena. It is all grazed, or eaten up.

Cạrpiṛ. Wide-spreading, as horns.
Dereń do cạrpiṛgetaea. His horns are wide spreading.

Caṭać cuṭuć. } Noise produced by slip-
Ciṭaṭ caṭeť. } pers hitting the heel when walking. (imitative.)
Caṭać cuṭuće taṛameda.

Caṭa cuṭu. To frizzle, to be crisp, to crackle.
Ma ãṛgoepe caṭa cuṭuǩkana. Take it off the fire it is frizzling.
Caṭa cuṭu rohoṛena. It is dry and crisp.
Caṭa cuṭu goćena. It is dead and crisp.

Caṭaǩ cuṭuǩ. To lick the lips.
Caṭaǩ cuṭuǩ baṛaekanae. He is licking his lips.

Caṭapạṭ. Quickly, rapidly, hurriedly, hastily.
Caṭapạṭko kạmi caba goťkeda. They quickly finished the work.
Caṭapạṭko isin goťkeda. They did the cooking hurriedly.

Cạukhũṭ. The four points of the compass, all round, every where.
Cạukhũṭe daǩkeda. It rained all round.

Cạukidar. A watchman, a village watchman.

Cạukidạri. Of or belonging to a chaukidar, to act as a cạukidar or watchman.
Cạukidạriedae. He does the work of a watchman.

Cạuraha. One who by certain incantations becomes possessed by a spirit.

Cạuwạị. To tell tales about one.
Hoṛaǩe cạuwaieťkana. He is telling tales about people.

Cawaǩ cawaǩ. To be agitated as liquid in a vessel being carried.
Daǩ cawaǩ cawagoǩkana. The water is being agitated.

Ceḍo ceḍo. Imitative of the call of partridges.

Cehel cehel. Flowing in full flood, brimful, overflowing.

Cehor behor. With demonstration of affection and welcome, heartily, warmly.
Cehor behorko daramkedińa. They received me with demonstration of affection and welcome.

Cehor behor. Cry of a species of quail. Cf. oṛe.

Cẽk. Having a counterfoil, as a receipt, cheque, &c., cor. of the English word cheque.
Cẽk rạsid. A receipt having a counterfoil.

Celkot. Smooth or sleek, as the hair when well oiled and brushed, applied also to the smoothness of feathers on the head of a starling Cf. cerkot.

Celpeń. Sunk, subsided, hollow, as the bridge of the nose.
Celpeń mũ. A hollow nose.

Cemel cemel. Quickly and lightly, applied to walking. Cf. cemeṛ cemeṛ.
Cemel cemele taṛameda. He walks quickly and lightly.

Cenḍa. Arriving at adolescence.

Cenḍa bayar. Almost full grown, applied to male buffaloes.

Cendkoť. Smooth, sleek.
Cendkoťe nạkićakaťa. She has combed her hair smooth.

Ceńcuriạ. Children, little ones, small, young.
Ekenko ceńcuṛiạgea. There are only children.

Ceńṛa. M. } A child about 9 or 10 years
Ciṅṛi. F. } of age.
Ekenko ceńṛagea. They are only children.

Cepel. } To fill full, brimfull,
Cepel cepel. } quite full, heaving as the water in a pond or tank when full.

Khub cepel cepel peređakana. (The tank) is well filled, or is very full.
Cedak cepel cepelpe peređkeda? Why did you fill it brimfull?
Cepelkedam kanḍa do. You filled the water-pot brimfull.
Cepel cepel rạskạteye peređena. He was filled with joy.

Cepel. Low, as ridge of rice field, &c., flat.

Cepṭhe. To stick or adhere together.
Cepṭheĕna ḍombok piṭhạ do. The bread balls are sticking together.

Cerca bayar. Stunted, small and lean.

Cercer. Cry of alarm of partridges.

Cerḍha. } Thick.
Cerḍha cerḍha. }
Cerḍha cerḍha cepa magpe. Cut the turf very thick.

Cere peṭe. Noise produced by grain bursting when being roasted, explosive sound produced by the wood of the Indian Ebony tree when burning.
Cerepeṭe oṭejokkana. It is bursting and cracking

Ceṛo ceṛo. Imitative of the call of partridges.

Ceṭepeṭe. Cf. cerepeṭe.

Ceṭe sahan. Firewood of the Indian Ebony tree (Cf. terel), which when burning produces slight explosions followed by sparks.

Ceṭeteṫ. Applied to the thin skin on the bark of the Indian Ebony tree (Cf. terel), which when burning produces slight explosions followed by sparks.

Ceṭha. To revive, good looking, healthy appearance.
Onko ńelte mon ceṭhaentaea. By seeing them his spirits revived.

Cethra. A rag, old worn out cloth.
Cethrakote menaklea. We are in old worn out clothes.

Ceweć ceweć. Imitative of the cry of the Night-jar. Cf. hạpuk.

Chạbur. } Splashing.
Chạbur chạbur. }
Chạbur chạbure don idikeda. He went jumping away splashing.

Chạbur marte. } With a splash.
Chạbur mente. }
Chạbur marteye donkeda. He jumped with a splash.

Chaćchuć. To be in a strait or difficulty.
Chaćchućkeḱleako peṛako, ạyuḅko hećente. Visitors put us in a strait by coming in the evening.

Chạchi. Cf. cạchi.

Chaklachạk. To surfeit, to give more than one can eat, to entertain hospitably.
Chaklachạkko emaḱlea. They gave us more than we could eat.
Ceḱlekae jom ocokeḱpea? Khub chaklachạke jom ocokeḱlea. How did he feed you? He entertained us most hospitably.
Emkateko chaklachạkkeḱkoa. They gave and surfeited them.

Chạldari. } A small one-ply tent.
Choldori. }

Chamak damak. Giving oneself airs, to show off, applied to females.
Chamak damakem calakkana. You are going about giving yourself airs.

Chanaṅ nandaṅ. Going about instead of working.
Chanaṅ nandaṅ baṛaekanae. He is going about instead of working,

Chanban. } Exact likeness, close resem-
Chanman. } blance.
Chanman uni lekaṅ ńelekana. He appears to me to bear a close resemblance to him.

Chand. } Pattern, sample, form, repres-
Chond. } entation.
Niạ chand benaome. Make it according to this pattern,

Chankạ chạnki. To season. to apply spices cooked in oil to food, mainly to a relish.
Chankạ chạnki kateko emaḱlea. They gave it to us spiced.

Chankao. To season, to add spices cooked in oil to food.
Utu chaukao ńogme. Season the relish a little more.

Chanman. Cf. chanban.

Chaoṛa. Immature, not full grown.
Chaoṛageae kạḍru do. The young buffaloe is immature.
Chaoṛa gidrạ. An immature lad.

Chapaḍao. The reciprocal form of chaḍao (q. v.)
Nukin bakin chapaḍaoa. These two will not separate from each other.

Chapar bandhi. A roof tax, a house tax.

Ato ato chapar bandhiko uthaua. They collect a house tax from each village.

Chapar chupur. } Applied to fairly
Chupur chupur } heavy rain which does not run off but makes a noise when one walks in it.

Bes chapar chupure dakkeda. It rained fairly heavily.

Chapar chupur dak. Fairly heavy rain.

Chap chap. Shallow, just covering the surface, as water.

Gabhatet do chap chap tahẽkana. Water just covered the surface of the middle of the tank.

Chapit. Secret.

Noa katha reak chapit banukanah. There is no secret about this matter.

Chapit alope dohoea. Do not keep it secret.

Chapka chapki. } Crouching, stealthi-
Chapka chupka. } ly, as a beast of prey.

Chaporae. } Low.
Cheporae. }

Chaporaegeye benaoakata orak do. He has made the house low.

Chapur chapur. Cf. capur capur.

Charchar. } To tear, to rend, imita-
Charcharao. } tive of the sound produced by tearing cloth, paper, &c.

Kicrić charcharaoe orećkeda. He tore the cloth and made a tearing sound.

Kicriće charcharaokeda. He tore the cloth.

Charchar kagoje orećkeda. He tore the cloth and produced a sound resembling charchar.

Char hatua. Childless, applied to females.

Char hatuageae. She is childless.

Chatabar. } Applied to a field of
Ir chatabar. } grain of larger or smaller area which a farmer leaves till the last and allows all who come to reap and carry away the grain.

Okatak khet ir chatabar lagitbo dohoea? Which field will we set apart for the people to reap?

Chata daṅ. The high pole on which the umbrella is hoisted at the *chata* or umbrella festival.

Chati jarao. } To burst the heart, to
Chati phatao. } rend the heart, to burst or rend the bosom, as sorrow, grief.

Chati phataokkantiña bhabnate. My heart is bursting with grief.

Cheporae. Low. Cf. chaporae.

Chidga chidgi. Throwing from side, to spatter from side to side, carelessly.

Chidga chidgiye joketkana. She is sweeping and spattering from side to side. [his way.

Chidga chidgiye calakkana. He is going and pushing all to one side or the other out of

Chidgai. To throw forward with force as slush, water, &c., to spatter, to to cause to spatter.

Chidgai pasiradiñae. He caused the slush to spatter over me.

Chidgai marte. } With a spatter.
Chidgai mente. }

Chidgai marteye calaoena. He went off with a spatter.

Chirbitir. To spread, to disperse, to divide. Cf. cirbitir. [as blood, &c.

Chir chir. Spurting, flowing quickly,

Chir chir mayam odokokkana. Blood is coming out spurting.

Chiria chit. To scatter, to disperse, to spread.

Chiria chitko pasnaoakana. They are dispersed here and there.

Begar chiria chitenako. The household has dispersed, the members of the family have set up for themselves and are dispersed.

Chirić chirić. Breaking up as a liquid substance falling on a hard surface, to spatter.

Chirić chirić dak pasirokkana. Water is falling on a hard surface and spattering.

Chob chob. Drenched, well moistened. Cf. cobcob.

Chob chob lohotakana daka utute. The rice is well moistened with the relish.

Chochna. M. } Niggardly, parsimonious,
Chuchni. F. } especially in the matter of giving food.

Chochnaha. M. } Cf. chochna.
Chochnahi. F. }

Choha. } One of a series.
Coha. }

Mit chohale pokeda, ar mit choha do bah. We hoed one sowing, and not the other sowing.

Mit choha pohoko paromena, ar mit chohako hijukkana. One flight of locusts passed and another flight is coming.

Mit chohako jomkeda, ar mit choha auriko joma. One section (portion, division,) of the company partook of food, and one section has not yet partaken of food.

Bar chohako seterena. Two detachments have arrived.

Chokchok. Gobbling, sound of eating voraciously.

Chokchokko jomeda. They are eating gobblingly.

Choldori. Cf. chạldạri.

Cholkao. To pare, to skim along the surface, obliquely, slantingly. Cf. chalgao.

Cetan cetante cholkao calaḱa. It will go skimming along the surface.

Chonbon. } **Chonmon.** } Exact likeness, close resemblance.

Chonbon uni lekạń ńelekana. He appears to me to bear a close resemblance to him.

Chond. } **Chand.** } Pattern, sample, form, representation, shape.

Niạ chond benaome. Make it this shape.

Choṅ. } **Choṅ choṅ.** } To frizzle, imitative of the sound produced when water falls into a fire.

Ṭukuć khon daḱ choṅ choṅ ńuroḱkana. Water is falling from the pot into the fire frizzling.

Choṅ marte. } **Choṅ mente.** } With a frizzle.

Choṅ marteko khadlekedako. They threw it in with a frizzle.

Chopao. To cut off the tops or ears of grain.

Gele geleko chopaoakaḱa. They have cut off the ears of the grain.

Chop chop. Sound of sucking (imitative.)

Chop chop mihũko nunua. The calves produce a sound resembling chop chop when sucking.

Chopor bạndhi. Cf. chapar bạndhi.

Chor. } **Chor chor.** } Imitative of the phizzing sound pruduced by anything red hot when put into water.

Chor chor sạḍekana. It is fizzing

Chor marte. } **Chor mente.** } With a fizzing sound.

Chor marte sạḍeena. It sounded phiz.

Dhipạu meṛheṭ daḱre cạḍolekhan chor mente sạḍea. If red hot iron be put into water it sounds phiz.

Chorchorao. To irritate, to sting, to rile, to wound to the quick, to sting to the quick.

Eger chorchoraokediñae. She scolded and stung me to the quick.

Choṭ. Immediately, instantly.

Chucạ. Mean, stingy, niggardly.

Chuchạ. Only, all.

Noa ul do jojo chuchạ. This mango is all bitter.

Chuchni. F. } **Chochna. M.** } Cf. chochna.

Chuṭạhạ. Ceremonially defiled, as vessels for domestic use.

Chuṭạliạ. Cf. chuṭaha.

Chuṭạlia. Free, disengaged, unemployed, superfluous, not in use, unbetrothed.

Ciḍor coḍor. Spilling when pouring out.

Ciḍor coḍor daḱko duleda. They spill the water as they pour it out.

Cidrạ. Loose in the bowels.

Nui ḍahra cidrạgeae. This bullock is loose in the bowels.

Cĩ ghoṛa. The neigh of a horse.

Ciknar. Delicate, as food; smooth.

Ciknạr jojomić kanae. He is a delicate feeder.

Cilcilạu. To frighten, to dragoon.

Sipạhi cilcilạukeḱlea. The bailiff dragooned us.

Toyo sime cilcilạukeḱkoa. The jackal frightened the hens.

Cimkiciṭiń. Lightly, trippingly, applied to females.

Cimkiciṭiń calaḱkana. She is going trippingly.

Cimṭạ dereń. Horns resembling callipers in shape, applied mainly to buffaloes.

Cindạr condor. } **Cindar candar.** } **Cindor condor.** } Wide or broad, as a piece of cloth, long and reaching to the feet as a garment.

Cindạr condore bandeakaḱa. She has fastened her cloth so that it reaches down to her feet.

Cindor condor osara. It is very wide.

Cindor condor baṛaekanae. She is going about with her garment reaching her feet.

Cinḍka cilaḱ. Here and there, in patches, not in a continuous stretch.

Cinḍka cilaḱe poakaḱa. He has hoed here and there.

Cindor candor. } **Cindor condor.** } Cf. cindạr condor.

Ciṅgul. A variety of rice or dhan.

Ciṅṛi. F. } **Ceṅṛa. M.** } A child about nine or ten years of age.

Cipạ. To press down, to oppress, to cause difficulty or hardship.

Khajnako baṛhaolekhanko cipạlea. If they raise our rents they will oppress us.

Cipạ cipi. Cf. cipạ.

Cipinhạu. The reciprocal form of cinhạu. (q. v.)

Cirbitir. } To spread, to disperse, to
Chirbitir. } divide.
Sanamko cirbitirena. They are all dispersed.
Sanam dhonko cirbitirkeda. They divided all the property.

Cirhoć. To shuffle the feet.
Cirhoćkedae. He shuffled his feet.

Ciṭaha. } Clayish, having the properties
Ciṭahi. } of clay.
Nonḍenak hasa ciṭahagea. The soil of this place is clayish.
Ciṭaha hasa. Clay.

Ciṭać caṭeć. Noise produced by slippers hitting the heel when the wearer walks. Cf. caṭać cuṭuć.

Cithạ. } A note, a written order.
Hat cithạ. }
Hat cithạe emadińa. He gave me a written order.
Hat cithạ menaka, ona iạte poesa reak botor bạnukan. There is a written order so there is no fear about the money.

Ciṭić ciṭić. Scaling off.
Ciṭić ciṭić paṛakena. It has cracked and is scaling off.

Citil bitil. } To divide, to apportion, to
Citir bitir. } break in pieces.
Oṛakpe citil bitilkeda.
Otko citir bitirkedako. They divided the land into pieces or shares.

Ciwạk cawak. To spill over as liquid agitated in a vessel when being carried.
Ciwak cawak dake hiriċeda. She is agitating the water and spilling it.

Cobcob. } Drenched, well moistened,
Chobchob. } slushy.
Cobcob lohoćakana daka do utute. The rice is well moistened with the relish.
Cob cobe sunumakawaća matkom ata. She has well moistened the roasted matkom (q. v.) with oil.

Cobhor cobhor. Imitative of the sound produced when pounding Indian corn or the unripe jạnum (q. v.) in the ḍhinki.

Cobhor marte. } With a splash.
Cobhor mente. }
Cobhor menteye donkeda. He jumped with a splash.

Cobor marte. } With a splash. Cf.
Cobor mente. } cobhor marte.

Cocko. The female organ, human and bestial.

Coeta. Lean, lanky, bony.
Coeta ḍahra. A lean bullock.

Coghe. To climb up on, to mount.
Nonḍem cogheakana. You are mounted here.

Coha. A kind of small bat.

Coha. Cf. choha.

Cokṛo. To get out of shape, to curl up as a leaf, to be crushed as a tin vessel, to crease, to crumple, to dent, &c. *Scottice*, bashed.
Thạri cokṛo cabaena. The brass plates are all out of shape.
Sakam rohoṛ cokṛoena. The leaf is dry and curled up.
Kagoje sạp cokṛokeda. He handled and creased the paper.

Con. To respect, to honour, to obey.
Oka hõ bae conaka. He respects nothing.
Jahātinakem metae, enrehõ bae conaka. Speak to him as much as you may, still he will not obey.

Corcor. A cry of alarm of barndoor fowls.

Coromokoć. Slightly acid. Cf. comkoroć.

Corońṭo. Stunted, puny, untidy, ill-looking.
Onḍe dare emanteakko do ạḍi corońṭogea. The trees and other such things there are very much stunted.

Coroṛiń. Cf. caroṛiń.

Coṭ. } Immediately, instantly.
Choṭ. }
Hoho coṭe heć goćena. Immediately on being called he came.

Cothao. To do, used only when quarrelling.
Cećem cothaotińa? What will you do to me?

Cucumguć. To sit on the heels, to hunker. Cf. cucuṅguć.
Cucumguće duṛupakana. He is sitting on his heels.

Cucumhuć. The sand-fly.

Cuḍur buḍur. Saying one thing to-day and another to-morrow, word not to be depended on.
Nui hoṛ do cuḍur buḍurgeae. This man does not stick to his word.

Cugli capaṭi. To tell tales, to inform against, to speak ill of behind one's back, to traduce, to calumniate.
Nui do cugli capạṭi bae baḍaea. This (man) does not know to traduce.
Okoehõ bae cugli capạṭiakoa. He tells tales of no one.

Cuhlạ cuhli. To the brim.
Cuhlạ cuhli pereċakana band do dakte. The tank is filled to the brim with water.

Cuhlạu. To fill to the brim.
Pereć cuhlạuena. It is full to the brim.
Khube dak̀keda, band cuhlạuena. There has been good rain, the tank is filled to the brim.

Cukạk̀ ghao. A deep ulcer with a hard, elevated edge, as in cancer, etc.

Cukri. A small earthenware vessel smaller than a cukạk̀. (q. v.)

Cukuć. To touch slightly to draw attention.
Cukućkediñae. He touched me slightly.

Culhạ kuḍạm. The back part of a native fireplace or cooking stove.

Culhạ koṛam. The front part of a native fireplace or cooking stove.

Culha ocoṭ. Small protuberances on the edge of the opening of a native cooking stove which prevent the pot when placed on the fire from closing the opening.

Culti. Cạlti. Well-to-do, in easy circumstances.
Bes culti awala hoṛ kanae. He is a well-to-do man.

Culti. Customary, usual.

Culur bulur. Culur buṭur. Without a settled habitation.
Culur bulure dạṛã baṛaekana. He is wandering about.

Cumcumba. A children's game.

Cunḍạ. M. Cunḍi. F. The youngest of a family.
Ale do baro boeha, cunḍạk̀ić do apuń ṭhen menaea. We are twelve brothers, the youngest is with my father.

Cunḍul bhuṭul. Roaming here and there, going from place to place, restless.
Bir pakaṛe sendraea cunḍul bhuṭul. He roamed over the country hunting.

Cuṅgur muṅgur. Restless and staring about.
Cuṅgur muṅgur baṛaekanae. He is restless and staring about.

Cupuikuṭ. To contract, to shrivel, as certain fruits when dry.
Netar rohoṛ cupuikuṭenae. At present he is emaciated.

Cupuruć. The reciprocal form of curuć (q. v.)

Curạmạr. Curemar. Quickly, fast, rapidly. Cf. curmạr.

Curcuṛia. To fry in oil.
Cuṛcuṛiạko isinakaṭa. They have cooked it by frying in oil.

Curcuṛia. Thin, narrow.
Cuṛcuṛia pinḍheko rakapakaṭa. They have raised the ridge of the rice field very narrow.

Curemar. Cf. curạmạr.

Curkạk̀ bhurkạk̀. In little heaps.,
Curkạk̀ bhurkạk̀e dohoakaṭa. He has put it down in little heaps.

Curu. To fill and heap up.
Khub cuṛue sohkeda. He measured it and heaped it well up.
Ma nitok̀ cuṛuiena. Now it is full.
Khạclạk̀reye pereć cuṛuakaṭa. He has filled and heaped up the basket.

Cusạu. To suck, to absorb.
Mahajon doe cusạu rehgeokedea. The money-lender sucked him poor.
Mạli lagaoadeae, bạṛić mayame cusạu oḍokkeda. He cupped him, and sucked out the bad blood.
Kuilạ do joto bạṛić so cusạua. Charcoal absorbs all the bad smells.

Cuṭki. A little piece, a fragment.
Miṭ cuṭki emadiñae. He gave me a fragment.

Cuṭki. To snap the fingers.
Cuṭkiadiñae. He snapped his fingers at me.

D

Dạb. An accident.
Dạb reak̀ okoe hõ bako badae darama. No one foresees an accident.
Dạb paṛaoena. An accident occurred.

Dạbte. Accidentally, by chance.
Dạbteye tuń ńamkedea. He accidentally shot him.

Dạbri maṅgal. To put down, to harass, to badger, to wherret, to bait.
Sanamkope dạbri maṅgalediña. You are all badgering me.

Dadka. Equivalent to dak̀ka, (q. v.) to be cooking, cooking.
Dadka oṛak̀. Cookhouse, kitchen, Cf. dak̀ka oṛak̀.
Ceṭe cekaeda? Dadkakanae. What is she doing? She is cooking.

Ḍaeka. Long, widespread, with an upward turn, as horns.
Ḍaeka dereń. Long, spreading horns with an upward turn.
Ḍaeka kaḍa. A buffaloe having long, spreading horns with an upward turn.

Dahap̃ duhup̃. Imitative of the sound produced by an elephant, or a heavy footed person when walking.
Dahap̃ duhup̃e taṛameťkana hạthi do. The elephant goes thudding along.

Ḍahar. A variety of rice or dhan.

Dảhgao. To blaze, to flare up, to increase. Cf. dahngao.

Dạhnạ. The right side, the right hand.
Dạhnạ ḍahra. The right hand bullock.
Dạhnạ dạhnạ. To the right, to the right, said to cause bullocks to turn to the right when ploughing.

Ḍạibuṅ. To be emaciated and weak.
Ōsoǩ ḍạibuṅenae. He is emaciated and weak.
Haṛam ḍạibuṅenae. He is emaciated and weak being old.
Daṛe hoṛ hõ osoǩlenkhanko mena ḍạibuṅenae. When even an able bodied man loses flesh they say he is emaciated and weak.

Dakaṛ dokoṛ. To shake, to be unsteady, from side to side, to wobble.
Baṅ bạisạulena, dakaṛ dokoṛ baṛaǩkana. It is not steady, it is shaking.
Ona do dakaṛ dokoṛoǩa niạṭaǩ do baṅ. That one wobbles, not this one.

Dạkhnạ. The south.
Dạkhnạ khone daǩeda. The rain is from the south.

Dạkhnạhi. Southern, southerly, of or belonging to the south.
Dạkhnạhi hoe kana. It is southerly wind.
Dạkhnạhi hoṛ kanae. He is a south country man.

Dalmal. } To shake, to reverberate,
Dalmalao. } to excite or agitate, to disturb, to sway as a crowd, to quiver, as a bog, mud, &c. when disturbed. Cf. dalmal.

Dạlsiń tạlsiń. Untidy, slatternly, dirty, not in working order, broken, unserviceable.
Ceť leka amgem ńeloǩkana dạlsiń tạlsiń.

Ḍamạnạ. A kind of large drum.

Ḍambaǩ ḍomboǩ. Lumpy, not pulverized.
Ḍambaǩ ḍomboǩko si lạhuťakaťa. They have not pulverized the soil when ploughing.

Dạni. Generous, liberal.

Danpun. To acquire merit.
Bese dan punakaťa. He has acquired great merit.

Dapadopo. Slow, sluggish in movement.
Balea dapadopogeae. Balea is slow.

Ḍapanḍom. The reciprocal from of ḍanḍom q. v.)

Ḍapka ḍupkạ. A succession of jungle patches. Cf. ḍupkạ.

Dara. Direction.
Oka darare menaǩa? In what direction is it?

Daradạri. Closely following, at the heels of, with little interval between.
Daradạriye pańjakedea. He followed close on his heels.
Daradạriye hećena. He came immediately after (him.)

Daṛadoṛo. To be unsteady, to wobble, as anything placed on the ground.
Kanḍa daṛadoṛoǩkana. The waterpot is wobbling.

Daṛa duṛuć. To become a cluster of large fruits, as those of the palmyra palm, papita, (q. v.) &c.

Dạṛiạ dapať. Thick, layer upon layer. Cf. dạṛiạ.

Dạris. Inclination, desire, appetite.
Jojom dạris baṅ tahena. There will be no desire to eat.
Sioǩ reaǩ dạris bạnuǩtaea. He has no inclination to plough.

Darońja. Large, imposing, huge.
Ạḍi maraṅ oṛaǩe benaoakawana darońja. He has built for himself a very large house, huge.
Darońja oṛaǩ. A large house.

Dasãe koṛa. Young men who have undergone a short training in medicine, exorcism, and divining, who go singing and begging during the dasãe (q. v.) festival.

Ḍaṭop̃. } Full or exact measure, full
Raṭop̃. } measure and nothing more or less.
Moka ḍaṭop̃. } Full lineal measure, by the moka
Moka raṭop̃. } (q. v.) or cubit.
Soṅ ḍaṭop̃. } Full measure, liquid or dry.
Soṅ raṭop̃. }

Dedar. Very much, very many, an immense quantity, an immense number.
Dedar nes hoṛo hoeaǩana. There is an immense quantity of rice this year.
Dedar netar hoṛećko ereda. They are sowing a great quantity of hoṛeć (q. v.) at present.
Dedar hoṛko jarwalena. An immense number of people were assembled.

Ḍeḍeń. } Applied to the sound
Ḍeḍeń ḍeḍeń. } produced when the ḍhak drum is beaten. Cf. ḍheḍheń.
Ḍeḍeń ḍeḍeńko ruieda. They are beating (the drum) and producing a sound resembling ḍeḍeń ḍeḍeń.

Degen. } To become hard, to
Degen degen. } harden.
Popokadale degen degen bań poka. We attempted to hoe it, it is very hard it will not hoe.
Degen goćena. It became hard.
Degenokkana. It is hardening.

Deloi. Come.

Ḍeć. Small, little.
Ḍećgeae ḍańra do. The bullock is small.

Dhab dhaba. Broad, wide.
Uniak jańga dhabdhabagetaea. His feet are broad.
Pạrlọkteć dhabdhabagea. The border (of the cloth) is wide.

Ḍhaba ḍhubu. Sound of splashing in water.
Ḍhaba ḍhubuko paerakkana. They are swimming splashingly, they are splashing while swimming.

Ḍhab ḍhob. Beautifully, well, excellently.
Ḍhabḍhobko dạpakaća. They have thatched it beautifully.

Ḍhabe ḍhobe. Well, beautifully, excellently.
Khub ḍhabe ḍhobeko benaoakaća. They have made it very beautiful, it is beautifully made.

Ḍhabos. Sound of plunging into water as of anything heavy.

Ḍhabos marte. } With a plunging
Ḍhabos mente. } sound.
Dhiri dakre ńur tora ḍhabos mente saḍe goćẹna. Immediately the stone fell into the water it sounded plunge.

Ḍhaḍnasiạ. A pretender, feigning, pretending.
Nui do ḍhaḍnasia kanae, menaktaerebõe meneda bạnuktińa. This man is a pretender, although he has (money) he says I have not any.

Ḍhak. A kind of drum. Cf. rahaṛ.

Ḍhạkuṛ. } Imitative of the
Ḍhạkuṛ ḍhạkuṛ. } sound produced when working a ḍhiṅki (v. v.
Ḍhiṅkiko lebećeda ḍhạkuṛ ḍhạkuṛ.

Ḍhạkuṛ marte. } With a thudding
Ḍhạkuṛ mente. } sound. Cf. ḍhạkuṛ.

Ḍhạlu. Slope, to slope.
Ḍhạluipe. Make it sloping.

Ḍhambo. } Large, mainly appli-
Ḍhambo ḍhambo. } ed to fruit.
Noa tale ạḍi ḍhambogea. This Palmyra palm fruit is very big.
Ḍhambo matkom. Large matkom (q. v.) flowers.

Ḍhambo ḍhạmbu. Cf. ḍhambo.

Ḍhambosak. Fat to unsightliness.
Ḍhambosake moṭaakana. He is fat and unsightly.
Ḍhambosakgeae. He is fat to unsightliness.

Dhạmcuk. } To bound, bound-
Dhạmcuk dhạmcuk. } ing, to spring, springing.
Dhạmcuk dhạmcukko don baṛaea roṭeko.

Dhạmcuk marte. } With a bound, with
Dhamcuk mente. } a spring.
Dhạmcuk marteye ḍonkeda. He jumped with a spring.

Dhamkhum. To dragoon, to force by threats, bluster, or violence.
Uni gidrạ ạḍiko dhamdhumkedea. They dragooned that boy.

Ḍhanḍhan. Buzzing round about, as a fly at a carcase, &c.
Reńgeće ḍhan ḍhan baṛaekanae. He is buzzing about (like a fly) through hunger. Cf. ḍhan ḍhanao.

Dhanghara. Rich, wealthy.

Ḍhạṅkuṛ ḍhạṅkuṛ. Imitative of a thudding sound as that produced when a long piece of timber, &c., is pressed down at one end and the raised end allowed to fall to the ground with a thud.

Ḍhanka ḍhạnki. Wandering about, going from place to place.
Reńgeće ḍhanka ḍhạnki baṛaekanae. He is going from place to place through hunger.

Ḍhankao. To wander about, to roam, to range.
Reńgeće ḍhankao baṛaekanae. He is wandering about through hunger.
Ḍhankao gujukam. You will die wandering about.

Ḍhapaka. The reciprocal form of ḍhaka (q. v.)

Dhapao. To fill in, to fill up.
Gaḍlakko dhapaokeda. They filled up the pit.

Ḍhapaṛ. } Imitative of the sound
Ḍhapaṛ ḍhapaṛ. } produced by anything flapping.
Ḍhapaṛ ḍhapaṛ saḍekana. It sounds flap, flap.

Ḍhapaṛ marte. } With flap, with a flapp-
Ḍhapaṛ mente } ing sound. Cf. ḍhapaṛ.

Dhapra. M. } Rough-headed, having a
Dhạpri F. } rough thick head of hair, shock headed.
Dhaprageae. He is shock headed.
Dhạprigeae. She is shock headed.

Dhara dhuṛa̤. } To dun, to dragoon, to
Dhaṛa dhuṛa̤. } force by threats or bluster.
Khajna la̤giťko dhara dhura̤ťlea. They are dragooning us about our rent.

Dharamara. To dragoon, to force by threats or bluster, to insist.
Dharamarakediňako. They dragooned me.

Dharao. To apprehend, to arrest, to seize.
Kanasṭae dharaokedea. The constable arrested him.

Dharapkia̤. } A receptacle for sindur
Darapkia. } (q. v.) Cf. kia̤.

Dhaṛpaṛ. Quickly, hurriedly, hastily.
Dhaṛpaṛ jahãnaǩe ňam baṛaeda. He is searching hurriedly for something.

Dhaṛphaṛao. To hurry, to haste.
Dhaṛphaṛao baṛae kanae. He is hurrying.

Dhaṛpilaǩ. Towsy, towzled, dishevelled, rumpled, as hair, applied to females.
Dha̤rpilaǩ ṳbe aṛaǩakaťa. She has let loose her hair dishevelled.
Dha̤rpilaǩgeae. She is dishevelled.

Dhatpat. Quickly, rapidly, hurriedly.
Khan unre dhatpate benaokeťkina. Then she made them hurriedly.

Dhatar patar. Quickly, hastily, hurriedly.
Dhatar patar ṭa̤nḍi senkate heraň petaňe a̤ruṗ baṛaena.

Ḍha̤ulia̤. Relationship between brother-in-law and sister-in-law.
Ḍha̤ulia̤ kanakin. They are brother-in-law and sister-in-law.

Ḍha̤ulia̤ sa̤gai. Relationship between brother-in-law and sister-in-law.
Great freedom is accorded to these in their intercourse with each other, and what is regarded as criminal intercourse in others is propriety with them.

Dhawa. To attack, to seize, to range, to roam.

Ḍheḍheń. } Applied to the
Ḍheḍheń ḍheḍheń. } sound produced when the ḍhak (q. v.) drum is beaten.

Ḍheke. } Rich, wealthy, fat, corpu-
Ḍhekela. } lent, very, applied to fatness.
Ḍhekelae moṭa̤akana. He is very fat.

Dhigdha̤. Cf. digdha̤.

Dhina̤ň. A future part of the same day.
Dhina̤ň hijuǩme. Come later on in the day.

Dhina̤ň tikin. Mid-day to-day.

Dhina̤ň tarasiń. About 3 p. m. to-day.

Dhipni A stopper, a lid.

Ḍhopko. A mound, a hillock.

Dhoṛos. } Owing to, in consequence
Dhoṛoste. } of.
Nia̤ dhoṛosteye rṳaǩkana. He has fever owing to this.

Ḍhõya ḍhape. } To become emaciated,
Ḍhoya ḍhape. } emaciated.
Rengeéte ḍhõya ḍhapeẽnae. He is emaciated through starvation.
Ḍhoya ḍhape osóǩenae. He is lean as a skeleton.

Dhuňṛa̤ dhuňṛi. To search for here and there.

Dhurpa̤u. To be at the maximum, utmost height, highest pitch or culminating point, to be in full swing.
Hoṛo rohoeko dhurpa̤uena. The planting of rice is in full swing.
Setoh dhurpa̤uena. The heat of the sun is at its height.

Dhuṛsa̤u. To singe, to slightly burn.
Ḍa̤kuko dhuṛsa̤ukedea. The thieves singed him (to cause him to give up his money.)

Dhusri. A variety of dhan or rice.

Dhuwa̤ bhua̤. Doubtful, uncertain, hesitating.

Ḍighi. To doubt, to suspect, to be uncertain; suspicion, uncertainty.

Ḍigoha. To fail. Cf. ḍiga̤u.
Suluk dulaṛ bae ḍigohaǩa. Charity fails not.

Ḍigor. Obstinate, self-willed.

Ḍigra̤li. } Obstinate, self-willed.
Ḍigra̤lia̤. }

Ḍigri piṭa̤u. To proclaim a civil court decree by beat of drum.
Ḍigri piṭa̤ukedako. They proclaimed, or made public, the decree of the court by beat of drum.

Ḍihdar. An official whose duty it is to look after the interests of a landholder in the villages on his estate.

Ḍihe ḍa̤nḍi. Hamlet and boundaries.

Dindirsič. Untidy, slatternly, careless of attire, hair in disorder, said of females.

Dinṭa̤. Daily.
Dinṭare pe dhao jomme. Eat three times daily.
Dinṭageye hijuǩkana. He is coming daily.

Dipisa̤. The reciprocal form of disa̤ (q. v.)

Dob.
Dob dosa. } Condition, state.

Pea gate uniak̇ dob reaḥ añjomkate jiwi rar̥ej-taea menteko heċena. Three friends heard of his state and came to comfort him.

Ḍobea.
Ḍobeoċ. } Emaciated and having a protuberant belly.

Har̥am ḍobeoċenae. He is old, emaciated and big-bellied.

Ruạ ruạteye ḍobeoċena. He is emaciated and big-bellied owing to continued fever.

Dobnao. To chide, to check, to curb, to restrain.

Noko bako dobnaolekokhan dolre suluk baḥ tahena. If they do not restrain these (people) there will not be harmony in the community.

Ḍoḍhor. A hole, a hollow, a cavity, hollow.

Dare ḍoḍhorre. In a hole of a tree.

Dokạni.
Dokạnia. } A shopkeeper.

Nui do dokạnia kanae. This is a shopkeeper.

Ḍola. To be damp, limp, lean, poor, to lose freshness.

Ḍolaena. It is damp.

Dolbadol.
Odolbodol. } Exchange, alteration, to exchange, to swop, to barter, to confuse, to displace.

Domdom. Heaped up, rising above the surrounding surface.

Domdomko puñjiakata. They have heaped it higher than the surrounding surface.

Domo. To swell.

Tor̥ domokediñako. They stung me and caused a swelling.

Domok̇ domok̇. Swaying, shaking or rhythmical movement of the body.

Domok̇ domok̇e calak̇kana. He is going swaying.
Domok̇ domok̇e hur̥uḥeda. She is working the ḍhiṅki and moving her body as she does so.

Dondkor̥o. Squatting, cowering, sitting close to the ground.

Dondkor̥o kulạiye oborakana. The hare is sitting cowering.

Dondorkole.
Dondorpole. } Dishevelled and out of sorts, applied to females.

Dondor kokor. A species of owl.

Dor marao. To fix or settle a price or rate.

Doriñ maraokeda. I fixed the rate.

Doroṅ soroṅ. Ailing, out of sorts, indisposed. Cf doro soro.

Dorpaṭ. Flaw.

Dorpaṭ janamena, noa do baḥ hoyok̇a. A flaw has appeared, this will not do.

Dorpoċ. Hollow, flawed, cracked, chipped.

Dub dan. To give a piece of *dub* grass (*Cynodon Dactylon*) as a proof that a bargain has been made. Cf. dub dhan.

Ḍublạu. To cover, as water, to overflow.

Dak̇te ḍublạuena. It is covered with water.

Dublạu. To become thin, to be emaciated.

Ruạte dublạuena. He is emaciated through fever.

Ḍubuk.
Ḍubuk ḍubuk. } To nod the head, to bow the head, as when making obeisance. Cf. ḍubuk̇ ḍubuk̇.

Dudr̥umte ḍubuk ḍubukok̇kanae. He is nodding owing to drowsiness.

Dudhkạni A variety of dhan or rice.

Dukdukuạs. Affliction, trouble.

Duk dukuạsre bae hirilea. He will not visit us in trouble.

Dukhar. Necessitous, needy, pinched.

Dukharok̇ jokheċ. At a pinch.
Dukharok̇ jokheċ dom cekaea? jahãn lekan kuḍige. What can you do at a pinch? any sort of a kuḍạli will do.

Dulkạu. To go out of the way, to keep out of the way.

Dulkạu heċenae. He has come to get, or be, out of the way.

Ḍumḍhukạk̇.
Ḍuḍumḍhukạk̇. } A kind of drum beaten on both ends, a kind of earthenware bottle shaped like the drum bulging in the middle and the ends like the neck of a bottle.

Dumdumi. Rough, uneven, as a road.

Noa rasta do ạdi dumdumigea. This road is very rough.

Durduri. To oppress, to exact by bluster or threats, to dragoon, to terrorize.

Ạdi durduriko sapeċlea. They oppress us greatly.

Ḍur̥hi ghãs.
Ḍuḍhi ghãs. } A kind of tall grass, *Apluda aristata, Linn.*

Durkarak̇. An exclamation of annoyance.

Durkarak̇, bạñ disạleda. How stupid, I forgot.

Ḍuru ḍuru. } A call to young buffaloes.
Ḍuruh ḍuruh. }

Dusạu. Faulty, blamable, defective, to blame, to find fault with.
Noa kiorić do dusạugea. This cloth is faulty.

Duṭhạk. An exclamation of annoyance, how foolish, dear me.
Duṭhạk iñ hiṛiñleda. Dear me, I forgot.

E

Eḍeṭhompo. Cf. eḍeṭhompe.

Eḍgejak. Cf. eṛgejak.

Egor ogor. Cf. ogor ogor.

Ẽhẽk. An emphatic negative.
Ẽhẽk, noa do bañ añjomoktama. Certainly not, this of yours will not be listened to.

Eho. Used to call attention.
Eho, añjomme.

Ẽhõ. Imitative of the crying of an infant.

Ektaraha. Masterful, impertinent, insolent, insulting.
Ektaraha kathatae. His impertinent remark.
Ektaraham roṛkeda. You spoke impertinently.

Enẽlgo. Cf. enẽlgol.

Ekam. One.
Ekam, dukam, tinik, lạkuṛ, salse, sapai, ḍenḍ, kõṛ, kiṭiñ, koṛok, ṭhakṛok. One, two, three, four, five, six, seven, eight, nine, ten, eleven, used by children to count the seeds in the pod of *Bauhinia Vahlii.*

Ekan. } Privately, alone, solitary.
Ekant. }
Ekanre idikateye galmarsaodea. He took him aside and talked to him.

Elaka. Province, district, jurisdiction.
Aleak elaka do bạnukanah. It is not within our jurisdiction. Cf. ilaka.

Eneseć. A stopper, a covering, any thing which covers, or closes an opening. Cf. eseć.

Eñgol. To pretend, to feign, to make a shew of.
Jom eñgol. To make a shew of eating.
Dal eñgol. To pretend to strike.
Ger eñgol. To feign to bite.

Epem. The reciprocal form of em to give. Cf. em.

Er tepeć. To throw a handful of dust in the eyes, to fill the eyes by throwing, as by throwing dust.
Kombṛo do hortenko meṭre dhuṛi er tepeckate cijko ạtkirtakoa. Thieves fill the eyes of travellers by throwing dust at them, and steal their property.

Eṛem eṛem. Cravingly, hankeringly, longing for, looking wistfully on.
Guṛ lạgitko eṛem eṛemokkana. They are looking wistfully at the sugar.
Jom lạgić eṛem eṛemokkanae. He is longing to eat.

Eṛeñ beṭeñ. To speak much, to boast.
Nui hoṛ do ạḍi eṛeñ beṭeñokkanae. This man is speaking much.
Eṛeñ beṭeñem roṛeć tahẽkana, okarem daṛelena? You were speaking boastingly, where did you conquer?

Etka. A climbing plant, *Mucuna puriens, D. C.*

G

Gab. Stain.
Gab lagaoena. It is stained.

Gab marte. } Deeply.
Gab mente. }
Losoṭreñ thạliena gab mente. I sunk deeply into the mud.

Gabcao. To pierce, to penetrate.
Kuḍi bañ gabcaoka hasare. The kudali will not penetrate the soil.
Laser kuḍi do gabcaokgea. A sharp kudali will penetrate.
Baheć bañ gabcaolente dare do goćena. The tree has died because the roots did not penetrate (the soil.

Gaḍa coḍa. A species of fish.

Gaḍa citi. A species of water snake.

Gaḍea guḍiạ. Struggling one on the top of another, leaning on.
Gaḍea guḍiạ mićtogeko calaoena. They left leaning on each other.
Gaḍea guḍiạ baṛakkanako. They are struggling together (as young pigs, &c, to get at the dam's dugs.)

Gaḍi. } A seed bed.
Aphor gaḍi. }

Gaḍlak godlok. Having a number of holes or depressions, as an earthen floor, &c.
Goṛa gaḍlak goḍlokakana. The floor of the cowshed is full of holes.

Gaḍoe saḍoe. To mix, to mingle, intermix, intermingle.
Utuko do thoṛa gaḍoe saḍoeoka. Relish will be slightly mixed.
Isạị ar bedin mić ṭhenko jomlekhan gaḍoe saḍoeẽnako. If Christians and heathen eat together they are mixed.

Gạ̃hjur. Baggy, baggy in the centre, as an awning not drawn tight, hanging loose or over, bulging, pendulous.
Jal gạ̃hjur teñme. Weave the net bulging in the centre.
Khub gạ̃hjurae nui sukri do. This pig has a good baggy belly.

Gạhńjur. Cf. gạhjur.
Gạhńjur laċ. A baggy or pendulous belly like a sow's.

Gạigum. Sensation produced by anything touching the skin, to scratch. Cf. gaegam.

Gaj. To pierce, to penetrate.
Borlomte banae gaj maraokedea. He pierced the bear with a spear, he speared the bear.

Gajgaj. Close, oppressively hot and steamy, perspiring and dirty, damp, moist. Cf. gijgij.

Gajha gạjhi. To be displeased, to sulk, to refuse to comply with the wish of another through ill temper.
Ajoam kankhan ạdim gajha gạjhiḱkana. When I put it to your lips you refuse to eat it through ill temper.

Gajhao. To be displeased, to be dissatisfied, to sulk, to contrary through ill temper.
Ạdi gajhaoḱkanae. He is very sulky.

Gal bajoṛiạ. Funny, joking, jesting, humourous.

Galgaeatiń. Smooth and glossy like the plumage of a crow.

Galgalao. To make a noise, to make a row, din or tumult, Cf. galgal.

Gal goppo. To tattle, to gossip.
Nonḍe ceṫpe gal goppoeda? What are you gossipping about here?

Gạńjliić. The fifth of a family when there are six or more children.

Gapegupe. To suppress, to keep secret, privily.
Katha dole gapegupekeda. We kept the matter secret.

Gạsuạ rambṛa. } A kind of early rambṛa (q. v.)
Ghạsuạ rambṛa. }

Gendṛaḱ cetṛaḱ. Rags, tattered clothes.

Gene phene. } Applied to nasal whining as of a cross child, nasal pronunciation.
Ghene phene. }

Gesoṭiạ. } Slovenly, dirty, filthy.
Ghesoṭiạ. }
Ḍaṭa bań saphalekhan hoṛ gesoṭiạko metakoa. If they do not clean the teeth people call them dirty.

Gesṭaha. M. } Dirty, filthy, untidy, uncleanly.
Gesṭahi. F. }

Ghạì. Opportunity, suitable time or season.
Kul ghạiye ńamleńneć doe jojoma. Only when, the tiger gets an opportunity he devours.

Ghajeṛ. To go or turn aside. Cf. ghańjeṛ.

Ghaṭwek. One in charge of a ghaṭ (q. v.) who collects royalties.
Bir ren ghaṭwek. The person in charge of the road to and from the forest by which timber is taken away.
Buru ren ghaṭwek. The person in charge of the road to and from the hills by which hill produce is taken away.

Ghesoṭiạ. Cf. gesoṭiạ.

Ghesṭahi. F. } Dirty, filthy, untidy, uncleanly.
Ghesṭaha M. }

Ghisạli. A variety of dhan or rice.

Ghisghisạu. } To rush at, to rush forward, to charge.
Gisgisau. }
Bana ghisghisạu heć goćenae. The bear came charging.

Ghuṛci gạì. Cf. gạì ghuṛạ.

Girạbas. } Residence, to settle, to take up one's residence.
Girobas. }
Nonḍe girạbas menaḱtińa. My residence is here.

Gisgisạu. Cf. ghisghisạu.

Gob. To steal, to purloin, to put out of the way.

Godogodo. Noise of falling water.

Goḍogoḍo. Sound of boiling or bubbling.

Gońj. Cf. goja.

Gop. } To hide, to keep back, to suppress, to keep secret.
Gopao. }
Gopkedako. } They suppressed it.
Gopaokedako. }

Goppo. To tattle, to gossip.
Duṛupkateko goppo joha. They sit and gossip.

Gorji. Need, occasion, want, necessity, wish, intention, interest, inclination.
Nui do bạhu reah gorji bạnuḱtaea. This man has no need of a wife.

Gorob. Heavy, indigestible.
Ona do ạdi gorobgea, laɛre do ạditeć besuauka. That is very indigestible, it makes the stomach very uncomfortable.

Gulki mạric. Round pepper. Cf. golmạric.

Gutạ. } To prod, to jab.
Gutạu. }

Gutạ guti. To prod, to jab.
Gutạ guti baṛaenakin. They prodded each other.

Guṭi. }A veiled name for a tree on
Guṭi dare. } which Tassar (q. v.) silkworms are being reared.

H

Hạdiạu. To long for, to sigh for, to crave for.
Bań ńamle hiloke hạdiạuka. When he does not get it he will sigh for it.
Misọr disom reak jel celańko hạdiạuaća. They sighed for the flesh pots of Egypt.

Hạdrap̣. Violent, headstrong, forceful, obstinate.

Hākar phukar̤. }To shout, as when
Hākar pukar̤. } watching crops at night.

Hạluć bạkuć. To limp, to walk totteringly as one weak, a child learning to walk or as one intoxicated.
Hạluć bạkuće dar̤ankana. He is walking totteringly.

Hanḍe nanḍe. Here and there.

Hańgor hako. }
Hońgor hako. }A shark.

Hạpu hara. To be without resource, to be reduced to the last extremity.
Kombr̤oko idi cabakettae iạte hạpu haraenae. He is resourceless owing to thieves having taken all he had.
Or̤ak loentae iạte hạpu haraenae. He has been reduced to the last extremity through his house having been burnt.

Har. Fully, a little over, applied to ripeness.
Bele harena. Fully ripe, or a little over ripe.

Hara hurạ. Damaged, broken, mixed, confused.
Hara hurạe ror̤keda. He spoke confusedly.

Har̤am gad. The first scum of sugarcane juice when being boiled.

Harbhańj. Remnant of an animal or human being killed by a wild beast.
Har bhańj ceṭ hõ bah ńamlena. No remnant whatever was found.

Hār̤u. The small flies found in the fruit of the Loa fig tree, *Ficus conglomerata, Roxb.*

Hạsi kusi. Jubilant, rejoicing, in high spirits.
Hạsi kusi ńeńelko calakkana. They are going in high spirits to the fair.

Hathea. Cf. daya.

Hebajot. To take care of, to preserve, to defend, to protect, to guard.

Heḍge hesak. To be polluted, to be filthy, to be dirty, dirty and untidy as a house; to lose taste or strength, as malted grain.
Ona ṭhạ̄i do dhorage heḍge hesagoka. That place will certainly become filthy.
Dak dul dulte sanamle heḍge hesakkeda hạnḍi do. With repeated watering we made the malted grain tasteless.

Hejleć pejleć. Dirty, untidy, slatternly, slovenly.
Hejleć pejleć dak mạnḍiye emadińa. She gave me food in an untidy manner.

Hemca. A variety of dhan or rice.

Hende kaṭ oṭ. A non-edible black fungus which grows on timber.

Henḍkok. }To throw oneself upon the
Her̤kok. } pity or charity of another, to attach oneself to another to be fed of his charity.
Iń ṭhenem heć henḍkokakana? Have you come to attach yourself to me to be fed of my charity?
Miṭṭah kisār̤ ṭhene henḍkokente sukri gupi tạnḍiteye kolkadea. He joined himself to a rich man who sent him to the field to herd swine.

Hene phene. Cf. jenephene.

Heńgla. Cf. henla.

Her̤agesa. Cf. her̤aghesa.

Her̤kok. Cf. henḍkok.

Hēsaliạ. Spiteful, envious, injuring another through envy.
Hēsaliạ hor̤ kanae. He is a spiteful man.

Hēslaha. Cf. hēsaliạ.

Hir̤ić. }Stounding, or shooting,
Hir̤ić hir̤ić. } as pain.
Hir̤ić hir̤ić hasoedińkana. It pains me stoundingly.

Hir̤ić marte. }
Hir̤ić mente. }With a stound.
Hir̤ić marte hasokedińa. It pained me with a stound.

Hir̤iṭ. }
Hir̤iṭ hir̤iṭ. }Cf. hir̤ić.

Hir̤iṭ marte. }
Hir̤iṭ mente. }Cf. hir̤ić marte.

Hirohi. To long for, to sigh for, to hanker after, to crave for, used with regard to food.
Misọr disom reak jel celahko hirohiaća. They sighed for the flesh pots of Egypt.

Hiwel hawal. To be weak, to be enfeebled.
Hiwel hawalgeń aṭkareda reṅgeċte. I feel weakened through hunger.
Hiwel hawalenae, bae tul daṛeaǩkana. He is weakened, he is not able to lift it.

Hoedoǩ kạpi. A kind of battle axe.

Holbol. Cf. halbal.

Hoṅhar. Father-in-law.
Hoṅhariń. My father-in-law.
Hoṅharme. Thy father-in-law.

Hordodo. } To overreach, to impose
Horododo. } upon, to cozen, to cheat.
Hordodokateye hataokeċtaea. He cheated him and took it from him.
Horododokateko eṛekedea. They over reached him and cheated him.

Hoṛ puṭkạ. An edible from of puff ball, which is eaten before it ripens.

Hū. To express assent, to assent to.
Hū ooekedińae. He caused me to assent.
Ma hūgme. Come, say hū, come, assent.
Baṅkhan ohoń hūlea. Else I would not have assented.

Huḍrạǩ. } To splash, to make
Huḍrạǩ huḍrạǩ. } a noise by plunging into or jumping in water.
Noa pukhrire katla hakoe huḍrạǩ maraokeda. A katla fish jumped and splashed in this tank.

Huḍrạǩ marte. } With a plunging or
Huḍrạǩ mente. } splashing sound.
Huḍrạǩ marte oḍok goċenae. He rushed out with a splash.

Huḍrạǩ huḍrạǩ. The peculiar coughing sound produced by Indian bulls.
Huḍrạǩ huḍrạǩkō hukạia sanḍko.

Hujut. To oppress, to annoy.

Huloṛ. To injure, to damage.
Ạḍi huloṛako. They will cause much damage.

Humdhum. To bully, to browbeat, to intimidate, to dragoon.
Ạḍiko humdhumkeċlea khajna lạgiċ. They bullied us greatly about our rent.

Huń marte. } Quickly, hurriedly.
Huń mente. }
Huń mente kulhite oḍokenae. He went out hurriedly into the street.

Huṛ. To engage, to hire, to order, employed in sarcasm.
Okoeye huṛaċmea? Who told you to do it?
Aċtege huṛanae. He engaged in it himself.

Huruċ oċ. } A fungus which grows
Kaṭ oċ. } mainly on tree stumps, some forms of which are edible.

Hutlaṅ. } Throwing out the leg
Hutlaṅ hutlaṅ. } when walking as one who has a stiff hip joint.
Hutlaṅ hutlaṅe calaǩkana. He walks throwing out his leg.

Hutlaṅ marte. } With a throw out of
Hutlaṅ mente. } the leg. Cf. hutlaṅ.

Huḍgạr. To agitate, to stir up, as water.

Huṭer. } A common plant, *Indi-*
Dare huṭer. } *gofera pulchella, Roxb.*
The flowers of this plant are eaten.

Huṭer gundri. A species of quail so named from its call.

I

Igor ogor. Cf. ogor ogor.

Ikoṭ. To decide, to settle, to sum up.
Galmaraokateko ikoṭakada. They have discussed and settled it.

Is. An exclamation of pain or annoyance.
Is! bạṛiċena. Oh dear! it is injured.
Is! ạḍi hasolediń. Oh! it pained me greatly.

J

Ja. To fix, to settle, to fix certain areas by estimation.
Rek jaakaċale. We have divided the land into reks (q. v.)
Kuni jaakaċale. We have fixed the area of the kuni, or we have divided the land into kunis. (q. v.)

Jab. A kind of grass.

Jabe Kisku. A sub-sept of the Santal sept Kisku. (q. v.)

Jahat johot. Slowly, dilatory, leisurely, snail-like.

Jahbaj. Huge, big, stalwart, obstinate, headstrong.
Jahbaj hoṛ kanae. He is an obstinate man
Ạḍi jahbaj hạthi kanae. He is a very huge elephant.

Jaṅre. Trousers.

Jạnti. To inform, to tell, to apprize, to acquaint.
Bako jạntiadiń. They did not inform me.

Jaro. Stock, line, race, ancestry.

Jeṭhwa. A variety of the cotton plant.

Jhahat jhohot. Slowly, dilatory, leisurely, snail-like.

Jhãora jhãuri. Weeping, crying.
Jhãora jhãuri baṛae kanako gidrę do. The children are crying.

Jhaṛni. One who cures snake bites, and scorpion stings by charms and incantations.

Jharoć jhapoć. Dilapidated, as a house, torn, old, worn out, as cloth or clothes,
Cet lekan jharoć jhapoć oṛakreko tahenkana. What a dilapidated house they are living in.

Jhiṅgạ sạl. A variety of dhan or rice.

Jhiṅji jhuri. Insignificant, poor, of no standing or consequence.
Noko jhiṅji jhuri cetko cekaea? What will these insignificants do?

Jhohot mohot. Slowly, leisurely, dilatory.

Jiạu. To kill the chrysalis in a cocoon, which in the case of Tussar cocoons is performed by steaming.

Jimtạu. To stick together, to adhere together, to form lumps by sticking together.
Bạlis reak tulạm hakopako jimtạukte keṭejoka. The cotton (stuffing) of a pillow through quickly sticking together gets hard.

Jion. The Tailor-bird. Cf. jiạm.

Jirlạ. A district, a division of a country for administrative purposes. Cf. jilạ.

Joboć. }
Joboć joboć. } Wet, slushy.
Ḍher dak paṭaokkhan ot do joboć jobocte seaka. If it be too heavily irrigated it will rot through the soil being wet.

Johot mohot. Slowly, dilatory, leisurely, snail-like.

Jom laṛ. A large jungle climbing plant, *Bauhinia Vahlii.*

Jopok. }
Ayup jopok. } A little after nightfall.

Joṛao. To join, to add together, to reckon, to add up, to fabricate, to unite, to invent, to cement, to solder, to yoke.
Sereñ joṛao. To compose a song.
Nahel joṛaome. Yoke the plough.
Gạḍire ḍaṅra joṛaokinme. Yoke the bullocks to the cart.
Joṛaoak kana. It is a pieced thing.
Bareako joṛaoakata. They have joined two together.
Sereñe joṛaoakata. He has composed a song.

Jugi Ṭuḍu. A sub-sept of the Santal sept Ṭuḍu (q. v.)

Juktạu. To amass, to accumulate, to lay up.
Sermare dhon juktạu lagit. For the purpose of laying up treasure in heaven.

Juṅgi. The unripe fruit of the *rol* tree, *Terminalia Chebula, Retz.*

Jurguḍạ. A variety of the cotton plant.

Jusi. }
Hãsi jusi. } Impropriety.
Hãsi jusi jemon alo hoyok. So that there may be no impropriety.

K

Kabra runḍạ. A species of wild cat.

Kacrat. A sapling of a year's growth.

Kạhtur. Tradition, traditional lore.
Kạhtur katha. Tradition.

Kạidạ. A big thick sickle, used to pollard trees or to cut branches.

Kalak. }
Kalaṅk. } Suspicion, reflection, scandal, fault, reproach, accusation.
Koloṅk. }
Kalak cakem hạra? Why should you incur reproach?
Bin kạlirenkin kalaṅkadea. They threw suspicion on one who was without reproach.
Bin kạlirenkin koloṅkadea. They threw suspicion on one who was without reproach.

Kalbhag. Unexpectedly, unawares, unwarned, unanticipated.
Kalbhag leka. It so happened.

Kalbokos. A species of fish.

Kạli piạj. Onions raised from bulbs.

Kamal. To finish, to complete, to perfect.
Ạurile kamala. We have not yet perfected it.
Ot bale kamalakata. We have not completed the reclamation of the land.

Kạmạni. A variety of dhan or rice.

Kanakcur. A variety of dhan or rice.

Kaṅdoṛ. To famish, to clem; famishing; famine, scarcity.
Noko gidrạ kaṅdoṛ baṛae kanako. These children are famishing.
Kaṅdoṛ aṭkarokkana, cetho̐ bạnukanaḥ. It seems to be a famine, there is nothing

Kãṛã. To be blasted, to be dried up through having been attacked by insects, applied to pods of the cotton plant which do not burst when ripe through having been injured by insects.

Kaṛibaṅki. A variety of dhan or rice.

Kaṛimsaḷ. A variety of dhan or rice.

Kasmi. Active, energetic, diligent.

Kasoeya. Cf. **kosoeya.**

Kaṭh piaj. Onions raised from seed.

Kaṭri. The beam or pole of a sugar cane press to which the cattle are yoked.

Kaṭrire duṛuḅkate daṛrae lagakoa. He sits on the beam and drives the bullocks.

Kecet̤ mecet̤. } Any way, inefficiently,
Kecot̤ mecot̤. } perfunctorily.

Kecet̤ mecet̤le rohoekeda. } We planted it any
Kecot̤ mecot̤le rohoekeda. } way.

Kele. A variety of dhan or rice.

Khab khub. Imitative of a thudding sound, thud thud.

Khab khuble tuṅketkoa. We shot them (with arrows) thud thud.

Khab khubko don boloena. The jumped into (water) thud thud.

Khạisạ. } To get angry, to become
Khạisạu. } irritated.

Bae khạisạ hodoka. He does not become quickly irritated.

Khạisạha. Short-tempered, easily angered.

Khạisạha hoṛ kanae. He is a short-tempered man.

Khạisạ khạisi. Short tempered, angry, irritated.

Khạisạ khạisi godokae. He gets easily angry.

Khajạnti. A treasury, a treasurer.

Khạṛgo. High, lofty, tall.

Khạṛgo dare. A high tree.

Khaṭạli. } Work, labour, earnings.
Khaṭạni. }

Khemota. Ability, power.

Khento. To decrease, to become less.

Khijạu. To mix, to intermingle, to pulverise.

Ḍaṅrako lebet khijạukeda. The bullocks trod it and pulverised it.

Hasa hõ bah khijạulena. The soil also was not pulverised.

Khilkam. Whole, well, not ailing.

Khilkamko lạgit do baha, dukhạliko lạgitge ojha do. The doctor is not for the unailing, but for the suffering.

Khirwạ. A cultivated plant so called.

Khober. News, intelligence.

Khondlak. } A pit, a gully.
Khonḍlak. }

La khondlakakaṭako. They have dug it into a pit.

Khoṛdeṭ. } To limp, limping,
Khoṛdeṭ khoṛdeṭ. } lame.

Jaṅga khoṛdeṭgetaea. His foot is lame.

Khoṛdeṭ khoṛdeṭe calakkana. He goes limping.

Khorna. } Saline, applied to a cer-
Khornaha. } tain kind of clayish soil.

Khorna dak. Saline water. Cf. **khorna.**

Khuṅgi. An open-woven little bag in which Tassar silk moths are incarcerated till they deposit their eggs.

Khupạ kạpi. A kind of battle axe. Cf. kạpi.

Kitạ ke kitạ. Like piece with like piece, like with like.

Kitạ ke kitạko dohoakaṭa. They have placed like with like.

Kokkoḍro. Uncomfortable owing to the presence of smoke, perplexed.

Kolonk. Cf. **kalak.**

Kos. To tan leather.

Kokosić. A tanner.

Kosle. } Sulkingly, crossly, sul-
Kosle kosle. } lenly, scowlingly, frowningly.

Kosle mosle. Cf. **kosle.**

Kosoeya. } The name of an insect to
Kasoeya. } which decay in the front teeth of cattle is attributed.

Kosoeyako jomekana. His front teeth are decayed.

Kosta. Red thread, employed in making the borders of cloth.

Kosṭo mosṭo. Sorely pressed, hard pressed, with great difficulty, with great hardship, with much suffering.

Kulạṅ. } Aimlessly, without settled
Alaṅ kulạṅ. } purpose.

Kuṛmbi selep jel. A species of deer.

L

Lạbni. The vessel into which the juice of the toddy palm is collected, and the measure by which it is sold.

Lacak lucuk. To limp, to hobble, limpingly.
Lacak lucuke taṛameṭkana. He is walking limpingly.

Lạdgu pạdgu. In large clusters in which the fruits touch each other.
Ul lạdgu pạdgu joḱkana. The mango has fruited in clusters.

Lahaṅga. M. } **Lahạṅgi** F. } Tall.

Lạhṭi. Shellac, lac after having been melted and strained through a cloth.
Lạhṭi caṛi. Wristlets made of lac.

Laṭać luṭuć. Insufficiently cooked.

Lạṭkum. Protuberant, rising above the surrounding surface.

Lekman. Full grown, able bodied.
Neke lekmanoḱkanae. He is just now reaching full growth.

Leṭreć. M. } **Liṭrić.** F. } Small, little.
Leṭreć gidrạ. A small boy.
Liṭrić gidrạ. A small girl.
Leṭreć mihü. A little bull calf.

Liṛoć toṛoć. Mucilaginous, applied also to the taste of the flesh of animals that have died a natural death.
Liṛoć toṛoćgea jel do. The flesh meat is insipid.

Liṭrić. Cf. leṭreć.

Loeya khạṇḍit. Newly reclaimed rice growing land.

Logbhog. Close, near, about, almost.
Kunạmi log bhog. About full moon.
Sohrae log bhog iạte choń senlena.. As it is near the Sohrae (q. v.) festival I cannot go.

Lohor pohor. To delay, to dilly daly, to put off time.

Loro boto. Slavering at the corners of the mouth, inefficiently, perfunctorily.

Loṛoḱ toroḱ. To drop, to spill, as liquid being carried.
Ạdi loṛoḱ toroḱem joro ocoeda.

Loṭoć. } **Kạṛã loṭoć.** } A kind of fly very troublesome to cattle, mainly during the rains.

Loṭoć. } **Seta loṭoć.** } A kind of small fly very troublesome to dogs on whom they are mainly found.

Loton. A variety of dhan or rice.

Ludgup̣. Very plump and fat, applied to children.
Ludgup̣e moṭaakana. He is very plump and fat.

Ludgup̣. } **Ludgup̣ ludgup̣.** } In clusters, one resting on or touching another, as fruit in a cluster.

Luihạ. An iron vessel or pot used for cooking and other purposes.

Lumbạk. } **Ạyup̣ lumbạk.** } A little after nightfall, about one hour after sunset.
Ạyup̣ lumbạkle seṭerena. We arrived a little after nightfall.

Lusur phusur. To whisper, whisperingly.
Lusur phusur joḱkanakin. They are whispering together.
Lusur phusurko galmarao joḱkana. They are conversing together in a whisper.

Luṭuć suṭuć. Fingering and turning over every thing as when searching.
Goṭa oṛaḱ luṭuć suṭućko ńam baṛakeda. They searched the whole house turning over everything.

M

Mal. A wrestler, an athlete.

Mande. A ridge to prevent water raised from a lower level flowing back.
Bar pe ṭhenko mandeakaṭa. They have raised ridges at two or three places to prevent water flowing back.

Meramot. To mend, to repair. Cf. maramat.

Merlaṅ mirliṅ. Sad, dejected, pitiable, miserable looking.

Mer sitruć. Small, insignificant, petty. paltry, trivial, unimportant.
Mer sitruće ńeloḱkana. He looks insignificant.

Mirạ. } **Mirạ mirạ.** } New, unknown.
Mirạ mirạ kathae oḍokeda. He is raising new matters.

Mirsiṭạr. Trivial, frivolous, unimportant.

Mõhjam. To have or be in readiness, to exist, to be present. Cf. mohńjam.
Sanam mõhjamena. All is in readiness, or all has been provided.

Momblot. All, completely.
Momblotko jom ocabakeda. They ate it all up.

More. To lean on or against.
Racare jaṅge tahẽkana onareñ moreka. There was a horizontal bar resting on posts in the courtyard and I would lean against that.

Moṭiao. To appropriate, to take possession of, to collect together.

Munḍ moron. Lazy, disinclined to make effort, a great hardship.
Aḍiteć munḍ moronko ạikạueda. They feel it to be a great hardship.
Laṛaok do munḍ morone aṭkareda. He feels moving to be a great hardship.

Muṭiạu. To appropriate, to possess oneself of, to collect together.

N

Nạgi. A variety of dhan or rice.

Nanha. A variety of dhan or rice.

Nạthu phoṛao. To snort, to make a noise through the nostrils.
Sadom nạthu phoṛaoedae. The horse snorts.

Nekra. Offensive, vile, polluted, defiled, dirty, filthy. Cf. nakara.

Nem. To sanctify, to observe certain prohibitions previous to officiating at certain sacrifices.
On the day previous to that on which his services are required at the Baha porob, or Flower festival and the Sohrae porob, or Harvest festival the Naeke or priest bathes and washes his clothes, and sleeps on a mat on the ground. He fasts on the day of the festival until he can partake of his share of one of the sacrifices. This he must consume himself, and in the event of his not being able to do so he must reduce it to ashes by fire.
On the day preceeding that on which Abge Boṅga or the household deity is to be worshipped all the male members of the family and invited relatives bathe and wash their clothes and pass the night lying on the ground on mats or straw. They fast until they can partake of the sacrifice offered to Abge Boṅga.
Teheñ do boṅgak burak reakko nemakaća. They have to-day sanctified themselves for the worship of the boṅgas (q. v.)

Nẽṛak. A little past the meridian, a little past mid-day.
Nẽṛakena nitok do. The sun is now past the meridian.
Tikin nẽṛakena. It is a little past mid-day.

Neskar. This year, the present year.
Neskar moto tahẽ ocoaeme. Allow her to stay for only this year.
Neskar din tahẽ ocoaeme. Allow her to remain this year.

Net puri. Applied to presents brought by invited guests to a marriage.
Net puri hạnḍi. Liquor brought by an invited guest to a marriage.

Nia. } By means of, through, owing
Niạte. } to.
Am niạte noań ńamkeda. I got this owing to, or through you.
Mạńjhi niạteń ḍanḍomlena. I was fined through the village chief.

Ni-ḍaṅgiria. Having no cattle to attend to in the morning and therefore in a position to sleep till late.
Nui do ni-ḍaṅgiria hoṛ lekae gitićakana. This (person) is lying (in bed) like a person who has no cattle.

Ninyạu. To cry poverty although well off.
Ninyạukkanae. He is crying poverty.

Ninyạ ninyī. To cry poverty, to pretend not to possess.
Ninyạ ninyī baṛae kanae. He is crying poverty.

Nirot. Calm, breezeless, still.
Teheńe nirotakaća. It is calm to-day.

Nisoṭ. Dry, sapless, moistureless.
Bah nisoṭ cabaakana. It has not all dried up, or evaporated, it is not perfectly dry, or sapless.

Niṭhur. Clearly, distinctly.
Okoekin orońeda tirio? khub niṭhur sadekana. Who are the two who are playing flutes? the sound is very distinct.

Nona. A variety of dhan or rice.

Ńumbạk.
Ạyup ńumbạk.
Ńupạk.
Ạyup ńupạk.
} A little after nightfall, about one hour after sunset.
Ạyup ńupạkle seterena. We arrived a little after nightfall.

O

Oḍhoń. } Cheap, low, as price or
Anḍhoń. } rate.
Noa dorteń ạkriṅkeda, ạḍi oḍhoṅgea. I sold at this rate, it is very cheap.

Ojoḍ. To anoint.
One okare mitṭeć cinhạ khunṭim ojoḍleć. Where thou anointedst a memorial pillar.

Okkodro. To be smoked when being cooked, stifling owing to the presence of smoke.

Omnete. Gratis, for nothing, free.
Omnetegeye emadińa. He gave it to megratis

Oṅ. To blow, as the breath; to breathe on.
Seṅgele oṅ jolkeda. He blew the fire into a flame.
Biṅe oṅadea. A snake breathed on him.

Onosar. } Breadth, width.
Onosarteć.
Ona reak onosarteć do pe muka. Its breadth is three cubits.

Osusar. Resourceless, in a strait, in a difficulty.
Osusarakanaṅ, niṭ susar calaokatiṅme. I am without resource, help me through this difficulty.

Ot ukṭaić. A rooter of the soil, a veiled name for a pig.

P

Pachtao. To be sorry, to grieve, to repent.

Pạcuk. } To finish, added to other
Phạcuk. } verbs gives the idea of completely, entirely, all.
Phạcukkedako. They finished it.
Eṛe pạcukkediṅae. He completely deceived me.
Jom pạcukkedae. He ate all.

Padar podor. Drizzle, fine rain.
Ale seć padar podore dakkeda. Over our way there was a drizzling rain.

Pãeṛẽ. To clandestinely give away to relatives articles belonging to the joint family, used mainly of wives.
Bạhukogeko pãeṛẽa. Wives clandestinely give away articles belonging to the joint family.

Pahak. } To clear away as mist, to
Pohok. } shine as the sun on the clearing away of mist,
Nitok doṅ calaka, pohokkedae. Now I will go, the mist has cleared away.

Pahaṭ. Side, strip, piece, direction. Cf. pahṭa.

Pahla pạhli. For the first time.
Pahla pạhli ne uṭạre bijukkana. This is the very first time he is coming.

Pahpaha. First signs of dawn approaching.
Pahpahakkana. There are signs of the dawn approaching.
Pahpahaakana. Signs of the dawn are apparent.

Pạhrạu. To put on the person as a garment, ring, ornament, &c. &c.

Pạhrạuạ. That which has been put on the person, as a garment, ring, ornament, shoes, &c. &c.

Pạliạu. To spread or smear clay in a soft state, as over a threshing floor, courtyard, &c.

Parmonosal. A variety of dhan or rice.

Phadar phodor. } Imitative of non-re-
Phodor phodor. } sonant sounds.
Tumdak sạḍekana phadar phodor. The tumdak drum sounds phadar phodor.
Maejiu ãṭṭeko calakkhan kicrić sạḍea phodor phodor. When women walk quickly their garments sound phodor phodor.

Pheṭ. To recover flesh after having been emaciated, to change, to alter.
Pheṭkateye heṅena. He changed (his clothes) and came.

Phećeć phećeć. Imitative of the sound produced when sifting with the haṭak (q. v.)
Gumedako phećeć phećeć. They are sifting with the haṭak and producing a sound resembling phećeć phećeć.

Pheṭek pheṭek. Flapping. Cf. pheṭe pheṭe.

Phicir. } To fly off as chips of
Phicir phicir. } wood from an axe, or water falling on a hard surface, to splash, to sprinkle. Cf. picir.

Phicir marte. } With a splash, with a
Phicir mente. } spray, Cf. picir marte.
Phicir marte ṅurena. It fell and broke up into spray.

Phodor phodor. Cf. phadar phodor.

Phodor phodor. To chatter, to jabber.
Tinạkpe roṛeda, phodor phodor? How long will you speak chatter chattering?

Phokok. } Imitative of the
Phokok phokok. } sound produced by any thick substance when boiling or any yielding substance when pierced.
Jondra daka hedejokre phokok phokok sạḍea. When Indian corn porridge boils a sound resembling phokok phokok is produced.

Phokok marte. } With a sound resem-
Phokok mente. } bling phokok.
Phokok menteṅ tuṅkedea. I shot him with an arrow and produced a sound resembling phokok.

Phola. A skein, the amount of thread wound on to the winder from the spinning axle of the carkha. Cf. laṭi.

Pholon. Increase.
Mihū meromko ren pholon. Increase of cattle.

Phula khasia. Joking, humour, fun.
Phula khasiatem galaocediń kana. You are dissolving me with humour.

Phuṭ. A part of the roof of a rat's hole the covering of earth on which is very thin and can easily be burst through and afford a way of escape when the ordinary way of egress is closed.

Pilpilau. To quake, as with fear,
Botorteko pilpilauk̃kana. They are quaking with fear.
Auritegeko pilpilauk̃kana. They are quaking without cause.

Piriń. A cultivated pot herb.

Piṭi khanḍa. A kind of cutting weapon which folds up.

Piṭna sakom. A kind of wristlet worn by women.

Podor. Dry.
Bhitrire podorgea. It is dry inside.

Podor podor. Fine, drizzling, as rain.
Podor podore dak̃eda. It is drizzling.

Pohok. To clear away as mist, to shine as the sun after mist has cleared away.

Puṭi. To contract, as a rope when wet.
Jaṛi baber lohoťlenkhan puṭik̃a. A rope of fibre when wet contracts,

Puṭrić. To become big or swollen as the belly, (of females.)

Puṭuryuć. Small, diminutive.

R

Rabać ribić. / Rabać rubuć. Drizzlingly, fine, as rain.
Rabać ribiće dak̃eda. It is raining fine, it is drizzling.

Race pace. / Race pacete. Carefully, discriminatingly.
Race pace k̃horocpe. Expend it carefully.

Raṭpaṭao. In comp, firmly, tightly, securely.
Tol raṭpaṭao. To tie tightly or securely.
Sap raṭpaṭao. To hold tightly or firmly, to detain.

Rawić. In comp, implies stealthily, surreptitiously, without authority.
Racak̃ rawidedako hoṛo. They are stealthily stripping the ears of rice.

Repe cirić. / Ripi cirić. To crowd, to be close together, to be packed together in little space, crowded.
Mić then ḍher hoṛ ripi cirić gitić do bań leka. It is not right for many people to sleep crowded together in one place.

Ribić. / Ribić ribić. Drizzle, fine rain.

Rohḍoć. To become emaciated, lean.
Netar kaḍru do aḍiye rohḍoćena. At present the young buffaloe is greatly emaciated.

Rubuć. / Rubuć rubuć. Drizzle, fine rain.

Rugḍai. / Rugḍai rugḍai. All shouting together.
Rugḍai rugḍaiko hohokeda. They all shouted at once.

Rugḍai marte. / Rugḍai mente. With a shout together.
Aḍi garte rugḍai menteko hohokeda. They shouted together with a loud shout.

S

Sajot. To conspire, to be in league with, to collude.
Sajotakanako. They are in league together.

Samta. / Se samta. / Ona samta. Rather than that.
Gidra cedak̃em dalekantińa? Ona samta ińge ma daleńme. Why are you striking my child? Rather than that strike me.

Samthul. Full, complete, undiminished.
Nes do samthul hoṛo bań ñamakana. A full crop of rice has not been got this year.
Nes jondra hoeśna samthul. This year there is a full crop of Indian corn.
Samthulle baeakaťa. We have stored it undiminished, we have stored all there was of it.

Sarua. To suffer from the effects of overeating, to surfeit.
Jom saruaenae. He has eaten till he is surfeited.
Jom saruak̃te goć hoko goć utarok̃a. They die from a surfeit of food, death often follows a surfeit of food.

Sealom. A fresh water Alga, *Mongeotea immersa, West.*

Sili. A neck ornament of plaited hair and small white heads, worn by females.

Siṅ munḍ. Head and horns, head, as of cattle, remains of an animal, generally head and horns, devoured by wild beasts.
Tinak̃ siṅ munḍ menak̃kotaea? How many head of cattle has he?

Soḍgo boḍgo. Applied to the sound produced by water when agitated in a hole or cavity.

Coḍgoć hakoe soḍgo boḍgoeda bhugạkre. The coḍgoć (q. v.) fishes in the hole are making a sound resembling soḍgo boḍgo.

Sodo bodgo. Hairy, hirsute, rough.

Sodo bodgo baberko uṅakaṭa. They have spun the string roughly

Soesoe. Indecently, applied to females.

Soesoeye duṛupakana. She is sitting indecently.

Soner gidi. A mythical vulture.

Soro soro. Applied to the fizzing or hissing sound produced by green wood burning.

Soro sorokkana. / Soro soro sadekana. } It is hissing or fizzing.

Soyoć soyoć. Sound of puffing produced by blowing out smoke from the mouth when smoking a pipe, cigar, &c.

Suạr jaṅghiạ. A short legged species of buffaloe.

Suć. To act as an intermediary, to explain, to inform, to inform one party of the views or intentions of another, to still, to allay excitement.

Raebarić kathae sućaḱkoa. The go-between informed them of the views of the other party.

Musạ samahre horkoe sućaḱkoa. He stilled the people in the presence of Moses.

Sulạ. To reduce the dimensions of the end of a piece of wood so that it may be inserted or fitted into another piece, The part of a piece of wood reduced in dimensions to fit into another; to tenon, to carry tales, to backbite.

Suruj muni. A variety of dhan or rice.

T

Talga tạwạḱ. / Talga tạuạḱ. } To crush, to smash.

Togoć talga tạuạḱkedeae. He bit and crushed him.

Taphat. Distance, difference, distinction, disparity, distant, separate, far away, remote. Cf. tophad.

Taṛaste. / Taraste. } Owing to, in consequence of.

Ghao taraste gaṇḍ rakapakawadea. Owing to the sore a swelling has arisen in the groin.

Ghao taṛaste ruạḱkanae. In consequence of the wound he has fever.

Ṭhal ṭhalao. Cf. ṭhal ṭhal.

Ṭipoṅ ṭoroṅ. The Grey partridge, *Ortygornis Ponticerrianus*. Cf. citri.

Ṭokar. To answer a shout by a shout, used mainly of shouting in response when watching crops by night.

Hohokedaṅ, cele hõ ṭokar bako emleda. I shouted, and no one gave a shout in response.

Cedaḱ bape ṭokar ruạṛlediṅa? Why did you not shout in response to me?

Tulsi phul. / Tursi phul. } A variety of dhan or rice.

Ṭuryuć. Small, diminutive.

Ṭuryuć ḍahra. A small bullock.

U

Unimre. Then. Cf. unre.